The Neurology
of Schizophrenia

Other volumes in the series

Handbook of Schizophrenia

Edited by H.A. NASRALLAH

VOLUME 1

The Neurology of Schizophrenia

Editors:

Henry A. NASRALLAH

Chairman, Department of Psychiatry,
The Ohio State University,
Columbus, OH, U.S.A.

Daniel R. WEINBERGER

Chief, Section on Clinical Neuropsychiatry and Neurobehavior,
Intramural Research Program, National Institute of Mental Health,
Director, Behavioral Neurology Service, Saint Elizabeth's Hospital,
Washington, DC, U.S.A.

1986

ELSEVIER

Amsterdam – New York – Oxford

ISBN 0 444 90415 8
ISBN SERIES 0 444 90437 9

Library of Congress Cataloging-in-Publication Data

The Neurology of schizophrenia.
  (Handbook of schizophrenia ; v. 1)
  Includes bibliographies and index.
  1. Schizophrenia--Physiological aspects. 2. Brain--
Diseases. 3. Brain--Radiography. I. Nasrallah, Henry A.
II. Weinberger, D. R. (Daniel Roy) III. Series.
[DNLM: 1. Nervous System--physiopathology. 2. Schizo-
phrenia. WM 203 N4937]
RC514.N445 1986   616.89'82   86-6305
ISBN 0-444-90415-8 (U.S.)

Published by:
Elsevier Science Publishers B.V.
P.O. Box 1527
1000 BM Amsterdam

Sole distributors for the USA and Canada:
Elsevier Science Publishing Co. Inc.
52 Vanderbilt Avenue
New York, NY 10017

Printed in the Netherlands by Casparie, Amsterdam

Contributors

K.F. BERMAN
   Section on Clinical Neuropsychiatry and Neurobehavior, Neuropsychiatry Branch, Intramural Research Program, National Institute of Mental Health, Saint Elizabeth's Hospital, William A. White Building, Washington, DC 20032, U.S.A.

J.L. CADET
   Section on Clinical Neuropsychiatry and Neurobehavior, Neuropsychiatry Branch, Intramural Research Program, National Institute of Mental Health, Saint Elizabeth's Hospital, William A. White Building, Washington, DC 20032, U.S.A.

J.A. COFFMAN
   Department of Psychiatry, The Ohio State University, College of Medicine, 473 West 12th Avenue, Columbus, OH 43210, U.S.A.

L.E. DELISI
   Clinical Neurogenetics Branch, The National Institute of Mental Health, Room 3N/220, Building 10, The National Institutes of Health, Bethesda, MD 20205, U.S.A.

T.E. GOLDBERG
   Section on Clinical Neuropsychiatry and Neurobehavior, Neuropsychiatry Branch, Intramural Research Program, National Institute of Mental Health, Saint Elizabeth's Hospital, William A. White Building, Washington, DC 20032, U.S.A.

J.A. GREBB
   Nathan Kline Institute, Orangeburg, NY 10962, and Department of Psychiatry, New York University Medical Center, 550 First Avenue, New York, NY 10016, U.S.A.

D.V. JESTE
   Section on Clinical Neuropsychiatry and Neurobehavior, Neuropsychiatry Branch, Intramural Research Program, National Institute of Mental Health, Saint Elizabeth's Hospital, William A. White Building, Washington, DC 20032, U.S.A.

Ch.A. KAUFMANN
   Columbia University College of Physicians and Surgeons, New York State Psychiatric Institute, 722 West 168th Street, New York, NY 10032, U.S.A.

Contributors

D.G. KIRCH
Section on Clinical Neuropsychiatry and Neurobehavior, Neuropsychiatry Branch, Intramural Research Program, National Institute of Mental Health, Saint Elizabeth's Hospital, William A. White Building, Washington, D.C. 20032, U.S.A.

J.E. KLEINMAN
Section on Clinical Brain Studies, Neuropsychiatry Branch, Intramural Research Program, National Institute of Mental Health, Saint Elizabeth's Hospital, William A. White Building, Washington, DC 20032, U.S.A.

J.B. LOHR
Neuropsychiatry Branch, Intramural Research Program, National Institute of Mental Health, Saint Elizabeth's Hospital, William A. White Building, Washington, DC 20032, U.S.A.

T.C. MANSCHRECK
Laboratory for Clinical and Experimental Psychopathology, Department of Psychiatry, Massachusetts General Hospital, Erich Lindemann Mental Health Center, Boston, MA 02114, U.S.A.

J.M. MORIHISA
Department of Psychiatry, Georgetown University School of Medicine, and Department of Psychiatry, VAMC, Washington, DC 20422, U.S.A.

H.A. NASRALLAH
Department of Psychiatry, The Ohio State University College of Medicine, 473 West 12th Avenue, Columbus, OH 43210-1228, U.S.A.

K.C. RICKLER
Section on Clinical Neuropsychiatry and Neurobehavior, Neuropsychiatry Branch, Intramural Research Program, National Institute of Mental Health, Saint Elizabeth's Hospital, William A. White Building, Washington, DC 20032, U.S.A.

R.C. SHELTON
Department of Psychiatry, Vanderbilt University School of Medicine, Medical Center North, Room A-2215, Nashville, TN 37232, U.S.A.

E.F. TORREY
Neuropsychiatry Branch, Intramural Research Program, National Institute of Mental Health, Saint Elizabeth's Hospital, Washington, DC 20032, U.S.A.

D.R. WEINBERGER
   Section on Clinical Neuropsychiatry and Neurobehavior, Neuropsychiatry Branch, Intramural Research Program, National Institute of Mental Health; Behavioral Neurology Service, Saint Elizabeth's Hospital, William A. White Building; and Department of Neurology and Psychiatry, George Washington University School of Medicine, Washington, DC 20032, U.S.A.

A. WISNIEWSKI
   Neuropsychiatry Branch, Intramural Research Program, National Institute of Mental Health, Saint Elizabeth's Hospital, William A. White Building, Washington, DC 20032, U.S.A.

R.F. ZEC
   Department of Psychiatry, Andrew McFarland Mental Health Center, Southern Illinois University School of Medicine, Springfield, IL 62708, U.S.A.

Contents

Contents

Introduction

The objective of the *Handbook of Schizophrenia* series is to provide a comprehensive overview of all aspects of schizophrenia, the most serious and disabling psychiatric disorder. The authors are investigators who are directly involved in basic and clinical schizophrenia research, biological as well as psychosocial.

The first volume in this series is, appropriately, devoted to the *Neurology of Schizophrenia.* Following the psychodynamic and the pharmacological eras earlier in this century, psychiatry is currently undergoing what may be considered its third major phase in less than 100 years: the neuroscience revolution. There are few scientific disciplines or medical specialties that are evolving as rapidly as psychiatry, with its almost breathtaking rate of new discoveries and insights.

Schizophrenia has been at the center of brain research over the past two decades. The discovery of effective antipsychotic medications in the 1950s triggered a vigorous search for the neurochemical basis of schizophrenia, which has led to numerous other discoveries along the way. However, it was the technological revolution which has provided the necessary impetus for the current momentum of brain research and its future promise in psychiatry. The quantum leap in computer technology has facilitated the development of brain imaging techniques which now allow, for the first time, the in vivo assessment of the brain's structures and functions. In less than a decade several types of brain imaging techniques have been developed and implemented, providing remarkable new insights into the last biological frontier, the brain.

The future course of psychiatry is obviously linked to advances in brain research and the unraveling of the brain-behavior link at the biopsychosocial levels. Significant progress is expected to shed new light, not only on schizophrenia but probably on many normative brain functions as well. Over the next few years, psychiatry is expected to undergo significant growth spurts of knowledge that will carry it into legitimate maturity as a scientific discipline.

This volume presents the impressive scientific evidence for the neurological basis of the schizophrenic syndrome. It provides not only facts, but also many conceptual frameworks for defining subtypes of schizophrenia and relating clinical phenomenological findings to disorders of brain structure and function. The first several chapters follow roughly the same sequence as does a neurologist's clinical examination of a schizophrenic patient (history, physical examination, differential diagnosis, laboratory tests, EEG evoked potentials, neuropsychological testing, etc.). Chapters 9 through 13 cover the state of the art in brain imaging findings in schizophrenia with the use of computerized tomography, magnetic resonance imaging, computerized mapping of electrophysiological data, cerebral blood flow studies and positron emission tomography. Finally, several chapters propose various theoretical models of schizophrenia based on current neuropathophysiological findings and provide a framework for future directions in research.

This book is intended to be a useful resource for clinicians, teachers and researchers who are interested in schizophrenia as a neurological syndrome. Psychiatrists, neuroscientists, physicians in general, as well as psychologists, neurologists, educators and rehabilitation specialists will find this book of particular value in their work. Future volumes in the series will provide overviews of advances in other areas of brain dysfunction and biopsychosocial treatment in schizophrenia.

HENRY A. NASRALLAH

CHAPTER 1

The clinical neurologic examination in schizophrenia

JEAN LUD CADET, KENNETH C. RICKLER AND
DANIEL R. WEINBERGER

Recent advances in clinical neuroscience and in neurological technology have led to a reevaluation of the early literature on the neuropathology of schizophrenia and have stimulated a more rigorous neurological approach to the study of this group of disorders. Schizophrenia has traditionally challenged clinicians and basic scientists and both groups have profited from renewed efforts to define its neural substrates.

These efforts reflect a wider resurgence of interest in neuropsychiatry, an orphaned discipline that at times has proved frustrating for both psychiatrists and neurologists. Many psychiatrists are uncomfortable with the medical concepts and techniques involved in neurological diagnosis; their neurological colleagues may feel ill-equipped to examine the difficult psychiatric patient or to deal with the complex psychosocial issues which surround even organically based behavioral disorders. As a result, relevant subtle aspects of the neurological exam may be neglected, resulting in a declaration of 'no acute neurological disorder' or 'no localizing signs.' In a similar fashion, the traditional mental status examination in psychiatry often fails to detect the presence of organic dysfunction. These deficits have the ability to impact negatively upon clinical care as well as to inhibit the potential for significant clinical collaboration in the further investigation of schizophrenia.

In this chapter, a selective formulation of the neurological examination will be presented. Whenever possible, the techniques of the examination will be interwoven with the available data relating to schizophrenia. When relevant, differential diagnosis and underlying pathogenic mechanisms will be discussed. For the sake of clarity and convention we have chosen to use the traditional format for the neurological examination. A number of standard neurological texts use the same format and afford the interested reader further opportunity to review these matters in greater detail (1, 2).

The process of neurological diagnosis involves a systematic attempt to examine anatomy in relation to function. The application of this process to schizophrenic patients presumes that their symptoms and behavior(s) have some type of anatomic and physiologic substrate. Such a presumption does not ignore theoretical concepts which accord a role to psychodynamic processes or environmental stressors; rather,

Handbook of Schizophrenia, Vol. 1: The Neurology of Schizophrenia.
H.A. Nasrallah and D.R. Weinberger, editors.
© Elsevier Science Publishers B.V., 1986.

these processes and stressors are seen as resulting from and/or impacting upon a state of brain dysfunction.

Since this presumption draws our focus to the nervous system, some organizing principles must be applied to the interpretation of data derived from a systematic neurological examination. The absence of demonstrable neurological abnormality does not necessarily exclude organic dysfunction. Like other efforts at physical diagnosis, the neurological examination suffers from limitations; however, recent advances in other clinical tools such as brain imaging techniques, evoked potential and electroencephalography (EEG) have broadened and enriched the clinical neurological data base about schizophrenia beyond these limitations. Conversely, the demonstration of an abnormal finding on neurological examination does not always have clinical relevance or significance. Nonetheless, from a research viewpoint it remains important to continue to document the nature and extent of neurological abnormalities in schizophrenia with the hope that the relevance of findings will eventually unfold.

The neurological examination in schizophrenia also serves another important function: the opportunity to diagnose illnesses which may appear at first glance to be schizophrenia but, in fact, are not. The performance of a thorough neuropsychiatric evaluation both addresses differential diagnosis and leads to a more accurate characterization of the psychiatric symptomatology. For example, in its early stages Wilson's disease may mimic schizophrenia, the detection of Kayser-Fleischer rings during the performance of a thorough examination will help to make the diagnosis.

General approach to the patient

The neuropsychiatric history

Medical diagnosis relies heavily on the patient's history. This anamnesis, in part, depends on the clinician's skills at directing the interview in an empathic and productive way. The schizophrenic patient may task these skills heavily and in most cases it is imperative to carry out follow-up interviews. In all cases, it is felt that close relatives or significant others should participate to some degree in that process. The medical history of the schizophrenic patient is essential to the formulation of a differential diagnosis and in characterizing nervous system dysfunction. Standard textbooks of psychiatry have dealt with this issue at length (3).

The interview begins by eliciting the chief complaint. This is usually followed by inquiring about the date of onset, nature, and severity of presenting signs and symptoms; associated symptomatology; provoking and alleviating stimuli; treatment modalities and their effects; and the course of the illness.

In order to form a neurological differential diagnosis, it is important for the clinician to obtain answers to questions regarding the location and the nature of the disease process. Are the symptoms related to the cerebral cortex, the basal ganglionic structures, long white matter tracts, the brainstem, the cerebellum, peripheral nerves, or other structures of the neuraxis? Inquiries about language and speech disturbances, disturbances of state of consciousness, involuntary movements, gait difficulty, weakness, or pain may help in directing the flow of the interview and localizing lesions. Those neurological disorders that may simulate schizophrenia often have symptoms referable to the cortex (e.g. memory, and language impairment), the basal ganglia (e.g. rigidity, slowness of movement, and extra movements), and/or cerebellum (e.g. coordination).

The tempo of the illness whether episodic, cyclic, or progressive may suggest its nature. Seizure disorders, vascular lesions, syncope, intoxications, and certain sleep disorders (e.g. narcolepsy) produce symptoms that are relatively sudden in onset. Brain tumors, neurodegenerative diseases, and viral encephalitides are progressive. In pursuing a history suggestive of a seizure, the examiner inquires about disturbances of sleep; persistent daytime sleepiness; and periods of intermittent confusion, restlessness, or incoherence. History of loss of consciousness should stimulate questions about the frequency and length of attacks; sequence of events including premonitory symptoms (anxiety, lightheadedness or malaise); specific auras (e.g. hallucinations, autonomic sensations, fear, embarrassment, etc.) and presence or absence of urinary or fecal incontinence. Differentiating syncope from a seizure may be difficult. Patients with true syncope may suffer from myoclonic jerks of the arms and legs or from tonic extension of the whole body. In a small number of cases there may be a tonic-clonic attack. The presence of incontinence does not rule out syncope and depends on the rapidity with which consciousness is regained. Post-ictal confusion is common and may be prolonged; post-syncopal confusion is rare and brief. It is important to elicit the presence of associated symptoms, drug history, and family history. Cerebral ischemia may be secondary to cerebrovascular disease, to vasovagal syncope, carotid sensitivity, central autonomic failure (Shy-Drager syndrome, some cases of parkinsonism), drugs (phenothiazine, levodopa), and cardiac diseases.

In general, headache is a frequent complaint in patients who visit their physician but may be ignored in the evaluation of the neuropsychiatric patient. It requires careful analysis because it may be the only clue to underlying pathologies. These include brain tumors, ophthalmic and nasopharyngeal diseases, or systemic disorders. Headache occurring in the morning suggests hypertension, migraine, and neoplasms. Migraine is unilateral, recurrent, throbbing, and often associated with blurriness of vision, migrating scotomas, and fortification spectrum. It tends to be familial. Complicated migraine (migraine associée) may be accompanied by transient neurologic deficits including hemiplegia and aphasia. Muscle contraction headaches are usually bilateral, dull, and often unremitting. Cluster headaches are nocturnal and usually awaken the patient. Posterior fossa tumors may produce pain in the occipital nuchal area, whereas supratentorial lesions cause frontal or parietal pain. Consistent unilateral headache suggests an intracranial lesion. So-called 'psychotic headache' is characterized as bizarre in nature and usually unremitting, but the possibility of psychotic elaboration of bona fide cephalalgia must be considered.

Abnormal involuntary movements or dyskinesias may be seen in a variety of neuropsychiatric and systemic illnesses, such as Huntington's chorea, Wilson's disease, systemic lupus erythematosus (SLE), thyrotoxicosis, Sydenham's chorea, as well as in pregnancy. They may also be associated with drugs including anticonvulsants, neuroleptics, and stimulants. The presence of these abnormalities at rest, during action, or maintenance of posture is determined. History of other associated symptoms including subjective restlessness and loss of function is also elicited. The drug history prior to the development of the illness is crucial to the differential diagnosis of these disorders. Abnormalities of gait, lack of control of extremities, history of dystonic posturing or myoclonus, and of localized or generalized weakness are documented in the initial assessment.

Peripheral nervous system disorders may be associated with impotence and/or incontinence. Diabetes mellitus (DM) is the most common cause of autonomic polyneuropathy. Impotence may be the presenting symptom in DM. Other neurological causes of impotence include pandysautonomia, Shy-Drager syndrome, familial dysautonomia, amyloidosis, alcoholic polyneuritis, and Guillain-Barré syndrome. The history of associated symptoms such as sweating irregularities and incontinence may be very helpful in distinguishing neurologic from psychiatric impotence. Inquiry about nocturnal erections is also helpful. Patients with temporal lobe tumors or epilepsy may also be hyposexual. Drugs such as the phenothiazines and anticholinergic agents, endocrine abnormalities (e.g. hypothyroidism, Addison's disease, and Cushing's syndrome) may all be associated with sexual impotence.

The neurodevelopmental history

The neurodevelopmental history is one of the most significant aspects of the neuropsychiatric patient's history because it provides clues to premorbid neurological dysfunction and/or injury. It includes specific drug intake, presence of infections, and other difficulties that might have occurred during the pregnancy. The clinician also inquires about premature delivery, induction and length of labor, neonatal infections, seizures or hypoxia, icterus, twin or multiple births, and APGAR score. The physician asks about nutrition; the presence of delayed milestones, hyperactivity, pervasive reading, speaking, learning, or communicating difficulties; and the appearance of choreiform movements, (e.g. Sydenham's chorea), hemiparesis, abnormal tone, gait abnormalities as well as difficulties in acquiring motor skills. It is important to inquire about febrile seizures, central nervous system (CNS) infections, and head traumas.

History of past illness and review of symptoms

This usually consists of a checklist that can be used to take a detailed but focused review of systems. Particular attention is paid to those conditions with neuropsychiatric implications. SLE, vasculitides, endocrine abnormalities, exposure to neurotoxic substances, seizures, and vitamin deficiencies etc., are to be considered.

Family and genetic history

Many neuropsychiatric diseases of the CNS are familial. These include Huntington's chorea (4), neurofibromatosis (5), Wilson's disease (6), tuberous sclerosis (7), metachromatic leukodystrophies (MLD) (8), Kufs' disease, idiopathic cerebral ferrocalcinosis (Fahr's disease) Alzheimer's disease etc. This is reviewed in detail elsewhere (9).

Clinical neurological examination

General physical examination

The general physical examination is an integral part of the neurological evaluation. It is discussed at length in standard physical diagnostic books (10). However, certain aspects of the exam need to be re-emphasized because of their potential importance in the neuropsychiatric population. For example, changes in skin texture, color, or moisture may be a sign of an endocrinologic and metabolic disorder (10). Patients who have postencephalitic Parkinson's disease may be especially seborrheic (11). The neurocutaneous syndromes show characteristic skin abnormalities: sebaceous adenomas and hypopigmental patches in tuberous sclerosis (7); neurofibromas and café-au-lait spots in Von Recklinghausen's syndrome (5); portwine facial nevus flammeus in Sturge-Weber-Dimitri syndrome; and conjunctival telangiectasias in ataxia-telangiectasia (12). Hypertrophy of gingiva might reveal chronic treatment with dilantin. In nicotinic acid deficiency, there may be glossitis and angular fissuring of the tongue (13). Vitamin deficiencies may be associated with various neuropsychiatric symptoms including irritability, depression, psychosis and cognitive disturbances (13). Dysmorphic facial appearance, epicanthal folds, bone and joint irregularities, hypertelorism, torso and spinal malformations, and abnormalities of hands and feet such as coarse skin, clinodactyly and syndactyly may be associated with neurodevelopmental disorders including autism, attention deficit disorder with hyperactivity and learning disabilities (14, 15). These signs are thought to be related to first trimester insults (14). Head size (macro- or microcephaly), the presence of bruit on auscultation (arterio-venous malformation), or any area of unilateral protuberance of the skull (meningiomas) should be documented.

Mental status

A complete mental status examination should be carried out in all neuropsychiatric patients. The 'mini mental state' may be used as a screening device (16). The examination is carried out in a non-confronting, conversational manner. During the anamnesis, observation is made of the patient's mental abilities and of his use of language. Disturbances in these functions may be related to diffuse or localized involvement of the brain. The cognitively oriented mental status exam can assist in differentiating diffuse from focal cerebral disease. While it is possible to formulate hypotheses about possible brain dysfunction on the basis of the patient's history, it is nonetheless imperative to test the subject's performance on specific sub-categories of the exam. Interpreting the mental status exam in neurological terms is particularly challenging in patients with schizophrenia. Aspects of the exam may suggest diagnosable focal or diffuse disease of the CNS. Nevertheless, diagnostically important associated findings will usually be absent.

Level of consciousness

The level of consciousness is evaluated first. This term embodies an amalgamation of processes that allow the organism to be aware of itself and its environment. The degree of awareness will affect the rest of the examination. Several terms which describe the degree of arousal have been used. They include alertness, clouding of consciousness, lethargy or somnolence, delirium, stupor, and coma (17).

The *alert* patient appears awake and is able to cooperate fully except in cases of aphasia, paralysis, or malingering. Patients with the locked-in syndrome, which is usually secondary to bilateral ventral pontine lesions, are usually alert, but because of paralysis of bulbar and limb musculature they are mute and only able to communicate through vertical eye movements (18).

Clouding of consciousness refers to patients who show reduced awareness of their environment. They may show hyperexcitability, irritability, or belligerence. Excitement may alternate with marked drowsiness, with subsequent progression to lethargy or somnolence. In these states, the patient is unable to sustain arousal, which prohibits full participation in the rest of the neurological evaluation.

In *delirium,* the patient is disoriented and fearful. He misperceives sensory stimuli and hallucinates. There may be periods of lucidity that alternate with those of agitation and suspiciousness. These states usually last less than 2 weeks; but there may be lingering and intermittent hallucinatory experiences.

In *stupor,* the patient looks like he is asleep, but he responds to vigorous stimulation. After arousal, the patient is unable to maintain alertness if the stimulus is stopped. He usually groans, moves somewhat restlessly in bed, and may progress to coma. Stupor has to be differentiated from catatonia (19, 20). In *catatonia* the patient looks awake and typically manifests catalepsy, grimacing, mutism, posturing, and rigidity. It is significant that catatonia may be secondary to a multitude of factors which include affective disorders, schizophrenia, encephalitis, or drug-induced psychosis (19). The eyes of the catatonic patients are usually open, the skin is greasy, the pulse is rapid, the temperature may be elevated, but the respiration pattern is regular. Although they may not respond to visual threats and even painful stimuli, caloric tests of vestibular functions show normal oculomotor response.

Coma is a state of complete unarousability. Comatose patients show no response to any external stimuli including deep pain. When one encounters a patient with an altered level of consciousness, a description of the patient's actual behavioral responses should be recorded instead of a non-informative label (e.g. coma). This allows for more objective criteria by which to follow the subject's progress.

Although schizophrenic patients are usually alert, their level of consciousness may at times resemble the various symptoms listed above. Even when alert, they may have difficulty cooperating because of intrusion of psychotic thoughts or hallucinations. The presentation may be similar to an acute confusional state. The differential diagnosis, is made on the basis of a lack of other associated signs and symptoms. Other ancillary tests, including EEG, do not show evidence of other causes for a disturbance in consciousness.

Attention

After assessing the level of consciousness, the clinician needs to evaluate the patient's ability to initiate, sustain, and shift attention. This is done early in the examination because attention and concentration will affect other higher intellectual functions as well as cooperation. Four quantifiable tests may be used to evaluate attention: the digit span, subtraction of serial sevens, reverse spelling, and the 'A' test.

In the *digit span test,* the patient is asked to listen carefully to a list of numbers and to repeat them after the examiner. The digits are repeated at a rate of one per second. The average individual is able to repeat five to seven digits. The subjects also may be asked to repeat a number of given digits in reverse order. Three to five correct reverse digits is normal. It should be noted that this test is not a test of memory.

The *serial 7 subtraction* is presented in the following manner: 'Start with 100 and subtract 7, take 7 from the answer and keep on subtracting sevens. If I were doing it with 5, it would be 100, 95, 90, etc'. The time taken to accomplish the test and the number of errors are noted. The patient is then asked to spell 'earth' or 'world' forwards and backwards. If the patient fails, shorter words may be tried: 'hand', 'hold', 'cat', or 'bat'. Bender suggested that defects in *reverse spelling* are a sign of brain dysfunction implicating the dominant hemisphere or of diffuse cerebral abnormality (21). Interpretation of these tests depends on the age, level of education, and the social history of the subject. Patients who have had little verbal education or who calculate poorly may be asked to perform serial 3 subtractions and to recite the months of the year backwards as substitutes. Since virtually everyone knows the months of the year forwards, inability to recite them backward may indicate an attentional deficit.

The *'A' test* is made up of a random number of letters among which the letter 'A' appears frequently (see appendix to this chapter). The patient is asked to indicate by tapping or raising a finger whenever 'A' appears in the sequence. Abnormal responses include errors of omission, commission, or perseveration.

It is also very important to observe the patient for any signs of hemi-inattention or neglect as they may suggest parietal lobe dysfunction. Denial of hemiparesis is the best known and most often described (22). In that disorder the examiner is unable to convince the patient of the existence of his hemiplegia even though the patient is unable to execute any task with the affected limbs. Other disorders of the body schema include conscious and unconscious hemiasomatognosia, autotopagnosia, macro- and microsomatognosia, and autoscopia (23). Subtle impairment may present as lack of concern for an obvious disability, a common feature of frontal lobe disease.

Conscious hemiasomatognosia is characterized by the reporting of loss of sensation on one side of the body. It is usually transient and is thought to be of paroxysmal subcortical origin (23). In the unconscious type, the patient may behave as if one side of the body is non-existent but does not report any deficit. He fails to shave or dress one side. This form is less transient and may persist for months. It is usually seen as part of the right parietal lobe syndrome (see Table I).

TABLE 1   *Frontal and parietal lobe syndromes*

Frontal	Parietal
Right	
1. Left hemiplegia	1. Cortical discrimination deficit (astereognosis, two-point discrimination), extinction phenomena
2. Affective changes, mood swings, hypomania	
3. Attentional deficits	
4. Sexual erethism	2. Muscle atropy and wasting, hemiparesis
5. Difficulty with initiating task, loss of drive	3. Hemianopia
6. Anosmia	4. Dressing and constructional apraxias
	5. Confusional states, attentional deficits, psychotic symptoms
	6. Loss of topographical memory
Left	
1. Right hemiplegia	1. Gerstmann's syndrome
2. Broca's aphasia, agraphia, apraxia	2. Autotopagnosia
3. Same as right-sided lesions (see above)	3. Asymbolia for pain, ideomotor and ideational apraxia
	4. Same deficits as in 1, 2, and 3 above
Bilateral	
1. Pseudobulbar palsy	1. Autotopagnosia
2. Dementia (Pick's disease) with reduced speech production, inappropriate behavioral patterns, and incontinence	2. Perceptual spatial impairments (position, distance, and direction in space)
3. Akinetic mutism and placidity (bilateral cingulate gyrus)	3. Loss of topographical memory
4. Memory deficit, Korsakoff-like syndrome (bilateral cingulate lesion)	4. Balint syndrome (psychic paralysis of gaze, optic ataxia, visual inattention)

Autotopagnosia is characterized by inability to localize and name body parts. Finger agnosia (inability to name fingers) and right-left disorientation are probably special cases of autotopagnosia. In evaluating right-left orientation, the patient is asked to identify various body parts on himself or on the examiner e.g. show me your (or my) left foot, right ear etc. Right — left disorientation is usually associated with acquired lesions of the dominant temporo-parieto-occipital area in the neighborhood of the angular gyrus. The examination may be rendered more difficult by testing the patients with hands crossed, using a mirror, or using objects in external space.

The parietal lobe syndromes described above are not typical of schizophrenia. Nevertheless, features suggestive of a parietal lobe lesion may exist, including errors in right — left orientation, unconcern about illness etc. The meaning of such features is not known. They probably reflect problems in concentration, attention, and possibly dysfunction of frontal cortex (see below). The accurate assessment of these syndromes requires a relative degree of cooperation both in the specific areas of assessment as well as in other related areas involving language functions. Schizophrenic patients may report delusional thought about their body parts and may also demonstrate bizarre ways of dressing or have inadequate concern for shaving etc. Thus, the accurate assessment of these and other specific cortical dysfunctions may be seriously compromised in the patient with schizophrenia.

Arousal and attention in schizophrenia The proposition that schizophrenia involves an arousal dysfunction has a long history. Bleuler suggested that individuals with this disorder show deterioration in attention and that most of the psychotic symptoms are related to an associative disconnection (24). Kraepelin wrote that these patients have difficulty staying attentive for a long period of time and that registration of information was defective (25). In clinical practice, the schizophrenic patient is alert, responsive, but may show some difficulty focusing. He may score in the defective range in the digit span and the 'A' test, gives idiosyncratic answers while performing the 'serial sevens' test, and does well on reverse spelling.

Various attempts have been made to further characterize the attention deficit in schizophrenia. A comprehensive review of that field is beyond the scope of this chapter. Many of these studies have used neuropsychological tools.

The *Continuous Performance Test* (CPT) is thought to be a test of vigilance (sustained attention) (26). As in the 'A' Test described above, the subject responds only when a critical stimulus is heard or seen. Kornetsky and co-workers have shown that between 40 and 45% of patients with schizophrenia show deficits in their performance on the CPT which improved somewhat on neuroleptic medication (27 – 29). Poor performance on the CPT correlated with a family history of psychiatric illness especially in siblings, but not with diagnostic subtype, duration of illness and/or hospitalization, intelligence, or education (29).

Of the various models advanced to explain this deficit (30, 31), the hypervigilance model has attracted the greatest interest. It is postulated that schizophrenics attend to all stimuli without being able to filter less significant ones. Mirsky suggested that hyperarousability is related to a dysfunction in the brainstem's ascending reticular activation system (32). Kornetsky and Eliasson have shown that mesencephalic reticular lesions in animals lead to attention deficits which are reversed by chlorpromazine (33). Using data from clinical experience and animal studies, several investigators have proposed a cortico-subcortical loop that is important in maintaining attention (34, 35). More recently Mesulam (36) suggested that a system composed of reticular structures (arousal), cingulate (motivation), posterior parietal (sensory), and frontal (motor) cortices is involved in the maintenance of attention. He further suggested that a lesion anywhere in the system including basal forebrain, cingulate cortex, polymodal cortex, frontal eye fields, or brainstem nuclei may lead to deficits in directed attention; all of these structures have been cited as showing possible neuropathologic changes in schizophrenia (see Chapter 8). In humans, attentional deficits or neglect frequently occur after right-sided lesions of both cortical and subcortical origin (37, 38). Does this imply that a right-sided brain dysfunction explains the attentional deficits seen in schizophrenia? This is in part not consistent with the data that suggest left-sided abnormalities in schizophrenia patients (39). Dysfunction of limbic diencephalic (40) or brainstem (41) structures that project diffusely to these areas might be a more parsimonious explanation, since neuropathological changes have been demonstrated in some of these regions (42, 43). In addition, there is increasing evidence of frontal lobe dysfunction in schizophrenia that may also be related to the attentional disorder (44).

Orientation

Orientation involves the assessment of a patient's ability to learn new information regarding his surroundings. Specifically, enquiries are made about time, date, day, month, season, year, and location. Schizophrenia does not usually involve gross degrees of disorientation, but bizarre responses or a disinclination to respond are not uncommon. Disorientation to person in the absence of impaired consciousness is almost certainly not a manifestation of *bona fide* neurologic disease.

Mood and affect

Disorders of mood are well described in psychiatric texts (3). The range, intensity, and stability of affect are evaluated. Expressions of anger, anxiety, happiness, or sadness are all noted. Changes in mood are common in patients with cerebrovascular accidents (45), basal ganglia disease (46), and may be the presenting symptoms of cerebral neoplasms (47). They may also be seen as late effects of head injuries. Patients with right hemispheric lesions may have laughing or crying spells associated with clinical depression (48), though a catastrophic depressive reaction is more often associated with left hemisphere injury (45). Patients with progressive supranuclear palsy show marked emotional responses to non-significant stimuli. Patients with amyotrophic lateral sclerosis, lacumar state, multiple sclerosis, and frontal lobe dysfunction may also show incontinence of affective response.

Schizophrenic patients often have flat or blunted affect. They may also show irritability, belligerence, and may even be aggressive at times. It is very important, though difficult, to differentiate post-psychotic depression from akinesia secondary to neuroleptic drugs.

Perceptual disturbances

Perception depends on normal functioning of pathways from the sensory receptors (auditory, olfactory, visual, etc.) on the one hand and on final integration at the level of the neocortex on the other. Perceptual abnormalities are thus classified according to the affected modalities. These disturbances include hallucinations and illusions. Hallucinations occur without external stimuli and may be elementary (unformed) or complex (formed). Unformed visual hallucinations have been related to the occipital lobe whereas formed visual and auditory ones suggest temporal lobe damage. Illusions refer to distortions of existing stimuli. Often hallucinations and illusions may occur in the same subject. At times it may also be difficult to differentiate them solely on the basis of a patient's complaint. There are several types of hallucinations (see Table 2), some of which may have localizing values (peduncular hallucinations). Others such as hypnagogic hallucinations, in which the human face is the most commonly reported object, have no localizing value.

Auditory hallucinations occur in association with temporal lobe lesions and usually consist of music or speech. Deaf patients may also suffer from auditory hallucina-

TABLE 2   *Perceptual disturbances*

Hallucinations

Auditory	(temporal lobe, schizophrenia)
Gustatory	(complex partial seizures, Briquet's syndrome, schizophrenia)
Heautoscopic	(parieto-occipital)
Lilliputian	(temporal lobe, toxic states, hypnogogic, schizophrenia)
Peduncular	(intoxication, encephalitis upper brainstem, pulvinar)
Olfactory	(epilepsy, migraine, Alzheimer's disease, alcoholic psychoses, manic-depressive illness, schizophrenia)
Somatic	(phantom limb, phantom breasts, toxic encephalopathies, schizophrenia)
Visual	(retinal diseases, optic nerve lesion, epilepsy, migraine, toxic-metabolic, Briquet's syndrome, sensory and sleep deprivation, schizophrenia)

Illusions*

Cinematographic vision	Paliacousis (seizures in temporal lobe)
Eidetic imagery	Palinopsia (occipital lesions)
Macropsia, micropsia (also parainsular cortex)	Phosphenes
Metachromatopsia	Polyopsia
Metamorphopsia	Teichopsia
	Teleopsia

* Most of them occur with parieto-occipital lesions.

tions. Auditory hallucinations have been thought to represent the patient's inner thought and Morel (49) has termed this phenomenon 'echo de la pensée'. Indeed, many patients with schizophrenia report that their hallucinations are 'heard' inside their head, an experience that is distinctly different from hallucinations heard externally in, for example, partial seizure disorders. The schizophrenic patient may report that he is receiving messages from television, parents, or God. The voices may be pejorative causing the patient much discomfort. The neurological basis for auditory hallucinations in schizophrenia is not known.

Visual hallucinations, though perhaps less common than auditory ones, do occur in schizophrenia. They also occur with temporal lobe lesions. A patient who has a hemifield defect, may report hallucinatory experiences on that side. The content of visual hallucinations may vary in size (micro- or macropsia, lilliputian), or shape (metamorphopsia). Occipital lesions cause unformed images which may be restricted to a superior or inferior quadrant. In addition, visual hallucinations have been reported in ophthalmic disorders, epilepsy, migraine, acute confusional syndrome, and sleep deprivation. The neuropathological substrate for visual hallucinations in schizophrenia is not understood.

Somatic hallucinations which include alteration of body size or shape may be part of a migrainous aura (50). They are also seen in hallucinogenic intoxication. Schizophrenics may also report similar experiences (51). Tactile hallucinations are seen in a high proportion of patients with schizophrenic and affective disorders (52). Formication (feelings of small animals crawling in the skin) occur in alcohol, hypnotic drug, cocaine withdrawal as well as in advanced cases of dementia.

Gustatory hallucinations may occur in schizophrenia, complex partial seizures, and in manic-depressive illness (52). Olfactory hallucinations occur in uncinate seizures, migraine, alcoholic psychosis, and Alzheimer's disease. Patients with schizophrenia or manic-depressive illness may report that they are emitting a foul odor.

Language and speech

Language involves a set of complex phonological and syntactic rules, whereas speech involves the neuromuscular events necessary in verbal communication. Interpretation of language function depends on first establishing the integrity of the speech process, namely respiration patterns, phonation, prosody, and articulation.

Examination of speech processes Abnormalities in respiration may be secondary to weakness or disturbed tone (hypertonicity) of the respiratory muscles. There may also be spasms of the vocal cords in dystonia and pseudobulbar palsy leading to short phrases interrupted by breathing pauses. Patients with dyskinetic abnormalities may show sudden interruption in their speech or changes in speech rhythm. Characteristic strained or harsh quality of the voice may be due to spasms of the abductors of the vocal cords. Some patients with bulbar palsy or chorea may show hypernasality. Patients with tardive dyskinesia (TD) involving oropharyngeal and/or diaphragmatic muscles may also exhibit disruption of speech patterns.

Prosody refers to the melody of speech. Dysprosody is thus a disorder of the rhythm and rate of speech production. Cerebellar lesions may cause scanning speech (53). Patients with Parkinson's disease may show festination of speech characterized by short rushes of speech interrupted by brief pauses (54). Patients with nondominant cortical lesions may also show dysprosody (48).

Articulation depends on the strength and timing of movements of the tongue and lips. Systematic errors in articulation have been termed lingual, labial, or guttural. The lingual sounds are t, d, l, s, sh, and th; the labials are b, p, m, and w; and the gutturals are formed in the back of the pharynx and include g, k, ng. The examiner listens carefully for any deviation in speech production and asks the patient to repeat the sounds listed above in order to evaluate the location of any articulatory difficulty. Disorders of speech, especially dysarthria and dysprosodia are seen in some patients with schizophrenia. Their significance is unclear.

Examination of language processes   After evaluating the patient's speech pattern, the clinician tests his language functions. The examiner listens for grammatical errors, word finding difficulties or substitution, or inappropriate use of words. These are usually seen in aphasia, a disorder of language which is usually associated with reading and writing difficulties. Constructional problems and impairment of gesture are sometimes seen. Aphasic disorders may be either fluent (Wernicke's) or nonfluent (Broca's) (55). Fluent aphasics produce a flowing speech that is devoid of content and replete with paraphasias. Such patients usually seem unconcerned or unaware of their language difficulties and may be mistakenly diagnosed as psychotic when first seen. Paraphasias may be semantic (word substitution) or phonemic (syllable substitution). Neologisms are also a form of paraphasia. Non-fluent aphasics show a restricted non-grammatic verbal output, have difficulty finding words, and pause frequently. They frequently become frustrated and disconsolate.

The comprehension of language is tested by asking the patient to follow specific instructions. These include yes-no questions and object identifications. Motor commands are tests of both comprehension and praxis. The normal execution of a command implies comprehension but the inability to execute it may only indicate a deficit in praxis. The patient is then asked to repeat single words, simple sentences, and more syntactically complex phrases. Errors include additions, omissions, and/or paraphasias. In some cases, the patient's answers may be totally unrelated to the examples given.

The examiner then asks him to name body parts, colors, and objects or parts of objects. The ability to name is disturbed in all subtypes of aphasia. Patients may have great difficulty with uncommon items but none with common ones. Reading ability is often overlooked in the language evaluation; aphasic patients usually have difficulty with reading as well. The patient is asked to read aloud and his comprehension is also tested. Errors include paralexias (word substitutions) or omissions. The clinician then asks the patient to write sentences with variable degree of difficulties. Both spontaneous writing and writing to dictation are tested. In interpretating the findings in these tests, the clinician must take the patient's education level into consideration.

Speech and language in schizophrenia   Kraepelin mentioned several types of communication disorders in schizophrenic patients (25). These include: *paralogia* or evasion in which the train of 'thought' is felt to be suppressed and replaced by another; *verbigeration* or frequent recurrence of single words or phrases; *derailment; word finding difficulties; phoneme substitutions;* and *neologisms.* He also mentioned *akataphasia* which is the production of sequential, similar sounding words by patients who were felt incapable of expressing their thoughts adequately. Abnormal constructions of sentences, telegraphic speech, and at times total disappearance of sentence structure were also described (25). Bleuler felt that it was the content of language that was disordered, but not language itself (24). Subsequently, various studies have been conducted to evaluate the nature of the communication deficits seen in some schizophrenic patients.

Rumke and Nijam suggested that confused language and neologisms may be reducible to an aphasic disturbance (56). However, Critchley (57) stated categorically that, despite certain 'superficial similarities', the deficits observed in schizophrenia are quite different from those seen in aphasia. He pointed out that in schizophrenia there is a qualitative abnormality, characterized by disturbance in the thought processes, whereas in aphasia there is a quantitative deficit, due to inaccessibility to verbal symbols. He further suggested that, in contrast to aphasics, schizophrenics may become totally mute and do not seem to strive to converse. He did add, however, that it is harder to differentiate between the two groups when jargon aphasia and neologisms are evaluated (57). While we agree with Critchley's arguments, there are a few problems. First, he writes about schizophrenic patients as if they were a homogenous group. Second, his suggestion that patients with schizophrenia do not strive to communicate, while true for many patients, is not a universal phenomenon. We have seen schizophrenic patients who show a degree of frustration with their communication difficulties similar to patients with aphasia. A case in point is that of an 18-year-old patient whose speech showed derailment, neologisms, and some word finding difficulties. During spontaneous conversation laden with paraphasic errors, she would interrupt herself several times by saying 'no, no that is not what I meant to say'. She would then make a great effort to find the right words, and at times, frustrated, would burst into tears.

Chaika suggested that these patients may suffer from an intermittent aphasia (58). She lists six characteristics of schizophrenic language: (1) sporadic disruption in the ability to match semantic features, (2) preoccupation with too many of the semantic features of words; (3) inappropriate noting of phonological features of words; (4) production of sentences according to phonological and semantic features of previously uttered words; (5) disruption in the ability to apply rules of syntax; and (6) failure to self-monitor. Fromkin pointed out that these patterns may occur in normal speech (59). Lecours and Vannier-Clement argued that these are also seen in jargon aphasia (60).

Other authors have approached this issue by using psycholinguistic tests, Carpenter studied the performance of 48 schizophrenic patients on three items: (1) word strings, (2) a connected discourse passage, and (3) click sentences (61). The patients were then compared to undergraduate students at Columbia University and 11-year-old children from a private school. The undergraduate students recalled significantly more unconnected words than the other groups. The good premorbid tested better than the poor premorbid patients. However, the groups showed no difference in recall due to syntactic structure (61). The schizophrenic patients did as well as university students, who are usually chosen for their ability to do well on standardized tests. Knight and Sims-Knight (62) demonstrated that patients with good premorbid adjustment were able to integrate linguistic ideas in long-term memory better than those with poor premorbid status. Both studies suffer from the introduction of memory-related variables which were not adequately addressed. Patients with schizophrenia do not ordinarily demonstrate any abnormalities on standard tests of memory, but may show memory falsification (63); others have stated that poor recent memory, memory gaps, and so-called negative hallucinations (failure to perceive existing stimuli) may occur in some patients (25). In a recent study, Grove and Andreasen have suggested that these patients have a short term memory deficit because they did poorly on the digit span test (64). As noted above, abnormality in this test reflects primarily attentional dysfunction and not memory deficit.

Bleuler's contention that schizophrenic communication patterns are secondary to loose associations has been the accepted dogma for many years (24). Recently, however, it has come under closer scrutiny (65 – 67). Chaika suggested that neologisms, word salads, abnormal associations, and gibberish are all instances of abnormal speech (65). We agree with her contention that abnormal thought (e.g. paranoid delusions) may be expressed through normal language processes and that speech production does not always reflect the speaker's thought processes (65). This position also is consistent with Andreasen's assessment (66). However, Schwartz stated that the abnormal utterances of these patients are related to defects in information processing and in selective attention, but not in language itself (67). Chaika's argument is more convincing because it is somewhat less inferential, and parsimony would dictate studying the abnormalities at the level of phenomena. However, her unifying theory of speech in schizophrenia fails to address the degree of heterogeneity in this group of disorders (68).

The tendency to compare schizophrenic communication with well-defined patterns of verbal output secondary to known neurological lesions might inhibit the development of new hypotheses to evaluate and/or explain schizophrenic language. Such an approach may have resulted in premature conclusions about lateralized cortical abnormalities in schizophrenia and might fail to consider the fact that aphasia may also occur with strictly subcortical lesions (69, 70). The study of communication disorders is still in its early infancy. Neuropsychiatrists befudled by the complexity of this endeavour may find solace in the fact that new technological advances have opened to question many accepted notions about the so-called classic neurologic aphasic syndrome (71, 72). In the case of schizophrenia, there are clearly disturbed verbal communication patterns. The relationship of this disturbance to classic aphasic syndromes is, however, weak.

Examination of praxis

Disorders of praxis may be defined as inability to carry out purposeful, complex movements by a person who has normal neuromuscular skills and normal understanding of the act to be performed. There are four major types of apraxia: ideomotor, ideational, constructional, and dressing apraxias (67, 68).

Ideomotor apraxia refers to disorders related to simple gestures: 'blow out a match', 'wave good-bye', 'bow' etc. This disorder is often associated with aphasic disturbances, thus care must be taken to ensure that the patient has understood the commands. *Ideational apraxia* relates to more complex tasks. The single elements of a gesture are carried out successfully but there is a breakdown in the performance of the entire act. They may have difficulty with the following task: 'put a cigarette in your mouth, take the match out of the box, light the cigarette, blow out the match'. It is usually associated with bilateral parietal lobe dysfunction. Aphasia, constructional apraxia, and disorientation are more often associated with the ideational variety.

Constructional apraxia is difficulty in drawing or in performing constructional tasks to commands or imitation. The patients are unable to draw or construct simple or more complex three-dimensional objects. The deficits may be variable appearing only during complex tasks. In *dressing apraxia,* the patient is unable to dress himself. He handles the clothes in a haphazard fashion and is unable to carry out the semi-automatic act of dressing. In some mild cases, he may have difficulty tying his shoe laces. Associated symptoms include sensory, somatognosic, and visuospatial deficits which are seen in non-dominant hemisphere dysfunction.

Patients with schizophrenia often have a variable degree of difficulty in carrying out tasks on command. This has often been attributed to negativism. Unlike the deficits described above, the schizophrenic patient's performance to motor commands is often variable, suggesting the possibility of an intermittent physiological apraxia, though other explanations involving attention, and cooperativeness seem more probable. Traditionally, some types of apraxia have been regarded as a manifestation of frontal lobe dysfunction; it is thus of interest in this regard that other frontal lobe abnormalities have been described in schizophrenia.

Memory

Memory, in terms of the ability to learn new information, is tested by asking the patient to repeat three unrelated words immediately and after 3 minutes. Remote memory or recall is tested by asking about personal and historical facts. Recent memory is assessed by asking about events of the preceding day (e.g. news, meals, etc.). More complex tests of memory include a verbal story (e.g. The Cowboy

Story), visual memory for objects hidden in patient's proximity, and design reproduction (73). Disorders of recall are seen in dementing illness, and are the central features of Korsakoff's syndrome, Alzheimer's disease, as well as in lesions affecting the hippocampus and associated structures in the temporal lobes and diencephalon. It is important to note that memory is a complex function which depends on intact arousal, attention, and concentration. Patients with schizophrenia do not show any consistent disorder of memory; abnormalities in this area of cognition most likely relate to an attentional deficit.

Calculations

Calculations are evaluated by testing performance in simple addition or multiplicative tasks; word problems which involve more complex conceptual abilities are also tested. Disorders of verbal quantitative reasoning are associated with dominant cerebral lesions. Dyscalculia is a component of the left angular gyrus syndrome (Gertsmann's syndrome) (74) and problems in calculating accompany most forms of dementia. Calculation is normal in schizophrenia; however, responses may be idiosyncratic.

Abstract thinking

The ability to think abstractly is assessed in the process of securing the history and by asking the patient to draw similarities between various objects, 'How are a chair and a table similar; an apple and an orange.' Proverb interpretations are also tested. The clinician notes bizarreness, concreteness, and idiosyncrasies. These tests are highly dependent on educational level, social class, and culture. In schizophrenia answers are frequently self-referential, bizarre, and fragmented, depending on the severity of illness.

Cranial nerves

Examination of the cranial nerves is an important part of the neurological evaluation. Understanding of their peripheral distribution and their central relationship to other neuroanatomic structures allows the clinician to recognize certain syndromes and to localize lesions with the brainstem (75). In what follows, the emphasis will be on those cranial nerves in which abnormalities have been reported in neuropsychiatric patients.

Olfactory nerve

The clinician closes one of the patient's nostrils and presents an odoriferous agent to the other (e.g. coffee, cinnamon etc.). Alcohol and other pungent stimuli probably test primarily pain and not smell. The patient is first asked if he perceives an odor and, if the answer is affirmative, to identify it. The most common cause of

17

anosmia is trauma, but meningioma arising at the base of the frontal lobe may be a cause. Disorders of the olfactory nerve have not been described in schizophrenias, even though such patients may report the presence of foul odors related to their own body parts.

Optic nerve (II)

Visual acuity is tested with the Snellen chart which is situated 20 feet away from the patient or with hand-held (Rosen) cards. The visual fields are tested by confrontation with the examiner facing the patient. The clinician covers one of the patient's eyes and asks him to fix his gaze on the examiner's eye. The perimetry of the visual field is tested in each eye separately. Various types of deficits may occur and are associated with different localizations along the visual pathway. Patients with psychogenic deficits many show contraction of the field of vision in a gun-barrel or tunnel fashion. Formal tangent screen visual field documentation should be determined in such cases. Some neurological illnesses such as frontal lobe meningioma, Wilson's disease and suprasellar masses (e.g. 3rd-ventricle tumor, pituitary adenoma, and sarcoidosis), may present with neuropsychiatric symptoms. These disorders may have demonstrable abnormality on a thorough examination of the visual system. Such findings are not encountered in schizophrenia and, when present, lead the examiner toward a neurologic diagnosis. Patients with Wilson's disease may have Kayser-Fleischer rings, which may require slit-lamp examination for documentation (6). In any patient with schizophrenia, an attentional defect can lead to an apparent field defect which is not fixed and which varies with the patient's mental state. Ophthalmoscopic examination may also reveal retinal hemorrhages, optic atrophy, a 'cherry red spot', or papilledema. These findings are associated with neurological disorders, not with schizophrenia.

Oculomotor nerves (III, IV, VI)

The nerves of eye movements (III, IV, VI) and pupillary responses (II, III) are usually examined together. The eyes are examined for exophthalmos, retraction of the upper lid, or lid lag. These abnormalities suggest endocrinopathies.

Pupillary responses   The size of the pupils and their reaction to light and accommodation is evaluated. Both direct and consensual responses are noted. Impairment in one optic nerve will show an afferent defect in that eye, that is the eye will constrict to consensual stimulation, but not to direct stimulation. Impaired parasympathetic innervation leads to a dilated, unreactive pupil whereas sympathetic disturbances (Horner's syndrome) cause a small, but reactive pupil. Argyll-Robertson pupils of syphilis are *small,* irregular pupils which react on accommodation but not to bright light. *Large* pupils that show similar characteristics may be seen in chronic alcoholism, diabetes, encephalitis, and syringomyelia. Other pathological but not diagnostic pupillary signs include sluggish response to light, small excursion, paradoxical dilation instead of constriction, constriction followed by dilation, and phasic constriction ('hippus'). Adie's syndrome consists of large pupils that react very slowly to light and normally to accommodation in association with anhidrosis and areflexia (76).

Both Bleuler and Kraepelin mention the existence of pupillary abnormalities in schizophrenia (24, 25). Kraepelin described wide, oval, and irregular pupils that lost the light reaction and the ciliospinal reflex (25). The irregularity was described as rarely persistent, varying during the day, and reversible. Schilder reported that the pupillary abnormalities ('catatonic pupils') are more common in black patients and are due to inhibition of the parasympathetic system (77, 78). These abnormalities may indeed be secondary to functional disturbances in the parasympathetic (Edinger-Westphal nucleus) or sympathetic systems which are responsible for pupillary constriction and dilation, respectively. In our experience such pupillary abnormalities are not common features of the neurological exam in schizophrenia, and it is doubtful whether they reflect a primary pathological disturbance of relevance to this disorder.

Eye movements Conjugate eye movements may be classified into two types: slow and rapid. *Slow eye movements* (optokinetic and vestibular) function to maintain image stability during head rotation. They are induced by slow moving visual or vestibular stimuli. They serve to maintain gaze constancy by producing compensatory opposite phases during head motion. Lesions of the cerebellum or brainstem – cerebellar pathways lead to dysfunction in that system and the appearance of saccadic movements. *Rapid eye movements* (saccades, pursuit, vergence) are brought about by changes in the position of the objects of interest. Saccades include the fast components of nystagmus and rapid eye movements (REM) during sleep. They serve to keep peripherally sighted objects on the fovea. Pursuit movements keep moving objects focused on the fovea and vergence movements move the eyes in order to maintain binocular vision as objects move towards (convergence) or away from (divergence) the patient.

Normal eye movements are maintained through the integration of visual, proprioceptive, and vestibular inputs. They also depend on a set of complex interactions that involve the cerebral cortex (frontal eye fields and visual cortex), superior colliculus, cerebellum, the brainstem, and the vigilance level of the organism (79). Disturbance in any of these structures or their connections may produce abnormal eye movements.

The clinician tests the oculomotor system by having the patient move his eyes in all directions of gaze. He makes note of any weakness, abnormalities of conjugate and vergence movements, diplopia, and the presence of nystagmus. Pursuit is tested by having the patient follow a moving target laterally and vertically. Abnormal saccadic intrusions may be observed instead of smooth pursuit. The patient's head is moved side to side or he may be rotated on a swivel stool to test for vestibuloocular integration. Optokinetic nystagmus is tested by having the patient watch a tape measure or any object with a repeatable pattern move in front of his eyes. This is done in both the horizontal and the vertical planes.

Eye movement abnormalities include monocular paresis, convergence and divergence paralysis, disturbances in conjugate movements, saccadic dysmetria and disorder of saccadic initiation, impaired smooth pursuit, vertical and horizontal gaze paresis, and nystagmus (79). Eye movements abnormalities are among the most consistent findings reported in schizophrenia. These include disturbances in eye blink rates, glabellar reflex, and smooth pursuit.

Eye blinks and glabellar reflex in schizophrenia   Stevens studied 44 schizophrenic patients who were drug-free for over one month (80). She reported that 34 subjects had at least one sign of oculomotor abnormality. Twenty-three patients showed difficulty moving the eyes independent of head movement (eye-head synkinesia); 20 had increased blink rates; and 17 had decreased glabellar response. Five patients showed rapid blinking during periods when they seemed dazed or to be hallucinating (80). Cegalis and Sweeney also reported high blink rates in their study (81). Recently, Karson reported that blink rates were increased in schizophrenia and decreased in subjects with Parkinson's disease (82). Monkeys showed dose-dependent increases in blink rate after apomorphine and bromocriptine injection, a response which was blocked by the dopaminergic antagonist sulpiride (82). Other studies have shown that spontaneous blinking is accentuated by L-dopa treatment (83). The results of these studies suggest that spontaneous blink rate varies directly with brain dopamine activity. The data also indicate that blinking is dependent on the functional integrity of the basal ganglia, as initially suggested by Ponder and Kennedy (84). However, blinking has been reported after stimulation of the nucleus accumbens, midbrain, or parietal cortex (85). From a strictly clinical perspective, increased blinking is often observed in the neurologic exam of schizophrenic patients on or off medication.

Smooth pursuit in schizophrenia   Several studies have reported impaired smooth pursuit in psychotic patients (see ref. 86 for review). In an effort to better categorize the eye movement disorders, Levin and his associates used an infrared recording technique in 6 patients (87). Three subjects showed saccadic intrusions during smooth pursuit, visual fixation, and vergence motion, and head – eye pursuit (88). However, the vestibulo-ocular reflex was normal (88). One patient had frequent blinks associated with the saccadic intrusions (88). Stark, using bioengineering techniques, has suggested that there are two abnormal patterns of eye movement: saccadic intrusions and saccadic smooth pursuit (89). In 50 – 80% of schizophrenics these impairments manifest themselves during both exacerbation and remission of the disease process, whereas only 8% of normals show similar patterns (89). The suggestion has recently been put forward that the region of dysfunction is probably situated above the brainstem (86, 89). Similar findings have been reported in patients with cerebellar disease, dyslexia, strabismus, intoxications, various degenerative neurologic conditions and normal aging (90 – 92). Eye movements need to be studied in conjunction with other neurological functions so as to determine the etiological significance of these reports. In one such report, Weinberger and Wyatt (93) found an association between pursuit irregularities and large ventricles on CT scan.

Oculomotor control involves a complex network that includes the brainstem – cerebellar system as well as the frontal and parieto-occipital cortices. Pathological involvement anywhere along the visual pathway may lead to dysfunctional eye movements. The results reported so far in schizophrenia are not specific to that disorder and are consistent with a number of interpretations. More research needs to be carried out before the pathogenesis of the smooth pursuit dysfunction in schizophrenia is elucidated.

Trigeminal nerve (V)

The fifth cranial nerve is evaluated by testing corneal reaction with a cotton swab and by checking pain, touch, temperature sensation in all three distributions of the nerve. Motor V is tested by palpating the bulk of the masseter and temporalis muscles with the patient's jaws closed against resistance. No abnormalities have been reported in schizophrenic patients.

Facial nerve (VII)

In testing the seventh nerve, the clinician looks for facial asymmetry, size of the palpebral fissure, and lacrimation. He asks the patient about hyperacusis. He may also test taste in the anterior two-thirds of the tongue, though this is a difficult task. Both sides of the tongue are tested with the tongue extended and care should be taken that the tongue is not pulled. Corticobulbar (upper motorneuron) lesions cause weakness of the lower part of the face, whereas those involving the facial nucleus or nerve (lower motoneuron) cause weakness of the whole side of the face. Bell's palsy is unilateral facial paralysis secondary to a lower motoneuron type lesion. Abnormal regeneration of the nerve may lead to synkinesis; 'crocodile tears', tearing during eating or talking, is one example of this phenomenon (94). Schizophrenia is not associated with any disturbances of facial nerve functions.

Acoustic and vestibular nerve (VIII)

The eight nerve consists of two subdivisions. The *cochlear* subserves hearing and the *vestibular* innervates the vestibular apparatus. The former is tested by bringing a watch slowly into hearing range of one ear while the other one is closed. The *Rinne test* compares air-to-bone conduction. Air conducts longer than bone in a normal ear. The *Weber test* compares bilateral hearing with the tuning fork vibrating in the middle of the forehead. In middle ear diseases, the sound is lateralized to the abnormal side; but in nerve dysfunction the sound is lateralized to the normal side. The vestibular division is tested by irrigating the ears with mildly cool water while the eyes are observed for nystagmus. The patient is queried about dizziness or nausea, which may be considerable. (For detailed description of the test see ref. 1). The normal response consists of a small excursion of the eyes toward the stimulus, followed immediately by rapid jerks from it. In contralateral cerebral lesions, the nystagmoid response is defective or absent; in ipsilateral peripheral or brainstem lesions, there is no deviation to that side. Hearing abnormalities are not related to schizophrenia.

Vestibular system abnormalities in schizophrenia   Studies of vestibular function in schizophrenia have reported various abnormalities. Claude and his co-workers described diminished vestibular response to caloric stimulation in four catatonic patients but not in eight hebephrenics (95). Argyal and Blackman studied 58 male patients and 20 normal controls using caloric stimulation and the Barany Maneuver (96). In 23 untreated patients there was decreased frequency of nystagmoid beats on all tests. There was no correlation with subtype, chronicity, or length of hospitalization. Those with the least vestibular response had hypotonia, were apathetic, and had poverty of thought content (96). Other authors have reported more dysrythmic ocular responses in chronic schizophrenics (97). These findings have been reviewed by Levy and her co-workers (98).

The neurological basis of these findings is not known. It is conceivable that subcortical systems that integrate oculomotor and vestibular functions might be dysfunctional in schizophrenia. Comparing these patterns to those seen in patients with known neuropathological lesions might help to clarify these issues. However, on routine clinical exam, vestibular dysfunction is rarely appreciated in patients with schizophrenia.

Glossopharyngeal and vagus nerves (IX and X)

The ninth nerve is tested by touching the posterior wall of the pharynx with a tongue depressor, observing the movement of the soft palate, and the ability to swallow. Unilateral damage to the X cranial nerve may lead to hoarseness and nasal speech due to weakness of the soft palate. Bilateral lesions may cause dysphagia and regurgitation.

Gag reflex abnormalities in schizophrenia   Gag reflex impairment was reported in 40% of psychiatric patients but in only 9% of normals in one study (99). In a more recent report (100) Craig et al. reported a 25.7% prevalence rate of depressed gag reflex. Drug-free patients had a rate of 31.3%. A subgroup of patients who suffered from neuroleptic-induced parkinsonism but not from tardive dyskinesia and who were not on anticholinergic drugs showed a significantly higher rate (50%). This is consistent with the findings that subjects with Parkinson's disease suffer from swallowing difficulties which improve with L-dopa therapy (101). It has been suggested that dopaminergic transmission affects the pharyngeal phase of swallowing (102). In schizophrenia, the meaning and etiology of gag reflex dysfunction is uncertain at the present time.

Spinal accessory nerve (XI)

The 11th nerve is tested by asking the patient to turn his head against the examiner's hand. The belly of the sternocleidomastoid contralateral to the direction of turning is observed and palpated. He is also asked to shrug his shoulders against resistance. Unilateral damage may lead to inability to raise one shoulder (trapezius muscle). Abnormalities of the function of this nerve are not related to schizophrenia.

Hypoglossal nerve (XII)

The 12th nerve is examined by having the patient protrude his tongue laterally and medially. The tongue is observed for atrophy and fasciculation. Strength is tested by having the patient push his tongue against resistance applied through each cheek. In supranuclear lesions, the tongue deviates contralateral to the side of cerebral abnormalities. Atrophy and vermiform fibrillations may be seen in amyotrophic lateral sclerosis. Choreoathetoid movements accompany tardive dyskinesia and other choreiform disorders. Tongue dyskinesia is best observed with the tongue resting inside the mouth. It is important to note the state of dental hygiene in interpreting tongue movements; dyskinesia may occur in the edentulous state. Schizophrenic patients without tardive dyskinesia show no abnormalities of the 12th nerve.

Motor examination

The motor examination is very important in the evaluation of the psychiatric patient. Testing of individual muscle function is usually not productive in that population; the interested reader is referred to the seminal monograph from the British Medical Research Council (103).

Normal motor function depends on the integration of various functional systems. These include the pyramidal system, the extrapyramidal system, peripheral neuromuscular system, the muscles, as well as sensory feedback. The pyramidal system consists of neurons that arise from the rolandic (area 4; 30%), adjacent frontal (area 6; 30%), and parietal (areas 1, 2, 3, 5; 40%) cortices. They travel through the internal capsule, cross in the medullary pyramids, and form the corticospinal tracts. Corticobulbar neurons synapse on brainstem nuclei while the corticospinal tracts reach motoneuron in the anterior horn of the spinal cord. The extrapyramdal system is made up primarily of the basal ganglia, the cerebellum, and various brainstem nuclei.

Muscle tone

Abnormalities in muscle tone may result from dysfunction of the motor system. Tone may be increased (rigidity, spasticity) or decreased (hypotonia). In *rigidity* both flexor and extensor groups contract, causing increased resistance to passive movements. The degree of resistance to movement is consistent throughout the range of the movement. The tendon reflexes are normal unless there is also involvement of the corticospinal tract. *Cogwheel rigidity,* in which the hypertonicity is interrupted by a frequent brief, and sudden give ('ratchet'), is thought to be secondary to concomitant tremor which may be occult. It is a common finding in idiopathic and secondary parkinsonism. In *spasticity,* there is a differential involvement of the opposing muscle groups with flexors in the upper extremities and extensors in the lower extremities primarily involved (i.e. anti-gravity musculature). The hypertonicity varies according to the speed and the direction of movement. There is also a *clasp-knife phenomenon,* characterized by relative relaxation after initial resistance. Patients with spasticity may develop contractures. Spasticity is a sign of corticospinal tract disease. In hypotonia, the muscles are somewhat flabby and do not resist passive displacement. The position of the extremities is influenced primarily by gravity; hyperextension of the joints may occur in severe hypotonia. Hypotonia is seen in Huntington's chorea, cerebellar disease, and peripheral neuropathy. Some schizophrenic patients may suffer from hypotonia; the neurological basis for this finding is not known. Catatonic excitement and the neuroleptic malignant syndrome may be associated with increased tone. *Paratonia* is a term used to describe increased tone that is neither spasticity nor rigidity, but seems to be a voluntary, though unconscious, resistance to passive movements. *Gegenhalten* is a form of paratonia seen with frontal lobe disease and diffuse encephalopathies. Paratonia is occasionally seen in schizophrenia, although its significance is not known.

Examination of the motor system   During the examination of the patient's tone, it is important that he be totally relaxed. Diversion may be very helpful. The examiner may ask questions unrelated to his illness. The clinician tests various muscle groups through their range of motion. The degree of resistance is noted. In Foment's maneuver, there is an increase in rigidity in association with movements of the contralateral side. Hypotonia of the extremities is elicited by having the patient sit on the edge of an examining table. After raising the legs, they are dropped and observed for the degree of swinging. *Postural fixation* is tested by asking the patient to close his eyes, hold his arm in front of him, with his fingers extended. The examiner looks for arm or hand drift. This test brings out weakness, hypotonia, tremor, choreic and athetoid movements. Abnormalities of this test may also be related to proprioceptive loss. Unmedicated schizophrenics do not show any significant disturbances in these tests.

Coordination

Abnormalities of coordination may be due to lesions of the cerebellum and cerebellar pathways, dorsal columns and related structures, and of frontal and parietal cortices. In basal ganglia disease, slowness of movement may appear as incoordination. The tests of coordination include the finger – nose test, heel – Shin test, toes – Finger test, and the pronation – supination test.

In the *Finger-to-Nose test,* it is important that the arm be fully extended at the elbow. With the eyes closed, the patient is asked to touch his nose with his index finger and to go back to the original position. The examiner changes the position after a few sequences. A variation on this test is using the examiner finger as a target with the subject's eyes open. In the *Heel-to-Shin test,* while supine, the patient is asked to lift the leg being tested high in the air and after touching his knee, to run it down his shin. This should be done in one smooth motion. In the *Toes-to-Finger test,* the patient, while supine, is asked to touch the examiner's fingers with his toes. The patient is also asked to draw a figure eight with his legs. In the *Supination – Pronation test,* the patient alternates tapping his knees with the palm and dorsum of his hand. Abnormalities in this test are called dysdiadokinesia. The clinician notes abnormalities of rhythm, rate, and amplitude of movement. Dysmetria (overshooting or undershooting of target) and dyssynergy (breaking down of movements in component parts) may be observed in any of these tests. Schizophrenic patients have been reported to show variable degrees of abnormalities on these tests. They are discussed below under the subheading 'Neurologic soft signs'.

Fine motor tests

At times the only abnormalities in the examination of the motor systems involve subtle differences in regularity, rhythm and amplitude of movements. Deficits in the rate of motion tend to appear before weakness or abnormalities in tone supervenes. In the *finger-wiggle test* the patient is told to move his fingers as if he were playing the piano. Another test involves the patient tapping the interphalangeal joint of the thumb with the tip of his first finger very rapidly; the two extremities are then compared. In the *foot-tap test,* the patient taps the floor with the ball of his feet without moving his heels. The number of taps per 10 seconds may be counted. The patient may also be asked to imitate screwing a light bulb while holding both of his arms at shoulder's height. Inability to carry out those tasks may be related to abnormalities of the extra-paranoid motor systems, but in the absence of other signs they usually implicate either corticospinal tracts or suggest a disorder of higher integrative (cortical) function. However, we have seen subtle dysfunctions in patients with major localizable lesions including cerebrovascular accidents and tumors, especially if they are confined to frontal lobes. Schizophrenic patients often have difficulty with fine motor tests (see below).

Involuntary movements

Involuntary movements most often are secondary to disorders of the basal ganglia. However, the exact nature of the functional disturbance causing the various abnormalities is not fully understood (104). Observation in an informal setting is an important part of the motor examination. The stress associated with a more formal

exam may at times enhance the appearance of involuntary movements. The association of abnormal movements with schizophrenia has a long history. Both Bleuler and Kraepelin have described in great detail the changes in motor behavior seen in these patients. Many of the movements may resemble those seen in diagnosable neurologic illnesses.

Tremors   Tremors are *rhythmic oscillations* of a body part secondary to abnormal contractions of antagonist muscles. They may occur primarily at rest (Parkinson's disease), while holding a posture (e.g. familial or essential tremor) or during a motor task (e.g. brainstem – cerebellar system lesions). Tremors usually cease during sleep. Most tremors are exacerbated by apprehension, or by tension or other physical discomfort. Certain drugs, including lithium, neuroleptics, tricyclic antidepressants, valproic acid, amphetamines, and coffee or tea may accentuate or produce tremors, of the so-called physiologic variety. Similar tremor is seen in anxiety, fatigue, thyrotoxicosis, pheochromocytoma, etc.

The resting tremor of Parkinson's disease has been called 'pill-rolling' or 'bread crumbing' because of a characteristic repetitive motion of the thumb on the first two fingers, which occurs typically in concert with tremor at the wrist. At times, parkinsonian patients may show both intention and resting tremors. Hyperthyroidism is characterized by very fine tremors which may be seen only when the arms are stretched and the fingers extended. Rosenbach's sign refers to fine tremors of the closed eyelids which are seen in anxious subjects and in hyperthyroidism. A 'flapping' or 'wing beating' type of tremor of the upper extremities is seen in Wilson's disease. Patients who are being treated with neuroleptic drugs may show a parkinsonian type tremor which often responds to anticholinergic therapy. Tremor is not typically seen in untreated patients with schizophrenia.

Chorea and athetosis

Chorea is characterized by brief, purposeless jerky movements which are abrupt in onset and rapid. They are not rhythmical, repetitive or stereotypic. They are typically random and appear in an unpredictable sequence. In advanced cases there are abrupt displacements of the limbs and bizarre grimaces of the patient's face. The milkmaid's grip refers to the patient's inability to sustain a firm grip. He may have difficulty keeping the tongue protruded. There may be fidgeting of the feet. These abnormal movements are seen in Huntington's disease, Syndenham chorea, SLE, thyrotoxicosis, tardive dyskinesia, L-dopa-induced dyskinesia, and dilantin intoxication.

Ballism is related to chorea, but the movements are of greater amplitude and, may sometimes be violent, leading to flailing motions. It is usually secondary to a vascular lesion in the subthalamic nucleus (105). *Athetosis* is a continuous, slow, writhing movement that is more sustained than chorea. Athetotic movements typically involve the face, tongue, and upper extremities. The involved part is seen to move through a sequence of extension – flexion, pronation – supination movements. *Choreoathetosis* refers to movements that are intermediate between the two, or that combine elements of both.

Dystonia

Dystonia is characterized by sustained spasms of agonist and antagonist muscles, which may be exacerbated during voluntary action. The spasms often are so slow as to represent sustained postures which appears as still frames from the athetoid sequence. There may be rhythmic interruptions during attempts by the patients to interrupt the abnormal movements. The dystonias are divided into primary and secondary (106). The primary or idiopathic dystonias are usually hereditary and typically begin with dystonic posturing of a body part during action (inversion of a foot during walking). The secondary or symptomatic dystonias are associated with juvenile Huntington's disease (Westphal variant), various congenital encephalopathies, Wilson's disease, Leigh's syndrome, Reye's syndrome, perinatal injury or infections, and various drugs and toxins (106). Writer's cramp, cranial dystonias, and torticollis are thought to be localized types of dystonia (107).

Chorea, athetosis, and dystonia in schizophrenia Description of choreiform movements of the face, including wrinkling of the forehead ('parakinesia'), irregular movements of the lips and tongue, and of the outstretched hands and fingers ('athetoid ataxia') were found in the early literature before the advent of neuroleptic drugs (25, 63). These movements tend to be more repetitive, patterned, and less random than true chorea. In this respect, they may be very difficult to differentiate on clinical grounds from tardive dyskinesia. Bleuler did not describe any chorea in his clinical reports (24). Most of the recent literature, including the study by Manschreck, fail to mention any true chorea in schizophrenia (108, 109). The presence of choreoathetosis or dystonia is usually associated with neurologic disorders and should raise the suspicion of Huntington's chorea, Wilson's disease, or other symptomatic dystonias including those induced by neuroleptics (110).

Spasms

Spasms refer to a variety of sudden muscle contractions that may be mistaken for dystonia. They can be clonic (rapid and repetitive) or tonic (prolonged). Metabolic disorders that lead to alkalosis or hypocalcemia may cause carpopedal spasm *(main d'accoucheur)* in which the fingers are approximated, flexed at the metacarpophalangeal joints, and extended at the interphalangeal joints. The thumb is extended, the wrist flexed, and the elbow pronated. There is a similar reaction at the ankle which may end in flexion or extension. Hemifacial spasm is a syndrome of unilateral facial nerve pathology that may look like an intermittent unilateral facial dystonia.

Mannerisms, stereotypies, and tics

A *mannerism* is defined as a bizarre, idiosyncratic way of carrying out purposeful acts. It may be difficult at time to separate mannerisms from tics. Traditional definitions suggest that mannerisms involve the ritualistic incorporation of purposeless, stereotypic movements into goal-directed activity. *Stereotypies* are quasi purposeful rhythmic, complex movements which have become somewhat autonomous.

Tics are involuntary, purposeless, coordinated, patterned movements which are repeated in a stereotypic fashion. Motor tics may be simple, such as twitching of the mouth, blinking or grimacing or head turning, or more complex such as suddenly bending over while walking, compulsive touching of objects or people, or making obscene gestures (copropraxia). These complex tics merge into the realm of mannerisms. Vocal tics may include the utterance of simple sounds, words, phrases, or involuntary obscenity (coprolalia). The words or phrases spoken by others may be repeated (echolalia) or their gestures imitated (echopraxia). The Gilles de la Tourette syndrome is an uncommon disorder characterized by multiple motor and vocal tics, which change over time. Less variable (and often milder) forms appear to be more common (111). Tics may also be seen following encephalitis with drug intoxications or use of antipsychotics, and following carbon monoxide poisoning.

Stereotypies and mannerisms in schizophrenia   A variety of stereotypic movements have been described in schizophrenia. These include hand clapping, bed beating, foot tapping, or circling around (24). Patients may repeat various phrases in the same exact sequence. Others may have simple motor tics or spasms (25). Manneristic behavior is very common. Fish noted a tubular movement of the rounded lips (snout spasm) which is thought to be a stereotypic posture (63). Morrison reported that of 250 catatonic patients, 24% showed stereotypies and 14% mannerisms (112). In a more recent study, Manschreck et al. reported that 25 of 37 patients had some abnormalities of spontaneous movements, including mannerisms, stereotypies, clumsiness, and motor blocking (108). Untreated patients were reported to have more abnormalities on their exam. On routine clinical exam, manneristic and stereotypic movements are very frequently observed. They often lead to diagnostic debates about other disorders, especially tardive dyskinesia (TD). These issues are discussed further in Chapter 4.

Myoclonus

Myoclonus is a shock-like contraction of an extremity, a part of an extremity, or of the trunk or face. It is usually spontaneous but is often inducible by auditory, tactile, or visual stimulation. *Action myoclonus* refers to myoclonus induced by voluntary movement. It is often a delayed effect of anoxic encephalopathy. Myoclonus has been divided into four major types: physiological, essential, epileptic, and symptomatic (113). *Physiological myoclonus,* involving usually the extremities, occurs during early stages of sleep and also includes hiccoughs. *Essential myoclonus* refers to repetitive jerks of the extremities which occur during deep sleep. In *epileptic myoclonus,* the myoclonic jerks may have EEG correlates. Variants include infantile spasms, Lennox-Gastaut syndrome, and photosensitive epileptic myoclonus. Symptomatic myoclonus may be seen in ceroid lipofuscianosis, Friedreich's ataxia, Wilson's disease, Huntington's disease, Alzheimer's disease, subacute sclerosing panencephalitis (SSPE), and Jakob-Creutzfeldt disease. Typically it is not seen in schizophrenia.

Palatal myoclonus refers to synchronous and rhythmic contractions of the palate which may or may not disappear during sleep. It is usually secondary to brainstem infarct or an injury which affects the pathways connecting the cerebellar dentate nucleus, the red nucleus, and the medullary olivary bodies. These connections have been termed the Guillain-Mollaret triangle (114).

Asterixis has been suggested to represent 'negative myoclonus' (113). It is, however, a sudden loss of postural tone, which can be elicited by having the patient stretch his arms at the elbow and extend his wrists and fingers. An abnormal response consists of intermittent irregular flexion – extension of the fingers and wrists. It is seen especially in hepatic encephalopathy, uremia, and phenytoin intoxication.

Paroxysmal dyskinesias

These complex abnormal movements usually occur in a sudden burst (115) and often appear non-neurologic. Three types will be discussed briefly: paroxysmal dystonia, kinesigenic choreathetosis, and hyperekplexia. In the first type, the dystonic reaction may be induced by coffee and alcohol and last up to several hours. It may occur two to three times per day. In *kinesigenic choreathetosis,* there are brief episodes of abnormal choreoathetoid movements that are induced by fatigue or emotional stimulation. *Hyperekplexia* (the *'jumping Frenchmen'* of Maine) is characterized by excessive startle response to verbal or tactile stimuli. These are not reported in schizophrenia.

Tardive dyskinesia

Tardive dyskinesia (TD) may be characterized as a variety of chorea-like movements with some dystonic features. TD patients do not show the *stuttering* gait of Huntington's disease, and hardly ever have a choreiform grip (milkmaid maneuver). These issues are discussed in the Chapter 4.

Motor blocking in schizophrenia   Slater and Roth report that there may be sudden transient episodes of akinesia during normal voluntary movement or during speech (116). At other times there may be intermittent hyperkinetic activities during long intervals of hypokinesia (116). This phenomenon bears some resemblance to the freezing or festinating episodes that may occur in Parkinson's disease. In our experience, motor blocking is rare in untreated schizophrenics and not well characterized.

Automatic obedience, negativism, and disorders of posture in schizophrenia: Automatic obedience is associated with abnormally increased compliance whereby the subject follows every instruction (24, 25). Kraepelin described schizophrenic patients who continued to stick out their tongues on commands after being pricked with needles (25). It is a feature of waxy flexibility (flexibilitas cerea), catalepsy, echolalia, echopraxia, and 'mitgehen'. *Waxy flexibility* is not synonymous with *catalepsy* (perseveration of posture). In the former there is a plastic resistance whereas in the latter there is no resistance to passive movements. In *mitgehen,* a body part is moved in the direction on very slight pressure. In *mitmachen* or cooperation, the displaced body part moves to a position without resistance to follow slight pressure by the examiner. The neurologic basis of such behaviors is not known but the basal ganglia have been implicated.

Automatic negativism refers to an abnormal level of opposition. The patient does not cooperate with any instructions, may lie or sit motionless, and refuses to communicate. Muscle tone is variable but may increase during passive movements ('gegenhalten'). Marked hypotonia has also been reported in some cases of schizophrenia (117). Similar features may be seen in patients with diffuse cortical and/or frontal lobe disease. Motor impersistence, the inability to maintain a posture or act (e.g. tongue protrusion) is associated with frontal and/or temporal lobe disease. It is seen in schizophrenia, but it may also represent voluntary uncooperativeness.

Catatonia is a symptom complex that may include stereotypic posturing, automatic negativism, waxy flexibility, and catalepsy (19, 20). It has classically been divided into three types: retarded, excited, and mixed (118). Both Bleuler and Kraepelin reported a significant number of catatonics in their clinical material. During the past 50 years there has been a decrease in the incidence of the catatonic subtype (111). Gelenberg reported that catatonia is more often associated with affective disorders and other medical and neurological illnesses (19). It is thus conceivable that many cases were misdiagnosed or associated with neurological illness with cyclic epidemiology, such as encephalitis lethargica. Diseases of the basal ganglia may present as catatonia (21), suggesting a role for these structures in the pathogenesis of the syndrome.

Gait and stance   Gait and stance result from a complex interaction between various levels of neural mechanisms and the psychological make-up of the individual. However, some gait disorders are very characteristic of certain diseases, for example hemiplegic gait or parkinsonism gait. During the examination, the examiner observes from all sides the patient walking; the way he gets up from a chair; the pace at which he walks and the way he turns around. The clinician also observes the attitude of the trunk and associated movements, such as arm swing. Having the patient walk backwards may help to bring out or accentuate subtle abnormalities seen on the examination. Tandem gait, (walking heel to toe), is useful in demonstrating ataxia.

In *parkinsonian gait,* the patient walks in a stooped fashion with the spine bent forward and the head bent down. The arms and the legs are somewhat flexed. He shows a marked paucity of movements and decreased arm swing during walking. He takes very small steps (marche à petit pas), but may suddenly take rapid small steps (festination). He may also freeze in place while attempting to start walking or go through a door. It is as if the parkinsonian patient suffers a inertial guidance problem, with difficulty both starting and stopping. Lateropulsion (falling to the side), retropulsion (falling backwards), and anteropulsion (falling forward) may also be observed. These are elicited by a sudden push or pull of the patient. Care is taken to prevent the patient from falling and hurting himself. Drug-induced parkinsonism due to neuroleptic treatment may have many of the features described above, particularly loss of associated movement while walking.

In *chorea,* sudden sideway or forward movement of the pelvis associated with twisting movements of the extremities lead to a dancing-like gait. Patients with dystonia, however, walk on the lateral side of their feet because of inversion at the ankle. They may show elevation of the shoulders and hips, twisting of the trunk, and marked lordosis and scoliosis. Dystonic gaits often appear very bizarre (119).

The patient with a frontal lobe lesion walks with his feet spread apart, takes small shuffling steps, and then stops. This cycle is usually repeated. This pattern has been called gait apraxia because of no demonstrable muscular weakness (120). It is most likely secondary to loss of integration between the cortical and basal ganglionic systems. This type of gait abnormality is often seen in patients with normal pressure hydrocephalus (NPH) and dementia. C.M. Fischer has suggested that this gait abnormality might be one of the earliest signs of NPH (121). Hemiplegic gait is characterized by circumduction and abduction of the involved lower extremity; the upper extremity on the affected side is held in flexion. Because of spasticity there is decreased range of motion in all affected joints.

Hysterical gait is inconsistent in its manifestations. At times, it may be very difficult to differentiate from a true neurologic disorder, especially dystonia. Although the term astasia – abasia has been applied to all forms of psychogenic gait abnormalities, it specifically refers to the inability to stand and walk by a patient who retains normal use of the lower extremities while supine. The clinician should keep in mind that this pattern may be seen in lesions of the anterior cerebellar vermis.

Sensory examination

The superficial sensory evaluation is one of the most difficult aspects of the clinical neurological examination. Since it depends almost entirely on the patient's reliability, it is not often productive in the evaluation of neuropsychiatric patients. A useful rule of thumb is that sensory findings on exam that are not related to subjective complaints are rarely important. In what follows, we shall concentrate on the cortical sensory exam. While abnormalities on these tests may reflect disruption of sensory transmission anywhere within the sensory pathways, when primary sensation (i.e. touch, pain) are intact, a cortical lesion is implicated.

Two-point discrimination

Two-point discrimination (TPD) is tested by using a pair of dull compasses or calipers. The lips, palms of the hand, and the fingertips are areas usually tested. Variable capacity to discriminate distances between two points: Lips (2 – 3 mm); palms (8 – 15 mm); and fingertips (2 – 5 mm). After demonstrating the test to the patient with his eyes open, he is asked to close them and to identify whether he feels one or two stimuli. The two sides of the bodies are then compared. TPD has been reported to be abnormal in some patients with schizophrenia and has been referred to as a 'soft' neurologic sign. The reason for the abnormality is unclear, but a lesion in the proprioceptive sensory system is unlikely.

Traced figures

In the traced figures test (graphesthesia), the patient is asked to identify various numbers or other common symbols or shapes drawn on his fingertips or other areas of the body. The figure does not have to be traced right side up. In *direction of cutaneous kinesthesia* (DCK), the patient is asked to tell the direction of the stimulus drawn on his skin. In a patient with normal peripheral sensation and good cooperation, abnormality in this test implies either contralateral parietal lobe or diffuse cerebral dysfunction (123).

Stereognosis

Stereognosis refers to the ability to recognize an object by feel. Common objects (e.g. safety pins, paper clips, keys) are used. Stereognosis, like two point discrimination and graphesthesia, test overlapping cortical sensory systems.

Localization

In localization, the patient is asked to localize a tactile stimulus. Difficulty in localization (topagnosia) is seen in parietal lobe disorders and dementia.

Extinction

Extinction refers to inability to perceive stimuli on one side when both sides are stimulated (double simultaneous stimulation: DSS). Tactile, painful, or other modalities of stimuli may be used. Diffuse cerebral dysfunction and parietal lobe lesions cause abnormalities in this test. A special case of the DSS is the *face – hand test*. In that test combinations of face and hand stimulation are used. Patients with diffuse encephalopathy consistently extinguish the hand percept, whereas patients with parietal lobe lesions extinguish the contralateral side. There may also be displacement to other body parts or into external space (exosomesthesias) (124). Abnormalities in these tests have been reported in some schizophrenic patients and are discussed together with the other neurologic 'soft' signs.

Reflexes

The elicitation of the muscle stretch reflexes depend on the patient's degree of relaxation and the proper application of the stimuli. Several reflexes may be tested (see Appendix). They are evaluated for hyperactivity, lateralized differences, and grossly pathological responses. Here, the focus will be on the so-called primitive or pathological reflexes. The appearance of these reflexes implies interruption of higher-order (usually cortical) inhibitory neural function. In isolation they are not as meaningful as when they are associated with other neurologic signs (124).

The *glabellar reflex* is elicited by tapping over the glabella which causes reflex closing of the eyes. Care is taken not to be in the patient's field of vision. In normals, there is disappearance of the response after a few taps (1). It can be exaggerated in corticospinal lesions rostral to the seventh cranial nerve nucleus and in extrapyramidal disorders (Myerson's sign). Neuroleptics may cause abnormalities similar to those of parkinsonian patients. The *grasp reflex* is characterized by flexion of the fingers and hand during stimulation of the palmar surface. In advanced dementia, grasp may increase as the examiner attempts to withdraw his hand (forced grasping), or a foot grasp may be present. At times a slight tough of the patient may elicit the response which is accompanied by a reaching motion (groping). A grasp response may be associated with contralateral frontal lobe disease or diffuse cortical dysfunction.

The palmo-mental or pollico-mental reflexes are characterized by contraction of the ipsilateral mentalis and/or orbicularis oris after noxious stimulation (usually a scratch) of the palms or thumbs respectively. It is seen in corticospinal tract lesions, diffuse cortical disorders, and frontal lobe dysfunction; however, the palmomental may be elicited in up to 30% of normals. A sizeable percentage of schizophrenic patients show abnormalities on these tests.

The *snout reflex* refers to pucking and protrusion of the lips in response to forceful pressure to the upper lip. It can also be seen in some normals. The *sucking* response is seen in more advanced cases of dementia when the patient may suck, chew, and even make swallowing movements when a stimulus is presented to his mouth.

In the *cornio-mandibular reflex,* a gentle touch of the patient's cornea leads to slight *opening* of the jaws and lateral deviation of the contralateral mandible.

The head retraction reflex refers to involuntary withdrawal of the head in response to tapping of the upper lip. It is usually seen in diffuse cerebral disorders. Of the tests mentioned above, the grasp and sucking reflexes have the greatest predictive value in terms of identifiable, gross cortical disease.

Neurologic soft signs in schizophrenia

Most of the authors who have used the neurological examination to evaluate patients with schizophrenia have dichotomized the findings into 'hard' and 'soft' neurologic signs (125 – 135). 'Hard' signs have predictive localizing power, usually referrable to specific nuclei, tracts, or nerves. 'Soft' signs represent non-normative performance on less specific tests, none of which by themselves indicate a clearly localizable CNS lesions. Included under 'soft' signs are such phenomena as dysdiadochokinesia, astereognosis, mirror phenomena, choreiform movements, primitive reflexes, diminished dexterity, sensory extinction, and cortical sensory loss. The isolated appearance of a mild 'hard' abnormality such as an extensor plant or response in the absence of other corticospinal tract signs might also be regarded as a 'soft' sign (see Table 3).

Kennard reviewed the charts of 123 psychiatric patients who had complete neurologic examinations including details of various 'soft' neurologic signs (125). She reported that patients with organic features on their examination and those with thought disorders had the highest number of so-called 'soft' or equivocal signs. The organic patients had 5.3 'soft' signs, the schizophrenics 4.6, and the neurotics 2.11. She suggested that these signs are significant and are probably related to dysfunction in subcortical integrating systems such as the basal ganglia or the brainstem (125). Hertzig and Birch reported that neurologic abnormalities occur at a higher frequency in psychotic adolescents of both sexes (126). There was also a strong correlation with sociopathy in adolescent boys (126). Neurologic abnormalities were defined as

TABLE 3   *Neurologic 'soft signs'*

Mental status

Right – left disorientation (self, examiner)	Attention deficit
Extinction on face – hand test	Speech defect
Perseveration, impersistence	

Motor system

Dysdiadokinesia	Impaired hand sequence test
Impairment in finger apposition	Motor and/or postural asymmetries
Poor hopping	Spooning, hypotonia, choreoathetoid
Abnormal gait − inverted feet	movements, mirror phenomena
Abnormal finger tapping	Isolated Babinski sign
Difficulty in manipulating objects	

Cortical sensory signs

Joint kinesthesia − directional kinesthesia	Impaired two-point discrimination
Topognosia	Astereognosis
Agraphesthesia	

Primitive reflexes

Glabellar	Snout
Crasp	Suck
Palmo – mental	

at least one 'hard' sign or two 'soft' signs. Using similar criteria, Rochford and co-workers (127) studied 65 patients (26 schizophrenics, 27 personality disorders, 12 depressives). The authors reported that 29.3% of their patients had neurologic impairments (127). The reviewed studies have consistently reported a frequency that varies between 29% to 80%.

In other studies, patients with schizophrenia have shown more neurologic soft signs than psychiatric patients with affective illness (131, 132) but not more than those with a history of sociopathy (132). Affected monozygotic twins demonstrated more impairment than their discordant siblings (133, 134). These abnormalities also correlated with lower birthweights and neonatal problems (134), premorbid asociality (132), low IQ and severity of illness, chronicity and organicity and large cerebral ventricles on CT (135). Torrey has failed to replicate the asociality data (136). In his study, however, he used 2 items (face – hand test and graphesthesia) (136) while the other authors tested 16 (132). He reported agraphesthesia in the right hand of 10 patients, suggesting left-sided dysfunction in these cases (136).

It has been suggested that these neurologic findings are probably related to intra-uterine or perinatal hypoxia or infections (137, 138). Bellak has postulated that these patients form a neurological subgroup and may be related to minimal brain dysfunction (139). This contention is consistent with the findings of higher frequency of minor physical dysmorphias in some patients (139) similar to those reported in attention deficit disorder (15). However these neurological dysfunctions are probably more consistent with first-trimester intra-uterine damage than with perinatal damage. Most of these studies were done before the advent of the RDC or DSM III. They need to be replicated using modern classification and much larger number of patients. Some 'soft' signs suggest dysfunction of basal ganglia, others of frontal cortex. While the exact meaning of many of these signs is often unclear, they are commonly observed during the clinical exam in schizophrenia.

Conclusion

In this chapter we have presented those features of the clinical neurological examination which might help to detect subtle deficits in neuropsychiatric patients. We have also tried to integrate the reported data on neurologic impairments in schizophrenic patients using that examination paradigm. The application of this examination will facilitate the collection of data about cranial nerve dysfunction, disturbances in motor behavior, and other neurologic signs which can be used for longitudinal and cross-sectional studies in schizophrenia and other psychiatric disorders. By allowing better neurologic subtyping of patients, this approach would assist in the formulation of new etiological hypotheses that would be testable using the available technological advances in neurobiology. A thorough neuropsychiatric examination is recommended in all patients who present with their first psychotic episodes in order to evaluate issues of motor dysfunction which may later be marred by the prolonged use of neuroleptics. Also, we wish to point out that in the presentation of the exam, we have described the so-called 'soft' signs under the systems were we think they belong even though we lumped them together when discussing their presence in schizophrenia. Non-localizability does not imply 'softness' of thinking; only our lack of knowledge has prevented us from deciphering their possible importance.

In the final analysis, however, clinical and research scientists must develop criteria that are of predictive value in practice. In the case of schizophrenia, there has been a multitude of reported abnormalities in the performance of the neurological examination. The findings are often reported in isolation and not integrated with the rest of the examination. This methodological approach has resulted in a confusing array of seemingly disjointed reports, which under closer scrutiny may form the basis for a more comprehensive neurologic hypothesis of schizophrenia. It is hoped that the approach delineated in this chapter will help to further such an understanding.

REFERENCES

1. DeJong RN (1979) *Neurological Examination.* Harper and Row, New York.
2. Strub RL, Black FW (1977) *The Mental Status Examination in Neurology.* F.A. Davis, Philadelphia.
3. Lehman HE (1980) Schizophrenia: clinical features. In: Kaplan HI, Freedman AM, Sadock BJ (Eds), *Comprehensive Textbook of Psychiatry, 3rd Ed, Vol 11*, pp. 1153 – 1192. Williams and Wilkins, Baltimore.
4. Hayden MR (1981) *Huntington's Chorea.* Springer-Verlag, New York.
5. Riccardi VM (1981) Von Recklinghausen neurofibromatosis. *N. Engl. J. Med., 305,* 1617.
6. Scheinberg IH, Sternlieb I (1984) *Wilson's Disease.* W.B. Saunders, Philadelphia.
7. Pampligione G, Moynahan EJ (1976) The tuberous sclerosis syndrome: clinical and EEG studies in 100 children. *J. Neurol. Neurosurg. Psychiatry, 39,* 666.
8. Austin J (1979) Some mechanisms of disease in metachromatic leukodystrophy (MLD). In: Goldens E, Appel S (Eds), *Scientific Approaches to Clinical Neurology,* pp. 342 – 362. Lea and Febiger, Philadelphia.
9. Myrianthropoulos NC (1981) Neurogenetic Directory, Part I. In: Vinken PJ, Bruyn GW (Eds), *Handbook of Clinical Neurology, Vol 42.* Elsevier/North-Holland Publishing Co., Amsterdam.
10. DeGowin EL, DeGowin RL (1981) *Bedside Diagnostic Examination.* MacMillan, New York.
11. Duvoisin RC, Yahr MD (1965) Encephalitis and Parkinsonism. *Arch. Neurol., 12,* 227.
12. Coulam CM, Brown LR, Reese DF (1976) Sturge-Weber syndrome. *Semin. Roentgenol., 11,* 55.
13. Farmer TW (1979) Neurologic complication of vitamin and mineral disorders. In: Baker AB, Baker LH (Eds), *Clinical Neurology, Vol IV, Ch 60,* pp. 1 – 31. Harper and Row, Philadelphia.
14. Waldrop M, Bell R, McLaughlin B, Halverson CF (1978) Newborn minor physical anomalies predict short attention span, peer aggression, and impulsivity at age 3. *Science, 199,* 563.
15. Rapoport JL, Ruinn PO, Lamprecht F (1974) Minor physical anomalies and plasma

dopamine beta hydroxylase activity in hyperactive boys. *Am. J. Psychiatry, 131,* 387.

16. Folstein MF, Folstein SW, McHough (1975) 'Mini-Mental State': a practical method of grading the cognitive state of patients for the clinician. *J. Psychiatr. Res., 12,* 189.
17. Plum F, Posner JB (1980) *The Diagnosis of Stupor and Coma.* F.A. Davis, Philadelphia.
18. Hawkes CH (1974) 'Locked in' syndrome: report of seven cases. *Br. Med. J., 4,* 372.
19. Gelenberg AJ (1976) The catatonic syndrome. *Lancet, 1,* 1339.
20. Frickhione GL (1985) Neuroleptic catatonia and its relationship to psychogenic catatonia. *Biol. Psychiatry, 20,* 304.
21. Bender MB (1979) Defects in reversal of serial order of symbols. *Neuropsychologia, 17,* 125.
22. Weinstein EA, Kahn RL (1955) *Denial of Illness.* Charles C Thomas, Springfield, IL.
23. Frederiks JAM (1969) Disorders of the body schema. In: Vinken PJ, Bruyn GW (Eds), *Handbook of Clinical Neurology, Vol 4,* pp. 207 – 240. Elsevier/North-Holland Publishing Co., Amsterdam.
24. Bleuler E (1950) *Dementia Praecox or the Group of Schizophrenias.* International University Press, New York.
25. Kraepelin E (1919) In: Robertson GM (Ed), *Dementia Praecox and Paraphrenia.* E.S. Livingstone, Edinburgh.
26. Rosvold HE, Mirsky AF, Sareson I, Bransome ED, Beck LH (1956) A continuous performance test of brain damage. *Psychology, 20,* 343.
27. Kornetsky C (1972) The use of a simple test of attention as a measure of drug effects in schizophrenic patients. *Psychopharmacologia, 8,* 99.
28. Wohlberg GW, Kornetsky C (1973) Sustained attention in remitted schizophrenics. *Arch. Gen. Psychiatry, 28,* 533.
29. Kornetsky C, Orzack MH (1978) Physiological and behavior correlates of attention dysfunction in schizophrenia. In: Wynne LC, Gromwell S, Matthysse (Eds), *The Nature of Schizophrenia: New Approaches to Research and Treatment,* pp. 196 – 204. John Wiley and Sons, New York.
30. Zahn TP (1975) Psychophysiological concomitants of task performance in schizophrenia. In: Kretzman ML, Sutton S, Zubin J (Eds), *Experimental Approaches to Psychopathology.* Academic Press, New York.
31. Venables PH (1978) *Schizophrenia: Towards a New Synthesis,* pp. 117 – 137. Academic Press, Inc., London.
32. Mirsky AF (1969) Neuropsychological bases of schizophrenia. *Annu. Rev. Psychol., 20,* 321.
33. Kornetsky C, Eliasson M (1969) Reticular stimulation and chlorpromazine: an animal model for schizophrenic over arousal. *Science, 165,* 1273.
34. Heilman KM, Valenstein E (1972) Frontal lobe neglect in man. *Neurology, 22,* 660.
35. Mesulam MM, Geschwind N (1978) On the possible role of neocortex and its limbic connections in the process of attention and schizophrenia: clinical cases of inattention in man and experimental anatomy in monkey. *J. Psychiatr. Res., 14,* 249.
36. Mesulam MM (1981) A cortical network for directed attention and unilateral neglect. *Ann. Neurol., 10,* 309.
37. Damasio AR, Damasio H, Chui HC (1980) Neglect following damage to frontal lobe or basal ganglia. *Neuropsychologia, 13,* 123.
38. Watson RT, Valenstein E, Heilman KM (1981) Thalamic neglect: possible role of the medial thalamus and nucleus reticularis in behavior. *Arch. Neurol., 38,* 501.

39. Flor-Henry P (1979) On certain aspects of the localization of the cerebral systems regulating and determining emotion. *Biol. Psychiatry, 14,* 677.

40. Weinberger DR (1984) Computed Tomography (CT) findings in schizophrenia: speculation on the meaning of it all. *J. Psychiatr. Res., 18,* 477.

41. Cadet JL (1984) Disorders of the isodendritic core of the brainstem. *Schizophr. Bull., 10,* 1.

42. Stevens J (1982) Neuropathology of schizophrenia. *Arch. Gen. Psychiatry, 39,* 1131.

43. Bogerts B, Hantsch J, Herzer M (1983) A morphometric study of the dopamine-containing cell group in the mesencephalon of normals, Parkinson patients, and schizophrenics. *Biol. Psychiatry, 9,* 951.

44. Weinberger DR, Berman KF, Zec RF (1986) Physiological dysfunction of dorsolateral prefrontal cortex in schizophrenia. I: Regional cerebral blood flow (rCBF) evidence. *Arch. Gen. Psychiatry, 44,* 114.

45. Heilman KM, Watson RT, Bowers D (1983) Affective disorders associated with hemispheric diseases. In: Heilman KM, Satz P (Eds), *Neuropsychology of Human Emotion.* pp. 45 – 64. The Guildford Press, New York.

46. Albert ML, Feldman RG, Willis AL (1974) The subcortical dementia of progressive supranuclear palsy. *J. Neurol. Neurosurg. Psychiatry, 37,* 121.

47. Binder RL (1983) Neurologically silent brain tumors in psychiatric hospital admissions: three cases and a review. *J. Clin. Psychiatry, 44,* 94.

48. Ross ED (1981) The aprosodias - functional anatomic organization of the affective components of language in the right hemisphere. *Arch. Neurol., 38,* 571.

49. Morel F (1936) Des bruits d'oreille, des bourdonnements, des hallucinations auditives élémentaires, communes, et verbales. *Encéphale, 31,* 81.

50. Lippman GW (1952) Certain hallucinations peculiar to migraine. *J. Nerv. Ment. Dis., 116,* 346.

51. Lukianowicz N (1967) 'Body image' disturbances in psychiatric disorders. *Br. J. Psychiatry, 113,* 31.

52. Goodwin DW, Alderson P, Rosenthal R (1971) Clinical significance of hallucinations in psychiatric disorders. *Arch. Gen. Psychiatry, 24,* 76.

53 Lechtenberg R, Gilman S (1978) Speech disorders in cerebellar disease. *Ann. Neurol., 3,* 285.

54. Critchley EMR (1981) Speech disorders of Parkinsonism: a review. *J. Neurol. Neurosurg. Psychiatry, 44,* 751.

55. Benson DF (1979) *Aphasia, Alexia, and Agraphia.* Churchill Livingstone, New York.

56. Rumke HC, Nijam SJ (1958) Aphasia and delusion. *Folia Psychiatr. Neurol. Neurochir. Neerl., 61,* 623.

57. Critchley M (1964) The neurology of psychotic speech. *Br. J. Psychiatry, 110,* 353.

58. Chaika E (1974) A linguist looks at 'Schizophrenic' language. *Brain Lang., 1,* 257.

59. Fromkin VA (1975) A linguist looks at 'schizophrenic language'. *Brain Lang., 2,* 498.

60. Lecours AR, Vanier-Clement M (1976) Schizophasia and jargonophasia: a comparative description with comments on Chaika's and Fromkin's respective looks at 'schizophrenic' language. *Brain Lang., 3,* 516.

61. Carpenter MD (1976) Sensitivity to syntactic structure: good versus poor premorbid schizophrenics. *J. Abnorm. Psychol., 85,* 41.

62. Knight RA, Sims-Knight JE (1979) Integration of linguist ideas in schizophrenics. *J. Abnorm. Psychol., 88,* 191.

63. Fish FJ (1967) *Clinical Psychopathology.* Wright, Bristol.

64. Grove WM, Andreasen NC (1985) Language and thinking in psychosis: is there an input abnormality? *Arch. Gen. Psychiatry, 42,* 26.
65. Chaika E (1977) Schizophrenic speech, slips of the tongue and jargonophasia: a reply to Fromkin and to Lecours and Vannier Clement. *Brain Lang., 4,* 464.
66. Andreasen NC (1979) Thought, language, and communication disorders: clinical assessment definition of terms, and evaluation of their reliability. *Arch. Gen. Psychiatry, 36,* 1315.
67. Schwartz S (1982) Is there a schizophrenic language? *Behav. Brain Sci., 5,* 579.
68. Chaika E (1982) A unified explanation for the structural deviations reported in the speech of adult schizophrenics. *J. Commun. Disord., 15,* 167.
69. Gur RE (1978) Left hemisphere dysfunction and left hemisphere overactivation in schizophrenia. *J. Abnorm. Psychol., 87,* 226.
70. Mazzochi F, Vignolo LA (1979) Localization of lesions in aphasia: clinical CT scan correlations in stroke patients. *Cortex, 15,* 627.
71. Mohr JP, Walters W, Duncan GW (1975) Thalamic hemorrhage and aphasia. *Brain Lang., 2,* 3.
72. Damasio AR, Damasio H, Rizzo M, Varney N, Gersh F (1982) Aphasia with non-hemorrhagic lesions in the basal ganglia and internal capsule. *Arch. Neurol., 39,* 15.
73. Lezak MD (1983) *Neuropsychological assessment.* Oxford University Press, New York.
74. Critchley M (1955) *The Parietal Lobes.* Hafner Press, New York.
75. Adams RD, Victor M (1981) *Principles of Neurology.* McGraw-Hill, New York.
76. Harriman DGF, Garland H (1968) The pathology of Adie's syndrome. *Brain, 91,* 401.
77. Schilder P (1931) Pupillary disturbances in schizophrenic negroes. *Arch. Neurol. Psychiatry, 25,* 838.
78. Schilder P (1942) The effects of drugs on the catatonic pupil. *J. Nerv. Ment. Dis., 96,* 1.
79. Bender MB, Rudolph SH, Stacy CB (1984) The neurology of the visual and oculomotor system. In: Baker AB, Baker LH (Eds), *Clinical Neurology. Vol I, Ch 12.* Harper and Row, Philadelphia.
80. Stevens J (1978) Disturbances of ocular movements and blinking in schizophrenia. *J. Neurol. Neurosurg. Psychiatry, 41,* 1024.
81. Cegalis JA, Sweeney JA (1979) Eye movements in schizophrenics: a quantitative analysis. *Biol. Psychiatry, 14,* 13.
82. Karson CN (1983) Spontaneous blink rates and dopaminergic systems. *Brain, 106,* 643.
83. Klawans HL, Goodwin JA (1962) Reversal of the glabellar reflex in Parkinsonism by L-dopa. *J. Neurol. Neurosurg. Psychiatry, 25,* 93.
84. Ponder E, Kennedy WP (1927) On the act of blinking. *Q. J. Exp. Physiol., 18,* 89.
85. Hiraoka M, Shimamura M (1977) Neural mechanisms of the corneal blinking reflex in cats. *Brain Res., 125,* 265.
86. Levin S (1984) Frontal lobe dysfunction in schizophrenia. I. Eye movements impairments. *J. Psychiatr. Res., 18,* 27.
87. Holtzman PS, Proctor LR, Levy DL, Yasillo NJ, Meltzer HY, Hart SW (1974) Eye tracking dysfunctions in schizophrenic patients and their relatives. *Arch. Gen. Psychiatry, 31,* 143.
88. Levin S, Jones A, Stark L, Merrin EL, Holzman PS (1982) Saccadic eye movements of schizophrenic patients measured by reflected light techniques. *Biol. Psychiatry, 17,* 1277.
89. Stark L (1983) Abnormal patterns of normal eye movements in schizophrenia. *Schizophr. Bull., 9,* 55.

90. Baloh RW, Konrad HR, Honrubia V (1975) Vestibulo-ocular function in patients with cerebellar atrophy. *Neurology, 25,* 160.
91. Avanzini G, Girotti F, Caraceni T, Spreafico R (1979) Oculomotor disorders in Huntington's chorea. *J. Neurol. Neurosurg. Psychiatry, 42,* 581.
92. Leigh JR, Zee D (1982) The diagnostic value of abnormal eye movements: a pathophysiological approach. *Johns Hopkins Med. J., 151,* 122.
93. Weinberger DR and Wyatt RJ (1982) Computed tomography (CT) findings in schizophrenia: clinical and biological implications. In: Perris C, Struwe G, Jansson B (Eds), *Biological Psychiatry 1981,* pp. 255 – 258. Elsevier/North-Holland, Amsterdam.
94. Chorobski J (1951) The syndrome of crocodile tears. *Arch. Neurol., 65,* 299.
95. Claude H, Baruk H, Aubry M (1927) Contribution a l'étude de la démence précoce: inexcitabilité labysinthique au cours de la catatonie. *Rev. Neurol., 1,* 976.
96. Angyal A, Blackman N (1940) Vestibular reactivity in schizophrenia. *Arch. Neurol. Psychiatry, 44,* 611.
97. Levy DL, Holtzman PS, Proctor LR (1981) Vestibular responses in schizophrenia. *Arch. Gen. Psychiatry, 35,* 972.
98. Levy DL, Holtzman PS, Proctor LR (1983) Vestibular dysfunction and psychopathology. *Schizophr. Bull., 9,* 383.
99. Moore MT, Bask MH (1970) Sudden death in phenothiazine therapy. *Psychiatr. Q., 44,* 383.
100. Craig TJ, Richardson MA, Pass R, Haugland G (1983) Impairment of the gag reflex in schizophrenic inpatients. *Comp. Psychiatry, 24,* 514.
101. Duvoisin RC (1984) *Parkinson's Disease: a Guide for Patient and Family.* Raven Press, New York.
102. Bieger D, Giles SA, Hockman CH (1977) Dopaminergic influences on swallowing. *Neuropharmacology, 16,* 245.
103. Medical Research Council (1976) *Aids to the Examination of the Peripheral Nervous System.* Her Majesty's Stationary Office, London.
104. Young AB, Penney JB (1984) Neurochemical anatomy of movement disorders. *Neurol. Clin., 2,* 417.
105. Klawans HL, Moses H, Nausieda PA, Bergen D, Weiner WJ (1976) Treatment and prognosis of hemiballismus. *N. Engl. J. Med., 295,* 1348.
106. Fahn S (1982) Torsion dystonia: clinical spectrum and treatment. *Semin. Neurol., 2,* 316.
107. Sheehy MP, Marsden CD (1982) Writers' cramp - a focal dystonia. *Brain, 105,* 461.
108. Manschreck TC, Maher BA, Rucklos ME, Vereen DR (1982) Disturbed voluntary motor activity in schizophrenic disorder. *Psychol. Med., 12,* 73.
109. Manschreck TC, Ames D (1984) Neurological features and psychopathology in schizophrenic disorders. *Biol. Psychiatry, 19,* 703.
110. Marsden CD, Tarsy D, Baldessarini RJ (1975) Spontaneous and drug-induced movement disorders in psychotic patients. In: Benson DF, Blumer D (Eds). *Psychiatric Aspects of Neurologic Disease,* pp. 219 – 266. Grune and Stratton, New York.
111. Butler IJ (1984) Tourette's syndrome: some new concepts. *Neurol. Clin., 2,* 571.
112. Morrison JR (1975) Catatonia: retarded and excited types. *Arch. Gen. Psychiatry, 28,* 39.
113. Marsden CD, Hallett M, Fahn S (1982) Nosology and pathophysiology of myoclonus. In: Marsden CD, Fahn S (Eds), *Movement Disorders.* Butterworth, London.
114. Matsuo F, Ajax ET (1979) Palatal myoclonus and denervation supersensitivity in the central nervous system. *Ann. Neurol., 5,* 72.

115. Lance JW (1977) Familial paroxysmal dystonic choreoathetosis and its differentiation from related syndromes. *Ann. Neurol., 2,* 285.
116. Slater E, Roth M (1969) *Clinical Psychiatry.* Bailliere, Tindall, and Cassell, London.
117. Cantor S, Pearce J, Pezzot-Pearce T, Evans J (1981) The group of hypotonic schizophrenics. *Schizophr. Bull., 7,* 1.
118. Taylor MA (1976) Catatonia: a prospective clinical study. *Arch. Gen. Psychiatry, 33,* 579.
119. Lesser RD, Fahn S (1978) Dystonia: a disorder often diagnosed as a conversion reaction. *Am. J. Psychiatry, 153,* 349.
120. Meyer JS, Barron WD (1960) Apraxia of gait: a clinical physiological study of frontal lobe apraxia. *Brain, 83,* 261.
121. Fisher CM (1982) Hydrocephalus as a cause of gait disturbance in the elderly. *Neurology, 32,* 1358.
122. Bender MB, Stacy C, Cohen J (1982) Agraphesthesia: a disorder of cutaneous kinesthesia or a disorientation in cutaneous space. *J. Neurol. Sci., 53,* 531.
123. Shapiro MF, Fink M, Bender MB (1952) Exosomesthesia or displacement into external space. *Arch. Neurol. Psychiatry, 68,* 481.
124. Jenkyn LR, Walsh DB, Culver CM, Reeves AG (1977) Clinical signs in diffuse cerebral dysfunction. *J. Nerv. Ment. Dis., 40,* 956.
125. Kennard M (1960) Value of equivocal signs in neurologic diagnosis. *Neurology, 10,* 753.
126. Hertzig ME, Birch HG (1968) Neurologic organization in psychiatrically disturbed adolescents: a comparative consideration of sex differences. *Arch. Gen. Psychiatry, 19,* 528.
127. Rochford JM, Detre T, Tucker GJ, Hanow M (1970) Neuropsychological impairments in functional psychiatric diseases. *Arch. Gen. Psychiatry, 22,* 111.
128. Cox SM, Ludwig AM (1979) Neurologic soft signs and psychopathology: findings in schizophrenia. *J. Nerv. Ment. Dis., 167,* 161.
129. Hertzig ME, Birch HG (1968) Neurologic organization in psychiatrically disturbed adolescents: a comparative consideration of sex differences. *Arch. Gen. Psychiatry, 19,* 528.
130. Tucker GJ, Campion EW, Kelleher PA, Silberfarb P (1974) The relationship of subtle neurologic impairments to disturbances of thinking. *Psychother. Psychosom., 24,* 165.
131. Walker E (1981) Attentional and neuromotor functions of schizophrenics, schizoaffectives and patients with other affective disorders. *Arch. Gen. Psychiatry, 38,* 1355.
132. Quitkin F, Rifkin A, Klein DF (1976) Neurologic soft signs in schizophrenia and character disorders: organicity in schizophrenia with premorbid asociality and unstable character disorders. *Arch. Gen. Psychiatry, 33,* 845.
133. Mosher LR, Pollin W, Stabeneau JR (1971) Identical twins discordant for schizophrenia. *Arch. Gen. Psychiatry, 29,* 422.
134. Pollin W, Stabeneau JR, Mosher L (1966) Life history differences in identical twins discordant for schizophrenia. *Am. J. Orthopsychiatry, 36,* 492.
135. Weinberger DR, Wyatt RJ (1982) Cerebral ventricular size: a biological marker for subtyping chronic schizophrenia. In: Hanin PI, Usdin E (Eds), *Biological Markers in Psychiatry and Neurology,* pp. 485 – 493. Pergamon Press, Ltd, New York.
136. Torrey EF (1980) Neurological abnormalities in schizophrenic patients. *Biol. Psychiatry, 15,* 381.
137. Handford HA (1975) Brain hypoxia, minimal brain dysfunction and schizophrenia. *Am. J. Psychiatry, 132,* 192.

138. Bellak L (1979) Schizophrenic syndrome related to minimal brain dysfunction: a possible neurologic sub-group. *Schizophr. Bull., 5,* 480.
139. Guy JD, Majorski LV, Wallace CJ, Guy MP (1983) The incidence of minor physical anomalies in adult male schizophrenics. *Schizophr. Bull., 9,* 571.

APPENDIX

Neurologic examination

Skull
microcephaly	epicanthal folds
macrocephaly	proptosis

Neck

tone   carotid exam

Spine

scoliosis
lordosis
spasm

Skin

neurocutaneous syndrome stigmata

Mental status

Alertness   Alert   lethargic   stuporous   comatose

Attention

'A' test: ANBAIFSAMRZEOAD PAKLAUCJTOEABAH
Digit span
Serial '7' or '3' subtraction
Backward spelling (earth, world, hold, bat)

Hemi-inattention, hemi-neglect (double simultaneous stimulation), denial

Face – hand test

Orientation

Person	name	birthdate	age		
Place	home	hospital unit	country		
Time	date	day	month	season	year
Visuospatial	map localization				

Affect   Appropriate   yes   no

Mood

happy   sad   depressed   normal

Thought content

Thought organization

To be continued

Appendix (*cont.*)

Perceptual disturbances

Hallucinations   unformed   formed
  auditory
  gustatory
  somatic
  olfactory
Illusions
  micropsia   macropsia
  teleopsia   palinopsia

Language testing
Spontaneous speech
  slurred
  articulation   fluency   grammar
  paraphasias

Comprehension
  Is it sunny, today?
  Is Carter from Louisiana?
  3 point command: Raise your hand, close your eye, stick out your tongue

Repetition
  United States of America
  No ifs, ands, or buts

Confrontation naming
  Colors
  Body parts   eye   wrist   elbow   foot
  Objects   ceiling   coat lapel   watch stem pen belt buckle

Reading
  aloud (paralexias, other aphasic errors, etc.)
  comprehension

Writing
  Spontaneous
  To dictation

Spelling

Praxis
  Blow out a match
  Comb your hair
  Drink through a straw
  Put toothpaste on a brush and brush your teeth

  Copy diagrams   △   □   ∿

To be continued

Appendix (*cont.*)

Memory

3 words	immediate	5 minutes	10 minutes
Remote	last war	5 presidents	breakfast, current events

Cowboy story

Hidden objects

Calculations

Addition:

$$53 \qquad 58 \qquad 8$$
$$+\,32 \qquad +\,27 \qquad +\,9$$

Subtraction:

$$782 \qquad 78 \qquad 9$$
$$-\,8 \qquad -\,54 \qquad -\,6$$

Multiplication: $6 \times 7 = \qquad 13 \times 5 = \qquad 12 \times 13 =$

Division: $6 : 2 \qquad 81 : 3 \qquad 483 : 21$

Proverbs
Don't cry over spilled milk
A golden hammer breaks an iron door
The hot coal burns; the cold one blackens

Similarities
car − airplane
desk − bookshelf
poetry − novel

Differences
water − store
summer − winter

Right − left orientation
Show me your right foot/left arm
Touch your left ear with your right thumb
Show me my left hand/right knee
Point to my left knee with your left thumb

Perseveration of speech and/or actions

Impersistence of speech and/or actions

Cranial nerves

I.   *Olfactory*

II.   *Optic*
            Visual acuity corrected   OS   OD
                          uncorrected

To be continued

Appendix (*cont.*)

Fundoscopy
Keyser-Fleischer rings
Confrontation fields

III, IV, VI.   *Oculomotor, trochlear, abducens*
     Ptosis   Horner's syndrome
     Pupils   shape   size   reflexes   consensual   accommodation
       R
       L

     Eye movements
       Pursuit   saccades   nystagmus

V.   *Trigeminal*
     Corneal reflex   sensory   motor
       R
       L

VII.   *Facial*
     emotional
     volitional

VIII.   *Acoustic*
     hearing

     Vestibular
     nystagmus

IX, X.   *Glossopharyngeal, vagus*
     gag reflex
     palate movement
     swallowing

XI.   *Spinal accessory*
     Trapezius, sternocleistomastoid

XII.   *Hypoglossal*
     Atrophy/fasciculations

     Tongue protrusion   Spontaneous protrusion
       R midline L
     dyskinesia

Motor

Fasciculations	size	bulk	asymmetries
Contracture	tenderness	atrophy	

To be continued

45

Appendix (*cont.*)

Tone	Hypotonia	Hypertonia
	Rigidity	Spasm
	Spasticity	Paratonia

Strength 0 – 5
Drift 0–5

Coordination
   Finger-nose
   Finger-nose-finger
   Past pointing
   Skilled actions, fine motor
   Rapid alternating movements
   Hand sequence
   Heel to shin

Gait and station

   Standing
      on one foot

   Romberg

   Walking
      Arm swing
      Tandem
      Hopping

Involuntary movements

Tremor	sustention	resting	action
chorea			
athetosis			
myoclonus		palatal	
dystonia			
torticollis	retrocollis	anterocollis	
Paroxysmal dyskinesia			

Sensation

Primary
   pin   light touch   vibration   position

Cortical
   Two-point
   Graphesthesias
   Localization
   Extinction
   Stereognosis

To be continued

Appendix (*cont.*)

Reflexes	Right	Left
Deep tendon		
Biceps		
Brachioradialis		
Triceps		
Patellar		
Achilles		
Plantar		
Finger flexors		
Hoffman		
Release signs		
Snout		
Suck		
Grasp		
Glabellar		

CHAPTER 2

The differential diagnosis of schizophrenia: genetic, perinatal, neurological, pharmacological and psychiatric factors

HENRY A. NASRALLAH

Schizophrenia is a heterogeneous syndrome (1). This fact was originally acknowledged by Bleuler (2), who coined the term 'schizophrenias' to describe a group of disorders of divergent etiologies which share a common clinical presentation. However, the criteria used to diagnose schizophrenia have been generally vague and unreliable for most of the past hundred years. Until the development of operational criteria such as the Research Diagnostic Criteria (RDC) (3) or DSM-III (4), almost any patient presenting with psychotic features, including bipolar affective illness, was labeled schizophrenic. It is not surprising, therefore, that research findings were frequently inconsistent and unreplicable, as the 'schizophrenic' populations studied were usually quite different and heterogeneous in composition.

It is now widely accepted that schizophrenia is a manifestation of a brain disease (5) in a final common pathway for many disorders of genetic and/or acquired origin, all of which impair brain function in a similar manner to produce some or many of the psychotic and non-psychotic signs and symptoms that are now included in the diagnosis of schizophrenia.

Attempts to 'localize' schizophrenia in the brain have generally fallen short, although there is considerable evidence for frontal, temporal and limbic involvement, and a general impairment of the brain's integrative functions (6). Yet, it seems that lesions in almost any part of the brain, be they traumatic, cerebrovascular, neoplastic, degenerative or metabolic, can produce schizophrenia-like illness. Thus, the issue of localization remains confusing and elusive.

In this chapter, an overview of a variety of genetic and non-genetic neurological, medical and psychiatric disorders which constitute the differential diagnosis of schizophrenia will be presented. The thrust of the review is to underline the pitfalls of the clinical diagnosis of 'true schizophrenia' and the serious difficulties which diagnostic problems may impose on the conduct of valid and meaningful research into the neurobiology of schizophrenia. Emphasis is laid on the need to carefully assess a psychotic patient for genetic disorders, perinatal brain insults, neurological disorders, medical illnesses and drug-intake history, because a wide variety of disorders in these areas may masquerade as schizophrenia, both cross-sectionally and longitudinally, and may receive inappropriate treatment because of a misdiagnosis that can, at times, be very hard to avoid due to the subtlety of the cues.

Handbook of Schizophrenia, Vol. 1: The Neurology of Schizophrenia.
H.A. Nasrallah and D.R. Weinberger, editors.
© Elsevier Science Publishers B.V., 1986.

Genetic disorders that may resemble schizophrenia

There exists a substantial body of evidence from family, twin and adoption studies that schizophrenia, especially the chronic, 'process' hebephrenic subtype, is hereditary (7). However, the nature of the genetic transmission is still uncertain, and different studies disagree on the extent of genetic transmission in schizophrenia. As will be seen in the rest of this chapter, the fact that a variety of acquired disorders may present with a schizophrenia-like picture is certainly a common source of 'false-negative' findings in the genetic studies of schizophrenia. Conversely, the various genetic disorders which may present with features similar to schizophrenia (i.e. a schizophrenia phenotype) probably contribute a serious confounding factor of 'false-positive' in some genetic studies of schizophrenia. A number of genetic disorders have been reported in the literature to present, occasionally, with psychotic manifestations that may be difficult to distinguish from schizophrenia; these are listed in Table 1.

All the genetic disorders listed in Table 1 have been reported at least once to present with psychotic features resembling schizophrenia. Given the genetic transmission of these disorders, their chronic course, and that more than one member of the family may present with schizophrenia-like features, it may be very easy to diagnose such patients as having 'true' familial schizophrenia.

It is also possible that some of the old reports of dysmorphic facial and body shape and appearance in some schizophrenic patients may have been due to patients with other genetic disorders presenting (and misdiagnosed) as schizophrenia, prompting an association between schizophrenia and dysmorphic body patterns.

TABLE 1   *Genetic disorders that may present with a schizophrenia-like psychosis*

1. Albinism (8)	15. Kartagener's syndrome (24)
2. Asperger's syndrome (9)	16. Klinefelter karyotype (25, 26)
3. Ataxia, dominant type (10)	17. Laurence-Moon-Biedl syndrome (27)
4. Congenital adrenal hyperplasia (11)	18. Metachromatic leukodystrophy, adult type (28 – 30)
5. Erythropoietic protoporphyria (12)	
6. Fabry's disease (13)	19. Niemann-Pick's disease, late type (31)
7. Familial basal ganglia calcification (14, 15)	20. Phenylketonuria (32 – 34)
8. Glucose-6-phosphate dehydrogenase deficiency (16, 17)	21. Porphyria, acute intermittent type (35 – 37)
9. Gaucher's disease (18)	22. Porphyria variegata (38)
10. Hemochromatosis (19)	23. 18q or r (18) constitution (39 – 40)
11. Homocystinuria (20)	24. Turner or Noonan syndrome (41 – 46)
12. Huntington's chorea (21)	
13. Hyperasparaginemia (22)	25. Wilson's disease (47 – 48)
14. Ichthyosis vulgaris (autosomal dominant type) (23)	26. XXX Karyotype (49 – 51)
	27. XXX Karyotype (52 – 54)

Perinatal factors that may contribute or lead to the development of a schizophrenia-like illness in adulthood

There are numerous obstetric pre-, peri-, and neonatal problems that may directly or indirectly compromise brain structure and function, and that may lead to the development of a schizophrenia-like disorder in adulthood in otherwise non-predisposed individuals. On the other hand, many investigators have assumed that there is a higher frequency of such perinatal brain insults in the children of schizophrenic parents, i.e. that adverse perinatal events may facilitate the development of schizophrenic psychosis in genetically predisposed 'at-risk' individuals. McNeil and Kaij (55) comprehensively reviewed the literature as well as their own studies on this subject to test the following hypotheses that they constructed: (a) there is no relationship between obstetric complications (OC) and schizophrenia; (b) OC may decrease the risk for schizophrenia; (c) OC increase the risk for schizophrenia as well as for other disorders; (d) there is a specific type of OC that increase the risk for all types of schizophrenia; (e) OC increase the risk for one sub-type of schizophrenia but not others; (f) OC are 'organic phenocopies' of true 'genetic' schizophrenia; (g) OC combined with a genetic loading for schizophrenia have an additive, not a multiplicative effect, for the development of schizophrenia; (h) OC and genetic factors combine in more than an additive manner to increase the risk for schizophrenia i.e. OC 'trigger' the genetic predisposition for schizophrenia; (i) OC interact with or add to other environmental factors to increase the risk for schizophrenia; (j) OC have an independent 'stressful' effect on the offspring, thus increasing the risk for schizophrenia; (k) OC are a non-etiological epiphenomenon, i.e. they are a direct consequence of other factors associated with schizophrenia (e.g. genetic) and have no independent stressful effects that increase the risk for schizophrenia; and (l) OC are a secondary consequence of other factors associated with schizophrenia (such as maternal medications, environmental conditions etc.) but that OC have etiologic effects that increase the risk for schizophrenia in the offspring.

McNeil and Kaij concluded that while OC are not the only factor in the etiology of schizophrenia, they are a 'risk-increasing factor to be taken seriously in the etiology of schizophrenia', and that further studies are needed to clarify how OC interact with other factors such as genetic loading, premorbid characteristics of schizophrenics, and environmental factors. Table 2 shows some of the obstetric and perinatal complications that should be considered in research of the role of OC in the development of schizophrenia-like psychosis.

In the study of McNeil and Kaij (1978), the obstetric complications which were significantly more frequent in process schizophrenia than in controls included low birthweight, asphyxia, respiratory distress, jaundice, pre-eclampsia, inertia of labor and pre-term/immaturity.

Jacobson and Kinney (56) reported that long labor was the most frequent complication in adopted and non-adopted schizophrenics compared to control subjects.

Parnas et al. (57) reported that in a prospective study of the offspring of

51

schizophrenic mothers, those offspring who became schizophrenic in adulthood were found to have had significantly more pregnancy and birth complications than the offspring who did not suffer from mental illness or were diagnosed as having 'borderline' schizophrenia.

In the study of the neurobiological antecedents of schizophrenia in children, Fish (58) presented evidence for a fluctuating dysregulation of maturation or 'pan-developmental retardation', which includes physical growth, gross motor, visual-motor, and cognitive development, proprioceptive and vestibular responses, muscle tone and arousal. However, she found that this pan-developmental retardation was significantly related to a genetic history for schizophrenia but not to obstetric complications. These findings would suggest that if certain perinatal complications do predispose to schizophrenia-like disorders in adulthood, then early neurodevelop-

TABLE 2   *Obstetric and perinatal complications that may be associated with the development of schizophrenia-like psychosis*

Prenatal factors (during pregnancy)

Maternal age above 39 years	Albuminuria
Nulliparous parity (first pregnancy is at higher risk)	Generalized edema
	Medication intake other than vitamins
Viral infection	Maternal diabetes or seizure disorder
Previous abortions	Venous thrombosis
Anemia	Psychiatric illness requiring medical attention
Bleeding	
Physical injury	Gestation under 36 weeks
Hypertension	

Perinatal (labor and delivery) factors

Long labor	Meconium in the amniotic fluid
Breech presentation	Meconium aspirated
Cesarean section	Physical trauma ex. fractures to the newborn
Twins or multiple births	
General or epidural anesthesia	Large placental infarcts
Abruptio placentae	Calcified placenta
Occult prolapse or neck-knot of cord	Birthweight under 2500 g or above 4000 g
Vacuum extraction	
Use of forceps	Postmaturity (greater than 44 weeks)
Apgar score under 6	Hemolytic disease

Neonatal factors

Respiratory distress	Convulsions
Septicemia/meningitis	Difficulty regulating temperature
Hyperbilirubinemia	Clinical dysmaturity
Anemia requiring transfusion	Hypoxia
Irritable or floppy infant	Oxygen treatment

mental antecedents may not be observed in infancy, and thus cannot be used for predicting development of psychotic illness in adulthood.

The issue of pregnancy and birth complications and their possible role in the development of schizophrenia-like illness in adulthood was taken a step further by Boklage (59), who postulated that discordance for schizophrenia in some monozygotic twins (frequently attributed to psychosocial influences) may be due to changes in cerebral asymmetry, possibly related to intrauterine or birth-stress factors. He points to the discordance for handedness in monozygotic twins discordant for schizophrenia (with the left-handed over-reported among the schizophrenic twins) which is not observed in dizygotic twins discordant for schizophrenia. Furthermore, in monozygotic twins concordant for schizophrenia, both twins tend to be concordant for handedness (usually right). The implication of Boklage's model is that anomalous motoric lateralization in monozygotic twins discordant for schizophrenia suggests the possibility of an intrauterine or neonatal brain insult (60) in the schizophrenic twin, or perhaps as a result of 'mirror-imaging' which is not uncommon in monozygotic twins (61).

Luchins et al. (62) confirmed Boklage's findings and reported that schizophrenia in discordant monozygotic twins is related to anomalous cerebral lateralization, has a less severe course and better prognosis than the schizophrenia observed in concordant monozygotic twins, which tends to be of the poor prognosis 'process' type. Such observations may assist in the differential diagnosis of schizophrenia-like illness that may be associated with early bio-environmental (obstetrical) factors vs. 'true' schizophrenia, which is probably an inherited disorder (63).

Finally, the author speculates that the remarkable strides achieved in the developed countries in reducing the infant mortality rates may be an unrecognized contributing factor to the increase in schizophrenia-like disorders. The salvaging of infants with perinatal complications, who, in the past, might otherwise have died may be allowing an increasing number of brain-injured children to survive into adulthood and to manifest a wide spectrum of psychopathology including schizophrenia (64).

Neurological disorders that may present with schizophrenia-like illness

Davison and Bagley (65), in an exhaustive review of the literature, presented an impressive body of evidence that numerous organic disorders of the central nervous system are associated with schizophrenia-like psychoses at a frequency that exceeds chance expectations. After an exhaustive examination of the prevalence of psychotic clinical manifestations, response to treatment, course of illness, the genetic history of psychiatric illness and issues of pathogenesis, Davison and Bagley concluded that: (a) lesions in the temporal lobe and diencephalon are particularly important in generating psychotic symptoms; (b) the psychoses produced by organic CNS lesions are of a wide range that covers all the schizophrenias; (c) it is very difficult to distinguish 'true schizophrenia' from psychoses associated with CNS lesions; (d) there are not enough data to make definitive conclusions about the treatment and outcome of these psychoses; and (e) these psychoses occur without a genetic predisposition to schizophrenia.

The various CNS disorders that Davison and Bagley found to be associated with schizophrenia-like psychoses include:

Epilepsy, especially in temporal lobe (66, 67).

Cerebral trauma, which has been shown in follow-up of large series of war-injuries, to produce psychotic features (68). The site of injury, duration of initial coma or the development of seizures have not been found to be predictive of psychosis.

Cerebral tumors frequently present with schizophrenia-like features. A review of several mental hospital autopsy studies in the first half of this century showed a CNS neoplasm frequency of $1.7 - 11.2\%$ (69) (compared to $1 - 1.5\%$ for the general population at autopsy). Up to 72% were not recognized before autopsy. This reflects the importance of a complete neurological work-up including a CAT scan (70) for a first life-time psychotic episode in a previously healthy person. As for the site of the tumor, the highest association with psychosis has been found in pituitary and temporal lobe tumors.

CNS infections frequently lead to the development of schizophrenia-like psychoses later on. These infections include encephalitides, meningococcal, viral herpes, inclusion body, spring-summer, Japanese B, Vilyuisk, subacute sclerosing, measles, rabies-post-vaccinal, typhus, toxoplasma, cryptococcal, malaria, trypanosoma, tuberculous and cysticercosis. Encephalitis in children is a definite risk factor for the development of psychosis in adulthood (71).

A well-known example of a CNS infection that produced a large number of psychotic disorders is the encephalitis lethargica of the 1920s (72). Sydenham's chorea, which is a specific form of rheumatic encephalitis in children, has been shown to produce a schizophrenia-like disorder in adulthood (73). Syphilis in its tertiary form has long been known to produce schizophrenia-like symptoms (74). Finally, 'true' schizophrenia has been postulated to be a result of a slow virus (75).

Degenerative CNS disorders are frequently associated with schizophrenia-like disorders. Idiopathic parkinsonism (76), Wilson's disease (77), Huntington's disease (21), Alzheimer's and Pick's disease (78), have all been reported to be associated with psychotic features. Other degenerative CNS disorders associated with schizophrenia-like symptoms include basal ganglia disorders, torsion spasm, essential familial tremor, mid-brain reticulosis, Leber's hereditary optic atrophy, cerebral lipidosis, Niemann-Pick disease, corticostriate and cortico-cerebellar atrophy, Friedreich's ataxia, other hereditary ataxias and motor neurone disease.

Demyelinating diseases such as multiple sclerosis and Schilder's disease (diffuse sclerosis) have been shown to present with psychotic symptoms, or to be unexpectedly found in psychotic patients at autopsy (79). Other demyelinating disorders such as metachromatic leukodystrophy (80), adrenoleukodystrophy (81) and Marchiafava-Bignami disease (82) have also been reported to show schizophrenia-like psychoses.

Narcolepsy is a disorder of the sleep – wake cycle which can be idiopathic or secondary to other CNS disorders such as encephalitis, hypothalamic tumor or the Kleine-Levin syndrome. It is frequently misdiagnosed as schizophrenia (83), due to the hallucinatory phenomena that occur during cataplexy, as well as the paranoid state that may occur with narcolepsy (84).

Cerebrovascular disease usually occurs after midlife, and does not usually present with schizophrenia-like psychoses. However, there are reports of psychotic symptoms following subarachnoid hemorrhage (85), cerebral fat embolism, bilateral carotid artery occlusion (86), arteriovenous malformation (87), stroke (88, 89), or subdural hematoma (90).

Aqueduct stenosis and hydrocephalus was reported by Reveley and Reveley (91) to present with psychotic illness. This was further supported by other reports (92).

Normal pressure hydrocephalus (93) has been associated with psychosis.

Cerebellar degeneration and atrophy appears to be associated with psychotic disorders. This was initially observed by Heath et al. (94), and later confirmed by other post-mortem and CT scan findings (95, 96) as well as clinical observations (97).

Septum pellucidum cavities, which have been regarded as incidental findings of little clinical importance, were recently reported to be strongly associated with psychotic disorders (98).

In summary, it appears that numerous neurological conditions, hereditary, congenital, or acquired (during childhood or adulthood) may produce schizophrenia-like symptoms. Such a wide variety of organic etiologies for the schizophrenic syndrome probably has confounded many of the studies in the literature, especially in the past, and even recently. The advent of non-invasive, brain imaging techniques has substantially improved the recognition of gross or subtle cerebral factors that may be clinically silent and could present as 'functional psychoses'.

Medical disorders that may present with schizophrenia-like psychoses

There are many systemic illnesses that may produce psychotic symptoms at some point in the course of the illness (99). The following are some well-known examples of medical illnesses with associated psychotic features, which should be considered in the differential diagnosis of schizophrenia:

Infections, by various agents, resulting in encephalitis or meningitis as discussed earlier.

Inflammatory disorders, such as systemic lupus erythematosus (100), which can produce a cerebritis and subsequent psychoses.

Endocrinopathies, including Addison's disease (101), hypothyroidism (102), hyperthyroidism (103), hyperparathyroidism (104), hypoparathyroidism (105), and parahypopituitarism (106).

Systemic illnesses, including uremia (107), hepatic encephalopathy (108), hyponatremia (109), hypercalcemia (110), hypoglycemia (111), and myasthenia gravis (112), which may also be associated with thymoma (113).

Deficiency states, such as of thiamine (Wernicke-Korsakoff Psychoses) (114), B12 and folate (115) and niacin (116) may be associated with psychotic features.

Recently, Wilcox and Nasrallah (117) reported that patients with catatonia, all of whom are psychotic, had a significantly higher frequency of a systemic medical illness in the week prior to admission than patients with schizophrenia or bipolar affective disorder. This may indicate that catatonic symptoms (may) reflect medical or organic factors in the development of schizophrenia-like illness.

Drug-induced psychotic syndromes

It is now widely acknowledged that numerous prescription and street drugs and other toxic agents may produce psychotic features that may be misdiagnosed as schizophrenia if the drug-intake or poisoning history is not obtained. The following are some classes of drugs which have been known to produce psychotic symptoms, frequently of a toxic nature, but sometimes, as in amphetamine psychosis for example, a psychosis highly similar to schizophrenia:

Depressants, including alcohol (118), hypnotics (119), and benzodiazepine anticonvulsants (120).

Stimulants, such as amphetamine (121), cocaine (122), as well as others such as ephedrine, methylphenidate, fenfluramine, diethylpropion and phenmetrazine (123).

Hallucinogens, most notably lysergic acid diethylamide (LSD), mescaline, psilocybine and dimethyltryptamine (124).

Phencyclidine, which is sufficiently different from hallucinogens to be classified separately, is well known to produce severe psychotic symptoms (125).

Anticholinergic drugs, which are numerous and include atropine, tricyclic antidepressants, neuroleptics, and drugs used for neuroleptic-induced extrapyramidal side effects (e.g. benzatropine, trihexyphenidyl); all of these can produce a toxic psychosis that may be confused with schizophrenia (126).

Catecholaminergic drugs, such as L-dopa, amantadine, ephedrine (127 – 128).

Glucocorticoids are well-known to produce psychotic symptoms (129).

Heavy metals such as lead, mercury, manganese, arsenic, and thallium (130).

Other drugs such as digitalis (131), disulfiram (132), cimetidine (133), and bromide (134).

Psychiatric disorders that may be misdiagnosed as schizophrenia

For many years, the most common source of error in the diagnosis of schizophrenia was the misdiagnosis of other psychiatric disorders as schizophrenia. This occurred most commonly with bipolar affective disorders, in which either the manic phase or the psychotic depressive phase were frequently misdiagnosed as schizophrenia (135). Other psychiatric disorders that are sometimes misdiagnosed as schizophrenia include mental retardation, paranoid disorders, pervasive developmental disorder, obsessive-compulsive disorder, hypochrondriasis, phobic disorder, factitious disorder with psychological symptoms and transient psychotic symptoms in schizotypal, histrionic, narcissistic, borderline and paranoid personality disorders (4).

Conclusions

The above review indicates that there are numerous disorders, perinatal/obstetric complications, neurological diseases, medical illnesses and pharmacological syndromes, all of which may be associated with psychotic symptoms. These should all be considered as part of the differential diagnosis of schizophrenia because there has always been a tendency, (even nowadays, despite more rigorous diagnostic criteria) to loosely diagnose most psychoses as schizophrenia or schizophreniform.

A careful assessment, including psychiatric and medical history, family history, review of systems, physical and neurological exams and mental status examination is indispensible for an as reliable as possible diagnosis of schizophrenia. However, the pitfalls are many, as suggested by the fact that even a first degree relative with psychosis does not necessarily mean that a patient has 'true' schizophrenia because there are many genetic disorders with a schizophrenia-like phenotype that may manifest in several family members.

It is clear that a significant portion of the published research into schizophrenia may be of questionable reliability due to the issue of diagnosis and over-inclusiveness. One wonders whether the epidemiological studies of the incidence and prevalence of schizophrenia are inflated due to the erroneous inclusion of many schizophrenia-like psychoses secondary to organic etiology, which should be considered 'symptomatic schizophrenia'. Another question that arises because of that possibility is whether many of the unreplicated biological findings in schizophrenia research are due to sampling variability and loose diagnostic criteria that include many different psychoses under the rubric of schizophrenia. Even current DSM-III criteria, operational and reliable as they are, may fail to distinguish clinically subtle symptomatic from true schizophrenia because phenotypically they can be identical, although they are etiologically diverse. Perhaps, psychiatrists should be more rigorous in ferreting out organic factors in psychotic patients by taking a more detailed and systematic medical history, and conducting a more comprehensive physical and neurological examination. Advances in brain imaging techniques can be judiciously used to reveal gross or subtle brain pathology that may masquerade as schizophrenia-like illness.

The literature reviewed in this chapter represents a strong body of evidence that:
1. Schizophrenia is a brain disease.
2. Schizophrenic and other similar psychoses may have a final common neuropathophysiological pathway for which psychosis is a clinical syndrome.
3. Progress of research into 'true schizophrenia' can be made only when rigorous diagnosis assures homogenous patient samples.
4. Research into schizophrenia-like psychosis with recognized organic etiologies may eventually help in the understanding of 'true schizophrenia'.

REFERENCES

1. Tsuang MT (1975) Heterogeneity of schizophrenia. *Biol. Psychiatry, 10,* 465.
2. Bleuler E (1911) *Dementia Precox.* International University Press Inc., New York.
3. Spitzer RL, Endicott J, Robins E (1975) *Research Diagnostic Criteria (RDC) for a selected group of functional disorders.* Biometrics, New York.
4. American Psychiatric Association, DSM-III (1980) *Diagnostic and Statistical Manual of Mental Disorders, 3rd Ed.* APA, Washington, DC.
5. Henn FA, Nasrallah HA (Eds) (1982) *Schizophrenia as a Brain Disease.* Oxford University Press, New York.
6. Flor-Henry (1983) *The Cerebral Basis of Psychopathology.* John Wright PSG, Boston.
7. Gottsman II, Shields J (1982) *Schizophrenia: the Epigenetic Puzzle.* Cambridge University Press, Cambridge.
8. Baron M (1976) Albinism and schizophreniform psychosis: a pedigree study. *Am. J. Psychiatry, 133,* 1070.
9. Wing L (1981) Asperger's syndrome: a clinical account. *Psychol. Med., 11,* 115.
10. Keddie KM (1969) Hereditary ataxia, presumed to be of the Menzel type, complicated by paranoid psychosis, in a mother and two sons. *J. Neurol. Neurosurg. Psychiatry, 32,* 82.
11. Rashkis HA, Harris C (1964) Schizophrenia with adrenal hypercorticolism. *Dis. Nerv. Syst., 25,* 624.
12. Gibney GN, Jones IH, Meek JH (1972) Schizophrenia in association with erythropoietic protoporphyria. Report of a case. *Br. J. Psychiatry, 121,* 79.
13. Liston EH, Levine MD, Philippart M (1973) Psychosis in Fabry disease and treatment with phenoxybenzamine. *Arch. Gen. Psychiatry, 29,* 402.
14. West A (1973) Concurrent schizophrenia-like psychosis in monozygotic twins suffering from CNS disorder. *Br. J. Psychiatry, 122,* 675.
15. Francis A, Freeman H (1984) Psychiatric abnormality and brain calcification over four generations. *J. Nerv. Ment. Dis., 172,* 166.
16. Forrest CR, Lee TTY, Tsang WK, Yu SY (1969) Typhoid fever in Hong Kong junk family. *Br. Med. J., 4,* 279.
17. Nasr SJ (1976) Glucose-6-phosphate dehydrogenase deficiency with psychosis. *Arch. Gen. Psychiatry, 33,* 1202.
18. Neil JF, Glew RH, Peters SP (1979) *Genetics of Epilepsy: a Review.* Raven Press, New York.
19. Ott B (1957) Über psychische Veränderungen bei Hämochromatose. *Nervenarzt, 28,* 356.
20. Bracken MG, Coll P (1985) Homocystinuria and Schizophrenia. Literature review and case report. *J. Nerv. Ment. Dis., 173,* 51.
21. McHugh PR, Folstein MF (1981) Psychiatric syndromes in Huntington's chorea. In: Benson DF, Blumer D (Eds), *Psychiatric Aspects of Neurologic Disease.* Grune and Stratton, New York.
22. Perry TL, Wright, JM, Hansen S (1983) Hyperasparaginemia in a schizophrenic patient. *Biol. Psychiatry, 18,* 89.
23. Mochizuki H, Tobo M, Itoi K (1980) A case of ichthyosis vulgaris associated with schizophrenia-like psychosis and spike-wave stupor. *Folia Psychiatr. Neurol. Jpn., 34,* 392.
24. Glick ID, Graubert DN (1964) Kartagener's syndrome and schizophrenia: a report of

a case with chromosomal studies. *Am. J. Psychiatry, 121,* 603.

25. Sorensen K, Nielsen J (1977) Twenty psychotic males with Klinefelter's syndrome. *Acta Psychiatr. Scand., 56,* 249.

26. Pomeroy JC (1980) Klinefelter's syndrome and schizophrenia. *Br. J. Psychiatry, 136,* 597.

27. Weiss M, Meshulam B, Wijsenbeek H (1981) The possible relationship between Laurence-Moon-Biedl syndrome and a schizophrenia-like psychosis. *J. Nerv. Ment. Dis., 169,* 259.

28. Besson JAO (1980) A diagnostic pointer to adult metachromatic leucodystrophy. *Br. J. Psychiatry, 137,* 186.

29. Mahon-Haft H, Stone RK, Johnson R, Shah S (1981) Biochemical abnormalities of metachromatic leukodystrophy in an adult psychiatric population. *Am. J. Psychiatry, 138,* 1372.

30. Manowitz P, Goldstein L, Nora R (1981) An arylsulfatase. A variant in schizophrenia patients: preliminary report. *Biol. Psychiatry, 16,* 1107.

31. Fox JT, Kane FJ (1971) Niemann-Pick's disease manifesting as schizophrenia. *Dis. Nerv. Syst., 28,* 194.

32. Pitt D (1971) The natural history of untreated phenylketonuria. *Med. J. Aust., 1,* 378.

33. Perry TL, Hansen S, Tischler B, Richards FM, Sokol M (1973) Unrecognized adult phenylketonuria: implications for obstetrics and psychiatry. *N. Engl. J. Med., 289,* 395.

34. Fisch RO, Hosfield WB, Chang PN, Barranger J, Hastings DW (1979) An adult phenylketonuric with schizophrenia. *Minn. Med., 62,* 243.

35. Kaelbling R, Craig JB, Pasamanick B (1961) Urinary porphobilinogen: results of screening 2500 psychiatric patients. *Arch. Gen. Psychiatry, 5,* 494.

36. Peters HA (1962) Porphyric psychosis and chelation therapy. *Res. Adv. Biol. Psychiatry, 4,* 204.

37. Roth N (1968) Psychiatric syndromes of porphyria. *Int. J. Neuropsychiatry, 4,* 32.

38. Pepplinkhuizen L, Bruinvels J, Blom W, Moleman P (1980) Schizophrenia-like psychosis caused by a metabolic disorder. *Lancet, 1,* 454.

39. Lejeune J (1977) Mental retardation in trisomy 21. *Paediatrician 6,* 331.

40. Krag-Olsen B, Hoeg Brask B, Jacobsen P, Nielsen J (1981) Is there an increased risk of psychoses in patients with ring 18 and deletion long arm 18? In: Schmid W, Nielsen J (Eds), *Human Behavior and Genetics,* pp. 211–220. Elsevier/North-Holland Biomedical Press, Amsterdam.

41. Slater E, Zilkha K (1961) A case of Turner mosaic with myopathy and schizophrenia. *Proc. R. Soc. Med., 54,* 674.

42. Milcu SM, Stancescu V, Ionescu V, Forea I, Poenaru S, Maximilian C (1964) Turner-Syndrome mit Schizophrenie und XO-Karyotypus. *Fiziol. Norm. Patol., 10,* 139.

43. Mellbin G (1976) Neuropsychiatric disorders in sex chromatin negative women. *Br. J. Psychiatry, 112,* 145.

44. Kaplan AR, Cotton JE (1968) Chromosomal abnormalities in female schizophrenics. *J. Nerv. Ment. Dis., 147,* 402.

45. Beaumont PJV, Mayon R (1971) Schizophrenia and XO/XX/XXX mosaicism. *Br. J. Psychiatry, 118,* 349.

46. Krishna NR, Abrams R, Taylor MA, Behar D (1977) Schizophrenia in a 46,XY male with the Noonan syndrome. *Br. J. Psychiatry, 130,* 570.

47. Beard AW (1959) The association of hepatolenticular degeneration with schizophrenia. *Arch. Psychiatr. Neurol. Scand., 34,* 411.

48. Scheinberg IH, Sternlieb I, Richman J (1968) Psychiatric manifestations in patients with Wilson's disease. *Birth Defects, IV/2,* 85.
49. Olanders S (1968) Excess of Barr bodies in patients in mental hospitals. *Lancet, 2,* 1244.
50. MacLean N, Court Brown WM, Jacobs PA, Mantle DJ, Strong JA (1968) A survey of sex chromatin abnormalities in mental hospitals. *J. Med. Genet., 5,* 165.
51. Forssman H (1970) The mental implications of sex chromosome aberrations. *Br. J. Psychiatry, 117,* 353.
52. Clark GR, Telfer MA, Baker D, Rosen M (1970) Sex chromosomes, crime, and psychosis. *Am. J. Psychiatry, 126,* 1659.
53. Faber R, Abrams R (1975) Schizophrenia in a 47,XYY male. *Br. J. Psychiatry, 127,* 401.
54. Dorus E, Dorus W, Telfer MA (1977) Paranoid schizophrenia in a 47,XYY male. *Am. J. Psychiatry, 134,* 687.
55. McNeil TF, Kaij L (1978) Obstetric factors in the development of schizophrenia: complications in the births of preschizophrenics and in reproduction by schizophrenic parents. In: Wynne L, Cromwell R, Matthysse S (Eds), *The Nature of Schizophrenia: New Approaches to Research and Treatment,* pp. 401 – 429. John Wiley and Sons, New York.
56. Jacobsen B, Kinney DK (1980) Perinatal complications in adopted and non-adopted schizophrenics and their controls: preliminary results. *Acta Psychiatr. Scand., Suppl., 285,* 337.
57. Parnas J, Schulsinger F, Teasdale TW, Schulsinger H, Feldman PM, Mednick SA (1982) Perinatal complications and clinical outcome within the schizophrenia spectrum. *Br. J. Psychiatry, 140,* 416.
58. Fish B (1977) Neurobiologic antecedents of schizophrenia in children. *Arch. Gen. Psychiatry, 34,* 1297.
59. Boklage CE (1977) Schizophrenia, brain asymmetry development, and twinning: cellular relationship with etiological and possibly prognostic implications. *Biol. Psychiatry, 12,* 19.
60. Satz P (1972) Pathological left-handedness: an explanation. *Cortex, 8,* 121.
61. Raney ET (1938) Reversed lateral dominance in identical twins. *J. Exp. Psychol., 23,* 304.
62. Luchins DJ, Weinberger DR, Wyatt RJ (1979) Anomalous lateralization associated with a milder form of schizophrenia. *Am. J. Psychiatry, 136,* 1598.
63. Crowe RR (1982) Recent genetic research in schizophrenia. In: Henn FA, Nasrallah HA (Eds), *Schizophrenia as a Brain Disease,* pp. 40 – 60. Oxford University Press, New York.
64. Murray RM, Lewis SW, Reveley AM (1985) Towards an aetiological classification of schizophrenia. *Lancet, 1,* 1023.
65. Davison K, Bagley CR (1969) Schizophrenia-like psychoses associated with organic disorders of the CNS: a review of the literature. (Part II of Current Problems in Neuropsychiatry - (Ed. Herrington). *Br. J. Psychiatry, Spec. Publ. No. 4,* 113.
66. Flor-Henry P (1969) Psychosis and temporal lobe epilepsy: a controlled investigation. *Epilepsia, 10,* 363.
67. Ounsted C (1981) Adult psychiatric health of children who had experienced chronic temporal lobe epilepsy. *Br. J. Psychiatry, 139,* 249.
68. Lewin W, Marshall TF de C, Roberts AH (1979) Long term outcome after severe head injury. *Br. Med. J., 2,* 1533.
69. Waggoner RW, Bagchi BK (1954) Initial masking of organic brain changes by psychic

symptoms. *Am. J. Psychiatry, 110,* 904.

70. Weinberger DR (1984) Brain disease and psychiatric illness: when should a psychiatrist order a CAT scan. *Am. J. Psychiatry, 141,* 1521.
71. Greenbaum JV, Lurie LA (1948) Encephalitis as a causative factor in behaviour disorders of children. *J. Am. Med. Assoc., 136,* 923.
72. Menninger KA (1926) Influenza and schizophrenia. An analysis of post-influenzal 'dementia precox', as of 1918, and five years later. *Am. J. Psychiatry, V/4,* 470.
73. Wertheimer NM (1963) A psychiatric follow-up of children with rheumatic fever and other chronic diseases. *J. Chronic Dis., 16,* 223.
74. Dewhurst KL (1969) The neurosyphilitic psychoses today. *Br. J. Psychiatry, 115,* 31.
75. Torrey EF, Peterson MR (1973) Slow and latent viruses in schizophrenia. *Lancet, 2,* 22.
76. Tyrell DAJ, Parry RP, Crow TJ, Johnstone E, Ferrier IN (1979) Possible virus in schizophrenia and some neurological disorders. *Lancet, 1,* 839.
77. Beard AW (1959) The association of hepatolenticular degeneration with schizophrenia. *Acta Psychiatr. Neurol. Scand., 34,* 411.
78. Winkelman NW, Book MH (1949) Asymptomatic extra-pyramidal involvement in Pick's disease. *J. Neuropathol. Exp. Neurol., 8,* 30.
79. Ferraro A (1934) Histopathological findings in two cases of clinically diagnosed dementia praecox. *Am. J. Psychiatry, 90,* 883.
80. Betts TA, Smith WT, Kelly RE (1968) Adult metachromatic leukodystrophy (sulphatide lipidosis) simulating schizophrenia. *Neurology, 18,* 1140.
81. Powell H, Tindall R, Schultz P, Paa D, O'Brien J, Lampert P (1975) Adrenoleukodystrophy. *Arch. Neurol., 32,* 250.
82. Freeman AM III (1980) Delusions, depersonalization and unusual psychopathological symptoms. In: Hall, RCW (Ed), *Psychiatric Presentations of Medical Illness.* SP Medical and Scientific Books, New York.
83. Shapiro B, Spitz H (1976) Problems in the differential diagnosis of narcolepsy versus schizophrenia. *Am. J. Psychiatry, 133/11,* 1321.
84. Coren HZ, Strain JJ (1965) A case of narcolepsy with psychosis. (Paranoid State of Narcolepsy). *Compr. Psychiatry, 6/3,* 191.
85. Silverman M (1949) Paranoid reaction during the phase of recovery from subarachnoid haemorrhage. *J. Ment. Sci., 95,* 706.
86. Shapiro SK (1959) Psychosis due to bilateral carotid artery occlusion. *Minn. Med., 42,* 25.
87. Vallant G (1965) Schizophrenia in a woman with temporal lobe artiovenous malformation. *Br. J. Psychiatry, 111,* 307.
88. Levine DN, Finklestein S (1982) Delayed psychosis after right temporoparietal stroke or trauma: relation to epilepsy. *Neurology, 32,* 267.
89. Peroutka SJ, Sohmer BH, Kumer AJ, Folstein M, Robinson RG (1982) Hallucinations and delusions following a right temporoparieto-occipital infarction. *Johns Hopkins Med. J., 151,* 181.
90. Cunningham Owens DG, Johnstone EC, Bydder GM, Reel LK (1980) Unsuspected organic disease in chronic schizophrenia demonstrated by computer tomography. *J. Neurol. Neurosurg. Psychiatry, 43,* 1065.
91. Reveley AM, Reveley MA (1983) Aqueduct stenosis and schizophrenia. *J. Neurol. Neurosurg. Psychiatry, 46,* 18.
92. Roberts JKA, Trimble MR, Robertson M (1983) Schizophrenic psychosis associated with aqueduct stenosis in adults. *J. Neurol. Neurosurg. Psychiatry 46,* 892.

93. Lying-Tunell U (1979) Psychotic symptoms in normal-pressure hydrocephalus. *Acta Psychiatr. Scand., 59,* 415.
94. Heath RG, Franklin DE, Shraberg D (1979) Gross pathology of the cerebellum in patients diagnosed and treated as functional psychiatric disorders. *J. Nerv. Ment. Dis., 167/10,* 585.
95. Weinberger DR, Kleinman JE, Luchins DJ, Bigelow LB, Wyatt RJ (1980) Cerebellar pathology in schizophrenia: a controlled postmortem study. *Am. J. Psychiatry, 137/3,* 359.
96. Nasrallah HA, Jacoby CG, McCalley-Whitters M (1981) Cerebellar atrophy in schizophrenia and mania. *Lancet, 1,* 1102.
97. Kutty IN, Prendes JL (1981) Single case study: psychosis and cerebellar degeneration. *J. Nerv. Ment. Dis., 169/6,* 390.
98. Lewis SW, Mezey GC (1985) Clinical correlates of septum pellucidum cavities: an unusual association with psychosis. *Psychol. Med., 15,* 43.
99. Jefferson JW, Marshall JR (1981) *Neuropsychiatric features of medical disorders.* Plenum Medical Book Company, New York.
100. Gonzalez-Scarano F, Lisak RP, Bilaniuk LT, Zimmerman RA, Atkins PC, Zweiman B (1979) Cranial computed tomography in the diagnosis of systemic lupus erythematosus. *Ann. Neurol., 5/2,* 158.
101. Cleghorn RA (1951) Adrenal cortical insufficiency: psychological and neurological observations. *Can. Med. Assoc. J., 65,* 449.
102. Sanders V (1962) Neurologic manifestations of myxedema. *N. Engl. J. Med., 266,* 547.
103. MacCrimmon DJ, Wallace JE, Goldberg W et al (1979) Emotional disturbance and cognitive deficits in hyperthyroidism. *Psychosom. Med., 41,* 331.
104. Alarcon RD, Franceschini JA (1984) Hyperparathyroidism and paranoid psychosis: case report and review of the literature. *Br. J. Psychiatry, 145,* 477.
105. Mikkelson EJ, Reider AA (1979) Post-parathyroidectomy psychosis: clinical and research implications. *J. Clin. Psychiatry, 40,* 352.
106. Hanna SM (1970) Hypopituitarism (Sheehan's syndrome) presenting with organic psychosis. *J. Neurol. Neurosurg. Psychiatry, 33,* 192.
107. Schreiner GE (1959) Mental and personality changes in the uremic syndrome. *Med. Ann. D.C., 28,* 316.
108. Read AE, Sherlock S, Laidlaw J, Walder JG (1967) The neuropsychiatric syndromes associated with chronic liver disease and extensive portal-systemic collateral circulation. *Q. J. Med., 36,* 135.
109. Burnell GM, Foster TA (1972) Psychosis with low sodium syndrome. *Am. J. Psychiatry, 128,* 133.
110. Weizman A, Eldar M, Shoenfeld Y, Hirschorn M, Wijsenbeck H, Pinkhas J, Hypercalcaemia-induced psychopathology in malignant diseases. *Br. J. Psychiatry, 135,* 363.
111. Nash JL (1983) Delusions. In: Cavenar JO Jr., Brodie HKH (Eds), *Signs and Symptoms in Psychiatry.* Lippincott, Philadelphia.
112. Dorrell W (1973) Myasthenia gravis and schizophrenia. *Br. J. Psychiatry, 123,* 249.
113. Ananth J, Davies R, Kerner B (1984) Single case study: psychosis associated with thymoma. *J. Nerv. Ment. Dis., 172/9,* 556.
114. Cutting J (1978) The relationship between Korsakov's syndrome and alcoholic dementia. *Br. J. Psychiatry, 132,* 240.
115. Reynolds EH (1976) Neurological aspects of folate and vitamin B12 metabolism. *Clin.*

Haematol., 5, 661.

116. Spivak JL, Jackson DL (1977) Pellagra: an analysis of 18 patients and a review of the literature. *Johns Hopkins Med. J., 140,* 295.

117. Wilcox JA, Nasrallah HA (1985) Organic factors in catatonia, schizophrenia and affective disorders. In: *Abstract Volume, Society of Biological Psychiatry Annual Meeting, Dallas, TX,* p. 145. Society of Biological Psychiatry.

118. Cook BL, Winokur G (1985) Separate heritability of alcoholism and psychotic symptoms. *Am. J. Psychiatry, 142,* 360.

119. Roman D (1978) Schizophrenia-like psychosis following 'Mandrax' overdose. *Br. J. Psychiatry, 121,* 619.

120. Browne TR (1978) Clonazepam. *N. Engl. J. Med., 299,* 812.

121. Snyder SH (1973) Amphetamine psychosis: a 'model' schizophrenia mediated by catecholamines. *Am. J. Psychiatry, 130,* 61.

122. Cohen S (1984) Cocaine: acute medical and psychiatric complications. *Psychiatric Ann., 14,* 747.

123. Angrist B, Sudilovsky A (1978) Central nervous system stimulants: historical aspects and clinical effects, In: Iverson LL, Iverson SD, Snyder SH (Eds), *Handbook of Psychopharmacology,* p. 99. Plenum Press, New York.

124. Schuckit MA (1979) Drug and alcohol abuse. Plenum Press, New York.

125. Showalter CV, Thornton WE (1977) Clinical pharmacology of phencyclidine toxicity. *Am. J. Psychiatry, 134,* 1234.

126. Dysken MW, Merry W, Davis JM (1978) Anticholinergic psychosis. *Psychiatr. Ann., 8,* 30.

127. Klawans HL (1978) Levodopa-induced psychosis. *Psychiatr. Ann., 8,* 19.

128. Borison RL (1979) Amantadine-induced psychosis in a geriatric patient with renal disease. *Am. J. Psychiatry, 136,* 111.

129. Ling MH, Perry PJ, Tsuang MT (1981) Side effects of corticosteroid therapy: psychiatric aspects. *Arch. Gen. Psychiatry, 38,* 471.

130. Lishman WA (1978) *Organic Psychiatry: The Psychological Consequences of Cerebral Disorder.* Blackwell Scientific Publications, Oxford.

131. Gorelick DA, Kussin SZ, Kahn I (1978) Paranoid delusions and auditory hallucinations associated with digoxin intoxication. *J. Nerv. Ment. Dis., 166,* 817.

132. Nasrallah HA (1979) Vulnerability to disulfiram psychosis. *West. J. Med., 130,* 575.

133. Adler LE, Sadja L, Wilets G (1980) Cimetidine toxicity manifested as paranoia and hallucinations. *Am. J. Psychiatry, 137,* 1112.

134. Raskind MA, Kitchell M, Alvarez C (1978) Bromide intoxication in the elderly. *J. Am. Geriatr. Soc., 26,* 222.

135. Pope HG, Lipinski JF (1978) Diagnosis in schizophrenia and manic depressive illness. *Arch. Gen. Psychiatry, 35,* 811.

CHAPTER 3

Motor abnormalities in schizophrenia

THEO C. MANSCHRECK

Motor abnormalities in schizophrenia, often neglected in the past, are now the focus of considerable research and clinical interest. They include a spectrum of voluntary and involuntary disturbances of varying frequency and severity, affecting such features as gait, general movement, and intentional action. As a rule, they have been difficult to study because of a lack of guiding hypotheses and effective measures, their fluctuating nature, and, to be sure, a reluctance to interpret their occurrence in terms of brain dysfunction. Yet, they have been observed repeatedly and well before the development of modern pharmacologic therapies. Dramatic features like catalepsy, posturing, excitement, and more common ones, often subtle, like stereotypies, mannerisms, clumsiness, and incoordination have been described for years (1 – 4). Beyond classification and description, however, we know little about them; and there have been remarkably few studies to change this situation. Despite extensive commentary on motor behavior in schizophrenia, no systematic explanation has been put forward, nor have there been many attempts to evaluate the relationship between motor features and other classes of symptoms, both of which seem essential to a satisfactory account of schizophrenia.

The study of motor disturbances could permit relating observable, measurable behavior to other aspects of brain function and anatomy so that localization of pathology may become possible. This potential contrasts with the limitations that plague the assessment of delusional, hallucinatory, and other subjective disturbances of schizophrenic illness. Indeed, a clearer understanding of the neurology of schizophrenic motor behavior holds the promise of advances in differential diagnosis, etiology, pathogenesis, and treatment. This chapter presents a summary of described motor abnormalities of schizophrenia, and reviews relevant clinical, high risk, and laboratory studies. While our understanding of the neurology of such abnormalities is limited, this knowledge provides a foundation and direction for further development.

Motor features of schizophrenia

Although there is little specific knowledge about the motor features of schizophrenia, they have been consistently observed in a remarkable variety over the

Handbook of Schizophrenia, Vol. 1: The Neurology of Schizophrenia.
H.A. Nasrallah and D.R. Weinberger, editors.
© Elsevier Science Publishers B.V., 1986.

TABLE 1   *Disturbances associated with decreased motor activity in schizophrenia*

Diffuse	
Retardation	Slowed in all activities, voluntary and vegetative, and often slowed in thinking and speech as well. Patients show little spontaneity and goal-directed behavior is reported to be exhausting.
Poverty of movement	Reduction in the amount or quantity of motor activity, sometimes called hypokinesia.
Stupor	A severe form of decreased motor activity. There may be almost no animation, spontaneous movement, or locomotion at the extreme. In milder cases, only some movements may be transiently blocked (cf. below).
Patterned	
Motor blocking (Obstruction)	A disorder of the execution of movement. Obstruction usually occurs episodically when movement suddenly is reduced or halted in the midst of normal or increased activity. Later, the patient may be able to resume the movement. Following such episodes, the patient may report the subjective experience of thought withdrawal, or that the intended movement was forgotten. Movement may appear stiff and awkward.
Cooperation	There are two forms: (1) *Mitmachen:* A displaced body part returns to its original position when released, after having passively acquiesced to movements made by the examiner. (2) *Mitgehen:* A more severe or extreme form of this disturbance in which the patient's body part continues to move in a given direction in response to light pressure.
Opposition (Gegenhalten)	Refers to the presence of muscular resistance to passive movement of the extremities. The opposite of cooperation.
Automatic obedience	The patient carries out all instruction, regardless of merit or propriety.
Negativism	A broad spectrum of motor behavior which is characterized by an apparently unmotivated failure to do what is suggested. This may lead to varying degrees of akinesia, or lack of movement. In its most severe form, it is also aptly described as stupor. Often it is called a disorder of volition.
Ambitendency	A form of negativism. In response to a request to carry out a voluntary action, the patient makes a series of tentative movements but does not reach the goal. For example, the patient may walk toward the examiner in response to a request to come forward and then halt halfway and return to his original position.
Echopraxia	The patient imitates the behavior of the examiner or other patients. (In *echolalia* speech is imitated.)
Last minute responses	The patient (often mute) is unable to reply to questions or initiate conversation until the examiner is leaving the bedside. Then the patient may blurt out a response to a prior question.

TABLE 2   *Disturbances associated with increased motor activity in schizophrenia*

Diffuse Restlessness	A persistent or generalized increase in bodily movement.
Excitement	Prolonged bursts of energy, often chaotic and disorganized, frenzied in character.
Tremor	Involuntary, purposeless contractions of muscle groups which produce oscillating movements near a joint or of the head. They may occur at rest, with arms extended (postural), resting, or with movement (intentional). They may be described as fine or coarse; regular or irregular; rapid or slow.
Patterned Stereotyped movements (Stereotypies)	Repeated performances of spontaneous non-goal-directed behavior in a uniform manner, often with some remnant of purposive behavior in the movement. Repeated gestures or actions (sometimes thought to have symbolic significance), including continuous movement in and out of a chair, crossing oneself, waving repeatedly in the air, touching objects over and over, (*handling* I--II a form of stereotypy) and grasping one's hands or clothes continuously (*intertwining*). *Complex stereotypies*: eating a bite of food and closing the eyes five times.
Spasms	Involuntary contractions of muscles or groups of muscles, sometimes associated with pain, embarrassment, and fear. Examples: habit spasm, spasms of swallowing or of the tongue, of the eyelids (blepharospasm).
Choreiform movements	Short, jerky movements which may affect the whole body. They may affect the periphery more than the trunk. They may be fine or coarse. Also, they may appear to be fragments of expression or gesture and áre often disguised in this manner.
Athetoid movements	Spontaneous movements that are slow, writhing and twisting (wormlike – hence athetoid) involving generally distal muscles but possibly proximally also, and bringing strange postures to the body, especially to the hands.
Parakinesia	Spontaneous, continuous, irregular muscular movements – often jerky in character. Persistent grimacing, twitching, and jerking may be present. They may superficially resemble tics.
Myoclonic movements	Rapid contraction of either proximal or distal muscles, usually in an unrhythmic fashion but sometimes with bilaterally symmetrical presentation.
Perseverative movements (Perseveration)	The involuntary continuation or recurrence of a movement more appropriate to a prior stimulus (e.g. request, command, etc.) whose purpose is already served, in response to a succeeding stimulus. Perseverative movement may be detected by asking the patient to close the eyes, stick out the tongue, or write for the examiner, as well as by close observation of interview behavior.

TABLE 2 *continued*

Impulsive movements	Sudden, apparently purposeless or involuntary acts including screaming, biting, exhibition of genitals.
Carphologic movements	These include picking at bedclothes, skin, clothing in a purposeless manner.
Agitation	The subjective report of anguish, psychic tension or anxiety of very unpleasant proportions *and* one or more of the following: pacing, fidgetiness, inability to sit still, wringing of the hands, pulling at skin, hair, or clothing, shouting or complaining in outbursts.
Tics	Short, sudden, repetitive, jerky movements of small groups of muscles of face, neck, or upper trunk, often worsened by psychological circumstances. Most commonly affecting the face, tics may be part of an unusual blink or distortion of the forehead, nose or mouth. Swallowing, grunting, coughing or shoulder movements may also be tics.
Mannerisms	These consist in an unusual, frequently stilted variation in the performance of a normal, goal-directed movement. Examples include unusual movements in greeting, shaking hands, or writing, strange uses of words, unusual verbal expressions out of keeping with the situation. Stereotypies are often difficult to distinguish from mannerisms. Stereotypies generally do not have a goal or form part of goal-directed behavior. Manneristic behavior may take the form of collecting or hoarding.

TABLE 3 *Postural disturbances associated with schizophrenia*

Increased muscle tonus in isolated area of body	Parts of the body are held rigidly in one position. For example, there may be increased tension in the jaws (clenched tightly together), the eyes tightly shut, or the head held rigidly just above the pillow (*psychological pillow*).
Manneristic postures	Stilted, often awkward postures, which usually are not maintained. Such posture may be seen to express a turning away or withdrawal from surroundings.
Stereotyped postures	Bizarre postures often maintained for hours.
Waxy flexibility (catalepsy)	The patient allows himself to be placed in any position and then maintains this position for at least several minutes.
Clumsiness	Awkward, uncoordinated, or poorly made movements substantially lacking ease, smoothness, nimbleness, dexterity, or grace. Also ungainly postural positions.

TABLE 4 *Catatonia*

Excitement	Catalepsy
Stupor	Negativistic motor behavior
Stereotypies	Echopraxia
Mannerisms	Last minute responses
Rigidity	

years. Despite the current confounding factor of antipsychotic drug treatment in most cases, their discovery clearly preceded the use of chlorpromazine (1, 2, 5). Attempts to classify them must, to some extent, be arbitrary. The scheme used here divides examples of reported abnormal behavior (regardless of specificity, frequency, or uniqueness to schizophrenia) into those associated with increased movement (hyperkinesia) and those associated with decreased movement (hypokinesia) in relation to normal behavior (Tables 1 and 2). These categories are then subdivided into diffuse or patterned the features. Disorders of posture (Fish, 1967) (6) are usually considered a form of motor disturbance, (Table 3). The features of catatonia, a classic syndrome of motor disturbance (Table 4), overlap several of these categories.

TABLE 5 *Neuroleptic-induced motor behaviors*

Tremor	As already defined
Dystonic movements	Usually acute. Bearing similarity to athetoid movements, but usually involving larger areas of the body musculature. Slowed hypertonic, occasionally grotesque movements with maintenance of peculiar postures.
Akathisia	Motor restlessness, often subjectively experienced as centered in the lower extremities and accompanied by muscular or somatic tension, a feeling of having to move, and an intolerance of sitting still. In milder states, shuffling or tapping movements, shifting, rocking to and fro. In severer states, an inability to sit still at all and incessant movement.
Parkinsonian effects	Slowed movements (*bradykinesia*) with expressionless facies, slow initiation of movements, loss of associated movements. A tremor at rest is often present as well as a 'cog-wheel rigidity' of the limbs.
Tardive dyskinesia	Literally this is a late disorder of motility. There are choreiform movements of the extremities, orofacial movements (such as flycatcher's tongue, unusual grimacing, snouting, and so forth), and dystonic postures. Younger patients may be more affected in the extremities and trunk, while in older patients, there is a greater restriction to the oral region.

Although it is sometimes difficult in practice to distinguish drug-induced effects (Table 5) from those associated with psychiatric illness itself, both have distinct characteristics.

Early observations

Emil Kraepelin's description of the motor features of dementia praecox emphasized their intermittent, variable, subtle, and occasionally dramatic nature. Among the patients with diagnosed dementia praecox (Table 6), Kraepelin noted multiple motor features, including echopraxia, catalepsy, forms of negativism, stupor, and reduced efficiency of fine movements. These patients were characterized by a marked clumsiness, jerkiness, or loss of smooth muscular coordination. Kraepelin described the gait of the patient as having the appearance of walking through snow. Although the catatonic subtype of dementia praecox was dominated by motor disturbance features, Kraepelin observed similar features in the hebephrenic and paranoid forms of the disorder as well. Kraepelin discovered that motor efficiency in a specific task deteriorated rapidly. In handiwork and crafts, particularly those involving fine work, he and others (7, 8) noted a general decline in ability.

Kraepelin also recognized that movement disorders suggestive of dementia praecox could be the consequence of known neurological diseases including encephalitis, syphilis, and epilepsy; he emphasized the value of differential diagnosis and careful follow-up to sort out such alternative explanations.

Eugen Bleuler (5) described many of the same motor features that Kraepelin had identified among dementia praecox patients, noting that motor anomalies were seldom absent. He also commented on 'idiomuscular contractions,' spasms, and a 'will 'o the wisp' gait, with irregular timing and spacing of steps.

Although his ideas concerning the hierarchical organization of the central nervous

TABLE 6 *Emil Kraepelin's dementia praecox (c. 1896)*

Onset	Adolescence
Clinical picture	*Always* Disturbance of emotion Disturbance of volition Weakening of judgment
	Usually Hallucinations Delusions Motor behavior disturbance
Prognosis	Complicated Generally deterioration (psychological enfeeblement or dementia) Temporary improvements

system derived from the study of neurological disease, James Hughlings Jackson (9) considered his concepts applicable to mental disorders. In mental illness, he maintained, there is a dissolution of the highest cerebral centers. Complex functions normally under voluntary control are lost. Consequently, less complex and undamaged central nervous system components produce the striking manifestations of mental disorder. Jackson proposed that, in psychosis, clinical features can be classified according to whether they result from dissolution (so-called negative symptoms) or from activity in the remaining undamaged nervous components (so-called positive symptoms). Negative symptoms of schizophrenia would include withdrawal, blocking, disturbances of identity, and passivity experiences. Positive symptoms would include hallucinations, delusions, stereotypies, mannerisms, and catalepsy.

Similar views were put forward by Carl Wernicke and Karl Kahlbaum, who argued that focal cerebral pathology was the basis for the motor features of psychotic disorders. The idea that subcortical mechanisms produce these features when deprived of the influence of higher centers has been popular. Kleist (1), for example, felt that schizophrenic motor disturbances had a source identical to that of neurological disease with similar motor manifestations. Other writers have echoed this theme (4, 10 – 12).

Karl Jaspers noted certain remarkable characteristics of schizophrenic motor features. For instance, while there is increased muscle tone in certain limbs or areas, such as the face of a patient maintaining a catatonic posture, there is decreased or normal tone in other areas of the body, a kind of incoordination or fragmentation of motor function. Jaspers also observed that the 'immobile' catatonic patient could initiate such basic activities as care of toileting, feeding, and dressing, but was often unable to respond to verbal requests (13). Jaspers coined the term 'psychomotor disturbance' and applied it to schizophrenia to suggest that the similarity between schizophrenic motor features and the features of certain neurological syndromes did not necessarily reflect a common set of causes or pathogenesis (14). In catatonic excitement, for example, patients may identify with their behavior and attempt to construct rationalizations for it. When outwardly similar behavior occurs in encephalitis lethargica, on the other hand, patients tend to be distressed, bewildered, and occasionally confused by their motor symptoms.

Thomas Freeman (15) also compared the clinical motor phenomena characteristic of chronic schizophrenia and those characteristic of organic mental disorder. In schizophrenia, particularly the catatonic and hebephrenic subtypes, disturbances in such voluntary movements as blocking, overly repetitive activity, and difficulty in switching to new movements can be observed frequently in spontaneous behavior and elicited on examination (e.g. using Luria's tests of motility). Disturbed movement is more likely to occur when the patient is inattentive, distractible, and generally unresponsive. The same characteristics are frequently found in other organic conditions, although the appearance of normal motility is rare in progressive degenerative disease. Even in schizophrenia, Freeman argues, normal motility is uncommon. The movements that recur in so-called normal fashion in schizophrenia are those that could be described as highly practiced.

The promising potential of these early observations was not realized because of the widespread view that motor features are secondary to more primary psychological disturbances; a paucity of useful performance measures for reliably defining the motor capacities of schizophrenic patients; the inconsistent nature of motor disturbances, which suggests they are not essential characteristics; and, fundamentally, the absence of a model that could predict and explain the relationships between thought, will, emotion, and motor anomalies (16).

The following sections summarize the variety and complexity of motor abnormalities in schizophrenia and indicate some of the gaps in our knowledge.

Catatonia and catatonic schizophrenia

Although Kahlbaum (17) as well as Kraepelin and Bleuler, stressed that catatonic behavior has a number of different possible etiologies, there has been a tendency to regard catatonic behavior as signifying schizophrenia. It is, of course, well known that fluorides, hyperparathyroidism, viral encephalitides, manic-depressive disorder, tuberculosis, and other diseases can be the source of catatonic behavior (18). Indeed, immobility, stupor, catalepsy, posturing, grimacing, stereotypic behavior, and negativism – that is, catatonia – constitute a syndrome that has been described in numerous psychiatric and medical disorders (see Table 4). Classically, there are two extreme patterns of catatonic behavior: a retarded or withdrawn stupor, and a hyperkinetic, occasionally aggressive, excitement. Kraepelin believed that, when these patterns were persistent, not diagnosable as part of known disease and associated with disturbances of will, judgment, and emotion, they formed a subtype of dementia praecox. Slater and Roth (14) claim, as do others, that the more prevalent type of catatonic behavior in schizophrenia is retarded or withdrawn.

Certainly, catatonic schizophrenia has been associated with the most obvious and dramatic motor disturbances. Yet motor anomalies of schizophrenia are not limited to this subtype. As Kraepelin and Bleuler both observed, motor disturbances occur in all subtypes of schizophrenia. When motor disturbances predominate, most cases are diagnosed catatonic. When motor disturbances are not detectable, or less striking, other characteristics (e.g. thought disturbance or paranoid thinking) have tended to determine subtype classification.

Matters are considerably less clear in contemporary clinical settings. Most schizophrenic patients manifest a mixture of catatonic, hebephrenic, and paranoid features, and fewer qualify for the classic subtype labels. This has resulted in the increased diagnosis of undifferentiated schizophrenia. Indeed, there has been a reduction in the diagnosis of catatonic and hebephrenic subtypes over the last 50 years, although the overall prevalence (about 1%) of schizophrenia appears to be stable (19). For instance, it is increasingly uncommon to find obvious catatonic slowing, rigidity, or related classic features. When they do occur, they usually are short-lived, often subtle, and frequently not associated with schizophrenic disorder (20, 21).

Some authors, e.g. Mahendra (22) and Marsden (23), have suggested that certain neurological disorders with varied epidemiologic patterns (e.g. encephalitis of Parkinson's disease) may have contributed to such changes. Others, e.g. Guggenheim and Babigan (24), have documented patterns of assigning the catatonic subtype diagnosis that indicate poor reliability. Whatever the source, shifts in the incidence of symptoms and signs make attempts to determine the frequency and nature of motor features in schizophrenia more difficult.

Not surprisingly, knowledge of incidence, prevalence, and natural history of motor features is sketchy because few reliable estimates appear in either the older or more recent literature (4, 25). Much of the relevant information concerns specific motor anomalies (such as stereotypies) as discussed below.

Specific motor abnormalities

Descriptive studies of specific abnormal movements, such as stereotypies, are complicated by problems of definition and interpretation. Lacking standard terminology, investigators have relied on their own concepts. Generally, only major or clinically obvious manifestations have been examined. Little work has attempted to explore more subtle features, such as clumsiness or incoordination, or the impact of motor disturbance on skilled performance (26). Most investigators have failed to assess these anomalies longitudinally.

The incidence and prevalence of choreiform and athetoid movements in psychiatric patients remains somewhat controversial. Mettler and Crandell (27) estimated that choreiform movements occurred frequently among schizophrenic patients and especially among chronic patients in psychiatric hospitals. Marsden et al. (4), however, have claimed that these movements occur in neurological disease, especially of the basal ganglia, and should not be considered part of the schizophrenic syndrome. Their frequent occurrence in tardive dyskinesia has been used to support this argument.

Perseveration is a well-known clinical sign of disturbed motor and speech behavior among neurologically and psychiatrically disordered individuals. Allison (28) documented that perseveration occurs in a wide variety of conditions. Freeman and Gathercole (29) examined perseveration in chronic schizophrenia and dementia. Extensive testing, using a number of methods to elicit forms of perseverative behavior, was undertaken in a group of schizophrenic and demented patients. The result provided no evidence for a unitary trait of perseveration.

Knowledge of echopraxia and echolalia has progressed in limited ways. Stengel (30) showed that echo reactions were common in a number of different conditions, although they have been considered a classic feature of catatonic disorder. Transcortical aphasia, mental deficiency, chronic epilepsy, delirium, early speech development in children, and states of fatigue and inattention in normals were the main disorders associated with echo phenomena. Echo phenomena tended to be associated in these conditions with an urge to act or speak, a tendency to repetition, and incomplete development or impairment in perception and expression of speech.

Jones and Hunter (25) reported a 2-year longitudinal study of abnormal movements in a group of 127 (90 females, 37 males) chronic institutionalized psychiatric patients, one-third of whom had not received antipsychotic medication. Of the 127, 111 (87%) were diagnosed as schizophrenics. Approximately 25% of the entire sample had diagnosed brain disorder and/or subnormal intelligence. Unfortunately, this group was not separated from the larger group in reporting observations. These investigators looked at four kinds of movements: tremor, choreoathetosis, tics, and stereotypies (by which they meant any form of movements, apart from the other categories, that became abnormal because of repetition). Tremor, found in 30% of the sample, was equally common among men and women. Choreoathetoid movements were found in 18% of the women but only 5% (2) of the men. Tics were discovered in 21% of the females and 11% of the men. Stereotypies occurred in 47% of the women and 5% of the men. These included rocking (18 patients), hand movements (19 patients), and oral movements (19 patients). Thirty patients exhibited only one form of stereotypy, and 15 had two or more such movements. Other findings included the observation that choreoathetoid movements occurred primarily in the older age groups and particularly in those aged 71–80. Observations of patients never treated with antipsychotic medication were made on 21 women and 24 men; 62% of the men had abnormal movements at some time during their illness. Examination of records showed that 75% of all patients had experienced catatonic posturing at least once previously, and all had records indicating 'manneristic and grimacing' behavior.

The authors concluded that there is a high incidence and variability of pattern of abnormal movements among long-stay psychiatric patients. Tics, stereotypies, and choreoathetosis occurred more frequently in those who at some time had received antipsychotic medication. However, examination of records disclosed that abnormal movements of all types had been present in patients never treated with neuroleptics. In some patients, abnormal movements developed only after years of exposure to drugs, and in others, only after drugs had been discontinued for months. Choreoathetosis, though least common, was the most persistent. Its occurrence in older patients as well as its association with neurological impairment suggests that it is not typically part of schizophrenia. Tics, tremors, and stereotypies tended to occur transiently, although continuous patterns of stereotypy were also evident. Episodes of restlessness, nowadays usually associated with neuroleptic treatment, were common in the early stages of mental disorder and recurred in some patients over many years, independent of treatment.

This report is one of the few systematic attempts to evaluate the incidence and natural history of reported motor disturbances in schizophrenia. The inclusion of patients with known organic impairment makes interpretation difficult because motor anomalies are common in brain disease. Moreover, the study failed to examine the full range of motor abnormalities in schizophrenia. Nevertheless, the findings clearly indicate that motor disturbances occur frequently, variably, and usually subtly in schizophrenia.

A British study (31) has examined spontaneous involuntary disorders of movement in a sample of 411 hospitalized patients with chronic schizophrenia (32). The findings, based on standardized rating techniques, the Abnormal Involuntary Movement Scale (AIMS) and the more detailed Rockland Scale, indicate a high prevalence of involuntary movement abnormalities in the sample. With at least moderate degrees of severity, 50.6% of the patients had demonstrable anomalies on one or more of AIMS items; the corresponding Rockland Scale figure was 67.6%. The major component of abnormality was contributed by rating of facial movements. Of particular interest was the opportunity to assess a subsample of 47 patients with no history of exposure to neuroleptic drugs. The authors found no differences in the prevalence and severity of movement disturbances and few differences in regional distribution of abnormality. They concluded that spontaneous involuntary movements can be a feature of chronic schizophrenia unmodified by drugs.

The study unfortunately did not report on disturbances in voluntary patterns of movement disorder. Assessment of neurological abnormalities resulted in relatively few, and generally minor peripheral findings. An important additional observation was that the movements considered in the study exhibited considerable stability in gross distribution and severity during a 12 – 18 month period of follow-up.

Onset and relationship to prognosis

No one knows precisely when abnormal movements have their onset in schizophrenia (See High Risk Studies below). Typically, motor manifestations have been reported to occur after the appearance of other symptoms. Schneider (33) offered an approach to diagnosis of schizophrenia in its early stages, in part because dramatic observable motor disturbances in acute cases are uncommon. His first-rank symptoms reflect subjective experiences of an unusual and incomprehensible sort from the standpoint of normal human experience. Auditory hallucinations, delusional perception, and several forms of passivity experience constitute the symptoms that Schneider believed were pathognomonic for acute schizophrenia, if coarse brain disease was not present. Two of the passivity experiences (i.e. made impulses, made acts) suggest disturbances affecting motor functions. They reflect a sense of loss of control and coordination of movement not necessarily discernible to others. Like other first-rank symptoms, they tend to be reported by patients early in the course of illness, whereas they may be uncommon in fully established schizophrenia. Mellor (34) found made impulses and made acts in 2.9% and 9.2%, respectively, of a group of 173 schizophrenics, independently diagnosed by two consultant psychiatrists. While the claim to pathognomonicity has been criticized (35, 36), there is general agreement that first-rank symptoms are highly discriminating symptoms for the diagnosis of schizophrenic disorder.

Chapman (37) decided to evaluate changes in subjective experience among a group of 40 schizophrenics early in the course of illness to learn specifically which features of behavior were altered. Many of the patients (75%) reported difficulty coordinating the motor sequences necessary for simple specific activities, such as walking, eating, and sitting down. Chapman named this disturbance ideokinetic apraxia. Movements seemed slow, required more deliberation and concentration, and felt more restricted than normal. Patients described a loss of automaticity of movements associated with heightened awareness of bodily processes. In 14 patients, motor and thought blocking, characterized by transient immobility, blank expression, and fixed gaze were common. Echolalia and echopraxia also occurred in a number of these patients. Mutism was encountered at some point during the course of illness in 16. In some patients, prolonged catatonic behavior and gross visual perceptual disturbances were associated with a deteriorating course.

These findings raise the possibility that objective assessment techniques, such as motor performance tests, might succeed in detecting early motor difficulties. Subjective accounts are helpful, but objective means would be more satisfactory to extend our knowledge of the natural history of motor phenomena in schizophrenia.

The relationship between prognosis and motor disturbance is unclear. Kraepelin (2), of course, believed that dementia praecox has a poor outcome. The natural history of the disorder was variable in pattern if not in result. He (and Bleuler) noted, that stereotypic movements could persist for many years, to become progressively more simplified, possibly to occur independent of apparent expressive purpose, and to become preoccupying. These movements often were associated with verbigeration or thought disorder (Kleist, 1908) (1). Many have held the view that motor disturbances, such as stereotypies, that may occur early in the course of schizophrenia, portend a poor prognosis. There have been few studies to confirm or refute such opinions. Jones (38) found no relationship between complexity of stereotypies and age of onset, length of illness, or duration of hospitalization in 13 chronic schizophrenics with stereotypic behavior.

In investigating the idea that an earlier onset of movement disorder is associated with poor prognosis, Yarden and Discipio (39) did a follow-up study of young schizophrenic patients who exhibited abnormal movements. The movements were primarily choreiform and athetoid, but included tics, stereotypies, and mannerisms. The patients were described as free of neurological disease, retardation, or history of chronic hospitalization. These patients, compared with a control group of schizophrenics without abnormal movements, had an earlier age of onset of changes in mental state and longer hospitalizations. Patients with abnormal movements also showed significantly more severe thought disorder, purposeless activity, negativism, and neglect of personal hygiene. This group was less affected than the control group by pharmacologic interventions. Moreover, the presence of abnormal movements was associated with a significantly poorer prognosis for the period of study.

An investigation of motor movements in schizophrenic disorders

We investigated the occurrence of the classic reported motor disturbances in schizophrenics and their relationship to other features of the illness (3). We were particularly interested in the relationship with subtype diagnosis, affective blunting, neurological non-localizing signs, delusions, and formal thought disorder.

We examined 37 patients who met the DSM III criteria for the diagnosis of schizophrenic disorders, including 13 paranoid, 10 disorganized, 13 undifferentiated, and 1 catatonic. The affective disorder group totaled 16 and consisted of 3 manic subjects, 4 schizoaffective (manic subtype), 1 schizoaffective (depressed subtype), and 8 psychotic depressives. These groups did not differ by age, education, length of illness, or neuroleptic drug treatment. Thirty of the schizophrenic and 10 of the affective subjects were taking antipsychotic medication. Of the 7 unmedicated schizophrenics, 2 had never received drug treatment; of the 6 unmedicated affective controls, 3 had been free of medication for at least 1 year, several for many years. The examination consisted of observations of spontaneous behavior and behavior elicited by the examiner (Table 7). We looked for features of disorganization, delayed response, postural persistence and lengthy completion. Evidence of drug-related extrapyramidal disturbance and/or tardive dyskinesia was found in 11 of the 30 schizophrenics and 4 of the 10 affective subjects on neuroleptics. The number and severity of the effects were in all cases minimal.

Disturbances in voluntary motor behavior were detectable in all but one schizophrenic (subtype paranoid) and were infrequent among affective subjects, except for the schizoaffective subtype (Table 8). The most common form of spontaneous motor abnormality in schizophrenics was clumsiness or awkwardness, a postural disturbance. The second most common were stereotypic and manneristic movements, followed by motor blocking. Not observed in this sample were ambitendency, catalepsy, automatic obedience, choreoathetoid movements, excitement, and stupor. Of the subtypes, a smaller proportion of the paranoid group exhibited spontaneous motor abnormalities (31%), whereas all of the disorganized (hebephrenic) subjects showed such anomalies. On the other hand, with the exception of the schizoaffective group, the performance of affective subjects was generally normal. The schizoaffective group displayed the major proportion of abnormalities among the affective controls. Indeed, four of the five schizoaffective subjects exhibited at least one feature of abnormal motor behavior on examination.

The effect of antipsychotic medication on motor movements was examined. The results suggest that neuroleptics tended to reduce the number and/or severity of such abnormalities.

The relationship of disturbance of voluntary motor activity to other features was

TABLE 7   *Techniques used to elicit motor disturbances*

Shake your head
Open and then close the eyes
Clap the hands three times
Grasp the examiner's hand three times
Ozeretski's test
Fist – Ring test
Fist – Edge – Palm test
Tests of coordination, including rapid alternating movements and finger – nose – finger
Station and gait

TABLE 8   *Evidence of disturbance of voluntary motor activity according to diagnosis and subtype (or subgroup) diagnosis*

Abnormal motor features	No. schizophrenics with feature by subtype					No. affective disorders by subgroup			
	Paranoid	Dis-organized	Undiff.	Cat.	Total	Manic	Depr.	Schiz. Aff.	Total
	n = 13	n = 10	n = 13	n = 1	n = 37	n = 3	n = 8	n = 5	n = 16
Spontaneous									
Motor blocking	0	4	3	1	8	0	0	0	0
Stereotypies/mannerisms	3	8	5	1	17	0	0	0	1
Clumsiness	3	9	9	1	22	0	0	1	1
Other (e.g. negativism, poverty of movement)	2	3	7	1	13	0	0	0	0
At least one feature	4 (32%)	10 (100%)	10 (76%)	1 (100%)	25 (67%)	0	0	1	1 (7%)
At least two features	4	9	8	1	22				
At least three features	1	6	1	1	9				
Elicited									
Motility									
Delayed response	1	3	1	1	5	0	0	0	0
Lengthy completion	1	4	3	0	7	0	0	0	0
Disorganization of movement	0	5	4	0	9	0	0	0	0
Postural persistence	0	2	4	0	6	0	0	1	1
Ozeretski test	2	5	8	1	16	1	0	1	1
Fist – Ring	8	9	9	2	27	0	0	1	1
Fist – Edge – Palm	5	6	7	1	19	0	0	0	0
Coordination	3	5	1	1	10	0	0	1	1

	2	3	2	0	7	0	0	1	1
Station and gait									
At least one feature	2 (92%)	10 (100%)	12 (92%)	1 (100%)	35 (95%)	0	0	4	4 (25%)
At least two features	5	8	7	1	20	0	0	1	1
At least three features	5	8	7	1	20	0	0	0	0
Spontaneous and elicited									
At least one feature	12 (92%)	10 (100%)	13 (100%)	1 (100%)	36 (98%)	1 (33%)	0 (0%)	4 (80%)	4 (25%)
At least two features	5	10	13	1	29	0	0	1	1
At least three features	5	10	12	1	28	0	0	0	0

interesting (Table 9). There was a positive and significant association between motor features and affective blunting and between non-localizing neurological signs and motor features. But the most striking association was the one between totaled abnormal intrinsic motor features and formal disturbances of thinking (r = 0.62, p < 0.0005, one-tailed). There was no evidence of a relationship between voluntary motor disturbances and delusional thinking.

The main finding was that disturbances in voluntary motor behavior (i.e. those that were not attributable to drug effects or known neurological disorder) occur in virtually all cases of conservatively defined schizophrenic disorder. The observed abnormalities were generally short-lived phenomena that, without careful scrutiny, might easily be missed. The fact that additional procedures for eliciting motor disturbance increased the number of observed abnormalities indicates that routine examination or occasional observation may not detect their presence. Indeed, the optimal method for discovering motor disturbances is clinical observation of patients over extended periods. Notably, the techniques for examination overlap only somewhat with the standard neurological examination.

It is also worth noting that certain dramatic features were not evident (e.g. automatic obedience, catalepsy, or excitement). Only 1 of the 37 schizophrenics qualified for the subtype diagnosis of catatonia. These observations are consistent with current reports of reduced incidence of catatonic schizophrenia. Yet abnormal movements were ubiquitous among the schizophrenic subjects, regardless of subtype, tempting the suggestion that they have been neglected largely because the search for motor manifestations has been focused on fairly uncommon and unusual features to the exclusion of more common ones (40).

The relative absence of motor disturbances in affective subjects suggests that while these features are certainly not pathognomonic for schizophrenia they tend to be significantly concentrated among individuals bearing that diagnosis. Of considerable interest is the fact that it was among the schizoaffective subgroup of affective subjects (a grouping that is controversial and based on the presence of both schizophrenic and affective features) that most of the voluntary motor disturbances occurred.

TABLE 9   *Interrelationships of abnormal features in schizophrenia (n = 37) (Pearson product – moment coefficients)*

	Affect	FTD	Delusions	Soft
Motor features	0.32**	0.54***	0.002	0.37**
Neurologic signs	0.01	0.27*	−0.002	−
Delusions	0.24	0.10	−	−
Formal thought disorder (FTD)	0.19	−	−	−

*p < 0.05, one-tailed
**p < 0.025, one-tailed
***p < 0.0005, one-tailed

The fact that affective blunting and non-localizing neurological signs also were associated with disturbed motor features points to interesting implications. The latter features have been considered evidence for subtle neurological impairment in schizophrenia. The frequency of affective blunting and neurological sign incidence is also consistent with published reports (41).

A second finding of the study was the significant, positive association of motor abnormality and disturbance in the form of thinking. The coincidence among schizophrenics of features from both these dimensions of behavioral functioning suggests that they may have a common pathogenetic basis.

The potentially difficult problem of neuroleptic drug effects was dealt with by the careful measurement of drug-induced motor activity and its exclusion from the computation of the motor behavior abnormality that was related to thought disorder. The incidence of neuroleptic side effects was consistent with previous reports and thus argues against a systematic underestimation of such effects. Moreover, we found significant differences between disturbed voluntary movement scores of medicated and non-medicated schizophrenics, suggesting that drugs tend to reduce those anomalies. On the other hand, in the paired comparisons of medicated schizophrenic and affective subjects, schizophrenic patients had significantly more voluntary motor disturbances, suggesting that motor impairment is more closely associated with schizophrenia.

It is naturally possible that some drug effects not detected by the rating scale methods we employed might be present (while other dramatic extrapyramidal features were absent), which could interfere with the programmed sequence of motor acts and the initiation of voluntary motor activity. The elicited motor activity assessments would be most susceptible to such effects; a separate analysis of the schizophrenic motor features observed in spontaneous behavior and formal thought disorder proved consistent with the hypothesized relationship between language and motor disturbance.

High-risk studies

Information is limited regarding the natural history of motor abnormalities. While follow-up studies will undoubtedly augment our knowledge, evidence from high-risk studies makes an important contribution.

Barbara Fish (42) reports that motor symptoms are often found in children who suffer psychiatric disturbance at a later age. For example, Robins (43, 44), observed that difficulty in walking differentiated preschizophrenic children from others. Watt (45) found that neurological disturbance and severe organic handicaps were more common at an earlier age among children who later developed schizophrenia than among classroom controls. Ricks and Nameche (46) discovered slow motor development and non-specific neurological symptoms twice as often in preschizophrenics as in controls, and more frequently in the group that became chronically disordered compared with that which experienced a more benign course of schizophrenia (47). Such prominent symptoms as hyperactivity, rigidity, abnormal gait, poor coordination, and impaired attention were typical among those who later became chronically withdrawn schizophrenics.

Marcus (48) investigated so-called neurological 'soft' signs in a group of 7 – 14 year-olds born of schizophrenic parents and a group of matched controls whose parents had no mental disease. He determined that facial asymmetry, fine motor coordination, left – right orientation, and evidence of disturbances of visual perception and auditory – visual integration were significantly more common among the high-risk sample. In the obstetric studies of high-risk individuals, conducted by Mednick, Mural, Schulsinger, and Mednick (49), retarded motor development at 5 days and 1 year differentiated offspring of schizophrenics from controls. Dozenko and Fatovi (42), using Ozeretski's method of studying motor maturity of children of schizophrenics, found that disturbances in speed, simultaneous movements, time and rhythm were the maximally decreased skills of motor function that distinguished the high-risk children. Fish's own work on infants at risk shows a spectrum of mild to severe irregularities and disruptions of physical growth as well as gross motor and visual – motor developmental abnormalities. These anomalies are associated with the later development of a spectrum of psychiatric disturbances. The presence of developmental disorders and complications thereof were significantly related to being at genetic risk for schizophrenia and not to pregnancy and birth complication history.

Hanson, Gottesman, and Heston (50) completed a prospective study of children of schizophrenic parents. At age 4, 30% of these children demonstrated poor motor skills in hopping, walking a line, catching a ball, and finer tasks, such as stringing beads. Three variables – poor motor skills, the presence of large intra-individual inconsistency of performance in various cognitive tasks, and observations of apathy, withdrawal, flatness, instability of relationships, irritability, and negativism – were chosen as predictors of vulnerability to schizophrenia on the basis of previous reports. These variables at extreme thresholds characterized 5 of 116 children, an incidence of about 10 times chance expectation. These 5 were all offspring of schizophrenic parents, and their case histories showed enduring forms of maladjustment of the types reported in the premorbid history of schizophrenia.

In another longitudinal study (51) evidence of premorbid neuromotor deviancies (e.g. poor gross and fine motor abilities) has also been associated with vulnerability to psychopathology among high-risk adolescents.

In summary, studies of high-risk populations suggest that delays in motor development and impairment of motor abilities, especially fine motor coordination, are detectable at an early age and may be associated with later development of schizophrenia, possibly of a more severe form.

Other neuropsychiatric investigations

Electromyographic studies

Practically since the development of electromyography, there has been an interest in the relationship between motor tension levels and schizophrenia. Part of this interest has been based on psychological views of development and cognition that stress the close relationship between motor behavior and thinking (52). Whatmore and Ellis (53) examined electromyographic activity in a group of schizophrenic patients at rest and compared these measures with a control population. Their findings disclosed that in all sites − forehead, jaw, forearm, and leg − significantly higher motor activity was present intermittently and/or continuously in the schizophrenic subjects. Malmo and Shagass (54) and Malmo, Shagass, Belanger, and Smith (55) showed similar high levels of response in patients under conditions of stress and performing a specific activity.

A series of electromyographic studies of auditory hallucinations in schizophrenia (56, 57) has produced evidence that electromyographic changes in the orofacial and laryngeal regions occur in close temporal association with the report of hallucinatory activity. There is no evidence that this phenomenon can be accounted for on the basis of generalized arousal, since control sites for electromyographic activity remain stable during hallucinations.

Studies of neuromuscular mechanisms

Meltzer and colleagues have investigated the incidence of various types of neuromuscular dysfunction in patients with schizophrenic and affective disorders and in their first-degree relatives. Meltzer (58) points to the long-known association of neuromuscular dysfunction and central nervous system disease, an association present in a number of neurological illnesses. Studies have demonstrated a variety of pathological changes in the neuromuscular system of psychotic patients, including alterations in creatine kinase levels in acute psychotic states, morphological changes in muscle fibers and subterminal motor nerves, and physiological abnormalities in nerve conduction velocity and spinal cord (Hoffman) reflex mechanisms. Crayton et al. (59) have extended these observations to single-fiber electromyographic recordings; their data suggest that psychosis is associated with responses characteristic of denervation or reinnervation of single muscle fibers by collateral sprouting. Studies have shown that acute schizophrenics have decreased recovery of the Hoffman reflex and chronic schizophrenics have increased recovery (60). These findings are consistent with increased dopaminergic influences on the alpha motor neuron system among acute schizophrenics and decreased dopaminergic influence on the same system among chronic schizophrenics. Hence, these findings may point to a link between neuromuscular dysfunction and the neurotransmitter theories of major psychoses (61).

A recent report (62) supports this general view through observations that the classic finding of slowed reaction time in schizophrenia, usually interpreted as resulting from central, specifically cognitive disturbances, may require a more complex explanation. They found that the disturbances (slowing) in reaction time could be partitioned into deviant peripheral and central components, thus challenging the notion of 'neuromuscular sameness' usually assumed by reaction time researchers.

Neuropharmacologic studies

Neuropharmacologic studies have been extremely fruitful in developing hypotheses and increasing understanding of the relationship between motor functioning and central nervous system disturbance believed to be present in schizophrenia. One source of evidence linking the motor anomalies of schizophrenia with central nervous system mechanisms are observations of motor effects following neuroleptic administration.

The dopamine hypothesis in schizophrenia, for example, is based in large part on the (blocking) effects of neuroleptic drugs on apomorphine- and amphetamine-induced stereotyped behaviors in laboratory animals (63, 64). Since these drugs interfere with the effects of dopamine, studies of the role of dopamine in psychomotor activity have flourished (65). It is clear that dopamine mechanisms are involved in spontaneous and purposeful motor activity. The anatomy relevant to this activity may be indicated by the high concentrations of dopamine found in the neostriatum but particularly in nigro – striatal pathways.

Lesions in the neostriatum can lead to symptoms involving postural mechanisms and spontaneous motor activity. Ancillary evidence supporting the proposal that dopamine and motor behavior are closely linked comes from studies of Parkinson's disease, which is known to be associated with damage to the nigro – striatal pathways. Such disturbance or damage leads to reduction or delay of spontaneous motor activity. In a study of Sernyl (phencyclidine, a dopamine agonist) effects on normal subjects, Holzman (66) reported the simultaneous occurrence of thought disturbance and a pronounced inability to coordinate movements. All subjects interviewed said that psychomotor integration and control were disrupted. Stevens (67) has hypothesized that blink rate is modulated by central dopamine activity, and Karson et al. (68) have found evidence in support of that view through the study of neuroleptic effects on blink rate. This area promises to provide useful data about central dopamine functions.

Work designed to elucidate the central nervous system mechanisms of motor behavior and their relationship to neuropharmacologic data remains at an early stage. However, evidence seems to be mounting to point to a close relationship between the neurotransmitters and basal ganglia and frontal lobe structures (69, 70). Among the pieces of evidence brought forward to establish this connection is the frequent association of schizophrenia-like disorders and basal ganglia disease. Such disorders as encephalitis, Huntington's disease, Wilson's disease, midbrain reticulosis, and essential hereditary tremor frequently result in psychotic manifestations.

A number of studies have demonstrated neurological impairment in psychiatric disorder (71 – 73). These studies have usually examined the incidence of so-called 'soft' or non-localizing neurological signs in hospitalized patients. Findings suggest that as many as three-quarters of schizophrenic patients demonstrate such disturbances on careful examination (74, 75). Longitudinal data are not available to determine whether such findings persist, remit, or become episodic. Tucker et al. (75)

showed that cognitive impairments, particularly thought disorder, occur more often in psychiatric patients with sensorimotor 'soft' signs than in controls and that neurological impairment and schizophrenia have a strong association. Gur (76) has suggested that findings of increased left-handedness in schizophrenics may reflect left-hemisphere dysfunction. Studies of non-localizing signs, handedness, and laterality have also pointed to possible left-hemisphere dysfunction in a significant proportion of schizophrenic patients (76 – 78). Those patients with greatest laterality impairments were also those manifesting the greatest motoric abnormalities (77).

Studies of ocular movement

In 1908, Diefendorf and Dodge reported that some schizophrenic patients exhibited ocular movement abnormalities, which could be photographed and which are detectable on careful neurological examination. Their work was extended only recently through a series of studies of oculomotor function in schizophrenia undertaken by Holzman and colleagues (79 – 82). The results indicate that 65 – 80% of schizophrenic patients and about 45% of their first-degree relatives have disturbed horizontal pursuit eye movements; that the impairment is largely independent of voluntary efforts to improve performance; that it is stable and independent of clinical state or antipsychotic medication; and that it appears to have a strong genetic component. Less than 10% of normal subjects show similar abnormalities.

An additional study (83) has demonstrated that pursuit impairments may be due to cortical dysfunction and that examination of specific optokinetic nystagmus responses (i.e. partial-field optokinetic nystagmus, OKN) in schizophrenics also reveals disordered movements compared to normals. The full import of such findings remains unclear, although certainly the association between schizophrenic disorder and oculomotor dysfunction adds considerable interest to the study of other motor abnormalities likely to be present among schizophrenics. Moreover, the study of ocular movements is sufficiently precise to permit sensitive analyses of factors that might alter the movements, including drug treatment. Such study, exemplified by the work of Latham et al. (83), promises progress in the anatomic localization of schizophrenic disturbances.

Additional studies

The findings of the investigation of motor abnormalities in schizophrenic disorder (3), reported above, led to two additional studies (84 – 85). In the first, we examined the relationship between formal thought disorder and clinical motor disturbance with more objective measures of language disorganization. In the second, we developed a laboratory measure of motor function, to compare disorganization in motor performance among schizophrenic and control subjects with assessments of thinking and motor behavior.

In the first study, we decided to measure the type-token ratio (TTR) because it is a simple, reliable, and quantifiable index of language deviance, unbiased by clinical judgment, and because in prior reports the TTR as an index of spoken language disorganization is statistically lower for formal thought-disordered schizophrenics compared to non-thought-disordered schizophrenics and psychiatric controls (84). Also age, education, and medication status do not appear to substantially influence this difference. The TTR is a measure of variability (or repetitiousness) in lexicon usage and is computed by dividing the total number of words (tokens) into the number of different words (types) in samples of uniform length.

Thus, the first study extending the survey, examined the hypothesis that disruptions in language behavior, as indicated by the TTR, would be associated with clinical evidence of disruptions in motor movement. Samples of language (at least 100 words) were assessed using the mean segmental type-token ratio (MSTTR) measure, which represents the average of TTRs for consecutive segments of 100 words. The motor response testing was the same as described in the survey study. The subjects included 21 schizophrenics (10 with evidence of formal thought disorder: 5 disorganized and 5 undifferentiated phenomenological subtypes). The 11 non-thought-disordered schizophrenics included 8 paranoid and 3 undifferentiated subtypes. There were 12 affective subjects (6 major depressives, 3 manics, and 3 schizoaffectives, manic type) and 12 normals. Non of the affective or normal controls had clinical evidence of formal thought disorder. Each schizophrenic subject and several affective (schizoaffective types in particular) showed evidence of disruption of skilled motor performance in the testing procedure. The relationship between scores summarizing evidence of disruption in skilled motor movements and MSTTRs was analyzed and the results indicated a negative association ($r = -0.59$, $df = 32$, $p < 0.001$).

The main finding then was that indices of disorganized motor behavior and language are strongly associated. Age and education appear to have little impact on the basic correlation. The results point to a potentially important relationship between disruptions in speech and movements behavior especially in, but not limited to, schizophrenics, particularly among the thought-disordered subgroup. The use of an index of language disturbance, the TTR, more reliable than the usual clinical ratings, represents an extension of and further support for the association between formal thought disorder and disrupted movements, a feature of schizophrenia not confounded by language. This study also pointed to the need for assessments of motor behavior that would be free of the inherent bias of clinical evaluation techniques in order to complement the greater reliability of language measures, such as the TTR.

The laboratory study of motor deficit (85) in schizophrenic disorders poses two problems: one is to establish that a reliable relationship exists between clinically observed motor phenomena and laboratory measurements of the deficit; the second is to establish that the motor anomalies have a reliable relationship with some other important aspect of the psychopathological syndrome, including evidence of structural or physiologic change.

Workers investigating the components of skilled motor performance have made extensive use of the concept of redundancy. From the standpoint of information theory, any event can be regarded as redundant to the extent that it is predictable from observation of a chain of immediately prior events. An object moving through space with fixed course and velocity is moving with high redundancy, whereas an insect flitting unpredictably from one point to another is moving with low redundancy. Simple rhythmic movements, such as are seen in the repeated hammering of a nail or the polishing of a surface, are examples of high-redundancy activities. Such patterns of motor activity permit adaptive responsiveness to other stimuli in the environment. Where an individual is deficient in the adaptive use of redundancies, we should expect rhythmic performance to be impaired. Indeed, some investigations reported elsewhere (86, 87) suggest that this is the case.

There is substantial evidence that schizophrenic patients fail to make use of redundancy (88) and that this is associated with the presence of thought disorder in these patients (89, 90). On this basis it seems reasonable to study rhythmic behavior in schizophrenic patients. We predicted that schizophrenics would be less able than non-schizophrenic controls to synchronize a motor movement with rhythmic stimuli. However, defective performance among schizophrenic patients on almost any task is practically axiomatic. Hence, we needed to be sure that by varying the difficulty of the rhythm task we could detect a differential deficit in the performance of schizophrenic subjects and not a uniform depression of adequacy of response across all conditions. We also expected that those patients who showed the most marked deficit would show deficits in the non-motor sphere (i.e. in thought disorder).

We decided to select rates of response that ranged from too low to permit accuracy to too high to do so. In this respect the investigation offered the possibility of establishing the task limits that would serve to detect differential deficit in schizophrenic and other psychiatric patients. We hypothesized that (a) schizophrenic performance on a rhythm synchronization task would reflect a relative incapacity to automate a motor performance (i.e. to rhythmize repetitive motor behavior) and would not be explicable by task difficulty; (b) clinical evidence of motor disturbance would be associated with evidence of poorer relative performance on the laboratory tasks; and (c) laboratory motor abnormality would be associated with severity of formal thought disorder.

Subjects were selected by strict diagnostic criteria (32) and by Research Diagnostic Criteria (RDC) (91). Sixteen schizophrenics were studied, including 5 paranoid, 7 disorganized, and 4 undifferentiated subtypes. Eight normal and 8 psychiatric (affective psychosis) controls were studied, including 5 major depressives and 3 schizoaffectives. Eleven of 16 schizophrenic subjects and 6 of 8 affective controls were taking neuroleptic medication. Dosages were matched according to chlorpromazine equivalents.

The procedure for clinical assessments of motor, thinking, and neuroleptic effects followed that of the survey investigation. Language samples were also obtained for TTR assessment of language disorganization. The synchronization task took place in a quiet, windowless laboratory. An Esterline Angus variable speed signal generator was used to produce rhythmic stimuli – uniform acoustic clicks. Unaccented (i.e. uniform) clicks create what is called a tremolo-rhythmic pattern (92). For each trial, a randomly ordered series of standard volume acoustic clicks of one rate (8, 12, 20, 40, 80, 120, 200, or 400 beats per minute) was presented. A wide range of rates was employed because it was not clear at which one the predictability of clicks would influence performance; although it was thought likely that at extremely slow and fast rates this factor would exert less influence on accuracy than on the ability to estimate intervals and tapping speed, respectively. To ensure that the effects of change in the rate were not confounded by changes in the pattern of rhythm, only the rate of clicks varied across trials. Synchronization was defined as simultaneous stimulus and subject response.

To determine the extent of the relationship between clinical and laboratory findings, the following strategy was applied. Disturbed motor activity scores, formal thought disturbance, and type – token ratios were compared among all subjects with synchronization accuracy at the rate that most distinguished the subject groups.

The results of this study can be summarized as follows. First, 15 of 16 schizophrenic subjects manifested one or more of the features of formal thought disorder, while 3 of the psychiatric controls showed such disturbance. Second, clinical motor disturbances were evident among all but 2 schizophrenics, whereas only 3 psychiatric controls showed such evidence. Normal controls showed no evidence of thought or motor abnormality. Third, evidence of neuroleptic side effects occurred in 2 of the 8 (25%) affective psychotic controls and in 5 of the 11 (45%) schizophrenic subjects taking neuroleptics. Within each group, subjects with neuroleptic side effects did not differ from those without side effects on ratings of other disturbed motor behavior. Medicated (11) and non-medicated (5) schizophrenic subjects did not differ in clinical motor ratings. On the other hand, medicated schizophrenic subjects and medicated affective controls were significantly different in clinical motor ratings ($t(14) = 3.05$, $p < 0.005$).

Fourth, our initial hypothesis, i.e. that schizophrenic group performance would be distinctive and not explained by task difficulty, was supported. The schizophrenic group was as able as normal or psychiatric control groups to rhythmize (or synchronize) performance at the slower rates (i.e. at 40 or slower) and at the faster rate of 200. This suggests that difficulty cannot account for these results and that other factors can operate to distinguish performance at the intermediate rates.

Fifth, clinical and laboratory measures of motor features were inversely related at a significant level, indicating that anomalous motor behavior is associated with reduced synchronization accuracy ($r = -0.53$, $p < 0.005$). Hence, our second hypothesis, i.e. that clinical measures of motor abnormality would be associated with evidence of lower laboratory performance in motor tasks, was also supported.

The relationship between clinical evidence of formal thought disorder, as defined in this report, and laboratory measures was also analyzed. Synchronization at 80 beats per minute, the rate showing the greatest spread among groups, correlated highly with formal thought disorder ($r = 0.50$, $p < 0.005$). The relationship between formal thought disorder and synchronization at other rates was also calculated and indicated generally the same relationship, namely, that formal thought disorder was related to poorer synchronization. Hence, our third hypothesis, that performance on the laboratory task is associated with degree of formal thought disorder, was also supported. The relationship is negative and significant. The MSTTR and synchronization accuracy were correlated at a significant level ($r = 0.35$, $0.025 < p > 0.05$), indicating that reduced accuracy on the motor task is associated with evidence of language impairment.

The major finding of this study is that measures of synchronization with auditory stimuli appear to distinguish the performance of schizophrenics and controls. Because schizophrenic performance overlaps with that of controls at some rates and diverges markedly at others, neither low motivation, the effect of general psychosis, difficulty of the procedure, motor dexterity, drug effects, nor tapping speed ability satisfactorily account for the observed differences. The plausibility of these explanations depends fundamentally on their ability to operate consistently across the experimental procedures. Failing that, other explanations must be considered.

These results are, however, consistent with predictions based on the hypothesis that schizophrenics are less able than controls to take advantage of the redundancy (in the information-processing sense of the term) of the auditory stimuli in order to synchronize tapping efficiently and accurately, a process similar to that required to automate any skilled motor activity (93, 94). The ability to be aware of and make use of the redundancy or predictability of the clicks has the effect of decreasing the need to attend to estimating click occurrence and selecting and coordinating the tapping response. Prior work summarized by Maher (95) has suggested that a disturbance in attentional focusing operates to impair the production of comprehensible speech in schizophrenics. In the synchronization procedure, a similar difficulty may disrupt performance. Specifically, we might expect that schizophrenics fail to adapt their attentional processes to the redundancies intrinsic to the task and hence exhibit relatively inefficient tapping and inaccurate synchronization. Indeed, schizophrenic performance, like that of controls, is aided by the redundancy of the stimuli, but to a significantly lesser degree.

Much work in experimental psychology has also shown that the performance of motor responses depends critically upon the operation of attentional processes (96 – 98). Particular importance has been attached to the effects of attention on the timing of sequential movements (99). The results of the present investigation, which demonstrate a strong association between motor and language disorders that clinically have certain similarities (e.g. repetition in speech and movement) in schizophrenia, can reasonably be considered within an attentional deficit frame of reference.

This view is supported by the work of Sternberg et al. (100), who demonstrated a connection between language and motor control in an investigation of speech and typewriting, Barlett's observations about the connections between language, thought, and motor movement, and their elaboration by Posner (101) into a sophisticated model pointing to the processes of attention involved in the sequencing and shifting of motor acts and thoughts. Yet other views may be appropriate as well and a skeptical attitude toward this as well as other explanatory models is warranted until it is better supported. Nevertheless, the possible relationship between such features and cortical and subcortical atrophy, which could be understood in the framework of an attention deficit, should be explored.

We replicated and extended the motor synchrony study with a computer-based measuring technique (102). The results indicate a relationship between deficient motor synchrony and the presence of negative symptoms of schizophrenia, such as blunted affect, emotional withdrawal, and refusal to speak. Additional work is needed to understand the nature of motor synchrony, but it appears that deficient performance in this task is related to disturbances in thinking and clinical motor abnormality in schizophrenic disorders.

Comment

The study of motor abnormalities must progress substantially to make a significant contribution to the neurology of schizophrenia. A critical step toward that goal will be to overcome the indirect nature of measurement of neurologic (central) abnormality through the study of behavioral (peripheral) features. Classic neurology successfully dealt with this limitation through the study of neuropathology. Investigators of schizophrenia may be able, through the use of imaging technologies, to relate behavior to central nervous system structure and/or physiology (103). A related critical step not to be overlooked is the establishment of better, quantifiable, reliable, experimentally useful, (ideally) laboratory-based techniques for motor performance investigation. Advances of both sorts should enrich the prospects for a mature neurology of schizophrenia.

Conclusions

The clinical and experimental literature on psychopathology of motor behavior and schizophrenia is sketchy at best. Nevertheless, important observations have been made that suggest avenues for further investigation.

1. Motor abnormalities intrinsic to schizophrenic disorder occur more frequently than is generally believed and are not limited to the catatonic schizophrenia. Yet dramatic and unusual motor anomalies, such as catalepsy, are not common currently, and this fact may contribute to the widespread belief in low incidence. On the other hand, more subtle features, such as clumsiness and repetitive movements (e.g. stereotypies, perseveration, as well as disorganization, delayed response, postural persistence, and lengthy completion of movements), are frequent, occurring in virtually all conservatively diagnosed cases. These features require either longitudinal and frequent assessment or examination techniques designed especially to elicit them in a systematic manner. Traditional examination approaches may simply miss them.

2. Certain movement abnormalities, such as choreiform and athetoid movements, are probably not a part of schizophrenic disorder at least in its early stages. Other basal ganglia diseases, brain damage, and drug effects are likely sources for these motor abnormalities.

3. Antipsychotic medications produce many motor effects, but they tend to reduce voluntary motor anomalies intrinsic to schizophrenic disorder and may not modify the occurrence of certain spontaneous involuntary disordered movements, at least among chronic cases. Further research, preferably in drug-free patients, could be an important step to clarification and extension of knowledge on this matter. The relationship of what is designated as tardive dyskinesia in schizophrenic patients to other movement abnormalities should be investigated further.

4. Motor disturbances, as currently understood, are not pathognomonic for schizophrenic disorder. Indeed, most schizophrenic motor abnormalities occur in a variety of diseases involving basal ganglia and other subcortical structures. Nevertheless, the concentration of motor abnormalities, both voluntary and involuntary, among schizophrenic patients compared to affective patients, suggests that certain specific relationships between motor disturbance and schizophrenic disorders exist. The coincidence of motor features, psychotic features, and cognitive impairment in schizophrenic disorders is also characteristic of some cases of hepatolenticular degeneration (Wilson's disease), Huntington's chorea, Parkinson's disease, and related disorders. Comparative studies involving schizophrenic patients might generate useful information about the pathogenesis, anatomy, and treatment of such disorders.

5. Schizophrenic motor disturbances are associated with formal thought disorder, certain neurological signs, and affective blunting. The connection between formal thought disorder and motor disturbances is congruent with predictions based on the attentional deficit hypothesis in schizophrenia. Assessments of subcortical and cortical atrophy in patients evaluated for motor disturbances might prove useful in extending our knowledge.

6. The exact relationship of motor features to prognosis is unclear. It appears, however, that the more severe the profile of motor disturbance, the more grave the illness. Observations of developmental motor difficulty in high-risk children also suggests that motor abnormalities detectable at an early age and prior to the onset of illness may portend a more severe and serious outcome.

7. Studies attempting to examine the motor and language deficits with laboratory techniques indicate an association between the two dimensions of behavior in schizophrenic disorder. They suggest parallel breakdowns in the capacity to utilize redundancy in behavior. The source of such breakdown, which can be conceptualized cognitively (attention) or neurologically (brain damage), remains a focus for research.

8. The relationships between motor and other psychopathologic features described occur predominantly, but not exclusively, in the schizophrenic patient groups, suggesting that further investigation of these findings may lead to knowledge applicable to a broader range of psychopathologic disorders.

9. A broad range of neuropsychiatric studies have centered on motor disturbances. The results, however preliminary, provide important support for the view that investigations attempting to integrate clinical and laboratory dimensions of motor abnormality may significantly extend our understanding of schizophrenic

disorders. Considerable potential exists for studies integrating laboratory measures of motor behavior and central (imaging) measures of brain structure and function.

REFERENCES

1. Kleist K (1908) *Untersuchungen zur Kenntnis der psychomotorischen Bewegungsstörungen bei Geisteskranken.* W. Klinkhart, Leipzig.
2. Kraepelin E (1919) *Dementia praecox.* Livingstone, Edinburgh.
3. Manschreck TC, Maher BA, Rucklos ME, Vereen DE (1982) Disturbed voluntary motor activity in schizophrenic disorders. *Psychol. Med., 12,* 73.
4. Marsden C, Tarsy D, Baldessarini R (1975) Spontaneous and drug induced movement disorders in psychotic patients. In: Benson D, Blumer D (Eds), *Psychiatric aspects of neurological disease.* Grune and Stratton, New York.
5. Bleuler E (1911) *Dementia praecox or the group of schizophrenias.* Reprinted in 1950 by: International Universities Press, New York.
6. Fish F (1967) *Clinical Psychopathology.* John Wright, Bristol.
7. Mailloux NW, Newberger M (1941) The work curves of psychotic individuals. *J. Abnorm. Soc. Psychol., 36,* 110.
8. Wulfeck W (1941) Motor function in the mentally disordered. *Psychol. Rec., 4,* 271.
9. Jackson J (1894) In: *Selected Writings of James Hughlings Jackson. Vol. 2.* Reprinted in 1958 by: Basic Books, New York.
10. Arieti S (1945) Primitive habits and perceptual alterations. *Arch. Neurol. Psychol., 53,* 378.
11. Jelliffe S (1928) The mental pictures in schizophrenia and in epidemic encephalitis. *Res. Publ. Assoc. Nerv. Ment. Dis., 5,* 204.
12. Orton ST (1930) Some neurologic concepts applied to catatonia. *Arch. Neurol. Psychiatry, 23,* 114.
13. Jaspers K (1963) *General psychopathology.* University of Chicago Press, Chicago.
14. Slater E, Roth M (1969) *Clinical Psychiatry.* Balliere, London.
15 Freeman T (1969) *Psychopathology of the psychoses.* International Universities Press, New York.
16. Manschreck TC (1983) Psychopathology of motor behavior in schizophrenia. *Prog. Exp. Pers. Res., 12,* 53.
17. Kahlbaum K (1874) *Catatonia.* Reprinted in 1973 by: Johns Hopkins Press, Baltimore.
18. Regenstein Q, Alpert J, Reich P (1977) Sudden catatonic stupor with disastrous outcome. *J. Am. Med. Assoc., 238,* 618.
19. Morrison JR (1973) Catatonia. Retarded and excited types. *Arch. Gen. Psychiatry, 28,* 39.
20. Andrews E (1981) Catatonic behavior: recognition, differential diagnosis, and management. In: Manschreck TC (Ed), *Psychiatric Medicine Update: Massachusetts General Hospital Revisions for Physicians.* Elsevier North Holland, New York.
21. Gelenberg A (1976) The catatonic syndrome. *Lancet 2,* 1339.
22. Mahendra B (1981) Where have all the catatonics gone? *Psychol. Med., 11,* 669.
23. Marsden CD (1982) Motor disorders in schizophrenia. *Psychol. Med., 12,* 13.
24. Guggenheim F, Babigian H (1974) Diagnostic consistency in catatonic schizophrenia. *Schizophr. Bull., 11,* 103.
25. Jones M, Hunter R (1968) Abnormal movements in patients with chronic psychiatric ill-

ness. In: Crane G, Gardner R (Eds), USPHS Pub. No. 1936.

26. King HE (1976) Psychomotor correlates of behavior disorder. In: Kietzman ML, Sutton S, Zubin J (Eds), *Experimental Approaches to Psychopathology.* Academic Press, New York.
27. Mettler FA, Crandell A (1959) Neurologic disorders in psychiatric institutions. *J. Nerv. Ment. Dis., 128,* 148.
28. Allison R (1966) Perseveration as a sign of diffuse and focal brain damage. I, II. *Br. Med. J.,* 1027, 1095.
29. Freeman T, Gathercole C (1966) Perseveration, the clinical symptom in chronic schizophrenia. *Br. J. Psychiatry, 112,* 27.
30. Stengel E (1947) A clinical and psychological study of echo reactions. *J. Ment. Sci., 93,* 598.
31. Owens DGC, Johnstone EC, Frith CD (1982) Spontaneous involuntary disorders of movement. *Arch. Gen. Psychiatry, 39,* 452.
32. Feighner J, Robins E, Guze S, Woodruff RA, Winokur G, Munoz R (1972) Diagnostic criteria for use in psychiatric research. *Arch. Gen. Psychiatry, 26,* 57.
33. Schneider K (1959) *Clinical psychopathology.* Grune and Stratton, New York.
34. Mellor CS (1970) First rank symptoms of schizophrenia. *Br. J. Psychiatry, 117,* 15.
35. Carpenter WT, Jr, Strauss JS, Muleh S (1973) Are there pathognomonic symptoms in schizophrenia? An empiric investigation of Kurt Schneider's first rank symptoms. *Arch. Gen. Psychiatry, 28,* 847.
36. Pope HG, Lipinski JF (1978) Manic depressive disorder and schizophrenia. *Arch. Gen. Psychiatry, 35,* 1.
37. Chapman J (1966) The early symptoms of schizophrenia. *Br. J. Psychiatry, 112,* 225.
38. Jones IH (1965) Observations on schizophrenic stereotypies. *Compr. Psychiatry, 6,* 323.
39. Yarden PE, Discipio WJ (1971) Abnormal movements and prognosis in schizophrenia. *Am. J. Psychiatry, 128,* 317.
40. McGhie A (1969) *Pathology of attention.* Penguin, Baltimore.
41. Tucker G, Silberfarb P (1978) Neurologic dysfunction in schizophrenia. In: Akiskal H, Webb W (Eds), *Psychiatric diagnosis.* Spectrum, New York.
42. Fish B (1975) Biological antecedents of psychosis in children. In: Freedman DX (Ed), *Biology of the major Psychoses.* Raven, New York.
43. Robins L (1966) *Deviant children grow up.* Williams and Wilkins, Baltimore.
44. O'Neal P, Robins L (1958) Childhood patterns predictive of adult schizophrenia. *Am. J. Psychiatry, 115,* 385.
45. Watt N (1974) Childhood and adolescent routes to schizophrenia. In: Ricks D, Thomas A, Roff M (Eds), *Life history research in psychopathology (Vol. 3).* University of Minnesota Press, Minneapolis.
46. Ricks D, Nameche G (1966) Symbiosis, sacrifice, and schizophrenia. *Ment. Hyg., 50,* 541.
47. Ricks D, Berry J (1970) Family and symptom patterns that precede schizophrenia. In: Roff M, Ricks D (Eds), *Life history research in psychopathology (Vol. 1).* University of Minnesota Press, Minneapolis.
48. Marcus J (1974) Cerebral functioning in offspring of schizophrenics. *Int. J. Ment. Health, 3,* 57.
49. Mednick SA, Mural M, Schulsinger G, Mednick B (1971) Perinatal conditions and infant development in children with schizophrenic parents. *Soc. Biol., 18,* 108.
50. Hanson D, Gottesman I, Heston L (1976) Some possible childhood indicators of adult

schizophrenia inferred from children of schizophrenics. *Br. J. Psychiatry, 129,* 142.

51. Erlenmeyer-Kimling L, Cornblatt B, Friedman D, Marcuse Y, Rutschmann J, Simmens S, Devi S (1982) Neurological, electrophysiological, and attentional deviations in children at risk for schizophrenia. In: Henn F, Nasrallah H (Eds), *Schizophrenia as a brain disease.* Oxford University Press, New York.
52. Jacobson E (1938) *Progressive relaxation.* University of Chicago Press, Chicago.
53. Whatmore GB, Ellis Jr RM (1958) Some motor aspects of schizophrenia: EMG study. *J. Psychiatry, 114,* 882.
54. Malmo R, Shagass C (1949) Physiologic studies of reaction to stress in anxiety and early schizophrenia. *Psychosom. Med., 11,* 9.
55. Malmo R, Shagass C, Belanger D, Smith A (1951) Motor control in psychiatric patients under experimental stress. *J. Abnorm. Psychol., 46,* 539.
56. Gould LN (1948) Verbal hallucinations and activity of vocal musculature: an electromyographic study. *Am. J. Psychiatry, 105,* 367.
57. McGuigan FJ (1966) Covert oral behavior and auditory hallucinations. *Psychophysiology, 3,* 73.
58. Meltzer H (1979) Neuromuscular dysfunction in schizophrenia. *Br. J. Psychiatry, 117,* 15.
59. Crayton J, Stalberg E, Hilton-Brown P (1977) The motor unit in psychotic patients: a single fiber EMG study. *J. Neurol. Neurosurg. Psychiatry, 40,* 455.
60. Goode DJ, Meltzer HY, Crayton JW, Mazura TA (1977) Physiologic abnormalities of the neuromuscular system in schizophrenia. *Schizophr. Bull., 3,* 121.
61. Meltzer H (1979) Biochemical studies in schizophrenia. In: Bellak L (Ed), *Disorders of the schizophrenic syndrome.* Basic Books, New York.
62. Schneider RD, Grossi V (1979) Differences in muscle activity before, during, and after responding in a simple reaction time task: schizophrenic vs. normals. *Psychiatry Res., 1,* 141.
63. Matthysse S (1974) Dopamine and the pharmacology of schizophrenia. *J. Psychol. Res., 11,* 107.
64. Snyder S, Banerjee S, Yammura A, Greenberg D (1974) Drugs, neurotransmitters, and schizophrenia. *Science, 21,* 1243.
65. Papeschi R (1972) Dopamine, extrapyramidal system and psychomotor function. *Psy. Neur. Neurochirurgia, 75,* 13.
66. Holzman P (1972) Assessment of perceptual functioning in schizophrenia. *Psychopharmacology, 25,* 29.
67. Stevens JR (1978) Eye blink and schizophrenia: psychosis or tardive dyskinesia. *Am. J. Psychiatry, 135,* 223.
68. Karson C, Fried WJ, Kleinman JE, Bigelow LB, Wyatt RJ (1981) Neuroleptics decrease blinking in schizophrenic subjects. *Biol. Psychiatry, 16,* 679.
69. Glassman R (1976) A neural systems theory of schizophrenia and tardive dyskinesia. *Behav. Sci., 21,* 274.
70. Munkvad I, Pakkenberg J, Randrup A (1968) Aminergic systems in basal ganglia associated with stereotyped behavior and catalepsy. *Brain Behav. Evol., 1,* 89.
71. Hertzig MA, Birch HC (1968) Neurologic organization in psychiatrically disturbed adolescent girls. *Arch. Gen. Psychiatry, 19,* 528.
72. Larson V (1964) Physical characteristics of disturbed adolescents. *Arch. Gen. Psychiatry, 10,* 55.
73. Rochford J, Detre T, Tucker G, Harrow M (1970) Neuropsychological impairments in

functional psychiatric diseases. *Arch. Gen. Psychiatry, 22,* 114.

74. Pincus J, Tucker G (1974) Behavioral neurology. Oxord University Press, New York.
75. Tucker G, Campoin E, Silberfarb P (1975) Sensorimotor functions and cognitive distur-
    bance in psychiatric patients. *Am. J. Psychiatry, 132,* 17.
76. Gur R (1977) Motoric laterality imbalance in schizophrenia. *Arch. Gen. Psychiatry, 34,*
    33.
77. Manschreck TC, Ames D (1984) Neurologic features and psychopathology in
    schizophrenic disorders. *Biol. Psychiatry, 19/5,* 703.
78. Nasrallah HA, Keelor K, Van Schroeder C, McCalley Whitters M (1981) Motoric
    lateralization in schizophrenic males. *Am. J. Psychiatry, 138/8,* 1114.
79. Holzman P, Proctor L, Hughes D (1973) Eye-tracking patterns in schizophrenia.
    Science, 181, 179.
80. Holzman P, Proctor L, Levy D, Yasillo N, Meltzer H, Hurt S (1974) Eye-tracking
    dysfunctions in schizophrenic patients and their relatives. *Arch. Gen. Psychiatry, 31,*
    143.
81. Holzman P, Levy D (1977) Smooth pursuit eye movements and functional psychoses:
    a review. *Schizophr. Bull., 3,* 15.
82. Holzman P, Kringlen E, Levy D, Haberman S (1980) Deviant eye tracking in twins
    discordant for psychoses: a replication. *Arch. Gen. Psychiatry, 37,* 627.
83. Latham C, Holzman P, Manschreck TC, Tole J (1981) Optokinetic nystagmus and pur-
    suit eye movements in schizophrenia. *Arch. Gen. Psychiatry, 38,* 997.
84. Manschreck TC, Maher BA, Ader DN (1981) (a) Formal thought disorder, the type-
    token ratio, and disturbed voluntary motor movement in schizophrenia. *Br. J.*
    Psychiatry, 139, 7.
85. Manschreck TC, Maher BA, Rucklos ME, Vereen DR, Ader DN (1981) (b) Deficient
    motor synchrony in schizophrenia. *J. Abnorm. Psychol., 90/4,* 321.
86. Breil MS (1953) Graphologische Untersuchungen über die Psychomotorik in den Hand-
    schriften Schizophrenen. *Monatschr. Psychiatr. Neurol., 125,* 193.
87. Kneutgen J (1976) Experimentelle Analyse einer Wahrnehmungsstörung bei Schizophre-
    nie: Desynchronisation von Handbewegungen mit einer gleichformigen akustischen Fre-
    quenz. *Fortschr. Neurol. Psychiatr., 44,* 182.
88. Cromwell RL (1968) Stimulus redundancy in schizophrenia. *J. Nerv. Ment. Dis., 146,*
    360.
89. Maher BA, Manschreck TC, Rucklos M (1980) Contextual constraint and the recall of
    verbal material in schizophrenia: the effect of thought disorder. *Br. J. Psychiatry, 137,*
    69.
90. Manschreck TC, Maher BA, Rucklos ME, White M (1979) The predictability of thought
    disordered speech in schizophrenic patients. *Br. J. Psychiatry, 134,* 595.
91. Spitzer R, Endicott J, Robins E (1975) *Research Diagnostic Criteria for a Selected*
    Group of Functional Disorders (RDC). Biometrics Research, New York.
92. Lundin R (1967) *An Objective Psychology of Music.* Ronald Press, New York.
93. Posner M, Keele SW (1969) Attention demands of movements. In: *Proceedings of the*
    17th Congress of Applied Psychology. Swets & Zeitlinger, Amsterdam.
94. Schmidt RA (1968) Anticipation and timing in human motor performance. *Psychol.*
    Bull., 70, 631.
95. Maher BA (1972) The language of schizophrenia: a review and interpretation. *Br. J.*
    Psychiatry, 120, 3.
96. Ells JG (1973) Analysis of attentional and temporal aspects of movement control. *J.*
    Exp. Psychol., 99, 10.

97. Rosenbaum DA (1980) Human Movement Initiation: specification of arm, direction, and extent. *J. Exp. Psychol., 109,* 444.
98. Stelmach GF (Ed) (1978) *Information Processing in Motor Control and Learning.* Academic Press, New York.
99. Rosenbaum DA, Pastashnik D (1980) A mental clock setting process revealed by reaction time. In: Stelmach GE, Requin J (Eds), *Tutorials in Motor Behavior.* North-Holland Publishing Company, Amsterdam.
100. Sternberg S, Monsell S, Knoll TL, Wright CE (1978) The latency and duration of rapid movement sequences: comparisons of speech and typewriting. In: Stelmach GF (Ed), *Information Processing in Motor Control and Learning.* Academic Press, New York.
101. Posner MI (1980) Orienting of attention. *Q. J. Exp. Psychol., 32,* 3.
102. Manschreck TC, Maher BA, Waller NG, Ames D, Latham CA (1985) Deficient motor synchrony in schizophrenic disorders: Clinical correlates. *Biol. Psychiatry, 20,* 990.
103. Guenther W, Breitling D, Banquet JP, Marcie P, Rondot P (1986) EEG mapping of left hemisphere dysfunction during motor performance in schizophrenia. *Biol. Psychiatry, 21,* 249.

CHAPTER 4

Neurological aspects of tardive dyskinesia

JAMES B. LOHR, ALEX WISNIEWSKI AND DILIP V. JESTE

The emergence of tardive dyskinesia (TD) in the late 1950's was probably one of the factors stimulating a reawakening of interest in neurological aspects of psychiatric disorders. Here was a movement disorder that appeared similar in form to other choreoathetoid disorders studied by neurologists for many years, yet it occurred in psychiatric patients (mainly schizophrenic patients) after treatment with pharmacological agents for their psychiatric problems. These agents have come to be called either antipsychotic or neuroleptic medications − terms which highlight, respectively, the psychiatric and neurological effects of these drugs. Thus, TD has become a focus of interest for both psychiatrists and neurologists and, much like the outbreak of postencephalitic parkinsonism decades earlier, has stimulated interest in the neurology of psychiatric disorders.

The first reported cases of TD were probably those of Schönecker (1) in Germany, approximately five years after the initial reports of the efficacy of chlorpromazine in psychiatric disorders. Three of the patients in this report were elderly women who developed orobuccal dyskinesias after exposure to chlorpromazine, although the dyskinesias appeared within less than two months of treatment. What was distinctive about the movements of these patients was that in two of the cases the dyskinesia persisted for up to almost three months following discontinuation of the neuroleptic. This was in marked contrast to the acute short-lived neuroleptic-induced movements described up to that time.

Following Schönecker, reports of a persistent neuroleptic-related dyskinesia usually involving the orofacial musculature began to appear throughout Europe and America in the late 1950s and early 1960s. These included the reports of Sigwald et al. (2) in France, Kruse (3) and Druckman (4) in the USA, Uhrbrand and Faurbye (5) in Denmark, and Hunter et al. (6) in England. In 1964 Faurbye et al. (7) first used the term 'tardive dyskinesia' to describe the syndrome.

In spite of the growing number of reports, TD was for a number of years thought to be quite uncommon. Then, in the late 1960s some studies began to report rather high prevalence rates of TD. In a review in 1973, Crane (8) noted that reports of the prevalence of TD ran as high as 40% among neuroleptic-treated patients.

The decade of the 1970s witnessed further characterization of the syndrome along with the first large-scale attempts at treatment. Nevertheless, even today the true dimensions of the disorder remain sketchy and an effective treatment has proven to be elusive.

Handbook of Schizophrenia, Vol. 1: The Neurology of Schizophrenia.
H.A. Nasrallah and D.R. Weinberger, editors.
© Elsevier Science Publishers B.V., 1986

Definition and description

TD is usually defined as a syndrome consisting of abnormal involuntary movements that are most often choreoathetoid in appearance and in which neuroleptic drug treatment is a necessary etiological factor (9). The movements occur relatively late in the course of treatment, usually after at least three months of therapy. The orofacial and upper extremity musculature is most commonly involved, although the trunk, lower extremities, pharynx and diaphragm are also affected in some patients. Orofacial movements (mainly involving the tongue) occur in approximately 80% of patients. Approximately 11% of patients exhibit movements in all the major body regions (9).

The facial movements usually consist of repetitive outward thrusting of the tongue, chewing movements of the jaw, lip smacking or pouting, and blinking, grimacing, sucking or frowning. In the upper extremities, finger movements are most often seen ('piano player's fingers') but choreoathetoid movements can involve any part of the limb or its entirety. In the lower extremities the movements involve the toes, often with spreading, retroflexion or combined movements. Stamping of the foot is seen, as well as inversion, eversion and lateral movements of the ankle. The trunk may exhibit rocking or twisting movements and respiratory or gastrointestinal symptoms may develop as a result of diaphragmatic, intercostal and abdominal muscle contractions. Axial movements can also occur in the neck as well as shoulders and pelvis. These movements may resemble dystonic contortions except that in TD they generally last for shorter periods of time.

The reported prevalence of TD has ranged from 10 to 40% in certain subgroups of patients. The variation in anatomical distribution and in the course of illness of different patients has prompted a number of investigators to propose subclassification schemes for TD. Kidger et al. (10) and Barnes et al. (11, 12), on the basis of studies of the somatic distribution of movements in TD patients, have proposed that TD may occur in both a central (i.e. orofacial) and peripheral form. The peripheral syndrome may occur more frequently in younger patients while orofacial movements may occur more often in the elderly (12, 13). The validity of such a classification has not yet been well established, however.

The course of the syndrome may vary among individuals, and there may be reversible, intermittent and persistent varieties. About 33% of cases of TD are reversible, with remission of the signs within 3 months of drug withdrawal (9). The intermittent form may be dependent on the stage of illness and neuroleptic status. A disorder probably related to TD is 'withdrawal-emergent dyskinesia' which as a rule disappears within one to three weeks of discontinuing medications, and most often occurs in children (14, 15). This withdrawal-emergent dyskinesia may at times represent a forerunner of the full syndrome.

Although neuroleptics are usually implicated in the etiology of TD, they are only one of a variety of drugs that may be involved. Some of the different drugs that have been reported to cause choreoathetoid movements and possibly TD are listed in Table 1. It should be noted that persistent TD has only been reported with the use of neuroleptic medications, however.

TABLE 1   *Drugs implicated in dyskinetic disorders including TD*

Neuroleptics:
  Phenothiazines
  Thioxanthines
  Butyrophenones
  Indolones
  Dibenzazepines
  Diphenylbutylpiperidines
	Antiparkinsonian agents:
	  Amantadine
	  Bromocriptine
	  L-DOPA

Antihistamines	Antidepressants:
	  Tricyclic antidepressants
	  Monoamine oxidase inhibitors

Stimulants:
  Amphetamines
  Methylphenidate
  Fenfluramine
	Lithium
	
	Metoclopramide
	
	Alpha-methylDOPA
	
	Anticonvulsants
	
	Estrogens

Age, gender and diagnosis are among factors reportedly related to the prevalence and prognosis. Based on a review of 19 studies, Jeste and Wyatt (16) calculated that women may have a 41% higher mean prevalence than men. The reasons for this difference are unclear. Patients between ages 40 and 70 appear to have more severe dyskinesias as well as a higher prevalence of the syndrome than younger patients (17, 18). Additionally, the older age group shows a lower rate of remission than the younger patients (19).

TD can occur in a number of different diagnostic categories outside of schizophrenia. Patients with unipolar depression (20) and bipolar affective disorder (21) have been identified as high-risk groups for TD. Other high risk groups include retarded patients, especially those with phenylketonuria (22). However, the issue of organicity and brain damage as a risk factor is controversial (23).

Other factors that may be associated with TD are high-dose neuroleptic treatment and high-potency neuroleptic medications as well as depot neuroleptics (9). Because the use of these agents may be reserved for special subgroups of patients who may be resistant or show poor response to neuroleptics, the higher incidence of dyskinesia could, in some way, be related to the underlying illness itself. Finally, other factors that may be associated with TD are parkinsonism, dental problems, or dentures (9).

Neurochemical and neuroendocrinological aspects

Current neurochemical theories of TD generally involve the dopaminergic system and its interactions with cholinergic mechanisms. In addition, investigators have postulated abnormalities in the noradrenergic and GABAergic systems, as well as in certain systems involving putative peptidergic neurotransmitters. We will briefly review the evidence for the involvement of these systems in TD.

Dopamine

The main factors pointing to dopaminergic overactivity in TD are pharmacological, as follows:

1. Withdrawal of neuroleptics (which are known to block dopamine receptors) results in worsening of symptoms and signs.

2. Dopaminergic agonists like L-DOPA and amphetamine aggravate the movements.

3. Dopamine depleting agents (e.g., reserpine, tetrabenazine) and dopamine receptor blocking agents (e.g., butyrophenones and phenothiazines) may lessen the movements.

4. The findings that Parkinson's disease and TD show opposite responses to dopaminergic agents (Parkinson's disease improves whereas TD worsens with L-DOPA), and the fact that dopamine is known to be reduced in Parkinson's disease may indirectly indicate that there exists a relative dopaminergic hyperactivity in TD.

Additionally, the interaction between dopamine and acetylcholine in Parkinson's disease provides clues to the underlying etiology of TD, as anticholinergic agents usually worsen the dyskinetic movements of TD presumably by further increasing dopaminergic transmission, whereas in Parkinson's disease anticholinergic agents improve the dysfunction.

Until recently, the favored neurochemical theory of TD revolved around supersensitivity of striatal dopamine receptors, but at present the relevance of this finding to TD is unknown. It is clear that probably all neuroleptic-exposed individuals develop some degree of supersensitivity, yet only a minority develop tardive dyskinetic movements. Additionally, there is little evidence of any generalized overactivity of the dopaminergic system in TD. Most studies comparing CSF dopamine metabolites have reported no differences between dyskinetic and non-dyskinetic patients (24). The prolactin and growth hormone responses indicative of tubero-infundibular dopaminergic activity show no differences between normal and dyskinetic patients (25, 26). Also, the coexistence of TD and drug-induced parkinsonism in some patients (which will be discussed in more detail later) is difficult to explain, based on the above theory, although it is possible that dopaminergic hyperfunction and hypofunction may coexist, but in different areas of the brain. As will be discussed later, the different patterns of TD may suggest involvement of different neurochemical systems.

Norepinephrine

The evidence for noradrenergic hyperactivity in TD to a large extent overlaps the evidence for dopaminergic hyperactivity. Drugs such as amphetamine and methylphenidate, which worsen TD, are both dopaminergic and noradrenergic stimulants. Also, neuroleptics are thought to exert some blockade on noradrenergic receptors (27).

A subgroup of patients with TD has been shown to have high serum dopamine beta-hydroxylase (DBH) activity (DBH is the enzyme that converts dopamine to norepinephrine), low platelet and lymphocyte monoamine oxidase (MAO) activity (MAO is the enzyme that inactivates norepinephrine), and elevations in CSF norepinephrine (28 – 30). This evidence suggests that noradrenergic hyperfunction may be a factor in the pathogenesis of TD.

A number of drugs involved in reducing noradrenergic activity have been used with limited success in TD. These include beta-adrenergic blockers such as propranolol, presynaptic alpha-adrenergic blockers such as clonidine, and DBH inhibitors such as fusaric acid (see Ref. 9). Indirect evidence for a relationship of TD with the noradrenergic system has been provided by recent reports of state-dependent dyskinesia in bipolar patients (31). As many etiological theories of bipolar disorder postulate abnormalities within the noradrenergic system, the reported amelioration or abolition of symptoms during depressed or manic periods is of considerable theoretical importance.

GABA

Gamma-aminobutyric acid (GABA) is thought to be involved in the regulation of the activity of norepinephrine as well as in that of two other neurotransmitters implicated in the etiology of TD – dopamine and acetylcholine (32, 33). With such complex interactions, it should be pointed out that the over- or underactivity of any of these systems may be absolute or relative, i.e. due to an absence or reduction of antagonistic systems. GABAergic agents have been shown to benefit some patients with TD (34, 35) although results have been conflicting in many cases. There have been recent reports in animal models of TD of a reduction of glutamic acid decarboxylase (GAD; an enzyme that synthesizes GABA) in the substantia nigra, medial globus pallidus and subthalamic nucleus, and this reduction may be related to the development of neuroleptic-induced dyskinesias (36, 37).

Neuropeptides

Endorphins, enkephalins, substance P, somatostatin and cholecystokinin have all been postulated to be involved in dyskinetic disorders, including TD. Partly, this is because most of these peptides are found in abundance in the striatum (see Refs 38 and 39). Basically there are very few studies concerning the contributions of neuropeptides to TD, and, when they have been studied, in most cases the focus has been on their interactions with dopaminergic mechanisms. Later in this chapter we will discuss an alternative way in which certain neuropeptides (in particular substance P) may be involved in TD.

Neuropathological studies

The earliest reported pathological findings linked to TD were those of Grunthal and Walther-Buhl (40). These authors reported chromatolysis of neurons in the inferior olive of a patient who developed perioral dyskinesias after treatment with 550 mg of perphenazine a day. The duration of neuroleptic treatment was, however, very short (only 13 days), which raises the question of whether this patient truly had TD.

Hunter et al. (41) reported neuropathological findings in three patients (aged 77, 85 and 69 years, respectively), all of whom had been treated primarily with chlorpromazine and who had exhibited mainly orofacial dyskinesias for four to five years before death. Although gliosis of the striatum, moderate loss of Purkinje cells in the anterior vermis of the cerebellum and neuron loss in the substantia nigra were reported, there were no consistent findings and these subjects were not considered to have any pathological changes that could not be accounted for by the aging process.

Gross and Kaltenbach (42) reported autopsy results on three patients who had developed persistent hyperkinesias following neuroleptics. In their first case, a man who developed perioral choreiform movements was found to have satellitosis and neuronophagia predominantly of large neurons in the medium portion of the caudate nucleus. Their second patient, also with perioral dyskinesia, demonstrated caudate atrophy and pathological changes in the 'oral parts' of the substantia nigra. In the third case, a diagnosis of Huntington's disease was suspected ante-mortem because of the characteristics of the movement disorder. On autopsy, atrophy of the head of the caudate nucleus, putamen and globus pallidus was noted. There was a history of alcohol abuse in the first two cases.

Dynes (43) reported generalized cortical atrophy as well as extensive degenerative changes bilaterally in the substantia nigra and globus pallidus of 76-year-old patient with mainly perioral dyskinesias for over 10 years. This patient was an alcoholic and at one time Korsakoff's syndrome was suspected. Moderate to marked neuron loss was seen in the pyramidal layer of the hippocampus as well.

Christensen et al. (44) performed the first controlled study of neuropathological changes associated with TD. They studied the brains of 28 dyskinetic patients (all of whom had perioral dyskinesias, but 10 had other dyskinesias as well) and compared them to the brains of 28 patients with no movement disorder but with identical diagnoses (16 with schizophrenia, 8 with senile dementia and 4 with other organic mental syndromes). The authors reported midbrain and brainstem gliosis in 25 of the brains from dyskinetic patients but in only 4 of the control brains. Also, they noted degeneration of cells in the substantia nigra of 27 of the brains from dyskinetic patients, but only in 7 of the controls. There are problems in the interpretation of these results, however, as the dyskinetic patients were older (with a mean age of 74 years, as compared with 69 years in the control group), and all were women (the control group consisted of 4 women and 24 men). Also, the dyskinesias were related to neuroleptics in only 21 of the 28 cases. In one case the dyskinesia was believed to be related to electroconvulsive therapy and in the other six cases it was thought to be 'spontaneous.'

Jamielity et al. (45) noted atrophic changes primarily in the substantia nigra of a 54-year-old man who was presumed to have TD.

Jellinger (46) performed a controlled neuropathological study of TD. His material included brains from 14 patients (10 men and 4 women) with drug-induced movement disorders. Most patients had carried a diagnosis of schizophrenia, although some had suffered from affective and organic psychoses. Of the 14 patients, 9 had developed perioral dyskinesias, the rest had drug-induced parkinsonism. The control group consisted of 14 non-dyskinetic patients (6 men and 8 women) most of whom had suffered from schizophrenia, with a few subjects having had affective disorders. These two groups had received similar amounts of neuroleptic medications. In 5 of the 9 dyskinetic subjects there was moderate caudate pathology (primarily involving swelling of large neurons and increased glial satellitosis bilaterally in the rostral two-thirds of the caudate nuclei) but none of the non-dyskinetic control subjects had this finding. Few pathological changes were noted in the globus pallidus or other subcortical nuclei. It is not clear if the putamen was included in the group of 'other subcortical nuclei,' however.

Ule and Struwe (47) described degenerative changes in the nigrostriatal area of a 66-year-old woman with abnormal movements.

In summary, it appears that there may be pathology in basal ganglia of patients with TD, especially of the striatum and the substantia nigra. The exact nature is unclear, although in some patients the larger cells of the striatum (particularly of the caudate nucleus) may be involved to a greater extent than other cell types.

Neuroradiological studies

Faurbye et al. (7) reported that out of 7 patients with TD, 6 demonstrated evidence of cortical or diffuse cerebral atrophy, but that this was no different from age-matched control subjects with schizophrenia.

Duvoisin stated in a personal communication to Gelenberg (48) that he had noted ventricular dilatation consistent with caudate atrophy on pneumoencephalography in a woman with TD. The dilatation was apparently greater contralateral to the side with the most severe dyskinetic signs.

Gelenberg (48), stimulated by the above finding, looked at the CT scans of 8 patients with TD, but reported no significant abnormalities, although 1 patient had evidence of mild generalized cortical atrophy. The patients were described as having mildly to moderately severe TD and there was no control group.

Famuyiwa et al. (49) measured CT scans of schizophrenic patients both with and without TD. When 17 patients with TD were compared with 33 age- and sex-matched controls, it was noted that the TD group fell into the pathological range on a measure for ventricular enlargement (the Ventricular Index) and the non-TD group did not, although there were no significant differences between the two groups. These authors also noted a difference in performance between the two groups on a neuropsychological learning test, with the performance of the TD group being significantly poorer than the non-TD group.

Jeste et al. (50) failed to find any difference on CT scan measurements for caudate and cerebral atrophy (bifrontal/bicaudate ratio and lateral ventricle/brain ratio, respectively) between a group of 12 elderly patients with TD and a group matched for age, race, diagnosis and length of neuroleptic treatment. There were also no differences when the scans were assessed for cortical or cerebellar atrophy. Although no significant differences between the TD and non-TD groups were found, the TD group did fall between the non-TD group and a group of patients with Huntington's disease (HD) on the bifrontal/bicaudate ratio.

Pandurangi et al. (51) performed pneumoencephalography on 5 patients with TD and 3 non-TD patients comparable for age, gender and diagnosis. All patients with dyskinesia carried a rating of at least 3 on the 0 – 4 point AIMS scale, and 4 out of 5 of the dyskinesia patients had upper extremity movements as well as orofacial movements. The investigators found a septum-caudate distance of more than 15 mm and a loss of caudate shadow convexity in 3 out of the 5 TD patients. In addition, these same 3 patients demonstrated 'small blobs of air . . . at the level of the foramen of Monro in the lateral films and overlapping the body of the lateral ventricle in the anteroposterior films.' These findings, which were taken as evidence of caudate atrophy, were not seen in any of the 3 non-TD control subjects. Interestingly, in the 2 dyskinetic patients without these findings, the dyskinesia disappeared when neuroleptics were stopped, whereas in the 3 dyskinetic patients with evidence of caudate atrophy, the dyskinesia remained unchanged after neuroleptic discontinuation.

Bartels and Themelis (52) evaluated CT scans of 29 patients with severe TD and 29 control patients matched for age, gender, diagnosis and length of neuroleptic treatment. All patients had orofacial movements and 14 patients had limb and trunk movements as well. In the TD group, these investigators reported significantly larger third-ventricle width and bicaudate distance, and significantly smaller caudate and lenticular nucleus areas. These differences were noted bilaterally and suggested atrophy of the striatum and possibly of the globus pallidus in TD patients.

Brainin et al. (53) reported no differences between 21 dyskinetic patients under the age of 60 and a population of normal controls of CT scan measurements for cortical atrophy and ventricular enlargement. Linear rather than areal measurements of ventricular size were used, and it is not clear how well-matched the normal controls were. The average global AIMS rating was 2.4 on the 0 – 4 scale, and only 1 patient had a rating of 4.

Kaufmann et al. (30) reported that enlarged ventricles occurred in only a subgroup of patients with TD – those with a normal plasma activity of dopamine-beta-hydroxylase (DBH). Patients with elevated DBH did not appear to have enlarged ventricles. This finding will be discussed further in the last section of this chapter.

Although some of the results are conflicting, it appears that there is neuroradiological evidence for atrophy of the striatum, and particularly of the caudate nucleus in some patients with TD. We should add, however, that structures such as putamen and substantia nigra are not well visualized on CT scans. As will be discussed in more detail later in this chapter, one of the reasons for the inconsistency of the results may be that different subpopulations of TD patients or different subtypes of TD were being looked at by the different investigators.

Electroencephalographic studies

There have been few studies of EEG abnormalities in patients with TD. Out of 30 patients with TD, Paulson (54) reported diffuse or focal slowing in 7 and epileptiform bursts in another 4, but no matched control group was included in the study. Gardos et al. (55) carried out a discriminant function analysis of variables separating patients with TD and without TD, and found 'abnormal EEG' to be one of five important variables. When these investigators considered EEG abnormalities alone, however, no difference was observed between patients with and without TD.

Simpson et al. (56) did not find a significant difference in the incidence of EEG abnormalities between patients with or without TD, and Jeste et al. (57) reported no difference in abnormal EEG findings in patients separated according to whether their dyskinesia was persistent or reversible.

In some studies, TD has been found to be associated with a particular EEG pattern known as the 'B-Mitten' pattern. This pattern consists of a sharp transient followed by a higher voltage slow wave, so that the form of the tracing resembles the thumb and fingers of a mitten. It is usually only observed in Stages 3 and 4 of sleep and is rare among normal subjects, especially children and the elderly. Wegner et al. (58) compared 21 patients with TD to 21 non-TD psychiatric control patients and noted that 95% of the TD patients had the B-mitten pattern in comparison with only 33% of the controls. Further experiments by these investigators (59) showed that the mitten pattern remains associated with TD on long-term follow-up, although in this latter report only 21 out of 37 TD patients were reported to have the mitten pattern, compared with 14 of 44 controls. As these authors point out, the B-mitten pattern may be associated with subcortical pathology, but the exact significance of these findings is not clear. Also, this finding remains to be replicated by other researchers.

Other localization studies

In addition to the more direct approaches to pathological change in the brains of TD patients such as those described in the sections above, other investigators have tried more indirect approaches. One of these involves the issue of lateralization of brain function, which may be altered by neuroleptic medications (60). After an initial promising study demonstrating more severe dyskinesias on the right side of the body in TD patients (61), two subsequent reports failed to find any difference in the prevalence of right- vs. left-sided signs of TD (62, 63).

A possible clue to the pathophysiology of TD in some patients may be provided in the case report of McEntee and Newman (64) of a 69-year-old woman who developed left unilateral dyskinetic movements after five years of perphenazine, methylphenidate and diphenhydramine treatment. This patient had a probable embolic infarction resulting in damage to a region near the left inferior precentral gyrus 25 years before presentation, evidence of which was still visible on CT scan. At the time of the infarct, she developed a right-sided hemiparesis, but this quickly cleared.

The authors believed that this infarct was the reason for the unilateral presentation of the TD, and further postulated that interruption of connections between the cortex and the striatum was the likely reason for the lack of dyskinetic movements on the patient's right side. This report raises interesting possibilities as regards the anatomical pathways involved in the mediation of the dyskinetic movements, and implies that input from the cortex may be a necessary factor for the development of such movements.

Differential diagnosis

One of the major problems in the diagnosis of TD is the many forms that the dyskinesia can take. Although the movements are usually choreoathetoid in form and follow a perioral distribution, many different types of hyperkinetic motor signs have at one time or another been reported to occur as a part of the syndrome. These include chorea, hemiballism, dystonia, tic; in fact, almost every type of hyperkinesis except tremor. We have frequently observed some of these different signs to coexist simultaneously in the same patient (especially choreoathetoid movements, dystonias and tics). There are now a number of reports in the literature of tardive syndromes dominated by one particular form of hyperkinesis, including reports of tardive dystonia (65, 66), tardive akathisia (67), and tardive Tourette's or tardive tic disorders (68). There have even been reports of persistent drug-induced parkinsonism lasting for up to one year following neuroleptic discontinuation (69). The relationship of all these different tardive syndromes to one another is unclear and, though the possibility exists that they may all simply be variants of TD, further investigation is necessary. It seems that, rather than a mere notation of whether or not a patient has TD, a careful description of the movements would prove to be more helpful both in terms of diagnosis and treatment.

Another problem concerns the coexistence of TD and parkinsonism. This phenomenon is probably common but tends to be ignored by practitioners for two principal reasons: (a) TD and parkinsonism may tend to mask each other, or the one may be so striking that signs of the other are not actively sought and (b) the most widely accepted etiological theories of drug-induced parkinsonism and TD (those of dopaminergic blockade and dopaminergic supersensitivity, respectively) are popularly thought to give rise to mutually exclusive clinical manifestations. This has very likely influenced clinical observations.

There are, nevertheless, a growing number of studies reporting the coexistence of TD and parkinsonism (70–72), with the reported prevalence of the coexistence of the two disorders being anywhere from 12.5% to 17.4% of patients treated with neuroleptic medications. An increase in the use of neuroleptics does not appear to be an important factor in the coexistence of these two syndromes (73).

TD has also been reported to coexist with other movement disorders in addition to parkinsonism. For example there are reports of the co-occurrence of TD with oculogyric crises (74) as well as with blepharospasm-oromandibular dystonia or Meige's syndrome (75).

The fact that TD can coexist with so many other types of hyperkinetic and hypokinetic movement disorders can make the differential diagnosis most difficult, but an attempt should be made to distinguish it from other dyskinesias, and especially those associated with neuroleptic medications. Akathisia in particular may cause problems in differential diagnosis. Munetz and Cornes (76) offer the following guidelines for differentiation of these two disorders:

1. Subjective distress is often present in akathisia and usually not in TD.

2. Akathitic movements are voluntary responses to subjective distress whereas tardive dyskinetic movements are largely involuntary, though susceptible to small amounts of voluntary control (it should be noted, however, that in the present authors' experience it is not clear if all cases of akathisia are responses to subjective distress).

3. Akathisia usually begins much sooner after institution of neuroleptic treatment than TD (akathisia may occur within less than three days of institution of oral neuroleptics).

4. Akathitic movements occur predominantly in the lower extremities, whereas the movements of TD tend to involve more orofacial musculature.

5. Other extrapyramidal signs such as tremor and akinesia more frequently accompany akathisia than TD.

6. In terms of pharmacological response, akathisia often improves whereas TD may actually worsen in response to anticholinergic agents. Akathisia usually improves with a reduction in neuroleptic dose and worsens with an increase, while the opposite is often true of TD.

In addition to drug-induced akathisia, drug-induced parkinsonian tremor should be distinguished from TD. This can be difficult at times because some patients with TD manifest a significant rhythmical or stereotypical component to their movements. We have observed this component to usually be in the range of 2 c.p.s., which separates it from the coarse parkinsonian tremor that usually appears in the range of 4 to 7 c.p.s. This rhythmical component to TD needs to be more fully explored, but appears to be similar to the rhythmical component described in other athetoid disorders (such as in cerebral palsy) which has been noted to be in the 2.5 c.p.s. range and clinically resemble a rubral tremor (77).

Another drug-induced syndrome that involves primarily orofacial muscles is the so-called rabbit syndrome. Here there are fine, rhythmic movements of lips at about 5 c.p.s., sometimes accompanied by a popping sound when the lips are separated (78, 79). Unlike TD, the tongue is often not involved, and there is a good therapeutic response to anticholinergic agents. TD and rabbit syndrome may coexist, however, and the combination may be difficult to treat (80).

Because TD tends to be more common in elderly individuals, it should be carefully differentiated from other bucco – linguo – masticatory (BLM) dyskinetic disorders which occur in this age group. These include the common spontaneous BLM dyskinesias of the elderly, which may reach a prevalence of 6% to 8% between the seventh and ninth decades of life (81) and the BLM dyskinesias that commonly accompany edentulous states (82). Also, Meige's syndrome may resemble TD in the elderly, as it usually begins in the sixth decade (83). Meige's syndrome is more dystonic in nature than TD, however. A careful history of exposure to neuroleptics must be obtained from any geriatric patient, as some individuals may not remember having taken these medications in the past, or may merely consider them to be 'sleeping pills' and therefore not mention them when questioned. A significant number of elderly patients have had low-potency antipsychotic medications (such as thioridazine) prescribed for sleep disturbances or anxiety.

Disorders of the basal ganglia must be considered in the differential diagnosis of *TD, especially those disorders such as Huntington's disease, Wilson's disease and Sydenham's chorea, which may present with psychiatric symptomatology early in the course of the illness. A number of these patients are prescribed neuroleptic medications for the psychiatric symptoms, and when the movement disorder appears these patients may appear to have developed TD. In these cases a positive family history for Huntington's disease, prior history of rheumatic fever, and appropriate laboratory tests such as serum ceruloplasmin, serum and urinary copper, ASO titers, etc., are helpful in making the correct diagnosis.

Other neurological conditions to be considered in the differential diagnosis of TD include dystonic disorders such as the Hallervorden-Spatz syndrome, dystonia musculorum deformans and nonhereditary idiopathic dystonias; Tourette's syndrome and other idiopathic tic disorders (especially multifocal tic disorders); and miscellaneous choreoathetoid disorders including familial paroxysmal choreoathetosis, chorea-acanthocytosis, chorea gravidarum and chorea in association with oral contraceptives, hyperthyroidism, polycythemia, systemic lupus erythematosus, stimulants (such as amphetamine, methylphenidate and pemoline), and L-dopa.

Finally, TD should be differentiated, where possible, from stereotypies and mannerisms which occur in schizophrenia, catatonia, mental retardation and autism.

TABLE 2   *Features useful in distinguishing stereotypies from tardive dyskinesia*

Stereotypy	Tardive dyskinesia
Highly repetitive	Less repetitive
Often involves complex movements of muscles in their normal synergistic relationships	Usually simple movements
Often appears to be a fragment of an action or a pseudo-purposeful behavior	Usually purposeless movements
Often involves contact between widely separated body parts (such as hand and head) or involves movement of the body as a whole	Usually involves movements limited to localized parts of the body such as face or hands
Tends to be more asymmetrical in distribution	Tends to be more symmetrical in distribution

This is often very difficult to do, but the guidelines offered in Table 2 may be of help in differentiating between these conditions.

Tardive dyskinesia — Where is the lesion?

Although most investigators today believe that there is an association of TD with dysfunction of the basal ganglia as well as with dopaminergic systems of the brain, the exact nature of the pathology is yet to be elucidated. In proposing a lesion site for TD, we should take into consideration the following: (a) the pattern of distribution of the hyperkinesis of TD, (b) neuropathological and other localizing studies, (c) neuropathological findings in conditions that are clinically similar to TD, (d) neurochemical evidence which may be indirectly localizing, and (e) recent hypotheses on the structure and functional circuitry of the striatum. We will consider each of these in the remainder of this section.

a. The pattern of hyperkinesis in TD. In many patients TD involves primarily the orofacial musculature and, to a lesser extent, muscles of the distal upper extremities. Other patients may show involvement of lower extremity and trunk muscles. It is not clear why so many patients with TD should show an orofacial distribution of movements, but it is possible that in some patients TD represents dysfunction of an area of the motor system more devoted to orofacial muscle control (84). It has been shown that somatotopic patterns of organization exist not only in the motor cortex, but throughout the striatum, globus pallidus, substantia nigra, subthalamus and thalamus as well (85 – 87). For example, of the two major striatal output stations – the globus pallidus (GP) and the substantia nigra pars reticulata (SNr) – the SNr has been found to be associated almost exclusively with orofacial movements (85). In the putamen, the 'face' area appears to be ventro-medial in monkeys, but the 'face' area of the human caudate is not known. In a recent report of a case of spontaneous orofacial dyskinesia, most of the histopathological abnormalities were noted to be limited to the dorsal halves of the caudate and putamen (88). Regardless of the exact location of the striatal area subserving the orofacial musculature, it is conceivable that, in those cases of TD marked by predominantly orofacial dyskinesias, certain portions of the striatum are likely to be pathologically affected to a greater extent than others.

b. Neuropathological studies. We reviewed these studies earlier in the chapter. Basically, the evidence indicates involvement of the striatum (especially the caudate nucleus) and the substantia nigra. Of importance are the studies of Jellinger (46) where pathological changes of large striatal cells were reported, a finding noted by other investigators as well (42). Investigators have also reported pathological changes with cell loss and gliosis in the substantia nigra, although it is not clear what part of the substantia nigra was most involved (42, 44, 45). In contrast to the direct neuropathological studies, some neuroradiological studies have reported much more extensive pathological changes in the brains of patients with TD, including ventricular enlargement and striatal atrophy (30, 51, 52). Other neuroradiological studies have not noted any difference between TD and non-TD patients, however (48, 50, 53).

c. Pathological changes in other disorders sharing clinical features with TD. Of all the choreoathetoid disorders, Huntington's disease has been studied most extensively. The most consistent pathological changes have been noted to be in the basal ganglia, especially in the smaller cells of the striatum (89). It has recently been determined that medium-sized spiny neurons are specifically altered in Huntington's disease, whereas medium and large aspiny neurons may be relatively unaffected (90). These medium-sized spiny neurons have been proposed to contain GABA (91). Interestingly, this relative sparing of larger neurons is in contrast to the neuropathological findings in some cases of TD, in which larger neurons appeared to be more affected. In fact, it has been found that the rigid variant of Huntington's disease may be marked by survival of large striatal neurons (92).

d. Neurochemical evidence. The theory of dopaminergic-cholinergic imbalance in the basal ganglia has long been invoked to explain the contrasting features of TD and Parkinson's disease. In this scheme, TD is thought to represent a state marked by a relative excess of dopaminergic over cholinergic activity, while the opposite situation is thought to hold for Parkinson's disease or drug-induced parkinsonism. Certainly, in some cases anticholinergic agents appear to worsen TD and dopamine receptor blocking agents may improve it (even if only transiently), whereas these

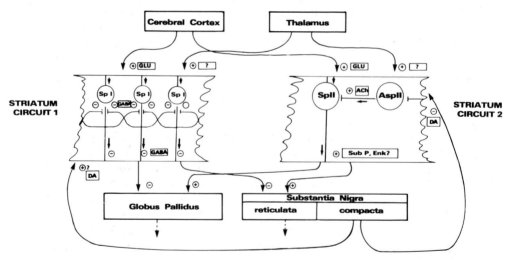

FIG. 1   *Diagram illustrating striatal Circuits 1 and 2 according to Groves (91). These circuits are described in greater detail in the text. The output of the globus pallidus and the substantia nigra pars reticulata (represented dashed arrows) returns to the cerebral cortex and thalamus to complete both the circuits. + or − refers to whether a given pathway is thought to be mainly excitatory or inhibitory, respectively. Putative neurotransmitters are shown in small boxes. GLU = glutamate, GABA = gamma-aminobutyric acid, ACh = acetylcholine, DA = dopamine, Enk = enkephalin, Sp I = Spiny Type I neuron, Sp II = Spiny Type II neuron, Asp II = Aspiny Type II neuron.*

agents have an opposite effect on parkinsonism. Unfortunately, available cholinergic agonists do not benefit most patients with TD, so the neurochemistry of the disorder must be more complicated than this simple balance theory. This is not surprising, considering the presence and probable importance of other neurotransmitters in the striatum, such as substance P, enkephalins and GABA. Nevertheless, any theory of the pathophysiology of TD must in some way explain the above findings relating to the effects of drugs known to alter dopaminergic and cholinergic neurotransmission. Furthermore, the evidence reviewed earlier implicating noradrenergic hyperfunction and GABAergic hypofunction in at least some patients with TD, must also be taken into account.

e. Striatal circuitry. Groves (91), drawing upon his own studies as well as the neurohistological findings of Pasik et al. (93), has proposed what is probably the first coherent hypothesis of striatal functioning. According to Grove's innovative scheme, there may be two main types of circuits in the striatum, and these are illustrated in schematic form in Figure 1. The first, which is the more abundant one, involves Spiny Type 1 neurons that are thought to utilize GABA as a neurotransmitter (94). Axons from the cerebral cortex and thalamus synapse on the Spiny I cells which in turn are inhibitory to neurons in the globus pallidus (GP) and substantia nigra pars reticulata (SNr). The GP and SNr complete the circuit by transmitting impulses back to the thalamus and cortex.

The second circuit, which involves fewer striatal neurons, consists primarily of the larger Aspiny Type II and Spiny Type II neurons, thought to contain acetylcholine (Aspiny II) and substance P (Spiny II) (94). The Aspiny II cells contain D2 receptors and may receive inhibitory fibers from the dopaminergic cells of the substantia nigra pars compacta (SNc). These Aspiny II cells are believed to be excitatory to the Spiny II cells, which in turn are excitatory to neurons in the SNr and GP.

An hypothesis

It is likely that both of the circuits described above are important in the etiology of TD. One of the major problems that has plagued studies of TD concerns the fact that TD may exist in different forms. TD has been subtyped according to many different criteria including somatic distribution of the abnormal movements (i.e. central vs. peripheral) (10, 11), response to anticholinergic agents (i.e. 'classical' responders with symptomatic worsening compared to atypical responders with no change or actual symptomatic improvement) (95), plasma DBH activity and presence of ventricular abnormalities (30), and reversibility or persistence (96). It is therefore possible that one of the reasons for differences in the observed neuropathology has to do with different forms of TD being studied.

From our review, it appears that pathology of the basal ganglia, including the striatum and its input and output pathways, is likely to be involved in the pathophysiology of TD. Some studies (30, 51, 52) indicate that the striatal pathology may be fairly pervasive, manifesting as ventricular enlargement somewhat comparable to that seen in Huntington's disease. Other studies have indicated that the pathology may be much more restricted, involving predominantly the large cells of the striatum, which is in contrast to the smaller cell involvement seen in Huntington's disease.

If striatal pathology is involved in the etiology of TD, then it is probable that these different observations may reflect different subtypes of TD. The evidence of widespread striatal damage along with evidence of GABAergic dysfunction in some patients with TD implies damage to the Spiny I cells of the striatum. The evidence of more specific damage to the large cells of the striatum would be consistent with the observations that dopaminergic agonists and anticholinergic agents usually exacerbate the clinical signs of TD. It is possible that TD could result from both of these different types of striatal pathology, but that the clinical form of the TD would be different. In the first case where there may be damage to the GABAergic Spiny I circuit, the TD would more closely resemble Huntington's disease and the choreoathetoid movements would be more generalized. In the second case the Spiny II and Aspiny II neurons of the second circuit described above may be involved. This second circuit has been postulated to be important in the pathophysiology of Parkinson's disease (91, 97) in terms of the presence of an increase in the output of Spiny II cells. In TD, there could be a decrease in output from the Spiny II cells, either directly because of pathological changes in these cells, or indirectly because of a loss of the excitatory input of Aspiny II cells (Spiny II and Aspiny II cells probably comprise the bulk of the large cells in the striatum). In comparison with the first circuit, which is abundant in the striatum and includes large numbers of medium-sized neurons (Spiny I cells comprise the majority of striatal neurons) the second circuit involves the relatively few dopaminergic neurons of the SNc as well as the Spiny II and Aspiny II neurons. Thus, motoric dysfunction relating to damage to the second circuit could theoretically appear with much more restricted tissue or cell destruction than that necessary to produce clinical signs relating to the first circuit.

It has been proposed that the observations concerning the 'dopamine-acetylcholine balance' may be related to the inhibitory connection of dopaminergic cells of the SNc and the acetylcholine-containing Aspiny II cells of the striatum (91, 97). In Parkinson's disease, the reduction of DA neurotransmission would, in this scheme, lead to an increase in cholinergic and ultimately to an increase in substance P neurotransmission that could underlie the production of some of the clinical signs of parkinsonism (91, 97). In TD the opposite might occur, for there could be a decrease in cholinergic transmission resulting in a decrease in substance P transmission that could be related to the production of the dyskinesia. This is highly speculative of course, but does suggest the need for further investigation into neuropeptide involvement in TD and in other movement disorders as well.

Given all of the above observations, another area deserving further study is that of the precise neuroanatomical locus of TD. For example, the somatotopic organization of the basal ganglia leads to the speculation that most cases of TD do not involve the basal ganglia as a whole, but only certain sections of it. The orofacial distribution of some cases of TD is most consistent with the hypothesis of damage to the second circuit of the striatum. It is of interest that the studies describing pathology of large striatal neurons in TD have reported fairly localized cell involvement of either the medial portion or the rostral two-thirds of the caudate nucleus (42, 46).

The available evidence may indicate that one form of TD may involve pathology predominantly of large striatal neurons, i.e. Spiny II and Aspiny II neurons which contribute to the second striatal circuit of Groves (91), in specific areas of the striatum that may subserve orofacial musculature. This 'orofacial' form could conceivably be more responsive to cholinergic agonists and show little evidence of ventricular enlargement on neuroradiological studies. Also, because of the possible loss of the output from large striatal cells, a substance P agonist might be of benefit in this form. Another form of TD may involve more generalized pathology of the striatum, including the abundant Spiny I GABAergic neurons of Circuit 1. This 'generalized' form of TD could possibly be more responsive to GABAergic agents and show more evidence of ventricular enlargement on neuroradiological studies. We should add that these two hypothesized forms of TD are neither mutually exclusive nor totally exhaustive. Also, direct neuropathological proof for our postulate is still lacking.

Such an hypothesis, in addition to offering a possible explanation for some of the conflicting results of neuropathological and neuroradiological studies reported earlier, may also help explain the conflicting results obtained in different medication trials of TD. For example, a wide variety of responses to different cholinergic agonists have been reported in TD (9). However, in the double-blind study of the efficacy of deanol in TD performed by Bockenheimer and Lucius (98) it was noted that the oral dyskinesia improved following administration of deanol, whereas the limb dyskinesia remained unchanged. The study of Klawans and Rubovits (99) offers an example of differential response to another cholinergic agonist, physostigmine. Here it was reported that in 10 out of 12 patients tongue movements improved after treatment, whereas limb movements improved in only 2 out of 6 cases. Finally, in a recent study of the effects of anticholinergic drug withdrawal on TD, it was noted that improvement in the dyskinesia was much more pronounced in the oral region than in limb or trunk regions (100).

The studies reporting possible involvement of the noradrenergic system in TD (28 – 30) are difficult to explain with this hypothesis at this time. The striatum contains very little norepinephrine except for the ventral striatum or nucleus accumbens (101, 102). There have, however, been reports of the presence of very large numbers of NE receptors (especially beta-receptors) throughout the striatum of the rat, and rats too have very little striatal NE (103, 104). These paradoxical observations are as yet unexplained, although it is possible that the receptors are on glial cells and not directly involved in neurotransmission. If they are involved in neurotransmission, their function is unknown, although it is possible that they may serve a neuromodulatory role. It has been shown in the rat brain that stimulation of the locus ceruleus (causing NE release) results in a marked reduction of the excitatory response of neurons to substance P in the cingulate cortex (105). It is conceivable that this phenomenon may occur elsewhere in the brain, possibly in areas which receive substance P output from the striatum (such as the GP and SNr). In accord with our earlier hypothesis of decreased substance P output from the striatum, it is possible that patients with elevated NE activity may effectively have a reduction of neuronal responsiveness to substance P. We referred earlier to the observations of Kaufmann et al. (30) who recently determined that a subgroup of TD patients with elevated DBH activity had normal ventricles on CT scans, whereas enlarged ventricles were noted in a subgroup of TD patients with normal DBH activity. This supports the idea that patients with elevated NE may manifest the signs of TD without gross brain atrophy being present, whereas patients with normal NE activity may need to have greater structural damage before the clinical signs of TD appear. Of interest is the observation of these same authors that the severity of orofacial dyskinesias was significantly correlated with CSF norepinephrine, but that there was no such correlation of norepinephrine with overall dyskinesia severity (i.e. orofacial + limb + trunk dyskinesia scores).

Whether or not the above hypothesis is substantiated, we are nevertheless left with the idea that we should refine our approach to the 'site of lesion' in TD and probably some other disorders of the basal ganglia as well. It appears that, in studying movement disorders, we can no longer consider the basal ganglia as a whole, but must instead investigate its finer structure in terms of different anatomical regions and different functional circuits of neurons. It is possible that in one form of TD Spiny I neurons (Circuit 1 of Groves, 91) may be predominantly involved, while in another form Spiny II and Aspiny II (Circuit 2) neurons may be the major site of pathology. TD patients with Circuit 1 damage may more closely resemble patients with Huntington's disease and therefore may have more generalized movements as well as greater evidence of GABAergic deficiency. Patients with Circuit 2 damage may have more anatomically restricted and less severe deficits and show more responsiveness to cholinergic agents. Of course, if these two different forms of TD exist, it is unlikely that they would commonly occur in pure form, because both forms would involve damage to the striatum, and it is unlikely that striatal damage would be so specific in most persons. Nevertheless, the notion that TD may exist in more than one form may help explain the considerable variability observed in neurological and treatment studies. It must be stressed that there is no direct neuropathological evidence so far to support this hypothesis. Further work along these lines will be of considerable interest.

REFERENCES

1. Schönecker M (1957) Ein eigentümliches Syndrom im oralen Bereich bei Megaphenapplikation. *Nervenarzt, 28,* 35.
2. Sigwald J, Bouttier D, Raymondeaud C, Piot C (1959) Quatre cas de dyskinésie facio-bucco-linguo-masticatrice à l'évolution prolongée secondaire à un traitement par les neuroleptiques. *Rev. Neurol., 100,* 751.
3. Kruse W (1960) Persistent muscular restlessness after phenothiazine treatment: report of

3 cases. *Am. J. Psychiatry, 117,* 152.

4. Druckman R, Seelinger D, Thulin B (1962) Chronic involuntary movements induced by phenothiazines. *J. Nerv. Ment. Dis., 135,* 69.
5. Uhrbrand L, Faurbye A (1960) Reversible and irreversible dyskinesia after treatment with perphenazine, chlorpromazine, reserpine, and electroconvulsive therapy. *Psychopharmacologia, 1,* 408.
6. Hunter R, Earl CJ, Thornicroft S (1964) An apparently irreversible syndrome of abnormal movements following phenothiazine medication. *Proc. R. Soc. Med., 57,* 758.
7. Faurbye A, Rasch P-J, Petersen PB, Brandborg G, Pakkenberg H (1964) Neurological symptoms in pharmacotherapy of psychoses. *Acta Psychiatr. Scand., 40,* 10.
8. Crane GE (1973) Persistent dyskinesia. *Br. J. Psychiatry, 122,* 395.
9. Jeste DV, Wyatt RJ (1982) *Understanding and Treating Tardive Dyskinesia.* The Guilford Press, New York.
10. Kidger T, Barnes TRE, Trauer T, Taylor PJ (1980) Sub-syndromes of tardive dyskinesia. *Psychol. Med., 10,* 513.
11. Barnes TRE, Kidger T, Trauer T, Taylor PJ (1980) Reclassification of the tardive dyskinesia syndrome. *Adv. Biochem. Psychopharmac., 24,* 565.
12. Barnes TRE, Rossor M, Trauer T (1983) A comparison of purposeless movements in psychiatric patients treated with antipsychotic drugs, and normal individuals. *J. Neurol. Neurosurg. Psychiatry, 46,* 540.
13. Bucci L (1971) The dyskinesias – A new therapeutic approach. *Dis. Nerv. Syst., 32,* 324.
14. Winsberg BC, Hurwic MJ, Perel J (1977) Neurochemistry of withdrawal-emergent symptoms in children. *Psychopharmacol. Bull., 13,* 38.
15. Polizos P, Engelhardt DM (1978) Dyskinetic phenomena in children treated with psychotropic medications. *Psychopharmacol. Bull., 14,* 65.
16. Jeste DV, Wyatt RJ (1981) Changing epidemiology of tardive dyskinesia: an overview. *Am. J. Psychiatry, 138,* 297.
17. Kane JM, Smith JM (1982) Tardive dyskinesia – Prevalence and risk factors, 1959 to 1979. *Arch. Gen. Psychiatry, 39,* 473.
18. Toenniessen LM, Casey DE, McFarland BH (1985) Tardive dyskinesia in the aged. *Arch. Gen. Psychiatry, 42,* 278.
19. Smith JM, Baldessarini RJ (1980) Changes in prevalence, severity, and recovery in tardive dyskinesia with age. *Arch. Gen. Psychiatry, 37,* 1368.
20. Rush M, Diamond F, Alpert M (1982) Depression as a risk factor in tardive dyskinesia. *Biol. Psychiatry, 17,* 387.
21. Yassa R, Ghadirian AM, Schwartz G (1983) Prevalence of tardive dyskinesia in affective disorder patients. *J. Clin. Psychiatry, 44,* 410.
22. Richardson MA, Pass R, Craig TJ, Fickers E (1984) Factors influencing the prevalence and severity of tardive dyskinesia. *Psychopharmacol. Bull., 20/1,* 33.
23. Wolf ME, Ryan JJ, Mosnaim AD (1982) Organicity and tardive dyskinesia. *Psychosomatics, 23,* 475.
24. Nagao T, Ohshimo T, Mitsunobu K (1979) Cerebrospinal fluid monoamine metabolites and cyclic nucleotides in chronic schizophrenic patients with tardive dyskinesia or drug induced tremor. *Biol. Psychiatry, 14,* 509.
25. Meltzer HY, Goode DJ, Fang VS, Shyve P, Young M (1976) Dopamine and schizophrenia. *Lancet, 2,* 1142.
26. Jeste DV, Neckers LM, Wagner RL, Wise CD, Staub RA, Rogol A, Potkin SG, Bridge

TP, Wyatt RJ (1981) Lymphocyte monoamine oxidase and plasma prolactin and growth hormone in tardive dyskinesia. *J. Clin. Psychiatry, 42,* 75.

27. Peroutka SJ, Snyder SH (1980) Relationship of neuroleptic drug effects at brain dopamine, serotonin, alpha-adrenergic and histamine receptors to clinical potency. *Am. J. Psychiatry, 137,* 1518.

28. Jeste DV, Linnoila M, Fordis CM, Phelps BH, Wagner RL, Wyatt RJ (1982) Enzyme studies in tardive dyskinesia. III. Noradrenergic hyperactivity in a subgroup of dyskinetic patients. *J. Clin. Psychopharmacol., 2,* 318.

29. Wagner RL, Jeste DV, Phelps BH, Wyatt RJ (1982) Enzyme studies in tardive dyskinesia. I. One-year biochemical follow-up. *J. Clin. Psychopharmacol., 2,* 312.

30. Kaufmann CA, Jeste DV, Shelton RC, Linnoila M, Kafka MS, Wyatt RJ (1986) Noradrenergic and neuroradiologic abnormalities in tardive dyskinesia. *Biol. Psychiatry,* in press.

31. Cutler NR, Post RM (1982) State-related cyclical dyskinesias in manic-depressive illness. *J. Clin. Psychopharmacol., 2,* 350.

32. Scatton B, Bartholini G (1982) Gamma-aminobutyric acid (GABA) receptor stimulation. IV. Effect of progabide (SL 76002) and other GABAergic agents on acetylcholine turnover in rat brain areas. *J. Pharmacol. Exp. Ther., 220,* 689.

33. Scatton B, Zivkovic B, Dedek J, Lloyd KG, Constantinidis J, Tissot R, Bartholini G (1982) Gamma-aminobutyric acid (GABA) receptor stimulation. III. Effect of progabide (SL 76002) on norepinephrine, dopamine and 5-hydroxytryptamine turnover in rat brain areas. *J. Pharmacol. Exp. Ther., 220,* 678.

34. Casey DE, Gerlach J, Magelund G, Christensen TR (1980) Gamma-acetylenic GABA in tardive dyskinesia. *Arch. Gen. Psychiatry, 37,* 1376.

35. Thaker GK, Hare TA, Tamminga CA (1983) GABA system: clinical research and treatment of tardive dyskinesia. In: Ban TA, Picot P, Poldinger LW (Eds), *Modern Problems in Pharmacopsychiatry,* p. 155. S. Karger, Basel.

36. Gunne L-M, Haggstrom J-E, Sjoquist B (1984) Association with persistent neuroleptic-induced dyskinesia of regional changes in brain GABA synthesis. *Nature (London), 309,* 347.

37. Gunne L-M, Haggstrom J-E (1985) Experimental tardive dyskinesia. *J. Clin. Psychiatry, 46,* 48.

38. Tamminga CA, Frohman LA (1979) Neuroendocrine approach to the study and treatment of tardive dyskinesia. In: Muller EE, Agnoli A (Eds), *Neuroendocrine Correlates in Neurology and Psychiatry,* p. 139. Elsevier/North-Holland, Amsterdam.

39. Blum, I, Korczyn AD (1983) Peptide neurotransmitters and their implications for the treatment of tardive dyskinesia. In: Ban TA, Picot P, Poldinger LW (Eds), *Modern Problems in Pharmacopsychiatry,* p. 187. S. Karger, Basel.

40. Grunthal VE, Walther-Buhl H (1960) Über Schädigung der Oliva inferior durch Chlorperphenazin (Trilafon). *Psychiatr. Neurol., 140,* 249.

41. Hunter R, Blackwood W, Smith MC, Cumings JN (1968) Neuropathological findings in three cases of persistent dyskinesia following phenothiazines. *J. Neurol. Sci., 7,* 263.

42. Gross H, Kältenbach E (1969) Neuropathological findings in persistent hyperkinesia after neuroleptic long-term therapy. In: Cerletti A, Bove FJ (Eds), *The Present Status of Psychotropic Drugs.* Excerpta Medica, Amsterdam.

43. Dynes JB (1970) Oral dyskinesias – Occurrence and treatment. *Dis. Nerv. Syst., 31,* 854.

44. Christensen E, Moller JE, Faurbye A (1970) Neuropathological investigation of 28

brains from patients with dyskinesia. *Acta Psychiatr. Scand., 46,* 14.

45. Jamielity F, Kosc B, Lukaszewicz A (1976) Zmiany neuropathologiczne w dyskinezji twarzowojezykowej prawdopodobnie polekowej. *Neurol. Neurochir. Pol., 26,* 399.

46. Jellinger K (1977): Neuropathologic findings after neuroleptic long-term therapy. In: Roizin L, Shiraki H, Grcevic N (Eds), *Neurotoxicology,* p. 25. Raven Press, New York.

47. Ule G, Struwe O (1978) Hirnveränderungen bei Dyskinesie nach Neuroleptica-Medikation. *Nervenarzt, 49,* 268.

48. Gelenberg AJ (1976) Computerized tomography in patients with tardive dyskinesia. *Am. J. Psychiatry, 133,* 578.

49. Famuyiwa OO, Eccleston D, Donaldson AA, Garside RF (1979) Tardive dyskinesia and dementia. *Br. J. Psychiatry, 135,* 500.

50. Jeste DV, Wagner RL, Weinberger DR, Rieth KG, Wyatt RJ (1980) Evaluation of CT scans in tardive dyskinesia. *Am. J. Psychiatry, 137,* 247.

51. Pandurangi AK, Devi V, Channabasavanna SM (1980) Caudate atrophy in irreversible tardive dyskinesia (a pneumoencephalographic study). *J. Clin. Psychiatry, 41,* 229.

52. Bartels M, Themelis J (1983) Computerized tomography in tardive dyskinesia: evidence of structural abnormalities in the basal ganglia system. *Arch. Psychiatr. Nervenkr., 233,* 371.

53. Brainin M, Reisner T, Zeitlhofer J (1983) Tardive dyskinesia: clinical correlation with computed tomography in patients aged less than 60 years. *J. Neurol. Neurosurg. Psychiatry, 46,* 1037.

54. Paulson GW (1968) An evaluation of the permanence of the 'tardive dyskinesias.' *Dis. Nerv. Syst., 24,* 692.

55. Gardos G, Cole JO, Labrie RA (1977) Drug variables in the etiology of tardive dyskinesia: application of discriminant function analysis. *Prog. Neuropsychopharmacol., 1,* 147.

56. Simpson GM, Varga E, Lee JH, Zoubok B (1978) Tardive dyskinesia and psychotropic drug history. *Psychopharmacologia, 58,* 117.

57. Jeste DV, Potkin SG, Sinha S, Feder S, Wyatt RJ (1979) Tardive dyskinesia – Reversible and persistent. *Arch. Gen. Psychiatry, 36,* 585.

58. Wegner JT, Struve FA, Kantor JS, Kane JM (1979) Relationship between the B-mitten EEG pattern and tardive dyskinesia. *Arch. Gen. Psychiatry, 36,* 599.

59. Struve FA, Willner AE (1983) A long term prospective study of electroencephalographic and neuropsychological correlates of tardive dyskinesia: initial findings at five year follow-up. *Clin. Electroencephalogr., 14,* 186.

60. Mintz M, Tomer R, Myslobodsky M (1982) Neuroleptic-induced lateral asymmetry of visual evoked potentials in schizophrenia. *Biol. Psychiatry, 17,* 815.

61. Waziri R (1980) Lateralization of neuroleptic-induced dyskinesia indicates pharmacological asymmetry in the brain. *Psychopharmacologia, 68,* 51.

62. Wilson RL, Waziri R, Nasrallah HA, McCalley-Whitters M (1984) The lateralization of tardive dyskinesia. *Biol. Psychiatry, 19,* 629.

63. Myslobodsky MS, Holden T, Sandler R (1984) Asymmetry of abnormal involuntary movements: a prevalence study. *Biol. Psychiatry, 19,* 623.

64. McEntee WJ, Newman GC (1981) A case report of tardive hemidyskinesia. *Am. J. Psychiatry, 138,* 1380.

65. Burke RE, Fahn S, Jankovic J, Marsden CD, Lang AE, Gollomp S, Ilson J (1982) Tardive dystonia: late-onset and persistent dystonia caused by antipsychotic drugs. *Neurology, 32,* 1335.

66. Giménez-Roldán S, Mateo D, Bartolomé P (1985) Tardive dystonia and severe tardive dyskinesia: a comparison of risk factors and prognosis. *Acta Psychiatr. Scand., 71,* 488.
67. Weiner WJ, Luby ED (1983) Tardive akathisia. *J. Clin. Psychiatry, 44,* 417.
68. Stahl SM (1980) Tardive Tourette syndrome in an autistic patient after long-term neuroleptic administration. *Am. J. Psychiatry, 137,* 1267.
69. Aronson TA (1985) Persistent drug-induced parkinsonism. *Biol. Psychiatry, 20,* 795.
70. Crane GE (1972) Pseudoparkinsonism and tardive dyskinesia. *Arch. Neurol., 27,* 426.
71. Richardson MA, Craig TJ (1982) The coexistence of parkinsonism-like symptoms and tardive dyskinesia. *Am. J. Psychiatry, 139,* 341.
72. Bitton V, Melamed E (1984) Coexistence of severe parkinsonism and tardive dyskinesia as side effects of neuroleptic therapy. *J. Clin. Psychiatry, 45,* 28.
73. Richardson MA, Craig TJ (1982) Reply to letter to the editor. *Am. J. Psychiatry, 139,* 1526.
74. Nasrallah HA, Pappas NJ, Crowe RR (1980) Oculogyric dystonia in tardive dyskinesia. *Am. J. Psychiatry, 137,* 850.
75. Weiner WJ, Nausieda PA, Glantz RH (1981) Meige syndrome (blepharospasm-oromandibular dystonia) after long-term neuroleptic therapy. *Neurology, 31,* 1555.
76. Munetz MR, Cornes CL (1983) Distinguishing akathisia and tardive dyskinesia: a review of the literature. *J. Clin. Psychopharmacol., 3,* 343.
77. Lance JW, McLeod JG (1981) *A Physiological Approach to Clinical Neurology,* p. 178. Butterworths, London-Sydney.
78. Villeneuve A (1972) The rabbit syndrome, a peculiar extrapyramidal reaction. *Can. Psychiatr. Assoc. J., 17* (SS-II), SS69.
79. Todd R, Lippmann S, Manshadi M, Chang A (1983) Recognition and treatment of rabbit syndrome, an uncommon complication of neuroleptic therapies. *Am. J. Psychiatry, 140,* 1519.
80. Weiss KJ, Ciraulo DA, Shader RI (1980) Physostigmine test in the rabbit syndrome and tardive dyskinesia. *Am. J. Psychiatry, 137,* 627.
81. Klawans HL, Barr A (1982) Prevalence of spontaneous lingual – facial – buccal dyskinesia in the elderly. *Neurology, 32,* 558.
82. Koller WC (1983) Edentulous orodyskinesia. *Ann. Neurol., 13,* 97.
83. Marsden CD (1976) Blepharospasm-oromandibular dystonia syndrome (Brueghel's syndrome). *J. Neurol. Neurosurg. Psychiatry, 39,* 1204.
84. Gerlach J (1977) Relationship between tardive dyskinesia, L-DOPA-induced hyperkinesia and parkinsonism. *Psychopharmacol., 51,* 259.
85. DeLong MR, Georgopoulos AP (1981) Motor functions of the basal ganglia. In: Brooks VB (Ed), *Handbook of Physiology. The Nervous System II,* pp. 1017 – 1061. American Physiological Society, Bethesda, MD.
86. DeLong MR, Georgopoulos AP, Crutcher MD (1983) *Cortico-basal ganglia relations and coding of motor performance. Experimental Brain Research, Suppl. 7,* pp. 30 – 39. Springer-Verlag, Berlin-Heidelberg.
87. Crutcher MD, DeLong MR (1984) Single cell studies of the primate putamen. I. Functional organization. *Exp. Brain Res., 53,* 233.
88. Altrocchi PH, Forno LS (1983) Spontaneous oral-facial dyskinesia: neuropathology of a case. *Neurology, 33,* 802.
89. Bruyn GW (1969) Huntington's chorea: historical, clinical and laboratory synopsis. In: Vinken PJ, Bruyn GW (Eds), *Handbook of Clinical Neurology, Vol. 6, Diseases of the Basal Ganglia,* Chapter 13, pp. 298 – 378. North-Holland Publishing Company, Amsterdam.

90. Graveland GA, Williams RS, DiFiglia M (1985) Evidence for degenerative and regenerative changes in neostriatal spiny neurons in Huntington's disease. *Science, 227,* 770.
91. Groves PM (1983) A theory of the functional organization of the neostriatum and the neostriatal control of voluntary movement. *Brain Res., 286,* 109.
91. Bugiani O, Tabaton M, Cammarata S (1984) Huntington's disease: survival of large striatal neurons in the rigid variant. *Ann. Neurol., 15,* 154.
93. Pasik P, Pasik T, DiFiglia M (1979) The internal organization of the neostriatum in mammals. In: Divac I, Oberg RG (Eds), *The Neostriatum,* pp. 5 – 37. Pergamon Press, New York.
94. Carpenter MB (1984) Interconnections between the corpus striatum and brain stem nuclei. In: McKenzie JS, Kemm RE, Wilcock LN (Eds), *The Basal Ganglia: Structure and Function,* pp. 1 – 68. Plenum Press, New York.
95. Moore DC, Bowers MB Jr (1980) Identification of a subgroup of tardive dyskinesia patients by pharmacologic probes. *Am. J. Psychiatry, 137,* 1202.
96. Jeste DV, Jeste SD, Wyatt RJ (1983) Reversible tardive dyskinesia: implications for therapeutic strategy and prevention of tardive dyskinesia. In: Ban TA, Picot P, Poldinger LW (Eds), *Modern Problems in Pharmacopsychiatry,* pp. 34 – 48. S. Karger, Basel.
97. Beart PM (1984) Transmitters and receptors in the basal ganglia. In: McKenzie JS, Kemm RE, Wilcock LN, (Eds), *The Basal Ganglia: Structure and Function,* pp. 261 – 296. Plenum Press, New York.
98. Bockenheimer S, Lucius G (1976) Zur Therapie mit Dimethylamino-ethanol (Deanol) bei neuroleptikainduzierten extrapyramidalen Hyperkinesen. *Arch. Psychiatr. Nervenkr., 222,* 69.
99. Klawans H, Rubovits R (1974) Effect of cholinergic and anticholinergic agents on tardive dyskinesia. *J. Neurol. Neurosurg. Psychiatry, 27,* 941.
100. Greil W, Haag H, Rossnagl G, Ruther E (1984) Effect of anticholinergics on tardive dyskinesia – A controlled discontinuation study. *Br. J. Psychiatry, 145,* 304.
101. Fahn S, Libsch LR, Cutler RW (1971) Monoamines in the human neostriatum: topographic distribution in normals and in Parkinson's disease and their role in akinesia, rigidity, chorea, and tremor. *J. Neurol. Sci., 14,* 427.
102. Farley IJ, Hornykiewicz O (1977) Noradrenaline distribution in subcortical areas of the human brain. *Brain Res., 126,* 53.
103. Alexander RW, Davis JN, Lefkowitz RJ (1975) Direct identification and characterisation of beta-adrenergic receptors in rat brain. *Nature (London), 258,* 437.
104. Palacios JM, Kuhar MJ (1980) Beta-adrenergic-receptor localization by light microscopic autoradiography. *Science, 208,* 1378.
105. Jones RSG, Olpe H-R (1984) Activation of the noradrenergic projection from locus coeruleus reduces the excitatory responses of anterior cingulate cortical neurones to substance P. *Neuroscience, 13,* 819.

CHAPTER 5

Electroencephalogram and evoked potential studies of schizophrenia

JACK A. GREBB, DANIEL R. WEINBERGER AND
JOHN M. MORIHISA

Electroencephalograms (EEGs) and evoked potential (EP) studies are standard tests that assess selected aspects of the electrophysiologic activity of the central nervous system (CNS). Their primary clinical applications are in the evaluation of epilepsy by EEG and in the assessment of demyelinating diseases with EPs. Their popularity in neuropsychiatric research is enhanced by their non-invasiveness, relatively low cost, and also by their adaptability to relevant animal models. The power of EEG and EP data to reflect brain function, however, is limited by the fact that scalp electrodes record the activity probably only of the uppermost cortical cell layers. How, or even whether, these measurements reflect functioning of other brain areas is the subject of active investigation.

This chapter reviews the EEG and EP studies of patients with schizophrenia. First, the techniques, terminology and neurophysiologic correlates of EEG and EP are outlined. Second, the data from EEG and EP studies are presented, as much as possible, without allusion to theoretical constructs. Third, the various hypotheses that have evolved from this data are summarized. Finally, we attempt a critical assessment of the data and discuss its implications for clinical application and further research.

Basic principles of EEG and EP

The number and placement of the scalp electrodes for both EEG and EP studies need to be considered in evaluating research reports. An increase in the total number of electrodes or a greater density of electrodes over one particular brain region can increase the probability of finding differences between groups of specific brain regions. Most recent studies conform to the International '10 – 20' System of electrode placement. Earlier studies, however, did not have this convention to follow, thereby making comparisons with more recent studies problematic.

Recording artifact is the major problem in both EEG and EP interpretation. Besides myriad specific technical issues (e.g. an electrode loosening because a psychotic patient is agitated, the specific settings on amplifiers and filters, etc.), the two major sources of artifact remain scalp muscle activity and eye movement. Mus-

Handbook of Schizophrenia, Vol. 1: The Neurology of Schizophrenia.
H.A. Nasrallah and D.R. Weinberger, editors.
© Elsevier Science Publishes B.V., 1986.

cle activity can be confused with beta activity, especially if the record is analyzed by computer without prior visual inspection. Eye movement can produce slow delta waves in the frontal leads potentially indistinguishable from pathologic slow activity unless eye movement is monitored concurrently during an EEG or EP recording.

Electroencephalogram

The two fundamental measures from visual inspection of EEG are frequency and amplitude of wave form. Visual inspection of an EEG also detects paroxysmal events, such as fast or slow wave bursts, spikes, or other isolated abnormalities. Frequencies have been divided, essentially arbitrarily, into delta activity (less than 4 Hz), theta activity (4 – 8 Hz), alpha activity (8 – 13 Hz), and beta activity (greater than 13 Hz). Visual inspection of the EEG assesses the amount, amplitude, and spatial distribution over the scalp of activity in each of these frequency ranges. The estimation of these qualities by eye provides a somewhat subjective approximation. The utilization of computers, however, has provided a quantitative, reproducible measure of the 'power' of each frequency, a summary of its amplitude and the amount of time it is present in the record.

Alpha activity has been the most actively investigated EEG frequency. This electrical activity is most marked over the parietal – occipital cortex in the adult when in the resting, eyes-closed state. Alpha activity is eliminated from the EEG if the subject is stimulated or if the eyes are opened. This is variously called alpha blocking, desynchronization, arousal response, or alerting response. The principle neurophysiologic pacemaker for alpha rhythm probably is the thalamus although isolated cortex itself is capable of producing an alpha-like rhythm (1).

The other EEG frequencies are less well understood than alpha activity. Beta activity in under 20 μV in amplitude in almost 100% of normal adult subjects (2). The most common etiologies for increased beta amplitude are drug ingestion or defects in the dura, bone or scalp that enhance beta activity preferentially over lower frequencies. Depressions in beta voltage are seen following focal cortical injury, subdural or epidural fluid collections, or transiently following focal epileptic seizures. Although theta activity is usually minimal in normal adults, approximately 35% of normal awake adults have low voltage frontal theta activity with their eyes closed (2). Drowsiness and hyperventilation can further bring out this rhythm. Although beta (3) and theta (4) activity appear to have genetic determinants, their physiologic basis is not known.

The EEG patterns of sleep require a separate description. Sleep can be divided into two phases, one accompanied by rapid eye movements (REM) and the other characterized by the absence of rapid eye movements (Non-REM). Non-REM sleep is divided into stages 1 through 4, representing increasing 'depth' of sleep. In Stage 1, alpha activity becomes fragmented and then disappears. The remaining activity decreases slightly in frequency and increases slightly in amplitude. Stage 2 is characterized by the appearance of high-voltage notched slow waves, 'K-complexes,' and 14-c.p.s. 'sleep spindles.' In Stage 3, high-amplitude delta waves begin to appear, and then in Stage 4, the delta activity becomes essentially constant. In REM sleep the high-amplitude slow waves are replaced by activity resembling that for awake and alert states, consisting of rapid, low-voltage, irregular activity.

Evoked potentials

Evoked potentials are also called averaged evoked potentials, cortical evoked potentials, or event-related potentials. Sometimes the word 'response' is substituted for 'potential.' All these terms essentially describe similar phenomena although arguments have been made concerning which is most accurate. The evoking event is usually either a somatosensory, auditory or visual stimulation, resulting in somatosensory evoked potentials (SEPs), auditory evoked potentials (AEPs) or visual evoked potentials (VEPs). The basis for EP studies is the relatively reproducible CNS electrophysiologic response to simple sensory stimuli. Averaging the scalp EEG during the first second following multiple identical sensory stimulations (often 20 – 200 ms) produces a characteristic wave form with the non-stimulus-related electrical activity averaged out of the summary recording.

Evoked potential recordings consist of positive and negative peaks spread along a time axis. Because of the usual polarity of the electrodes, positive waves are by

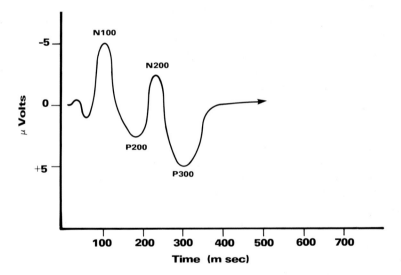

FIG. 1   *Idealized average evoked potential pattern.*

convention designated as down-going and negative waves up-going; however, this can vary with the specific setup of recording equipment. The peaks are named by two different systems in the literature. One system labels the positive (P) and negative (N) peaks from first to last (e.g. P1, P2, P3 . . .Px; N1, N2, N3 . . .Nx). This system makes comparison between reports difficult because of uncertainty that the 'N4', for example, of one report is really the same wave as the 'N4' in another report. The second convention is labeling the waves either positive (P) or negative (N) along with the approximate time that peak appears after the stimulus (e.g. P300, a positive wave appearing approximately 300 ms after the stimulus) (see Fig. 1).

Each peak or wave is individually assessed by a number of measures. Amplitude is the height of the wave; latency is the length of time from stimulus to wave. A 'faster latency' means that the wave appeared sooner, and a 'slower latency' means that that wave appeared later. Other EP measures are the shape of the wave, the variability of the EP from one trial to the next, and the distribution of different peaks over the scalp.

The timing of the EP pattern has been somewhat arbitrarily divided into 'early' or 'fast' potentials (occurring in the first 50 ms), middle potentials (50 – 250 ms), and 'late' or 'slow' potentials (occurring after 250 ms). A late potential, the P300, is also called the 'late positive wave' (LPW), or part of the 'late positive component' (LPC). Other EP waves considered as late potentials are the 'contingent negative variation' (CNV) and the 'post-imperative negative variation' (PINV). The CNV is a negative shift in electrical potential that precedes an expected event (5). The paradigm for eliciting CNVs often consists of a warning stimulus (S1) followed by an expected stimulus (S2) that often signals the subject to perform some 'imperative' task. It is before S2 that the CNV is recorded. The PINV is the continuation of the negativity of the CNV following S2 (6). Another EP, the readiness potential (RP, also called the movement-related potential (MRP) or the Bereitschaftspotential (BP)), is a slowly increasing negative potential that begins 0.5 to 1 second before self-initiated movement (7).

The early, middle, and late EPs are thought to have different neurophysiological meanings. The early EP waves are the best understood and are felt to represent anatomically specific events in the relay of sensory information to cortex. The neuroanatomic bases for the waves in the first 50 ms are well worked out for the auditory (8), visual (9) and somatosensory (10) EPs. After 50 ms, the anatomic generator of the waves is basically unknown, but is generally ascribed to cortical events. The pervasive assumption throughout the EP literature is that after 50 ms, the later an event is, the more it reflects 'psychological' or 'cognitive' processing. The division between middle and late EPs in this regard is arbitrary.

The most commonly identified middle and late waves are the N100, P200, N200 and P300. The N100 occurs with a latency of 120 – 200 ms, is often paired with a subsequent positive potential, the P200, and described as the N100 – P200 complex. The P300 occurs with a usual latency of 250 – 350 ms. Some studies, however, have considered waves as late as 600 ms as equivalents of the P300. The P300 is often preceded by the N200.

As mentioned previously, the middle and late EPs, the CNV and the PINV have been the subject of much research and speculation as to what cognitive or psychological processes they represent. Although research continues to attempt to label the underlying cognitive processes (e.g. selective attention, expectancy) for each of the waves after 50 ms, there is also increasing evidence that virtually every measure of these components is subject to experimental manipulation (11). Other variables that also affect EP studies, often not controlled for in experimental designs, are fatigue, coffee and cigarette consumption, age (12), and diurnal variation (13).

Although nagging uncertainties about validity remain, there is some general agreement assigning specific cognitive operations to various peaks. The N100 – P200 complex is basically similar across sensory modalities and is thought to represent 'attention' and 'selective filtering for stimulus attributes' (14, 15). The N100-P200 wave is augmented by increased attention by the subject or enhancement of specified stimulus characteristics. The amplitude of the P300 – N200 is inversely related to the subject's expectancy of an event. It would, therefore, seem that the P300 – N200 might be seen as representing another facet of 'attention.' More recently the P300 has been divided into separate components, P300a, P300b, etc. (16), with each component varying independently according to the design of the paradigm, and potentially having different physiological significance. The CNV has been interpreted as representing attention, arousal (17), personality traits (18), 'response set' (19), preparation for planned activity (20), and motivation (21). The RP seems to more straightforwardly represent intention to make a voluntary, spontaneous movement (22).

Data from EEG and EP studies of patients

The evaluation of EEG and EP studies of patients with schizophrenia involves many of the usual methodological concerns. Patient selection, diagnostic rigor, specification of subtype and medication status, and an adequate control group are basic requisites of a well-designed study. Much of the old EEG and EP literature does not meet these standards. A description of the clinical state of the patient is necessary to evaluate whether electrophysiologic abnormalities represent the current clinical state of the illness or, more significantly, a marker or trait of the illness.

EEG data

The most basic finding from EEG studies of schizophrenia is that these patients have a higher percentage of abnormal records (23, 24). Because of a wide range of study designs, the percentages reported range from 5 to 80% (25). A review based on ten early well-controlled studies, nevertheless, did conclude that the rate of EEG abnormalities in schizophrenia is higher than that for normals (26). The most consistent specific finding of these pre-1977 studies is that EEG records from schizophrenic patients have a disorganized alpha frequency with less alpha activity and a lower mean alpha frequency than normals (27, 28). In one of the best designed studies, patients with schizophrenia also had more delta, theta and fast beta activity (27). Other abnormalities included paroxysmal abnormal wave forms, epileptic-like spikes and waves, and 'choppy activity' (29), referring to a low-amplitude, disorganized record with an apparent increase in fast activity. As is often the case with studies of schizophrenia, the range of test values is increased. For example, in these early studies that reported abnormal records there was also a subgroup of 'hypernormal' EEGs associated with a poor response to neuroleptics (30).

Itil (24) and Shagass (23) reviewed the studies that show that schizophrenic patients are more sensitive to activation procedures such as hyperventilation, pentathol administration, or sleep. The most consistently reported abnormality seen with these activation procedures is the B-mitten pattern that consists of a sharp transient followed by a slow wave, thereby resembling the thumb and hand of a mitten. This pattern occurs in about 35% of patients with schizophrenia, and has been associated more with 'reactive' patients than 'process' patients (31) and also with the presence of tardive dyskinesia (32). The B-mitten also occurs in patients with epilepsy and affective disorders (33), although perhaps at a lower rate for the latter group than for patients with schizophrenia. The physiological meaning of this pattern, however, or even whether it is pathological at all, is unknown.

Five studies published since 1977 further support some of the earlier findings, offering new information as well. These newer studies all use more restrictive definitions of schizophrenia. One study comparing 27 schizophrenic patients with 132 affective patients found twice as many abnormal records (e.g. slowing, sharp waves, slow bursts) in the schizophrenic group (48%) compared with the affective group (24%) (34). Among the schizophrenic patients, the abnormalities were more often over the temporal regions; among the affective patients, the abnormalities were more frequent in the parieto – occipital region. The abnormalities in the schizophrenic group were not correlated with age, sex, severity of illness or past or present drug administration. Another recent study used computer-derived spectral analysis to define EEG differences among subtypes of schizophrenia (35). This group reported that acute patients (n = 26 with 13 drug-free) had less alpha power especially over the bilateral temporal regions. Chronic outpatients (n = 30 all on medications) had less power in both alpha and beta frequencies. A final group of chronic inpatients (all drug-free) had an excess of delta activity, but no abnormalities of alpha and a non-significant trend toward increased beta. The abnormalities in the two chronic groups were diffusely distributed about the scalp. Not surprisingly, the inpatient chronic group had the most 'negative' or deficit symptoms of the illness. This last finding may complement a report describing a correlation between EEG abnormalities and poor performance on neuropsychological testing, especially the Halstead-Reitan Neuropsychological Test Battery (36).

A novel approach to EEG assessment utilized 24-hour telemetry of EEG with power spectral analysis (37). This report studied 18 patients, 8 of whom were drug-free. The findings generally supported the previous reports of more delta activity (especially over right temporal regions) and less alpha activity. These authors were particularly interested in the presence of 'ramp' spectra (characterized by a smooth decline in power from highest to lowest frequencies) that previously have been reported to be associated with subcortical spike activity in epileptic patients. Nine of the 18 patients had ramp spectra whereas none of the controls did. These ramp spectra were associated twice as often as not with episodes of abnormal behavior, including catatonic episodes, hallucinatory periods or stereotyped darting horizontal saccades. These findings support the early reports of a high incidence of EEG abnormalities in schizophrenia including many records with epileptic-like activity, a finding that was particularly pronounced in patients with hebephrenia (38) and in catatonia, especially during acute attacks (39).

One comprehensive recent study puts many of the previous reports in a different perspective (40). This group reviewed the clinical and EEG records of 759 patients seen in 1965 – 1972 and bearing DSM-I or DSM-II diagnoses of schizophrenia. Analysis of the EEGs of this total group completely supported earlier studies showing a high incidence of EEG abnormalities and a lower mean alpha frequency. Furthermore, as previously mentioned, 'hypernormal' records were associated with a poor prognosis, whereas the presence of EEG abnormalities predicted a better prognosis. All of the patients were re-diagnosed according to strict Feighner criteria, resulting in a change of diagnosis for one-third of the patients. The presence of EEG abnormalities in a DSM-I/II schizophrenic predicted change to another diagnosis and a better prognosis. Although the incidence of abnormal EEGs among the Feighner schizophrenics was lower, 38% still had abnormal records. Feighner schizophrenics with normal EEGs tended to have a more chronic course, perhaps consistent with earlier reports of 'hypernormal' EEGs in neuroleptic non-responsive schizophrenics. The mean alpha activity among Feighner organic, schizo-affective and schizophrenic disorders was lower than that for other groups, including patients with affective disorders. The patients were also re-diagnosed according to the Research Diagnostic Criteria (RDC). Analysis of this approach supported the finding of the low mean alpha frequency in schizophrenia inasmuch as affective pathology was correlated with high alpha frequency. One subgroup of high-functioning RDC schizophrenics had had affective symptoms early in the course of their illness, normal EEGs and high alpha frequency.

A large number of studies have looked for asymmetries in the EEG as a possible reflection of abnormal functioning of one hemisphere. One hypothesis has been that there is a left hemisphere dysfunction in schizophrenia, as suggested by a number of non-electrophysiologic measures, e.g. lateralization of skin conductance, psychotic phenomena associated with left hemisphere lesions in epilepsy (41), and greater incidence of left-handedness in schizophrenia (42). The major argument against this theory is that the demonstration of a difference in left hemispheric functioning by any method does not prove that the initial, or even current, pathology is on that side. A number of studies, nevertheless, have reported increased left-sided EEG abnormalities in schizophrenia, particularly temporal – frontal, and have associated these with symptoms of thought disorder (34, 43 – 45). More recent reports have hypothesized variations in the asymmetry to be related to specific symptoms with left-sided lesions associated with thought disorders and right-sided lesions associated with anxiety (46). It is relevant to mention that visual (47 – 49) and auditory EP studies (50 – 51) are consistent with the hypothesis of left-sided dysfunction in schizophrenia. These same data also have been used to support the hypothesis that there is dysfunction of the corpus callosum in patients with schizophrenia (52 – 53). There are at least two studies which do not support a left-sided dysfunction in schizophrenia, one using spectral analysis of EEG (35) and one assessing VEP response to neuroleptics (54).

All studies discussed so far have been awake EEGs. Despite many practical and technical problems, there is a large body of literature on the sleeping EEG of patients with schizophrenia. The most solid finding from all-night sleep studies of patients with schizophrenia is a decrease in the amount of deep sleep (Stages 2, 3 and 4) (55). Although some investigators have reported decreased REM activity during acute illness or exacerbations of chronic illness and absence of normal REM rebound following REM deprivation (56 – 57), other reports have found normal REM sleep (58).

In conclusion, despite numerous studies and many findings, the most consistent EEG observations have been an increased percentage of patients who have abnormal records and increased sensitivity to activation procedures, such as hyperventilation. There is no clear finding of specific abnormalities that are associated with either the illness in general, or a specific state of the illness (see Table 1).

EP data

There are a number of recent general reviews of EPs in schizophrenia (59 – 62). There also are specific reviews of early (63), middle (64) and late EPs (65). There are three relatively consistent findings. First, the early EPs tend to be increased in amplitude and show less wave shape variability, especially in chronic patients. This is most true with the N60 wave of the SEP, and least true with VEPs. Second, the middle evoked potentials, particularly P100, N140, and P200, are reduced in amplitude with most stimulus paradigms. Third, the late EPs, notably the P300, also are reduced in amplitude. The CNV is reduced in patients with schizophrenia, and it has been suggested that this may be a trait marker, inasmuch as amplitude remains decreased in clinically improved patients. EPs in schizophrenic patients also demonstrate a prolonged PINV and a reduced RP. An oversimplification of this data is that EPs before 100 ms are larger and less variable, whereas EPs after 100 ms are smaller and more variable. The major problem with this generalization is that it represents summaries across many studies which utilize different paradigms. Not

TABLE 1   *EEG findings in patients with schizophrenia*

Well established	1. Higher incidence of abnormal records.
	2. More sensitive to activation procedures.
Frequently seen abnormalities	1. Alpha activity decreased and lower in mean frequency.
	2. Delta and theta activity increased.
Controversial findings	1. More epileptiform activity.
	2. More left-sided abnormalities.

all the studies, moreover, were controlled for medication status (66) or the many other environmental variables than can effect EPs (e.g. shape of visual stimulus, caffeine or tobacco consumption).

EP studies published since 1980 have extended and perhaps solidified some of the previous findings. The finding of decreased wave shape variability and increased amplitude before 100 ms, and increased variability and decreased amplitude after 100 ms in the SEP was confirmed in a comprehensive study involving SEP, AEP and VEP paradigms in multiple patient and control groups (67). This finding, however, was present only in the SEP and not in the AEP or VEP, and only in chronic schizophrenics. Although most earlier studies have reported reduced amplitude recovery following repeated stimuli (59, 60), a series of well designed studies have reported an opposite finding. Using a longer interstimulus interval (ISI) (0.5 – 2 s) than in previous studies, medication-free schizophrenic subjects demonstrated a markedly increased amplitude recovery of the AEP P50 (68). The authors suggested that their ISI took into account the long inhibitory intervals of the cerebral cortex. The same result was found in medicated schizophrenics (69). It is noteworthy that although medication did normalize the baseline P50s of the schizophrenics it did not normalize the increased amplitude recovery. This group of investigators used the same paradigm on manic patients and found a similar increase in amplitude recovery. There was, however, more variability among the manic patients, and the recovery measurement reverted to normal with stabilization on lithium carbonate.

In a complex AEP paradigm looking at middle and late EPs, investigators were able to demonstrate decreased N140 with slow rates of repetitive stimulation and an increased N140 for fast rates of stimulation in schizophrenic patients (70), again emphasizing the importance of paradigm design in affecting EP data. This same study supported the finding of a decrease in P300 amplitude, but also demonstrated a prolonged latency which is not consistent with earlier reports. Because of suggestions that the P300 might have diagnostic power in discriminating dementia, schizophrenia and depression, a group of investigators employed AEP and VEP paradigms in these three patient groups (71). The AEP and VEP both showed changes in P300 latency and amplitude; however, these were neither large enough nor specific enough to differentiate the patient groups.

Three recent studies have explored use of the CNV as a marker for the stage of illness. Earlier reports had described a decreased CNV amplitude and presence of a PINV in acute schizophrenics. The CNV returns toward, but does not reach, normal with successful medication. These results were replicated in a study of 14 acute patients (72); however, this same study showed an abnormal CNV in both medication-free, residual schizophrenics and in medicated chronic patients with intermittent exacerbations. These chronic groups did not exhibit a PINV. The CNV has more recently been divided into four factors or components (73), and a pilot application of such an analysis suggests that the factors may have potential for discriminating subtypes of schizophrenic pathology, for instance, negative symptoms being associated with specific CNV factors distributed frontally (74).

TABLE 2   *EP findings in patients with schizophrenia*

Well established	1. Decreased amplitude of late components (e.g. CNV, P300)
Frequently seen abnormalities	1. Increased amplitude of early (< 100 ms) and decreased amplitude of middle (> 100 ms) SEPs 2. Decreased variability of early and increased variability of middle EPs
Controversial findings	1. Reduced amplitude recovery after repeated stimuli 2. Left-sided abnormalities

The variety of paradigms reported in this literature makes it difficult to distill the major EP findings. The two most consistent findings, however, are increased amplitude in the early SEPs and decreased amplitude of the P300 and CNV (Table 2).

EEG and EP data from childhood psychosis and first-degree relatives

The presence of similar EEG and EP findings in childhood psychosis might add validity to electrophysiologic measures as markers of psychotic processes. One major problem with such a conclusion is that baseline normal EEGs and EPs of adults and children are quite different. Another problematic assumption is that 'psychosis' is a unitary phenomenon. These differences in baseline normal EEGs can make seemingly similar abnormalities very difficult to compare in a meaningful way. A second source of information about the validity of EEG and EP markers of schizophrenia might come from an investigation of non-affected first-degree relatives of schizophrenic patients. It is possible to conceptualize such markers as indicative of a predisposition to schizophrenia. The major problem with this conclusion is the assumption that the shared EEG and EP measures were relevant to the pathophysiology of the illness and not merely representative of the general genetic loading between relatives having nothing to do with the illness.

The two most restricting problems in electrophysiological studies of childhood psychosis are diagnosis and maturational changes. In the existing studies, childhood psychosis, autism and schizophrenia occurring in childhood are very difficult to separate with confidence. The fact that EEG and EP (12) recordings change throughout development further confounds comparative studies when even a limited range of ages is involved. The most recent summary of the psychophysiology of childhood psychosis (75) reviews a large number of EEG studies of psychotic children and reports a range of 30–83% of the patients as having abnormal records, variously correlated with a positive family history of psychiatric illness, lower age of the patient, severity of illness or presence of a seizure disorder. The only spectral analysis of childhood psychosis with mixed diagnoses reported less alpha activity and increased slow and fast activity. Visual inspection of the records also indicated fewer alpha bursts when compared with the normal controls. The authors pointed out the similarities of these findings with their own findings in adult schizophrenic patients (76). Studies of EPs have been limited to patient groups with autism and are not reported here.

A 1982 review of electrophysiologic studies in children 'at risk' for schizophrenia concluded that the available EEG data did not lend itself to interpretation (77). EP studies that were reviewed also reported conflicting findings. There were relatively consistent reports, however, of longer latencies and reduced amplitude late positive components in the high-risk children. This is similar to the findings regarding P300 in adult schizophrenia. A more recent study of AEPs in children at risk replicated the finding of decreased amplitude in late positive waves (77).

There have been two recent studies of first-degree relatives of schizophrenic probands, both suggesting potential electrophysiologic markers of the schizophrenic trait. An AEP paradigm was used to assess schizophrenic patients, their siblings, and normal controls (78). Though the siblings and the normals had similar N100s which were different from that of the patients, the siblings were different from the normals in their failure to augment the LPCs of their EP when they detected the target stimulus. The amplitude of their LPC, in fact, was quite close to that of their schizophrenic siblings. The authors point out the similarities of the LPC in adult schizophrenic patients and in children at risk. One of the most recent EP investigations of genetic concomitants of schizophrenia utilized an AEP paradigm with paired stimuli, measuring not only amplitude and latency of the P50, but also the percent reduction or inhibition of the P50 for the second stimulus (S2) (79). This group reported on 15 schizophrenic patients and their parents. Whereas normal controls inhibited their S2 P50 to less than 20% of the S1 P50, the schizophrenic probands had a S2 P50 greater than 85% of the amplitude of their S1 P50. Among the first-degree relatives 57% (vs. 11% normals) had non-reducing S2 P50s similar in non-reduction to the schizophrenic probands. Of the 15 families tested, 14 had at least one parent with a non-reducing response. The abnormal response of the relatives differed from that of the schizophrenics by having a normal shape and latency, whereas these measures were abnormal in the patients with schizophrenia. The presence of a non-reducing response in relatives was associated with abnormalities on the MMPI and a positive family history of schizophrenia. The presence of more EP abnormalities in first-degree relatives of families with more than one schizophrenic member is not consistent with one report of a higher incidence (72.3%) of abnormal EEGs in patients without a family history than the incidence (43%) of abnormal EEGs in patients with a family history (80).

Theoretical formulations from EEG and EP data

The data summarized above have been used in the literature to generate or support hypotheses about the etiology and pathophysiology of schizophrenia. The theories that schizophrenia is associated with a left hemisphere or corpus callosum dysfunction are examples. The following sections discuss proposed pathophysiologies (e.g. epileptic activity, deficits in attention) and potential anatomic locations for pathology (left temporal, frontal, thalamic).

Left temporal lobe epileptic foci

The EEG data is weakly consistent with the hypothesis that epileptic-like activity, particularly in the left temporal lobe, may be involved in the pathophysiology of schizophrenia (41). Perhaps the genesis of this theory came from the clinical observation that both the ictal and interictal phenomena in complex partial seizures (formerly called temporal lobe epilepsy) could approximate some aspects of the clinical presentation of schizophrenia. Further implicating data are that epilepsy and schizophrenia co-exist more often than one would expect by chance (81), and the proposal that dominant hemisphere temporal epileptic foci tend to result in disorders of thinking, in contrast to non-dominant foci which produce affective symptoms (82).

This review of EEG data illustrates the high incidence of abnormal EEG patterns in schizophrenic patients. These abnormalities often include paroxysmal activity and other epileptic-like events. The increased sensitivity of patients with schizophrenia to activation procedures also might support an epileptic diathesis. The presence in some studies of increased slow activity over temporal lobes may reflect a hypometabolism of these areas, perhaps similar to the hypometabolic areas which have been identified by positron emission tomographic (PET) scanning coinciding with interictal epileptic foci (83). The possibility of subcortical seizure activity is also supported by the 'ramp' spectra reported from sporadic telemetered EEG data (37) as well as from reports of clinical improvement in non-epileptic schizophrenic patients with paroxysmal EEGs when treated with anticonvulsants in combination with antipsychotics (84). These associations, however, are supported only by circumstantial evidence.

Electrophysiologic recordings using depth electrodes in patients with schizophrenia have demonstrated spikes and waves in the thalamus (85), onset of rapid synchronized waves in the frontal – parietal and temporal lobes (86) and paroxysmal slow discharges in the deep areas of the frontal lobes (87). Paroxysmal discharges in the septal region have been reported using depth electrodes in schizophrenic patients (88). These deep spikes which reportedly are associated with agitated and hostile behavior, may not be reflected in the surface EEG. As interesting as these studies are, their interpretation is limited by the absence of normative data concerning deep electrical activity and the improbability of acquiring replication data.

Deficits in attention, sensory and cognitive processing

Evoked-potential studies have suggested many theoretical formulations regarding the pathophysiology of schizophrenia. The majority of models which have evolved from the EP data are concerned with 'attention,' 'sensory filtering,' 'arousal,' and 'processing speed.' These words are placed in quotes because they represent abstractions, and do not have absolute innate meaning as descriptors of brain function. The process of attention (89) is often measured via the middle EPs. Related to hypotheses stating a deficit of attention in schizophrenia are theories about increased distractability (90), and various subsets of attention-selective attention, focused attention, attention maintenance, and shifting attention (91). A hypothesis that patients with schizophrenia have defective filtering of input is supported by the augmented early EPs (19, 59, 63). The reduced amplitude of middle and late EPs as well as their greater variability are hypothesized to represent the variable abilities of the neuromodulatory systems to dampen or inhibit the spread of this initial overload of information. Such a condition has been further hypothesized to lead to 'sensory overload,' and a pathological defense mechanism of 'reducing' response to increased stimulus intensity (64). This work has since been criticized as inadequately controlling for major sources of artifact (92). Deficient motivation (93) and slow processing speed (94, 95) also have been hypothesized to represent pathophysiologic models of schizophrenia.

Frontal lobe dysfunction

A more recently suggested unifying theory involves frontal lobe dysfunction in schizophrenia and is discussed elsewhere in this volume. This hypothesis is supported by some of the EP findings. The increased early EPs would be explained by decreased cortical inhibition of early sensory processing. In fact, the more general finding of decreased EP amplitude after 100 ms could be explained by decreased motivation and apathy from frontal cortex dysfunction. Although 'engagement' in a test procedure is monitored by task performance, it is quite likely that even with equal performance between a schizophrenic patient and a normal or other patient control, the schizophrenic was less engaged than the other subject. The regional distribution of abnormal late EPs (e.g. CNV) has more directly implicated frontal cortex (see above), although generation of these potentials may be located at a point distant to the frontal cortex.

Thalamic dysfunction

The thalamus also is implicated by the EEG and EP data since it is the major contributor to the alpha rhythm of the EEG, the major conduit of messages from brainstem to cortex, as well as the relay station for evoked potentials. The thalamus is critically situated with reciprocal connections to dorsolateral and orbitomedial frontal cortex (96), input from the hippocampus (probably via septum) (97), and a functional role in the basolateral limbic system (98). There are even single thalamic neurons in the rat which project to cerebral cortex, striatum and intrathalamically (99). Lesion studies in animals (100) and descriptions of human thalamic syndromes (101) provide provocative behavioral and electrophysiologic parallels with schizophrenia. Consistent with a hypothesis of thalamic dysfunction in schizophrenia are the reports that bilateral stereotaxic destruction of the medial nuclei were performed as an alternative to prefrontal leukotomies (102).

Summary

The single most consistent finding from EEG studies in schizophrenia has been a higher incidence of abnormal records, both in adult patients and in psychotic children. This observation alone implicates brain pathophysiology in at least the symptoms of schizophrenia. Also fairly consistent is the finding that alpha activity is decreased (particularly in acute patients) and delta activity is increased (perhaps more so in chronic patients). There may be subgroups with epileptiform activity, left-sided prominence of abnormalities, or temporal prominence of abnormalities. There is some indication that EEG abnormalities suggest a better prognosis and more affective pathology, whereas normal EEGs suggest a more chronic course. The most consistent findings in the EP literature are increased amplitude of the early SEPs and decreased amplitude of the P300 and CNV. These findings appear most markedly in patients who are either severely ill acutely or chronically. It should be noted that no single or specific EEG or EP finding characterizes schizophrenia. Furthermore, the generic notion of 'EEG abnormalities' is potentially misleading as different abnormalities may implicate distinct pathophysiological processes. Nevertheless, the results of the studies reviewed above suggest that to the extent that EEG and EP data reflect cerebral physiology, there are abnormal cerebral physiological events associated with schizophrenia.

A broad interpretation of the EEG and EP findings supports the presence of brain disease in many patients with this disorder. The pattern of these electrophysiologic abnormalities would seem to represent either the presence of multiple different pathophysiologies or, possibly, the varied manifestations of an earlier common pathologic insult. The mutual interactions within the brain and the plasticity of its organization produce a system in which the identification of a particular location or marker as aberrant in a clinical condition could be quite far removed in time and space from the original pathologic insult. For example, animal experiments have demonstrated that focal cortical seizures in the rat can produce distant thalamic lesions (103), a pathophysiologic process which has also been reported in human complex partial seizures (104–105).

A number of directions for future research studies are also suggested. First, diagnosis, subtype and clinical state should be carefully assessed. Second, activation procedures (EPs, cognitive testing, drug infusions, etc.) may be more powerful at exposing pathology than tests in the 'resting' state. Third, an attempt should be made to correlate electrophysiologic measures with other biologic measures or symptom complexes less comprehensive than DSM-III diagnoses. Fourth, the emphasis on the topography of EEG and EP abnormalities should continue.

Clinical implications

Clinically, in a patient with a presumptive diagnosis of schizophrenia, it is prudent to get a sleep-deprived EEG, preferably with nasopharyngeal leads, in an attempt to rule out a contributing epileptic disorder. *All* other research findings from EEG and EP studies are statistical in nature and *should not* be used to assess individual cases. Specific indications for an EEG include young age (under 25), first episode of psychosis, and any documented or likely history of injury to the brain (e.g. accidents, infection, birth complications).

REFERENCES

1. Andersen, P, Andersson SA (1968) *Physiological Basis of the Alpha Rhythm.* Appleton-Century-Crofts, New York.
2. Klass DW, Daly DD (Eds) (1979) *Current Practice of Clinical Electroencephalography.* Raven Press, New York.
3. Vogel F (1970) The genetic basis of the normal human electroencephalogram (EEG). *Humangenetik, 10,* 91.
4. Cohn R, Nardini JE (1958) The correlation of bilateral occipital slow activity in the human EEG with certain disorders of behavior. *Am. J. Psychiatry, 115,* 44.
5. Walter WG, Cooper R, Aldridge VJ, McCallum WC, Winter AL (1964) Contingent negative variation: an electric sign of sensorimotor association and expectancy in the human brain. *Nature (London), 103,* 380.
6. Tismit-Berthier M, Delaunoy J, Rousseau JC (1973) Slow potential changes in psychiatry. I. Contingent negative variation. *Electroencephalogr. Clin. Neurophysiol. 35,* 355.
7. Grunewald-Zuberbeit E, Grunewald G (1978) Goal-directed movement potentials of human cerebral cortex. *Exp. Brain Res., 33,* 135.
8. Hillyard S, Woods D (1979) Electrophysiological analysis of human brain function. In: Gazzaniga M (Ed), *Handbook of Behavioral Neurology, Vol 2,* pp. 345 – 378. Plenum Press, New York.
9. Goff WR, Allison T, Vaughan HG, Jr (1978) The functional neuroanatomy of event-related potentials. In: Callaway E, Teuting P, Koslow S (Eds), *Event Related Brain Potentials in Man.* Academic Press, New York.
10. Arezzo JC, Vaughan HG, Jr, Legatt AD (1981) Topography and intracranial sources of somatosensory evoked potentials in the monkey. II Cortical components. *J. Electroencephalogr. Clin. Neurophysiol., 51,* 1.
11. Bumgartner J, Epstein CM (1982) Voluntary alteration of visual evoked potentials. *Ann. Neurol., 12,* 475.
12. Allison T, Hume AL, Wood CC, Goff WR (1984) Developmental and aging changes in somatosensory, auditory and visual evoked potentials. *Electroencephalogr. Clin. Neurophysiol., 58,* 14.
13. Zimmermann P, Gortelmeyer R, Wiemann H (1983) Diurnal periodicity of lateral asymmetries of the visual evoked potential in healthy volunteers. *Neuropsychobiol., 9,* 178.
14. Hillyard S, Picton T, Regan D (1978) Sensation, perception and attention: analysis using ERP's. In: Callaway E, Teuting P, Koslow S (Eds), *Event Related Brain Potentials in*

Man, pp. 223 – 332. Academic Press, New York.

15. Picton TW, Stuss DT (1980) The component structure of the human event-related potentials. In: Kornhuber HH, Deeck L (Eds), *Motivation, Motor and Sensory Processes of the Brain: Electrical Potentials, Behavior and Clinical Use,* pp. 17 – 42. Elsevier, Amsterdam.

16. Teuting P (1978) Event-related potentials, cognitive events, and information processing: a summary of issues and discussion. In: Otto DA (Ed), *Multidisciplinary Perspectives in Event-Related Brain Potential Research,* pp. 159 – 169. U.S. Environmental Protection Agency, Washington.

17. Tecce JJ, Savignano-Bowman J, Cole JO (1978) Drug effects on contingent negative variation and eye blinks: the distraction-arousal hypothesis. In: Lipton MA, DiMascio A, Killam KP (Eds), *Psychopharmacology,* pp. 745 – 758. Raven Press, New York.

18. Bachneff SA, Engelsmann F (1983) Correlates of cerebral event-related slow potentials and psychopathology. *Psychol. Med., 13,* 763.

19. Broadbent DE (1970) Stimulus set and response set: two kinds of selective attention. In: Mostofsky DJ (Ed), *Attention: Contemporary Theory and Analysis.* Appleton-Century-Crofts, New York.

20. Gaillard AW (1978) *Slow Brain Potentials Preceding Task Performance.* Academische Pers B.V., Amsterdam.

21. Rowland V (1968) Cortical steady potential (D.C. potential) in reinforcement and learning. In: Stellar E, Sprague J (Eds), *Progress in Physiological Psychology,* pp. 1 – 77. Academic Press, New York.

22. Loveless N (1979) Event-related slow potentials of the brain as expression of orienting function. In: Kimmel HD, Van Olst EH, Orlbeke J (Eds), *The Orienting Reflex in Humans,* pp. 77 – 100. L. Erlbaum, Hillsdale.

23. Shagass C (1975) EEG and evoked potentials in the psychoses. In: Freedman DX (Ed), *Biology of the Major Psychoses, Research and Public Association of Research in Nervous and Mental Disease, Vol 54,* pp. 101 – 127. Raven Press, New York.

24. Itil TM (1977) Qualitative and quantitative EEG findings in schizophrenia. *Schizophr. Bull., 3,* 61.

25. Small JG, Small IF (1965) Re-evaluation of clinical EEG findings in schizophrenia. *Dis. Nerv. Syst., 26,* 345.

26. Ellingson RJ (1954) The incidence of EEG abnormality among patients with mental disorders of apparently nonorganic origin: a critical review. *Am. J. Psychiatry, 111,* 263.

27. Itil TM, Saletu B, Davis S (1972) EEG findings in chronic schizophrenics based on digital computer period analysis and analog power spectra. *Biol. Psychiatry, 5,* 1.

28. Giannitrapani D, Kayton L (1974) Schizophrenia and EEG spectral analysis *Electroencephalogr. Clin. Neurophysiol., 36,* 377.

29. Davis PA (1940) Evaluation of the electroencephalograms of psychotic patients. *Am. J. Psychiatry, 96,* 851.

30. Igert C, Lairy GC (1962) Prognostic value of the EEG in the course of the development of schizophrenics. *Electroencephalogr. Clin. Neurophysiol., 14,* 183.

31. Struve FA, Becka DR (1968) The relative incidence of the B-mitten EEG pattern in process and reactive schizophrenia. *Electroencephalogr. Clin. Neurophysiol., 24,* 80.

32. Wegner JT, Struve FA, Kantor JS, Kane JM (1979) Relationship between the B-mitten EEG pattern and tardive dyskinesia. *Arch. Gen. Psychiatry, 36,* 599.

33. Gibbs FA, Gibbs EL (1963) The mitten pattern: an electroencephalographic abnormality

correlating with psychosis. *J. Neuropsychiatry, 5,* 6.

34. Abrams R, Taylor MA (1979) Differential EEG patterns in affective disorder and schizophrenia. *Arch. Gen. Psychiatry, 36,* 1355.

35. Fenton GW, Fenwick PBC, Dollimore J, Dunn TL, Hirsch SR (1980) EEG spectral analysis in schizophrenia. *Br. J. Psychiatry, 136,* 445.

36. Selin CL, Gottschalk LA (1983) Schizophrenia, conduct disorder and depressive disorder: neuropsychological, speech sample and EEG results. *Percept. Mot. Skills, 57,* 427.

37. Stevens JR, Livermore A (1982) Telemetered EEG in schizophrenia: spectral analysis during abnormal behavior episodes. *J. Neurol. Neurosurg. Psychiatry, 45,* 385.

38. Kennard MA, Levy S (1952) The meaning of the abnormal electroencephalogram in schizophrenia. *J. Nerv. Ment. Dis., 116,* 413.

39. Bonkalo A, Lovett Doust J, Stokes AM (1955) Neurologic concomitants of the phasic disturbances seen in periodic catatonia. *Am. J. Psychiatry, 122,* 114.

40. Small JG, Milstein V, Sharpley PH, Klapper M, Small IF (1984) Electroencephalographic findings in relation to diagnostic constructs in psychiatry. *Biol. Psychiatry, 19,* 471.

41. Flor-Henry P (1969) Psychosis and temporal lobe epilepsy: a controlled investigation. *Epilepsia, 10,* 363.

42. Nasrallah HA (1982) Laterality and hemispheric dysfunction in schizophrenia. In: Henn FA, Nasrallah HA (Eds), *Schizophrenia as a Brain Disease,* Oxford University Press, New York.

43. Serafetinides EA (1972) Laterality and voltage in the EEG of psychiatric patients. *Dis. Nerv. Syst., 32,* 622.

44. Abrams R, Taylor MA (1980) Psychopathology and the electroencephalogram. *Biol. Psychiatry, 15,* 871.

45. Etevenon P (1984) Intra and inter-hemispheric changes in alpha intensities in EEG's of schizophrenic patients versus matched controls. *Biol. Psychiatry, 19,* 247.

46. Serafetinides EA (1984) EEG lateral asymmetries in psychiatric disorders. *Biol. Psychiatry, 19,* 237.

47. Roemer RA, Shagass C, Straumanis JJ, Amadeo M (1978) Pattern evoked potential measurements suggesting lateralized hemispheric dysfunction in chronic schizophrenics. *Biol. Psychiatry, 13,* 185.

48. Connolly JF, Gruzelier JH, Manchanda R, Hirsch SR (1983) Visual evoked potentials in schizophrenia. *Br. J. Psychiatry, 142,* 152.

49. Jutai JW, Gruzelier JH, Connolly JF, Manchanda R, Hirsch SR (1984) Schizophrenia and spectral analysis of the visual evoked potential. *Br. J. Psychiatry, 145,* 496.

50. Roemer RA, Shagass C, Straumanis JJ, Amadeo M (1979) Somatosensory and auditory evoked potential studies of functional differences between the cerebral hemispheres in psychosis. *Biol. Psychiatry, 14,* 357.

51. Hiramatsu K, Kameyama T, Saitoh O, Niwa S (1984) Correlations of event-related potentials with schizophrenic deficits in information processing and hemispheric dysfunction. *Biol. Psychiatry, 19,* 281.

52. Connolly JF (1982) The corpus callosum and brain function in schizophrenia. *Br. J. Psychiatry, 140,* 429.

53. Shaw JC (1982) The corpus callosum and brain function in schizophrenia *Br. J. Psychiatry, 140,* 429.

54. Mintz M, Tomer R, Myslobodsky MS (1982) Neuroleptic-induced lateral asymmetry of

visual evoked potentials in schizophrenia. *Biol. Psychiatry, 17*, 815.

55. Itil TM, Shapiro D (1968) Computer classification of all-night sleep EEG (sleep prints). In: Gestaut J, Berti Ceroni G, Collagna G (Eds), *Abnormalities of Sleep in Man*, pp. 45–53. Aulo, Bologna.
56. Wyatt R, Termini BA, Davis J (1971) Part II. Sleep studies. *Schizophr. Bull., 4*, 56.
57. Kupfer DJ, Foster FG (1975) The sleep of psychotic patients: does it all look alike? In: Freedman DX (Ed), *Research Publication of the Association of Research in Nervous and Mental Disease, Vol 54*, pp. 143–164. Raven Press, New York.
58. Hartmann E (1967) *The Biology of Dreaming.* Charles C Thomas, Springfield, IL.
59. Shagass C (1976) An electrophysiological view of schizophrenia. *Biol. Psychiatry, 11*, 3.
60. Vaughan HG (1978) Toward a neurophysiology of schizophrenia. *J. Psychiatric Res., 14*, 129.
61. Knott VJ (1983) Psychophysiological aspects of schizophrenia: a selective review. *Psychiatr. J. Univ. Ottowa, 8*, 51.
62. Spohn HE, Patterson T (1980) Recent studies of psychopathology in schizophrenia. *Schizophr. Bull.* Special Report.
63. Shagass C (1977) Early evoked potentials. *Schizophr. Bull., 3*, 80.
64. Buchsbaum MS (1977) The middle evoked response components and schizophrenia. *Schizophr. Bull., 3*, 93.
65. Roth WT (1977) Late event-related potentials and psychopathology. *Schizophr. Bull., 3*, 105.
66. Straumanis JJ, Shagass C, Roemer RA (1982) Influence of antipsychotic and antidepressant drugs on evoked potential correlates of psychosis. *Biol. Psychiatry, 17*, 1101.
67. Shagass C, Roemer RA, Straumanis JJ, Amadeo M (1979) Temporal variability of somatosensory, visual, and auditory evoked potentials in schizophrenia. *Arch. Gen. Psychiatry, 36*, 1341.
68. Adler IE, Pachtman E, Franks RD, Pecevich M, Waldo MC, Freedman R (1982) Neurophysiological evidence for a defect in neuronal mechanisms involved in sensory gating in schizophrenia. *Biol. Psychiatry, 17*, 639.
69. Freedman R, Adler LE, Waldo MC, Pachtman E, Franks RD (1983) Neurophysiological evidence for a defect in inhibitory pathways in schizophrenia: comparisons of medicated and drug-free patients. *Biol. Psychiatry, 18*, 537.
70. Baribeau-Braun J, Picton TW, Gosselin J-Y (1983) Schizophrenia: a neurophysiological evaluation of abnormal information processing. *Science, 219*, 874.
71. Pfefferbaum A, Wenegrat BG, Ford JM, Roth WT, Kopell BS (1984) Clinical application of the P3 component of event-related potentials. II. Dementia, depression and schizophrenia. *Electroencephalogr. Clin. Neurophysiol., 59*, 104.
72. Rizzo PA, Albani GF, Spadaro M, Morocutti C (1983) Brain slow potentials (CNV), prolactin, and schizophrenia. *Biol. Psychiatry, 18*, 175.
73. McCallum WC, Curry SH (1981) Late slow wave components of auditory evoked potentials: their cognitive significance and interaction. *Electroencephalogr. Clin. Neurophysiol., 51*, 123.
74. Van den Bosch RJ (1984) Contingent negative variation: components and scalp distribution in psychiatric patients. *Biol. Psychiatry, 19*, 963.
75. James AL, Barry RJ (1980) A review of psychophysiology in early onset psychosis. *Schizophr. Bull., 6*, 506.
76. Itil TM, Hsu W, Aletu B, Rudman S, Vlett G, Mednick S, Schulsinger F (1974) Computer EEG and evoked potential investigations in children at high risk for schizophrenia.

Am. J. Psychiatry, 131, 892.

77. Friedman D, Vaughan HG, Jr, Erlenmeyer-Kimling L (1982) Cognitive brain potentials in children at risk for schizophrenia: preliminary findings. *Schizophr. Bull., 8,* 514.

78. Saitoh O, Niwa S-T, Hiramatsu K-I, Kameyana T, Rymar K, Itoh K (1984) Abnormalities in late positive components of event-related potentials may reflect a genetic predisposition to schizophrenia. *Biol. Psychiatry, 19,* 293.

79. Seigel C, Waldo M, Mizner G, Adler LE, Freedman R (1984) Deficits in sensory gating in schizophrenic patients and their relatives. *Arch. Gen. Psychiatry, 41,* 607.

80. Kendler KS, Hays P (1982) Familial and sporadic schizophrenia: a symptomatic, prognostic, and EEG comparison. *Am. J. Psychiatry, 139,* 1557.

81. Parnas J, Korsgaard S (1982) Epilepsy and psychosis. *Acta Psychiatr. Scand., 66,* 89.

82. Bear DM, Fedio P (1977) Quantitative analysis of interictal behavior in temporal lobe epilepsy. *Arch. Neurol., 34,* 454.

83. Engel J (1984) The use of positron emission tomographic scanning in epilepsy. *Ann. Neurol., 15 (Suppl),* S180.

84. Kameyama T, Anzai N, Saito O, Niwa S-I (1980) Schizophrenia-like psychosis with paroxysmal abnormal EEG. *Folia Psychiatr. Neurol. Jpn., 34,* 333.

85. Wycis HT, Lee AJ, Spiegel EA (1949) Simultaneous records of thalamic and cortical (scalp) potentials in schizophrenics and epileptics. *Confin. Neurol., 7,* 264.

86. Sem-Jacobsen CW, Petersen MC, Dodge HW, Jr, Lynge HN, Lazarte JA, Holman CB (1956) Intracerebral electrographic study of 93 psychotic patients. *Acta Psychiatr. Scand., 106 (Suppl),* 222.

87. Sem-Jacobsen CW, Petersen MC, Lazarte JA, Dodge HW, Jr, Holman CB (1955) Electroencephalographic rhythms from the depth of the frontal lobes in 60 psychotic patients. *Electroencephalogr. Clin. Neurophysiol., 7,* 193.

88. Heath RG (1958) Correlation of electrical recordings from cortical and subcortical regions of the brain with abnormal behavior in human subjects. *Confin. Neurol., 18,* 305.

89. Silverman J (1967) Variations in cognitive controls and psychophysiological defense in the schizophrenias. *Psychosom. Med., 19,* 225.

90. Lawson JS, McGhie A, Chapman J (1967) Distractibility in schizophrenia and organic cerebral disease. *Br. J. Psychiatry, 113,* 527.

91. Zubin J (1975) Problem of attention in schizophrenia. In: Kietzman ML, Sutton S, Zubin J (Eds), *Experimental Approaches to Psychopathology,* Academic Press, New York.

92. Iacono WG, Gabbay FH, Lykken DT (1982) Measuring the average evoked response to light flashes: the contribution of eye-blink artifact to augmenting-reducing. *Biol. Psychiatry, 17,* 897.

93. Lang PJ, Buss A (1965) Psychological deficit in schizophrenia: II. Interference and activation. *J. Abnorm. Psychol., 70,* 77.

94. Yates A (1966) Psychological deficit. *Annu. Rev. Psychol., 17,* 111.

95. Callaway E, Naghdi S (1982) An information processing model for schizophrenia. *Arch. Gen. Psychiatry, 39,* 339.

96. Alexander GE, Fuster JM (1973) Effects of cooling prefrontal cortex on cell firing in the nucleus medialis dorsalis. *Brain Res., 61,* 93.

97. Meibach RC, Siegel A (1977) Efferent connections of the septal area in the rat: an analysis utilizing retrograde and anterograde transport methods. *Brain Res., 119,* 1.

98. Yakolev PI (1948) Motility, behavior and the brain. *J. Nerv. Ment. Dis., 107,* 313.

99. Cesaro P, Nguyen-Legros J, Pollin B, and LaPlante S (1985) Single intralaminar thalamic neurons project to cerebral cortex striatum and nucleus reticularis thalami. A retrograde anatomical tracing study in the rat. *Brain Res., 325,* 29.
100. Skinner JE, Lindsley DB (1973) The nonspecific mediothalamic-frontocortical system: its influence on electrocortical activity and behavior. In: Pribram KG, Luria AR (Eds), *Psychophysiology of the Frontal Lobes,* pp. 185 – 252. Academic Press, New York.
101. Martin JJ (1968) Thalamic syndromes. In: Vinken PJ, Bruyn GW (Eds), *Handbook of Clinical Neurology, vol 2,* pp. 469 – 496. North-Holland Publishing Company, Amsterdam.
102. Wada J (1951) Dorsomedial thalamotomy (I): the principles and methods particularly consulted with EEG records. *Folia Psychiatr. Neurol. Jpn., 4,* 309.
103. Collins RC, Olney JW (1982) Focal cortical seizures cause distant thalamic lesions. *Science, 218,* 177.
104. Glaser GH (1980) Treatment of intractable temporal lobe-limbic epilepsy (complex partial seizures) by temporal lobectomy. *Ann. Neurol., 8,* 455.
105. Olivier A, Gloor P, Andermann F, Ives I (1982) Occipitotemporal epilepsy studied with stereotaxically implanted depth electrodes and successfully treated by temporal resection. *Ann. Neurol., 11,* 428.

CHAPTER 6

Methodological issues in the neuropsychological approach to schizophrenia

TERRY E. GOLDBERG AND DANIEL R. WEINBERGER

A long-standing goal of neuropsychology has been to associate specific neurological conditions with their cognitive and emotional consequences. The experimental base of neuropsychology includes lesion studies in which well-defined areas of damage give rise to replicable behavioral states (1 – 6). Patients with structural lesions due to neoplasm, stroke, penetrating head wound, or neurosurgery (e.g. callosal section and hemispherectomy) comprise typical samples in these reports. In normal subjects techniques for presenting information to a hemifield, such as dichotic listening, tachistoscopic flashes, and dichaptic stimulation have been used to characterize hemispheric asymmetries in processing various material-specific stimuli (7 – 8). From such studies correlations between anatomical structure and neuropsychological function are made. The validity of the correlations is based on the assumption that behavioral changes relate directly to the lesion and are not due to non-specific factors involving motivation, arousal and attention, and response bias. Under circumstances close to ideal, neuropsychology may set forth rules governing transformations from one level of analysis to another: brain (anatomical and physiological) to mind (cognitive and emotional) to behavior (observable).

The endeavor has been considerably less successful when applied to disease states in which the pathophysiology is not known, particularly where there is no focal, structural lesion. In disorders where behavior may reflect subtle changes in arousal, slight perturbations in regional cerebral metabolism, altered activity in diffuse neurotransmitter systems, and/or congenital cytoarchitectonic abnormalities, the signal-to-noise ratio may be so low (9) that a consistent neuropsychological profile is difficult to identify or quantify. Alternatively, it may not exist.

The present chapter will attempt to chart progress in the neuropsychological study of schizophrenia. It will emphasize promising techniques and replicated results. In particular, the chapter will review results of standardized neuropsychological tests and test batteries, nearly all of which suggest that schizophrenia is a disorder of complex problem solving. Uses of non-standardized measures of cognitive processing and interhemispheric functioning will be reviewed and their problems considered. Issues concerning methodology will then be addressed and overall conclusions drawn.

Handbook of Schizophrenia, Vol. 1: The Neurology of Schizophrenia.
H.A. Nasrallah and D.R. Weinberger, editors.
© Elsevier Science Publishers B.V., 1986.

Standardized tests

Two research paradigms have been used when standardized neuropsychological tests are administered to schizophrenic patients. In one, a battery of tests is administered and the location of regional cerebral dysfunction is inferred, based on test profile analysis. In the second approach, which is atheoretical, a schizophrenic group is compared with 'organic' and/or normal groups in an effort to define neuropsychological discriminators (via 'hit rate').

Neuropsychological profiles

Studies using the Halstead-Reitan Battery (HRB) have usually found a wide range of impairments in schizophrenic patients. These include deficits in abstraction, language processing, mental flexibility, tactile problem solving, and psychomotor speed. Goldstein and Halperin (10) administered the HRB and Wechsler Adult Intelligence Scale (WAIS) to a sample of 140 schizophrenic patients. Length of institutionalization, rather than evidence of a neurological abnormality (by history, examination, or diagnostic procedure) or degree of paranoia, had the greatest impact on test performance. HRB tests were impaired globally, suggesting diffuse cortical dysfunction. In a large cross-national study, Townes et al. (11) found that type and extent of neuropsychological impairment were largely independent of DSM-III psychiatric diagnosis (organic brain syndrome, affective disorder personality disorder, schizophrenia). Nearly 500 psychiatric patients were administered the HRB. Q-type factor analysis classified 350 into distinct groups in which (a) performance was consistently normal (23% of the sample), (b) performance was consistently abnormal (26% of the sample), (c) adequate verbal, but poor problem-solving and motor abilities were present (7%), (d) adequate visual spatial functioning, but poor problem-solving abilities were present (7%), and (e) intact verbal and visual spatial skills, but impaired problem-solving abilities were displayed. The latter group, comprising 29% of the sample, was modal. Impaired problem-solving was clearly characteristic of many patients in the study.

Taylor and Abrams (12) administered a neuropsychological battery consisting of the WAIS, Hooper Visual Organization Test, Benton Visual Retention Test, Raven Matrices, and Double Simultaneous Stimulation and Purdue Pegboard to 17 patients. The sample performed much like a group of 8 patients with 'coarse' brain disease. However, failure to clarify units of measurement and incomplete description of the organic group made results of the study difficult to interpret. The authors, however, concluded that schizophrenic patients displayed bilateral hemispheric dysfunction. Taylor et al. (13) compared 62 patients with schizophrenia to 42 normal controls using neuropsychological tests of neurodevelopmental motor performance, aphasia screening, mental status, items from the HRB and Luria-Nebraska Battery (LNNB), and visual half-field identification of letters and shapes. Over 75% of the patients exhibited cognitive impairment that was thought to reflect bilateral dysfunction, though relatively more severe deficits were imputed to the dominant frontotemporal region. How ratings were derived was unstated. Age, sex, handedness, and drug status did not affect outcome.

Kolb and Whishaw (14) assessed 30 schizophrenic patients diagnosed by DSM-III criteria and 30 age, hand, and education matched controls. All patients were receiving neuroleptics. A battery of tests that reveal impairment in patients with localized cerebral damage (including category shifting, fluency, memory for stories and designs, dichotic listening, orientation span, and closure) was administered, as well as the WAIS. The pattern of results suggested bilateral frontal and temporal lobe dysfunction.

Other studies have attempted to delineate language dysfunction in schizophrenia and thereby implicate dominant perisylvian cortex. Taylor et al. (15) found that schizophrenic patients made more errors on an aphasia screening battery than controls. They interpreted the results as indicating left temporo-parietal dysfunction. Andreasen and Grove (16) suggested that schizophrenic patients with severely disorganized speech resemble fluent aphasics, especially in word-finding difficulty. Silverberg-Shaler et al. (17) used a battery of neuropsychological tests of language, memory, abstract thinking, visual spatial ability, and rate of information processing. They found that schizophrenic patients (especially those who had been ill over 15 years) differed from controls primarily on language tests, having more anomic and paraphasic responses.

Benson and Stuss (18) administered motor tasks suggestive of 'frontal release,' tests of praxis, and neuropsychological tests of psychomotor speed and inhibition to schizophrenic and leukotomized schizophrenic patients. Actively psychotic patients had difficulty with motor sequencing, inhibiting motor acts in the face of conflicting signals, and shifting response. These difficulties were independent of whether they had been leukotomized. Klonoff et al. (19) also found that severity of psychiatric symptoms had more influence on performance in patients with schizophrenia than did leukotomy per se.

On the basis of test pattern analysis it might be concluded that frontal and temporal cortical dysfunction is common in schizophrenia. However, there are difficulties with such a conclusion. Because a group of patients with a known lesion have a consistent pattern of cognitive deficit, other individuals with the same pattern do not necessarily have a similar lesion. For example, Malmo (20) found that patients with frank frontal lobe lesions and patients with schizophrenia do poorly on the Wisconsin Card Sort (WCS), a test in which subjects have to generate conceptual categories, respond to feedback, and shift sets. Weinberger et al. (21) reported abnormalities in metabolic activation as measured by regional cerebral blood flow in the dorsolateral prefrontal cortex of patients with schizophrenia during WCS performance. While this suggests that the cognitive deficit on the WCS is the result of a frontal cortical disorder, other explanations are possible. Indeed, 'neurotic' patients (20) and neurological patients with non-frontal pathology (22) also do not perform at normal levels on the WCS. Factors such as attention, anxiety, effort, and perceptual competence, possibly mediated by both subcortical and cortical structures, may influence performance.

Association of neuropsychological testing performance and CT scan abnormalities

In an effort to discount the possibility that cognitive deficits are secondary to non-specific factors such as inattention or effort, researchers have provided correlations between these higher-level impairments and objective evidence of CNS disease in schizophrenia as imaged by CT scan. Performance on neuropsychological test batteries including the HRB, LNNB, and Withers-Hinton has been associated with lateral ventricular enlargement and/or cortical atrophy (23 – 26). Overall there appears to be a relationship between CT scan abnormality and global neuropsychological dysfunction in schizophrenia. In conjunction with features of the disorder involving gait and minor neurological signs, electrophysiological abnormalities, and smooth pursuit eye movement impairments, the findings support the link between schizophrenia and central nervous system dysfunction (27). They also support the contention that neuropsychological test performance deficits are valid manifestations of brain pathology and, inversely, that CT scan findings (e.g. large ventricles) affect cognition.

Issues in intelligence

Researchers since Kraepelin (28) have considered the possibility that schizophrenia is associated with deterioration in intellectual functions or with premorbid limitations in intellect. Lubin et al. (29) readministered the US Army General Classification Test to veterans who were subsequently hospitalized for brain injury or schizophrenia. The schizophrenic patients displayed marked deterioration, though not as great as the organic group. Schwartzman and Douglas (30) reported that in 50 schizophrenic patients a significant loss in intellectual functioning occurred between premorbid and morbid scores on the Canadian Army M-Test. Most of the difference was due to deterioration in 30 chronic patients. Smith (31) administered the Wechsler-Bellevue and Weigl Sorting task (a precursor of the WCS) to 24 chronic schizophrenic patients and then retested the group eight years later. Scores were notably stable in both high- (FSIQ = 101) and low- (FSIQ = 80) functioning subgroups. Only on the Weigl test was deterioration reported. Klonoff et al. (19) found that WAIS scores improved over eight years in a group of 66 chronic patients. They suggested that intellectual impairment in schizophrenia occurs during the onset of the disease after which there is little further loss. Those investigators who have studied retrospectively the intellectual and academic performances of children who later manifested psychosis found that premorbid intellectual limitations were associated with the later emergence of schizophrenia (32 – 33). These studies have not provided a consistent answer to the question of intellectual deterioration. It appears that there are deficits in general intelligence present at the onset of the disorder, though it may be a relatively stable characteristic in schizophrenia thereafter. Moreover, intellectual deficit is an indicator of poor prognosis, both premorbidly and after diagnosis.

Patterns in verbal and non-verbal intelligence test measures have been used to infer lateralized cerebral dysfunction. Flor-Henry and Yeudall (34) reported that schizophrenic patients have more difficulty with language tasks and, specifically, have lower verbal than performance IQs on the WAIS. However, actual differences were small. Gruzelier and Hammond (35) administered the WAIS to stabilized schizophrenic patients (n = 24). Verbal IQ was lower than Performance IQ, though scores were not reported. The studies stand in contrast to many others in which Performance IQ was more impaired than verbal IQ (10, 14, 23). Goldberg et al. (36) found that Performance IQ was significantly reduced in 39 adolescent patients with schizophreniform psychoses compared to 41 psychiatric controls. Despite sporadic inconsistencies, the majority of studies indicate that the pattern of IQ is typical of 'brain-damaged' groups, i.e. lower Performance than Verbal IQ.

Neuropsychological tests to distinguish schizophrenia from coarse brain disease

A plethora of studies has attempted to determine whether standardized tests can be used to discriminate patients with schizophrenia from those with 'organic' conditions (usually diffuse). Initially, the impetus for the studies derived from the belief that cognitive dysfunction in schizophrenia, as a 'functional' disorder, somehow differed from that in neurological diseases. Classification accuracies, however, were not satisfactory and the findings were interpreted anew: schizophrenic patients perform like organic patients because they too have brain disease. In studies in which mixed psychotic groups were compared with 'organic' groups, single tests, including Memory-for-Designs, Bender-Background Interference, Stroop, Minnesota Perceptuo-Diagnostic, and Purdue Pegboard, have been used (37 – 42). Median accuracy ('hit') rate was 70% (43). Though results were often statistically significant, their clinical significance is dubious, as a 70% hit rate is not diagnostically useful. When the course of schizophrenia is considered, acute patients are more accurately differentiated than are chronic patients (43). Again, the majority of studies involve single tests or combinations of two or three: Bender-Background Interference, Goldstein-Scheerer Sorting, Critical Flicker Fusion, Pursuit Rotor, Raven Matrices, and Trail Making (44 – 49).

Studies using batteries of tests have sometimes claimed greater success, but overall, the results have been inconsistent. DeWolfe et al. (50) thought that pattern analysis of WAIS and HRB subtests revealed differences in categorization, comprehension, and coding between 25 young chronic patients and 25 patients with diffuse neurological conditions. Level of performance was similar between the groups. An attempt to cross-validate the diagnostic profiles was unsuccessful, however (51). Watson et al. (52) contrasted the performance of 50 schizophrenic and 50 neurological patients at different levels of chronicity. Neither WAIS IQs nor selected HRB tests were of value in discriminating the groups. Wysocki and Sweet (53) evaluated the performance of 25 normal, 25 brain-damaged, and 25 schizophrenic patients. Detailed information regarding chronicity, medication status, and symptom severity was not provided. Using a screening battery comprised of a wide range of auditory, tactile, visual, spatial, verbal, attention, and memory tasks, a decision rule based on overall functioning led to high accuracy in classification. Golden (54) compared the performance of 30 psychotic patients with groups of left-, right-, and diffusely brain-damaged subjects on the WAIS and complete HRB. Only three tests (Tactual Performance, Trail Making-B, and Block Design) as well as the Impairment Index distinguished the brain injured from the psychiatric sample at beyond the 70% level. The battery as a whole, however, had a classification accuracy of about 95%. The psychotic group tended to do best and the diffuse group worst. Chelune et al. (55), in a study using neurological patients with well documented lesions, found that the level of performance on the HRB and WAIS, rather than pattern of performance, best discriminated a schizophrenic group from acutely and chronically diffusely brain-damaged groups. The schizophrenic patients performed at a higher level.

Overall, those studies using batteries to discriminate organic from schizophrenic patients have produced decision rules that are unwieldy, sometimes inefficient, and attenuate rapidly upon cross-validation. Systematic patterns across studies have been unreplicable.

Unstandardized measures to assess hemispheric asymmetries and inter-hemispheric communication

Limitations in the results of standardized tests and test batteries, notably an inability to resolve problem solving deficits to more specific mental mechanisms, and the development of new techniques for the study of hemispheric dominance, led to the application of new approaches in research in patients with schizophrenia. Dichotic listening, transfer of tactile information, and visual field stimulation have been used in a number of studies. However, the parameters of even similar tasks have varied widely and their reliability is often unknown. Interpreting the sometimes conflicting data is fraught with difficulty.

In dichotic listening, auditory stimuli are presented simultaneously to the left and right ears. An individual whose left hemisphere is dominant for speech is usually more accurate in remembering material presented to the right ear. The technique thus offers a means of assessing cerebral speech lateralization. Lishman et al. (56) reported increased recall asymmetry both in schizophrenic and bipolar patients. Right-ear advantage was notably large in male patients with schizophrenia. An altered pattern of hemispheric function was proposed as an explanation, as well as differences in such general cognitive factors as attention and memory capacity. Nachson (57) suggested that marked right-ear superiority scores in schizophrenia (especially in the paranoid type) were indicative of left hemispheric overactivation. Other investigators (58 – 59), however, have reported that dichotic listening differences between schizophrenic patients and controls were insignificant. In another report asymmetries in dichotic listening were found to increase with recovery from acute psychoses (60). A loss of interhemispheric inhibition during psychotic episodes was offered as an interpretation. Given the fragility of ear asymmetry in normal subjects (61), the possible influence of non-specific state variables, and the impact of symptoms, the meaning of these results is obscure.

Green (62) reported that performance of schizophrenic patients in tasks involving bimanual tactile matching and interhemispheric transfer of tactile information was impaired. However, task difficulty may have accounted for the results because differences in the complexity of the tests were not controlled. Tactile shape and size recognition and naming have also been reported to be deficient in schizophrenia (63 – 64). Interhemispheric transfer of information was presumed faulty, though alternative explanations, including task difficulty (noted above), attentional deficits, and unilateral hemispheric dysfunction were also plausible. Torrey (65) reported poor performance of schizophrenic patients on graphesthesia and double simultaneous stimulation. Right-sided performance was especially poor. Beaumont and Dimond (66) reported that schizophrenic patients displayed poor matching of visual stimuli presented briefly by tachistoscope and suggested that impaired interhemispheric communication caused the deficit. However, results indicated that intrahemispheric matching was also impaired. Gur (67) assessed 24 patients and 24 control subjects on two tachistoscopic tasks believed to measure verbal and visual spatial information processing. The schizophrenic group exhibited superiority for both tasks when presented to the left visual field, unlike the control group. In a second study, 48 schizophrenic patients displayed significantly more rightward eye movement when presented with verbal, spatial, or emotional questions. Results were interpreted as indicating left hemispheric dysfunction and overactivation. Other interpretations of the data, such as bilateral involvement, are possible, given the fact that both left and right hemifield performance was poor. Furthermore, it is difficult to conclude from such studies whether one hemisphere is overactive; rather, the other hemisphere may be underactive. The basic validity of these paradigms is also problematic.

Fundamental neuropsychological processes

The foundations of higher-level cognitive processing, including attention, visual and auditory perception, and memory have been investigated. Few of the replicable findings are specific to schizophrenia.

Attention

Attentional processes have received intensive study in schizophrenia research. The concept of attention is complex. It involves reflection, persistence, concentration, vigilance, scanning, selection, and set maintenance (68). Two paradigms have been widely used to study attention, reaction time and continuous performance testing (CPT) (69).

Shakow (70) investigated schizophrenic patients' speed of response to a light or tone. This imperative stimulus was preceded by a warning signal. In addition to having slower simple reaction times, the patients did not benefit from longer, regularly spaced preparatory intervals as compared with performance on irregularly spaced preparatory intervals. Deficits in the ability to establish a set (70) or disattend to irrelevant prior preparatory intervals (71) were thought to explain the findings. The latter point led Zubin (72) to conclude that the effects of stimulation persist longer in schizophrenia, facilitating similar stimuli and inhibiting dissimilar stimuli.

The CPT has been used to study vigilance and sustained attention. Simple stimuli (letters or numbers) are presented randomly and the subject responds to a designated ('target') stimulus. CPT performance deficits are present in at least 40 to 50% of patients (73). Remitted drug-free subjects also display impairment on more difficult versions of the task (74). Whether attention represents a primary deficit in schizophrenia or is an epiphenomenon or state variable is unresolved. Attentional deficits are inordinately non-specific and are manifestations of numerous other neurological and psychiatric disorders.

Memory

Koh (75) found that schizophrenic patients were deficient in recall but not in recognition of words. When cued to use recall strategies (i.e. categories to cluster words) performance was normalized. Grove and Andreasen (76) attributed short digit spans in schizophrenic patients to lack of use of 'control' strategies in encoding. Raulin and Chapman (77) found that schizophrenic patients showed a greater recall deficit on random rather than semantically meaningful word lists. Wechsler Memory Scale performance has also been reported to be impaired (relative to IQ) (14). Cutting (101) found that patients with schizophrenia, especially those with chronic histories, had verbal and/or visual pattern memory impairments comparable to patients with confusional states, dementia, or Korsakoff's syndrome. In general, recognition superiority over recall is typical of schizophrenia. It is unclear whether this represents dysfunction of the cerebral memory system or is due to problems in concentration or generating control strategies.

Perception

Auditory perception and discrimination have been mentioned as relevant in the genesis of schizophrenic symptoms. For example, Moon et al. (78) linked loose associations with auditory misperception. Failure to filter irrelevant stimuli presented to one ear has been thought to impede performance in responding to target words in the other ear (79). Tone discrimination has also been examined, though results have been conflicting (80–81).

The ability of patients to process briefly presented visual material has been examined from several different standpoints. Braff and Saccuzzo (82) used a backward masking visual processing paradigm in an effort to measure speed of transfer from sensory to cortical association areas. In their procedure, a tachistoscopically presented test stimulus is prevented from reaching awareness by the near-simultaneous presentation of a second stimulus. Visual processing could be disrupted in patients with schizophrenia even when the second masking stimulus arrived after long delays. Iconic memory (the sensory registration of visual events) has been investigated by Knight et al. (83). As it is thought to be an automatic process, a deficit may be considered to reflect abnormalities in the posterior visual cortex rather than attentional or motivational influences. However, schizophrenic patients were not impaired on a task in which they were required to name a pictured object generated by brief successive presentations.

Methodological considerations

Methodological problems are commonplace in the literature reviewed. Difficulties in the consensual diagnosis of schizophrenia are well known. With the introduction of DSM-III, reliable criteria have been formulated, though validity remains a concern. Unfortunately, recent studies have still used vague or idiosyncratic diagnostic criteria. The bases for a neurological diagnosis in control groups are often unmentioned. This is especially important, as the term 'organic' (in those studies comparing schizophrenic patients with brain-damaged patients) is meaningless, given that such conditions do not have the same cause, location, extent, dynamics, or chronicity (4). Age, sex, education and premorbid IQ all may have impact on neuropsychological performance at a particular point in time (84 – 85). Furthermore, age at onset, chronicity, history of drug/alcohol abuse, and history of head trauma are variables that have not been adequately controlled in patients with schizophrenia. Use of normal as well as psychiatric samples as controls is also advisable, so that differences are attributable to the index condition rather than artifacts of a comparison.

Medication status may also be important. A patient stabilized on neuroleptics might be cooperative, but deficits may be selectively ameliorated; a patient not receiving medication may be agitated or non-responsive. In general, neuroleptics improve performance on tasks involving the conscious deployment of attention (86), have little effect on higher cognitive processes (87), and have adverse effects on motor speed (88). They may also differentially effect the cerebral hemispheres or interact with handedness to affect performance (89). The symptomatic status of patients is often unspecified. Only studies of attention in patients in 'residual' states have attempted to manage the problem (90). The degree of severity of the disorder and its effect on social functioning at the time of assessment should be reported (by, for example, Brief Psychiatric Rating Scale or Global Assessment Scale scores).

Chapman and Chapman (91) have demonstrated that differences between schizophrenic and control groups may be due to the psychometric characteristics of tasks and level of performance of the groups. Thus, to minimize attentional and motivational differences, tasks, rather than subjects, should be matched. In addition to similar difficulty levels, tasks should be similar in content, differing only in the parameter of interest. For example, it has been suggested that the crucial factor in WCS performance is the ability to respond to set shifts. Incrementally increasing patients' knowledge, by cueing to category or to the concept of set shifts, might clarify the nature of the schizophrenic deficit. Few studies, however, actually have used the recommended procedures.

Hughlings Jackson (92) proposed that diseases of the nervous system result in negative signs involving dissolution of function and/or positive signs of release from inhibition. Neuropsychology has been successful in identifying and quantifying both global and discrete loss of function, especially in the language and visual spatial domains. Identifying the existence of neuropsychological release phenomena has proven more difficult. Behavioral states involving the apparent exaggeration of a function (hyperkinesis, hypersexuality, compulsivity, aggression, logorrhea) or lack of modulation (impulsivity, intrusion, disinhibition) are difficult to quantify, as are the protean subcortical processes involved in deployment of attention (arousal, inhibition, drive), conditioning, set formation, and skill learning. Furthermore, disordered subcortical functioning is manifested in interactions with cortical functioning. For example, so-called subcortical dementias, in which there are recall deficits, impaired problem solving, and apathy or irritability, are phenomenologically similar to syndromes involving frontal lobe damage (93). The lack of emphasis on comprehensive assessment of memory function (which offers the opportunity to make inferences about various subcortical and deep temporal regions) is also unfortunate. Furthermore, the distinction between item-specific declarative memory and non-representational 'skill-based' procedural systems (94) has not been applied to schizophrenic populations. Overall, functions thought to be localized in the cortex have received more study than subcortical functions.

Another little explored issue is that the deficits examined in schizophrenia may not always remain stable. It is worth noting that about 25% of schizophrenic patients recover (95). Neuropsychological precursors or patterns of change are unknown, as is the utility of explanatory constructs of functional substitution or restitution.

The evidence that schizophrenia is accompanied by neurological, neurophysiological, and neuroanatomical abnormalities is strong. To determine if schizophrenic patients are more or less like other patients with neurologically based cognitive deficits provides little understanding of specific processing dysfunctions and their 'in vivo' analogs. It is notable that though the cognitive profile of schizophrenic patients may be similar to many neurological patients, the loss of goal-directed behavior or drive, thought disorder, and perceptual aberrations tend to distinguish them clinically. Thus, more reliable diagnoses of schizophrenia are still made by interview, behavioral observation, and history.

Given the recent interest in frontal lobe disease and schizophrenia (21) it may be valuable to directly compare schizophrenic patients with 'frontal lobe' patients on a variety of cognitive and social-cognitive tasks. A second patient group, high-functioning autistic adults (Asperger's syndrome), has not been compared to schizophrenic samples either in regard to social problem solving or on various neuropsychological parameters.

Seidman (96) reviewed the neuropsychological concomitants of schizophrenia. He defined 3 subgroups with different neuropsychological profiles. One was thought to display poor premorbid adjustment, affective blunting and other negative symptoms, intellectual deficits, and cerebral atrophy. A 'reactive' group was thought to have adequate premorbid adjustment, rapid onset of illness, positive psychotic symptoms, and neuropsychological hemispheric asymmetries during the acute phase of the disorder. The third group was believed to have minimal cerebral damage, attend well, and maintain primarily paranoid delusions. While information-processing paradigms have frequently found distinctions in performance between paranoid and non-paranoid schizophrenic patients (97), the neuropsychological literature provides stronger support for an acute/chronic distinction than for a paranoid/nonparanoid distinction.

From a statistical standpoint, cluster analytic techniques have been neglected. It might be possible to cluster patients at the level of biological variables (e.g. CT scan atrophy, spinal fluid homovanillic acid concentration), at the level of symptom, and at the level of neuropsychological profile. Consistency of membership across levels could then be compared, providing construct validity to subgrouping. In studies employing neuropsychological batteries, data reduction techniques such as factor analysis and the use of multivariate statistics could reduce the probability of Type I statistical error. Points of contact between neuropsychological functioning, information processing and phenomenological symptom study have been lacking. In one of the few such studies, Silverstein and Arzt (98) found that reaction time, but not measures of thought disorder, was deficient in a schizophrenic sample with impaired neuropsychological functioning.

It cannot be overemphasized that the interpretation of neuropsychological test performance is not straightforward. Response biases (e.g. tendency to guess), variance in attention, or generalized deficits may influence the results. It is unclear what reduction of function means in the absence of correlated structural or physiological changes and whether greater dysfunction contributes to greater behavioral variance (99). It should also be recognized that the interpretation of an asymmetry is not equivalent to the interpretation of a unilateral abnormality (99). Furthermore, lateralized functional asymmetries may reflect sensitivity and quantity of tasks (i.e. more and better language tasks) rather than lateralized dysfunction. In this regard, most studies have not revealed morphological differences between the left and right cerebral hemispheres of patients with cerebral atrophy (100).

Finally, a score on a neuropsychological test is the summary index of multiple microprocesses. For the most part, this index reflects a final common pathway, i.e. local cortical function. The impact of subcortical processes is not differentiated.

Conclusions

Do neuropsychological paradigms provide basic information about the nature of schizophrenia? We believe that these paradigms have assisted in the task. Neuropsychological test deficits represent useful phenomenological characteristics that can aid in the difficult task of reducing clinical heterogeneity. When used concurrently with neurobiological investigative techniques such as rCBF, positron emission tomography (PET), and evoked potentials, these tests stress the central nervous system so that cognitive activation anomalies can be recognized. The association of CT scan and neuropsychological abnormalities reduces the chance that results can be ascribed solely to attention and motivation.

In particular, problem solving deficits thought to be associated with frontal lobe dysfunction have been consistently identified in schizophrenic patients. Tests of set shifting, category formation, mental flexibility, and vulnerability to interference generally elicit poor performance. 'Real life' analogs of such deficits might involve lack of goal-directed behavior, an inability to select and substantiate frames of social knowledge, and fragmentation of thought. Impairment in recall memory has also been a relatively consistent finding: temporal lobe involvement is suggested, though deficits in frontal control functions might also have an impact. Decrements in Wechsler Performance IQ reflect limitations in the capacity to respond to stimuli presented in novel formats. Poverty in cortical reserve or power may be at their cause. The results from paradigms assessing hemispheric asymmetry have been conflicting; they are further compromised by low or unknown reliabilities.

REFERENCES

1. Geschwind N (1965) Disconnection syndromes in animals and man. *Brain, 88,* 237.
2. Luria AR (1966) *Higher Cortical Functions in Man.* Basic Books, New York.
3. Newcombe F (1969) *Missile Wounds of the Brain: A study of Psychological Deficits.* Oxford University Press, New York.
4. Sperry RW (1974) Lateral specialization in the surgically separated hemispheres. In: Schmitt FO, Worden FG (Eds), *Neuroscience Third Study Program,* pp. 5 – 19. MIT Press, Cambridge, MA.
5. Smith A (1975) Neuropsychological testing in neurological disorders. In: Freidlander WJ (Ed), *Advances in Neurology,* pp. 49 – 112. Raven Press, New York.
6. Benton AL (1979) Visuoperceptive, visuospatial, and visuoconstructive disorders. In: Heilman KM, Valenstein E (Eds), *Clinical Neuropsychology,* pp. 186 – 232. Oxford University Press, New York.
7. Bradshaw JL, Nettleton NC (1981) The nature of hemispheric specialization in man. *Behav. Brain Sci., 4,* 51.
8. Segalowitz SJ, Bryden MP (1983) Individual differences in hemispheric representation of language. In: Segalowitz SJ (Ed), *Language Functions and Brain Organization,* pp. 341 – 372. Academic Press, New York.
9. Levin S (1984) Frontal lobe dysfunctions in schizophrenia. II. Impairments of psychological and brain functions. *J. Psychiatr. Res., 18,* 57.
10. Goldstein G, Halperin MM (1977) Neuropsychological difference among subtypes of schizophrenia. *J. Abnorm. Psychol., 80,* 34.
11. Townes BD, Martin DC, Nelson D, Prosser R, Pepping M, Maxwell J, Peel T, Preston M (1985) Neurobehavioral approach to classification of psychiatric patients using a competency model. *J. Consult. Clin. Psychol., 53,* 33.
12. Taylor MA, Redfield J, Abrams R (1981) Neuropsychological dysfunction in schizophrenia and affective disease. *Biol. Psychiatry, 16,* 467.
13. Taylor MA, Abrams R (1984) Cognitive impairment in schizophrenia. *Am. J.*

Psychiatry, 141, 196.

14. Kolb B, Whishaw IQ (1983) Performance of schizophrenic patients on tests sensitive to left or right frontal, temporal, or parietal function in neurological patients. *J. Nerv. Ment. Dis., 171,* 435.
15. Taylor MA, Greenspan B, Abrams R (1979) Lateralized neuropsychological dysfunction in affective disorder and schizophrenia. *Am. J. Psychiatry, 136,* 1031.
16. Andreasen NC, Grove W (1979) The relationship between schizophrenic language, manic language and aphasia. In: Gruzelier J, Flor-Henry P (Eds), *Asymmetries of Function in Psychopathology,* pp. 373 – 390, Elsevier, Amsterdam.
17. Silverberg-Shaler S, Gordon HW, Bentin S, Aranson A (1981) Selective language deterioration in chronic schizophrenia. *J. Neurol., Neurosurg. Psychiatry, 44,* 547.
18. Benson DF, Stuss DT (1982) Motor abilities after frontal leukotomy. *Neurology, 32,* 1353.
19. Klonoff H, Fibiger CH, Hutton G (1970) Neuropsychological patterns in chronic schizophrenia. *J. Nerv. Ment. Dis., 150,* 291.
20. Malmo HP (1974) On frontal lobe functions: Psychiatric patient controls. *Cortex, 10,* 231.
21. Weinberger DR, Berman KF, Zec R (1986) Physiological dysfunction of dorsolateral prefrontal cortex in schizophrenia. I. Regional cerebral blood flow (rCBF) evidence. *Arch. Gen. Psychiatry, 43,* 114.
22. Robinson AL, Heaton RK, Lehman RAW, Stilson D (1980) The utility of the Wisconsin Card Sort in detecting and localizing frontal lobe lesions. *J. Consult. Clin. Psychol., 48,* 605.
23. Lawson WB, Waldman IN, Weinberger Dr (1986) Schizophrenic dementia: Results of neuropsychological testing and clinical correlates. *J. Clin. Psychiatry,* in press.
24. Johnstone EC, Crow TJ, Frith CD (1976) Cerebral ventricular size and cognitive impairment in chronic schizophrenia. *Lancet, 2,* 924.
25. Golden CJ, Moses JA, Zelazowski MA (1980) Cerebral ventricular size and neuropsychological impairment in young chronic schizophrenics. *Arch. Gen. Psychiatry, 37,* 619.
26. Zec RF, Weinberger DR (1985) The relationship between CT Scan findings and neuropsychological performance in schizophrenia. *Psychiatr. Clin. North Am.,* in press.
27. Berman KF, Weinberger DR (1985) Schizophrenic dementia. In: Jeste D (Ed), *Dementia.* American Psychiatric Association Press, Washington, in press.
28. Kraepelin E (1919) *Dementia praecox and paraphrenia.* Robert Krieger, Huntington.
29. Lubin A, Gieseking CF, Williams HL (1962) Direct measurement of cognitive deficit in schizophrenia. *J. Consult. Psychol., 26,* 139.
30. Schwartzman AE, Douglas VI (1962) Intellectual loss in schizophrenia Part I. *Can. J. Psychol., 16,* 1.
31. Smith A (1964) Mental deterioration in chronic schizophrenia. *J. Nerv. Ment. Dis., 139,* 479.
32. Lane EA, Albee GW (1965) Childhood intellectual differences between schizophrenics and their siblings. *Am. J. Orthopsychiatry, 35,* 747.
33. Offord DR (1974) School performance of adult schizophrenics, their siblings, and age mates. *Br. J. Psychiatry, 125,* 12.
34. Flor-Henry P, Yeudall LT (1979) Neuropsychological investigation of schizophrenia and manic-depressive psychoses. In: Gruzelier J, Flor-Henry P (Eds), *Hemisphere Asymmetries of Function in Psychopathology,* pp. 341 – 362. Elsevier, Amsterdam.
35. Gruzelier JH, Hammond IV (1976) Schizophrenia: A dominant temporal-limbic disorder? *Res. Commun. Psychol. Psychiatry, Behav., 1,* 33.

36. Goldberg TE, Karson CN, Weinberger DR: Patterns of intellect in adolescent psychosis, submitted for publication.
37. Graham FA, Kendall BS (1960) Memory-for-Designs Test: Revised general manual. *Percept. Mot. Skills, 11,* 147.
38. Uyeno E (1963) Differentiating psychotics from organics on the Minnesota Perceptuo-Diagnostic Test. *J. Consult. Psychol., 27,* 462.
39. Canter AA (1966) A background interference procedure to increase sensitivity of the Bender-Gestalt Test to organic brain disorder. *J. Consult. Psychol., 30,* 91.
40. Fernald LD, Fernald PS, Rines WB (1966) Purdue Pegboard and differential diagnosis. *J. Consult. Psychol., 30,* 279.
41. Small IF, Small JG, Milstein V, Moore JE (1972) Neuropsychological observations with psychosis and somatic treatment. *J. Nerv. Ment. Dis., 155,* 6.
42. Golden C (1976) The diagnosis of brain damage by the Stroop test. *J. Clin. Psychol., 32,* 654.
43. Heaton RK, Baade LE, Johnson KL (1978) Neuropsychological test results associated with psychiatric disorders in adults. *Psychol. Bull., 85,* 141.
44. McDonough JM (1960) Critical flicker frequency and the spiral aftereffect with process and reactive schizophrenics. *J. Consult. Psychol., 24,* 150.
45. Knehr CA (1962) Psychological assessment of differential impairment in cerebral organic conditions and in schizophrenics. *J. Psychol., 54,* 165.
46. Tutko TA, Spence JT (1962) The performance of process and reactive schizophrenics on a conceptual test. *J. Abnorm. Social Psychol., 65,* 387.
47. Orme JE, Lee D, Smith MR (1964) Psychological assessments of brain damage and intellectual impairment in psychiatric patients. *J. Soc. Clin. Psychol., 3,* 161.
48. King HE (1967) Trail making performance as related to psychotic state, age, intelligence, education and fine psychomotor ability. *Percept. Mot. Skills, 25,* 649.
49. Canter AA (1971) A comparison of the background interference procedure effect in schizophrenic, nonschizophrenic, and organic patients. *J. Clin. Psychol., 27,* 473.
50. DeWolfe AS, Barrell RP, Becker BL, Spaner FE (1971) Intellectual deficit in chronic schizophrenia and brain damage. *J. Consult. Clin. Psychol., 36,* 197.
51. Watson CG (1971) Separation of brain damaged from schizophrenic patients by Reitan-Halstead pattern analysis. *Psychol. Rep., 29,* 1343.
52. Watson CG, Thomas RW, Anderson D, Felling J (1968) Differentiation of organics from schizophrenics at two chronicity levels by use of the Reitan-Halstead Organic Test battery. *J. Consult. Clin. Psychol., 32,* 629.
53. Wysocki JJ, Sweet JJ (1985) Identification of brain-damaged, schizophrenic, and normal medical patients using a brief neuropsychological screening battery. *Int. J. Clin. Neuropsychol., 7,* 40.
54. Golden DJ (1977) Validity of the Halstead-Reitan Neuropsychological Battery in a mixed psychiatric and brain-injury population. *J. Consult. Clin. Psychol., 45,* 1043.
55. Chelune GJ, Heaton RK, Lehman RA, Robinson A (1979) Level versus pattern of neuropsychological performance among schizophrenic and diffusely brain damaged patients. *J. Consult. Clin. Psychol., 47,* 155.
56. Lishman WA, Toone BK, Colbourn CJ, McMeekan ERL, Mance RM (1978) Dichotic listening in psychotic patients. *Br. J. Psychiatry, 132,* 333.
57. Nachson I (1980) Hemispheric dysfunctioning in schizophrenia. *J. Nerv. Ment. Dis., 168,* 241.
58. Bull HC, Venables PH (1974) Speech perception in schizophrenia. *Br. J. Psychiatry, 125,* 350.

59. Yozawitz A, Bruder G, Sutton S, Sharpe L, Gurland B, Fleiss J, Costa S (1979) Dichotic perception: Evidence for right hemisphere dysfunction in affective psychosis. *Br. J. Psychiatry, 135,* 224.
60. Wexler BE, Heninger GR (1979) Alterations in cerebral laterality during acute psychotic illness. *Arch. Gen. Psychiatry, 36,* 278.
61. Blumstein S, Goodglass H, Tarttar V (1975) Reliability of ear advantage in dichotic listening. *Brain Lang., 2,* 226.
62. Green P (1978) Defective interhemispheric transfer and schizophrenia. *J. Abnorm. Psychol., 87,* 472.
63. Carr SA (1980) Interhemispheric transfer of stereognostic information in chronic schizophrenics. *Br. J. Psychiatry, 136,* 53.
64. Dimond SJ, Scammell R, Pryce IG, Huws D, Gray C (1980) Some failures of inter-manual and cross manual transfer in chronic schizophrenia. *J. Abnorm. Psychol., 89,* 505.
65. Torrey EF (1980) Neurological abnormalities in schizophrenic patients. *Biol. Psychiatry, 15,* 381.
66. Beaumont JG, Dimond SJ (1973) Brain disconnection and schizophrenia. *Br. J. Psychiatry, 123,* 661.
67. Gur RE (1978) Left hemisphere dysfunction and left hemisphere overactivation in schizophrenia. *J. Abnorm. Psychol., 87,* 226.
68. Ross DM, Ross SA (1976) *Hyperactivity.* John Wiley, New York.
69. Rosvold HE, Mirsky AF, Sarason I, Bransome ED, Beck LH (1956) A continuous per-formance test of brain damage. *J. Consult. Psychol., 20,* 343.
70. Shakow D (1962) Segmental set: A theory of the formal psychological deficit in schizophrenia. *Arch. Gen. Psychiatry, 6,* 1.
71. Zahn TP, Rosenthal D, Shakow D (1963) Effects of irregular preparatory intervals on reaction time in schizophrenia. *J. Abnorm. Soc. Psychol., 67,* 44.
72. Zubin J (1975) Problems of attention in schizophrenia. In: Kietzman ML, Sutton S, Zubin J (Eds), *Experimental Approaches to Psychopathology,* pp. 139–166. Academic Press, New York.
73. Garmezy N (1978) Attentional processes in adult schizophrenia and in children at risk. *J. Psychiatr. Res., 14,* 3.
74. Kornetsky C (1972) The use of a simple test of attention as a measure of drug effects in schizophrenic patients. *Psychopharmacologia, 24,* 97.
75. Koh SD, Kayton L, Schwartz C (1974) The structure of word storage in the permanent memory of nonpsychotic schizophrenics. *J. Consult. Clin. Psychol., 42,* 879.
76. Grove WJ, Andreasen NC (1985) Language and thinking in psychosis. *Arch. Gen. Psychiatry, 42,* 26.
77. Raulin ML, Chapman LJ (1976) Schizophrenic recall and contextual constraint. *J. Abnorm. Psychol., 85,* 151.
78. Moon AF, Mefferd RB, Wieland BA, Porkorny AD, Falconer GA (1968) Perceptual dysfunction as a determinant of schizophrenic word dysfunction. *J. Nerv. Ment. Dis., 146,* 50.
79. Korboot P, Damini N (1976) Auditory processing speed and signal detection in schizophrenia. *J. Abnorm. Psychol., 85,* 287.
80. Bahzin EG, Wasserman LI, Junkonogii IM (1975) Auditory hallucinations and left tem-poral lobe pathology. *Neuropsychologia, 13,* 481.
81. Hammond N, Gruzelier J (1978) Laterality, attention, and rate effects in temporal discrimination of chronic schizophrenics. *Q. J. Exp. Psychol., 30,* 91.

82. Braff DL, Saccuzzo DP (1985) The time course of information-processing deficits in schizophrenia. *Am. J. Psychiatry, 142,* 170.
83. Knight R, Sherer M, Putchat C, Carter G (1978) A picture integration task for measuring iconic memory in schizophrenics. *J. Abnorm. Psychol., 87,* 314.
84. Prigatano GP, Parsons OA (1976) Relationship of age and education to Halstead test performance in different patient populations. *J. Consult. Clin. Psychol., 44,* 527.
85. Finslayson MAJ, Johnson KA, Reitan RM (1977) Relationship of level of education to neuropsychological measures in brain damaged and non-brain damaged adults. *J. Consult. Clin. Psychol., 45,* 536.
86. Spohn HE, Lacoursiere RB, Thompson K, Coyne L (1977) Phenothiazine effects on psychological and psychophysiological dysfunction in chronic schizophrenics. *Arch. Gen. Psychiatry, 34,* 633.
87. Killian GA, Holzman PS, Davis JM, Gibbons R (1984) Effects of psychotropic medication on selected cognitive and perceptual measures, *J, Abnorm. Psychol., 93,* 58.
88. Heaton RK, Crowley TJ (1981) Effects of psychiatric disorders and their somatic psychiatric treatment on neuropsychological test results. In: Filskov S, Boll TJ (Eds), *Handbook of Clinical Neuropsychology,* pp. 481–525. John Wiley, New York.
89. Irwin I (1985) Greater brain response of left-handers to drugs. *Neuropsychologia, 23,* 61.
90. Asarnow RF, MacCrimmon DJ (1978) Residual performance deficit in clinically remitted schizophrenics: A marker of schizophrenia. *J. Abnorm. Psychol., 87,* 597.
91. Chapman LJ, Chapman JP (1978) The measurement of differential deficit. *J. Psychiatr. Res., 14,* 303.
92. Jackson JH (1887) Remarks on evolution and dissolution of the nervous system. *J. Ment. Sci., 33,* 25.
93. Albert ML (1978) Subcortical dementia. In: Katzman R, Terry RD, Bick KL (Eds), *Alzheimer's Disease: Senile Dementia and Related Disorders,* pp. 173–196. Raven Press, New York.
94. Cohen NJ (1984) Preserved learning capacity in amnesia: Evidence for multiple memory systems. In: Squire LR, Butters N (Eds), *Neuropsychology of Memory,* pp. 83–103. Guilford Press, New York.
95. Bleuler ME (1978) The long-term course of schizophrenic psychoses. In: Wynne LC, Cromwell RL, Matthysse S (Eds), *The Nature of Schizophrenia,* pp. 631–636. John Wiley, New York.
96. Seidman LF (1983) Schizophrenia and brain dysfunction. *Psychol. Bull., 94,* 195.
97. Magaro PA (1981) The paranoid and the schizophrenic: The case for distinct cognitive style. *Schizophr. Bull., 7,* 632.
98. Silverstein ML, Arzt AT (1985) Neuropsychological dysfunction in schizophrenia. *J. Nerv. Ment. Dis., 173,* 341.
99. Marin RS, Tucker GJ (1981) Psychopathology and hemispheric dysfunction. *J. Nerv. Ment. Dis., 169,* 546.
100. Weinberger DR, Torrey EF, Neophytides AN, Wyatt RJ (1979) Lateral cerebral ventricular enlargement in chronic schizophrenia. *Arch. Gen. Psychiatry, 36,* 935.
101. Cutting J (1979) Memory in functional psychosis. *J. Neurol. Neurosurg. Psychiatry, 42,* 1031.

CHAPTER 7

Cerebral hemisphere asymmetries and interhemispheric integration in schizophrenia

HENRY A. NASRALLAH

There is now a large literature indicating that many morphological and functional aspects of the normal human brain are lateralized either to the left or to the right hemisphere (1,2). The two cerebral hemispheres, which have been shown to be neuroanatomically asymmetric (3), appear to be differentially activated by cognitive, perceptual, emotional, motoric or linguistic tasks, based on the skills of each hemisphere for the particular task.

Although the evidence for the above dates back for over a century in the history of neurology, to Broca (4), the strongest and most elegant proof was provided by the commissurotomy studies in both animals (5) and humans (split-brain patients) (6,7). Those classical studies revolutionized the concepts of cerebral organization by showing that the right and left cerebral hemispheres contain different and independent spheres of consciousness, and that each was superior to the other in certain skills. Thus, neither hemisphere can be considered 'major' or 'minor', and both are needed for the effective execution of complex brain functions. The two hemispheres are very intimately integrated by millions of fibers connecting homologous areas on the right and left cortices. These fibers comprise the interhemispheric commissures (the largest of which is the corpus callosum) which assure the integration of the two spheres of consciousness into a unified 'self', 'mind' or 'consciousness'.

Over the past decade, it has become apparent that cerebral asymmetry and lateralization of function are involved in psychopathology (8), and that some psychiatric disorders, particularly schizophrenia, are associated with significant changes in the normal pattern of cerebral asymmetries (9). Perhaps many or most psychiatric disorders involve some disturbance of cerebral lateralization, but at the present time, schizophrenia is more widely investigated in this regard than any other disorder. The findings are quite contradictory at times, reflecting the methodological problems inherent in the measurement of laterality (10). However, the past decade has witnessed the emergence of several neurophysiological models for schizophrenia including left hemispheric dysfunction, right hemispheric impairment, bilateral hemispheric dysfunction and defective interhemispheric integration.

In this chapter, the current evidence for the above models will be highlighted and reviewed. In an area of research fraught with methodological inconsistencies, no

Handbook of Schizophrenia, Vol. 1: The Neurology of Schizophrenia.
H.A. Nasrallah and D.R. Weinberger, editors.
© Elsevier Science Publishers B.V., 1986.

definitive conclusions can be drawn, but many important questions can be generated.

The left hemispheric dysfunction model of schizophrenia

The hallmark of schizophrenia is a disturbance of thoughts and associations, expressed through language. Some investigators even consider schizophrenic language to be a form of aphasia (11). Thus, the earliest link between the left hemisphere and schizophrenia comes from the historically well-known studies of Broca (4), who concluded from post-mortem studies of aphasic patients that the left temporal lobe is crucial for language. The implication for schizophrenia is that it is associated with a dysfunction in the left temporal lobe. This notion was further supported by a large brain-injury literature in the first half of this century (12), which suggested a strong association between left temporal lobe trauma and schizophrenia-like symptoms (13).

Psychosis and lateralization of temporal lobe epilepsy

Over the past 20 years, several investigators have focused on the association of schizophrenia-like psychosis, which sometimes occurs in patients with temporal lobe epilepsy. This association was first studied by Slater (14), but was extensively investigated by Flor-Henry (15), who observed that when psychotic features occurred in conjunction with temporal lobe epilepsy, the psychosis was more schizophrenia-like when the seizure was on the left, and resembled affective illness when the focus was on the right. When the patient had bilateral foci, the psychotic symptoms were 'schizo-affective' in quality. These findings, which were replicated by some investigators (16 – 18), but not by others (19), have spawned a large literature of the relationship between psychopathology and cerebral asymmetries of structure and function, as discussed below.

Neuroanatomical asymmetries on computerized tomography

Many structural neuroanatomical abnormalities have been reported in schizophrenia over the past few years, including ventricular enlargement, cerebral atrophy, cerebellar vermian atrophy, reversed neuroanatomical asymmetries and density deficits (20). Findings in schizophrenia related to asymmetries include (a) larger left than right cerebral ventricles observed by several investigators, (b) decreased left hemispheric density compared to the right (21, 22), as well as higher grey and white density in the right hemisphere, which is not found in controls (23); (c) evidence for a subgroup of right-handed schizophrenics with reversal of normal cerebral asymmetry (right frontal lobes slighty more anterior than the left frontal lobe and vice versa occipitally), who in the absence of brain atrophy parameters tended to have a milder course of illness with fewer years of hospitalization (24). A similar reversal had been reported in children with autism (25) and with developmental dyslexia (26). However, although some subsequent studies confirm this reversal of cerebral asymmetry in schizophrenia (27,28), others fail to replicate the finding (29 – 33), while others found the reversal to occur in schizophrenics compared to manics (34), or more likely in non-paranoid than in paranoid schizophrenia (35). Further controlled studies are needed to explore neuroanatomical asymmetries in schizophrenia and their possible clinical significance.

Neurochemical asymmetry

Evidence for neurochemical asymmetries of various neurotransmitters in the normal human brain now exists including left-right asymmetries for GABA, dopamine and choline acetyl transferases (ChAT) (36). Dopamine and ChAT were found to be significantly higher in the left-versus-right globus pallidus which is similar to findings in the rat brain (37). Oke et al. (38) reported a strong lateral distribution of norepinephrine in the human thalamus (higher in the left pulvinar and in the somatosensory area).

Increased concentrations and lateral asymmetry of amygdala dopamine were reported in a post-mortem study of schizophrenics versus controls (39). The amygdala, which is part of the medial temporal lobe, is a mesolimbic dopaminergic tract innervating the nucleus accumbens and olfactory tubercle and is believed to be involved in psychosis and antipsychotic action. The finding of increased dopamine in the left amygdala serves as neurochemical evidence for the involvement of the left hemisphere in schizophrenia.

Tardive dyskinesia, an involuntary choreiform movement disorder that occurs in some schizophrenic patients after chronic neuroleptic treatment has been shown in one study (40) to be lateralized more to the right side of the body, suggesting that neuroleptics may produce asymmetric neurochemical changes in the left nigrostriatal tract. Parkinsonism is also well known to be frequently asymmetric in its symptoms (41), suggesting that the left basal ganglia (in a right-handed person) are differentially involved in this movement disorder as well.

Handedness

Handedness is a crude indicator of cerebral dominance, but it may be useful as a possible indicator of left hemispheric dysfunction in certain individuals. It has been hypothesized that since the majority of people are right-handed, i.e. left hemisphere-dominant for motoric skills, then left-handedness, especially in the absence of a family history, may reflect some form of left hemispheric insult during development (42).

Several studies of left-handedness in schizophrenia have been reported in the last ten years and have produced conflicting results of increased (43, 44), no difference (45, 47), or decreased (48) left-handedness. Lishman and McMeekan (49) reported a higher frequency of left-handedness only in young male delusional patients.

Nasrallah et al. (50) found that although male schizophrenic patients have significantly higher incidence of left-handedness than in matched controls, most of the left-handedness was accounted for by the paranoid subgroup of schizophrenia while the non-paranoid (hebephrenic) schizophrenic subgroup showed no difference from controls. Thus left-handedness may be associated with only certain schizophrenics, perhaps those with the less severe paranoid subtype as Boklage (51) and Luchins et al. (52) suggested from their studies of twins discordant for both handedness and schizophrenia, where the schizophrenic twin is usually the left-handed one as well. Thus the inconsistent findings in handedness research in schizophrenia may be in large part due to the different subtype and gender composition of the various samples reported.

Conjugate lateral eye movements

It has been hypothesized that conjugate lateral eye movements (LEM) to the right or to the left reflect activation of the cerebral hemisphere contralateral to the direction of the gaze (53, 54). Kinsbourne (55) reported that verbal tasks usually produced rightward LEM while spatial tasks produced leftward LEM, implying that the left and right hemispheres are activated by verbal and spatial tasks respectively. Schwartz et al. (56) also showed that emotionally laden tasks generally activate the right hemisphere.

Schweitzer et al. (57) found that schizophrenic patients had right LEM to both verbal and emotional tasks, suggesting an overall increase of left hemisphere activity in schizophrenia. Cultural background or education had no effect on this finding but gender did: women generally initiated cognition in the left hemisphere more often than men regardless of diagnosis. Tomer et al. (58) compared female schizophrenics and controls and suggested that hemispheric activation is not necessarily pathological.

Gur (54) also used LEM to show that schizophrenic patients showed more rightward movements than controls to both verbal and spatial-emotional tasks, suggesting an inappropriately over-stimulated left hemisphere in schizophrenia. However, there were also more 'stare' responses in schizophrenics, which were assumed to reflect activation of both or neither hemispheres.

Skin conductance

Luria and Homskaya (59) and Sourek (60) reported that there is absence of skin conductance response in the hand ipsilateral to a brain lesion. The neurophysiological basis for this observation remains ambiguous. Gruzelier and Venables (61 – 63) and Gruzelier (64) found that chronic schizophrenic patients had no response or significantly decreased response in the left hand. On the other hand, depressed patients were found to have the opposite pattern of skin conductance. These findings suggest that there may be a left hemisphere dysfunction in schizophrenia.

160

Dichotic listening

Kimura (65) used asymmetrical responses of the hemispheres to different simultaneous auditory stimuli as a method of indicating which hemisphere is dominant for language functions. Words are identified more frequently when heard by the ear contralateral to the linguistically dominant hemisphere. Several studies of dichotic listening in schizophrenia show a higher right- than left-ear absolute threshold. Specific studies demonstrate (a) temporal decrement in left hemisphere auditory functions (66–69) with possible temporal–limbic (especially hippocampal) involvement as a locus of dysfunction; (b) left hemispheric overactivation (exaggerated right-ear preface and fewer shifts of attention away from the right ear) in paranoid as compared with non-paranoid patients (70–72); (c) loss of ear asymmetry during acute psychosis and re-emergence of normal right-ear advantage after recovery (73), suggesting that laterality shifts in schizophrenia may be a state-dependent dynamic process; and (d) that neuroleptic drugs seem to influence asymmetry and produce a larger right-ear (left hemisphere) advantage (74).

Evoked potentials

Roemer et al. (75) found lower used visual evoked responses in finding lower left hemispheric stability suggestive of a left hemispheric desynchronization in schizophrenic patients compared with controls. Buchsbaum et al. (76) reported visual evoked response findings suggestive of a dysfunction of the left temporal lobe in schizophrenia and Connolly et al. (77) examined visual evoked potentials in unmedicated schizophrenics and found left temporal and left occipital dysfunction in schizophrenia. Shagass et al. (78) also reported left hemispheric evoked potential abnormalities in schizophrenia.

Electroencephalography (EEG)

Many studies – but not all – have reported possible asymmetries of EEG abnormalities in schizophrenia. Some show right-sided disorders to be more common (79), while others show more abnormalities on the left (80). Flor-Henry et al. (81) reported abnormal power distribution in the left temporal region of unmedicated schizophrenics. Coger et al. (82) reported a significant increase in power densities in frontal/temporal regions. Stevens et al. (83) used ambulatory telemetry and reported EEG desynchronization over the left temporal region during spatial tasks and the reduction of power in the alpha-frequency in the left temporal region during periods of auditory hallucinations simultaneously with right temporal lobes slowing.

Two subtypes of schizophrenia, paranoid and residual, were compared with control subjects by Etevenon et al. (84), who reported that EEG differences between paranoid schizophrenics and controls were only on the left while differences between residual schizophrenics and controls were mainly on the right. This difference in schizophrenia subtypes is also confirmed in other studies (85, 86).

Overall, studies of EEG and schizophrenia tend to implicate both hemispheres and perhaps the failure of many investigators to separate schizophrenics into diagnostic subtypes such as paranoid and non-paranoid produced mixed results (as in handedness research discussed previously).

Cerebral blood flow

The first cerebral blood flow studies in schizophrenia were conducted by Kety et al. (87) using nitrous oxide. Although they found no differences in overall flow compared with controls they did not rule out regional differences that their method could not detect. This conclusion was validated in 1974, when Ingvar et al. (88) reported that with intracarotid xenon, schizophrenic patients had lower anterior flow (hypofrontal), greater posterior flow (hyperoccipital), and normal overall cerebral blood flow compared to controls. The left hemisphere was used for those studies. More recent studies using ^{133}Xe inhalation found decreased right hemispheric mean flow for schizophrenics (89) and bilateral decrease in blood flow (90). In control subjects, asymmetrical cerebral blood flow was reported by gender and handedness and in response to specific tasks with greater increases in left hemispheric flow for verbal tasks and in right hemispheric flow for spatial tasks (91).

Gur et al. (92) found that regional cerebral blood flow differences in schizophrenics emerged during task performance. In contrast to the increase in left hemisphere flow for verbal and right hemisphere flow for spatial tasks in controls, schizophrenics showed no flow asymmetry for the verbal task and a greater left hemispheric increase for the spatial task. This finding was seen as consistent with the hypothesis of left hemispheric overactivation in schizophrenia (93) (as in conjugate lateral eye movement studies discussed earlier). Recently, Burns et al. (94) reported that with dynamic CT scanning, blood perfusion in brain tissue was asymmetric in the temporal lobe and in the cerebellum with a higher perfusion in the right hemisphere.

Positron emission tomography

Positron emission tomography (PET) is a recent brain imaging technique that has revealed asymmetries in hemispheric metabolic activity (95). Buchsbaum et al. (96) confirmed the hypofrontality that was first detected by cerebral blood flow studies but also reported diminished metabolism in the central gray matter areas on the left but not on the right side. Widen et al. (97) reported that in the young unmedicated schizophrenic patients the hypofrontal pattern was not found on PET scans and that on repeat PET scans done after 4 − 5 weeks of neuroleptic treatment there was reduction in left frontal glucose metabolism compared with temporal regions, a significant increase in glucose metabolism on the right lentiform nucleus, and a reduction in the left-right asymmetry of the lentiform nucleus which was significantly higher on the left before treatment. Widen and his colleagues (including Dr. Ingvar who discovered hypofrontality in schizophrenia) concluded that the previous findings of hypofrontality may be due to neuroleptic drug treatment and chronicity of illness which was characteristic of patients in earlier studies.

Frontal asymmetry in regional cerebral metabolic rate on PET scans in normal individuals was described by Phelps et al. (98). Brodie et al. (99) make a similar observation in the PET scans of schizophrenic patients (with drug washout), where they found decreased glucose metabolic rate in the left frontal region at the basal ganglia level. They reported that both regional asymmetry and hypofrontality were not altered after neuroleptic therapy.

Sheppard et al. (100) used ^{15}O PET scanning in unmedicated or never-treated acute schizophrenics to show that there was no reduction in frontal blood flow or metabolism and equivocal support for reduced metabolism in the basal ganglia in schizophrenics. Their most prominent finding, however, was an abnormality in hemispheric lateralization with the normal group showing significant left – right asymmetry while the schizophrenic patients generally showed absence of hemispheric asymmetry.

It should be emphasized that technical, methodological and cognitive considerations limit the reliability of PET scan investigation and interpretation at this time. However, some trends are emerging that may suggest the presence of lateralization abnormalities in schizophrenia.

Neuropsychological tests

Evidence for left hemispheric dysfunction in schizophrenic patients is provided by the neuropsychological test literature. However, pervasive neuropsychological impairment is usually found in chronic rather than acute schizophrenics (101). Flor-Henry and Yeudall (102) conducted extensive neuropsychological tests in patients with schizophrenia and affective disorders. Right hemispheric dysfunction was found in all groups but the schizophrenics had a left hemispheric (frontal temporal) dysfunction as well. Abrams and Taylor (80) confirmed some of those findings but found that, while both schizophrenics and affective patients had bilateral hemispheric impairment, there were far more left hemispheric temporal and parietal deficits in schizophrenia.

Golden et al. (103) found neuropsychological impairment on the Luria-Nebraska battery to be associated with cerebral ventricular enlargement in schizophrenia and with CT scan density deficits in the left frontal lobe (21).

Silverstein (104) used the Luria-Nebraska battery and found that schizophrenics with impairment were more likely to be unmedicated, non-Caucasian, left-handed and chronic. Left frontal dysfunction was found in some schizophrenics but also in some affective patients.

Overall, many schizophrenic patients show lateralized left hemispheric (usually frontal and temporal parietal) dysfunction on neuropsychological testing. However, when extensive tests are given, bilateral hemispheric impairment becomes more apparent in schizophrenia. On the other hand, impairment in patients is not detected if the tests used are not sufficiently sensitive.

The right (± left) hemispheric dysfunction model of schizophrenia

Most of the findings suggesting a deficit in right cerebral hemispheric function with or without left hemispheric dysfunction in schizophrenia were obtained by investigators who usually set out to test the left hemisphere dysfunction model of schizophrenia. Hartlage and Garber (105) found right hemispheric impairment on spatial vs. non-spatial reasoning. Schweitzer et al. (106) described right cerebral hemisphere dysfunction in the presence of left hemisphere overactivation (using a visual half-field presentation of verbal and spatial material), and suggested that the apparent left hemispheric activation for spatial tasks in schizophrenia (93) may actually be a compensatory mechanism for a primary deficit in the right hemisphere. Sandel and Alcorn (107) used conjugate lateral eye movements to show that schizophrenics, especially the non-paranoid type, tended to rely on the right hemisphere for most of their tasks, even when the left hemisphere was more suited for a given task.

Other studies that reported a bilateral hemispheric dysfunction (108 – 111) imply that schizophrenia is associated with impairment of function in both the right and left hemispheres, i.e. that it is a pervasive brain dysfunction.

The interhemispheric communication/integration defect model of schizophrenia

There is a considerable body of evidence suggesting that schizophrenia may be associated with a defect in interhemispheric integration which may be related to a lateralized dysfunction of the right, left or both hemispheres as described in the previous discussion. The following is a brief overview of the evidence.

Anatomical evidence

The two cerebral hemispheres are anatomically connected by several commissures, the largest of which is the corpus callosum, which is essentially a bundle composed of over 200 million fibers connecting homologous areas of the right and left hemispheres. In 1972, Rosenthal and Bigelow (112) reported a post-mortem study of significant thickening in the corpus callosum in 10 chronic schizophrenics as compared with 10 psychiatric controls. The only post-mortem replication of this finding was done by Nasrallah et al. (113) in an older group of schizophrenics. No differences between schizophrenics and normal controls were found but thicker mean corpus callosum in early-onset (non-paranoid) versus late-onset (paranoid) schizophrenics was detected. In a further analysis of the data (114), significant thickening was found in the anterior but not in the posterior part of the corpus callosum in schizophrenic patients as compared with psychiatric controls.

A recent magnetic resonance imaging study of the corpus callosum in young male schizophrenics by Nasrallah et al. (115) showed significantly thicker corpus callosum in female but not in male schizophrenic patients. In addition, when male schizophrenic patients were divided by handedness, the left-handers had significantly smaller callosal dimensions (area, anterior and mid-thickness) as compared with right-handers. These findings pointed to an association between gender handedness and callosal morphology which was not addressed in previous post-mortem studies.

Histological evidence

Nasrallah et al. (116) conducted the only histological study of the corpus callosum in schizophrenic patients. No differences were found in the numbers of glial cells and fibers per unit area, but significantly more fibrillary gliosis was found in the late-onset (paranoid) as compared with the early-onset (non-paranoid) group. The data, which need replication in a younger sample of patients, suggest that a chronic inflammatory process in the corpus callosum (and perhaps impaired callosal interhemispheric transfer) may be associated with the paranoid subtype of schizophrenia.

Neurological evidence

There is a large literature of schizophrenia-like symptoms in patients with tumors of the corpus callosum (117). However, Nasrallah and McChesney (118) found this to be true mainly for tumors involving the anterior part (genu) of the corpus callosum. Furthermore, the possibility that involvement of neighboring tissue may contribute to the symptomatology cannot be ruled out.

Callosal transfer of unilateral perceptual stimuli

Impairment of interhemispheric communication across the corpus callosum in schizophrenia was first reported by Beaumont and Dimond (119), who used tachistoscopy to show failure of visual cross-matching between the hemispheres in chronic schizophrenics. They hypothesized that there is interhemispheric disconnection in schizophrenia. Since then there have been several reports of impaired callosal transfer in schizophrenia involving other perceptual modalities such as tactile and intermanual errors (120 – 122), visual errors (93, 123), and auditory errors (124). However, most of these studies tend to suggest a model of a 'noisy' or 'inefficient' callosal channel rather than a 'disconnected' one, as Beaumont and Dimond originally suggested. In several of the studies, a left hemispheric dysfunction was also found to partially account for the results.

Evoked potentials

Somatosensory evoked potentials in response to tactile stimuli were studied by Tress et al. (125), who found that schizophrenic patients have a sensory processing deficit in callosal transmission of ipsilateral stimuli. Jones and Miller (126) measured interhemispheric time for ipsilateral and contralateral vibratory stimuli and, finding no difference, concluded that there was a failure of callosal transmission in schizophrenia. However, Shagass et al. (78) failed to replicate these findings.

Do neuroleptics produce an interhemispheric dysfunction?

Myslobodsky et al. (127) reviewed the literature of hemispheric disconnection in schizophrenia and made the important observation that evidence of disconnection was noted mainly when the patients were receiving neuroleptic treatment. Thus, it is vital that future control studies of hemispheric and interhemispheric function in schizophrenia be conducted on patients before and after neuroleptic treatment. Neuroleptic drugs may produce a 'disconnection syndrome' in schizophrenia, which may confound the results of laterality research.

Nasrallah (128) has suggested a hypothetical model for the production of schneiderian delusions based on the premise that in the schizophrenic brain, the unintegrated right hemispheric consciousness may become an 'alien intruder' on the verbally expressive left hemisphere. He proposes that impaired interhemispheric integration in schizophrenia involves the loss of a neurochemical (possibly dopamine-related) inhibitory process that normally prevents the realization by the left hemispheric consciousness that it actually receives and sends thoughts and intentions to and from another (right hemispheric) consciousness. The schizophrenic patient would thus complain, via the verbal left hemisphere, of being influenced by 'someone' or by a 'force' and that thoughts are being inserted into or withdrawn from or broadcast out of his head. This model postulates not a 'disconnection' between the hemispheres, but normal anatomical connections in the presence of defective neurochemical integration, which in many patients can be reversed with the use of antidopaminergic (neuroleptic) drugs. According to this model, neuroleptics may exert their therapeutic antidelusional effect by actually 'disconnecting' the brain of schizophrenics, and eliminating what the left hemispheric consciousness regards as 'external intrusion' i.e. the usual right hemispheric input and information exchange. As a test for the hypothesis, right intracarotid amobarbital injection should temporarily halt schneiderian delusions by transiently anesthetizing the right hemisphere, and surgical commissurotomy should permanently eliminate delusions of control and influence by an outside 'force'.

Conclusions

The evidence for a lateralized hemispheric dysfunction or an interhemispheric integration defect in schizophrenia is strongly suggestive but certainly not definitive. Some studies fail to find any specific hemisphere dysfunction in schizophrenia (129 – 134). What is probably more important, however, there remain several methodological problems in the laterality/psychopathology, comprising:
1. The *diagnosis* of schizophrenia is highly suspect in many of the studies, with no reliable or valid criteria used. Furthermore, only some studies separated schizophrenics into paranoid and non-paranoid subtypes, and those who did used unclear criteria.
2. *Gender* differences have not been given serious consideration in this literature. There are strong indications that there are important gender differences in both

psychopathology (135) and hemisphere asymmetries (136), and that males and females should be studied separately.

3. The *state* of the patient at the time of investigation is frequently ignored and should be considered an important variable. It is quite possible that schizophrenic patients in relapse may show a different laterality pattern as compared with those in remission. In fact, although there is evidence of a marked lateralization change (73), few studies have attempted to test schizophrenic patients before and after treatment.

4. The effect of *medication* status has not been controlled for. Some studies include medicated schizophrenics while others do not. It is essential that investigators attempt to study drug-free and medicated patient groups, especially in the light of the observation by Myslobodsky et al. (127) that neuroleptics may produce and account for many of the interhemispheric deficits described by various studies.

5. The *chronicity* of the schizophrenic patients is an important factor that is frequently ignored. It is quite likely that acute, moderately and severely chronic schizophrenic patients differ in brain function parameters including laterality. A study sample should be homogeneous for the duration of illness so that meaningful conclusions can be derived. The hypofrontality that was initially described on cerebral blood flow schizophrenia studies may be related to chronicity and long term neuroleptic treatment rather than to the illness itself (97).

6. The *measurements* of laterality may not be valid (10, 137). Or may not be measuring similar or comparable neurophysiological processes. This is a vital methodological issue that remains vague and has not been adequately addressed. The development of objective modes of valid measures of hemispheric function is critical for further advances in this area of research.

At this point in time, the evidence cited in this chapter should be used for generating and properly testing new hypotheses regarding the relationship of hemispheric asymmetries of function and schizophrenia, and for studying whether the changes observed are cause, effect or epiphenomena. This relatively new area of neuroscience investigation faces methodological challenges which, if overcome, may lead to remarkable advances in the understanding of brain function in health and in severe psychiatric illness such as schizophrenia.

REFERENCES

1. Hellige JB (Ed) (1983) *Cerebral Hemisphere Asymmetry: Method, Theory and Application.* Praeger, New York.
2. Bradshaw JL, Nettleton NC (1983) *Human Cerebral Asymmetry.* Prentice-Hall, New Jersey.
3. Galaburda AM, Le May M, Kemper TL, Geschwind W (1978) Right-left asymmetries in the brain. *Science, 199,* 852.
4. Broca P (1861) Remarques sur la siège de la faculté du langage articulé. *Bull. Soc. Anat., 6,* 330.
5. Sperry RW, Stamm J, Miner N (1956) Relearning tests for interocular transfer following

division of optic chiasma and corpus callosum in cats. *J. Comp. Physiol. Psychol., 49,* 529.

6. Sperry RW (1968) Hemisphere deconnection and unity in conscious awareness. *Am. Psychol. 23,* 723.
7. Gazzaniga MS (1970) *The Bisected Brain.* Appleton-Century-Crofts, New York.
8. Galen D (1974) Implications for psychiatry of left and right cerebral specialization. A neurophysiological context for unconscious processes. *Arch. Gen. Psychiatry, 31,* 572.
9. Gruzelier J, Flor-Henry P (Eds) (1979) *Hemisphere Asymmetries of Function in Psychopathology.* pp. 189 – 222. Elsevier/North-Holland Biomedical Press, New York.
10. Colbourn CJ (1978) Can laterality be measured? *Neuropsychologia, 16,* 283.
11. Andreasen NC (1982) The relationship between schizophrenic language and the aphasias. In: FA Henn, HA Nasrallah (Eds), *Schizophrenia as a Brain Disease,* pp. 99 – 111. Oxford University Press, New York.
12. Davison K, Bagley CR (1969) Schizophrenia-like psychoses associated with organic disorders of the central nervous system: a review of the literature. In: RN Herrington (Ed), *Current Problems in Neuropsychiatry,* pp. 113 – 184. Royal Medico-Psychological Association, Ashford, Kent.
13. Nasrallah HA, Fowler RC, Judd LL (1981a) Schizophrenia-like illness following head injury. *Psychosomatics, 22,* 359.
14. Slater E, Beard AW, Glithero E (1963) The schizophrenia-like psychosis of epilepsy. *Br. J. Psychiatry, 109,* 95.
15. Flor-Henry P (1969) Psychosis and temporal lobe epilepsy: a controlled investigation. *Epilepsia, 10,* 363.
16. Gregoriadis A, Fragos E, Dapslakis Z et al. (1971) A correlation between mental disorders and EEG and AEG findings in temporal lobe epilepsy. *Prensa Med. Mex., 36,* 325.
17. Taylor DC (1975) Factors influencing the occurrence of schizophrenia-like psychosis in patients with temporal lobe epilepsy. *Psychol. Med., 5,* 249.
18. Sherwin I (1981) Psychosis associated with epilepsy: significance of the laterality of the epileptogenic lesion. *J. Neurol. Neurosurg. Psychiatry, 44,* 83.
19. Shukla GD, Katisyar BC (1980) Psychiatric disorders in temporal lobe epilepsy: the laterality effect. *Br. J. Psychiatry, 137,* 181.
20. Nasrallah HA, Coffman JA (1985) Computerized tomography in psychiatry. An overview. *Psychiatr. Ann., 14,* 239.
21. Golden CJ, Graber B, Coffman J (1981) Structural brain deficits in schizophrenia. Identification by computed tomographic scan density measurements. *Arch. Gen. Psychiatry, 38,* 1014.
22. Coffman JA, Andreasen NC, Nasrallah HA (1984) Left hemispheric density deficits in schizophrenia. *Biol. Psychiatry, 19,* 1237.
23. Largen JW, Calderon M, Smith RC (1983) Asymmetries in the density of white and grey matter in the brains of schizophrenic patients. *Am. J. Psychiatry, 140,* 1060.
24. Luchins DJ, Weinberger DR, Wyatt RJ (1979) Schizophrenia: evidence of a subgroup with reversed cerebral asymmetry. *Arch. Gen. Psychiatry, 36,* 1309.
25. Hier DB, LeMay M, Rosenberger RP (1978) Autism: association with reversed cerebral asymmetry. *Neurology, 28,* 348.
26. Hier DB, LeMay M, Rosenberger RB, Perlo VP (1978) Developmental dyslexia: evidence for a subgroup with a reversal of cerebral asymmetry. *Arch. Neurol., 35,* 90.
27. Naeser MA, Levin HL, Benson DF (1981) Frontal leukotomy size and hemispheric

asymmetries on CT scans of schizophrenics with variable recovery. *Arch. Neurol., 38,* 30.

28. Luchins DJ, Weinberger CR, Wyatt RJ (1982) Cerebral asymmetry in schizophrenia determined by computed tomography. *Am. J. Psychiatry, 139,* 753.

29. Nasrallah HA, Rizzo M, Damasio H, McCalley-Whitters M, Kuperman S, Jacoby CG (1982) Neurological differences between paranoid and nonparanoid schizophrenia. II. Computerized tomographic neuroanatomical findings. *J. Clin. Psychiatry, 43,* 307.

30. Andreasen NC, Dennert JW, Olson JA (1982) Hemispheric asymmetries and schizophrenia. *Am. J. Psychiatry, 139,* 427.

31. Jernigan TL, Zatz LM, Moses JA, Cardellino JP (1982) Computed tomography in schizophrenics and normal controls. II. Cranial asymmetry. *Arch. Gen. Psychiatry, 139,* 771.

32. Weinberger DR, DeLisi LE, Perman GP et al. (1982) CT scans in schizophreniform disorder and other acute psychiatric patients. *Arch. Gen. Psychiatry, 39,* 778.

33. Luchins DJ, Meltzer HY (1983) A blind controlled study of occipital cerebral asymmetry in schizophrenia. *Psychiatry Res., 10,* 87.

34. Tsai L, Nasrallah HA, Jacoby CG (1983) Hemisphere asymmetry in schizophrenia and mania. A controlled study and a critical review. *Arch. Gen. Psychiatry, 40,* 1286.

35. Tsai LY, Nasrallah HA, Jacoby CG (1984) Cerebral asymmetry in subtypes of schizophrenia. *J. Clin. Psychiatry, 45,* 423.

36. Glick SD, Ross DA, Hough LB (1982) Lateral asymmetry of neurotransmitters in human brain. *Brain Res., 234,* 53.

37. Zimmerberg B, Glick SD, Jerussi TP (1974) Neurochemical correlate of a spatial preference in rats. *Science, 185,* 623.

38. Oke A, Keller R, Mefford I et al. (1978) Lateralization of norepinephrine in the human thalamus. *Science, 200,* 1411.

39. Reynolds GP (1983) Increased concentrations and lateral asymmetry of amygdala dopamine in schizophrenia. *Nature (London), 305,* 527.

40. Waziri R (1980) Lateralization of neuroleptic-induced dyskinesia indicates pharmacologic asymmetry in the brain. *Psychopharmacol., 68,* 51.

41. Liberman A (1974) Parkinson's disease: a clinical review. *Am. J. Med. Sci., 267,* 66.

42. Satz P (1972) Pathological left-handedness: an explanation. *Cortex, 8,* 121.

43. Walker HA, Birch HG (1970) Lateral preference and right – left awareness in schizophrenic children. *J. Nerv. Ment. Dis., 151,* 341.

44. Nasrallah HA, Schroeder C, Keelor K (1981) Motoric lateralization in schizophrenic males. *Am. J. Psychiatry, 138,* 1114.

45. Wahl OF (1976) Handedness in schizophrenia. *Percept. Mot. Skills, 42,* 944.

46. Bolin BJ (1953) Left-handedness and stuttering as signs diagnostic of epileptics. *J. Ment. Sci., 99,* 483.

47. Fleminger JJ, Dalton R, Standage KF (1977) Handedness in psychiatric patients. *Br. J. Psychiatry, 131,* 448.

48. Taylor PJ, Dalton R, Fleminger JJ (1980) Handedness in schizophrenia. *Br. J. Psychiatry, 136,* 375.

49. Lishman WA, McMeekan ERL (1976) Hand preference in psychiatric patients. *Br. J. Psychiatry, 129,* 158.

50. Nasrallah HA, McCalley-Whitters M, Kuperman S (1982) Neurological differences between paranoid and nonparanoid schizophrenia. I. Sensory and motoric lateralization. *J. Clin. Psychiatry, 43,* 305.

51. Boklage EC (1977) Schizophrenia, brain asymmetry development and twinning: cellular

169

relationship with etiological and possibly prognostic implications. *Biol. Psychiatry, 12,* 17.

52. Luchins DJ, Weinberger DR, Wyatt RW (1979) Anomalous lateralization associated with a milder form of schizophrenia. *Am. J. Psychiatry, 136,* 1598.
53. Bakan P (1971) The eyes have it. *Psychol. Today, 4,* 64.
54. Gur RE (1975) Conjugate lateral eye movements as an index of hemispheric activation. *J. Pers. Soc. Psychol., 31,* 751.
55. Kinsbourne M (1972) Eye and head turning indicates cerebral lateralization. *Science, 176,* 539.
56. Schwartz GE, Davidson RS, Maer F (1975) Right hemisphere lateralization for emotion in the human brain: interactions with cognition. *Science, 190,* 286.
57. Schweitzer L, Becker E, Welsh H (1978) Abnormalities of cerebral lateralization in schizophrenic patients. *Arch. Gen. Psychiatry, 35,* 982.
58. Tomer R, Mintz M, Levy A et al. (1981) Smooth pursuit pattern in schizophrenic patients during cognitive tasks. *Biol. Psychiatry, 16,* 131.
59. Luria AR, Homskaya EG (1966) *The Frontal Lobe and Regulation of Psychological Processes.* Moscow University Press, Moscow.
60. Sourek K (1965) *The Nervous Control of Skin Potentials in Man.* Nakladatelstvi Ceskoslovensa Akademic Ved., Prague.
61. Gruzelier JH, Venables PH (1972) Skin conductance orienting activity in a heterogenous sample of schizophrenics. *J. Nerv. Ment. Dis., 155,* 277.
62. Gruzelier JH, Venables PH (1973) Skin conductance response to tones with and without attentional significance in schizophrenic and non-schizophrenic psychiatric patients. *Neuropsychologia, 11,* 221.
63. Gruzelier JH, Venables PH (1974) Bimodality and lateral asymmetry of skin conductance orienting activity in schizophrenia: replication and evidence of lateral asymmetry in patients with depression and disorders of personality. *Biol. Psychiatry, 8,* 55.
64. Gruzelier JH (1973) Bilateral asymmetry of skin conductance orienting activity and levels in schizophrenia. *Biol. Psychiatry, 1,* 21.
65. Kimura D (1967) Functional asymmetry of the brain in dichotic listening. *Cortex, 3,* 163.
66. Gruzelier JH, Hammond N (1976) Schizophrenia: a dominant hemisphere temporal-limbic disorder? *Res. Commun. Psychol. Psychiatr. Behav., 1,* 33.
67. Gruzelier JH, Hammond NV (1979) Gains, losses and lateral differences in the hearing of schizophrenic patients. *Br. J. Psychol., 70,* 319.
68. Kugler BT, Caudry DJ (1983) Phoneme discrimination in schizophrenia. *Br. J. Psychiatry, 142,* 53.
69. Niwa S, Hiramatsu K, Makeyama T et al. (1983) Dichotic detection task and schizophrenic attention deficit. In: Flor-Henry P, Gruzelier JH (Eds), *Laterality and Psychopathology,* pp. 507–529, Elsevier/North-Holland Biomedical Press, Amsterdam.
70. Lerner J, Nachson I, Carmon A (1977) Responses of paranoid and non-paranoid schizophrenics in a dichotic listening task. *J. Nerv. Ment. Dis., 164,* 247.
71. Nachshon G (1980) hemispheric dysfunction in schizophrenia. *J. Nerv. Ment. Dis., 168,* 241.
72. Gruzelier JH, Hammond NV (1978) The effect of chlorpromazine upon psycho-physiological endocrine and information processing measures in schizophrenia. *J. Psychiatry Res., 14,* 167.
73. Wexler BE, Heninger GR (1979) Alterations in cerebral laterality during acute psychotic illness. *Arch. Gen. Psychiatry, 36,* 278.

74. Gruzelier JH (1978) Bimodal states of arousal and lateralized dysfunction in schizophrenia: the effect of chlorpromazine. In: Wynne L, Cromwell R, Matthyse S (Eds), *The Nature of Schizophrenia: New Approaches to Research and Treatment,* pp. 167 – 187. Wiley, New York.

75. Roemer RA, Shagass C, Straumanis JJ, Amadeo M (1978) Pattern evoked potential measurements suggesting lateralized hemisphere dysfunction in chronic schizophrenia. *Biol. Psychiatry, 13,* 185.

76. Buchsbaum MS, Carpenter WT, Fedio P et al. (1979) Hemispheric differences in evoked potential enhancement by selective attention to hemiretinally presented stimuli in schizophrenic, affective and post-temporal lobectomy patients. In: Gruzelier J, Flor-Henry P (Eds), *Hemispheric Asymmetries of Function in Psychopathology,* pp. 317 – 328. Elsevier/North-Holland Biomedical Press, New York.

77. Connolly JF, Gruzelier JH, Manchanda R et al. (1983) Visual evoked potentials in schizophrenia: intensity effects and hemispheric asymmetry. *Br. J. Psychiatry, 142,* 152.

78. Shagass C, Josiassen RC, Roemer RA et al. (1983) Failure to replicate evoked potential observation suggesting corpus callosum dysfunction in schizophrenia. *Br. J. Psychiatry, 142,* 471.

79. Small JG, Sharpley PH, Milstein V et al. (1979) Research diagnostic criteria and EEG findings in hospitalized schizophrenic patients. In: Obiols J, Gonzalezmonelus E, Pujol J (Eds), *Biological Psychiatry Today.* Elsevier/North-Holland Biomedical Press, Amsterdam.

80. Abrams, R, Taylor MA (1979) Laboratory studies in the validation of psychiatric diagnoses. In: Gruzelier JH, Flor-Henry P (Eds), *Hemisphere Asymmetries of Function in Psychopathology,* pp. 363 – 372. Elsevier/North-Holland Biomedical Press, Amsterdam.

81. Flor-Henry P, Koles ZJ, Howarth BG, Burton L (1979) Neurophysiological studies of schizophrenia, mania and depression. In: Gruzelier J, Flor-Henry P (Eds), *Hemisphere Asymmetries of Function in Psychopathology,* pp. 189 – 222. Elsevier North-Holland Biomedical Press, New York.

82. Coger RW, Dymond AM, Serafetinides ES (1979) Electroencephalographic similarities between chronic alcoholics and chronic non-paranoid schizophrenics. *Arch. Gen. Psychiatry, 38,* 91.

83. Stevens JR, Bigelow L, Denny D, Lipkin J, Livermore AH, Rauscher F, Wyatt RJ (1979) Telemetered EEG-EOG during psychotic behaviours of schizophrenia. *Arch. Gen. Psychiatry, 36,* 251.

84. Etevenon P, Peron-Magon P, Campistron D et al. (1983) Differences in EEG symmetry between patients with schizophrenia. In: Flor-Henry P, Gruzelier JH (Eds), *Laterality and Psychopathology,* pp. 269 – 290. Elsevier/North-Holland Biomedical Press, Amsterdam.

85. Stevens JR, Livermore A (1982) Telemetered EEG in schizophrenia spectral analysis during abnormal behavior episodes. *J. Neurol. Neurosurg. Psychiatry, 45,* 385.

86. Coger RW, Serafetinedes EA (1983) In: Flor-Henry P, Gruzelier JH (Eds), *Laterality and Psychopathology,* pp. 225 – 248. Elsevier/North-Holland Biomedical Press, Amsterdam.

87. Kety SS, Woodford RB, Hormel MH et al. (1948) Cerebral blood flow and metabolism in schizophrenia. *Am. J. Psychiatry, 104,* 765.

88. Ingvar DH, Franzen G (1974) Abnormalities of cerebral blood flow distribution in patients with chronic schizophrenia. *Acta Psychiatr. Scand., 50,* 425.

89. Mathew RJ, Meyer JS, Francis DJ et al. (1981) Regional cerebral blood flow in

schizophrenia: a preliminary report. *Am. J. Psychiatry, 138,* 112.

90. Mathew RJ, Ducan GC, Weinman ML et al. (1982) Regional cerebral blood flow in schizophrenia. *Arch. Gen. Psychiatry, 39,* 1121.

91. Gur RC, Gur RE, Obrist WD et al. (1982) Sex and handedness differences in cerebral blood flow during rest and cognitive activity, *Science, 217,* 659.

92. Gur RE, Skolnick BE, Gur RC et al. (1983) Brain function in psychiatric disorder. I. Regional cerebral blood flow in medicated schizophrenics. *Arch. Gen. Psychiatry, 40,* 1250.

93. Gur RE (1978) Left hemispheric dysfunction and left hemispheric overactivation in schizophrenia. *J. Abnorm. Psychol., 87,* 226.

94. Burns EM, Nasrallah HA, Kathol MH, Kruckeberg TW, Chapman SM (1985) Asymmetry of temporal lobe perfusion with dynamic CT scanning in schizophrenia. In: *Abstract Volume, Society of Biological Psychiatry Annual Meeting, May 15 – 19, 1985, Dallas, TX,* p. 79.

95. Sokoloff L, Reivich M, Kennedy C (1977) The [C^{14}] deoxyglucose method for the measurement of local cerebral glucose utilization: theory, procedure and normal values in the conscious and anesthetized albino rat. *J. Neurochem., 28,* 897.

96. Buchsbaum MS, Ingvar DH, Kessler R et al. (1982) Cerebral glucography with positron tomography. Use in normal subjects and in patients with schizophrenia. *Arch. Gen. Psychiatry, 39,* 251.

97. Widen L, Blomquist G, Greitz T et al. (1983) PET studies of glucose metabolism in patients with schizophrenia. *Am. J. Neuroradiol., 4,* 550.

98. Phelps ME, Mazziotta JC, Huang SC (1982) Study of cerebral function with positron computed tomography: a review. *J. Cereb. Blood Flow Metab., 2,* 113.

99. Brodie JD, Gomez-Mont F, Volkow ND et al. (1983) Analysis of positron emission transaxial tomography images in psychiatric disorders. In: Greitz T, Ingvar D, Widen L (Eds), *The Metabolism of the Human Brain Studied with Positron Emission Tomography,* pp. 441 – 451. Raven Press, New York.

100. Sheppard G, Gruzelier J, Manchander R et al. (1983) O positron emission tomographic scanning in predominantly never-treated acute schizophrenic patients. *Lancet, 2,* 1448.

101. Lezak M (1976) *Neuropsychological Assessment.* Oxford University Press, New York.

102. Flor-Henry P, Yeudall LT (1979) Neuropsychological investigation of schizophrenia and manic-depressive psychosis. In: Gruzelier JH, Flor-Henry P (Eds), *Hemisphere Asymmetries of Function in Psychopathology,* pp. 341 – 362. Elsevier/North-Holland Biomedical Press, Amsterdam.

103. Golden CJ, Moses JA, Zelazowski R et al. (1980) Cerebral ventricular size and neuropsychological impairment in young chronic schizophrenics. *Arch. Gen. Psychiatry, 37,* 619.

104. Silverstein ML, Meltzer HY (1983) Neuropsychological dysfunction in the major psychoses. In: Flor-Henry P, Gruzelier JH (Eds), *Laterality and Psychopathology,* pp. 143 – 152. Elsevier/North-Holland Biomedical Press, Amsterdam.

105. Hartlage LC, Garber J (1976) Spatial vs. nonspatial reasoning ability in chronic schizophrenics. *J. Clin. Psychol., 32,* 235.

106. Schweitzer L (1982) Evidence of right cerebral hemisphere dysfunction in schizophrenic patients with left hemisphere overactivation. *Biol. Psychiatry, 17,* 655.

107. Sandel A, Alcorn JD (1980) Individual hemisphericity and maladaptive behaviours. *J. Abnorm. Psychol., 89,* 514.

108. Eaton FM, Busk J, Maloney MP et al. (1979) Hemisphere dysfunction in schizophrenia: assessment by visual perception tasks. *Psychiatry Res, 1,* 325.

109. Serafetinides EA, Coger RW, Martin J et al. (1981) Schizophrenia symptomatology and cerebral dominance patterns: a comparison of EEG, AER and BPRS measures. *Compr. Psychiatry, 22,* 218.
110. Shaw JC, Brooks S, Cotler N et al. (1979) A comparison of schizophrenic and neurotic patients using EEG power and coherence spectra. In: Gruzelier JH, Flor-Henry P (Eds), *Hemisphere Asymmetries of Function in Psychopathology,* pp. 257–284. Elsevier/North-Holland Biomedical Press, Amsterdam.
111. Taylor PJ, Fleminger JJ (1981) The lateralization of symptoms in schizophrenia. *Br. J. Med. Psychol., 51,* 59.
112. Rosenthal R, Bigelow LB (1972) Quantitative brain measurements in chronic schizophrenia. *Br. J. Psychiatry, 121,* 259.
113. Nasrallah HA, Bigelow LB, Rauscher FP, Wyatt RJ (1979) Corpus callosum thickness in schizophrenia. In: *New Research Abstract Volume, American Psychiatric Association 132nd Annual Convention, May 11–18, 1979,* p. 15.
114. Bigelow LB, Nasrallah HA, Rauscher FP (1983) Corpus callosum thickness in chronic schizophrenia. *Br. J. Psychiatry, 142,* 284.
115. Nasrallah HA, Andreasen NC, Olson SC, Coffman JA, Dunn VD, Ehrhardt JC (1985) A magnetic resonance imaging study of callosal morphology in schizophrenia. In: *Abstract Volume, Society of Biological Psychiatry Annual Meeting, Dallas, TX,* p. 107.
116. Nasrallah HA, McCalley-Whitters M, Bigelow LB et al. (1983) A histological study of the corpus callosum in chronic schizophrenia. *Psychiatry Res., 8,* 251.
117. Elliot FA (1969) The corpus callosum, cingulate gyrus, septum pellucidum, septal area and fornix. In: Vinken PJ, Bruyn GW (Eds), *Handbook of Clinical Neurology, Vol 2,* pp. 758–765. Elsevier/North-Holland Biomedical Press, New York.
118. Nasrallah HA, McChesney CM (1981) Psychopathology of corpus callosum tumours. *Biol. Psychiatry, 16,* 661.
119. Beaumont JG, Dimond SJ (1973) Brain disconnection and schizophrenia. *Br. J. Psychiatry, 123,* 661.
120. Carr SA (1980) Interhemispheric transfer of sterognostic information in chronic schizophrenics. *Br. J. Psychiatry, 136,* 53.
121. Dimond SJ, Scammell RE, Pryce IG, Huws D, Gray C (1979) Callosal transfer and left hand anomia in schizophrenia. *Biol. Psychiatry, 14,* 735.
122. Nasrallah HA, Tippin J, McCalley-Whitters M (1983) Impaired callosal transfer in schizophrenic and manic patients. In: *Abstract Volume, Society of Biological Psychiatry Annual Meeting, April 27–May 1, 1983, New York,* p. 131.
123. Eaton EM, Busk J, Maloney MP, Sloane RB, Whipple K, White K (1980) Hemispheric dysfunction in schizophrenia: assessment by visual perception tasks. *Psychiatry Res., 1,* 325.
124. Green P, Kotenko V (1980) Superior speech comprehension in schizophrenics under monaural versus biaural listening conditions. *J. Abnorm. Psychol., 89,* 399.
125. Tress KH, Kugler BT, Caudrey DJ (1979) Interhemispheric integration in schizophrenia. In: Gruzelier JH, Flor-Henry P (Eds), *Hemisphere Asymmetries of Function in Psychopathology,* pp. 449–462. Elsevier/North-Holland Biomedical Press, Amsterdam.
126. Jones GH, Miller JJ (1981) Functional tests of the corpus callosum in schizophrenia. *Br. J. Psychiatry, 139,* 353.
127. Myslobodsky MS, Mintz M, Tomer R (1983) Neuroleptic effects and the site of abnormalities in schizophrenia. In: Myslobodsky MS (Ed.), *Hemisyndromes: Psychobiology, Neurology, Psychiatry,* pp. 347–388. Academic Press, New York.

128. Nasrallah HA (1985) The unintegrated right cerebral hemispheric consciousness as alien intruder: a possible mechanism for Schneiderian delusions in schizophrenia. *Compr. Psychiatry, 26,* 273.
129. Bull HC, Venables PH (1974) Speech perception in schizophrenia. *Br. J. Psychiatry, 125,* 350.
130. Clooney JL, Murray DJ (1977) Same-different judgement in paranoid and nonparanoid patients: a laterality study. *J. Abnorm. Psychol., 86,* 655.
131. Domino EF, Demetriou S, Tuttle T et al. (1979) Comparison of the visually evoked response in drug-free schizophrenic patients and normal controls. *Electroencephalogr. Clin. Neurophysiol., 46,* 123.
132. Yozawitz A, Bruder G, Sutton S, Sharpe L, Gurland B, Fleiss J, Costa L (1979) Dichotic perception: evidence for right hemisphere dysfunction in affective psychosis. *Br. J. Psychiatry, 135,* 224.
133. Toone BK, Cooke E, Laden MH (1981) EDA in the affective disorders and schizophrenia. *Psychol. Med., 11,* 497.
134. Iacono WG (1982) Bilateral electrodermal habituation-dishabituation and resting EEG in remitted schizophrenics. *J. Nerv. Ment. Dis., 170,* 91.
135. Seeman MV (1982) Gender differences in schizophrenia. *Can. J. Psychiatry, 27,* 107.
136. Flor-Henry P (1978) Gender, hemispheric specialization and psychopathology. *Soc. Sci. Med., 12B,* 155.
137. Schneider SJ (1983) Multiple measures of hemispheric dysfunction in schizophrenia and depression. *Psychol. Med., 13,* 287.

CHAPTER 8

Brain areas implicated in schizophrenia: a selective overview

RONALD F. ZEC AND DANIEL R. WEINBERGER

Early in this century many neuropsychiatric theorists, including Kraepelin (1), Bleuler (2), and even Freud (3), believed that schizophrenia was a brain disease (4). Kraepelin (1) hypothesized, on the basis of early reports of neuropathological changes, that frontal and temporal neocortex were principally involved. Kraepelin also argued that involvement of these brain areas could be inferred from the clinical symptoms of the illness.

However, the lack of consistency and specificity of the neuropathological findings reported in the first half of this century (4) led to proposals of many alternative theories of schizophrenia, some of which were psychogenic theories whereas others focused on sites other than the frontal and temporal neocortical areas. While it remains unproven that schizophrenia is a primary brain disease or that the frontal and temporal lobes are the principal sites of damage, evidence has accumulated over the years which strongly suggests that chronic schizophrenia involves brain pathology that very likely does affect frontal and temporal lobe functioning. However, other brain areas have also been proposed as primary lesion sites (5, 6).

Notions about a possible site in the brain where a lesion might produce schizophrenia have evolved in concert with new discoveries about regional brain function. Since at the turn of the century the frontal and temporal lobes were considered the cerebral foci for the regulation of behavior, it is not surprising that theorists such as Kraepelin implicated these structures in mental illness. Theories implicating extra-frontotemporal areas were primarily instigated by the recognition around 1950 of three previously unappreciated functional systems in the brain: the reticular activating system, the limbic system, and the reward and punishment systems. Rapidly expanding knowledge about some of the neurotransmitters involved in these systems also played a major role in the development of new hypotheses.

In 1949, Moruzzi and Magoun (7) described the role of the brainstem reticular formation in mediating arousal and attention. Since an important part of the clinical picture of schizophrenia has often been thought to involve disturbances of arousal and attention, it was logical to hypothesize that a defect in this system may play a role in the pathogenesis of the illness (8).

In 1953, Olds and Milner designed an experiment to study the effects of electrical stimulation of the reticular activating system on learning (9). Due to their mistaken-

Handbook of Schizophrenia, Vol. 1: The Neurology of Schizophrenia.
H.A. Nasrallah and D.R. Weinberger, editors.
© Elsevier Science Publishers B.V., 1986.

ly implanting an electrode in the medial forebrain bundle, they made the fortuitous discovery of the brain's 'reward system'. A year earlier, Delgado, Roberts and Miller had discovered that stimulation of certain brain sites could have punishing effects on an animal's behavior (9). Since anhedonia and a lack of goal-directedness have been considered core deficits in schizophrenia, damage to the medial forebrain bundle reward system could play a role in the etiology of this illness (10).

In 1952, MacLean extended the concept proposed earlier by Papez that a circuit of periventricular structures was the biological substrate for the experience and expression of emotion (11). MacLean coined the term 'limbic system' for this set of interconnected nuclei and regions. Since schizophrenia clearly involves disturbances in emotion and perceived reality, MacLean and others have theorized that schizophrenia is a disease of the limbic system (11 – 13).

A fourth major discovery was the finding by Delay and Deniker in 1952 that chlorpromazine could ameliorate psychotic symptoms without causing excessive sedation (14). The discovery of neuroleptic drugs coincided with major breakthroughs in the understanding of chemical neurotransmission, and together these discoveries propelled the search for a biochemical basis of mental illness (14). As late as 1950 there were still some physiologists who believed that synaptic transmission was predominantly an electrical phenomenon, but the development of sophisticated techniques for recording the electrical activity from the interior of single neurons and the use of the electron microscope helped make the case for neurochemical transmission at the synapse (15). The identification of different neurotransmitters, the mapping of neurotransmitter systems in the brain, and the study of the effects of pharmacological agents on these systems eventually led to the discovery that the psychotogenic effects of various amphetamine-like substances related to their dopamimetic properties, while the antipsychotic effects of neuroleptic medication were closely linked to their antidopaminergic properties (14).

These observations spawned the 'dopamine hypothesis', a proposal that schizophrenia was due to an overactivity of the dopaminergic systems in the brain (14, 16, 17). Since the nigrostriatal projection is the most prominent dopamine system, some researchers hypothesized that the basal ganglia were involved (18). The mesolimbic dopamine system, however, might be more relevant since this system projects to structures more directly related to the limbic system, e.g. the nucleus accumbens, amygdala and hypothalamus (19). More recently, studies of the mesocortical dopamine system, which innervates primarily the prefrontal cortex, have renewed interest in the frontal lobes and thus, via dopamine, have brought us back full circle to Kraepelin's notion that the frontal lobes are the key (20, 21).

In the first section of this chapter, several of the brain sites which have been hypothesized to be involved in schizophrenia and the arguments in support of each are reviewed. In the second section the neuroanatomical interconnections among the implicated structures are summarized. It is proposed that this seemingly disparate group of brain structures forms a highly integrated network of functional neuroanatomical systems, and that one or more strategically placed lesions, particularly if occurring early in development, could have widespread functional ramifications throughout this network.

Brain areas implicated in schizophrenia

Recent reviews of CT scan studies (13), neuropathological studies (4), and neuropsychological studies (8, 22 – 24), have concluded that chronic schizophrenia, as the
early theorists suspected, is probably a brain disorder. The data suggest that the
presumed brain pathology is subtle, rather than gross in nature, and perhaps
qualitatively non-specific. This has made precise localization of the primary site(s)
of the damage and/or dysfunction difficult.

The various brain structures implicated in schizophrenia by different research approaches are summarized in Table 1. The areas most often implicated are the frontal
and temporal neocortex (with perhaps a left hemisphere trend) (see Chapters 9 – 15),
the limbic system, especially the amygdala, hippocampus, and septum (which are
located deep inside the temporal and frontal lobes) (see Chapters 14, 15), and the
brainstem. The basal ganglia and the substantia innominata are the next most frequently incriminated, followed by the diencephalon (see Chapter 14). The parietal
lobe has been less frequently implicated; it is specifically the inferior parietal lobule
(which has intimate connections with the frontal and temporal lobes) that has been
mentioned. Recent evidence has also pointed to the cerebellum (see Chapters 9, 14).
The occipital lobe has only rarely been mentioned. Some of the evidence and
arguments implicating the fronto – temporal cortex, brain stem reticular formation,
and parietal cortex are discussed in this section.

Frontal and temporal lobes

Throughout this century, theorists have emphasized the frontal and temporal lobes
as particularly important in schizophrenia. Kraepelin (1) argued that deficits in
higher cognitive function, e.g. poor judgement and inability to plan, loss of the
'critical faculty', loss of creativity, etc., were most likely the result of frontal lobe
damage, whereas the peculiar speech disorders and auditory-verbal hallucinations
were more likely due to presumed irritative damage to the temporal lobe. Jacobi and
Winkler's pneumoencephalogram (PEG) findings in 1929 linking hallucinosis with
temporal lobe damage and intellectual deficits with frontal lobe damage (5) were
viewed as support for Kraepelin's speculations.

Almost half a century later, Parfitt (25) theorized from a psychodynamic perspective that the frontal and temporal lobes were involved in schizophrenia. Parfitt cited
work by Miskolczy, who had found neuropathological changes in the prefrontal and
inferior temporal areas to be consistent with his own clinically based inferences
about the sites of pathology. Parfitt argued that deteriorated patients with
schizophrenia very much resemble patients with frontal lobe damage. He pointed
out that both groups share an inability to plan, impoverishment of thought, failure
of insight, loss of the sense of adult responsibility, emotional flattening, and a
reduction of drive. Hallucinosis was attributed to temporal lobe disturbance as suggested by the work of Penfield and Jasper (26).

Mirsky (8) (see below) has proposed that a defect in the ascending reticular ac-

TABLE 1   *Brain structures implicated in schizophrenia by different research approaches*

Approaches	Brain structures implicated														
	Neocortex			Limbic system					Dien-cephalon		Limbic striatum		Basal ganglia	Brain-stem	Cere-bellum
	FL	TL	PL	Cg	Un	Am	Hp	Sp	Hy	Th	NAS	SI			
Neuropathology															
Older studies	neocortex			x					x						
Recent studies					x	x	x	x	x	x	x	x	x	x	x
CNS disorders with schizophrenia-like symptoms															
Neurological disorders	x	x*		limbic system					dien-cephalon				x	x	
Temporal lobe epilepsy		x				x	x								
Structural brain imaging (PEG, CT)	neocortex			limbic system					dien-cephalon						x
Functional brain imaging (CBF, BEAM, PET)	x												x		
Neurophysiology															
Scalp EEG abnormalities	x	x*													
Depth EEG abnormalities	x	x			x	x	x	x				x		x	
Electrical brain stimulation in man															
Older studies	x			limbic system											
Recent studies				x	x										

178

Neuropharmacology
Antidopaminergic neuroleptics   x   limb. str.   x   x
Amphetamine psychosis   x   x   limb. str.   x   x
Psychedelic drugs   x   limb. str.   x   x

                                         limbic system
                                         limbic system
                                         limb. syst.   x   x

Neuropsychology
Test batteries   x* x* ?
CPT studies   x   x   x
Eyetracking   x   x   x
Neurological signs x   x   x   x

* = Left hemisphere trend; FL, TL and PL = frontal, temporal, and parietal lobes, Cg = cingulate gyrus, Un = uncus, Am = amygdala, Hp = hippocampus, Sp = septum, Hy = hypothalamus, Th = thalamus, NAS = nucleus accumbens septi, SI = substantia innominata.

179

tivating system (ARAS) is the fundamental abnormality in schizophrenia, but that it is the presence or absence of additional damage to the inhibitory frontal and/or temporal corticofugal systems which determines how this ARAS defect is manifested clinically. According to this notion, frontal and perhaps temporal damage is presumed to be present in *chronic, nuclear* schizophrenia in which symptoms of blunted affect and withdrawal predominate (8). Temporal, septal, and hippocampal damage, and perhaps frontal damage as well, may be involved in *episodic, paranoidal* schizophrenia in which personality problems including aggressive, fragmented, and bizarre behavior are common (8). In *paranoid* schizophrenia cortical damage is presumed to be minimal or absent, and only the putative ARAS lesion is thought to be operative (8). Mirsky's proposal, though highly speculative, has stimulated a great deal of discussion in the psychological literature.

Early in this century, Hughlings-Jackson proposed that schizophrenia must involve the highest levels of brain function, i.e. the frontal and temporal cortices (27, 28). He believed that damage to the frontal and temporal lobes released sensory and perceptual systems from inhibition and produced dreaming during waking, i.e. hallucinations and illusions. Hughlings-Jackson (28) believed that brain damage produces both positive and negative symptoms. Negative symptoms were thought to be a direct result of the lost function of the brain-damaged area, whereas positive symptoms or disinhibited functions were attributed to intact brain areas normally inhibited by the damaged area.

This distinction between positive and negative symptoms has recently been reinstated in discussions about schizophrenia (6, 29 – 32). Seidman (6), after reviewing neurodiagnostic findings, proposed that the relative proportion of positive and negative symptoms reflects the extent and location of dysfunction in a cortico – subcortical, arousal-attention system which includes the frontal – temporal cortical regions, the limbic system, and the brainstem reticular activating system. Negative symptoms, including apathy, blunted affect, social withdrawal, avolition, and poor judgement and planning, were attributed to frontal lobe dysfunction. Positive symptoms were thought to result from dysfunction in the limbic, midbrain, and brainstem regions.

One theoretical rationale for the use of frontal leukotomies in the treatment of schizophrenia was the assumption that the frontal lobes were diseased and should be isolated (33). Although disturbed patients tended to become more friendly, calm, and cooperative after surgery, they also tended to retain their basic mode of thinking and their delusional ideas (34). Hallucinations were reduced in at most half of the cases (34). Undesirable behavioral effects of frontal leukotomies included a loss of drive and energy and an increase in stimulus-bound behavior (33).

Patients with high levels of emotional tension, fear, worry, and anxiety were the ones most likely to benefit from frontal leukotomy (33). It was theorized that a malfunction in the frontal lobes of these patients created a reverberating circuit or positive feedback loop in which anxiety and fixed patterns of thought were perpetuated (33 – 35). The frontal leukotomy was thought to lower anxiety levels by interrupting the reverberating circuit and vicious cycle (33 – 35). The anxiety-reducing effect of frontal leukotomies does support the notion that the frontal lobes are part of a neuroanatomical circuit involved in the mediation of arousal and emotion. It does not necessarily follow, however, that the brain abnormality which triggers the persistent anxiety must reside in the frontal lobes. It is equally possible that the abnormality exists in another part of this circuit, e.g. in the limbic system or brainstem, but that a frontal leukotomy can, nonetheless, effectively interrupt the vicious cycle of presumed overactivity.

Levin (36, 37) has recently argued that converging lines of evidence from clinical, cognitive – behavioral, neurochemical, and brain imaging studies suggest that there is frontal lobe dysfunction in schizophrenia, especially in patients with negative symptoms. Positive symptoms (e.g. auditory hallucinations, delusions, formal thought disorder, and bizarre behavior), on the other hand, are attributed to damage in the temporal – parietal area and the inferior parietal lobule.

Levin (37) seconds the notion that the negative symptoms of schizophrenia, including flat affect, alogia, mutism, apathy, anhedonia, social withdrawal, distractability, and impairments in volition, planning, and goal-directed behavior, are clinical manifestations of frontal lobe damage. He further notes that cognitive – behavioral studies have demonstrated a wide variety of attentional, information processing, and psychomotor deficits in schizophrenia which parallel impairments reported in experimental studies of frontal lobe damage in man and animals. For example, difficulty in maintaining and shifting set are deficits shared by both schizophrenic and frontal lobe damage groups. Levin (37) proposes that the diverse set of cognitive deficits in schizophrenia may all reflect a fundamental defect in a broadly defined attentional mechanism mediated primarily by the frontal lobes.

Unfortunately, as with other theorists, Levin's arguments that the clinical symptoms and neuropsychological deficits of schizophrenia closely resemble the behavioral consequences of frontal lobe damage are *not* based on any studies in which these two groups were directly compared. Clearer evidence on this point would come from studies using a double-dissociation design in which it is shown that on a variety of measures patients with schizophrenia are more similar to frontal lobe patients than to patients with damage to other brain areas. It does not necessarily follow that just because there are studies which have demonstrated attentional difficulties in schizophrenia and other studies which have demonstrated attentional difficulties in frontal lobe patients, that schizophrenia involves frontal lobe pathology, or even that the two groups have similar types of attentional problems. Attention is a complex cognitive process in which multiple brain areas participate (38). As discussed in later sections of this chapter, the attentional deficits in schizophrenia can be viewed as implicating other brain areas, such as the brain stem reticular activating system and the inferior parietal lobule (40).

A major part of Levin's argument for frontal lobe dysfunction in schizophrenia is based on eye movement impairments seen in this group (36). He suggests that the disruption of smooth pursuit eye movements (SPEM) by saccadic intrusions implies dysfunction in the frontal eye fields, an area in the prefrontal cortex involved in the feedback regulation of saccades during visual tracking. Levin speculates that a second, less specific kind of smooth pursuit impairment consisting of saccadic substitution may be due to a dysfunction in the temporal – parietal mechanism of task engagement. An alternative view is that the disturbance in SPEM may be caused by a dysfunction in the brainstem (8).

Goldberg (41) recently proposed two additional explanations for the 'frontal lobe hypothesis' of schizophrenia. One alternative view is that frontal lobe dysfunction may be the result of two recently alleged effects of antipsychotic medication: the 'akinesia' and 'tardive dysmentia' syndromes. These two supposedly iatrogenic phenomena appear to closely resemble two well-known frontal lobe syndromes: the dorsolateral prefrontal cortex (DLPFC) syndrome and the fronto-orbital/mediobasal syndrome. The second alternative explanation for frontal lobe dysfunction in schizophrenia is that it may be a secondary effect of primary pathology located elsewhere in the brain.

The 'akinesia' effect, like the DLPFC syndrome, is characterized by behavioral aspontaneity and apathy, while the 'tardive dysmentia' syndrome, like the orbitofrontal syndrome, is characterized by behavioral disinhibition and hypomania. Goldberg (41) points out, however, that the reports of these iatrogenic phenomena are preliminary and their apparent resemblance to the prefrontal syndromes needs to be experimentally verified. The 'akinesia' effect is the better established finding, having been reported in several double-blind studies (43, 44), while the 'tardive dysmentia' effect has thus far been reported in one uncontrolled study (44). Although 'akinesia' is usually reversible, Goldberg (41) speculated that in some individuals long exposure to neuroleptic drugs may lead to 'akinesia' which is persistent, analogous to the case of tardive dyskinesia.

Goldberg (41) argues that these neuroleptic-induced phenomena and their apparent resemblance to prefrontal lobe syndromes can be understood in terms of the distribution of the mesocortical dopamine system. The orbital and medial prefrontal cortex and the DLPFC receive projections from this dopamine system and have higher concentrations of dopamine than any other cortical area (46 – 48). Since the antipsychotic effects of neuroleptics have been linked to their effects on brain dopamine activity, it is possible that neuroleptics could in some cases cause a disturbance in the mesocortical dopamine system which could in turn disturb functioning in the frontal lobes (41). Against this proposal, however, is the observation by Kraepelin, Bleuler and others early in this century, that apathy syndromes were found in chronic schizophrenia before the advent of neuroleptic treatment.

Another explanation offered by Goldberg (41) for the apparent disturbance of frontal lobe functioning is that it may be a secondary effect of primary damage located elsewhere in the brain. For example, it has been shown that destruction of the ventral tegmental area, a midbrain area where the mesolimbic/mesocortical dopamine cell bodies are found, can 'simulate' the effects of lesions in prefrontal areas in both animals (48 – 50) and humans (51). Goldberg (41) suggests that damage to many locations in the brain could have repercussions on frontal lobe function because the frontal lobes are linked to a large and diverse set of brain areas.

He also notes that physiological brain imaging techniques and neuropsychological testing have provided the strongest evidence for frontal lobe involvement in schizophrenia, while structural measures like the CT scan and neuropathological techniques have not found predominantly frontal lobe pathology. Goldberg (41) argues that this discrepancy between the functional and structural measures is consistent with the view that frontal lobe dysfunction in schizophrenia may be the result of primary damage located at some other site in the brain.

Others have also speculated that altered frontal lobe functioning may be due to damage elsewhere in the brain (13, 52). Ingvar (52) proposed that a malfunction of one or more subcortico – cortical projection systems, e.g. the medial forebrain bundle, may be the culprit. Weinberger (13) suggested that frontal symptoms in schizophrenia may be due to limbic forebrain pathology and the resultant disruption of reciprocal limbic – frontal projections.

In favor of the hypothesis that the primary damage in schizophrenia is actually located in the frontal lobes, Goldberg (41) points to the frontal lobe's unique role as an integrator of many different functions, and to the dissociation of these functions in schizophrenia. Since the frontal lobes are connected to a large and diverse set of brain areas (41, 53), they are ideally situated to integrate diverse psychic functions. At the risk of mixing metaphors, it is interesting to note that the term 'schizophrenia' was coined by Bleuler to refer to the 'splitting' of the different psychic functions (54).

The argument was made earlier that damage to many different locations in the brain could possibly disturb frontal lobe functioning, but it is equally possible that frontal lobe damage could disrupt the functioning of other brain areas. It has been shown in the rat, for example, that damage to mesocortical dopamine system projections in the prefrontal cortex results in a disinhibition of activity in the mesolimbic and nigrostriatal dopamine systems (55, 56).

Davison and Bagley (5), in their archival review of schizophrenia-like psychoses associated with a wide variety of neuropathological disorders, concluded that lesions in the temporal lobe and diencephalon were especially correlated with these psychoses. Delusions were associated with left temporal lobe lesions, catatonia with lesions in the basal ganglia and left temporal lobe, auditory hallucinations with diencephalic lesions (including the basal ganglia), and thought disorder and schneiderian first-rank symptoms with brainstem lesions. No significant correlations were found between psychotic symptoms and lesions in the right hemisphere, the frontal, parietal and occipital lobes, or with the hypothalamus. It should be pointed out, however, that Davison and Bagley (5) largely ignored the defect state or negative symptoms of schizophrenia, including the intellectual deficits. The few times that symptoms like intellectual changes and loss of insight were mentioned, these symptoms were ascribed to the frontal lobes.

Achte, and co-workers (57) followed 3,552 men for 22 – 26 years, who suffered brain injuries in the Finnish wars of 1939 – 1945 and found that 317 persons, or 8.9%, developed a psychosis. Most had only one psychotic episode, and 42% did not develop a psychosis until 10 years after injury. Psychoses in general were more common after severe injuries, but schizophrenia-like psychoses were more frequent among those with mild injuries. The categories of localizable brain injury for the entire sample included the following: orbital frontal, non-orbital frontal, temporal, sensorimotor cortex, parietal, occipital, basal and cerebellar. Basal lesions were more frequent in the patients who became psychotic, while sensorimotor injuries were less frequent in the psychotic group. There was also a non-significant trend for temporal injury to be more frequent among the psychotic patients. However, no particular type of psychosis, e.g. schizophrenia, was associated with any particular location of brain injury, except that dementia was associated with frontal non-orbital injury, and Korsakoff's syndrome was associated with basal injuries. The investigators concluded that there was a higher-than-expected risk for psychosis among brain-injured persons, but that the location of the injury was for the most part irrelevant. They suggested that it was the stress associated with having one's coping ability compromised that increases the risk of psychosis after brain injury.

Other reports also support the view that whereas psychotic symptoms like hallucinations and delusions are rare after frontal lobe lesions, negative symptoms which comprise the 'defect state' of schizophrenia are common consequences (58 – 62). For example, the most frequent psychiatric symptoms associated with frontal lobe tumors are depression, apathy, loss of energy and interest, loss of planning ability, and problems with memory, attention, and orientation (59 – 62).

The literature on human brain disorders offers only rare anecdotal evidence for an association between psychosis and frontal lobe dysfunction. For example, Girgis (34) reported a case in which a slow growing tumor in the orbital surface of the frontal lobe was associated with intractable psychosis including visual and auditory hallucinations, paranoia, disorientation with respect to time and place, negativism, and a lack of insight and judgement.

In a review discussing the association between psychosis and water intoxication (63), it was pointed out that the vast majority of reported cases of compulsive drinking to the point of water intoxication were chronic schizophrenic patients, while other reported cases involved persons with apparent frontal or temporal lobe dysfunction. It could be argued that these two groups of patients make up the majority of water intoxication cases because schizophrenia may be a fronto – temporal disorder.

In Huntington's disease, psychiatric symptoms including a schizophrenia-like syndrome are often seen. This is a case in which both psychosis and dementia (i.e. both positive and negative symptoms) are associated with possible frontal lobe involvement (64, 65). While some neuropsychological studies have found specific 'executive deficits' early in the course of the disease, including impaired organizing, sequencing, and planning, and while it was proposed that Huntington's patients may have a 'frontal lobe syndrome', the consensus view seems to be that progressive degeneration of the basal ganglia is sufficient to account for most of the symptoms (66).

In general, while studies of brain damage in humans are consistent with the view that frontal lobe pathology may be responsible for the 'defect' state of schizophrenia, these studies provide very little support for the view that frontal lobe pathology alone can also account for the psychotic symptoms of schizophrenia such as auditory hallucinations, delusions, and thought disorders. Furthermore, it is possible that both the psychosis and dementia of schizophrenia could be due to subcortical damage, as appears to be the case with Huntington's disease (66).

Several recent neuropsychological studies using different test batteries support the frontal and/or temporal lobes hypothesis. Flor-Henry (67, 68), on the basis of both neuropsychological and electrophysiological findings, implicated the left frontotemporal lobe with a particular emphasis on left temporal – limbic dysfunction. Kolb and Whishaw (69) tested a sample of patients on a battery of tests emphasizing frontal, temporal and parietal functions. They interpreted their findings as indicative of bilateral frontotemporal dysfunction. Taylor and Abrams (70) examined a large sample of patients using a battery of standard cognitive tests and came to a similar conclusion, but with greater left than right frontotemporal impairment. Golden et al. (71) using the Luria-Nebraska Battery reported results that they interpreted as suggestive of left temporal lobe involvement. One limitation of these neuropsychological studies is that patients with schizophrenia were not directly compared with patients having frontotemporal damage and with other brain damage control groups.

Abrams and Taylor (72) compared patients with schizophrenia and affective disorder (all of whom had EEG abnormalities) and found that schizophrenia had more temporal abnormalities and affective disorder more parieto-occipital abnormalities. In another study, Abrams and Taylor (73) reported a correlation between thought disorder and EEG abnormalities in the left temporal lobe of a mixed schizophrenic and affective disorders group. The latter finding was interpreted in terms of the possible similarity between thought disorder and language dysfunction.

Many studies in the literature used neuropsychological and electrophysiological techniques to address the question of lateralization of dysfunction. In general, these studies have suggested perhaps greater bilateral dysfunction in the left hemisphere. The literature concerned with lateralized dysfunction in schizophrenia is reviewed elsewhere in this volume (Chapter 7).

The most compelling evidence for frontal cortex dysfunction has come from recent cerebral imaging studies. Ingvar and Franzen, in a series of regional cerebral blood flow (rCBF) studies of mostly elderly, medicated patients, found an abnormal 'hypofrontal' distribution of rCBF consisting of low blood flow frontally and high flow postcentrally (52, 74 – 76). The typical pattern for normal awake subjects at rest is a 'hyperfrontal' distribution with relatively greater rCBF in anterior brain regions. Since rCBF is a function of regional neuronal metabolism, the 'hypofrontal' pattern suggests that these patients have depressed frontal cortical activity (52, 74 – 76). The greatest degree of 'hypofrontality' was found in the most 'burned out' patients and correlated with 'negative' symptoms.

Consistent with this hypofrontal – hyperpostcentral rCBF distribution, two studies using computer-determined EEG topography, e.g., brain electrical activity mapping (BEAM), have reported increased slow frequency activity in frontal regions and increased fast frequency activity in post-central regions (77, 78). Buchsbaum et al. (79) have also reported increased frontal delta activity in schizophrenic patients as compared with controls.

While there are additional reports of greater delta activity in schizophrenic patients compared with controls (80 – 82), there have also been negative studies (83 – 85) and findings of decreased alpha activity instead (80, 83, 85, 86). The inconsistency among the studies may be due to methodological differences and/or due to the heterogeneity of patients with schizophrenia (77). A study by Morihisa and McAnulty (87) is particularly noteworthy. They reported greater frontal EEG abnormalities in those patients with marked frontal atrophy compared with those with no frontal atrophy as determined by CT scan. This finding suggests that there may be a relationship between regionally specific functional and structural abnormalities (87).

Morihisa, and co-workers (77) also suggested that there may be greater cortical irritability in the posterior portion of the left hemisphere in schizophrenic patients. They based this speculation on findings of increased beta activity and amplitude of visual evoked potentials in this region coupled with diminished P300 amplitudes in this same area – a set of signs which has been associated with cortical irritability (77). Morstyn et al. (88) reported deficient P300 activity in the left-middle and posterior temporal regions.

Consistent with these rCBF and tomographic EEG studies, several positron emission tomographic (PET) studies have found lower ratios of glucose metabolism in the frontal lobes relative to posterior regions (89 – 92). In one study, both medicated and drug-free schizophrenic groups were found to have lower frontal activity (90). A relative hypofrontal metabolic gradient appears not to be specific to schizophrenia, since a recent study found this pattern in patients with affective disorders (93). In addition, there have been several PET studies which have not found differences in regional metabolism between patients and controls (94 – 96), including one study of mostly never-medicated acute schizophrenic patients (94). Thus, although some PET studies have found deficient frontal activity, the specificity, clinical relevance, and generalizability of the finding is still open to question.

Inconsistent results also characterize recent attempts to replicate the Ingvar and Franzen rCBF studies (99 – 100). Using the non-invasive xenon-133 inhalation technique, one study found a bilateral anterior deficit (97), but another reported decreased frontal flow only in elderly patients (98). Two other studies did not specifically address the question of 'hypofrontality', but one of these reported decreased whole brain CBF (99), and the other found no differences during resting but laterality differences during cognitive activation (100).

In summary, each of the three functional brain imaging techniques (i.e. rCBF, BEAM, PET) have revealed in at least two studies lower frontal activity in schizophrenia as compared with control groups (52, 77, 78, 89, 90, 97). Unfortunately, there are also several studies using each technique which have not found these differences (83, 84, 94, 95, 97). Possible explanations for these discrepancies are discussed further in the chapters on rCBF and PET.

Caution is warranted in interpreting these studies because functional brain imaging is a relatively new field. The studies with schizophrenic patients generally used small sample sizes. The clinical significance of 'hypofrontality' is not yet fully understood. There has been very little work exploring what factors can affect the degree of 'hypofrontality' in patients with schizophrenia, or for that matter the degree of 'hyperfrontality' in normal subjects. Two studies reported that increasing the motivational level of normal subjects using a monetary incentive for correct performance increased (though non-significantly) the regionally specific CBF activation during cognitive testing (101, 102), including increased hyperfrontality in the left hemisphere (102). These findings raise the possibility that some extraneous or epiphenomenal 'state' difference between patient and control groups may be responsible for the relative 'hypofrontality' found in some studies of schizophrenia.

Only one cerebral imaging study attempted to examine frontal physiology during a specific frontal mediated behavior. Weinberger, Berman, and Zec (103, 104) studied rCBF during performance of the Wisconsin Card Sort (WCS) and found that young, unmedicated patients, unlike controls, failed to activate the dorsolateral prefrontal cortex (DLPFC) while engaged in this test. The WCS is especially sensitive to damage in the DLPFC (105 – 107). The results provide direct evidence for a link between pathophysiology and symptomatic behavior (i.e. cognitive dysfunction). Several hypotheses were proposed to explain the findings. It may reflect subtle structural damage to DLPFC. On the other hand, it may be an 'upstream effect' due to pathology in some subcortical connection of DLPFC. Although it is not possible to decide between these two alternative hypotheses simply on the basis of rCBF data, other recent evidence (discussed below) is more consistent with the notion of actual prefrontal damage. A third interpretation is that the findings may reflect some extraneous or artifactual difference, e.g. in attention or motivation, between the patient and control groups. Although it is difficult to rule out this possibility, various control procedures did not lend support for this interpretation.

On the basis of these findings and other recent evidence, Weinberger et al. (103) proposed that there may be subtle structural damage to the dopamine projections in or near the DLPFC and that such damage could possibly account for *both* the 'negative' and the 'positive' symptoms of schizophrenia. In support of a DLPFC damage-negative symptoms association, they cited evidence that DLPFC damage as a result of traumatic brain injury, for example, produces a set of 'defect' or 'negative' symptoms, including flat affect, withdrawal, poor insight, inattentiveness, and loss of goal-directed behavior, which appear to be strikingly similar to those described in schizophrenic patients (62, 63). This proposal is, of course, similar to that of others as described above.

The possibility of a link between prefrontal damage and positive symptoms is suggested by a recent report that 6-OHDA lesions in the prefrontal cortex in rats can cause overactivity in subcortical dopamine systems, and thus consistent with the 'dopamine' hypothesis of schizophrenia, could result in 'positive' symptoms, i.e. psychosis (55). In this experiment, selective destruction of dopamine terminals resulted in increased dopamine turnover and increased dopamine receptors in the nucleus accumbens and striatum. This atypical pattern of both pre- and postsynaptic dopamine hyperactivity in the nucleus accumbens and striatum has also been reported in some post-mortem studies of schizophrenic patients (108).

The proposal that prefrontal cortical damage can cause both prefrontal hypoactivity and limbic dopamine hyperactivity may also explain observations that neuroleptics ameliorate primarily the positive, as opposed to the negative, symptoms of schizophrenia (56), that with aging there is a tendency for positive symptoms to decline and negative symptoms to increase, and that the onset of schizophrenia typically occurs in late adolescence. Neuroleptics would be expected to improve mainly positive symptoms because the antidopaminergic effects of these drugs would tend to counter limbic dopamine hyperactivity, but increase prefrontal dopamine hypoactivity. Similarly, the normal decline in dopamine content and receptor activity with aging (109, 110) would also be expected to decrease limbic dopamine hyperactivity but increase prefrontal hypoactivity, and thus may explain the trend for decreasing positive symptoms but increasing negative symptoms in schizophrenic patients as they get older. Furthermore, recent findings that a perinatal lesion of the DLPFC impairs delayed-response performance in monkeys only after sexual maturity (111) may shed light on the pathogenesis of the tendency for the schizophrenic 'first break' to occur in late adolescence (see Chapter 18).

In summary, while the negative-defect symptoms of schizophrenia have generally been attributed to *underactivity* in the prefrontal cortex, positive-psychotic symptoms have been attributed to *overactivity* in the temporal cortex and/or limbic – subcortical structures which have intimate connections with the frontal and temporal cortical regions. Different theories regarding the site or sites of the putative lesion have been proposed to account for this pattern of frontal – temporal involvement. For example, Kraepelin suggested that there may be damage in frontal cortex and an irritative lesion in temporal cortex. Others have proposed a single lesion site which causes 'upstream' effects on connected structures. For example, pathology in the limbic system could partially deafferent frontal cortex and thus cause hypoactivity in that structure (13, 52). On the other hand, pathology in the frontal lobes may disinhibit activity in the temporal cortex and/or in limbic – subcortical structures (20, 103). Despite the many claims of frontal and temporal lobe involvement in schizophrenia, the evidence to date remains more circumstantial than definitive.

An additional note of skepticism regarding frontal involvement in schizophrenia seems warranted in view of the fact that there is no overwhelming evidence of structural damage to this area. While post-mortem and CT studies have revealed some evidence for frontal and/or temporal pathology (see Chapters 9, 14), signs of brain damage are as frequent or more frequent in other parts of the brain, e.g. in periventricular areas (4, 41). Furthermore, the subtle forms of brain damage which have been detected in some schizophrenic patients may be incidental to the illness, e.g. they may be due to a higher incidence of head trauma and poor self-care (112). However, even with these caveats in mind, it would be surprising, given all the suggestive evidence reviewed in this volume, if the frontal and temporal lobes were not involved in some primary way in this disorder.

Brainstem reticular formation

Since the brainstem reticular formation (BSRF) or ascending reticular activating system (ARAS) plays a central role in the regulation of arousal and attention (7, 113), it has been suggested that the arousal and attentional disturbances of schizophrenia (114, 115) may be due to a fundamental defect in this system (8, 116 – 118). Some theorists view the disturbances of arousal and attention as core deficits in schizophrenia which can lead to other characteristic symptoms (6, 116, 119, 120). Indeed, in reviewing the literature on schizophrenia-like sequelae after brain damage, Davison and Bagley concluded that thought disorder and schneiderian first-rank symptoms were most commonly associated with lesions in the brainstem (5). Similarly, the Scheibels (121) have argued that the BSRF is involved in the generation of hallucinations, and Kleist (122) speculated that brainstem dysfunction is reponsible for both hallucinations and paranoid delusions and plays a role in catatonia.

Various equivocal findings have been cited as support for a BSRF hypothesis. For example, non-specific EEG abnormalities reported in some patients during both waking and sleep have been interpreted as indicating BSRF dysfunction (123). However, reports of normal auditory brainstem evoked potentials imply that brainstem structures are grossly normal (124). Two recent post-mortem studies found gliosis in brainstem reticular formation of schizophrenic cases (125, 127). However, two other post-mortem studies which examined exclusively the brainstem were divided on this question, i.e. one reported pathology (127), the other did not (128). Clearly, these neurophysiological inferences and weak neuropathological findings do not provide compelling support for a BSRF lesion hypothesis.

The strongest behavioral evidence implicating the BSRF comes from studies using the continuous performance test (CPT) (6, 8, 129, 130). The finding that patients with schizophrenia as a group are impaired on this test of sustained attention has been replicated many times (8, 120, 130 – 132). The CPT deficit is reduced by neuroleptic treatment (120, 133), although residual impairment is found in remitted patients (132). The CPT deficit appears to be unrelated to cognitive functioning, diagnostic subtype, duration of illness or hospitalization, age of onset, age, sex, race, ethnic background, or education (120).

Mirsky and Kornetsky have argued that for many patients attentional deficits and susceptibility to distraction are the result of excessive central arousal due to dysfunction of the ARAS, while the attentional deficits of some other patients with schizophrenia may be due to extreme underarousal (8, 119, 129, 134). They suggest that chlorpromazine improves CPT performance by reducing high central arousal to a more optimal level (118, 129). These notions about 'arousal' in schizophrenia, while of considerable theoretical interest, are largely inferential and not based on empirical data.

Both animal and human studies have linked the CPT deficit to damage in the BSRF (6, 135). Lesions in the BSRF in monkeys cause CPT impairment along with high-voltage, slow-wave cortical EEG abnormalities (135, 136). CPT deficits have *not*, however, been found in alcoholic or Korsakoff patients, who often have damage to the mammillary bodies, dorsomedial nucleus of the thalamus, and cortex (130). Attention deficits are also *not* typically produced by lesions of the midline thalamic nuclei (130). Patients with seizure foci in the orbital frontal or temporal lobes also have been found to perform as well on the CPT as appropriately matched normal control groups (137). Even psychosurgery patients who have undergone either an anterior prefrontal lobotomy or a medial orbital leukotomy do not consistently show significant deficits on the CPT (137).

Further evidence of possible brainstem dysfunction in schizophrenia is the disorder of SPEM discussed earlier (6, 40). Although disordered SPEM may be a consequence of prefrontal dysfunction (36), the paramedian portion of the pontine reticular formation is crucial for the regulation of both saccadic and smooth pursuit eye movements (6, 36, 40). Deviations from normal tracking have been associated with damage in the brainstem, cerebellum, and basal ganglia (6, 36, 40), in addition to frontal lobe damage (36, 138).

As discussed earlier, Mirsky theorized that, while disturbed functioning of the ARAS may be a basic neurophysiological abnormality in schizophrenia, the expression of this ARAS disturbance in terms of clinical symptoms may be governed by the question of whether or not there is damage to the inhibitory frontal and/or temporal corticofugal systems (8). Also since the attentional system probably includes the prefrontal and cingulate cortex, and the posterior parietal cortex in addition to the mesencephalic reticular formation (6, 38, 130), structural or biochemical faults at one or more points of this sytem could conceivably result in attentional deficits (6, 138, 139). Nevertheless, it can safely be concluded that despite active theoretical discussion about the role of the ARAS in schizophrenia and some circumstantial evidence, there is virtually no empirical data to directly implicate this region.

Parietal lobe and the right hemisphere

The parietal lobe has only infrequently been implicated or hypothesized to be important in schizophrenia (see Table 1). Evidence has been accumulating in recent years, however, that the inferior parietal lobule (IPL) plays an important role in the mediation of selective attention (39, 139, 141). Since selective, as well as sustained attention, is believed to be impaired in schizophrenia (6, 140, 142), the IPL might be considered as a possible site of damage or dysfunction. Arguments for IPL involvement have been based on anatomical, pharmacological and on behavioral considerations (39, 139, 143).

Evidence that the IPL plays an important role in selective attention comes from work with both human subjects and rhesus monkeys (139, 140). Focal damage in either the parietal or prefrontal lobes of stroke patients, especially in the right hemisphere, can cause either global inattention or unilateral neglect (139). Each of these syndromes involves disturbance in attention and affect which cannot be attributed to more fundamental deficits in sensation, language, arousal, or motor function (139).

The global inattention syndrome includes marked impairments in the ability to direct or maintain attention, to maintain a coherent train of thought, and to perform a sequence of goal-directed behaviors (39, 139, 140). This syndrome also involves emotional abnormalities that range from apathy to severe agitation (139), and is associated with unconcern with or denial of illness (140). It is frequently misdiagnosed as dementia, aphasia, amnesia or psychosis (139, 140).

The unilateral neglect syndrome, in which there is inattention to the hemispace opposite the lesioned hemisphere, also is associated with IPL and DLPFC lesions, especially in the right hemisphere (38, 141). Why lesions of roughly the same brain areas result in unilateral neglect in some patients, and global inattention in others is not known, but unilateral neglect may be a milder disorder or involve the disruption of different neuroanatomical connections (139). Persons with unilateral neglect also often display a global lack of concern for their disability (139).

IPL lesions in the rhesus monkey result in a failure to attend to appropriate visual, auditory, or somatosensory stimuli in the contralateral hemispace (139). Furthermore, single neuron recordings in the IPL have revealed that some neurons fire only when motivationally significant stimuli are presented (139, 144). This reinforces the view that affective information reaches the IPL and helps direct selective attention.

Presumably, it is by virtue of the connections between the IPL and limbic structures that attention is influenced by motivationally relevant stimuli. The nucleus accumbens (NAS) receives input from the hippocampus, amygdala and the mesolimbic dopamine system and projects to the substantia innominata (SI), which receives gustatory, olfactory, and hypothalamic projections (139). The SI then sends cholinergic projections to the IPL (139). The IPL sends projections to the cingulate gyrus and parahippocampal gyrus, which in turn projects to the hippocampus; thus a feedback loop between the IPL and the limbic system is completed (38). Circuits from limbic sites to DLPFC and DLPFC to IPL complement this system.

Phylogenetic and myelogenetic evidence indicates that the IPL along with prefrontal and temporal neocortex are the latest brain areas to evolve and develop (139, 145). When compared with non-human primates, the IPL and DLPFC are the areas of the human brain which have shown the greatest relative growth (145, 146). If schizophrenia is the result of damage to the most human parts of the brain (25), then the IPL in addition to the frontal and temporal lobes is high on an ontogenically based list of possible sites.

The IPL has been termed the 'association cortex' of association cortices because it is situated between the visual, auditory, and somatosensory association cortices and receives direct input from each (145). The IPL also has direct and reciprocal connections with the dorsolateral prefrontal cortex (145), the anterior temporal neocortex (147), and other tertiary association cortices. In addition, as previously mentioned, the IPL receives inputs from the limbic system and hypothalamus via the NAS – SI pathway. It thus appears that IPL like DLPFC integrates emotional, visceral, and ideational information.

Recent evidence from electrophysiological studies cited above suggests that there

191

may be greater cortical irritability in the posterior portion of the left hemisphere, particularly in the parietal region, in patients with schizophrenia (77). While such data support arguments for parietal lobe involvement, they are circumstantial at best and not consistent with the evidence reviewed in this section emphasizing the right hemisphere. It is also not clear whether these as yet unreplicated observations involve IPL.

Other phenomenological associations between schizophrenia and parietal lobe damage include reports that patients with schizophrenia have deficits in cortical sensation (e.g. weight discrimination) and disturbances of body image (148 – 150), findings seen in patients with parietal lobe dysfunction (151). A recent study comparing these two groups, however, concluded that the neuroanatomical substrates for these deficits may be quite different (151). While both patient groups were found to have deficits in weight discrimination, a double dissociation was found when the groups were compared on tactile discrimination and body image tests. Only the group with parietal damage had deficits in tactile discrimination as measured by the Finger Agnosia Test, and only the schizophrenic group were found to have a body image disturbance when reality factors were taken into account in the brain damage group. These investigators concluded that the proprioceptive deficits in parietal syndromes are due to impaired somatosensory systems, while the proprioceptive deficits in schizophrenia are not.

In summary, anatomical and behavioral considerations suggest a possible role of the IPL in schizophrenia. The IPL is associated with four major brain areas or systems also implicated in schizophrenia: the limbic system, the mesolimbic dopamine system, the dorsolateral prefrontal cortex, and the temporal neocortex. IPL damage, especially in the right hemisphere, causes disturbances of selective attention and affect which bear a phenomenological resemblance to some clinical features of schizophrenia. The major weakness of the IPL theory is that it is totally speculative. There is almost no direct evidence bearing on this theory. Perhaps this is because the special role of the IPL and the right hemisphere in attention has only come to light in recent years, and so researchers have not yet specifically focused on this brain area. The theoretical arguments suggesting a possible role for IPL involvement, however, are persuasive enough that serious consideration should be given to this region in future investigations.

Anatomical interrelationships among brain areas implicated in schizophrenia

In this section, we will review some of the neuroanatomical relationships among the brain areas that have been cited. The view that the structures reviewed in this section form a well-integrated network is reinforced by a recently proposed neuropsychological model of how the brain regulates emotion (152). The list of brain structures implicated in this model included three cortical areas: prefrontal area, anterior and inferior temporal area, and the inferior parietal lobule; several structures in the limbic system, including cingulate gyrus, septum, hippocampus, and amygdala; and the reticular activating system, including its brain stem components.

It was proposed that damage to any one of these structures could disrupt essential neural feedback mechanisms, the consequence of which could be a psychiatric disorder like schizophrenia.

Cortico-cortical connections

The three major neocortical association areas implicated in schizophrenia (i.e. the dorsolateral prefrontal cortex, inferior parietal lobule, and the anterior temporal neocortex) send direct, reciprocal projections to each other (21, 53, 62, 76). In addition they converge on limbic cortex in the cingulate gyrus and parahippocampal gyrus, which thereby connects them to hippocampus, amygdala, and hypothalamus (21, 53, 62, 77).

Frontal, temporal, and parietal neocortex are mutually linked not only by direct connections, but also by important indirect routes. The uncinate fasciculus pathway connects the anterior temporal cortex (including the superior and middle temporal gyri, and to a lesser extent the inferior temporal gyri) to a large portion of frontal cortex (62). But the inferior temporal region is also connected specifically to the frontal cortex via the inferior thalamic peduncle and the dorsomedial nucleus of the thalamus (53). In the monkey, the inferior parietal lobule has a prominent direct connection to the ventral bank of the principle sulcus in the caudal frontal region in and around the 'frontal eye fields' (53). The principle sulcus region loosely corresponds to DLPFC in man. Since the inferior parietal lobule has extensive projections to the superior, middle, and inferior temporal gyri, other potential parietal-frontal pathways would be the temporo-uncinate fasciculus, temporo-thalamic, and temporo-amygdalo-thalamic pathways (62). The superior parietal lobule, on the other hand, has more limited connections with the temporal and frontal lobes (62).

The corpus callosum, the largest fiber bundle in the brain, provides the major link between mostly homologous neocortical areas in the left and right hemispheres (27). However, portions of the prefrontal cortex and inferior parietal lobule are not linked with the contralateral hemisphere (27), suggesting extreme lateralization of function in these areas. The anterior commissure is the interhemispheric connection for the amygdalae and portions of the anterior temporal lobe, while the hippocampal commissure joins the paired hippocampal formations (27, 155 – 158).

Cortico-limbic connections

In addition to their close association with the cingulate gyrus, parahippocampal gyrus, and hippocampus, each of these three neocortical areas share relationships with other limbic structures, particularly the amygdala (53, 146, 154, 158). The anterior temporal neocortex, especially the inferior temporal area, is reciprocally connected with the amygdala (53). The prefrontal cortex has both direct and indirect connections with the amygdala (146). The indirect connections are by way of an inferior temporo-uncinate fasciculus pathway, and by a thalamic pathway via the DMN. Although both the dorsolateral and orbital prefrontal areas have connections

193

with the amygdala (146, 154), the link to orbital prefrontal area by way of the temporal lobe is considered the primary connection (53).

The inferior parietal lobule also is linked to the amygdala by virtue of its extensive temporal lobe connections (62). In addition, the inferior parietal lobule is associated with the amygdala by indirect pathways through the substantia innominata. The inferior parietal lobule receives cholinergic innervation from the substantia innominata which in turn receives projections from the nucleus accumbens septi (39, 52). The substantia innominata also receives projections from the olfactory tubercle, the bed nucleus of the stria terminalis, the amygdala, and the peripeduncular nucleus, the latter structure being associated with auditory pathways (37). The basal nucleus of Meynert, which is part of the substantia innominata, has cholinergic projections to the entire cerebral cortex, as well as to the amygdala, hypothalamus, septum, habenula, ventral tegmental area, and the olfactory bulb (159 – 163). The nucleus accumbens receives inputs from both the amygdala and hippocampus, and also receives dopaminergic innervation from the ventral tegmental area (164, 165).

Limbic-subcortical connections

The limbic structures are intimately linked together and also closely connected with diencephalic and mesencephalic brain regions which are themselves intimately linked (83). Both the hippocampus and amygdala (interconnected limbic components in the temporal lobe) (166 – 169), have direct connections with the septum and hypothalamus (35, 158, 169), and as previously mentioned, with the nucleus accumbens septi (53). The septum and hypothalamus are also directly linked together (158, 169). The hypothalamus also has direct connections with the olfactory system (piriform cortex and olfactory tubercle), brain stem structures (midbrain tegmentum and central gray), other diencephalic nuclei (subthalamic region and thalamus), basal ganglia (substantia innominata-nucleus basalis of Meynert, and globus pallidus), and prefrontal neocortex (168). The amygdala also has connections with the olfactory bulb, thalamus, and midbrain (168).

The major pathways connecting the hippocampus, amygdala, and septum to the hypothalamus are the fornix, stria terminalis, and medial forebrain bundle, respectively (158, 166). The fornix connects the hippocampus to the septum, thalamus, and midbrain in addition to the mammillary body and lateral hypothalamus (158, 166). One of the better defined cholinergic pathways in the brain goes from septum to hippocampus (170, 171). The mammillothalamic tract projects from the mammillary bodies to the anterior nucleus of the thalamus which connects with the cingulate gyrus (34, 166). The amygdala is linked to the hypothalamus not only by the stria terminalis, but also by the ventral amygdalofugal pathway (17, 154). The amygdala and septal area are connected by both the stria terminalis and the diagonal band of Broca, and the septal area and habenula are connected by the stria medullaris (166). The anterior commissure interconnects the amygdala in the right and left hemispheres, and the hippocampal commissure joins the hippocampal formation in the two hemispheres (27). The medial forebrain bundle not only connects the septum and hypothalamus with each other, but also connects both structures directly to the midbrain tegmentum, and the hypothalamus with the orbitofrontal cortex (158, 169). Two other major fiber groups connecting the hypothalamus with the brainstem reticular formation are the mammillary peduncle and the dorsal longitudinal fasciculus (169).

Prefrontal-subcortical connections

The prefrontal cortex is the only neocortical area to send direct projections to the hypothalamus, preoptic region, septum, locus ceruleus, and raphe nuclei — the latter two brainstem structures receive projections only from the dorsolateral and dorsomedial regions of the prefrontal cortex (146, 172). While the frontal, temporal, and parietal neocortical areas all have multiple associations with the limbic system, only the prefrontal cortex projects to the same subcortical areas to which limbic structures project (53, 146). The prefrontal cortex receives direct afferents from the cingulate gyrus, amygdala, hypothalamus, hippocampus, thalamus, and midbrain tegmentum (146). The prefrontal cortex has additional links with the following limbic-related structures via the dorsomedial nucleus of the thalamus: the prepiriform cortex, septal area, amygdala, hypothalamus, ventral tegmental area, and the midbrain reticular formation (146).

The three major brainstem connections to the prefrontal cortex are the dopaminergic projections from the ventral tegmental area, the serotonergic projections from the raphe nuclei, and the noradrenergic projections from the locus ceruleus (146, 153, 172, 173). The raphe nuclei and locus ceruleus innervate widespread areas of cortex but receive a selective dorsal prefrontal cortical projection, whereas the ventral tegmental area and the substantia nigra primarily innervate the cingulate and prefrontal cortex but receive afferents from widespread cortical areas (172). The mesocortical dopamine system arises in cell bodies in the ventral tegmental area and substantia nigra and selectively innervates the prefrontal, anterior temporal, cingulate, piriform, and entorrhinal cortices (20, 21). The prefrontal cortex receives cholinergic input from the basal nucleus of Meynert as do other areas of the cerebral cortex, amygdala, septum, olfactory bulb, and ventral tegmental areas (37).

Two separate prefrontal areas are connected to the hypothalamus: the caudal orbitofrontal region and posterior DLPFC. It is the inferior thalamic peduncle via the dorsomedial nucleus of the thalamus which connects the orbital prefrontal cortex with the hypothalamus, inferior temporal region, and the prepiriform cortex (53). The olfactory input received from prepiriform cortex makes the frontal lobes the only neocortical region where sensory information from four sensory modalities converges (i.e. olfactory, visual, auditory, and tactile) (53). The prefrontal cortex, like other cortical areas, sends extensive efferent projections to the basal ganglia, including the caudate (especially the head of the caudate), putamen, globus pallidus, claustrum, and substantia nigra (53, 146, 153). Unlike most prefrontal projections, the efferent projects to the basal ganglia are unreciprocated (147).

Striatal connections

The dorsal striatum consisting of the caudate and putamen is distinguished from the ventral or limbic striatum which includes the nucleus accumbens, olfactory tubercle, and the bed nucleus of the stria terminalis (19, 61, 174). Both the dorsal striatum and the limbic striatum receive dopaminergic input from cell bodies in the brainstem. The caudate and putamen receive dopaminergic input from the substantia nigra via the nigrostriatal tract, whereas the limbic striatum is innervated by the mesolimbic dopamine system originating in the ventral tegmental area (Tsai) and ascending via the medial forebrain bundle (19, 61, 173). The mesolimbic dopamine system also projects to the amygdala, and both the amygdala and prefrontal cortex project to most of the striatum (19, 75, 173, 174).

The caudate and putamen are closely linked to the sensory and sensorimotor areas of the neocortex (61, 174). The limbic striatum, on the other hand, receives its major input from structures in the limbic system (19, 61, 75). The amygdala projects to the bed nucleus of the stria terminalis, the hippocampus to the nucleus accumbens, and piriform cortex to the olfactory tubercle (19). The nucleus accumbens sends projections to the substantia innominata which then projects to the frontal lobe and hypothalamus (19).

Comment

The diversity of brain areas and structures implicated in schizophrenia can be viewed as an integrated network of neural sytems. Reciprocally connected neocortical areas (i.e. prefrontal, temporal, and inferior parietal cortex) have links with inter-related structures of the limbic system (e.g. hippocampus, amygdala, and septum) which in turn are closely associated with the hypothalamus and the brainstem (including the reticular activating system), all of which have cortical connections, especially to prefrontal cortex. Although this discussion has focused on brain systems implicated in schizophrenia in particular, these systems are, in fact, those viewed as fundamental to emotional and cognitive behavior in general. Given the complexity of such behaviors, it is not surprising that the neural systems associated with them are numerous and tightly interwoven.

Site(s) of the lesion: single, variable, or multiple?

It is important to make the distinction between putative dysfunctional systems and alleged lesion sites in schizophrenia. The clinical symptoms and functional deficits of schizophrenia suggest that many brain systems may in fact be dysfunctional. But since these structures and systems form an integrated network, it is conceivable that damage at a single strategic location could cause widespread dysfunction, especially if the damage occurred during the ontological development of these systems.

The high degree of connectivity suggests that almost any location in this network could be considered a site of the lesion in schizophrenia. But on the basis of neuroanatomical considerations alone, a good case can be made that the prefrontal cortex is the leading candidate for a single lesion site. Although there are multiple interconnections among the diverse structures hypothesized in schizophrenia, the prefrontal cortex has more extensive, direct, and reciprocal connections with the implicated neural structures than any other brain area (35, 146, 153, 169).

It may also be that any one of several sites is sufficient to cause some variant of schizophrenia. Different lesion sites within this network or variation in the degree of damage may be responsible for different clinical subtypes, consistent with the clinical heterogeneity of the disorder. Other factors that may contribute to heterogeneity include time of onset of the injury, its exact etiology, and secondary psychosocial factors which probably interact with the underlying cerebral deficit. The variability and nonspecificity of the abnormal sites found in neuropathological studies of schizophrenic brains (4) is consistent with a 'variable site' theory.

New directions for research

In the last decade there have been revolutionary advances in the technologies associated with virtually every branch of the neurosciences. These technological advances afford us the opportunity to answer questions which could previously only be speculated about. The pneumoencephalogram and depth electrode recordings (176) provided important early clues about the condition of the brain in schizophrenia, but these techniques fell into disfavor because of their inherent invasiveness and risk (6, 12). The development of newer technologies, such as X-ray computerized tomography (CT), positron emission tomography (PET), nuclear magnetic resonance (NMR) imaging and regional cerebral blood flow (rCBF), are not only less invasive but more powerful and versatile techniques for studying directly during life brain structure and function. Advances in post mortem histopathology (38) and histochemistry have made it possible to detect subtle neuropathological and neurochemical abnormalities in autopsied brains. These new approaches are detailed elsewhere in this volume.

In the rapidly developing field of clinical neuropsychology, the single 'psychological' test approach is being replaced by the increasing use of comprehensive neuropsychological test batteries (177, 178). These test batteries provide more reliable, valid, sensitive, and complete information regarding the severity, extent, and nature of deficits in adaptive functioning, and also some clues regarding the lateralization and localization of the underlying cerebral dysfunction (178 – 180). A recent important development in the field has been the increasing attention given to the question of subcortical brain damage. A better understanding of the neuropsychological sequelae of subcortical lesions is important if the implications of functional and dysfunctional neuroanatomical and neurochemical systems in schizophrenia are to be understood.

REFERENCES

1. Kraepelin E (1971) *Dementia Praecox and Paraphrenia* (facsimile 1919 edition). R.E. Krieger Publishing Company, New York, NY.
2. Bleuler EP (1930) The physiogenic and psychogenic in schizophrenia. *Am. J. Psychiatry, 87,* 203.
3. Freud S (1964) *Analysis terminable and interminable, Vol. 23,* pp. 216 – 253. (Standard edition of the complete psychological works of Sigmund Freud). Hogarth Press, Ltd., Toronto.
4. Weinberger DR, Wagner RL, Wyatt RJ (1983) Neuropathological studies in schizophrenia: A selective review. *Schizophr. Bull., 9,* 193.
5. Davison K, Bagley CR (1969) Schizophrenia-like psychoses associated with organic disorders of the central nervous system: A review of the literature. *Br. J. Psychiatry, Special Publication No. 4,* 113.
6. Seidman LJ (1983) Schizophrenia and brain dysfunction: An integration of recent diagnostic findings. *Psychol. Bull., 94,* 195.
7. Moruzzi G, Magoun HW (1949) Brain stem reticular formation and activation of the EEG. *Electroencephalogr. Clin. Neurophysiol., 1,* 455.
8. Mirsky AF (1969) Neuropsychological bases of schizophrenia. *Ann. Rev. Psychol., 20,* 321.
9. Olds J (1956) Pleasure centers in the brain. *Sci. Am., 195,* 105.
10. Stein L, Wise CD (1971) Possible etiology of schizophrenia: progressive damage to the noradrenergic reward system by 6-hydroxydopamine. *Science, 171,* 1032.
11. MacLean PD (1952) Some psychiatry implications of physiological studies on frontotemporal portion of limbic system (visceral brain). *Electroencephalogr. Clin. Neurophysiol., 4,* 407.
12. Torrey EF, Peterson MR (1974) Schizophrenia and the limbic system. *Lancet, 2,* 942.
13. Weinberger DR (1984) CAT scan findings in schizophrenia: Speculation on the meaning of it all. *J. Psychiatr. Res., 18,* 477.
14. Davis JM (1985) Antipsychotic drugs. In: Kaplan HI, Sadock BJ (Eds), *Comprehensive Textbook of Psychiatry, 4th Ed., Vol. 2, Ch 30,* pp. 481 – 513. Williams and Wilkins, London.
15. Eccles Sir J (1965) The synapse. *Sci. Am., 212,* 56.
16. Brown RP, Mann JJ (1985) A clinical perspective on the role of neurotransmitters in mental disorders. *Hosp. Commun. Psychiatry, 36,* 141.
17. Snyder SH (1980) *Biological Aspects of Mental Disorder.* Oxford University Press, New York.
18. Lidsky TI, Weinhold PM, Levine FM (1979) Implications of basal ganglionic dysfunction for schizophrenia. *Biol. Psychiatry, 14,* 3.
19. Stevens JR (1973) An anatomy of schizophrenia? *Arch. Gen. Psychiatry, 29,* 177.
20. Glowinski J, Tassin JP, Theirry AM (1984) The mesocortico-prefrontal dopaminergic neurons. *Trends Neurosci., 7,* 415.
21. Goldman-Rakic PS (1984) The frontal lobes: uncharted provinces of the brain. *Trends Neurosci., 7,* 425.
22. Heaton RK, Baade LE, Johnson KL (1978) Neuropsychological test results associated with psychiatric disorders in adults. *Psychol. Bull., 85,* 141.
23. Goldstein G (1978) Cognitive and perceptual differences between schizophrenics and organics. *Schizophr. Bull., 4,* 160.

24. Malec J (1978) Neuropsychological assessment of schizophrenia versus brain damage: A review. *J. Nerv. Ment. Dis., 166,* 507.
25. Parfitt DN (1956) The neurology of schizophrenia. *J. Ment. Sci., 102,* 671.
26. Penfield W, Jasper H (1954) *Epilepsy and the Functional Anatomy of the Human Brain.* Little Brown, Boston.
27. Kolb B, Whisaw IQ (1980) *Fundamentals of Human Neuropsychology.* W.H. Freeman and Company, San Francisco.
28. Hughlings-Jackson J (1932) Remarks on dissolution of the nervous system as exemplified by certain post-epileptic conditions. In: Taylor J (Ed.), *Selected Writings of John Hughlings-Jackson, Vol. 2.* Hodder and Stoughton, London.
29. Strauss JS, Carpenter WT Jr, Bartko JJ (1974) The diagnosis and understanding of schizophrenia. Part III. Speculations on the processes that underlie schizophrenic symptoms and signs. *Schizophr. Bull., 11,* 61.
30. Crow TJ (1980) Positive and negative schizophrenic symptoms – the role of dopamine. Br. *J.* Psychiatry, 137, 383.
31. Andreasen NC, Olsen S (1982) Negative versus positive schizophrenia. *Arch. Gen. Psychiatry, 39,* 789.
32. Pogue-Gelle MF, Harrow M (1984) Negative and positive symptoms in schizophrenia and depression: A followup. *Schizophr. Bull., 10,* 371.
33. Greenblatt M, Solomon HC (1953) *Frontal Lobes and Schizophrenia – Second Lobotomy Project of Boston Psychopathic Hospital.* Springer Publishing Company, New York.
34. Girgis M (1971) The orbital surface of the frontal lobe of the brain and mental disorders. *Acta Psychiatr. Scand., Suppl. 222,* 1.
35. Fulton JF (1951) *Frontal Lobotomy and Affective Behavior.* W.W. Norton and Company, New York.
36. Levin S (1984) Frontal lobe dysfunction in schizophrenia – I. Eye movement impairments. *J. Psychiatr. Res., 18,* 27.
37. Levin S (1984) Frontal lobe dysfunction in schizophrenia – II. Impairments of psychological and brain functions. *J. Psychiatr. Res., 18,* 57.
38. Mesulam MM (1981) A cortical network for directed attention and unilateral neglect. *Ann. Neurol., 10,* 309.
39. Matthysse S (1977) Dopamine and selective attention. In: Costa E, Gessa GL (Eds), *Advances in Biochemical Psychopharmacology, Vol. 16,* pp. 667 – 669. Raven Press, New York.
40. Holtzman PS, Levy DL 1977: Smooth pursuit eye movements and functional psychoses. *Schizophr. Bull., 3,* 15.
41. Goldberg E (1985) Akinesia, tardive dysmentia, and frontal lobe disorder in schizophrenia. *Schizophr. Bull., 11,* 255.
42. Rifkin A, Quitkin F, Klein DF (1975) Akinesia. *Arch. Gen. Psychiatry, 32,* 672.
43. Rifkin A, Quitkin F, Kane J, Struve F, Klein D (1978) Are prophylactic antiparkinson drugs necessary? *Arch. Gen. Psychiatry, 35,* 483.
44. Wilson JC, Garbutt JC, Lanier CF, Moylan J, Nelson W, Prange AJ Jr (1983) Is there a tardive dysmentia? *Schizophr. Bull., 9,* 187.
45. Lindvall O, Bjorklund A, Moore RY, Stenevi V (1974) Mesencephalic dopamine neurons projection to neocortex. *Brain Res., 81,* 325.
46. MacBrown R, Goldman PS (1977) Catecholamines in neocortex of rhesus monkey: Original distribution and ontogenetic development. *Brain Res., 124,* 576.

47. Brown RM, Crane AM, Goldman PS (1979) Regional distribution of monoamines in the cerebral cortex and subcortical structures of the rhesus monkey: Concentrations and in vivo synthesis rates. *Brain Res., 168,* 133.
48. Tassin JP, Stinus L, Simon H, Blanc G, Theirry AM, LeMoal M, Gardo B, Glowinski J (1978) Relationship between the locomotor hyperactivity induced by A10 lesions and the destruction of the fronto-cortical dopaminergic innervation in the rat. *Brain Res., 141,* 267.
49. Simon H, Scratten B, LeMoal M (1980) Dopaminergic A10 neurones are involved in cognitive functions. *Nature (London), 286,* 150.
50. Oades RD (1982) Search strategies on a holeboard are impaired in rats with ventral tegmental damage: Animal model for test of thought disorder. *Biol. Psychiatry, 2,* 243.
51. Goldberg E, Mattis S, Hughes JEO, Antin P (1982) *Frontal syndrome without a frontal lesion: A case study.* Paper presented at the Fifth European Meeting of the International Neuropsychological Society, Deauville, France.
52. Ingvar DH (1980) Abnormal distribution of cerebral activity in chronic schizophrenia: A neurophysiological interpretation. In: Baxter C, Melnechuk T (Eds), *Perspectives in Schizophrenia Research,* pp. 107–130. Raven Press, New York.
53. Nauta WJH (1971) The problem of the frontal lobe: A reinterpretation. *J. Psychiatr. Res., 8,* 167.
54. Bleuler E (1950) *Dementia Praecox or the Group of Schizophrenias.* New York International Press, New York.
55. Pycock CJ, Kerwin RW, Carter CJ (1980) Effect of lesion of cortical dopamine terminals on subcortical dopamine receptors in rats. *Nature (London), 286,* 74.
56. Bannon MJ, Roth RH (1983) Pharmacology of mesocortical dopamine neurons. *Pharmacol. Rev., 35,* 53.
57. Achte KA, Hillbom E, Aalberg V (1969) Psychoses following war brain injuries. *Acta Psychiatr. Scand., 45,* 1.
58. Birnie CR (1966) The frontal lobes and psychoses. *Int. J. Neuropsychiatry, 2,* 27.
59. Avery TL (1971) Seven cases of frontal tumor with psychiatric presentation. *Br. J. Psychiatry, 119,* 19.
60. Selecki BR (1965) Intracranial space-occupying lesions among patients admitted to mental hospitals. *Med. J. Australia, 1,* 383.
61. Hecaen H (1964) Mental symptoms associated with tumours of the frontal lobe. In: Warren JM, Akert K (Eds), *The Frontal Granular Cortex and Behavior,* pp. 335–352. McGraw-Hill, New York.
62. Hecaen H, Albert ML (1978) *Human Neuropsychology.* John Wiley and Sons, New York.
63. Rosenbaum JF, Rothman RS, Murray GB (1979) Psychosis and water intoxication. *J. Clin. Psychiatry, 40,* 287.
64. Caine ED, Hunt RD, Weingartner H, Ebert MH (1978) Huntington's dementia: Clinical and neuropsychological features. *Arch. Gen. Psychiatry, 35,* 377.
65. Caine ED, Shoulson I (1983) Psychiatric syndromes of Huntington's disease. *Am. J. Psychiatry, 140,* 728.
66. McHugh PR, Folstein MF (1975) Psychiatric syndromes of Huntington's chorea: A clinical and phenomenologic study. In: Benson DF, Blumer D (Eds), *Psychiatric Aspects of Neurological Diseases,* pp. 267–287. Grune and Stratton, New York.
67. Flor-Henry P (1976) Lateralized temporal-limbic dysfunction and psychopathology. *Ann. N.Y. Acad. Sci., 280,* 777.

68. Flor-Henry P (1983) Neuropsychological studies in patients with psychiatric disorders. In: Heilman KM, Satz P (Eds), *Neuropsychology of Human Emotion,* pp. 193 – 220. The Guildford Press, New York.

69. Kolb B, Whishaw IQ (1983) Performance of schizophrenic patients on tests sensitive to left or right frontal temporal parietal function in neurological patients. *J. Nerv. Ment. Dis., 171,* 435.

70. Taylor MA, Abrams R (1984) Cognitive impairment in schizophrenia. *Am. J. Psychiatry, 141,* 196.

71. Golden CJ, Purisch A, Hammeke T (1979) *The standardized Luria-Nebraska Neuropsychological Battery: A Manual for Clinical and Experimental Uses.* University of Nebraska Press, Lincoln, NE.

72. Abrams R, Taylor MA (1979) Differential EEG patterns in affective disorder and schizophrenia. *Arch. Gen. Psychiatry, 36,* 1355.

73. Abrams R, Taylor MA (1980) Psychopathology and the electroencephalogram. *Biol. Psychiatry, 15,* 871.

74. Franzen G, Ingvar DH (1975) Abnormal distribution of cerebral activity in chronic schizophrenia. *J. Psychiatr. Res., 12,* 199.

75. Ingvar DH, Franzen G (1974) Abnormalities of cerebral blood flow distribution in patients with chronic schizophrenia. *Acta Psychiatr. Scand., 50,* 425.

76. Ingvar DH, Franzen G (1974) Distribution of cerebral activity in chronic schizophrenia. *Lancet 2,* 1484.

77. Morihisa JM, Duffy FH, Wyatt RJ (1983) Brain electrical activity mapping (BEAM) in schizophrenic patients. *Arch. Gen. Psychiatry, 40,* 719.

78. Mostyn R, Duffy FH, McCarley RW (1983) Altered topography of EEG spectral content in schizophrenia. *Electroencephalogr. Clin. Neurol., 56,* 263.

79. Buchsbaum MS, Cappelletti J, Coppolo R, et al. (1982) New methods to determine the CNS effects of antigeriatric compounds: EEG topography and glucose use. *Drug Dev. Res., 2,* 489.

80. Itil TM, Saletu B, Davis S (1972) EEG findings in chronic schizophrenics based on digital computer period analysis and analog power spectra. *Biol. Psychiatry, 5,* 1.

81. Stevens JR, Livermore A (1982) Telemetered EEG in schizophrenia: Spectral analysis during abnormal behavior episodes. *J. Neurol. Neurosurg. Psychiatry, 45,* 385.

82. Fenton GW, Fenwick PBC, Dollimore J, Dunn TL, Hirsch SR (1980) EEG spectral analysis in schizophrenia. *Br. J. Psychiatry, 136,* 445.

83. Giannitrapani D (1979) Spatial organization of the EEG in normal and schizophrenic subjects. *Electroencephalogr. Clin. Neurophysiol., 19,* 125.

84. Scott DF, Schwartz MS (1975) EEG features of depressive and schizophrenic states. *Br. J. Psychiatry, 126,* 408.

85. Rodin E, Grisell J, Gottlieb J (1968) Some electrographic differences between chronic schizophrenic patients and normal subjects. In: Wortis J (Ed.), *Recent Advances in Biological Psychiatry,* pp. 194 – 204. Plenum Press, New York.

86. Milstein V, Stevens J, Sachdev K (1974) Habituation of the alpha attentuation response in children and adults with psychiatric disorders. *Electroencephalogr. Clin. Neurophysiol., 36,* 377.

87. Morihisa JM, McAnulty GB (1985) Structure and function: Brain electrical activity mapping and computer tomography in schizophrenia. *Biol. Psychiatry, 20,* 3.

88. Morstyn R, Duffy FH, McCarley RW (1983) Altered P300 topography in schizophrenia. *Arch. Gen. Psychiatry, 40,* 729.

89. Buchsbaum MS, Ingvar DH, Kessler R, Waters RN, Cappelletti J, van Kammen DP, King AC, Johnson JL, Manning RG, Flynn RW, Mann LS, Bunney WE, Sokoloff L (1982) Cerebral glucography with positron tomography: Use in normal subjects and in patients with schizophrenia. *Arch. Gen. Psychiatry, 39,* 251.

90. Farkas T, Wolf AP, Jaeger J, Brodie JD, Christman DR, Fowler LS (1984) Regional brain glucose metabolism in chronic schizophrenia: A positron emission transaxial tomographic study. *Arch. Gen. Psychiatry, 41,* 293.

91. Delisi LE, Buchsbaum MS, Holcomb HH, Dowling-Zimmerman S, Pickar D, Boronow J, Morihisa JM, van Kammen DP (1983) Clinical correlates of decreased anteroposterior metabolic gradients in positron emission tomography (PET) of schizophrenic patients. *Am. J. Psychiatry, 142,* 7.

92. Katzman R (1985) The biology of Alzheimer disease: Clinical and neuropsychological implications. Paper presented at the 13th Annual International Neuropsychology Meeting. San Diego, California.

93. Buchsbaum MS, Delisi LE, Holcomb HH (1984) Anteroposterior gradients in cerebral glucose use in schizophrenia and affective disorders. *Arch. Gen. Psychiatry, 41,* 1159.

94. Sheppard G, Gruzelier J, Manchanda R, Hirsch JR, Wise R, Frackowiak R, Jones T (1983) 150 positron emission tomography scanning in predominantly never treated acute schizophrenic patients. *Lancet, 2,* 1448.

95. Widen L, Blomgrist G, DePaulis T 1984: Studies of schizophrenia with positron CT. *J. Clin. Neuropharmacol., 7,* 538.

96. Kling AS, Kuhl DE, Metter EJ, Kurtz N, Phelps ME, Reiger W, Hullet J (1984) Positron computer tomography and CT scans in schizophrenia and depression. (NR Abstract No. 102). American Psychiatric Association Annual Meeting, Los Angeles.

97. Ariel RN, Golden CJ, Berg RA, Quaife MA, Dirksen JW, Forsell T, Wilson J, Graber B (1983) Regional cerebral blood flow in schizophrenia with the 133-Xenon inhalation method. *Arch. Gen. Psychiatry, 40,* 258.

98. Mubrin Z, Krezevic S, Koretic D, Lazic L, Javarnik N (1982) Regional cerebral blood flow patterns in schizophrenic patients. *Reg. Cereb. Blood Flow Bull., 3,* 43.

99. Mathew RJ, Duncan GC, Weinman ML, Barr DL (1982) Regional cerebral blood flow in schizophrenia. *Arch. Gen. Psychiatry, 39,* 1121.

100. Gur RE, Skolnick BE, Gur RC, Caroff S, Rieger W, Obrist WD, Younkin D, Reivich M (1983) Brain functions in psychiatric disorder: I. Regional cerebral blood flow in medicated schizophrenics. *Arch. Gen. Psychiatry, 40,* 1250.

101. Risberg J, Halsey HN Jr., Wills EL, Wilson EM (1975) Hemispheric specialization in normal man studied by bilateral measurements of the regional cerebral blood flow: A study with the 133-Xe inhalation technique. *Brain, 98,* 511.

102. Warren LR, Butler RW, Katholi CR, McFarland CE, Crews EL, Halsey JH Jr (1984) Focal changes in cerebral blood flow produced by monetary incentive during a mental mathematics task in normal and depressed subjects. *Brain Cogn., 3,* 71.

103. Weinberger DR, Berman KF, Zec RF (1985) Physiological dysfunction of dorsolateral prefrontal cortex in schizophrenia. I. Regional cerebral blood flow (rCBF) evidence. *Arch. Gen. Psychiatry, 43,* 114.

104. Berman KF, Zec RF, Weinberger DR (1985) Physiological dysfunction of dorsolateral pre-frontal cortex in schizophrenia: II. Role of neuroleptic treatment, attention, and mental effort. *Arch. Gen. Psychiatry, 43,* 126.

105. Milner B (1971) Interhemispheric differences in the localization of psychological processes in man. *Br. Med. Bull., 27,* 272.

106. Milner B (1963) Effects of different brain lesions on card sorting. *Arch. Neurol., 9*, 90.
107. Malmo HB (1974) On frontal lobe functions: Psychiatric patient controls. *Cortex, 10,* 231.
108. Bracha HS, Kleinman JE (1984) Post mortem studies in psychiatry. *Psychiatr. Clin. N. Am., 7,* 473.
109. McGeer PL, McGeer EG (1981) Neurotransmitters in the aging brain. In: Darrison AM, Thompson RHS (Eds), *The Molecular Basis of Neuropathology,* pp. 631 – 648. Edward Arnold, London.
110. Wong DF, Wagner JH Jr, Dannals RF, Links JM, Frost JJ, Ravert HT, Wilson Alan A, Rosenbaum AE, Gjedde A, Douglass KH, Petronis JK, Folstein MF, Toung JK, Burns DH, Kuhar MJ (1984) Effects of age on dopamine and serotonin receptors measured by positron emission tomography in the living human brain. *Science, 226,* 1393.
111. Alexander GE, Goldman PS (1978) Functional development of the dorsolateral prefrontal cortex: An analysis utilizing reversible cryogenic depression. *Brain Res., 143,* 233.
112. Zec RF, Weinberger DR (1986) The relationship between CT scan findings and neuro-psychological performance in chronic schizophrenia. *Psychiatr. Clin. North Am.,* in press.
113. Lindsley DB, Bowden JW, Magoun HW (1949) Effect upon the EEG of acute injury to the brain stem activating system. *Electroencephalogr. Clin. Neurophysiol., 1,* 475.
114. Blum RH (1957) Alpha-rhythm responsiveness in normal, schizophrenic, and brain-damaged persons. *Science, 126,* 749.
115. McGhie A (1972) Attention and perception in schizophrenia. In: Cancro (Ed.), *Annual Review of the Schizophrenic Syndrome, Vol 2.* Brunner-Mazel, New York.
116. Fish F (1961) A neurophysiological theory of schizophrenia. *J. Ment. Sci., 107,* 828.
117. Venables PH (1964) Input dysfunction in schizophrenia. In: Maher BA (Ed.), *Progress in Experimental Personality Research,* pp. 1 – 47. Academic Press, New York.
118. Kornetsky C, Mirsky A (1966) On certain psychopharmacological and physiological differences between schizophrenics and normal persons. *Psychopharmacologia, 8,* 309.
119. Kornetsky C, Eliasson M (1969) Reticular stimulation and chlorpromazine: An animal model for schizophrenic overarousal. *Science, 165,* 1273.
120. Kornetsky C, Orzack MH (1978) Physiological and behavioral correlates of attention dysfunction in schizophrenic patients. *J. Psychiatr. Res., 14,* 69.
121. Scheibel ME, Scheibel AB (1962) Hallucinations and the brain stem reticular core. In: West (Ed.), *Hallucinations.* Grune and Stratton, New York.
122. Kleist K (1960) Schizophrenic symptoms and cerebral pathology. *J. Ment. Sci., 106,* 246.
123. Feinberg I (1969) Recent sleep research: Findings in schizophrenia and some possible implications for the mechanism of action of chlorpromazine and for the neurophysiology of delirium. In: Sankar (Ed.), *Schizophrenia – Current Concepts and Research.* PJD Publications, New York.
124. Brecher M, Begleiter H (1985) Brain stem auditory evoked potentials in unmedicated schizophrenic patients. *Biol. Psychiatry, 20,* 199.
125. Nieto D, Escobar A (1972) Major psychoses. In: Minckler J (Ed.), *Pathology of the Nervous System, Vol 3,* pp. 654 – 665. McGraw-Hill, New York.
126. Stevens JR (1982) Neuropathology of schizophrenia. *Arch. Gen. Psychiatry, 39,* 1131.
127. Fisman M (1975) The brain stem in psychosis. *Br. J. Psychiatry, 126,* 414.
128. Hankoff LD, Peress NS (1981) Neuropathology of the brain stem in psychiatric disorders. *Biol. Psychiatry, 16,* 945.

129. Mirsky AF (1978) Attention: A neuropsychological perspective. In: Chall JS, Mirsky AF (Eds), *Education and the Brain*, pp. 33 – 60. University of Chicago Press, Chicago, IL.

130. Mirsky AF, Bakay Pragay E (1983) Brainstem mechanisms in the processing of sensory information: Clinical symptoms, animal models and unit analysis. In: Sheer DE (Ed.), *Attention: Theory Brain Functions and Clinical Applications*. Earlbaum, Hillsdale, New Jersey.

131. Orzack MH, Kornetsky C (1966) Attention dysfunction in chronic schizophrenia. *Arch. Gen. Psychiatry, 14,* 323.

132. Wohlberg GW, Kornetsky C (1973) Sustained attention in remitted schizophrenics. *Arch. Gen. Psychiatry, 28,* 533.

133. Orzack MH, Kornetsky C (1971) Environmental and familial predictors of attention behavior in chronic schizophrenics. *J. Psychiatr. Res., 9,* 21.

134. Kornetsky C (1967) Attention dysfunction and drugs in schizophrenia. In: Brell H (Ed.), *Neuropsychopharmacology. Proceedings of the 5th International Colloqium Neuro-psycho-pharmacologicum.* Excerpta Medica Foundation, Amsterdam.

135. Bradley PB (1972) The action of drugs on single neurons in the brain. In: Bradley PB, Brimblecombe RW (Ed.), *Progress in Brain Research, Vol. 35,* p. 183. Elsevier, Amsterdam.

136. Mirsky AF, Oshima HI (1973) Effect of subcortical aluminum cream lesions on attentive behavior and the electroencephalogram in monkeys. *Electroencephalogr. Clin. Neurophysiol., 35,* 25.

137. Mirsky AF, Orren MM (1977) Attention. In: Miller LH, Sandman CA, Kastin AJ (Eds), *Neuropeptide Influences on the Brain and Behavior: Advances in Biochemical Psychopharmacology, Vol 17,* pp. 233 – 267. Raven Press, New York.

138. Stevens J (1978) Disturbances of ocular movements and blinking in schizophrenia. *J. Neurol. Neurosurg. Psychiatry, 41,* 1024.

139. Mesulam MM, Geschwind N (1978) On the possible role of neocortex and its limbic connections in the process of attention and schizophrenia: Clinical cases of inattention in man and experimental anatomy in monkey. *J. Psychiatr. Res., 14,* 249.

140. Geschwind N (1982) Disorders of attention: a frontier in neuropsychology. *Philos. Trans. R. Soc. London, 298,* 173.

141. Heilman KM, Watson RT, Valenstein E, Damasio AR (1983) Localization of lesions in neglect. In: Kertez A (Ed.), *Localization in Neuropsychology, Ch 20,* pp. 471 – 492. Academic Press, New York.

142. Schneider SJ (1976) Selective attention in schizophrenia. *J. Abnorm. Psychol., 85,* 167.

143. Venables PH (1977) Psychophysiology of Abnormal Behavior. *Br. Med. Bull., 37,* 199.

144. Lynch JC, Mountcastle VB, Talbot WH (1977) Parietal lobe mechanisms of directed visual attention. *J. Neurophysiol., 40,* 362.

145. Geschwind N (1964) The development of the brain and the evolution of language. In: Stuart CIJM (Ed.), *Report of the 15th Annual R.T.M. on Linguistic and Language Studies,* (Monograph Series on Languages and Linguistics, No. 17), pp. 155 – 169. Georgetown University Press, Washington, DC.

146. Fuster JM (1980) *The Prefrontal Cortex: Anatomy, Physiology, and Neuropsychology of the Frontal Lobe.* Raven Press, New York.

147. Petras JM (1971) Connections of the parietal lobe. *J Psychiatr. Res., 8,* 189.

148. Meehl PE (1962) Schizotaxia, schizotypy, and schizophrenia. *Am. Psychol., 17,* 827.

149. Rado S (1953) Dynamics and classification of disordered behavior. *Am. J. Psychiatry, 110,* 406.

150. Rosenbaum G (1971) Feedback mechanisms in schizophrenia. In: Tourney G, Gottlieb J (Eds), *Lafayette Clinic Studies in Schizophrenia.* Wayne State University Press, Detroit.
151. Erwin BJ, Rosenbaum G (1979) Parietal lobe syndrome and schizophrenia: Comparison of neuropsychological deficits. *J. Abnorm. Psychol., 88,* 234.
152. Schefft BK, Moses JA Jr, Schmidt GL (1985) Neuropsychology and emotion: A self-regulatory model. *Int. J. Clin. Neuropsychol., 7,* 207.
153. Stuss DT, Benson DF (1984) Neuropsychological studies of the frontal lobes. *Psychol. Bull., 95,* 3.
154. Singh MM (1985) Cholinergic Mechanisms, adaptive brain process and psychopathology: Commentary and a blueprint for research. In: Singh MM, Warburton DM, Lal H (Eds), *Central Cholinergic Mechanisms and Adaptive Dysfunction, Ch 12,* pp. 353–397. Plenum Press, New York.
155. Tinley F (1938) The hippocampus and its relations to the corpus callosum. *Bull. Neurol. Inst. N.Y., 7,* 1.
156. Blackstad TW (1956) Commissural connections of the hippocampal region of the rat, with special reference to their mode of termination. *J. Comp. Neurol., 105,* 417.
157. Jr GF Tucker, Alonso WA, Cowan M, Tucker JA, Druck N (1973) The anterior commissure revisited. *Ann. Otol. Rhinol. Laryngol., 82,* 625.
158. Isaacson RL (1982) *The Limbic System.* Plenum Press, New York.
159. Kievit J, Kuypers HGJM (1975) Basal forebrain and hypothalamic connections to frontal and parietal cortex in the rhesus monkey. *Science, 187,* 660.
160. Miodonski R (1967) Myeloarchitectonics and connections of substantia innominata in the dog brain. *Acta Biol. Excerpt., 27,* 61.
161. Jones EG, Burton H, Saper CB, Swanson LW (1976) Midbrain diencephalic and cortical relations of the basal nucleus of Meynert and associated structures in primates. *J. Comp. Neurol., 167,* 385.
162. Troiano R, Siegel A (1978) Efferent connections of the basal forebrain in the cat: The substantia innominata. *Exp. Neurol., 61,* 198.
163. Femano PA, Edinger HM, Siegel A (1979) Evidence of potent excitatory influence from substantia innominata on basolateral amygdaloid units: A comparison with insula-temporal cortex and lateral olfactory tract stimulation. *Brain Res., 177,* 361.
164. Swanson LW, Cowan WM (1975) Hippocampo-hypothalamic connections: Origin in subicular cortex, not Ammon's horn. *Science, 189,* 303.
165. Ungerstedt U (1971) Stereotaxic mapping of the monoamine pathways of the rat brain. *Acta Physiol. Scand., Suppl 367,* 1.
166. Everett NB (1971) *Functional Neuroanatomy, Sixth Edition.* Lea and Febiger, Philadelphia.
167. Rae AS (1969) Histology of the zone of contact between amygdala and hippocampus. *Confin. Neurol., 31,* 330.
168. Gloor P (1960) Amygdala. In: Field J (Ed.), *Handbook of Physiology, Section I. Neurophysiology, Vol 2,* pp. 1345–1372. Williams and Wilkins Co., Baltimore.
169. Nauta WJH, Haymaker W (1969) Hypothalamic nuclei and fiber connections. In: Haymaker W, Anderson E, Nauta WJH (Eds), *The Hypothalamus, Ch 4,* pp. 136–209. Charles C Thomas, Springfield, IL.
170. Robinson SE (1985) Cholinergic pathways in the brain. In: Singh MM, Warburton DM, Lal H (Eds), *Central Cholinergic Mechanisms and Adaptive Dysfunctions, Ch. 2,* pp. 37–61. Plenum Press, New York.

171. Lader M (1980) *Introduction to Psychopharmacology.* The Upjohn Company, Kalamazoo, MI.
172. Arnsten AFT, Goldman-Rakic PS (1984) Selective prefrontal cortical projections to the region of the locus coeruleus and raphe nuclei in the rhesus monkey. *Brain Res., 306,* 9.
173. Cotman CW, McGaugh JL (1980) *Behavioral Neuroscience.* Academic Press, London.
174. Mehler WR (1982) The basal ganglia — circa 1982. A review and commentary. In: Gildenberg AL (Ed.), *Applied Neurophysiology,* pp. 261 – 290. Karger, Basel.
175. Carlson NR (1977) *Physiology and Behavior.* Allyn and Bacon, Boston.
176. Heath RG (1970) Perspectives for Biological Psychiatry. *Biol. Psychiatry, 2,* 81.
177. Goldstein G (1984) Comprehensive Neuropsychological Assessment Batteries. In: Goldstein G, Hersen M (Eds), *Handbook of Psychological Assessment, Ch 10,* pp. 181 – 210. Pergamon Press, New York.
178. Gilandas A, Touyz S, Beumont PJV, Greenberg HP (1984) *Handbook of Neuropsychological Assessment.* Grune and Stratton, Orlando, FL.
179. Boll TJ (1981) In: Filskov SB, Boll TJ (Eds), *The Halstead-Reitan Neuropsychological Battery,* pp. 577 – 607. John Wiley and Sons, New York.
180. Golden CJ (1981) A standardized version of Luria's neuropsychological tests: A quantitative and qualitative approach to neuropsychological evaluation. In: Filskov SB, Boll TJ (Eds), *Handbook of Clinical Neuropsychology,* pp. 608 – 642. John Wiley and Sons, New York.

CHAPTER 9

X-ray computerized tomography studies in schizophrenia: a review and synthesis

RICHARD C. SHELTON AND DANIEL R. WEINBERGER

The first major advance in observing the actual structure of the brain in living subjects was the development early in this century of pneumoencephalography (1). This technique, in which the ventricular system and cortex are outlined on X-rays of the head by injecting air into the lumbar subarachnoid space, was used for better than half a century for studying abnormalities of brain structure in persons with schizophrenia (2, 3). Several observations were made in these studies, including that of enlargement of the lateral and third ventricle and atrophy of the cortical sulci. Furthermore, these findings appeared to co-vary with so-called defect symptoms (e.g. apathy, flattening of affect cognitive impairment, etc.), with a limited response to treatment, and with overall poor outcome, suggesting that such changes were markers of severity of the schizophrenic syndrome (3). The procedure was not without methodological problems, and was poorly suited to the study of psychiatric patients. Nevertheless, the findings do presage many of those later observed with computerized tomography (CT), a technique which, after its introduction in the early 1970s, quickly made pneumoencephalography obsolete.

The process of CT scanning involves the projection of X-rays through body structures in a flat plane by rotating the X-ray source around the subject. Images are created by a computer from X-ray attenuation information derived in this manner. The two-dimensional image is projected onto a screen or photographic plate, with individual points or 'pixels' in the picture corresponding to different tissue densities. The CT scan marked a major advance over previous methods of 'brain imaging' because it not only provided much improved image resolution, it also was noninvasive (except for radiation exposure). This made it particularly well suited to the study of psychiatric patients, as well as normal individuals needed to establish normative data.

Beginning with the report of Johnstone et al. (4) in 1976, literally dozens of CT studies of schizophrenia have emerged. Findings from these studies fall into six main areas which will be reviewed individually: lateral ventricular enlargement, third ventricular enlargement, increased cortical (sulcal) markings, cerebellar atrophy, reversed cerebral asymmetries, and abnormalities of brain density.

Handbook of Schizophrenia, Vol. 1: The Neurology of Schizophrenia.
H.A. Nasrallah and D.R. Weinberger, editors.
© Elsevier Science Publishers B.V., 1986.

Lateral ventricular enlargement

The lateral ventricles are cerebrospinal fluid-containing spaces in the brain bounded by structures such as the lenticular nuclei (caudate, putamen, and globus pallidus), thalamus, hypothalamus, hippocampus, fornix, and corpus callosum. These regions have been implicated in the neuropathology of schizophrenia (5), and certainly pathology of these structures could lead to increases in size of the ventricles. Lateral ventricular enlargement also can serve as a marker for more diffuse or distant pathology involving the central nervous system (CNS). Table 1 includes a partial list of conditions associated with diffuse changes on CT scan, including lateral ventricular enlargement. The non-specificity of ventricular enlargement has led some investigators to recommend caution in interpreting the findings (6, 7). Such caution is indeed warranted in evaluating any new research finding, but may fail to distinguish salient facts regarding the CT changes. Abnormalities on CT scans are not simply markers of putative CNS changes, they do in almost all instances indicate abnormalities of brain structure. Unlike peripheral markers of a putative brain disorder, CT changes are direct, first order approximations of CNS pathology (3, 8, 9). Similar CT changes have been observed in some cases of other psychiatric conditions such as affective disorder (7, 10 – 21), anorexia nervosa (22), and post-traumatic syndromes (23). This apparent lack of specificity has prompted some to argue against the importance of such CT findings in schizophrenia. In response to this argument is the fact that many etiologically and pathologically unrelated disorders have a common pattern of CT abnormalities. Perhaps what is most strik-

TABLE 1   *Conditions associated with generalized atrophic changes on CT scans*

Neurological	*Medical*
Epilepsy	Nutritional deficiencies
Migraine	Cushing disease
Parkinson's disease	Steroids
Huntington's disease	Intoxicants:
Wilson's disease	alcohol
Post-encephalitic states	solvents
Multiple sclerosis	heavy metals
Alzheimer's disease	Radiation exposure
Multi-infarct dementia	
Head injury	*Psychiatric*
Systemic lupus erythematosus	
Other degenerative CNS conditions	Schizophrenia
	Affective disorders
Other	Anorexia nervosa
	Post-traumatic syndromes
Normal aging	

ing is that abnormalities are seen in a variety of so-called 'functional' disorders and this may well indicate that all are associated with underlying pathological processes in the brain.

Methodological issues

Figure 1 demonstrates 'normal' and pathologically enlarged lateral ventricles in schizophrenic patients. Usually, such alterations are not so obvious. In fact, the CT scans of most schizophrenic patients are read as normal by neuroradiologists. The usual case involves subtle alterations of anatomy and requires special techniques of evaluation and comparison with control populations. Several methods have been devised to assess ventricular dimensions on CT scans. Linear measurements of ventricular size as a proportion of brain width were introduced to evaluate pneumoencephalograms. Evans (24), by dividing the width of the anterior horns of the lateral ventricles (easily seen on pneumoencephalograms) by the maximum width of the brain, created a ratio to assess ventricular size. Similarly, Huckman et al. (25) proposed an anterior horn span/brain width ratio for use with CT. Hansson et al. (26) used the anterior horn width/inner skull diameter ratios. Lastly, the so-called cella media index, a CT derived ratio of the maximum width of the bodies of the lateral ventricles and the brain width has been frequently cited (27). Such linear measurements, though quick and simple to determine, do not correlate well with

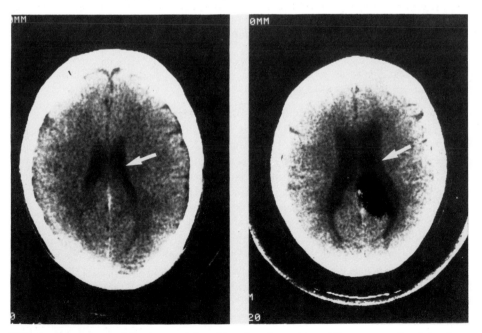

FIG. 1   *Lateral ventricles (arrows) in schizophrenic patients. The scan on the right shows clear enlargement.*

ventricular volumes and are not sensitive to suble changes (28). A more sensitive and reliable method is the lateral ventricular brain ratio (VBR) technique and variations thereof. VBR is an area measure that correlates well with total volume and is sensitive to small changes (28, 32). As first described by Synek and Reuben (29) in 1976, the area measurement is made with a planimeter, an engineering device used to measure circumscribed two-dimensional areas. The outlines of the lateral ventricles and brain are traced and the area contained within the ventricles is divided by the total area of the brain. This ratio is (usually) multiplied by 100, giving the VBR as a percentage value. Other techniques include tracing the outlines of the ventricles and brain on a video screen using a cursor linked to a computer to derive the ratios, and the use of CT pixel density numbers theoretically corresponding to ventricles and brain tissue to derive similar ratios (31). Each of these VBR techniques has certain errors. For example, errors can be introduced into the density number method (here and described below) from variations in energy transmitted via X-ray, thickness of the skull, scan artifacts, and changes over time in operation of the machinery (30 – 33). Another error involves the so-called 'partial volume effect.' Since the scan itself is a two-dimensional representation of a three-dimensional 'slice' of at least 5 millimeters thickness, the image is a 'compression' of the structures within that slice. Looking at the ventricles on a given scan, one might see within them evidence of both fluid *and* tissue. This 'partial volume' effect is a source of measurement variability (33). If the margins of the ventricles are outlined without consideration of the tissues 'within,' a spuriously large estimation of volume will result. This problem can be partially overcome with manual planimetry by excluding part of the area of the ventricle containing extra tissue, thereby compensating for the partial-volume effect.

Studies

We have reviewed 36 studies of lateral ventricular size on CT in schizophrenia; the results are summarized in Table 2. Of the 35 studies comparing schizophrenic patients to a non-psychiatric control population, 26 (about 75%) show significant enlargement in patients. As cited by Andreasen et al. (45), Jernigan et al. (50), and others, the differences between groups seems to be based on three factors: method of measurement, control group, and patient selection.

As discussed above, linear measures of ventricular size tend to underestimate subtle degrees of enlargement. Though it is possible to demonstrate differences using such methods, since ventricular dilatation is apparently subtle in schizophrenia, the chances for a type one statistical error are great. In fact, only four of seven studies (57%) using linear measures showed significant increases in size of lateral ventricles. This decrease in numbers of studies indicating significant enlargement may reflect diminished sensitivity of the measurements.

The second possible source of differences in findings is selection of control sample. As indicated in Table 1, many medial conditions can produce evidence of cortical atrophy on CT scans. Used as controls, such patients would tend to bias against

210

TABLE 2   *CT studies of lateral ventricular enlargement in schizophrenia*

Study	Ref. no.	Diagnostic criteria[a]	Sample Category	No.	Mean age	% of total Male	Female	Method	VBR mean	Sign. enl.[b]
Johnstone et al. (1976, 1978)	4, 35	Feighner	Schizophrenia chronic	17	57.7 ± 8.9	100	–	Planimetry	18.96 ± 4.22	+
			Normal volunteers	8	55.8 ± 8.4	100	–		10.51 ± 1.96	
Trimble and Kingsley (1978)	34	NR	Schizophrenics	11	34	NR	NR	Evans inex	NA	–[c]
Weinberger et al. (1979)	36	RDC	Schizophrenia, chronic	66	50	NR	NR	Planimetry	8.7 ± 3.9	+
			Schizophrenia, acute	7	50				7.0 ± 2.8	+
			Normal volunteers	56	50				3.5 ± 2.3	
Moriguchi (1981)	37	NR	Schizophrenics	55	NR	NR	NR	Volumetric reconstruction	NA	+
			Medically ill controls	65						
Weinberger et al. (1981)	38	Feighner + RDC	Schizophrenics	10	26.7 ± 3.9	NR	NR	Planimetry	11.1 ± 3.7	+
			Siblings	12	26.1 ± 6.9				5.5 ± 2.5	
			Normal controls	17	27.9 ± 7.2				NR	
Tanaka et al. (1981)	39	NR	Schizophrenia	49	35	63	37	Width of anterior horns & Cella media	NA	+
			Medical controls	38	44	66	34			

211

TABLE 2 (continued)

Study	Ref. no.	Diagnostic criteria[a]	Sample Category	No.	Mean age	% of total Male	% of total Female	Method	VBR mean	Sign. enl.[b]
Okasha et al. (1981, 1982)	40, 41	NR	Schizophrenia	43	33	81	19	Cella media index	NA	+
			Medical controls	39	33	61	39			
Takahashi et al. (1981)	42	IPSS	'Nuclear' schizophrenia	280	27.9 ± 8.4	53	47	Cella media index	NA	+
			Volunteers + Psychiatric controls	234	27.0 ± 8	60	40			
Pearlson and Veroff (1981)	12	DSM III	Schizophrenia	22	M	M	M	Densities	7.5 ± 2.9	+[d]
			Affective disorders	16					6.5 ± 3.3	
			Psychiatric controls	35					3.6 ± 2.6	
Johnstone et al. (1981)	13	NR	Institutionalized schizophrenics	111	NR	NR	NR	Planimetry	12.7	+[d]
			Outpatient schizophrenics	18					11.2	
			Institutionalized manic-depressives	10					11.7	
			Outpatient manic-depressives	22					11.3	
			'Neurotics'	8					10.2	

212

Study	Ref.	Diagnostic criteria	Group	N	Age	% M	%	Measurement	Value	Sig.
Benes et al. (1982)	43	Feighner	Schizophrenia	10	21.2 ± 5.5	NR	NR	Cella media index Planimetry	2.4 ± 1.1	–
			Medical controls	26	29 ± 6.3				2.4 ± 0.8	
Frangos et al. (1982)	44	NR	Schizophrenia	70	50	NR	NR	NR	NA	+[c]
Andreasen et al. (1982)	45, 46	DSM III + RDC	Schizophrenia, medical	52	29.96 ± 10.6	52	48	Planimetry (video cursor)	6.00 ± 3.91	+
			Controls	47	M	M	M		4.46 ± 3.05	
Reveley et al. (1982)	47	SADS	Schizophrenia	7	38.6 ± 9.5	86	14	Densities	8.6 ± 5.23	+
			Discordant twins	7	38.6 ± 9.5	86	14		6.5 ± 4.54	
Nasrallah et al. (1982)	48	Tsuang-Winkour	Schizophrenia	41	29.4	100	–	Bifrontal + bicaudate ratio	NA	–
			Medical controls	40	M	100	–			
Nyback et al. (1982)	49	RDC	Schizophrenia Probable schizophrenia	28 13	32 ± 75	54	46	Bifrontal ratio	NA	+
			Schizoaffective	2						
			Other psychoses	3						
			Normal volunteers	46	127 ± 1	52	48			
Jernigan et al. (1982)	50	DSM III + RDC	Schizophrenia	29	32.4 ± 8.2	100	–	Densities + planimetry	5.2 ± 2	–
			Normal controls	13	M	100	–		5.0 ± 2	
Nasrallah et al. (1982, 1983)	51, 52	DSM III + Feighner	Schizophrenia	55	29.9 ± 8.2	M	M	Planimetry	8.7 ± 4	+[d]
			Manic-depressive	24	31.8 ± 7.5				7.5 ± 3.2	
			Medical controls	27	29.7 ± 5.8				4.5 ± 2.6	

213

TABLE 2   (continued)

Study	Ref. no.	Diagnostic criteria[a]	Sample Category	No.	Mean age	% of total		Method	VBR mean	Sign. enl.[b]
						Male	Female			
Weinberger et al. (1982)	53	DSM III	Schizophreniform	35	20.7 ± 6.2	54	46	Planimetry	5.3 ± 3.6	+[d]
			Chronic schizophrenia	17	28.3 ± 9.7	65	35		6.0 ± 4.2	
			Affective disorders	27	30.3 ± 10.1	35	65		3.8 ± 2.9	
			Other psychiatric disorders	27	21 ± 9.6	59	41		3.2 ± 2.9	
			Medical controls	26	30.3 ± 6.9	50	50		2.9 ± 2.9	
Kling et al. (1983)	54	DSM III	Schizophrenia	26	33.5 ± 7.3	NR	NR	Planimetry	8.44 ± 3.9	+[e]
			Alcoholics	13	40.7 ± 6.9				9.88 ± 4.3	
			Neurological patients	9	36.8 ± 8.7				9.1 ± 2.8	
			Medical controls	20	36.8 ± 8.7				4.75 ± 2.0	
Rieder et al. (1983)	18	RDC	Schizophrenia	28	25.9 ± 0.1	46	54	Planimetry	3.7 ± 3.4	NA[e]
			Schizo-affectives	15	24.6 ± 4.3	73	27		3.9 ± 3.8	
			Bipolar	19	43.6 ± 14.6	53	47		5.3 ± 3.7	
Woods and Wolf (1983)	55	RDC	Schizophrenia	19	23.3 ± 8.5	74	26	Bifrontal and bicaudate ratios	NA	+
			Medical neurological controls	29	23.8 ± 4.4	52	48			

Study	Ref	Criteria	Group	N	Mean ± SD			Method	Value ± SD	Sig
Schultz et al. (1983)	56	DSM III	Schizophreniform	8	16.5 ± 1.55	60	40	Planimetry	8.4 ± 5.0	+
			Border-line	8	16 ± 0.88	37	63		2.9 ± 1.6	
Pearlson et al. (1984, 1985)	57, 58	DSM III	Schizophrenia	19	28.8 ± 5.8	58	42	Planimetry (computerized)	6.2 ± 2.6	+d
			Bipolar	27	30.8 ± 6.7	44	56		6.6 ± 3.4	
			Controls							
			vs. schizophrenia	19	29.7 ± 5.3	M	M		4.5 ± 1.0	
			vs. bipolar	19	30.7 ± 7.6				4.75 ± 2.1	
DeMeyer et al. (1984)	59	DSM III	Schizophrenia	8	26.3 ± 8.0	63	37	Planimetry	5.8 ± 2.8	−
			Other psychiatric disorders	7	25.1 ± 5.9	43	57		8.36 ± 2.9	
			Medical neurological controls	15	26.1 ± 3.99	NR	NR		4.26 ± 2.16	
Luchins et al. (1984)	60	RDC	Schizophrenia	45	29.0 ± 7.4	NR	NR	Planimetry	4.1 ± 2.7	+d
			Affective disorders	22					4.5 ± 2.7	
			Medical neurological controls	62	33.9 ± 11.5				3.0 ± 2.3	
Pandurangi et al. (1984)	61	DSM III	Schizophrenia	23	28	100	−	Planimetry	5.4 ± 1.1	−
			Normal volunteers + neurological controls	23	34	100	−		3.48 ± 0.5	

215

TABLE 2 *(continued)*

Study	Ref. no.	Diagnostic criteria[a]	Sample		Mean age	% of total		Method	VBR mean	Sign. enl.[b]
			Category	No.		Male	Female			
Schulsinger et al. (1984)	62	DSM III	Schizophrenia Schizotypal Medical controls	7 11 13	NR	NR	NR		9.76 5.41 7.48	+[e]
Largen et al. (1984)	63	RDC	Schizophrenia + schizo-affective Medical neurological	35 17	30.4 ± 8 26.8 ± 4.4	49 35	51 65	Planimetry (video cursor) + bifrontal bicaudate ratios	6.7 6.52	−[e]
Carr and Wedding (1984)	67	RDC + DSM III	Schizophrenia Medical controls	21 21	M M	M M	M M	Planimetry	1.84 ± 0.5 1.47 ± 0.5	+
Shima et al. (1985)	64	DSM III	Schizophrenia Normal volunteers neurological controls	46 46	36.6 ± 6.7 36.9 ± 6.9	52 50	48 50	Bifrontal (Evans index + cella media index	8.2 ± 2.3 7.6 ± 1.8	−
Boronow et al. (1985)	65	RDC	Schizophrenia + schizo-affective Medically ill controls	30 30	24.9 ± 4.4 M	67 M	33 M	Planimetry	5.7 ± 2.0 4.9 ± 1.7	−

Author	Ref	Criteria	Group	N	Age	±	SD			Method	VBR	Sign.
Williams et al. (1985)	66	RDC	Schizophrenia Schizoaffective disorders	31 9	32	±	8	75	25	Densities	4.58 ± 2.55	+
			Neurological controls	40	M		M	M			3.37 ± 1.96	
Turner et al. (in press)	68	DSM III	Schizophrenia Normal volunteers	30 26	24.9 26.4			73 38	27 62	Densities	5.0 3.6	+
Shelton et al. (1985)	69	DSM III	Schizophrenics Normal volunteers	73 30	28.7 28.7	± ±	5.5 7.8	70 47	30 53	Planimetry	5.5 ± 3.1 3.8 ± 2.7	+

a Key to diagnostic criteria: Feighner = Feighner Diagnostic Criteria (70); RDC = Research Diagnostic Criteria (71); IPSS = International Pilot Study of Schizophrenia (72); DSM III = Diagnostic and Statistical Manual of the American Psychiatric Association, Third Edition (73); SADS = Schedule for Affective Disorders and Schizophrenia (74); Tsuang and Winokur = Tsuang and Winokur Criteria for Schizophrenia (75).
b Key to abbreviations: NR = Not reported; NA = Neo applicable; VBR = Ventricular-Brain Ratio; M = Matched; Sign. enl. = significant enlargement.
c Compared to literature controls.
d No differences from affective disorder patients.
e No differences from other psychiatric patients.

demonstrating significant differences, again a potential type one error. For example, of the studies using patients with neurological illnesses as part of the control group only four out of eight (50%) revealed differences, whereas seven out of eight studies (88%) in which only normal volunteers served as the comparison group found demonstrable differences. Arguments have been ventured, however, that medically ill or chronically institutionalized subjects should be chosen as comparison samples in order to control for length of hospitalization, duration and type of treatment, intercurrent or co-existing medical illness, and so forth (75 – 77). Use of careful diagnosis and screening for other illnesses in many studies have helped to exclude superimposed medical or neurological causes for atrophy. Further, age, duration of illness, length of hospitalization, and so forth (reviewed in greater detail below) have not, in general, been correlated with ventricular dilatation in patients. It is also important to point out that the generic concept of 'medical illness' is potentially misleading and not relevant. Illnesses are not equipotent in terms of their impact on brain structure nor are their effects invariably 'non-specific.'

The previous two sources of variation represent biases potentially reducing the discriminating power of the analyses. The third source, selection of patient samples, is not simply a source of variability; it may also relate to the clinicopathological significance of the findings. The majority of studies of schizophrenic patients showing differences from control subjects utilized primarily a severely ill and often chronically institutionalized sample. Two controlled and carefully performed negative studies, those of Benes et al. (43) and of Jernigan et al. (50), both using variations of the ventricular – brain ratio method, demonstrate the importance of sample choice. The previous group was drawn from McLean Hospital, Belmont, Massachusetts, a private psychiatric institution. As compared to the sample of Weinberger et al. (79), the patients had received less overall hospital treatment and were not drawn from a chronic-treatment facility. It is interesting to note, however, that a repeat study from the same hospital found larger ventricles in patients with schizophrenia (55). In addition, other positive studies (45, 46) and our most recent study (70) show that less severely impaired subjects, thought still significantly different from controls, generally have lower mean VBRs and fewer patients outside the control range.

Important questions have been raised regarding the relationship of ventricular enlargement to such variables as age, prior treatment, duration of illness, and hospitalization. In general, no relationship has been found between the degree of ventricular dilatation and the extent of treatment with neuroleptics (4, 13, 35, 51, 62, 66, 80, 81) or ECT (4, 13, 36, 44, 62, 80), duration of illness (36, 44, 49, 51, 66, 80, 81), or total length of hospitalization (36, 44, 49, 51, 66, 80, 81). Coupling these studies with those of Weinberger et al. (53) Schultz et al. (56), and Nyback et al. (49), showing that lateral ventricular enlargement is present at or near onset of illness after little or no neuroleptic treatment, and that of Johnstone et al. (4) that included 4 patients who had never received treatment, suggests that enlargement cannot be accounted for by these variables.

Age has been found to be correlated with ventricular size in normal populations

(82 – 84), in control samples in CT studies of schizophrenia (37, 49, 60, 69), and in persons with affective disorders (18, 61). Though there remains minor controversy regarding the matter (55), the preponderance of data shows no relationship between age and lateral ventricular size in schizophrenia (3, 13, 18, 35, 37, 44, 49, 51, 55, 60, 62, 66, 69, 81, 82). Again, studies showing increased ventricular size early in the disease (49, 53, 54, 56, 57) are consistent with this conclusion. These findings indicate that ventricular enlargement in schizophrenia is either static and non-progressive from the onset of illness (and perhaps throughout the person's life), or at least that the majority of enlargements occur prior to the manifestations of the illness, with a lesser degree occurring later.

Theorizing that lateral ventricular enlargement might define a subpopulation of schizophrenic patients, a number of investigators proceeded to attempt to define the clinical parameters of this subgroup. Indeed, the original paper in the field, that of Johnstone et al. (4), began the process of relating ventricular enlargement to a specific syndrome of cognitive impairment. In their sample of 17 patients (including 9 selected because of so-called 'age disorientation'), there was a significant relationship between ventricular size and cognitive impairment on the Withers and Hinton test (85). This relationship held in a follow-up study on the same patients (35) using the Withers and Hinton battery, the Inglis paired associative learning test (86), and the 'digits backward test.' Additionally, these tests of cognitive impairment also related to the degree of so-called 'negative' symptoms of the illness (including affective flattening and poverty of speech) as defined by the Krawiecka scale for chronic psychiatric patients (87). It was proposed that these relationships defined a subgroup of patients with the 'dementia of dementia praecox' of Kraepelin (88) and Jaspers (89).

Though Weinberger et al. (36) were unable to link ventricular enlargement to abnormalities on the Wechsler Adult Intelligence Scale (WAIS) (90) in their initial study, they did so in a follow-up evaluation (91) in which 15 patients were divided into 'normal' (i.e. VBR falling within the control range) and 'abnormal' (VBR greater than 10.6, outside the control range) and compared on the WAIS and the Halstead Reitan Battery (HRB) (92), a more specific test of cortical impairment. The two groups were significantly different on both WAIS and HRB scores, with patients having enlarged lateral ventricles showing more impairment. Further, using an average impairment rating of 1.55 or above (scale 0 – 6) across the 12 subtests of the HRB as a 'cutting score' for cerebral impairment, they were able to predict in 12 of 15 cases whether a patient would fall into normal or abnormal groups on CT scan. Therefore, they felt that the HRB was a 'reliable predictor' of schizophrenic patients with an 'organic defect' (here, abnormalities on CT scans).

Two studies by Golden et al. (80, 93) further demarcated the relationship of neuropsychological deficits to apparent cerebral atrophy in schizophrenia. Applying the Luria-Nebraska Neuropsychological Battery (LNNB) (94), 42 patients diagnosed as having chronic schizophrenia by DSM III were tested, half of whom were referred for the possibility of 'brain damage' (but without demonstrable etiology) and half without. Each subject underwent a CT scan and VBR was determined. With considerable overlap between the so-called 'brain-damaged' and 'non-brain-damaged' groups on VBR, the ratio was correlated with the scores on the 14 subsets of the LNNB. Eight of the subsets correlated at the $p < 0.05$ level, with an overall correlation of 0.72, again indicating, in general, a relationship between degree of neuropsychological impairment and ventricular size in schizophrenia. In the second study (92), an attempt was made to predict ventricular enlargement (defined as VBR greater than 10) according to specified criteria of neuropsychological impairment on the LNNB. Abnormalities were accurately predicted in 15 of 15 patients with VBR greater than 10, but also in 10 of 20 patients when the VBR was less than 10, for an overall 'hit rate' (rate of accurate prediction) of 77%. One possible explanation of the high false-positive rate is that the arbitrarily defined 'abnormal' VBR of greater than 10 may be too high, and both neuropsychological impairment and ventricular size in schizophrenia may form continuums of severity, somewhat paralleling one another. On the other hand, the cause of the cognitive impairment may be multifactorial, just as it is in late life dementias. Taken at face value the studies seem to implicate a relationship between one test of brain pathology deficits on neuropsychological testing, with another, enlargement of lateral ventricles. In addition, those patients with VBRs outside the normal range tend to have the most severe neuropsychological impairment. At least one study failed to replicate these findings on the LNNB and HRB (67), but this may be attributable to the fact that significant neuropsychological impairment was found in essentially all of their chronically ill samples. Most studies of CT findings and cognitive impairment support a relationship between the two.

Other findings related to the degree of ventricular enlargement include poor premorbid adjustment (including presence of 'schizoid' traits) (66, 95, 96); poor outcome with more frequent hospitalization (96); persistent unemployment (57, 58); a lower incidence of so-called positive symptoms (delusions, hallucinations, etc.) (45, 60, 97); more negative symptoms (apathy, flat affect, social isolation, etc.) (45, 57, 58, 66); diminished antipsychotic response to neuroleptics (60, 79, 98 – 100); and greater incidence of extrapyramidal side effects to treatment (100, 101). Interestingly, in affective disorder patients there may also be an association between lateral ventricular enlargement and poor premorbid adjustment (58); greater severity of illness with a greater incidence of psychosis (7, 15 – 17, 19, 20); presence of negative symptoms (57, 58); worse outcome (10, 21); increased frequency of hospitalization (17, 21); and persistent unemployment (21, 57). In general, though negative reports exist (97, 102), ventricular size seems to relate to severity of psychopathology and degree of impairment in both patients with schizophrenia and affective disorder, though not necessarily because of the same etiology.

Third ventricular enlargement

The third ventricle is a midline component of the cerebrospinal fluid circulation system, connected rostrally to the anterior horns of the lateral ventricles through the foramina of Monro, and caudally to the fourth ventricle through the aqueduct of

Silvius. Surrounding the ventricles are structures such as thalamus, hypothalamus, fornix, and habenula. As with the areas abutting the lateral ventricles, pathology of these regions has also been implicated in schizophrenia (5, 107). Although literature regarding abnormalities of the third ventricle is more limited than that of the lateral ventricles, diffuse conditions such as those in Table 1 can be associated with pathological enlargement. Further, at least one study in neurological patients has linked increased size of the third ventricle selectively to impairment of memory (specifically, delayed recall) but not decline in overall intellectual performance (108).

Methodological issues

Figure 2 shows normal and pathologically enlarged third ventricles. Except in circumstances in which the ventricle is simply too narrow to be easily seen or measured, the diameter can be reliably determined. Since in pathological conditions expansion of the ventricle is primarily lateral, most investigators have simply measured the maximum width. Two groups (49, 63) used a variation of the VBR method, tracing the outline of the ventricle and the outer margin of the brain generating a third ventricular – brain ratio. Positive results have, however, been demonstrated with both methods.

Studies

Table 3 summarizes the 12 studies of third ventricular enlargement in schizophrenia. Of these, 10 (83%) demonstrated significant differences from controls. The two

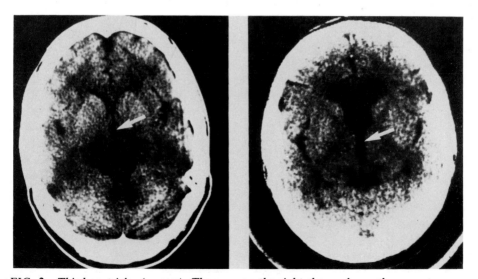

FIG. 2   *Third ventricles (arrows). The scan on the right shows clear enlargement.*

221

TABLE 3   CT studies of third ventricular enlargement in schizophrenia

Study	Ref. no.	Diagnostic criteria[a]	Sample Category	No.	Mean age	% of total Male	% of total Female	Mean width	Sign. enl.
Gluck et al. (1980)	103	NR[b]	Schizophrenia	68	M	59	41	3.3	−
Mundt et al. (1980)	104		Medical controls	68	M	M	M	4.0	
Moriguchi (1981)	37	NR	Schizophrenia	55	NR	NR	NR	5.1 ± 1.5	+
			Medical controls	65				4.5 ± 1.3	
Takahashi et al. (1981)	42	IPSS	Schizophrenia	280	27.9 ± 8.4	53	47	5.7 ± 1.6	+
			Medical controls	234	27.0 ± 8	60	40	5.2 ± 1.7	
Tanaka et al. (1981)	39	NR	Schizophrenia	49	35	63	37	−	+
			Medical controls	38	44	66	34	−	
Okasha et al. (1981, 1982)	40, 41	NR	Schizophrenia	43	33	81	19	5.23 ± 1.9	+
			Medical controls	39	33	62	38	1.64 ± 0.4	
Gattaz et al. (1981)	105	RDC	Schizophrenia	40	34.5 ± 10.3	40	60	4.82 ± 2.51	+
			Medical controls	40	M	M	M	3.3 ± 1.31	
Nyback et al. (1982)	49	RDC	Schizophrenia	28	32 ± 1.5	54	46	d	+
			Other psychiatric patients	18					
			Normal volunteers	46	27 ± 1	52	48		

Study	Ref.	Diagnostic criteria	Group	n	Age	%	%	VBR	Sign. enl.
Dewan et al. (1983)	106	DSM III							+
Pandurangi et al. (1984)	61		Schizophrenia	23	28.2	100	–	3.2 ± 0.2	+
			Neurological controls	23	34	100	–	2.1 ± 0.2	
DeMeyer et al. (1984)	18	DSM III	Schizophrenia	8	26.3 ± 8	63	37	2.62 ± 1.3	+
			Other psychiatric patients	7	25.1 ± 6	43	57	2.86 ± 1.6	
			Medical controls	15	26.1 ± 4	NR	NR	1.0	
Largen et al. (1984)	63	RDC	Schizophrenia	30	30.4 ± 8	49	51	d	–
			Schizoaffective disorders	5					
			Medical neurological controls	17	26.8 ± 4.4	35	65		
Boronow et al. (1985)	65	RDC	Schizophrenia	23	24.9 ± 4.4	67	33	1.1 ± 0.4	+
			Schizoaffective disorders	7					
			Medical controls	30	M	M	M	0.9 ± 0.2	
Shelton et al. (1985)	69	DSM III	Schizophrenia	73				3.26 ± 1.3	+
			Normal volunteers	30				2.75 ± 1.0	

[a] Key to diagnostic criteria: IPSS = International Pilot Study of Schizophrenia (72); RDC = Research Diagnostic Criteria (71); DSM III = Diagnostic and Statistical Manual of the American Psychiatric Association, Third Edition (73).
[b] Not reported.
[c] Matched.
[d] Used variation of ventricular-brain ratio method.
[e] Sign. enl. = significantly enlarged.

223

studies, using normal volunteers as the control sample, both showed significant differences (49, 69); however, even if these are factored out, eight of the remaining ten studies (80%) using medical or neurological controls were significant. In the study by Boronow et al. (65), in which a medically ill control group was used, significant enlargement of the third ventricle was shown even where no differences in lateral ventricles emerged. This was found even though the group discovered enlargement of the third ventricle in subsets of their medical controls, such as those receiving cancer chemotherapy. This may indicate that third ventricular enlargement is less sensitive to 'contamination' from medically ill controls, and that possibly it is a 'stronger' finding than lateral ventricular enlargement.

Age has been correlated with size of third ventricles in normal volunteer samples (49, 69, 109), though one study of medical controls failed to indicate a relationship (37). The findings in patients with schizophrenia have been mixed, with two studies showing a relationship (49, 99) and three studies not clearly exhibiting a correlation (37, 65, 69). A more common finding has been an association of ventricular enlargement with duration of illness and number of hospitalizations (18, 39, 49, 105). On the other hand, Moriguchi et al. (37), found no association with age of onset or duration of illness, and Boronow et al. (65), discovered no linkage to a wide variety of clinical variables, including length of illness, cumulative hospitalizations, prior treatment, premorbid adjustment, symptom complex, subtype of schizophrenia, and so forth. Though failure to reveal congruence is not an absolute indication of an absence of mutual relationships between third ventricular size and such clinical characteristics, a simple explanation of the discrepancies is that enlargement of the third ventricle may exist in a preponderance of the schizophrenic population. Again, expansion of the ventricles in schizophrenic patients seems to be a vigorous finding.

Increased cortical surface markings

The previous two categories, lateral and third ventricular enlargement, are referred to as signs of so-called central cerebral atrophy. The cortical surface is also sensitive to the processes listed in Table 1. Like ventricular enlargement, cortical atrophy has been associated with dementing illnesses, though atrophy on CT scan is not invariably present even when severe dementia exists (25, 113 – 120).

Atrophy of the cerebral cortex is associated with reduction in volume of the gyri. This process is manifested on CT scan by widening and deepening of the sulci, expansion of the fissures (especially the Sylvian and interhemispheric), and 'thinning' of the gyri themselves. Figure 3 displays CT scans of the cortex with and without atrophy present.

Methodological issues

No clearly superior method of evaluating cortical atrophy has emerged; therefore techniques have followed three different paths. First, a plurality of studies have used variations of measuring the widths of sulci and fissures (12, 39 – 41, 54, 61, 103,

104, 106, 110). These have ranged from measuring the Sylvian fissure alone to detailed assessments of widths of individual sulci.

The second most common method has been visual evaluations of degree of atrophy, both with (7, 18, 49, 65, 68, 69, 111) and without (42, 48, 112) use of a reference scale based on 'standard' CT scans. This allows judgement of presence or absence of atrophy in a gross fashion and, in the case of the studies that used reference scales, a ranking of degree of atrophy.

Another method of assessing atrophy is the use of a computer algorithm for summing the number of pixels with a value within a specific range as described by Jernigan et al. (49). This mode of evaluation is similar to that described for lateral ventricles earlier, in which a cutoff density number is used to correspond to tissue (all numbers in the cortex above the minimum pixel number) and fluid (all pixels below the value). The total pixels for tissue and fluid are summed for comparisons. This technique is affected by the problems described earlier, particularly energy output variations in the X-rays, differences in skull thickness, changes in sensitivity and recording in the CT machinery and so forth.

All methods of evaluation suffer from the so-called 'apical artifact' if the uppermost CT slices are used. When the X-rays pass through bone, a certain degree of distortion occurs. At the apex of the skull, the beams must pass through a considerable thickness of curved bone which distorts the image produced, somewhat magnifying the apical sulci. This difficulty can be largely avoided by focusing on lower CT slices.

FIG. 3   *Examples of cortex scans. The scan on the right is consistent with cortical atrophy.*

TABLE 4   CT studies of cortical surface atrophy in schizophrenia

Study	Ref. no.	Diagnostic criteria[a]	Sample		Mean age	% of total		Method	Sign. atr.
			Category	No.		Male	Female		
Johnstone et al. (1978)	35	Feighner	Schizophrenia	17	M[b]	100	–	Total area of sulci	+
			Normal volunteers	8	M	100	–		
Weinberger et al. (1979)	110	RDC	Schizophrenia	60	31	NR	NR	Width of sylvian and interhemispheric fissures + three largest sulci	+
			Normal volunteers	62	30	NR	NR		
Gluck et al. (1980)	103	NR	Schizophrenia	68	44.5	59	42	Width of anterior horns + number sulci, 3 × 1 mm, two top slices	–
Mundt et al. (1980)	104		Medical controls	68	M	M	M		
Tanaka et al. (1981)	39	NR	Schizophrenia	49	35	63	37	Width of sylvian fissures, visual assessment of cortical surface	+
			Medical controls	38	44	66	34		
Pearlson and Veroff (1981)	12	DSM III	Schizophrenia	22	M	M	M	Width three largest sulci	+[c]
			Affective disorders	16	M	M	M		
			Psychiatric controls	35	M	M	M		
Okasha et al. (1981, 1982)	40, 41	NR	Schizophrenia	43	33	81	19	Width of sylvian and interhemispheric fissures + three largest sulci	–
			Medical controls	39	33	61	39		

				N	Age				
Takahashi et al. (1981)	42	IPSS	Schizophrenia Volunteers + Psychiatric controls	169 169	27.9 27	53 60	47 40	Visual inspection	+
Nyback et al. (1982)	49	RDC	Schizophrenia Other psychiatric patients Normal volunteers	28 18 46	32 ± 1.5 27 ± 1	54 52	46 48	Visual assessment 0–3 scale	+
Nasrallah et al. (1982)	48	Tsuang-Winokur	Schizophrenia Medical controls	41 40	29.4 M	100 100	– –	Visual assessment	+
Nasrallah et al. (1982, 1983)	7, 111	DSM III + Feighner	Schizophrenia Affective disorders Medical controls	55 24 27	29.9 ± 8.2 31.8 ± 7.5 29.7 ± 5.8	M M M	M M M	Visual assessment 0–3 scale	+[c]
Jernigan et al. (1982)	50	DSM III + RDC	Schizophrenia Volunteer controls	29 13	32.4 ± 8.2 M	100 100	– –	Pixel densities	–
Kling et al. (1983)	54	DSM III	Schizophrenia Alcoholics Neurological patients Medical controls	26 13 9 20	33.9 ± 7.3 40.7 ± 6.9 36.8 ± 8.7 36.8 ± 8.7	NR	NR	Width of sylvian fissure	–[c]

TABLE 4 (continued)

Study	Ref. no.	Diagnostic criteria[a]	Sample Category	No.	Mean age	% of total Male	Female	Method	Sign. atr.
Rieder et al. (1983)	18	RDC	Schizophrenia	28	25.9 ± 8.1	46	54	Visual assessment, 0–2 scale	c
			Schizoaffective disorders	19	24.6 ± 4.3	73	27		
			Bipolar disorders	19	43.6 ± 14.6	53	47		
Dewan et al. (1983)	106	DSM III	Schizophrenia	23	28.2	100	–	Width of sylvian fissure	+
			Medical neurological controls	23	34	100	–		
Oxenstierna et al. (1983)	112	RDC	Schizophrenia	30	33.3	57	43	Visual assessment	+
Pandurangi et al. (1984)	61	DSM III	Schizophrenia	23	28	100	–	Width of sylvian fissures, width frontal, parietal occipital sulci	+
			Medical controls	23	34	100	–		
Largen et al. (1984)	63	RDC	Schizophrenia Schizoaffective disorders	30 5	30.4 ± 8 (mean for entire patient group)	49	51	Video cursor, 0–4 scale	–c
			Medical and neurological controls	17	26.8 ± 4.4	35	65		

Reference		Diagnostic criteria[a]	Group	N	Age		Matched	CT measure	Sign. atr.[b]
Boronow et al. (1985)	65	RDC	Schizophrenia	23	24.9 ± 4.4 (mean for all patients)		M	Visual assessment, 0–3 scale	−
			Schizoaffective disorders	7		67	M		
			Medical controls	30		33	M		
Shelton et al. (1985)	69	DSM III	Schizophrenia	73				Visual assessment parieto-occipital atrophy (0–3 scale)	+
			Normal volunteers	30				Prefrontal atrophy (0–3 scale)	
Turner et al. (in press)	68	DSM III	Schizophrenia	30	24.9	73	27	Sylvian fissure, interhemispheric fissure, cortical sulci, 0–6 scale	+
			Normal volunteers	26	26.4	38	62		

a Key to diagnostic criteria: Feighner = Feighner Diagnostic Criteria (70); RDC = Research Diagnostic Criteria (71); DSM III = Diagnostic and Statistical Manual of the American Psychiatric Association, Third Edition (73); IPSS = Internal Pilot Study of Schizophrenia (72); Tsuang and Winokur = Tsuang and Winokur Criteria for Schizophrenia (75).
b Key to abbreviations: NR = Not reported; M = Matched; Sign. atr. = significant atrophy.
c No difference from other psychiatric or neurological patients.

Studies

Table 4 reviews the 20 CT studies of surface atrophy, including the methods used in each. Fourteen (about 67%) revealed significant differences from control groups. Sensitivity does appear reduced by using medical or neurological patients as controls with six of 11 (55%) of such studies discovering differences where five of six (83%) of studies utilizing exclusively normal volunteers had positive findings.

In general, the presence and degree of cortical atrophy does seem to correlate with age and presence of dementia in normals and persons with other illnesses such as Alzheimer's disease (10, 25, 113 – 120). Age did not appear to relate to the presence or degree of cortical atrophy in most studies of schizophrenia (49, 69, 110, 111). On the other hand, at least two reports have uncovered relationships between cognitive impairment and apparent atrophy.

Rieder et al. (121), evaluated 4 schizophrenic patients with sulcal prominence and 4 matched schizophrenic controls without such atrophic changes on the Halstead-Reitan Battery (92). All four patients with atrophy performed in the so-called impaired range, while only 1 of 4 patients without atrophy did so, exhibiting only mild impairment.

Nasrallah et al. (111) divided patients into those with and those without signs of cortical atrophy. Of the 22 subjects with sulcal widening, 27% fell below the cutoff score (25) of the Mini Mental State Exam of Folstein and McHugh (122), implying cognitive impairment, while none of 33 patients without atrophy manifested impairment. Though these studies are few, they do indicate a possible relationship between cortical surface atrophy and cognitive impairment.

Studies of other clinical correlates of cortical atrophy are even more limited in number and therefore must be viewed as preliminary. Weinberger et al. (110) found no connection between presence of atrophy and length or duration of illness but did find a greater incidence of atrophic changes in patients treated with electroconvulsive therapy (ECT) (though a large number of their ECT-treated patients showed no abnormalities). Nasrallah et al. (111) also found no differences in duration of illness as well as severity, premorbid adjustment, family history of schizophrenia, response to neuroleptics, and positive and negative symptoms between patients with and without signs of cortical atrophy. The absence of correlations in these studies stands in striking contrast to the lateral ventricular research and indicates that cortical atrophy per se may be related primarily to cognitive impairment. On the other hand, since relatively few patients appear to have cortical atrophy alone, the samples may have been too small to yield statistically significant relationships. Only further research will help elucidate such relationships.

A final consideration is the location of the cortical atrophy; is it a non-localized phenomenon, as with Alzheimer's disease, or is the site more specific? Most studies looked at atrophy as a diffuse phenomenon, assessing diverse areas of the brain; several did, however, evaluate more selectively.

The area of the Sylvian fissure that is commonly measured on CT scan falls primarily between frontal and temporal cortex. A study by Pandurangi et al. (61)

evaluated both sulcal widening and Sylvian fissure width and found differences only in the latter. This is supported by other studies, including that of Dewan et al. (106), that looked exclusively at Sylvian fissure diameter. Takahishi et al. (42), in a study of 169 schizophrenic patients and 169 controls, found strongly significant differences in degree of dilatation of Sylvian fissures and frontal cortex bilaterally, with slight differences in right temporal areas and no distinction in left temporal, parietal and occipital regions. Similarly, Tanaka et al. (89), found atrophy localized to frontal and temporal regions (with absence of changes in parietal and occipital cortex, and Oxenstierna et al. (112), found atrophy localized in the dorsolateral, prefrontal cortex in 4 of their 10 patients with cortical atrophy. Because of these findings and the results of physiological studies implicating the prefrontal cortical area (123), we evaluated schizophrenic patients versus normal volunteer controls using a scale of generalized (primarily parieto-occipital) atrophy, and a novel scale of atrophy of the prefrontal cortex. The latter scale used the CT scan slice showing the third ventricle most prominently; this cut reveals prefrontal cortex clearly, allowing evaluation according to degree of separation of skull from brain substance and depth of fissure and sulcal markings (69). The generalized atrophy scale revealed no differences between patient and control samples; the prefrontal atrophy scale, on the other hand, demonstrated striking distinctions in numbers of patients affected and the degree of atrophy present. Over 50% of our sample showed some signs of atrophy in the prefrontal region. Taken together, these studies indicate that cortical atrophy may be especially apparent in prefrontal and to a lesser degree temporal areas.

Cerebellar atrophy

Cerebellar atrophy is a relatively uncommon condition in non-neurological patients, discovered in approximately 1% of routinely interpreted CT scans from large surveys (124, 125). Signs of atrophy can result from reductions in tissue of the cerebellar hemispheres, nuclei, or vermis. Primary degenerative diseases, carcinoma, alcoholism, and phenytoin use are commonly associated with atrophic changes.

Neuropathological studies of cerebellar atrophy in schizophrenia have been discussed elsewhere in this volume, and therefore will not be dealt with at length here. Suffice it to say that atrophic changes particularly affecting the cerebellar vermis have been discovered in post-mortem studies (126, 127). Further, in rare instances, disorders of the cerebellum, such as primary degeneration, tumors, cysts, and so forth, have been associated with schizophrenia-like illnesses (128, 129).

Because of its location in the posterior fossa the cerebellum is often visualized poorly and is prone to imaging artifacts. Whenever X-rays must traverse considerable amounts of bone to reach soft tissue, the bone – brain interface loses clarity on CT. Since there is relatively thick bone in the posterior fossa as compared with other areas, the cerebellum is especially prone to this artifact. Nevertheless, atrophy can be assessed with acceptable reliability. Various approaches have been used, both qualitative and quantitative. In particular, the dimensions of the fourth ventricle, cisterna magna, and cerebellar vermis have been made as well as pixel density measurements, demonstration of folia in the vermis, and visual inspection for presence of atrophy.

An overview of the CT studies of cerebellar atrophy is contained in Table 5. As can be readily seen, there are marked discrepancies in the percentages of patients with atrophy, ranging from zero to 50%. Though variations in patient sample may account for part of this, differences in measurement technique probably explain the majority of the variation. The presence of a 'criterion' for atrophy, such as enlargement of the fourth ventricle, presence of an arbitrary number of vermian folia, or other changes does not necessarily mean that atrophy is present. Further, any 'threshold' for atrophy is by definition arbitrary since variations in normal anatomy can, of course, exist. Therefore estimations of cerebellar atrophy are, in general, rough approximations of an atrophic process. Interestingly, however, in seven of the ten studies that attempted to assess the number of patients affected, the rates were between 5 and 17%. This may indicate that a replicable estimate of the rate of atrophy is about 10% in schizophrenia, substantially greater than in the general population. As with the post-mortem research, the bulk of atrophy seems to be localized to the cerebellar vermis. A quick reference to the table will reveal that schizo-affective and other affective disorder patients also have cerebellar atrophy. As with ventricular enlargement, this does not diminish the finding in schizophrenia but rather may indicate the presence of brain pathology in these disorders. It also does not necessarily imply a common pathogenic factor.

The etiology of the atrophy is unknown and there is little information about the relationship to clinical variables. Dewan et al. (135) found no association of atrophy with age and duration of hospitalization. Since the cerebellum, and especially the vermis, is sensitive to the chronic toxicity of drugs like phenytoin and alcohol, one possibility is that the effects seen in schizophrenia could be due to chronic neuroleptic exposure. This avenue bears further investigation. It should be noted that studies of first episode patients have not reported findings of cerebellar atrophy.

The possible physiological implications of cerebellar pathology in schizophrenia are intriguing. Connections from the vermis to limbic – diencephalic areas linked to regulation of autonomic activity and emotion has spurred speculation that cerebellar pathology could directly affect behavior (136).

Cerebral asymmetries

Anatomical asymmetry of the brain refers to differences in size of structures in the left and right hemispheres. Such variations in dimensions of paired structures have been known through much of this century, but the significance of the findings has been mired in controversy (137).

In general, among the most commonly reproduced findings from CT have been asymmetry of width or volume of the frontal and occipital lobes. In these areas, right-handed, normal individuals have a greater than expected incidence of larger

TABLE 5   *CT studies of cerebellar atrophy in schizophrenia*

Study	Ref. no.	Diagnostic criteria[a]	Sample Category	No.	Mean age	% of total Male	Female	Method	Results
Weinberger et al. (1979)	130	RDC	Schizophrenia Other psychiatric patients	60 15	31	NR	NR	Visual assessment	Atrophy: 10 (17%) 0 –
Heath et al. (1979)	128	NR	Schizophrenia Other psychoses	85 31	NR	NR	NR	2 vermian folia, enlargement of the cerebellar criteria	Atrophy: 34 (40%) 9 (29%)
Coffman et al. (1981)	131	DSM III	Schizophrenia Medical/ neurological controls	14 21	NR	NR	NR	Vermis/brain ratio	No differences from controls
Nasrallah et al. (1981)	132	DSM III	Schizophrenia Affective disorders Medical controls	43 15 36	NR	NR	NR	Hemisphere sulci 1 mm; 1 vermian folia present, enlargement of cerebellar cisternae or fourth ventricle	Meets 1 criterion: 5 (12%) 4 (27%) 1 (3%)

233

TABLE 5 (continued)

Study	Ref. no.	Diagnostic criteria[a]	Sample		Mean age	% of total		Method	Results
			Category	No.		Male	Female		
Pearlson and Veroff (1981)	12	DSM III	Schizophrenia	22	M	M	M	NR	Atrophy: 1 (5%)
			Affective disorders	16					0 –
			Psychiatric controls	35					0 –
Nasrallah et al. (1982)	48	Tsuang-Winokur	Schizophrenia	41	29.4	100	–	Visual assessment	Atrophy: 4 (10%)
			Medical controls	40	M	100	–		NR (sign. diff.)
Nasrallah et al. (1982)	7	DSM III + Feighner	Schizophrenia	55	29.9 ± 8.2	M	M	0 – 3 scale	Atrophy: 5 (9%)
			Affective disorders	24	31.8 ± 7.5				5 (21%)
			Medical controls	24	29.7 ± 5.8				1 (4%)
Lippman et al. (1982)	133	DSM III	Schizophrenia	54	M	NR	NR	1 – 3 scale	Atrophy: 16 (30%)
			Affective disorders	18	M				5 (28%)
			Unspecified controls	79					4 (5%)

Study	N	Criteria	Group	n	Age			Measure	Findings
Heath et al. (1982)	134	DSM III	Schizophrenia	50	NR	NR	NR	Size of cerebellar cisternae + pixel density vermis	Atrophy: 25 (50%)
			Other psychoses	64					34 (53%)
			Psychiatric controls	1586					74 (4.7%)
Weinberger et al. (1982)	53	DSM III	Schizophrenia	17	28.3	65	35	2 vermian folia	Atrophy: 2 (12%)
			Affective disorders	23	30.3	35	65		2 (9%)
			Other psychiatric patients	62	20.8	56	44		0 –
			Medical controls	26	30.3	50	50		0 –
Dewan et al. (1982)	135	DSM III	Schizophrenia	23	28.2	100	–	Width fourth ventricle and vermis, 'intermastoid ratio', pixel densities	Significant difference fourth ventricle and vermis width
			Medical/ neurological controls	23	34	100	–		
Rieder et al.	18	RDC	Schizophrenia	28	25.9 ± 8.1	46	54	Visual assessment	Atrophy: 2 (7%)
			Schizoaffective disorders	15	24.6 ± 4.3	73	27		1 (7%)
			Affective disorders	19					2 (11%)

a Key to diagnostic criteria: RDC = Research Diagnostic Criteria (71); DSM III = DSM III Diagnostic and Statistical Manual of the American Psychiatric Association, Third Edition (73); Tsuang and Winokur = Tsuang and Winokur Criteria for Schizophrenia (75); Feighner = Feighner Diagnostic Criteria (70).
b Key to abbreviations: NR = Not reported; M = Matched.

235

TABLE 6   CT studies of reversed cerebral asymmetries in schizophrenia

Study	Ref. no.	Diagnostic criteria[a]	Sample Category	No.	Mean age	% of total Male	% of total Female	Method	Reversed asymmetry controls
Luchins et al. (1979)	150	RDC	Schizophrenia	57	NR[b]	NR	NR	Widths frontal and occipital lobes	+
			Literature controls	80					
Nyback et al. (1982)	49	RDC	Schizophrenia	28	32 ± 1.5	54	46	Widths frontal and occipital lobes	+[c]
			Other psychiatric patients	18					
			Normal volunteers	46	27 ± 1.0	52	48		
Andreasen et al. (1982)	151	RDC + DSM III	Schizophrenia	43	29.9 M	NR	NR	Widths frontal and occipital lobes	−
			Medical controls	40					
Nasrallah et al. (1982)	48	Tsuang-Winokur	Schizophrenia	41	29.4 M	100	−	Widths frontal and occipital lobes	−
			Medical controls	40		100	−		
Luchins et al. (1982)	152	RDC	Schizophrenia + schizo-affective disorder	79	NR	NR	NR	Width occipital lobes	+
			Medical/neurological controls	100					
Jernigan et al. (1982)	153	DSM III	Schizophrenia	31	33 ± 9	100	−	Width frontal and occipital lobes	−
			Normal volunteers	32	NR	100	−		

Study	Ref.	Criteria	Group	n	Mean ± SD			Measure	Result
Weinberger et al. (1982)	53	DSM III	Schizophreniform	35	20.7 ± 6.2	54	46	Width of frontal and occipital lobes	−
			Chronic schizophrenia	17	28.3 ± 9.7	65	35		
			Affective disorder	23	30.3 ± 10.1	35	65		
			Other psychiatric patients	27	21 ± 9.6	59	41		
			Medical controls	26	30.3 ± 6.9	50	50		
Luchins et al. (1983)	154	RDC	Schizophrenia + schizoaffective disorders	45	NR	NR	NR	Planimetry of occipital lobes	−
			Medical controls	62					
Kling et al. (1983)	54	DSM III	Schizophrenia	26	33.9 ± 7.3	NR	NR	Widths of frontal lobes	−[c]
			Alcoholism	13	40.7 ± 6.9				
			Neurological patients	9	36.8 ± 8.7				
			Medical controls	20	36.8 ± 8.7				
Tsai et al. (1983)	155	DSM III	Schizophrenia	55	NR	100	−	Width of frontal and occipital lobes	+
			Affective disorders	27		100	−		

[a] Key to diagnostic criteria: RDC = Research Diagnostic Criteria (71); DSM III = Diagnostic and Statistical Manual of the American Psychiatric Association, Third Edition (73); Tsuang-Winokur = Tsuang and Winokur Criteria for Schizophrenia (75).
[b] Key to abbreviations: NR = Not reported; M = Matched.
[c] No difference from other psychiatric or neurological patients.

right frontal and left occipital lobes, a finding observed from a variety of studies including neuropathological (138), CT (139), fossil human cranium, and even non-human primates (140). It has been proposed that this asymmetry underlies lateralization of certain cerebral functions such as handedness and speech (141, 142). Increased frequency of reversed asymmetry (i.e. larger left frontal and/or right occipital lobes) has been reported in such disorders as autism (143), dyslexia (144), and in patients with verbal intellectual deficits (145), indicating a possible relationship between such reversals and cortical function, especially in disorders of language.

There has been considerable interest in the possibility of abnormal cerebral lateralization in schizophrenia. Findings such as increased frequency of left-handedness (146, 147), verbal intellectual deficits, and other observations led to a proposal that lateralization asymmetry might be a marker of a subgroup of patients, and that these patients may have a 'milder' form of the illness (148, 149). The use of CT scan assessments of anatomical asymmetries was a natural progression of this line of thought.

The CT evaluation of anatomical asymmetries is a relatively simple procedure. Most investigators have used a millimeter ruler to measure the width of the frontal and/or occipital lobes on each side, at the level of the third ventricle. Alternatives to this method have included projecting the image to 'life size' in order to maximize potential differences in the widths, and to measure the lobes on two or three different slices. Lastly, the dimensions of the individual lobes have been measured with the planimeter as described in the section on VBR above. One main source of error is incorrect positioning of the head in the scanner with a corresponding lateral tilt in the image; this spuriously produces differences in dimensions by creating varying planes of section corresponding to different levels on each side. This problem can be overcome by viewing the petrous portion of the temporal bone for symmetry, and excluding abnormally angled scans.

Table 6 lists the CT studies of asymmetry in schizophrenia. As shown, while positive studies have appeared, the majority have failed to reveal significantly greater numbers of schizophrenic patients with reversed anatomical asymmetries. The reasons for this are unclear, but do not seem to be related to differences in patient sampling (48) or clinical variables such as age, duration of illness, duration of hospitalization, premorbid adjustment, neuroleptic exposure, etc. (154). The existence and significance, if any, of reversed asymmetry in schizophrenia remain unestablished.

Brain density

The density of brain tissue has been estimated using the CT scan by taking the numerical X-ray attenuation values (CT numbers or Hounsfield units) from each pixel. This technique has, for example, revealed decreased densities of certain brain structures in patients with presenile dementia (156). The technique has been fraught with methodological problems such as variations in X-ray output, machinery differences, alteration due to bone, and so forth, discussed in greater detail earlier in this chapter. A number of methods have been used to assess density, and will be discussed along with the studies.

The earliest reports of brain densities in schizophrenia were a series of three articles comparing patients to medical and neurological controls (157 – 159). The first study (157) compared 22 schizophrenic patients with 21 matched controls and summed total pixel values in left and right hemispheres at three different levels. The patients were found to have lower densities overall at all levels, and both groups had lower values on the right as compared with the left. This normal left with higher values than right finding has not been observed by other investigators and may explain the left hemisphere differences between patients and controls described in the two later reports. The second report (158) was of 16 patients and the same 21 controls. Here the investigators divided the brain into four quadrants at the level of the lateral ventricles. Differences emerged with decreased relative density only in the left anterior distribution. Though there were no overall changes posteriorly, there were correlations of the absolute values of density and total neuroleptic exposure. Conceptually, this linkage is unclear, and probably reflects a chance correlation. Lastly (159) the group compared 23 patients and 24 controls, measuring every fourth pixel at three levels, and dividing into four separate brain regions at each level on each side for a total of 24 distinct regions. The main finding of this study was reduced density localized to the anterior aspect of the left hemisphere. The authors proposed that this represented structural abnormalities of the cortex in this distribution, possibly due to local atrophy.

Criticism arose regarding the methodology of the foregoing studies. Since the entire regions were evaluated, the pixels used could have fallen in the ventricles, fissures, and sulci, indicating enlargement of these structures and not abnormalities of tissue density per se. Several follow-up studies attempted to correct for this by outlining small areas in the brain parenchyma proper.

Largen et al. examined CT scans of 25 schizophrenic patients and 19 medical controls (160); in this study they visually outlined a 0.25 cm^2 area above the lateral ventricles bilaterally in anterior and posterior distributions in the gray and white matter. Though they found no differences from the controls, there was an indication of *higher* density of gray and white matter in the right hemisphere in schizophrenic patients. In a follow-up to their original report (63), the group found no differences between patients and controls on any measure when the relatively conservative Bonferroni's t-test was used, but univariate analysis showed evidence of some increased density in the white matter anteriorly, especially on the right and continued right.

Three other reports continued in the same vein of investigation. Kanba et al. (161), using a technique of visually placing a cursor around an area of interest, measured the mean pixel density in the parenchyma of the frontal, parietal, and occipital lobes at the level of the lateral ventricles. They discovered lower density in frontal and occipital areas bilaterally in 40 schizophrenic patients as compared with the same number of diagnostically unspecified controls. They found no correlation of density with age or neuroleptic exposure. Coffman and Nasrallah (162) compared 18 schizophrenic patients with 11 manic-depressives, assessing four areas from the left and right hemispheres at three different levels. They reported differences only in the uppermost slice, a fact that they attributed to cortical atrophy in schizophrenia. In a small study of 8 schizophrenic patients, 7 other psychiatric patients, and 15 medical controls, DeMeyer et al. (163), using a technique similar to that of Coffmann and Nasrallah (162), found the 'other psychiatric' patients to have greater overall densities than the schizophrenic and control groups, with no general distinctions between the latter two; the schizophrenic sample was found, however, to have somewhat lower density in the frontal distribution in the middle slice (corresponding to the dorsal aspect of the prefrontal cortex).

Finally, in a somewhat different study, Dewan et al. (106) examined the densities of 0.1 cm^2 areas in the caudate and temporal lobes, and 0.5 cm^2 of the thalamus in 23 patients and medical controls, all males. They found no differences in the cortical measures, but significantly greater density of the periventricular nuclei.

Taken together the studies present a confusing array of discrepant findings. Some reports indicate decreased density in patients, while others find density to be increased especially in the so-called subcortical regions. The only replicated finding is that of lowered values in the cortex, especially in the frontal distribution, which may simply be an indicator of cortical atrophy. This disparity in findings, as well as the methodological problems involved, warrant caution in interpreting any of these results.

Comment

In this chapter we have reviewed over 80 separate studies of CT scanning in schizophrenia. After all this, what do we know? First, and perhaps most importantly, we know that schizophrenia is a disorder involving the brain and that this is demonstrated by abnormalities of the cerebrum and cerebellum on CT scans. The findings are not, however, of equal strength. The studies of asymmetries and densities seem mired in problems of methodology and clinicopathological significance; cerebellar atrophy, though more frequently and consistently reproduced, still seems to require further elucidation. The most robust finding is that suggestive of cerebral atrophy, as revealed by enlarged lateral and third ventricles and an increase of cortical surface markings, perhaps clearest in the prefrontal cortex. In addition, atrophy of these areas may be related in some fashion to one another; enlargement of the third ventricle has been correlated with that of the lateral ventricle (37, 69), and in our recent study we found a significant association between degree of prefrontal atrophy and third ventricular size, and a trend toward significance with lateral ventricles. Further, prefrontal atrophy and ventricular enlargement have been linked to increased delta (slow) waves on EEG (164) and so-called hypofrontality of regional cerebral blood flow (165), suggesting a regional link between neuroanatomical and neurophysiological deficits.

The finding of cortical and subcortical pathology and its association with such clinical variables as cognitive impairment, resistance to neuroleptics, and poorer clinical outcome, has led some investigators to propose subtyping of the schizophrenic syndrome according to these variables (9). The chief among these concepts is that of the Type I and Type II dichotomy proposed by Crow (166). This scheme splits schizophrenia into a first group (Type I), characterized by an acute onset, remitting illness in which dopamine overactivity is prominent, and an absence of cerebral atrophy, and a second (Type II) typified by insidious onset, cognitive impairment, poor response to neuroleptics and poor outcome, and presence of cerebral atrophy. This inverse relationship between dopamine activity and signs of brain atrophy is supported by several reports. Nyback et al. (167), in a study of 26 schizophrenic patients and 43 normal volunteers found no differences in CSF homovanillic acid (HVA, a metabolite of dopamine), 3-methoxy-4-hydroxy-phenylglycol (MHPG, a byproduct of norepinephrine) and 5-hydroxyindoleacetic acid (5-HIAA, a metabolite of serotonin) between the groups. They did, however, find an inverse relationship between lateral ventricular size and both HVA and 5-HIAA in patients only, suggesting a relationship between ventricular enlargement and low central dopamine and serotonin activity. A study by Van Kammen et al. found an inverse relationship between both lateral ventricular enlargement and cortical atrophy, and central dopamine activity as evidenced by CSF HVA and dopamine beta-hydroxylase levels. Weinberger et al. (170) have reported that CSF HVA is inversely correlated specifically with prefrontal atrophy, the area of distribution of mesocortical dopamine neurons. Tachiki et al. (171) found that monoamine oxidase-B correlated with ventricular size in non-paranoid but not in paranoid patients, which lends support to the subtyping notion. Finally, in a study of eyeblinking (thought to reflect central dopamine activity), Kleinman et al. (172), found that patients with small lateral ventricles had suppression of blinks (indicating a change in central dopamine activity) with neuroleptics, while those with atrophy failed to do so.

Collectively, such studies support the notion of a subtype of schizophrenia with cerebral atrophy in which mesocortical dopaminergic activity may be reduced. There is, however, one powerful countering argument to the notion of a subtype. It is based on the fact that the magnitude of surface, third, or lateral ventricular anatomical deficits do not parcel out into distinct groups. Rather, the quantitative measures form a relatively uniform continuum with means above those of normal samples. The continuum notion is at least as compelling an explanation for the clinical correlations, with the patients having atrophy, poorer outcome, diminished response to neuroleptics, and the other characteristics noted earlier simply falling at the more severe end of the pathological continuum.

Atrophy on a CT scan does not tell us about etiology. There are some hints, however. Ventricular size has a powerful genetic determinant in normal individuals, with near parity in identical twins, and striking similarities within families (38, 173). Schizophrenic patients have been found to have larger ventricles than their twins and other siblings (though the mean for the entire sibling groups was somewhat larger than that of the control group) (38). Beyond these findings are the reports

241

that patients with ventricles within the normal range tend to have a stronger family history of schizophrenia than those with clearly enlarged ventricles (48, 62, 174), and that patients with clear-cut atrophy have a greater incidence of perinatal trauma (58, 62, 174, 175), a finding apparently also true of patients with bipolar disorder (58). This raises the intriguing possibility of at least two paths to schizophrenia; one associated with a genetic predisposition and a second related to birth injury or other early life trauma. Unfortunately, an inverse relationship between ventricular enlargement and a positive family history of schizophrenia has not been consistently observed (38, 52, 176).

Finally, it is important to note that while abnormalities of the brain are generally associated with poorer outcome, such findings are not *predictive* of bad results in any given patient (177). Therefore, a CT scan should be reserved for diagnosis of a remediable lesion (which may be found in patients with schizophrenia-like illnesses), not for outlining prognosis (178). It goes without saying that the CT scan is not used to 'rule-in' the diagnosis of schizophrenia.

REFERENCES

1. Dandy WE (1919) Roentgenography of the brain after the injection of air into the spinal cord. *Ann. Surg., 70,* 397.
2. Haug JO (1962) Pneumoencephalographic studies in mental disease. *Acta Psychiatr. Scand. Suppl. 165,* 38, 1.
3. Weinberger DR, Wyatt RJ (1982) Brain morphology in schizophrenia: In vivo studies. In: Henn FA, Nasrallah HA (Eds), *Schizophrenia as a Brain Disease,* pp. 148 – 175. Oxford University Press, New York.
4. Johnstone EC, Crow TJ, Frith DC, Husband J, Krel L (1976) Cerebral ventricular size and cognitive impairment in schizophrenia. *Lancet, 2,* 924.
5. Stevens JR (1982) Neuropathology of schizophrenia. *Arch. Gen. Psychiatry, 39,* 1121.
6. Snyder SH (1982) Schizophrenia. *Lancet, 2,* 970.
7. Nasrallah HA, McCalley-Whitters M, Jacoby GG (1982) Cortical atrophy in schizophrenia and mania: a comparative study. *J. Clin. Psychiatry, 43,* 439.
8. Weinberger DR (1984) Computed tomography (CT) findings in schizophrenia: speculation on the meaning of it all. *J. Psychiatric Res., 18,* 477.
9. Weinberger DR, Wyatt RJ (1982) Cerebral ventricular size: a biological marker for subtyping chronic schizophrenia. In: Hanin I, Usden E (Eds), *Biological Markers in Psychiatry,* pp. 505 – 512. Pergamon, New York.
10. Jacoby RJ, Levy R (1980) Computed tomography in the elderly. 3: Affective disorder. *Br. J. Psychiatry, 136,* 270.
11. Jacoby RJ, Levy R, Bird JM (1981) Computed tomography and the outcome of affective disorder: a follow-up of elderly patients. *Br. J. Psychiatry, 139,* 288.
12. Pearlson GD, Veroff AF (1981) Computerized tomographic scan changes in manic-depressive illness. *Lancet, 2,* 170.
13. Johnstone EC, Owens DGC, Crow TJ, Jagoe R (1982) A CT study of 188 patients with schizophrenia, affective psychosis and neurotic illness. In: Perris C, Struwe G, Jansson B (Eds), *Biological Psychiatry 1981,* pp. 237 – 240, Elsevier, Amsterdam.
14. Nasrallah HA, McCalley-Whitters M, Jacoby CG (1982) Cerebral ventricular enlarge-

ment in young manic males. A controlled CT study. *J. Affect. Disord., 4,* 15.

15. Standish-Barry HMAS, Bouras N, Bridges PK, Bartlett JR (1982) Pneumoencephalographic and computerized axial tomography scan changes in affective disorder. *Br. J. Psychiatry, 141,* 614.
16. Scott MZ, Golden CJ, Ruedrich SL, Bishop RJ (1983) Ventricular enlargement in major depression. *Psychiatry Res., 8,* 91.
17. Targum DS, Rosen LN, DeLisi LE, Weinberger DR, Citrin CM (1983) Cerebral ventricular size major depressive disorder. Association with delusional symptoms. *Biol. Psychiatry, 18,* 329.
18. Rieder RO, Mann LS, Weinberger DR, van Kammen DP, Post RM (1983) Computed tomographic scans in patients with schizophrenia, schizoaffective, and bipolar affective disorder. *Arch. Gen. Psychiatry, 40,* 735.
19. Targum DS, Rosen LN, Citrin CM (1983) Delusional symptoms associated with enlarged cerebral ventricles in depressed patients. *South. Med. Assoc. J., 76,* 985.
20. Luchins DJ, Meltzer HY (1983) Ventricular size and psychosis in affective disorder. *Biol. Psychiatry, 18,* 1197.
21. Pearlson GD, Garbacz DJ, Tompkins RH, Ahn HS, Gutterman DF, Veroff AE, DePaulo JR (1984) Clinical correlates of lateral ventricular enlargement in bipolar affective disorder. *Am. J. Psychiatry, 141,* 253.
22. Heinz R, Martinez J, Haenggli A (1977) Reversibility of cerebral atrophy in anorexia nervosa and Cushing's syndrome. *J. Comput. Assist. Tomograph., 1,* 415.
23. Jensen SJ, Genfke IK, Hyldebrandt N, Pedersen H, Petersen HD, Weile B (1982) Cerebral atrophy in young torture victims. *N. Engl. J. Med., 307,* 1341.
24. Evans WA (1942) An encephalographic ratio for estimating ventricular enlargement and cerebral atrophy. *Arch. Neurol. Psychiatry, 47,* 931.
25. Huckman M, Fox J, Topel J (1975) The validity of criteria for the evaluation of cerebral atrophy by computed tomography. *Radiology, 116,* 85.
26. Hansson J, Levander B, Liliequist B (1975) Size of the intracerebral ventricles as measured with computer tomography, encephalography and echoventriculography. *Acta Radiol., Suppl., 346,* 98.
27. Meese W, Lanksch W, Wende S (1976) Cerebral atrophy and computerized tomography aspects of a qualitative and quantitative analysis from cranial computerized tomography. In: Lanksch W, Kasner E (Eds), *Cranial Computerized Tomography,* pp. 222 – 232. Springer-Verlag, Berlin.
28. Penn RD, Belanger MG, Yasnoff WA (1978) Ventricular volume in man computed from CAT scans. *Ann. Neurol., 3,* 216.
29. Synek V, Reuben JR (1976) The ventricular-brain ratio using planimetric measurement of EMI scans. *Br. J. Radiol., 49,* 233.
30. Zatz LM, Jernigan TL (1983) The ventricular-brain ratio on computed tomographic scans: validity and proper use. *Psychiatry Res., 8,* 207.
31. Jernigan TL, Zatz LM, Naeser MA (1979) Semiautomated method for quantifying CSF volume on cranial computed tomography. *Radiology, 132,* 463.
32. Zatz LM, Alvarez RE (1977) An inaccuracy in computed tomography: the energy dependence of CT values. *Radiology, 124,* 91.
33. McCullough EC (1977) Factors affecting the use of quantitative information from CT scanner. *Radiology, 124,* 99.
34. Trimble M, Kingsley D (1978) Cerebral ventricular size in chronic schizophrenia. *Lancet, 1,* 278.

35. Johnstone EC, Crow TJ, Frith CD, Stevens M, Kreel L, Husband J (1978) The dementia of dementia praecox. *Acta Psychiatr. Scand., 57,* 305.
36. Weinberger DR, Torrey EF, Neophytides AN, Wyatt RJ (1979) Lateral ventricular enlargement in chronic schizophrenia. *Arch. Gen. Psychiatry, 36,* 735.
37. Moriguchi I (1981) A study of schizophrenic brains by computerized tomographic scans. *Folia Psychiatr. Neurol. Jpn., 35,* 54.
38. Weinberger DR, DeLisi LE, Neophytides AN, Wyatt RJ (1981) Familial aspects of CT scan abnormalities in chronic schizophrenic patients. *Psychiatry Res., 4,* 65.
39. Tanaka Y, Hazama H, Kawahara R, Kobayash K (1981) *Acta Psychiatr. Scand., 63,* 191.
40. Okasha A, Madkour O, Madg FA (1982) Cortical and central atrophy in chronic schizophrenia, a controlled study. In: Perris C, Struwe G, Jansson B (Eds), *Biological Psychiatry 1981.* Elsevier, Amsterdam.
41. Okasha A, Madkour O (1982) Cortical and central atrophy in schizophrenia. *Acta Psychiatr. Scand., 65,* 29.
42. Takahashi R, Inaba Y, Inanaga K, Kato N, Kumashiro H, Nishimura T, Okuma T, Otsuki S, Sakai T, Sato T, Shimazono Y (1982) CT scanning and the investigation of schizophrenia. In: Perris C, Struwe G, Jansson B (Eds), *Biological Psychiatry 1981.* Elsevier, Amsterdam.
43. Benes F, Sunderland P, Jones BD, LeMay M, Cohen BM, Lipinski J (1982) Normal ventricles in young schizophrenics. *Br. J. Psychiatry, 141,* 90.
44. Frangos E, Athanassenas G, Gregoriades A, Kapsalakis Z (1982) Lateral cerebral ventricular enlargement in chronic schizophrenia. *Enkephalos, 19,* 64.
45. Andreasen NC, Smith MR, Jacoby CG, Dennert JW, Olsen SA (1982) Ventricular enlargement in schizophrenia: definition and prevalence. *Am. J. Psychiatry, 139,* 292.
46. Andreasen NC, Olsen SA, Dennert JW, Smith MR (1982) Ventricular enlargement in schizophrenia: relationship to positive and negative symptoms. *Am. J. Psychiatry, 139,* 297.
47. Reveley AM, Reveley MA, Clifford CA, Murray RM (1982) Cerebral ventricular size in twins discordant for schizophrenia. *Lancet, 1,* 540.
48. Nasrallah HA, Rizzo M, Damasio H, McCalley-Whitters M, Kuperman S, Jacoby CG (1982) Neurological differences between paranoid and non-paranoid schizophrenia: Part II. Computerized tomographic findings. *J. Clin. Psychiatry, 43,* 307.
49. Nyback H, Wiegel F-A, Berggren B-M, Hindmarsh T (1982) Computed tomography of the brain in patients with acute psychosis and in healthy controls. *Acta Psychiatr. Scand., 65,* 403.
50. Jernigan TL, Zatz LM, Moses JA, Berger PA (1982) Computed tomography in schizophrenics and normal volunteers I. Fluid volume. *Arch. Gen. Psychiatry, 39,* 765.
51. Nasrallah HA, Jacoby CG, McCalley-Whitters M, Kuperman S (1982) Cerebral ventricular enlargement in subtypes of chronic schizophrenia. *Arch. Gen. Psychiatry, 39,* 774.
52. Nasrallah HA, Kuperman S, Hamra BJ, McCalley-Whitters M (1983) Clinical differences between schizophrenic patients with and without large cerebral ventricles. *J. Clin. Psychiatry, 44,* 407.
53. Weinberger DR, DeLisi LE, Perman GP, Targum S, Wyatt RJ (1982) Computed tomography in schizophreniform disorder and other psychiatric disorders. *Arch. Gen. Psychiatry, 39,* 778.
54. Kling AS, Kurtz N, Tachiki K, Orzeck A (1983) CT scans in sub-groups of chronic

schizophrenics. *J. Psychiatric Res., 17,* 375.

55. Woods BT, Wolf J (1983) A reconsideration of the relation of ventricular enlargement to duration of illness in schizophrenia. *Am. J. Psychiatry, 140,* 1564.

56. Schultz SC, Koller MM, Kishore PR, Hamer RM, Gehl JJ, Friedel RO (1983) Ventricular enlargement in teenage patients with schizophrenia spectrum disorder. *Am. J. Psychiatry, 140,* 1592.

57. Pearlson GD, Garbacz DJ, Breakey WR, Ahn HS, DePaulo JR (1984) Lateral ventricular enlargement associated with persistent unemployment and negative symptoms in both schizophrenia and bipolar disorder. *Psychiatry Res., 12,* 1.

58. Pearlson GD, Garbacz DJ, Moberg PJ, Ahn HS, DePaulo JR (1985) Symptomatic, familial perinatal, and social correlates of computerized axial tomography (CAT) changes in schizophrenics and bipolars. *J. Nerv. Ment. Dis., 173,* 42.

59. DeMeyer MK, Gilmor R, DeMeyer WE, Hendrie H, Edwards M, Franco JN (1984) Third ventricle size and ventricular brain ratio in treatment-resistant psychiatric patients. *J. Oper. Psychiatry, 15,* 2.

60. Luchins DJ, Lewine RRJ, Melzer HY (1984) Lateral ventricular size, psychopathology, and medication response in the psychoses. *Biol. Psychiatry, 19,* 29.

61. Pandurangi AK, Dewan MJ, Lee Sh, Ramachandran T, Levy BF, Boucher M, Yozawitz A, Major L (1984) The ventricular system in chronic schizophrenic patients, a controlled tomography study. *Br. J. Psychiatry, 144,* 172.

62. Schulsinger, F, Parnas J, Petersen ET, Schulsinger H, Teasdale TW, Mednick SA, Moller L, Silverton L (1984) Cerebral ventricular size in the offspring of schizophrenic mothers. *Arch. Gen. Psychiatry, 41,* 602.

63. Largen JW, Smith RC, Calderon M, Baumgarten R, Lu R-B, Schoolar JC, Ravichandran GK (1984) Abnormalities of brain structure and density in schizophrenia. *Biol. Psychiatry, 19,* 991.

64. Shima S, Kanba S, Masuda Y, Tsukumo T, Kitamura T, Asai M (1985) Normal ventricles in chronic schizophrenia. *Acta Psychiatr. Scand., 71,* 25.

65. Boronow J, Pickar D, Ninan PT, Roy A, Hommer D, Linnoila M, Paul SM (1985) Atrophy limited to third ventricle only in chronic schizophrenic patients: reports of a controlled series. *Arch. Gen. Psychiatry, 40,* 266.

66. Williams AO, Reveley MA, Kolakowska T, Ardern M, Mandelbrote BM (1985) Schizophrenia with good and poor outcome II: Cerebral ventricular size and its clinical significance. *Br. J. Psychiatry, 146,* 239.

67. Carr EG, Wedding D (1984) Neuropsychological assessment of cerebral ventricular size in chronic schizophrenics. *Int. J. Neuropsychol., 6,* 106.

68. Turner SW, Toone BK, Brett-Jones JR (1986) Computerized tomographic scan changes in early chronic schizophrenia − their relationship to perinatal trauma, family history and alcohol intake: preliminary findings. *Psychological Med.,* in press.

69. Shelton RC, Weinberger DR, Doran A, Pickar D (1985) Cerebral structural pathology in schizophrenia. Presented at the Fourth World Congress of Biological Psychiatry, Philadelphia, PA.

70. Feighner JP, Robins E, Guze SB, Woodruff RA, Winokur G, Munoz R (1972) Diagnostic criteria for use in psychiatric research. *Arch. Gen. Psychiatry, 26,* 57.

71. Spitzer RL, Endicott J, Robins E (1977) *Research Diagnostic Criteria (RDC) for a Selected Group to Functional Disorders, 3rd Ed.* Biometrics Research, New York.

72. Carpenter WT, Bartko JJ, Strauss JS (1980) A postscript on the 12-point flexible system for the diagnosis of schizophrenia: A report from the IPSS. *Psychiatry Res., 3,* 357.

73. American Psychiatric Association, Committee or Nomenclature and Statistics (1980) *Diagnostic and Statistical Manual of Mental Disorders, 3rd Ed.* American Psychiatric Association, Washington, DC.

74. Spitzer RL, Endicott J (1977) *The Schedule for Affective Disorders and Schizophrenia, Lifetime Version, 3rd Ed.* New York State Psychiatric Institute, New York.

75. Tsuang MT, Winokur G (1974) Criteria for subtyping schizophrenia. Clinical differentiation of hebephrenic and paranoid schizophrenia. *Arch. Gen. Psychiatry, 31,* 43.

76. Marsden CD (1976) Cerebral atrophy and cognitive impairment in chronic schizophrenia. *Lancet, 2,* 1079.

77. Jelinek EH (1976) Cerebral atrophy and cognitive impairment in chronic schizophrenia. *Lancet, 2,* 1202.

78. Garratt FN (1976) Cerebral atrophy and cognitive impairment in chronic schizophrenia. *Lancet, 2,* 1303.

79. Weinberger DR, Bigelow LB, Kleinman JE, Klein ST, Rosenblatt JE, Wyatt RJ (1980) Cerebral ventricular enlargement in chronic schizophrenia, an association with poor response to treatment. *Arch. Gen. Psychiatry, 37,* 11.

80. Golden CJ, Moses JA, Zelazowski R, Graber B, Zatz LM, Horvath TB, Berger PA (1980) Cerebral ventricular size and neuropsychological impairment in young chronic schizophrenics, measurement by the standardized Luria-Nebraska neurophysiological battery. *Arch. Gen. Psychiatry, 37,* 619.

81. Frangos E, Athanassenas G (1982) Differences in lateral brain ventricular size among various types of chronic schizophrenics, evidence basic on a CT study. *Acta Psychiatr. Scand., 66,* 459.

82. Barron SA, Jacobs L, Kunkel WR (1976) Changes in size of normal lateral ventricles during aging determined by computed tomography. *Neurology, 26,* 1011.

83. Haug G (1977) Age and sex dependence of the size of normal ventricles on computed tomography. *Neuroradiology, 14,* 201.

84. Earnest MP, Heaton RK, Wilkinson WE, Manke WF (1979) Cortical atrophy, ventricular enlargement and intellectual impairment in the aged. *Neurology, 29,* 1138.

85. Withers E, Hinton J (1971) Three forms of clinical tests of the sensorium and their reliability. *Br. J. Psychiatry, 119,* 1.

86. Inglis J (1959) A paired associative learning test for use with psychiatric patients. *J. Ment. Sci., 105,* 440.

87. Krawiecka M, Goldberg D, Vaughan M (1977) A standardized psychiatric assessment scale for rating chronic psychotic patients. *Acta Psychiatr. Scand., 55,* 299.

88. Kraepelin E (1971) *Dementia Praecox and Paraphrenia.* RM Krieger, New York.

89. Jaspers K (1963) *General Psychopathology.* Manchester University Press, London.

90. Wechsler D (1981) *WAIS-R Manual.* Psychological Corporation, New York.

91. Donnely EF, Weinberger DR, Waldman IN, Wyatt RJ (1980) Cognitive impairment associated with morphological brain abnormalities on computed tomography in chronic schizophrenic patients. *J. Nerv. Ment. Dis.*

92. Halstead WC (1947) *Brain and Intelligence.* University of Chicago Press, Chicago.

93. Golden CJ, MacInnes WD, Ariel RN, Ruedrich SL, Chu C-C, Coffman JA, Graber B, Bloch S (1982) Cross-validation of the ability of the Luria-Nebraska Neuropsychological Battery to differentiate chronic schizophrenics with and without ventricular enlargement. *J. Consult. Clin. Psychol., 50,* 87.

94. Golden CJ, Purisch AD, Hammeke TA (1979) *The Luria-Nebraska Neuropsychological Battery: A Manual for Clinical and Experimental Uses.* University of Nebraska Press,

Lincoln, NE.

95. Weinberger DR, Cannon-Spoor E, Potkin SG, Wyatt RJ (1980) Poor premorbic adjustment and CT scan abnormalities in chronic schizophrenia. *Am. J. Psychiatry, 137,* 1410.

96. DeLisi LE, Schwartz CC, Targum SD, Byrnes SM, Cannon-Spoor E, Weinberger DR, Wyatt RJ (1983) Ventricular brain enlargement and outcome of acute schizophreniform disorder. *Psychiatry Res., 9,* 169.

97. Naber D, Albus M, Burke H, Muller-Spahn F, Munch U, Reinertshofer T, Wissman J, Ackenheil M (1985) Neuroleptic withdrawal in chronic schizophrenia, CT and endocrine variables relating to psychopathology. *Psychiatry Res., 16,* 207.

98. Smith RC, Largen J, Calderon M, Schoolar J, Shvartsburd A, Ravichandran GK (1983) CT scans and neuropsychological tests as predictors of clinical response in schizophrenics. *Schizophr. Bull., 19,* 505.

99. Schulz SC, Sinicrope P, Kishore P, Friedel RO (1983) Treatment response and ventricular enlargement in young schizophrenic patients. *Psychopharm. Bull., 19,* 510.

100. Luchins DJ, Lewine RJ, Meltzer HY (1983) Lateral ventricular size in the psychoses: relation to psychopathology and therapeutic and adverse response to medication. *Schizophr. Bull., 19,* 518.

101. Luchins DJ, Jackman J, Meltzer HY (1983) Lateral ventricular size and drug-induced parkinsonism. *Psychiatry Res., 9,* 9.

102. Bishop RJ, Golden CJ, MacInnes WD, Chu C-C, Ruedrich SL, Wilson J (1983) The BPRS in assessing symptom correlates of cerebral ventricular enlargement in acute and chronic schizophrenia. *Psychiatry Res., 9,* 225.

103. Gluck E, Radu EW, Gerhardt P (1980) A computed tomographic prolective trohoc study of chronic schizophrenics. *Neuroradiol., 20,* 167.

104. Mundt C, Radu W, Gluck E (1980) Computer tomographische Untersuchungen der Liquorräume an chronisch schizophrenen Patienten. *Nervenarzt, 51,* 745.

105. Gattaz WF, Kasper S, Kohlmeyer K, Beckman H (1981) Die kraniale Computertomographie in der Schizophrenieforschung. *Fortschr. Psychiatr. Neurol., 49,* 286.

106. Dewan MJ, Pandurangi AD, Lee SH, Ramachandran T, Levy B, Boucher M, Yozawitz A, Major LF (1983) Central brain morphology in chronic schizophrenic patients: a controlled CT study. *Biol. Psychiatry, 18,* 1133.

107. Neito D, Escobar A (1972) Major psychoses. In: Minkler J (Ed), *Pathology of the Nervous System,* pp. 2654–2665. McGraw-Hill, New York.

108. Hyyppa MT, Lhra J, Makkonen R, Sarijavri S, Tenkku M (1982) Relation between central cerebral atrophy, memory defects, and prolactin secretion. *Psychoneuroendocrinology, 7,* 195.

109. Meese W, Kluge W, Grumme T, Hopfenmuller W (1980) CT evaluation of the CSF spaces of healthy persons. *Neuroradiology, 19,* 131.

110. Weinberger DR, Torrey EF, Neophytides AN, Wyatt RJ (1979) Structural abnormalities in the cerebral cortex of chronic schizophrenic patients. *Arch. Gen. Psychiatry, 36,* 935.

111. Nasrallah HA, Kuperman S, Jacoby CG, McCalley-Whitters M, Hamra B (1983) Clinical correlates of sulcal widening in schizophrenia. *Psychiatry Res., 10,* 237.

112. Oxenstierna G, Bergstrand G, Bjerkenstedt L, Sedvall G, Wik G (1984) Evidence of disturbed CSF circulation and brain atrophy in cases in schizophrenic psychosis. *Br. J. Psychiatry, 44,* 654.

113. Fox JH, Topel JL, Huckman MS (1975) Use of computerized tomography in senile dementia. *J. Neurol. Neurosurg. Psychiatry, 38,* 1948.

114. Roberts MA, Caird FI (1976) Computerized tomography and intellectual impairment in

the elderly. *J. Neurol. Neurosurg. Psychiatry, 39,* 986.

115. DeLeon MJ, Ferris SH, Blau I, George AE, Reisberg B, Kricheff II, Gershon G (1979) Correlations between computerized tomographic changes and behavioral deficits in senile dementia. *Lancet, 2,* 859.

116. Jacoby RJ, Levy R, Dawson JM (1980) Computerized tomography in the elderly I. The normal population. *Br. J. Psychiatry, 136,* 244.

117. Jacoby RJ, Levy R (1980) Computerized tomography in the elderly, 2. Senile dementia, diagnosis and functional impairment. *Br. J. Psychiatry, 136,* 256.

118. Naeser MA, Gebhardt C, Levine HL (1980) Decreased computerized tomography numbers in patients with pre-senile dementia. *Arch. Neurol., 37,* 401.

119. Bondareff W, Baldy R, Levy R (1981) Quantitative computed tomography in senile dementia. *Arch. Gen. Psychiatry, 38,* 1365.

120. Bird JM (1982) Computerized tomography, atrophy, and dementia: a review. *Progr. Neurobiol., 19,* 91.

121. Rieder RO, Donnelly EF, Herdt JR, Waldman IN (1979) Sulcal prominence in young chronic schizophrenic patients: CT scan findings associated with impairment on neuro-psychological tests. *Psychiatry Res., 1,* 1.

122. Folstein MF, McHugh PR (1975) Mini-mental state. *J. Psychiatry Res., 12,* 189.

123. Weinberger DR, Kleinman JE (in press) Observations on the brain in schizophrenia. In: Andreasen N (Ed), *American Psychiatric Association Annual Review, Vol 5.* APA Press, Washington, DC.

124. Allen JH, Martin JT, McLain LW (1979) Computed tomography in cerebellar atrophic processes. *Radiology, 130,* 379.

125. Koller WC, Glatt SL, Perlik S, Huckman MS, Fox JH (1981) Cerebellar atrophy demonstrated by computed tomography. *Neurology, 31,* 405.

126. Weinberger DR, Kleinman JE, Luchins DJ, Bigelow LB, Wyatt RJ (1980) Cerebellar pathology in schizophrenia: a controlled post-mortem study. *Am. J. Psychiatry, 137,* 359.

127. Luchins DJ, Morihisa JM, Weinberger DR, Wyatt RJ (1981) Cerebral asymmetry and cerebellar atrophy in schizophrenia: a controlled postmortem study. *Am. J. Psychiatry, 138,* 1501.

128. Heath RG, Franklin DE, Shraberg D (1979) Gross pathology of the cerebellum in patients diagnosed and treated as functional psychiatric disorders. *J. Nerv. Ment. Dis., 167,* 585.

129. Kutty IN, Prendes JL (1981) Psychosis and cerebellar degeneration. *J. Nerv. Ment. Dis., 169,* 390.

130. Weinberger DR, Torrey EF, Wyatt RJ (1979) Cerebellar atrophy in chronic schizophrenia, *Lancet, 1,* 718.

131. Coffman JA, Mefferd J, Golden CJ, Broch S, Graber B (1981) Cerebellar atrophy in chronic schizophrenia. *Lancet, 1,* 666.

132. Nasrallah HA, Jacoby CG, McCalley-Whitters M (1981) Cerebellar atrophy in schizophrenia and mania. *Lancet 1,* 1102.

133. Lippmann S, Manshadi M, Baldwin H, Drasin G, Rice J, Alrajeh S (1982) Cerebellar vermis dimensions on computerized tomographic scans of schizophrenia and bipolar patients. *Am. J. Psychiatry, 139,* 667.

134. Heath RG, Franklin DE, Walker CF, Keating JW (1982) Cerebellar vermal atrophy in psychiatric patients. *Biol. Psychiatry, 17,* 569.

135. Dewan MJ, Pandurangi AK, Lee SH, Ramachandran T, Levy BF, Boucher M,

Yozawitz A, Major L (1983) Cerebellar morphology in chronic schizophrenic patients: a controlled computed tomographic study. *Psychiatry Res., 10,* 97.

136. Snider SR (1982) Cerebellar pathology in schizophrenia - cause or consequence? *Neurosci. Biobehav. Rev., 6,* 47.
137. Von Bonin G (1962) Anatomical asymmetries of the cerebral hemispheres. In: Mountcastle VB (Ed), *Interhemispheric Relations and Cerebral Dominance,* pp. 6 – 14. Johns Hopkins University Press, Baltimore, MD.
138. Weinberger DR, Luchins DJ, Morihisa JM, Wyatt RJ (1982) Asymmetrical volumes of the right and left frontal and occipital regions of the human brain. *Ann. Neurol., 11,* 97.
139. LeMay M, Kido DK (1978) Asymmetries of cerebral hemispheres on computed tomograms. *J. Comput. Assist. Tomograph., 2,* 471.
140. LeMay M (1976) Morphological cerebral asymmetries of modern man, fossil man, and nonhuman primate. *Ann. N. Y. Acad. Sci., 280,* 349.
141. Galaburda AM, LeMay M, Kemper TL, Geschwind NW (1978) Right-left asymmetries in the brain. *Science, 199,* 852.
142. LeMay M (1977) Asymmetries of the skull and handedness. *J. Neurol. Sci., 32,* 243.
143. Hier DB, LeMay M, Rosenberger PB (1978) Autism associated with reversed cerebral asymmetry. *Neurology, 28,* 348.
144. Hier DB, LeMay M, Rosenberger PB, Perlo VP (1978) Developmental dyslexia: evidence for a subgroup with reversal of cerebral asymmetry. *Arch. Neurol., 35,* 90.
145. Rosenberger PB, Hier DB (1980) Cerebral asymmetry and verbal intellectual deficits. *Ann. Neurol., 8,* 300.
146. Oddy HC, Lobstein TJ (1972) Hand and eye dominance in schizophrenia. *Br. J. Psychiatry, 120,* 331.
147. Boklage CE (1977) Schizophrenia, brain asymmetry development, and twinning: cellular relationship with etiological and possible prognostic implications. *Biol. Psychiatry, 12,* 19.
148. Luchins DJ, Weinberger DR, Wyatt RJ (1979) Anomalous lateralization associated with a milder form of schizophrenia. *Am. J. Psychiatry, 136,* 1598.
149. Luchins D, Pollin W, Wyatt RJ (1980) Laterality in monozygotic schizophrenic twins: an alternative hypothesis. *Biol. Psychiatry, 15,* 87.
150. Luchins DJ, Weinberger DR, Wyatt RJ (1979) Schizophrenia, evidence of a subgroup with reversed cerebral asymmetry. *Arch. Gen. Psychiatry, 36,* 1309.
151. Andreasen NC, Dennert JW, Olsen SA, Damasio AR (1982) Hemispheric asymmetries and schizophrenia. *Am. J. Psychiatry, 139,* 427.
152. Luchins DJ, Weinberger DR, Wyatt RJ (1982) Schizophrenia and cerebral asymmetry detected by computed tomography. *Am. J. Psychiatry, 139,* 753.
153. Jernigan TL, Zatz LM, Moses JA, Cordellino JP (1982) Computed tomography in schizophrenics and normal volunteers II. Cranial asymmetry. *Arch. Gen. Psychiatry, 39,* 771.
154. Luchins DJ, Meltzer HY (1983) A blind controlled study of occipital cerebral asymmetry in schizophrenia. *Psychiatry Res., 10,* 87.
155. Tsai LY, Nasrallah HA, Jacoby CG (1983) Hemispheric asymmetries on computed tomographic scans in schizophrenia and mania. *Arch. Gen. Psychiatry, 40,* 1286.
156. Naeser MA, Gebhart C, Levine HL (1980) Decreased computerized tomography numbers in patients with pre-senile dementia. *Arch. Neurol., 37,* 401.
157. Golden CJ, Graber B, Coffman J, Berg R, Bloch S, Brogan D (1980) Brain density deficits in chronic schizophrenia. *Psychiatry Res., 3,* 179.

158. Lyon K, Wilson J, Golden CJ, Graber B, Coffman JA, Bloch S (1981) Effects of long-term neuroleptic use on brain density. *Psychiatry Res., 5,* 33.
159. Golden CJ, Graber B, Coffman J, Berg RA, Newlin DB, Bloch S (1981) Structural deficits in schizophrenia, identification by computed tomographic scan density measurements. *Arch. Gen. Psychiatry, 38,* 1014.
160. Largen JW, Calderon M, Smith RC (1983) Asymmetries in the density of white and gray matter in the brains of schizophrenic patients. *Am. J. Psychiatry, 140,* 1060.
161. Kanba S, Shima S, Tsukumo D, Masuda Y, Asai M (1984) Brain CT density in chronic schizophrenia. *Biol. Psychiatry, 19,* 273.
162. Coffman JA, Nasrallah HA (1984) Brain density patterns in schizophrenia and mania. *J. Affect. Disord., 6,* 307.
163. DeMeyer MK, Gilmor R, Hendrie H, DeMeyer WE, Franco JN (1984) Brain densities in treatment-resistant schizophrenic and other psychiatric patients. *J. Oper. Psychiatry, 15,* 9.
164. Morihisa JM, McAnulty GB (1985) Structure and function: brain electrical activity mapping and computed tomography in schizophrenia. *Biol. Psychiatry, 20,* 3.
165. Berman KF, Shelton RC, Weinberger DR (unpublished data).
166. Crow TJ (1980) Molecular pathology of schizophrenia: more than one disease process? *Br. Med. J., 28,* 66.
167. Nyback H, Berggren B-M, Hindmarsh T, Sedrall G, Wiesel F-A (1983) Cerebroventricular size and cerebrospinal fluid monoamine metabolites in schizophrenic patients and healthy volunteers. *Psychiatry Res., 9,* 301.
168. van Kammen DP, Mann LS, Sternberg DE, Scheinin M, Ninan PT, Marder SR, van Kammen W, Rieder RO, Linnoila M (1983) Dopamine-betahydroxylase activity and homovanillic acid in spinal fluid of schizophrenics with brain atrophy. *Science, 220,* 974.
169. Kling A, Kurtz N, Tachiki K, Connor S (1982) CAT scan measures in schizophrenics: correlations between brain atrophy, MAOs and diagnostic subgroups. *Neurosci. Soc. Abstr., 8,* 30.
170. Weinberger DR, Kaufmann C, Shelton R, Berman KF, Linnoila M (1985) *Reduced CSF dopamine metabolites and prefrontal atrophy in schizophrenia.* (Abstracts) ACNP, Maui.
171. Tachiki KH, Kurtz N, Kling AS, Hullett FJ (1984) Blood monoamine oxidases and CT scans in subgroups of chronic schizophrenics. *J. Psychiatr. Res., 18,* 233.
172. Kleinman JE, Karson CN, Weinberger DR, Freed WJ, Berman KF, Wyatt RJ (1984) Eye-blinking and cerebral ventricular size in chronic schizophrenic patients. *Am. J. Psychiatry, 141,* 1430.
173. Reveley AM, Reveley MA, Chitkara B, Clifford C (1984) The genetic basis of cerebral ventricular volume. *Psychiatry Res., 13,* 261.
174. Reveley AM, Reveley MA, Murray RM (1984) Cerebral ventricular enlargement in non-genetic schizophrenia: a controlled twin study. *Br. J. Psychiatry, 144,* 89.
175. Reveley AM, Reveley MA, Murray RM (1983) Enlargement of cerebral ventricles in schizophrenia is confined to those without known genetic predisposition. *Lancet, 2,* 525.
176. Owens DGC, Johnstone EC, Crow TJ, Frith CD, Jacoe JR, Kreel L (1985) Lateral ventricular size in schizophrenia: relationship to the disease process and its clinical manifestations. *Psychol. Med., 15,* 27.
177. Leigh H, Callahan WA, Einhorn D (1978) Good outcome in a catatonic patient with enlarged ventricles. *J. Nerv. Ment. Dis., 166,* 139.
178. Weinberger DR (1984) Brain disease and psychiatric illness: when should a psychiatrist order a CT scan. *Am. J. Psychiatry, 141,* 12.

CHAPTER 10

Magnetic resonance brain imaging in schizophrenia

JEFFREY A. COFFMAN AND HENRY A. NASRALLAH

Principles of magnetic resonance (MR)

Magnetic resonance (MR) imaging, based on principles long applied in chemistry, is the most recent technique to emerge utilizing the spatial data image reconstruction paradigms originally developed through computed tomography. Based on the interaction of low energy electromagnetic radiation with tissue, the technique offers excellent soft tissue anatomic information (see Fig. 1) as well as potential for metabolic studies. Beyond these desirable qualities in an imaging tool, the feasibility of mapping tissue distribution of certain pharmaceuticals is under development. In other words, it appears that many if not all of the physiologic and biochemical assessments possible with PET might eventually be readily accomplished with MR, which also offers the advantages of non-ionizing radiation and clear anatomic images unavailable with PET. Before outlining the specific intent of this proposal, a brief discussion based on several sources (1 – 3) of the principles of magnetic resonance imaging will be presented as a background.

The phenomena of magnetic resonance, when considered at the molecular or atomic level, are best understood by quantum mechanical principles. However, when such molecular or atomic level physical principles are applied to larger systems such as tissue samples, the rules of classical mechanics and magnetism usefully apply. Nuclear magnetic resonance is based on the interaction of certain nuclei (those of biological interest are ^{1}H, ^{13}C, ^{19}F, ^{23}Na, and ^{31}P) with an external magnetic field. These nuclei all have an odd number of protons or neutrons or both, and, as protons and neutrons each have an intrinsic angular momentum or 'spin', which cancels out when pairing of neutrons or protons is possible, they all possess a net quantity of 'spin'. Because each such nucleus is charged, this net spin of an electrical charge produces a small magnetic field. Each nucleus then behaves as a magnetic dipole, analogous to a small bar magnet or compass needle. Under normal conditions, the orientation of these magnetic dipoles is random (Fig. 2A). With the imposition of a uniform static magnetic field (labeled Ho), the dipoles will orient themselves so that their net magnetic force vector becomes aligned parallel to the external field (Fig. 2B). According to the convention, the coordinates of the external field and the net magnetization vector are given, using a three-dimensional system

Handbook of Schizophrenia, Vol. 1: The Neurology of Schizophrenia.
H.A. Nasrallah and D.R. Weinberger, editors.
© Elsevier Science Publishers B.V., 1986.

in which the z-axis is parallel to the force direction of the external field with x- and y-axes aligned perpendicularly.

The nuclear resonance phenomenon itself can be understood by analogy with a system involving two tuning forks. Provided both tuning forks have the same characteristic frequency, resonance is possible. If tuning fork No. 1 is given energy input by striking it with a mallet, this energy is given off as sound in the characteristic frequency. When this sound energy is transmitted to fork No. 2, it will begin to vibrate, as it is promoted from low to high kinetic energy, radiating out sound energy at the same frequency, which itself again is capable of re-exciting fork No. 1 if the impulses of No. 1 have been stopped. The tuning forks have been in resonance and have transferred a characteristic sound with a set frequency.

To excite the nuclear magnetic resonance phenomenon, a short pulse of electromagnetic energy in the radiofrequency (rf) range is given through a coil surrounding the sample. This rf radiation is selected for the characteristic energy of the target nuclei, which when they absorb this energy behave as if they were under the

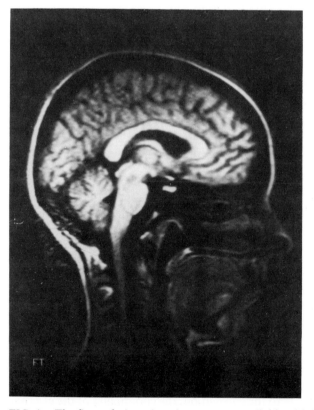

FIG. 1   *The fine soft tissue imaging contrast available with Magnetic Resonance Imaging as illustrated above. The midsagittal section shown was obtained at a field strength of 0.5 tesla.*

A

B

FIG. 2   *(A) Illustration of the random orientation of proton magnetic dipoles in the body. (B) With the imposition of a uniform external, static magnetic field (labeled each sub-0) the proton dipoles orient themselves so that the majority point in the direction of the external field, such that the net magnetic field vector is aligned parallel to the external field.*

influence of a smaller magnetic field which causes their magnetization vector to tip away from the z-axis and rotate in the x,y-plane with a frequency equal to the radio frequency. This displacement of a portion of the net magnetization vector produces a rotating magnetic field which describes the wall of a cone. This rotating field motion can be compared to that described by a spinning gyroscope whose axis has been tipped slightly away from the direction of the surrounding gravitational field. The angle between the direction of the static magnetic field and the net nuclear magnetization vector is dependent on the amount of energy delivered by the rf radiation and increases as long as the pulse continues.

Therefore, the angle can be increased by augmenting either the intensity or duration of the rf pulse. A pulse just strong or long enough to move the net magnetization vector from its equilibrium positron so that it precesses entirely in the x,y plane (where $\theta = 90°$) is called $\frac{\pi}{z}$ or 90° pulse. Applying such a pulse and turning it off allows one to observe the free induction decay (FID) signal (Fig. 3). Immediately following the pulse, the net magnetization vector lies wholly in the x,y-plane and the initial amplitude of the FID signal is maximal since only the x,y-component of the displaced vector contributes to the emitted signal. A pulse increased to twice the strength or length of the 90° pulse tips the net magnetization vector from equilibrium ($\theta = 0°$) to $\theta = 180°$ (the opposite direction), or entirely in the z-direction. This is a π or 180° pulse. In this there is no component in the x,y-plane and therefore an isolated 180° pulse provides no signal.

In a static magnetic field of H_0 the nuclei possessing spin (i.e. NMR sensitive nuclei) will respond only to excitation by an rf pulse of a specific frequency named the Larmor or resonant frequency (f) (Fig. 4). This resonant frequency is directly proportional to the intensity of the static magnetic field according to the following

$$f_0 = H_0 \, (\gamma/2\pi)$$

253

where H_0 again is the static field strength and γ is the gyromagnetic ratio, a constant for each specific nucleus with spin.

For hydrogen nuclei $\gamma = 2.675 \times 10^8 \text{ s}^{-1} \overline{\overline{T}}^1$ which indicates that in a magnetic field of one tesla (T) strength the resonant frequency for protons is 42.57 megahertz (million cycles per second, MHz). The same equation identifies the frequency of the emitted signal after the pulse is turned off. In application of NMR principles to imaging, the total magnetic field strength may vary between the absorption and emission of rf energy, leading to a consequent difference in the absorbed and emitted signal frequencies. Ordinarily the same antenna coil used to transmit the exciting signal is used to receive the emitted signal.

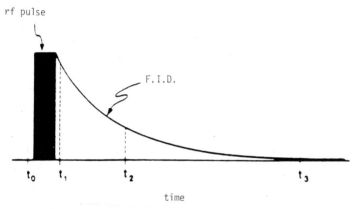

FIG. 3   *The decay of the radiofrequency signal in the z-direction following pulse application is shown above. Figs. 3, 4 and 6 have been reproduced from Pykett et al. (3), by courtesy of the Editors of Radiology.*

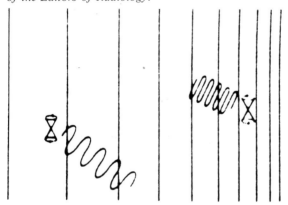

FIG. 4   *The above figure indicates the increase in resonant frequency with increasing strength of the external magnetic field with both field strength and frequency increasing as spacing of field lines decreases.*

254

In general, NMR signals comprise complex waveforms of multiple frequencies. In spectroscopic use, this waveform can be represented as a line graph with the coordinate showing signal amplitude and the abcissa showing time. In order to produce an image or more useful spectroscopic information, the amount of signal detected at each frequency must be known. This is accomplished through a mathematical exercise labeled Fourier transformation, which creates a curve showing signal strength vs. frequency. The FID signal following Fourier transformation provides the NMR frequency spectrum.

Having discussed the initial state of the FID signal, the behavior of the signal once the pulse has been turned off involves decay of the net magnetization vector to its original equilibrium, parallel to the static magnetic field. The involved decay phenomena are characterized by two target sample determined time constants: the spin-lattice or longitudinal relaxation time, T_1, and the spin-spin or transverse relaxation time, T_2.

An understanding of relaxation times is made easier by considering the motion of the net microscopic magnetization vector relative to a frame of reference located on the point of the vector as it spins about at the Larmor frequency. A useful analogy would be the frame of reference of a person standing stationary on the earth. In such a frame of reference, one appears to be standing still when in fact one is rotating about the earth's axis at a frequency of one cycle or revolution per day.

T_1 describes the time needed for the component of net magnetization in the z direction to return to its equilibrium value following its perturbation or excitation by the rf pulse (Fig. 5). This process depends on the nuclei transferring energy to their molecular environment or 'lattice' hence the label 'spin-lattice'. In a pure liquid this return follows an exponential function, therefore after $T_1 \times 3$, 95% of the reduction in net magnetization in the z-direction will have been restored. Should another rf pulse be applied following partial decay of the first signal, the total FID

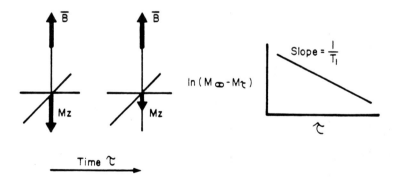

FIG. 5   *The relationship of declining magnetization in the z-direction to time is illustrated as described by the decay constant T_1. Reproduced from Partain et al. (27), by courtesy of the Publishers.*

following this second pulse will be reduced. This latter property can be applied to enhance the measurement of T_1 variations in the sample.

T_2 relaxation influences the decay rate of the FID signal and is best explained using the rotating reference frame mentioned above. Following the deflection of the net nuclear magnetization vector toward the transverse plane by an rf pulse, the component nuclear signals making up this vector all rotate or precess together 'in phase'. Therefore, they all appear to be stationary when viewed from the rotating reference frame (Fig. 5). However the precessing nuclei do not remain in phase. Slight local alterations of the magnetic field cause some nuclei to precess at different frequencies than others; the resulting rf waves from individual nuclei cancel each other out and the sum of nuclear magnetization vectors or net magnetization in the transverse plane decays to zero. The observed overall time constant characterizing this decay by dephasing is termed T_2^*. This observed parameter is in fact a composite relaxation time resulting from intrinsic interactions between neighboring nuclei (hence, spin-spin) and from heterogeneities in the applied magnetic field.

The intrinsic or target sample related portion of the transverse signal decay is characterized by the relaxation time constant T_2, of the specimen. This parameter reflects the mean magnitude of the internuclear magnetic interactions and is a result of energy interchange between spinning nuclei. The FID signal from a sample in a real, rather than ideal, magnetic field, decays according to the shorter time constant T_2^* due to the unavoidable small irregularities in the magnetic field. In addition, in the course of an NMR imaging experiment, T_2^* is further shortened through application of magnetic field gradients. Due to the fact that these inhomogeneities remain constant during the period of data acquisition, their contribution to dephasing and signal decay is reversible. The signal can be recalled as a 'spin-echo' or a series of such echoes through special patterns of rf pulses such as the Carr-Purcell sequence. In the latter, the initial FID and each of the individual spin echoes decay with a time constant T_2^* but the amplitudes or peak heights of the successive spin echoes decline with a time constant equivalent to the intrinsic T_2 constant of the sample. In NMR imaging, image intensity is derived primarily as a function of T_1 or T2 or both as well as the quantity of spins per unit volume of tissue (nuclear spin density), depending on the rf pulse sequence used.

Intrinsic sample values for T_1 or T_2 are affected by a number of factors, some of which are of particular interest when one considers biological systems. Foremost among the physiochemical properties altering T_1 and T_2 is the degree of molecular and intramolecular motion present. In solids and quasi solids such as liquids at low temperature or gel substances, there is little molecular motion and T_1 is long (many seconds) while T_2 is very short (microseconds). However in liquids or at higher temperatures, T_1 and T_2 are nearly equal. For example, in pure water at room temperature T_1 and T_2 are about two seconds. In general, T_2 is substantially shorter than T_1 and can never be longer. As a result, the ratio of T_2 to T_1 as it approaches 1 demonstrates 'liquid-like' behavior in a sample while a very small T_2/T_1 ratio shows 'solid-like' behavior. In the context of NMR imaging, rigidly bound nuclei give a very small, essentially zero signal so that only the signal from gel-like or liquid-like molecular regions can be observed.

Differences in T_1 proton relaxation times among different tissues are often related to free water content. Various abnormal tissues have been demonstrated to have higher T_1s than do corresponding normal tissues (4), which may (5) or may not (6) be the result of larger free water content. However, these tissue differences are often sufficient to distinguish between various normal and abnormal tissues.

Principles of NMR as applied to imaging

Magnetic resonance scanners produce images which portray the location and behavior of nuclei emitting NMR signals. The relative contributions of spin density (ϱ) and the relaxation time T_1 and T_2 to image contrast depends on the rf pulse sequence applied. Most current methods can be placed in one of two broad categories: (1) 'simple' pulse sequences in which the interpulse interval T_r is on the order of the average relaxation times of the sample (i.e. $T_r \simeq T_1, T_2$) and (2) steady state free precession sequences where the interpulse spacing is small when compared with the average tissue relaxation times (i.e. $T_r \ll T_1, T_2$).

Using the simple pulse methods, T_r and the pulse sequence can be selected to enhance image contrast by selectively emphasizing T_1 or T_2 contributions to signal intensity. These techniques have been especially useful in proton imaging studies as relaxation times are more sensitive parameters for soft tissue contrast than is pure mobile proton density alone. For instance, white and gray matter in the central nervous system differ in water content by only around 10%, while their T_1 values differ by about 150%. Certain imaging experiments can then be designed to usefully identify signal intensity contributions from T_1 and spin density and to display them separately. T_2 variation can also be identified in this manner as in multiple sclerosis (7).

One frequently used 'simple' pulse technique is the 'inversion-recovery' sequence, in which a 180° pulse is initially applied to invert the spin system. Following a delay time T_r (T_r T_1), during which some spin-lattice relaxation occurs, a 90 'read' pulse is given. The resultant free induction decay signal is stored to generate an image with signal intensity in this case given by:

$$I \alpha (1 - 2e^{-(T_r/T_1)})$$

Further, two or more data sets obtained with different interpulse delays can be mathematically combined to yield T_1 and/or spin density maps. The inversion-recovery pulse sequence highlights T_1 variation in the sample.

It is important to note that for most biological samples, given their multiplicity of constituents, relaxation times are characterized by multiexponential decays. Caution, therefore, appears prudent in interpreting relaxation data obtained from T_1 and T_2 maps, as results are generally weighted averages of a family of values each depending on the individual cellular and molecular microenvironments in which the nuclei reside.

NMR imaging equipment can be designed to receive data from a single point in the sample, from a line, a plane or a three dimensional volume all at once. The most efficient scanning method is one in which data are acquired from an entire volume simultaneously. The data can then be reconstructed as a three-dimensional map, or a series of tomographic planes which can be selected arbitrarily and then viewed. Most current scanners provide planar images. Imaging planes are selected by applying a magnetic field gradient at an angle of 90° to the plane selected. One way of generating such a gradient is to drive current in opposite directions in two adjacent circular coils. This provides an overall magnetic field equal to the primary field H only at the midline while differing elsewhere. Then the sample is irradiated with a very narrow band of rf frequencies, so that only those nuclei within a plane perpendicular to the direction of the gradient field will be excited (Fig. 6).

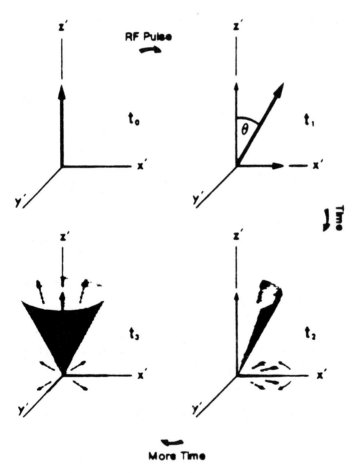

FIG. 6   *The spacial relationship of nuclear orientation to the response following a specifically directed rf pulse is illustrated above.*

Once the plane of interest is selected, several methods of mapping signal intensity within the slice can be applied. These methods are similar to those used in computed tomography and include iterative back projection and Fourier image processing. In the former, a magnetic gradient is applied to the plane of interest so that the field increases in one direction across the plane. The entire plane is stimulated by an rf pulse and the resulting NMR signal recorded. NMR signals from nuclei within the plane are recorded as a frequency spectrum with low field nuclei producing low frequency signals and nuclei in the high strength portion of the field giving off higher frequencies. In order to determine position of the individual nuclei, gradient derived spectra are produced for a number of different angles by rotating the field gradient. These multiple spectra are resolved into a spectral signal distribution map by computer processing techniques to result in a recognizable image.

Applications of magnetic resonance imaging to the study of schizophrenia

Historical background

The first NMR image was produced in 1973 by Lauterbur from the Department of Chemistry of the State University of New York at Stonybrook. The technical developments which form the basis of the above discussion were contributed by a variety of laboratories in the United States and Europe. Nearly all of the early work in the field was performed with conventional NMR spectroscopic instrumentation modified in various ways for imaging and making use of relatively small magnets. The technical developments necessary for practical magnetic resonance imaging centered primarily upon enlarging the sample aperture by provision for larger magnets of adequate homogeneity. These developments were complete to the point that production of radiographic quality images of the head became possible after 1979, although the initial images available were of rather poor quality, and practical experience with relatively high-quality NMR images did not become available in any but the initial centers of research development until 1983.

In contrast to the relatively slow response of psychiatric researchers to the availability of computed tomography − although the first scanner became available in the early seventies only one study of psychiatric patients was undertaken until the latter part of the decade − psychiatric researchers eagerly began to apply the new magnetic resonance imaging technique as soon as imaging units became available. Several of the groups involved in such research had had experience in computer tomography studies.

Early experience in the application of magnetic resonance imaging to schizophrenia research

The first studies of schizophrenics utilizing magnetic resonance imaging (MRI) techniques were reported at the December 1983 meeting of the American College of Neuropsychopharmacology in a preliminary report by Smith et al. The same data were reported more fully in 1984, in a study involving 9 patients who met RDC criteria for a diagnosis of schizophrenia and comparing these with 5 controls utilizing a 0.3-tesla magnetic resonance imaging system (8). Utilizing methodologies developed for evaluation of computer tomographic scans, bifrontal ratios, bicaudate ratios, lateral ventricular ratios and ventricular brain ratios were calculated from transverse images. No significant differences emerged on these parameters. In addition, image intensity value differences on a region of interest basis were examined and again no significant differences emerged, although there seemed to be trends toward a reduction in these values for gray and white matter. These reductions in image intensity values were reported for an inversion recovery sequence with a T_e of 30 ms.

Smith et al. (9), reported a further enlargement of their study group to 23 schizophrenics with diagnoses by DSM-III criteria and compared to 17 controls using the same instrumentation and pulse sequences. Again, they found no differences between the groups in the linear and area measurements mentioned above. However, differences did appear on comparison of certain region of interest image intensity measures. These values were lower for controls in right anterior white matter and left anterior gray matter while they were lower among schizophrenics for putamen/globus pallidus. They also observed that positive and negative symptoms correlated with ventricular size and the width of the third ventricle although no significant differences in these ventricular measurements were apparent between the total groups. In discussing the results of these region of interest samplings, Smith et al. commented that in the inversion recovery mode with 30-ms T_e, shorter T_1 relaxation times might be a possible cause for the observed increase in image intensity in frontal regions.

Besson and associates (10) reported a study of 23 schizophrenics diagnosed by RDC criteria compared with 15 controls utilizing a 0.08-tesla magnetic resonance imaging instrument and unspecified pulse parameters. They noted, again on a region of interest basis and presumably based on a measured T_1, that there appeared to be a significant increase in T_1 values in the right basal ganglia. They found no correlation of these changes with positive or negative symptoms based on the Krawiecka scale with this. They did, in addition, note an increase in T_1 values in the left basal ganglia which correlated positively with the negative symptom score and also that their rating scale for tardive dyskinesia tended to positively correlate with increases in T_1 times for both the right and left basal ganglia. On the other hand, although there were no absolute differences in the schizophrenic and control values for T_1 in frontal white matter, they did observe that high positive symptom scores were associated with the reduction in T_1 and that age and duration of illness were not correlated in any direction with their T_1 measurements.

Fujimoto (11) reported a study of 30 male and 16 female schizophrenics who were studied along with 10 male and 10 female controls whose ages ranged from 30 to 40, using 0.1-tesla imaging equipment. They reported that in all cases measured T_1 values differed between schizophrenics and controls although not always in the same direction. Specifically they noted that the T_1 values were reduced in frontal white matter in the schizophrenics as compared to the controls. They reported that T_1 values were increased in the putamen among schizophrenics compared to controls; that values for T_1 varied when compared for the thalamus and that with regard to the corpus callosum values for the genu were increased in schizophrenics. In addition they noted some right-left differences in the white matter and the thalamus. However, in examining their results, they used no statistical comparisons, instead relying upon descriptive statistics. In graphic presentation it appears that what they noted was a high degree of scatter among the patient group without any clear bimodality to the distribution of values.

A series of studies involving another large group of schizophrenics and the first study of utilize a 0.5-tesla magnet was performed at the University of Iowa in 1984 with the first reports by this group appearing late in that year and through 1985. Nasrallah et al. reported in 1984 an initial evaluation of the midline sagittal images derived from an inversion recovery sequence with T_e of 600 ms of the study group which examined a variety of parameters relating to the dimensions of the corpus callosum in groups subdivided for handedness (12). They noted that no differences appeared when right-handed male schizophrenics were compared with right-handed male controls. However when the left-handed males were compared to right-handed male controls, they were found to have significantly smaller callosal thickness, callosal area, callosal to brain ratio and splenial area, while when the left-handed patients were compared to left-handed controls, the primary significant difference was that they had smaller callosal area. The group was enlarged to 38 chronic schizophrenics, including 28 males, 23 of these right-handed and 5 left-handed and 10 females all right-handed (13). All patients had been diagnosed by DSM-III criteria and were compared to 41 normal volunteers with the group composed of 21 males (11 right- and 10 left-handed) and 20 females (10 right- and 10 left-handed). With regard to the results noted, this group reported that the total group of schizophrenics, compared with the controls, showed significantly larger callosal area, anterior and midcallosal thickness, as well as callosal-to-brain ratio. However, when right-handed males were compared with right-handed controls these differences disappeared. Similarly, when left-handed males were compared callosal area was found to be smaller in schizophrenics without differences in callosal thickness. A within-group comparison of the schizophrenics divided by handedness showed that the left-handed schizophrenics had significantly smaller callosal dimensions than the right-handed schizophrenic males. When the female groups were compared, both the anterior and midcallosal thicknesses were significantly increased among the schizophrenics in contrast to the absence of such a difference between schizophrenic and control males. The authors concluded that anatomical gender related differences in callosal dimensions described seemed to be consistent with the previous sex related differences reported in normal human brain, while the differences noted in the schizophrenic might relate to lateralization abnormalities and clinical differences noted in schizophrenics which relate in some as yet undetermined fashion with the psychopathology of schizophrenia.

Andreasen et al. (14) examined area measurements of a number of structures utilizing the midsagittal images provided by the instrumentation noted above in the same group of schizophrenic controls and found that the schizophrenic group had a significantly smaller frontal lobe area. These findings were noted in concert with those reported by Olson et al. (15), relating to reduction in midsagittal cerebral and cranial size among the schizophrenic patients. Examination of a subgroup which also underwent imaging procedures which allowed assessment of brain structures in the cranial dimension seemed to be confirmatory. The authors also noted that diminished cerebral cranial size seemed to be associated with prominent negative symptoms, although diminution in frontal size was not. In addition, decreased cranial, cerebral, and frontal size were significantly associated with impairment on cognitive tests designed to assess memory, attention and ability to shift response set. The authors concluded that their findings were consistent with the hypothesis that some schizophrenics might have an early development abnormality leading to prominent negative symptoms and cognitive impairment and that an additional group might have some demonstrable abnormality in frontal lobe structure.

Expanding further on the above mentioned finding of diminished cerebral and cranial size in their group of schizophrenics, Olson (15) observed that mean cerebral area was significantly smaller $p < 0.001$ among schizophrenics, while reduction of equipment magnitude was observed in cranial area, which led the authors to suggest that atrophy of the brain subsequent to cranial synostosis seemed not to account for the observed difference in brain size between the groups. These differences were noted only among the male schizophrenics and controls and did not appear when females were compared, although the small size of the female groups leaves any conclusions open to question. The authors observed that early writers, such as Kretschmer (16) had noted that anthropometric measurement of skull size in schizophrenics showed them to be smaller sized than the controls. The authors concluded that some developmental abnormality related to genetic factors or *in utero* environmental factors might be related to these differences. Interestingly, in examining skull size in the transverse dimension, these differences do not appear, either on NMR scans or on the previous CT scans which were available for some of the subjects.

With attention to image intensity values, Coffman et al. (17) noted a variety of differences between the schizophrenics and controls for whom region of interest data was available, specifically 28 schizophrenics and 36 controls. In order to account for instrumentation-related variability in subject-to-subject comparison, image intensity value ratios were calculated utilizing values for each patient for the posterior corpus callosum as a denominator. Utilizing this methodology, and examining the values for the midsagittal slice in the entire group of schizophrenics and controls, an increase in image intensity ratio was noted for the mid and posterior cingulate gyrus. When these ratios were examined with regard to coronal planes, image intensity ratios were found to be reduced in cortical gray matter, particularly in frontal regions, caudate, bilaterally, anterior temporal white matter, particularly on the left, and also in cerebellar regions in the vermis and the gray and white matter of the left cerebellar hemisphere. The authors have concluded that the most likely explanation for such a reduction in image intensity ratio for most of the regions examined, would likely relate to a lengthening or increase in T_1 values. By contrast, the increase in the image intensity ratio value for the cingulate gyrus found in schizophrenics was attributed to a partial volume effect incorporating adjacent white matter, with its higher image intensity value, suggesting perhaps some thinning of the cortical mantle of the cingulate gyrus in the schizophrenic group.

Mathew et al. (18) reported in a study of midsagittal images of 18 DSM-III diagnosed schizophrenics and 18 controls that they had noted an increase in the area of the septum pellucidum as well as an increase in the ratio of the septum area to the area of the brain in midsagittal section and an increase in the anterior to posterior length of the corpus callosum. In a later report, the same group noted no differences between 12 schizophrenics and controls in midsagittal areas of the cerebellum and 4th ventricle (19), a finding recently corroborated by Coffman et al. (20).

Smith et al. (21) reported mixed results in a further continuation of studies on schizophrenics, indicating that the findings they had noticed previously were not readily replicable and that some of their difficulty related to changes in imaging software. They did note that they continued to see no differences in the linear and area measurements which they had applied to their scans, and that their primary difficulty in replication was that the image intensity value measurements they had made were presently non-comparable with their previous data due to the change in software. They suggested that the use of ratios might increase the comparability of the data and offered that some external standard might be of use such as a vial of copper sulfate solution or some other external reference standard placed adjacent to the patient.

De Meyer et al. (22), in a study of 11 schizophrenics and 11 controls at 0.15-tesla noted that the schizophrenics tended to have higher values for T_1 in white matter regions and that the increase in T_1 occurred predominately in frontal and temporal white matter regions.

Overall, these early studies point to a number of abnormalities in the brains of schizophrenics as revealed by MRI techniques. These abnormalities can be grouped into two major categories: (1) indicators of gross structural changes at the anatomic level and (2) indicators of fine structural changes at the tissue or biochemical level. The former category has advanced in lock-step fashion with improvements in MRI technology while the latter's surface has just been scratched.

As has been indicated, MRI is rapidly gaining recognition as the foremost tool for the appreciation of soft tissue anatomy in vivo. With MRI, it is possible to use to advantage the large inherent differences in the T_1 and T_2 values of tissues in order to allow their discrimination. For instance, the T_1 values for gray and white matter differ by a factor of 1.3 while T_2 values for normal diseased tissues can differ by a factor of 2.0. It is not too difficult to see how such high-resolution images as have become available can be provided.

Utilizing the exquisite soft tissue imaging properties of MRI in examining the brain, the researchers whose work has been noted above have reported mixed results with regard to abnormal increases or diminutions in size of brain structures among schizophrenics. Most interesting are the apparent reductions in cerebral and cranial size and the alternations in callosal structure found in the studies by Nasrallah, Andreasen and their associates.

In studies which have begun to make use of the tissue assessment capabilities of MRI, there seems to be substantial agreement, although the meaning of such findings remains obscure. It has been noted elsewhere that most pathologic processes induce a lengthening of relaxation times, both T_1, and T_2. As increases in T_2 produce greater signal intensity in T_2 weighted pulse sequences, T_2 weighted images have begun to emerge as sensitive screening tools for a variety of disorders. However, such findings remain non-specific.

A similar non-specific lengthening of T_1 values for tissue has been noted above by various researchers to be present in a number of schizophrenic brain regions, notably frontal, temporal and cerebellar regions. Such non-specific findings are interesting in light of the increasing attention being drawn to neuropathologic findings on similar regions (23) and points to the possibility that MRI might be used to focus the search for the neuropathological underpinnings of schizophrenia.

Future directions

It can readily be seen that MRI is a significant development towards elucidating the understanding of the anatomic pathology of the brain in living individuals. Relatively minute structures previously visible only on post-mortem inspection can be viewed in situ. Work is underway as summarized previously, which may shed some light on the gross structure of the schizophrenic brain while T_1 and T_2 measurements may non-specifically point to more discrete regions of tissue affected by various pathologic processes, pointing out the need for further exploration.

It is in even more subtle examinations that the promise of MRI may lie. As noted earlier the process of NMR spectroscopy had its earliest application in the study of chemical compounds. Early studies are being undertaken to apply nuclear magnetic resonance spectroscopy to the evaluation of tissue in vivo. With relation to the brain, animal studies have been done examining anoxia related changes in ^{31}P spectroscopy (24), while excised brain tissue ^{13}C spectroscopy has revealed the possibility of tissue constituent characterization (25).

In addition, receptor localization and kinetic studies may become possible through attachment of compounds affecting the local MR signal to receptor ligands of interest. Coffman et al. (26) have reported promising initial studies of such a compound used to study benzodiazepine receptors in rabbits.

In summary, magnetic resonance appears to offer many avenues toward the investigation of heretofore inadequately understood structural – functional relationships in psychiatric disorders. The next several years will find increasing use of this technique by psychiatric researchers. It remains to be seen how well MRI will fulfil the potential that has been looked for from its early successes.

REFERENCES

1. House WV (1983) Theoretical basis for NMR imaging. In: Partain CL, James AE, Rollo FD, Price RR (Eds) *Nuclear Magnetic Resonance (NMR) Imaging*. WB Saunders, Philadelphia.
2. Willcott MR, Cook JP, Ford, JJ, Martin GE (1983) NMR in chemistry. In: Partain CL, James AE, Rollo FD, Price, RR (Eds) *Nuclear Magnetic Resonance (NMR) Imaging*. WB Saunders, Philadelphia.
3. Pykett IL, Newhouse JH, Brady TJ, Goldman MR, Kistler JP, Pohost GM (1982) Principles of nuclear magnetic resonance imaging. *Radiology, 143*, 157.
4. Eggleston JC, Saryan LA, Hollis DP (1975) Nuclear magnetic resonance investigations of human neoplastic and abnormal non neoplastic tissues. *Cancer Res., 35*, 1326.
5. Kiricuta IC Jr, Simplaceanu V (1975) Tissue water content and nuclear magnetic resonance in normal and tumor tissues. *Cancer Res., 35*, 1164.
6. Ranade SS, Shah S, Korgaonkar KS, Kasturi SR, Chaughule RS, Cijayraghavan R (1976) Absence of correlation between spin-lattice relaxation times and water content in human tumor tissues. *Physiol. Chem. Phys., 8,* 131.
7. Runge VM, Price AC, Kirshner HS, Allen JH, Partain CL, James AE Jr (1984) Magnetic resonance imaging of multiple sclerosis: a study of pulse-technique efficacy. *Am. J. Roentgenol., 43*, 1015.
8. Smith RC, Calderon M, Ravichandran GK, Largen J, Vroulis G, Shvartsburd A, Gordon J, Schoolar JC (1984) Nuclear magnetic resonance in schizophrenia: a preliminary study. *Psychiatr. Res., 12,* 137.
9. Smith RC, Calderon M, Baumgartner R, Ravichandran GK, Peters I, Schoolar JC, Gordon J (1984) Nuclear magnetic resonance studies of schizophrenia. In: *Abstract Volume: Society of Magnetic Resonance in Medicine, 3rd Annual Meeting*.
10. Besson JAO, Corrigan FM, Foreman EI, Aschroft GW, Smith FW (1984) T1 changes in schizophrenic disorders measured by proton NMR. In: *Abstract Volume: Society of Magnetic Resonance in Medicine, 3rd Annual Meeting*.
11. Fujimoto T, Yokoyama Y, Fumimoto A, Yamamoto K, Okada A, Asakura T, Igata A (1984) Spin-lattice relaxation time measurement in schizophrenic disorders. In: *Abstract Volume: Society of Magnetic Resonance in Medicine, 3rd Annual Meeting*.
12. Nasrallah HA, Andreasen NC, Olson SC, Coffman JA, Dunn VD, Ehrhardt JC (1984) A controlled magnetic resonance study of the corpus callosum in schizophrenia. In: *Abstract Volume: American College of Neuropsychopharmacology, December 10 – 14, San Juan, Puerto Rico*.
13. Nasrallah HA, Andreasen NC, Coffman JA, Olson SC, Dunn VD, Ehrhardt JC, Chapman SM (1986) A controlled magnetic resonance study of corpus callosum thickness in schizophrenia. *Biol. Psychiatry, 21,* 274.
14. Andreasen NC, Nasrallah HA, Dunn VD, Olson SC, Grove WM, Ehrhardt JC, Coffman JA, Crossett JHW (1986) Structural abnormalities in the frontal system in schizophrenia, a magnetic resonance study. *Arch. Gen. Psychiatry, 43,* 146.
15. Olson SC, Andreasen NC, Nasrallah HA, Coffman JA, Grove WM, Dunn VD, Ehrhardt JC (1985) Magnetic resonance imaging in schizophrenia: smaller cerebral area in schizophrenic males. In: *Abstract Volume, Society of Biological Psychiatry, 40th Annual Meeting, May 15 – 19, 1985, Dallas, TX*.
16. Kretschmer E (1925) *Physique and Character,* Harcourt, Brace and Co., New York.
17. Coffman JA, Nasrallah HA, Andreasen NC, Olson SC, Dunn VD, Ehrhardt JC (1985)

Magnetic resonance image intensity values in schizophrenia. In: *Abstract Volume, Society of Biological Psychiatry, 40th Annual Meeting, May 15 – 19, 1985, Dallas, TX.*

18. Mathew RJ (1985) Midsagittal brain section in schizophrenia with nuclear magnetic resonance. In: *Abstract Volume, American Psychiatric Association, 138th Annual Meeting, May 18 – 24, 1985, Dallas, TX.*

19. Mathew RJ, Partain CL (1985) Midsagittal sections of cerebellar vermis and fourth ventricle obtained with magnetic resonance imaging of schizophrenic patients. *Am. J. Psychiatry, 142,* 970.

20. Coffman JA, Nasrallah HA, Andreasen NC, Olson SC, Dunn VD, Ehrhardt JC (1985) Midsagittal dimensions of the cerebellum in chronic schizophrenics by magnetic resonance imaging. *Abstract Vol. American College of Neuropsychopharmacology, December 9 – 13, 1985, Manui, Hawaii.*

21. Smith RC, Baumgartner RN, Calderon M, Ravichandran GK, Peters ID, Scholar JC (1985) Nuclear magnetic resonance studies of schizophrenia. In: *Abstract Volume, American Psychiatric Association, 138th Annual Meeting, May 18 – 24, 1985, Dallas, TX.*

22. De Meyer MK, Gilmor RL, Hendric HC, Meiere FT, De Meyer WE (1985) Brain OT_1 in schizophrenics and normal controls. In: *Abstract Volume, American Psychiatric Association, 138th Annual Meeting, May 18 – 24, 1985, Dallas, TX.*

23. Bogerts B, Meertz E, Schonfeldt-Bausch R (1985) Basal ganglia and limbic system pathology in schizophrenia. *Arch. Gen. Psychiatry, 42,* 784.

24. Elliot GR, Barchas JD, Wade-Jardetzky N, Jardetzky O (1985) Magnetic resonance spectroscopy and brain research. In: *Abstract Volume, American Psychiatric Association, 138th Annual Meeting, May 18 – 24, 1985, Dallas, TX.*

25. Barany M, Arus C, Chang YC (1985) Natural abundance ^{13}C NMR of brain. *Magn. Reson. Med., 2,* 289.

26. Coffman JA, Barfknecht CF, Dunn VD, Neff N, Hunter W (1985) Benzodiazepine receptor site imaging by magnetic resonance techniques. *Abstract Vol. American College of Neuropsychopharmacology, December 9 – 13, 1985, Manui, Hawaii.*

27. Partain CL, James AE, Rollo FD, Price RR (Eds) (1983) *Nuclear Magnetic Resonance Imaging.* WB Saunders, Philadelphia.

CHAPTER 11

Computerized mapping of electrophysiologic data in schizophrenia research: two possible organizing strategies

JOHN M. MORIHISA

Computerized mapping of evoked potential and EEG activity has been used in neurology research to facilitate the presentation of the highly complex and topographically diverse information of electrophysiological studies acquired from multiple lead recordings (1). In the last three years this technique has been introduced into the investigation of schizophrenia (2). It has produced maps that have allowed a different presentation of summarized and condensed information as an aid in the analysis of this data. In this chapter we will focus on two groups of findings: (A) Those that support an organizing theory of frontal lobe dysfunction (3), and (B) Those that support an organizing theory of left hemispheric dysfunction (4, 5).

   Although a number of topographic mapping techniques have been used in medicine, only a few have been systematically applied to the study of schizophrenia. We will compare two basic topographic approaches that have been used. The first records 16 or 32 channels of information and displays data in maps of the left or right side of the brain (6, 7). The second collects 20 channels of data and presents information as a map of the entire cortical surface, looking down at the top of the head (1, 2).

Methodological considerations

In both techniques data is collected from gold cup electrodes secured with collodion and applied according to the 10 – 20 International System of Electrode Placement. Both techniques use EEG amplifiers to increase the microvoltage of brain electricity to the 1-Volt range. This amplified data is then recorded on a 28-track FM tape recorder or recorded on a Winchester drive of a 11 – 23 computer.

   In the first approach, data recorded on the 11 – 23 computer may then be stored on a magnetic tape cartridge for subsequent data analysis. This analysis consists of Fast Fourier Transform spectral analysis of EEG data that has been visually inspected with segments of EEG contaminated with artifact of muscle and eye movement excluded from analysis. For each point of the 16-lead graphic outline of the head a value is determined that represents the power for delta, theta, alpha or beta

Handbook of Schizophrenia, Vol. 1: The Neurology of Schizophrenia.
H.A. Nasrallah and D.R. Weinberger, editors.
© Elsevier Science Publishers B.V., 1986.

brain electrical activity. A matrix is created within the graphic outline defining picture elements or pixels. Each of these picture elements is given a value by interpolation between the four nearest electrodes. In this manner a gray-scale map of the activity of brain electricity may be created for either the left or right side of the brain (6, 7).

In the second basic technique, data recorded on the FM tape recorder is analyzed by a computer that subjects data to a Fast Fourier Transform spectral analysis of EEG data. In this case, data is also visually inspected and EEG segments with muscle artifact or eye movements are eliminated. Twenty electrode positions provide 20 data channels arrayed within a graphic outline of the head. For each point a value is determined that represents the power for delta, theta, alpha or beta brain electrical activity. A 64×64 matrix is created within the graphic outline, defining picture elements or pixels. Each of these picture elements is given a value by linear interpolation between the three nearest electrodes. In this manner a gray-scale map of the brain electrical activity may be created for the entire cortical surface, looking down from above. A color map is then formed by assigning separate colors to different voltage ranges (1, 2).

Arguments have been raised that the divided left and right view of the brain is more specifically related to the spherical anatomy of the brain (6). Each approach, however, appears to have both advantages and disadvantages. The topographic EEG techniques presently applied to schizophrenia research generally fall into one of these two categories of approach although modifications, such as different electrode arrangements, are relatively common.

Frontal lobe dysfunction in schizophrenia

In the first systematic application of Brain Electrical Activity Mapping applied to the investigation of schizophrenia, Morihisa and colleagues (8) studied schizophrenic patients who fulfilled DSM III and Research Diagnostic Criteria for schizophrenia. Both medicated (haloperidol, 0.4 mg/kg) and drug-free (4 weeks or more) inpatients were compared with normal controls. These groups were not significantly different for age, gender or handedness.

The most striking finding of this study was increased delta activity over the entire cortical surface of schizophrenic patients as compared with controls. This abnormal delta activity was greatest over the frontal lobes and was seen in both the medicated and drug-free patient groups. In Figure 1 we see a brain electrical activity mapping picture of a statistical comparison between schizophrenic patients (medicated and drug-free combined) compared with normal controls for delta activity. In this map, the white region delineates the greatest regional difference and highlights an area overlying the frontal lobes. This means that schizophrenic patients as a group had more delta activity over the entire cortical surface when compared with normal controls. Moreover, this difference was regionally greatest over the frontal lobes. In this same study (8), a large bifrontal group difference late in the visual evoked potential for medicated patients compared with controls was also noted. Although further

268

studies will be needed to clarify the effects of drugs on the evoked potential, this finding may represent another possible manifestation of frontal dysfunction in schizophrenic patients.

Subsequently, a different study using brain electrical activity mapping also found increased delta that was greatest frontally in a different group of schizophrenic patients (9). Thus, in a study using the same topographic technique in a different group of patients with schizophrenia, evidence of abnormally increased delta activity was also found to be most prominent frontally. Most recently (10), a group using a modified form of brain electrical activity mapping also reported increased bilateral delta that was greatest in frontal regions. In addition, a study using the 16-lead approach described above also found increased delta activity that was greatest frontally, although only the data from the left side was reported (11).

Thus, investigations of different groups of chronic schizophrenic patients as well as alternative topographic mapping techniques have demonstrated increased delta activity in patients with schizophrenia. Moreover, this abnormally increased delta is greatest in regions overlying the frontal lobes.

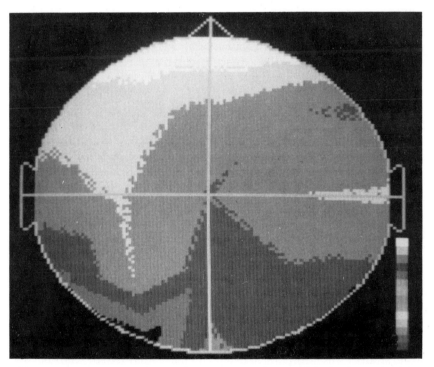

FIG. 1   *Brain electrical activity map of a statistical comparison between schizophrenic patients (medication and drug-free combined) compared with normal controls for delta activity. In this map the white region delineates the greatest regional difference and highlights an area overlying the frontal lobes. (Picture credit to John M. Morihisa, Veterans Administration Medical Center, Washington, DC and Frank H. Duffy, Children's Hospital Medical Center, Boston, MA).*

These findings are consistent with a recent spectral analytic investigation of schizophrenia that did not employ topographic mapping. In a 1980 study of schizophrenia, Fenton (12) reported that his chronic schizophrenic patients demonstrated greater delta activity than controls.

Thus, there is some supporting evidence from both topographic and non-mapping investigations of EEG in schizophrenia for abnormally increased delta activity in schizophrenia.

Furthermore, this finding of increased delta activity that is greatest in the frontal regions may be consistent with the work of Ingvar and Franzen (13). In this first study of the regional cerebral blood flow in schizophrenic patients compared to alcoholic controls, it was found that some patients with schizophrenia had a relative decrease in frontal blood flow. This was interpreted as indirect evidence that patients with schizophrenia have reduced neural metabolic activity in frontal regions.

In a different study, Ingvar et al. (14) demonstrated a correlation between mean EEG frequency and cerebral blood flow. On the basis of this finding, one might expect patients with decreased frontal blood flow to also demonstrate increased frontal delta. A recent application of the Xenon-133 inhalational regional cerebral blood flow technique by Weinberger and colleagues (15) replicates this relative decrease in the resting blood flow of patients with schizophrenia.

Recently, a more direct measure of regional brain metabolism, positron emission tomography (PET), has been applied to schizophrenia research. This technique utilizes radioactive isotopes to investigate brain metabolism. Recent findings using PET (16, 17) report an abnormality of the antero-posterior gradient of metabolic activity in schizophrenia, that could be consistent with our frontal findings.

It is important to point out, however, that brain imaging findings in schizophrenia research do not form a coherent pattern and, indeed, contradictory results have been reported in cerebral blood flow, PET and electrophysiological studies of this disorder (18 – 20). This has led to a lack of agreement as to what, if any, metabolic, structural and electrophysiological abnormalities might be characteristic or even important to our understanding of schizophrenia.

In an effort to address these questions several strategies have been developed. One has used increasingly powerful approaches to verify and expand upon the pioneering work of previous investigators. Another strategy has been to use multiple brain imaging approaches in concert in an attempt to better delineate possible patterns of pathophysiology (21).

An example of the first strategy is reported in Chapter 12, which replicates Ingvar and Morihisa's finding of resting state abnormalities of the frontal brain regions and uses activation procedures to focus attention upon a specific region of the frontal lobes (15, 22).

The second strategy was incorporated in a preliminary study (23) of schizophrenia that employed both brain electrical activity mapping and computed tomography (CT scan). Schizophrenic patients who fulfilled DSM-III and Research Diagnostic Criteria were divided according to whether they demonstrated marked frontal lobe atrophy or no apparent atrophy. These patients were then compared using brain electrical activity mapping methodology to determine whether the two groups differed across electrophysiological measures. When patients with and without evidence of frontal lobe atrophy were compared, only four regional differences were defined. In each case the electrophysiologic differences delineated involved regions that overlay the frontal lobes. Thus, this preliminary evidence suggests that in some patients with schizophrenia, functional differences in electrophysiology can be associated with gross structural abnormalities of the brain. In this manner, this combined anatomic and physiological approach to the investigation of schizophrenia yields further evidence implicating the frontal lobes as a site of dysfunction that may be basic to the schizophrenic process.

Topography-based statistics

A further extension of computerized topographic approaches to schizophrenia involves development of numerical representations of these maps that may then be subjected to further statistical analysis (1, 24). In a study by Morihisa et al. (8), the brain electrical activity mapping images were further analyzed into numerical representations that were used to develop diagnostic rules. These rules were then used for retrospective classification and in jack-knifing statistics which provide an estimate of prospective classification potential. For both medicated and drug-free patients these studies were over 90% successful in overall retrospective classification and over 80% successful in the jack-knifing classification. However, these findings do not suggest that the heterogeneous disorder of schizophrenia may be diagnosed by EEG or evoked potential studies. Rather these findings demonstrate the sensitivity of computerized topographic EEG and evoked potential approaches to differences in brain electrical activity that appear to be related to the pathophysiology of schizophrenia (8).

Left hemispheric dysfunction in schizophrenia

Prior to the application of computerized topographic techniques to the investigation of schizophrenia, a number of studies have implicated left hemispheric dysfunction in schizophrenia (4, 5). The introduction of topographic approaches to the study of EEG and evoked potential abnormalities in schizophrenia have provided further evidence to support a role for dysfunction of the left hemisphere in the pathophysiology of schizophrenia.

In 1983, brain electrical activity mapping was employed by Morstyn et al. to map the 'spatiotemporal evolution' of an auditory P300 evoked potential in 10 male chronic schizophrenic patients (25). When this patient group was compared with a normal control group, the schizophrenic subjects demonstrated an anterior and right-sided displacement of the P300 maximum and a left temporal deficit in brain electrical activity. When the statistical technique of significance probability mapping (24) was applied to these topographic findings, the left-middle and posterior temporal regions were delineated as topographic areas of maximal group separation. Furthermore, this finding was shown to have the potential to discriminate between schizophrenic patients and control subjects. Although neither the psychological concomitants of the P300 nor the nature of its neural generators are clearly defined, these findings do appear to support the hypothesis of left hemispheric dysfunction in schizophrenia. However, it should be noted that all of the patients in this study were medicated and further studies are needed to delineate the effect of drugs on the P300 evoked potential.

In a different study of evoked potentials in schizophrenia using brain electrical activity mapping, Morihisa et al. (8) did not find differences in the long latency components of the simple auditory evoked response in schizophrenic patients. This does not contradict the findings by Morstyn et al. because Morstyn (25) used a different stimulus paradigm specifically designed to evoke a P300 which Morihisa did not. Thus, these auditory evoked potential findings in schizophrenia, both using brain electrical activity mapping, are complementary in nature. Moreover, findings from the visual evoked potential study and the spectral analysis reported by Morihisa (8) can support the theory of left hemispheric dysfunction in schizophrenia. In this study (8) drug-free schizophrenic patients demonstrated increased fast beta activity and augmented visual evoked potential amplitude that were most prominent in the left posterior quadrant. This is the same topographic region in which Morstyn (25) reported diminished P300 amplitudes. When taken together these findings present elements of focal cortical arousal, and both augmented and diminished evoked potentials in schizophrenic patients as compared with controls. This combination of seemingly opposing findings is not without neurophysiological precedent (26) and adds further evidence for left hemispheric abnormalities in schizophrenia.

Furthermore, these findings of increased fast beta activity are theoretically consistent with the work of Ingvar and Franzen (13), who found relatively increased blood flow in post-central regions. In addition, a recent PET study by Delisi et al. (27) has reported increased temporal lobe glucose utilization in schizophrenic patients that is consistent with these findings. These findings are also consistent with the work of Gur (28), who found evidence of left hemispheric overactivation in schizophrenic patients with the use of regional cerebral blood flow. However, her work also emphasizes the important effects of medication, gender and specific cognitive activation tasks. Further research is needed to delineate the effects of these factors on the findings of the various studies described here.

Finally, Guenther and Breitling (10) in a recent study using a modified system of brain electrical activity mapping that employed a 16-electrode montage have reported that during multisensorimotor activation, schizophrenic patients demonstrate evidence of 'widespread left hemisphere dysfunction.' This spectral analytic study investigated French schizophrenic patients using a different topographic montage and mapping technique. This is the same study that also replicated the finding of increased delta activity in schizophrenic patients. Thus, a study using different technology in a crosscultural patient group supported findings of left hemispheric dysfunction as well as evidence of frontal lobe dysfunction.

Considerations of application

Common to the use of all the computer-assisted techniques in neuropsychiatry is a balance between the strengths and limitations of each of these approaches. Two major limitations of computerized topographic approaches are basic to electrophysiological research. First, the electrical activity of the brain is usually measured at the cortical surface and this limits the ability of this technique to resolve different neural generators and to detect electrical phenomena that do not occur close to the surface of the brain. In most cases, as a result, little can be determined concerning electrical activity deep within the brain parenchyma and a conservative interpretation of the topographic focus of electrical activity is warranted. Second, electroencephalography is sensitive to muscle artifact, eye movements and drug effects. For this reason these potential sources of artifact must be carefully controlled in all research applications. A special limitation that is inherent in computer brain imaging approaches is that the data may be biased both in its analysis and presentation by assumptions and rules incorporated into the computer software. This requires circumspect and conservative interpretation of computer maps of brain electrical activity.

A major advantage of computerized topographic EEG approaches is that it is non-invasive and does not involve radiation exposure. Moreover, it may therefore be repeated more easily and safely than other brain imaging techniques. Finally, these computer-assisted electrophysiological approaches have much greater chronologic resolution than other methods of investigating brain function (28). For example, these techniques can examine electrical events that occur in small fractions of a second and are therefore particularly well suited for the investigation of transient cognitive phenomena.

Summary

Computerized topographic EEG techniques have allowed us to further investigate electrophysiological abnormalities in schizophrenia. Although researchers reported abnormalities in brain electrical activity in schizophrenia early in the course of electrophysiological research, there remains no agreement concerning the clinical relevance of these findings. With the introduction of computerized techniques for the analysis and presentation of data new and powerful approaches have become available to schizophrenia research (29). These approaches have grown out of the expansion of neurological and neuroscience techniques into research psychiatry. It is therefore particularly appropriate that their findings should implicate basic neurostructural and neurophysiological abnormalities in this disorder. Specifically, findings of increased delta activity that are greatest in frontal regions provide further evidence for frontal lobe pathology in schizophrenia. When taken with supporting work employing neurostructural and neurometabolic approaches, a compelling body of research implicates the frontal lobes as a site of pathological dysfunction in this destructive disease of the brain (3). In a similar manner, a growing body of electrophysiological and cerebral metabolic evidence is accumulating that implicates left hemispheric dysfunction in the underlying pathophysiology of schizophrenia.

We have employed the approach of presenting findings in the context of two of the most investigated theories of pathological localization in computer-assisted EEG and evoked potential mapping research of schizophrenia. This is not meant to imply that all findings fit these particular constructs but rather to suggest that in the topographic mapping of brain electrical activity the use of these two theories as an organizing structure may facilitate the further elaboration and testing of these hypotheses concerning the pathophysiology of schizophrenia.

REFERENCES

1. Duffy FH, Burchfiel JL, Lombroso CT (1979) Brain electrical activity mapping (BEAM): a method for extending the clinical utility of EEG and evoked potential data. *Ann. Neurol., 5,* 309.
2. Morihisa JM, Duffy FH, Wyatt RJ (1982) Topographic analysis of computer processed electroencephalography in schizophrenia. In: Usdin E, Hanin I (Eds), *Biological Markers in Psychiatry and Neurology.* Pergamon Press, New York.
3. Morihisa JM, Weinberger DR (1986) Frontal lobe dysfunction in schizophrenia: an organizing theory of relevant anatomy and physiology. In: Andreasen N (Ed), *Can schizophrenia be localized in the brain?,* American Psychiatric Press, Washington, DC, in press.
4. Flor-Henry P (1976) Lateralized temporal-limbic dysfunction and psychopathology. *Ann. NY Acad. Sci., 280,* 777.
5. Gur RE (1977) Motoric laterality imbalance in schizophrenia: a possible concomitant of left hemisphere dysfunction. *Arch. Gen. Psychiatry, 34,* 33.
6. Buchsbaum MS, Rigal F, Coppola R et al. (1982) A new system for gray-level surface distribution maps of electrical activity. *Electroencephalogr. Clin. Neurophysiol., 53,* 237.
7. Coppola R, Buchsbaum MS, Rigal F (1982) Computer generation of surface distribution maps of measures of brain activity. *Comput. Biol. Med., 12,* 191.
8. Morihisa JM, Duffy FH, Wyatt RJ (1983) Brain Electrical Activity Mapping (BEAM) in schizophrenic patients. *Arch. Gen. Psychiatry, 40,* 719.
9. Morstyn R, Duffy F, McCarley R (1983) Altered topography of EEG spectral content in schizophrenia. *Electroencephalogr. Clin. Neurophysiol., 56,* 263.
10. Guenther W, Breitling D (1985) Predominant sensorimotor area left hemisphere dysfunction in schizophrenia measured by brain electrical activity mapping. *Biol. Psychiatry, 20,* 515.
11. Buchsbaum MS, Cappelletti J, Coppola R et al. (1982) New methods to determine the CNS effects of antigeriatric compounds: EEG topography and glucose use. *Drug Dev. Res., 2,* 489.
12. Fenton GW, Fenwick PBC, Dollimore J et al. (1980) EEG spectral analysis in schizophrenia. *Br. J. Psychiatry, 136,* 445.
13. Ingvar DH, Franzen G (1974) Abnormalities of cerebral blood flow distribution in patients with chronic schizophrenia. *Acta Psychiatr. Scand., 50,* 425.
14. Ingvar DH, Sjolund B, Ardo A (1976) Correlation between dominant EEG frequency,

cerebral oxygen uptake and blood flow. *Electroencephalogr. Clin. Neurophysiol., 41,* 268.

15. Weinberger DR, Berman KF, Zec RF (1986) Physiological dysfunction of dorsolateral prefrontal cortex in schizophrenia: I. Regional cerebral blood flow (rCBF) evidence. *Arch. Gen. Psychiatry, 43,* 114.

16. Buchsbaum MS, Ingvar DH, Kesseler R et al. (1982) Cerebral glucography with positron tomography: use in normal subjects and in patients with schizophrenia. *Arch. Gen. Psychiatry, 39,* 251.

17. Wolkin A, Jaeger J, Brodie J et al. (1985) Persistence of cerebral metabolic abnormalities in chronic schizophrenia as determined by positron emission tomography. *Am. J. Psychiatry, 142,* 564.

18. Gur RE (1984) Regional cerebral blood flow in psychiatry: the resting and activated brains of schizophrenic patients. In: Morihisa J (Ed), *Brain Imaging in Psychiatry,* pp. 65 – 76. American Psychiatric Press, Washington, DC.

19. Sheppard G, Gruzelier J, Mavchanda R et al. (1983) 150 positron emission tomographic scanning in predominantly never-treated acute schizophrenic patients. *Lancet, 2,* 1448.

20. Matthew RJ, Duncan GC, Weinman ML et al. (1982) Regional cerebral blood flow in schizophrenia. *Arch. Gen. Psychiatry, 39,* 1121.

21. Morihisa JM (Ed) (1984) Brain Imaging in Psychiatry. American Psychiatric Press, Washington, DC.

22. Berman KF, Zec RF, Weinberger DR (1986) Physiological dysfunction of dorsolateral prefrontal cortex in schizophrenia: II. Role of medication status, attention and mental effort. *Arch. Gen. Psychiatry, 43,* 126.

23. Morihisa JM, McAnulty GB (1985) Structure and function: brain electrical activity mapping and computed tomography in schizophrenia. *Biol. Psychiatry, 20,* 3.

24. Duffy FH, Bartels PH, Burchfiel JL (1981) Significance probability mapping: an aid in the topographic analysis of brain electrical activity. *Electroencephalogr. Clin. Neurophysiol., 51,* 455.

25. Morstyn R, Duffy FH, McCarley RW (1983) Altered P300 topography in schizophrenia. *Arch. Gen. Psychiatry, 40,* 729.

26. Morihisa JM, Duffy FH (1986) Focal cortical arousal in the schizophrenias. In: Duffy FH (Ed), *Topographic Mapping of the Brain.* Butterworth, Stonehan, MA, in press.

27. Delisi LE, Buchsbaum MS, Holcomb H et al. (1986) Increased temporal lobe glucose utilization in chronic schizophrenic patients. *Biol. Psychiatry,* in press.

28. Gur RE (1984) Regional cerebral blood flow in psychiatry: the resting and activated brains of schizophrenic patients. In: Morihisa JM (Ed), *Brain Imaging in Psychiatry,* pp. 65 – 76. American Psychiatric Press, Washington, DC.

29. Morihisa JM (1985) Computerized Topographic Mapping of Electrophysiologic Data in Psychiatry. *Psychiatr. Ann., 15,* 250.

CHAPTER 12

Cerebral blood flow studies in schizophrenia

KAREN FAITH BERMAN AND DANIEL R. WEINBERGER

Inherent in most contemporary approaches to the conceptualization and study of schizophrenia (as reflected in this volume) is the supposition that this illness is a brain disorder with underlying 'organic' (i.e. physical) pathology of structure, of function, or of both. The eventual localization and physiological characterization of this pathology may revolutionize our understanding of the normal human brain as well as the way we think about and treat disorders such as schizophrenia. Relatively recent advances in neuroradiological techniques that allow qualitative evaluation and quantitation of brain function in vivo (also, see Chapter 13) have increased the possibility that this goal may be realized. These functional brain imaging methodologies have the potential to localize and physiologically characterize mental processes in the living, working human brain. The ability to directly assess regional cerebral physiology in living human patients affords several important advantages: the results can be compared with concurrent clinical observations, correlations with results of other diagnostic evaluations (e.g. X-ray computed tomography, electroencephalography, neuropsychometric testing, etc.) can be made, and cerebral effects of therapeutic interventions can be assessed. This chapter focusses on a particular functional brain imaging technique, xenon-133 inhalation method, for measuring regional cerebral blood flow (rCBF), and the results of its application to schizophrenia research. The use of this technique is based on the fact that cerebral blood flow is tightly coupled to neuronal metabolic activity.

Characteristics of an ideal 'brain imaging' technique for studying regional physiology in schizophrenia would include the following: (a) it should be non-invasive so as not to create extraneous cognitive sets (i.e. those not of primary interest) that might contaminate the cerebral physiological 'landscape' being studied; (b) it should be easily applied to the study of patients who might be unable to cooperate with long or invasive procedures and who might resist motor restraint or other procedural inconveniences; (c) its temporal resolution should be short enough to facilitate study of transient mental phenomena; and (d) its spatial resolution should be sufficient to allow investigation of important structures such as the basal ganglia, limbic system, etc. Unfortunately, no currently available technique for functional brain imaging completely fulfills these criteria, and the application of each involves a 'trade-off.' For example, those techniques with the best spatial resolution sacrifice non-invasiveness, and vice versa.

Of the various methodologies now utilized to assess brain function in vivo (see

Handbook of Schizophrenia, Vol. 1: The Neurology of Schizophrenia.
H.A. Nasrallah and D.R. Weinberger, editors.
© Elsevier Science Publishers B.V., 1986.

also Chapters 11 and 13), the xenon-133 inhalation technique for measuring rCBF, a sensitive, albeit indirect measure of neuronal metabolic activity, has proven to be particularly well suited to the study of higher cortical function in schizophrenia. The method is quick and non-invasive, and there are no major procedural inconveniences. Its relatively short temporal resolution of less than ten minutes is particularly valuable both practically and theoretically. The hardware is relatively inexpensive (less than $150,000 for equipment and installation); the radioisotope is readily available and remarkably cheap (about $20 per study); and, unlike the positron-emitting radionuclides used in positron emission tomography (PET), xenon-133 does not require a cyclotron for its production. Because xenon is rapidly eliminated via the lungs, the radiation exposure involved is quite low (1), even if a series of several procedures is performed. This is a major advantage that enables multiple rCBF measurements to be made on a single individual in fairly rapid succession. Thus, rCBF can be determined during various cognitive or behavioral states. It is also possible to compare changing clinical states and medication conditions, with a subject serving as his or her own control.

Compared to other perhaps more sophisticated methods, this technique has important limitations. Unlike tomography, it yields only two-dimensional data representing superficial cortical metabolism and is unable to visualize deep subcortical structures. Another disadvantage is its relatively limited spatial resolution. Although not conclusively established, it is generally accepted that rCBF is capable of measuring a cone of tissue with an apex of cortical surface approximately 2 cm in diameter (2). The resolution of current PET scanners, on the other hand, is less than 1 cm (3). However, some investigators believe that the cerebral cortex participates in physiological brain work by activating large numbers of functionally and spatially related cortical columns comprising 'cortical fields' of approximately $3-6$ cm^2 (4). If this is indeed the case, the resolving power of rCBF technology would suffice to adequately measure regional cortical function.

Theoretical and historical background

The xenon-133 inhalation technique evolved from a series of developments over the past century. An appreciation of these theoretical and historical foundations is helpful in understanding and interpreting the rCBF literature as it applies to schizophrenia.

Preclinical foundations

In 1896 Charles Roy and Charles Sherrington observed that within seconds after the onset of an epileptic seizure, a swelling of the brain occurred, suggesting to them an increase in the supply of blood (5). About 25 years later, Joseph Barcroft refined the notion that blood flow to a tissue varies with its functional activity and metabolism (6). He hypothesized that enhanced functional level can only be sustained by increasing the rate of oxygen consumption and, thus, of the flow of oxygenated blood to the tissue. In 1937, Carl Schmidt and James Hendrix recorded a strictly localized increase in blood flow to the visual cortex when they applied a small spot of light to the retina of a cat (7).

These investigators all advanced the notion that enhanced functional activity in a tissue results in an augmentation of local metabolism, and that this requires increased oxygen consumption; to provide this and to eliminate metabolic waste products such as carbon dioxide, increased supply of oxygenated blood is necessary. An extensive body of basic research has now verified quite unequivocally that in the grossly intact brain, 'brain work,' neuronal metabolism and local blood flow are very tightly coupled (8 – 10). Thus, cerebral blood flow can be studied not just to elucidate cerebral hemodynamics per se, but, more importantly, as a marker for neuronal metabolism. The concept of these important homeostatic relationships was soon applied to investigating the physiology of the human brain by studying the exchange of nonmetabolized (i.e. inert), diffusible molecules between capillary and brain tissue. The rate of this exchange would be a function of blood flow.

Non-regional (invasive) CBF techniques

In 1944, Seymour Kety and Carl Schmidt made the first determination of *whole brain mean* blood flow in man using 15% nitrous oxide inhalation with venous and arterial sampling (11). The Kety-Schmidt technique, a modification of the familiar Fick Principle, requires repeated sampling of blood from both the femoral artery and the superior jugular bulb throughout a ten-minute period during which subjects breathe a mixture of 21% oxygen, 64% nitrogen, and 15% nitrous oxide. Mean cerebral blood flow (CBF), often expressed in milliliters per 100 grams of brain tissue per minute (ml/100 g/min), is calculated as an integrated function from the shapes of the arterial and internal jugular (i.e. venous) nitrous oxide concentration time curves. In 1955, Lassen and Munck (12, 13) used an inert, radioactive gas, krypton-85, as the tracer and bilateral venous sampling of cerebral blood to increase the accuracy of whole brain mean blood flow determinations. While useful for the measurement of blood flow and metabolism of the human brain as a whole, this technique is not able to measure these functions in individual structures or regions of the brain.

Regional invasive (intracarotid) CBF techniques

The objective of mapping blood flow to individual cortical areas was realized in 1961 when Ingvar and Lassen (14) extended the principles of the Kety-Schmidt technique to determine concentrations of inert radioactive tracers in small tissue regions. By injecting a radioactive tracer (dissolved in saline) into the carotid artery and monitoring gamma-ray emissions with extracranial radiation detectors, they were able to measure *regional* cerebral blood flow in humans. These measurements were initially made with krypton-85 as the tracer, but xenon-133 was soon found to be more satisfactory (15). Cortical blood flow was defined as the initial slope of a semi-logarithmically plotted curve of the clearance ('washout') of the tracer from the cortical regions being monitored (16).

One advantage of injecting the tracer directly into the internal carotid was that this minimized background radiation from the contralateral hemisphere and extracranial structures. This technique provided excellent spatial resolution. However, several limitations were inherent in the method. For instance, it restricted the delivery of the tracer, and thus rCBF measurements, to only cortical areas subserved by the anterior cerebral circulatory system and to only one hemisphere (usually the dominant hemisphere was studied). The invasive and traumatic nature of the procedure was probably its greatest drawback since this precluded the study of strictly normal volunteers. It also ran the risk of producing cerebral physiological epiphenomena corresponding to the metabolic effects of the uncomfortable conditions of the procedure. Thus, interpretation of these studies may be difficult. Nonetheless, important observations about cortical metabolism in general, and that of patients with schizophrenia in particular, emerged with the use of this technique.

One of the first indications that this technique was sensitive to functional activation of specific cortical areas occurred almost serendipitously (17). When a subject was asked to repeatedly open and close his fist against a blood pressure cuff (in order to increase blood pressure without using drugs), a marked increase in rCBF was seen in the contralateral hand motor cortex (18). This suggested that the measurement of rCBF could be a powerful tool for demonstrating brain regions that become active during specific stimulus conditions. Indeed, mapping of cortical function during a variety of sensory and motor tasks was subsequently accomplished using the intracarotid technique (17, 19, 20), and its application launched the field of functional brain imaging.

Regional non-invasive (xenon-133 inhalation) CBF techniques

A completely atraumatic rCBF technique was first proposed by Conn in 1955 (21); this milestone was accomplished in the 1960s when Veall and Mallett made the first *non-invasive* attempt to measure *regional* cerebral blood flow in man (22 – 24). They administered xenon-133 gas as a tracer via inhalation and, like Ingvar and Lassen, they used extracranial radiation detectors to monitor the time course of the concentration of radioactivity. They found that the cortical clearance curves had two distinct exponential components: (a) a fast-clearing compartment with a half-period of 1.5 minutes presumed to represent gray matter blood flow, and (b) a slow-clearing compartment with a half-period of 10 minutes thought to consist of blood flow to white matter plus extracranial tissues. Although an important achievement, their method had several problems; the procedure was relatively long (five minutes of xenon-133 inhalation plus an additional 20-minute 'washout period'), and the values obtained were considerably lower than those obtained with the intracarotid method. This was thought to be due to contamination by diffusion of xenon-133 into extracranial tissues (i.e. skin, muscle, scalp, skull, etc.), having a much slower rate of clearance, and also due to the arterial recirculation of xenon-133 after the five-minute inhalation. Since xenon is more soluble in air than blood, the majority of the blood xenon content is vented in the lungs with each circulatory pass. Nonetheless, a small amount is recirculated and redelivered to the brain, thus complicating determination of the clearance rate. This reloading of the brain with recirculated xenon-133 had not been a major problem with intracarotid bolus injection.

In 1967 Obrist et al succeeded in overcoming several of these obstacles by demonstrating that the end-expiratory xenon-133 concentration in expired air closely parallels the arterial concentration and that the former could be used to correct for recirculation (25). In addition, by extending the extracranial recording to 45 minutes or more, Obrist was able to factor out the contaminating extracranial blood flow. In 1971, Obrist and his colleagues (26) designed and computer-programmed a much quicker (one-minute inhalation plus ten-minute washout) two-compartmental theoretical model that yields accurate, reliable gray matter values (and less precise slow compartment values consisting of blood flow to both white matter and extracranial tissues). This model, in essence, remains the mainstay of current rCBF technology.

Current xenon-133 inhalation rCBF technique

It was Obrist's contribution that made the technique a practical and attractive one for research and clinical use. Gray matter rCBF thus obtained has been well validated. The currently used xenon-133 inhalation technique as developed by Obrist (25 – 28) and slightly modified by Meyer (1) and Risberg (29, 30) is entirely non-invasive and involves minimal discomfort and low radiation exposure. The theoretical aspects and mathematics have been described in detail by these investigators and others and are briefly summarized here.

This method utilizes a low-energy, gamma-ray emitting radioisotope, xenon-133 gas, which is inhaled in small concentrations (5 – 7 millicuries/liter of room air) for one minute. As mentioned above, xenon is an inert gas that in tracer doses does not participate in or affect biochemical or physiological processes in man; since it is a freely diffusible substance, it exchanges readily between blood and tissue. When inhaled, it passively diffuses from inspired air to lung tissue and the bloodstream. It is carried primarily by hemoglobin to cerebral capillaries where it diffuses into brain parenchyma. If a tissue (e.g. brain) is first saturated with this radioisotope and then allowed to desaturate, the blood flow to that tissue directly determines the rate of disappearance of radioactivity from it. External monitoring of the disappearance of radioactivity from a xenon-133-saturated brain is possible since xenon-133 gamma rays, especially those from superficial cortex, penetrate brain tissue and skull. Monitoring is carried out with extracranial scintillation detectors (thallium-activated sodium iodide crystals) applied to the scalp. These are housed in lead-shielded cases and are 'collimated' (i.e. focused) to insure that each detector records the arrival ('saturation') and disappearance ('desaturation' or washout) of radioactive tracer mainly from the area of cortex underlying it.

By taking radioactivity counts every six seconds during the one-minute xenon-133 inhalation period and the ensuing fourteen or so minutes during which the subject breathes room air, each extracranial radiation detector generates a saturation-desaturation curve (i.e. 'head curve') for the region of cortex it overlies. If the desaturation rates of a number of contiguous cortical regions are determined simultaneously, a regional distribution or topographical map of blood flow and, by inference, of cortical physiological activity and metabolism (31, 32) can be obtained. These 'head curves' can be subjected to various analyses to yield the desaturation rate and a number of rCBF parameters. From continuous monitoring of radioactivity in expired air, it is possible to construct an end-expiratory 'air curve' which approximates the time course of arterial xenon-133 concentration. The air curve is used to correct the head desaturation curves for arterial recirculation of xenon-133 (27).

Several measures reflecting gray matter flow can be derived from the corrected head curves. One approach is a biexponential mathematical analysis which identifies fast-clearing (gray matter) and slow-clearing (white matter plus extracranial) compartments. Another measure, the initial slope index (ISI) described by Risberg et al (29), is a monoexponential (i.e. one-compartmental) model, calculated as the slope constant of the head desaturation curve between the second and third minutes of the study. ISI is an index of blood flow to all tissues 'seen' by a given detector, but it largely reflects the fast-clearing gray matter compartment. Yet another parameter more exclusively reflecting gray matter rCBF is the initial slope (IS) of Obrist and Wilkinson (28). This measure is monoexponential and is defined as the tangent to the clearance curve at time zero for an equivalent bolus injection. It may be more accurate and dependable in pathological conditions and at low count rates than are some biexponential parameters, and it may be particularly sensitive to changes related to cognitive activity (33).

Methodological considerations in applied research

Despite the many advantages of xenon-133 inhalation rCBF, there are a number of technical limitations associated with this two-dimensional technique. These are discussed in detail elsewhere (1, 27, 30, 34 – 37), but are important to consider before discussing the rCBF data pertaining to schizophrenia. As will become apparent, these data are far from consistent. Reasons for the perplexing variability in the results of these studies may include technical problems and/or difficulties in the application of this method to schizophrenia research. Some of the familiar problems commonly encountered by all schizophrenia researchers – including the need for careful and reliable patient diagnosis, selection of appropriate control groups, rigorous statistical analysis, etc. – are no less important in rCBF studies. Other technical and methodological problems are unique or specific to this particular approach. Both 'generic' and specific issues in rCBF research design and implementation are discussed below.

Generic methodological issues

Subject selection: a number of group variables must be controlled in rCBF studies. First, since several studies have reported differences in rCBF between men and women (33, 38), patient and control groups should be matched for sex. Second, relatively recent investigations indicate that mean CBF (39, 40) as well as the relative increase in frontal rCBF over that to posterior areas (i.e. 'hyperfrontality,' which is seen in most normal individuals) decrease with age (41). Therefore, experimental groups of different ages cannot be directly compared. Third, although the effect of cerebral dominance on rCBF is not clear, differences between left- and right-handed individuals have been reported (33, 42), suggesting that patients and normal controls must also be matched for this variable.

Finally, although some studies have found no differences in rCBF or rCBF pattern between various subgroups of patients with schizophrenia (43, 44), other investigators have reported such differences. For example, patients with productive symptoms may differ from those with non-productive symptoms (45 – 47); rCBF of more withdrawn and deteriorated patients may be different from that of those more acutely disturbed (46); hallucinators may differ from nonhallucinators (47), etc. Thus, divergent findings in the literature may reflect different patient populations, diagnostic approaches, or variables related to stage of illness.

Medication status: although the acute and chronic effects on rCBF of neuroleptic and other pharmacological treatments in schizophrenia have not been definitively elucidated, it would be surprising if such effects did not exist. Therefore, medication state must be kept in mind in evaluating rCBF studies, and findings in medicated patients may differ from those in drug-free patients. Efforts to study medication-free patients as well as those who have never been treated are important. In addition, nicotine (48) and caffeine (48, 49) must be avoided prior to rCBF procedures since these have been shown to affect rCBF.

Statistical analysis: the statistical analysis of rCBF data is complex and somewhat controversial (36, 50). There is no perfect statistical approach. Each procedure yields as many as 32 rCBF values which are spatially and/or functionally inter-related to varying degrees. Some investigators have viewed multiple measurements from the same brain as 'repeated measures' and have used a repeated measures analysis of variance (ANOVA) to compare groups. Since this approach assumes that the measures have a special covariance structure (all possible pairs of measures must have the same variance and correlate to the same degree), small deviations may appear significant. Therefore, this approach is overly prone to Type I statistical error (i.e. falsely positive results) (51). rCBF data, in particular, are not likely to have this special covariance structure since the functional and spatial relationships between different cortical areas vary greatly. A more theoretically conservative approach would be a multivariate analysis of variance (MANOVA) that views each probe or brain region as a separate variable and takes into account a general covariance structure. While this approach is resistant to Type I error, it requires large samples to avoid Type II error (i.e. falsely negative results). Some investigators (52, 53) have performed analyses that represent a compromise between these two approaches, involving MANOVA for across-group comparisons of multiple regions and ANOVA for across group comparisons of individual regions. While this may constitute an improvement over some earlier studies, an ideal statistical approach has yet to be delineated.

Specific methodological issues

CBF testing conditions: rigorous control of the conditions (both internal and external to the subject) under which rCBF is measured is the single most essential prerequisite of obtaining meaningful and interpretable data. This cannot be overemphasized and is a critical consideration in any functional brain imaging paradigm. Since rCBF studies measure dynamic brain *function* rather than static brain *anatomy*, and since the brain may be expected to reflect and respond to its surround, a subject's mental state and behavior, sensory input, motor outputs, cognitive activity, and the ambient testing conditions all have impact on data obtained with this method. Thus, the very facet of these techniques that makes them so potentially valuable, their ability to measure physiological concomitants of mental phenomena, makes their application to clinical research complex.

One explanation for the lack of consensus among rCBF schizophrenia studies (as reviewed below) may be that in some cases ambient test conditions were not adequately controlled. It is important to evaluate and interpret the data with these conditions in mind. For example, having an intracarotid injection probably has different psychological impact, resulting in different physiological concomitants, than does inhaling through a mask or mouthpiece. Even the same technique applied in different laboratory settings may result in divergent cerebral functional landscapes.

Failure to appreciate the impact of testing conditions on studies of brain function is reflected in the fact that few investigators have attempted to control the cognitive state of subjects. In fact, many studies (e.g. 43, 47, 54, 55) have been carried out under conditions that are especially difficult to define and standardize from individual to individual or even within an individual – the so-called 'resting state.' Resting rCBF procedures involve no prescribed sensory, motor, or cognitive events. Nonetheless, the procedure itself exposes subjects to an uncontrolled variety of complex sensory and mental stimuli that produce highly variable subjective experiences (56). Thus, differences in cerebral physiology during resting may reflect the subjective experience of the procedure rather than primary differences in cerebral physiology.

Carefully executed activation studies in which cerebral function is measured while a subject is receiving controlled sensory input and/or carrying out a specified cognitive or motor task have been shown to be less randomly variable than resting studies (50, 56–58). This reduction in the 'noise' of the system increases the probability of uncovering meaningful neurophysiological correlates of psychopathology. An additional benefit of determining rCBF during prescribed behavioral, cognitive, or sensory conditions that predictably activate specific cortical regions in normal persons, is that these paradigms, if utilized in patient populations, may uncover subtle abberations in function that would not be detected during resting conditions. An analogous situation in clinical medicine is that subtle weakness of a skeletal muscle may not be apparent on physical exam unless the muscle is challenged. Similarly, cardiac stress tests yield much more useful information about cardiac function and reserve than do resting electrocardiograms. By analogy, 'cerebral stress tests' can be designed to challenge cerebral reserve and to test a specific hypothesis by imposing a selective physiological load on a cortical area of particular interest.

Arterial tension of carbon dioxide (pCO$_2$): gray matter CBF values may vary directly with changes in blood pCO$_2$ concentrations. Therefore, between group differences in CBF may be an artifactual result of group differences in ventilatory function. While it is clear that acute or extreme changes in pCO$_2$ will significantly alter CBF (59 – 62), the importance of chronic minor differences within the normal range is unclear and controversial (63). In fact, changes in CBF accompanying acute alterations of pCO$_2$ have been shown to be reversed when the change in pCO$_2$ is chronically maintained (64). The role of pCO$_2$ in rCBF studies of psychiatric patients is thus complicated by the possibility that group pCO$_2$ differences may represent not acute but chronic ventilatory patterns to which CBF has adapted (64).

One approach to handling pCO$_2$ differences is the application of an arbitrary pCO$_2$ correction factor (44, 59 – 62). However, the magnitude of the correction factor is controversial, and it does not adequately resolve the problem. Also, since pCO$_2$ values are usually derived from expired air, spurious values may arise from mask leakage. Other investigators have suggested that no correction may be necessary for pCO$_2$ values that are stable and within the normal physiological range (43, 55). While the effect of pCO$_2$ on rCBF remains unclear, pCO$_2$ must be monitored during rCBF studies to ensure that it does remain stable and within the physiological range and to determine whether group differences in ventilatory function exists. Possible effects of group pCO$_2$ differences must be considered if they might account for group differences in CBF, and efforts should be made to analyze rCBF data using pCO$_2$-independent parameters (such as rCBF values normalized to the hemisphere mean or expressed as a ratio of another region) as well as absolute values.

Detector placement: reliable and reproducible placement of the rCBF detectors with respect to cerebral cortex, both within and between individuals, is of obvious importance. However, this has been difficult to achieve for several reasons. One inescapable obstacle is that the cortical topography of each brain is unique, and its relation to external landmarks differs. A potentially remediable problem is that the number of detectors used by various investigators has varied from as few as 4 to as many as 16 per hemisphere; moreover, few attempts to standardize detector placement have been made. Thus, studies carried out with different numbers and positions of detectors may not be comparable. Even within the same laboratory and subject, precise localization is difficult to ensure.

Recent applications of the xenon-133 inhalation rCBF technique involve as many as 32 cortical radiation detectors, radially arranged in 16 homologous pairs per hemisphere. Several strategies have been employed to ensure reliable and reproducible detector placement. Some laboratories have adopted focused light markers to identify external cranial landmarks (65). Another approach is to measure and mark each subject's head to locate the Fp1 and Fp2 leads of the 10–20 international system of EEG placement (2, 52, 53). These marks serve as reproducible guides for applying the fronto-polar rCBF detectors. To ensure reproducible placement of the other detectors, the inferior margin of the helmet in which the detectors are mounted may be aligned parallel to the orbito-meatal line.

Technical artifacts: since the energy of xenon-133 radiation emissions is low (81 Kev for gamma), most of the activity comes from superficial cortex (4). This minimizes the contribution of sub-cortical tissue. Emissions from the opposite hemisphere ('interhemispheric cross-talk') can be minimized by orienting the probes in a radial rather than a parallel array (65). 'Airway artifact,' the contamination of the cortical clearance curves by radioactivity in the air passages, is limited by starting the mathematical analysis of the head curves at the time that the end-expiratory radioactivity concentration has fallen to 20% of its peak value (27). If not prevented, the effect of each of these contaminants would be to lower the rCBF values obtained (8, 66).

Mathematical artifacts related to 'slippage' (28), an occasional misassignment of radioactive counts into the gray or white matter compartment by the computer algorithm, must also be considered. Since the occurrence of slippage is randomly distributed throughout cortical areas, no systematic artifact in group data results. Nonetheless, slippages add 'noise' to the data, and their occurrence can be minimized by increasing the amount of data the computer algorithm has available to work with. This can be accomplished by lengthening the washout period measured and/or increasing the count rate (37). Low count rates must also be avoided because the standard deviation of the blood flow values has been shown to be inversely correlated with the square root of the counts (27), and low count rates, therefore, result in decreased stability of rCBF values. These problems can be minimized by careful laboratory technique and adoption of the strategies discussed above and elsewhere (37).

Gas delivery: while some rCBF laboratories employ a tight-fitting face mask for gas delivery, others have found that a snorkel-like mouthpiece and a soft, foam nose-clamp may serve at least as well (52, 53). Most subjects find the latter to be more comfortable and less threatening. More important, it may result in less gas leakage. It is also better suited to the administration of activation procedures because there is minimal visual field obstruction. An added feature of having the nose clamped is that subjects do not smell the potentially disturbing odor of the plastic tubing in the gas delivery system. While many studies have been and continue to be carried out with the subject laying supine, they may also be done with the subject seated in a semi-reclining position (Figure 1). This position may be better tolerated and more appropriate for performing cognitive tasks than is recumbency.

Review of the literature

A number of CBF studies of schizophrenia have appeared in the literature. Some of these studies are summarized in Table 1; several will be critically reviewed below. Methodological problems, conceptual limitations, and possible interpretations of the sometimes diverse results will be discussed and emphasized. Differences in instrumentation and application of these techniques in many cases make direct comparisons between studies difficult.

Non-regional invasive CBF studies

In 1948, Kety et al. (67) reported the first determinations of whole brain mean (i.e. non-regional) blood flow in patients with schizophrenia using his nitrous oxide method. They found no difference between 35 young normal male subjects and 22 patients with schizophrenia (7 females, 15 males; mean age 35 years, range 19–56; medication status unspecified). Furthermore, they found no difference in mean CBF between chronic patients and those with more 'acute aberrations.' They concluded that 'on the basis of these data a generalized change in circulation or oxygen utilization by the brain of schizophrenics may be safely ruled out although there remains

FIG. 1   *Artist's rendering of subject undergoing rCBF study while taking the WCS.*

TABLE I rCBF studies in schizophrenia

Study (Ref.)	Sample	Method/Condition	Results			Comment
			Decreased mean CBF	Altered laterality	Hypo-frontality	
Ingvar and Franzen (46, 68–71)	up to 31 patients (med.) 15 'controls'	Intracarotid ^{133}Xe -Resting -Activation	no no	n/a n/a	yes yes	Younger control group Dry alcoholic controls Premedication for all procedures
Mathew et al. (43)	23 patients (most med.) 18 normals	^{133}Xe inhalation -Resting	yes	no	no	No pCO_2 correction Metronome breathing
Ariel et al. (54)	29 patients (most med.) 22 normals	^{133}Xe inhalation -Resting	yes	n/a	yes	No pCO_2 correction Unusual statistics
Mubrin et al. (55)	17 patients (med.) 18 normals	^{133}Xe inhalation -Resting	(yes)	n/a	(yes)	Hypofrontality especially in patients older than 30
Gur et al. (44)	15 patients (med.) 25 normals	^{133}Xe inhalation -Resting -Spatial & verbal tasks	no no	no yes	no n/a	Acute patients only
Gur et al. (74)	19 patients (DF) 19 normals	^{133}Xe inhalation -Resting -Spatial & verbal tasks	no no	yes yes	no n/a	Acute patients only Tasks weakly lateralized in normals

Weinberger et al. (52)	17 patients (DF) 25 normals	^{133}Xe inhalation -Resting -Prefrontal & control tasks	no no	n/a n/a	yes yes	Decreased rCBF during specific cognitive demands in DLPFC only
Berman et al. (53)	24 patients (med.) 25 normals	^{133}Xe inhalation -Resting -Prefrontal & control tasks	no no	n/a n/a	yes yes	Results qualitatively similar to DF patients (52)
	18 patients (DF) 17 normals	^{133}Xe inhalation -Non-frontal tasks (CPTs)	no	n/a	no	No differences with non-frontal tasks
Kurachi et al. (47)	16 patients (med.) 20 normals	^{133}Xe inhalation -Resting	(yes)	(yes)	yes	No pCO_2 correction Increased left temporal only in auditory hallucinators

Key: DF = medication-free; med. = neuroleptic-treated; n/a = not applicable or not examined; (yes) = non-significant trends.

the possibility that local disturbances confined to small but important regions may still occur since the method used yields only mean values for the entire brain.'

Kety and colleagues also reported the effect on whole brain mean blood flow of several therapeutic interventions in use at that time (67). They found no difference in mean blood flow before and after seminarcosis produced by barbiturates in 8 patients, despite clinical response, and no effect of insulin hypoglycemia and coma on CBF in 7 patients before treatment, during hypoglycemia, and during coma. However, the small sample size and relatively large individual variation in baseline CBF, along with the fact that, in the latter study, CBF determinations for all three states were available only in 1 patient, may limit conclusions drawn from these data. Finally, in 7 patients studied before as well as 10 to 20 minutes after generalized convulsions produced by electroshock, a marked decrease in CBF was observed.

Hoyer and Oesterreich (45) studied 15 normal subjects (mean age 25 years, range unspecified) and 55 patients with schizophrenia (age 32 years, range 17 to 56 years) using the Kety-Schmidt technique with a different gas mixture (21% oxygen, 25% nitrous oxide, and 54% nitrogen). Most patients were receiving neuroleptic medication. 'From the clinical point of view,' the patients were divided into 3 groups: those having productive schizophrenia (n = 16), those with paranoia and schizophrenia simplex (n = 23), and those with non-productive schizophrenia (n = 16). Mean CBF was found to differ between the patient groups (101.4, 57.6, and 36.7 ml/100 g/min., respectively). Compared with controls (52.9 ml/100 g/min.), patients with productive schizophrenia had increased mean CBF while that of patients with non-productive schizophrenia was decreased. This report highlighted the potential importance of sub-grouping patients and correlation with clinical state. However, the validity of these findings must be questioned. Data for individual subjects are not given, but the reported range of 17.6 to 175.0 ml/100 g/min. obviously includes CBF values outside the range consistent with normal level of consciousness. Such 'non-physiological' values, along with the fact that the reported mean CBF of patients with productive symptoms almost doubled that for normal subjects (52.9 vs. 101.4 ml/100 g/min.) suggest technical problems in this study.

Regional invasive (intracarotid) CBF studies

Beginning in 1974, Ingvar and colleagues reported a series of landmark studies (46, 68 – 71) using the xenon-133 intracarotid injection technique. Before considering these studies, it is worth reiterating that the intracarotid technique of rCBF measurement has several drawbacks, as discussed above.

In their first report (46) they compared resting state rCBF of 10 control subjects and 31 patients with schizophrenia (mean age 39 years, range 17 – 72 years; mean duration of illness 30 years). A key observation was that in the non-schizophrenic ('control') population during the resting condition the highest blood flow (10 – 30% above hemispheric means) was consistently in premotor and frontal regions. The prevalence in normal individuals of this pattern, which they termed 'normal hyperfrontality,' has since been repeatedly confirmed for both hemispheres. In contrast, the patients with schizophrenia, while having normal mean hemispheric CBF during rest, showed a shift in regional blood flow distribution characterized by relatively lower blood flow to frontal structures and relatively greater flow to postcentral cortex. Among the more psychotic patients (n = 13, mean age 64 years) the degree of psychosis and the mean hemispheric blood flow were directly related. In addition, the most indifferent, inactive, and autistic patients showed the lowest frontal flow, while the most cognitively disturbed patients showed the highest postcentral rCBF, leading these investigators to postulate that schizophrenia includes a 'hypointentional' component related to hypofrontality and a 'hypergnostic' component related to increased postcentral blood flow.

During a simple picture test normals showed 'changes' in cerebral activity while the more deteriorated patient did not, suggesting that 'defective function of the non-specific mediothalamic frontocortical projection system' might underlie the behavioral and perceptual abnormalities of schizophrenia (46). While these findings paved the way for further speculation and experimentation in this area, their interpretation is somewhat beclouded by several methodological concerns. First of all, the control subjects were alcoholic. Second, although these investigators did not find age to be correlated with blood flow parameters, it has since been shown that hyperfrontality decreases with age in normal subjects (41). Therefore, the fact that those patients described as 'hypofrontal' were apparently the oldest may compromise their conclusion that hypofrontality was related to primary clinical variables.

In a more comprehensive report (68), Ingvar and Franzen studied 11 young patients with schizophrenia (4 women, 7 men; mean age 25 years; mean duration of illness 5 years) described as 'post-psychotic;' 9 older female patients with schizophrenia (mean age 61 years, mean duration of illness 40 years) who were described as 'highly deteriorated,' 'severely apathetic,' and 'burned-out;' 11 women with Alzheimer's disease (mean age 62 years); 11 patients with posttraumatic dementia (3 women, 8 men; mean age 46 years); and a 'reference group' of 11 male alcoholics (mean age 38 years). Studies were done during rest as well as during attempts at mental activation. All subjects were premedicated with 200 mg phenobarbital and 0.75 mg atropine, and all patients with schizophrenia were receiving neuroleptics as well as a variety of other psychoactive drugs. While resting, mean hemisphere gray matter blood flow for the young patients (75 ml/100 g/min.), the older patients (74 ml/100 g/min.), and the alcoholic reference group (81 ml/100 g/min.) did not differ, values for the Alzheimer's and post-traumatic dementia groups were significantly lower (50 and 47 ml/100 g/min., respectively). As in the previously described study (46), severity of psychosis was found to be directly correlated with mean resting CBF, especially in the older group, suggesting that 'the well-known variation in the clinical picture of schizophrenic psychosis is reflected in the cerebral blood flow (and metabolism).' Activation with attempting to solve either Raven's Progressive Matrices test (for the younger group) or a simple picture test (for the older patients), produced 'by and large normal flow augmentations' regionally in the younger group but 'only very slight flow changes, if any at all' in the older group. The older patients were found to be the most hypofrontal, with the younger patients being intermediate between the alcoholic controls and the older patients. In both patient groups, the higher the postcentral flow, the greater the cognitive impairment rating. These investigators speculated that the high blood flow found over para-auditory and para-visual cortex might be related to hallucinatory activity.

In 1975, Franzen and Ingvar (69), having added 11 elderly male patients (mean age 64 years, mean duration of illness 35 years) with various degrees of psychosis to the previously described sample of 20 (68), published a more detailed analysis of resting rCBF distribution. They again emphasized hypofrontality as well as increased posterior flow in schizophrenia.

Also in 1975 (70), they reported the change in rCBF between an initial resting study and activation studies in 27 patients and 15 controls. Different mental activation procedures were employed in the subject groups (a picture naming test in 13 older, deteriorated patients; Raven's Matrices in 14 less severely ill patients as well as in 9 control subjects; and digit-span-backward tests in 6 controls). While the controls increased rCBF during activation over that at rest, the patients failed to do so. The severely ill group, in fact, tended to decrease frontal flow with activation, but increased post-central flow in a manner similar to normals. Franzen and Ingvar put forth the important observation 'that this disorder implies not only a low resting activity in frontal structures, but also an inability to activate these structures. The results thus support the notion that in chronic schizophrenia a transmission failure might be present in a projection system activating frontal granular cortex'. A role for dysfunction of the median forebrain bundle was posited (71).

Regional noninvasive (xenon-133 inhalation) CBF studies

In 1980, the results of the application of noninvasive xenon-133 inhalation rCBF to schizophrenia research began to appear in the literature. In a preliminary study of 3 male and 3 female patients with schizophrenia and 6 matched normal controls studied at rest, Mathew and colleagues found decreased mean hemisphere CBF to the right hemisphere (72). They did not report regional values.

In a more comprehensive investigation (43), Mathew et al. reported rCBF during the resting state for 8 regions per hemisphere in 23 patients with schizophrenia (14 treated with neuroleptic medication, 9 medication-free for one week) and 18 age- and sex-matched normal subjects. No differences in relative rCBF for any region between the patient and control groups, no between-group laterality differences, and no differences between various patient subgroups (medicated vs. unmedicated, subchronic vs. chronic, paranoid vs. non-paranoid) were found. However, hallucinatory behavior correlated inversely with left parietal and temporal as well as right temporoparietal and occipital 'relative rCBF' (i.e. rCBF values normalized to mean hemispheric flow). Also, in contrast to most earlier studies using invasive methods, patients were reported to have 'reduced CBF to both hemispheres and most brain regions,' which these authors suggested might be consistent with findings of cerebral atrophy in schizophrenia. Moreover, patients were not found to be 'hypofrontal.' Mathew et al. speculated that inconsistencies with earlier results might be due to differences in technique as well as in age and the clinical picture of the patients studied.

Several limitations of this study (43) will be cited. First, only the resting state was studied. Furthermore, an unusual modification of the 'resting condition theme' was that subjects were asked to regulate their breathing to a metronome cue. It is unclear what effect this intervention might have on rCBF since controls and patients may have responded differently to this 'task.' Second, as these authors mentioned, the lower pCO_2 levels seen in the patients might be one explanation for their finding of decreased CBF. However, Mathew et al. felt that this could not fully account for the patients' lower overall blood flow, and they put forth a relevant discussion of the problems inherent in considerations of pCO_2 in rCBF (also, see the section on pCO_2 above). This is an important and controversial methodological consideration that to date has not been completely resolved.

In 1983 Ariel et al. (54) compared rCBF of 29 patients with schizophrenia (mean age 30 years) and that of 22 normals (mean age 33 years) during a resting condition using 8 detectors per hemisphere. All but 2 patients were treated with neuroleptic medication. After averaging rCBF for four brain quadrants (left and right, anterior and posterior), they analyzed their data using a MANOVA with a between-subjects factor of diagnosis (normal vs. schizophrenia) and within-subjects factors of CBF (gray vs. white matter), hemisphere (left vs. right), and position (anterior vs. posterior). As in some previous studies (43, 72), patients were found to have lower blood flow in all four quadrants. Also, consistent with other studies (46, 68 – 70), this reduction was found to be greatest anteriorly. No laterality differences in gray matter rCBF, no effect of sex, and no correlations between rCBF and education or neuroleptic dosage were found. However, in addition to the difficulties inherent in resting studies (as discussed above) and the fact that almost all patients were medicated, two problems further limit this study. First, no mention of pCO_2 measurement is made. Second, their statistical analysis included not only rCBF for gray matter, but also that for white matter. Unfortunately, white matter rCBF data derived from the two-compartmental analysis used, unlike gray matter rCBF data, are highly contaminated by blood flow to extracranial tissues (i.e. skin, muscle, etc.). Moreover, gray matter rCBF and white matter rCBF would be expected to differ significantly since the former has been shown to be approximately four times greater than that for white matter (1, 73). Thus, it is possible that the inclusion of this factor in the MANOVA might skew the overall results towards significance. Nonetheless, post-hoc Scheffe t-tests on gray matter alone did confirm significantly lower rCBF in the patients, particularly anteriorly.

Mubrin et al. in a preliminary report (55) compared resting rCBF of 17 male patients with schizophrenia (mean age 32 years), most of whom were outpatients and all of whom were medicated, with that of an age-matched normal group of 18 'mentally healthy inpatients.' Consistent with some previous reports (43, 54), the patients had slightly, but not significantly, lower mean hemispheric blood flow bilaterally.

In partial agreement with the findings of Ingvar and Franzen, decreased rCBF was especially evident in frontal and occipital areas. While only 1 of 8 patients younger than 29 was hypofrontal (i.e. frontal flow less than mean hemispheric flow), 5 of 9 patients older than 30 displayed this finding. These authors cited several technical limitations of their study and recommended caution in the interpretation of these data. Nonetheless, they suggested that the regional changes described, 'especially in the older subgroup, where withdrawal, emotional blunting etc. are more prominent . . . might be related to a defect of a thalamo-cortical frontal activating projection.' They speculated that in subsequent rCBF studies 'activation methods will be able to display more subtle changes connected with schizophrenia than a plain rest measurement can.'

In 1983, Gur and her colleagues (44) measured rCBF in 8 cortical regions per hemisphere during rest as well as during activation tasks – the performance of verbal and spatial tests – in 15 medicated patients with schizophrenia and a group of 25 controls matched for age, sex, socio-economic background, and level of education. The patient group was described as 'in an acute phase of schizophrenia,' with 5 patients having been ill for one year or less and 7 patients undergoing their first hospitalization. During the resting condition no differences in mean rCBF or anterior – posterior rCBF distribution between the two groups were found. However, mean hemisphere rCBF during cognitive activation did differentiate the two groups. During the verbal task, while normal subjects showed greater blood flow increases to the left hemisphere than to the right, patients did not show this hemispheric flow asymmetry. During the spatial task normals activated the right hemisphere to a greater degree than the left while patients showed the reverse pattern. Further, while male patiens showed activation changes similar to male controls, female patients had the highest resting flows and showed the greatest increase during the verbal task. These authors considered these complex findings to be evidence of left hemisphere overactivity in schizophrenia. They did not assess frontal blood flow or any regional blood flow differences between the two groups during cognitive activation.

In 1985, Gur et al. (74) compared rCBF during rest and during the same visual and spatial tasks in 19 medication-free patients and 19 matched control subjects. Whereas the medicated patients in the previous study (44) had shown normal rCBF at rest, the medication-free patients, particularly those most severely ill, showed higher mean left hemisphere resting flows than did normals. The authors viewed these data as indicative of left hemisphere overactivation in schizophrenia which may be 'normalized' by neuroleptic treatment. The results for verbal and spatial tasks were similar to those described in their earlier publication (43). Several issues in these studies deserve mention. The facts that 3 patients had never been hospitalized, that 9 had had only one admission, and that a number had never been treated with neuroleptics suggest that this patient population, like that in their earlier paper (44), was mildly ill and perhaps somewhat atypical. No information is given about the behavior and experience of patients during the tests. For example, perhaps patients talked to themselves during the spatial task, accounting for their increased left rCBF during this condition. Furthermore, the magnitude of the differences described is quite small, and the robustness of the lateralizing effect of their tasks on the normal population (at least in this study) seems questionable. These considerations render this study somewhat difficult to interpret, particularly with regard to differentiating primary pathophysiology from epiphenomena.

In 1985 Kurachi et al. (47) reported resting rCBF for 8 patients with auditory hallucinations (3 women, 5 men), 8 women patients without auditory hallucinations, and 20 age-matched controls. All patients were medicated. Only 7 detectors per hemisphere were used. Both patient groups showed lower relative (i.e. compared with the hemispheric mean) frontal flow bilaterally, and both had slightly but not significantly lower mean hemisphere blood flow than the normal group. Compared to the normal group, the non-hallucinators showed higher relative right temporal rCBF than the normals, while the hallucinators showed higher relative temporal flow bilaterally. Relative left temporal flow was higher in the hallucinators than in the non-hallucinators. These authors conclude that their 'results suggest that the negative symptoms of schizophrenics are related to bilateral hypofrontal activity and among positive symptoms at least auditory hallucination is related to hypertemporoparietal activity, predominantly in the left hemisphere.' These interpretations are similar to those of Ingvar et al. (68 – 71) and also in some ways perhaps consistent with those of Gur et al. (44, 74). However, several problems exist with this study. In addition to the use of only resting conditions and the fact that all patients were medicated, pCO_2 level was not mentioned. Furthermore, the statistical analysis was limited to multiple t-tests, apparently not adjusted for the approximately 50 comparisons made. It is also unclear how the presence or absence of auditory hallucinations was established.

NIMH rCBF researchers recently reported a series of rCBF studies designed specifically to test the hypothesis of dysfunction of a distinct region of frontal lobe, the dorsolateral prefrontal cortex (DLPFC) (52, 53). DLPFC dysfunction is suggested by many clinical and biological features of schizophrenia (51) and is consistent with some earlier rCBF findings (45, 55, 68 – 71, 74). These studies represent an attempt to avoid some of the methodological pitfalls outlined above. To directly evaluate DLPFC physiology in schizophrenia, Weinberger and colleagues (52) studied 20 medication-free patients and 25 normal controls each of whom underwent three separate xenon-133 inhalation rCBF procedures. After an initial rCBF procedure carried out at 'rest,' rCBF was then determined during two cognitive activation conditions that were presented in randomly counterbalanced order: (a) to assess the function of prefrontal cortex under conditions of behavioral demand, rCBF was measured while subjects were engaged in an automated version of the Wisconsin Card Sort (WCS), which selectively tests DLPFC cognitive function (75 – 79); and (b) to control for non-specific aspects of the WCS/rCBF procedure (such as the minimal finger movement necessary to make a response, the visual stimulation and eye scanning involved, and the experience of performing a task while having rCBF measured) subjects were also studied during a simple number matching test (NM) tailored for this purpose (37). It was hypothesized that by utilizing the WCS to impose a physiological load on prefrontal cortex, otherwise subtle or undetectible DLPFC abnormalities might be demonstrated. The number matching task provided a non-specific baseline activation state against which gray matter rCBF values during WCS were compared. These investigators found that during rest, although most patients were 'hyperfrontal,' as a group they had significantly reduced relative rCBF to DLPFC (Fig. 2).

Of greater importance were the results of the two activation conditions (52). During NM, no specific region differentiated patients from controls. During WCS, however, both absolute and relative rCBF to DLPFC significantly distinguished patients from controls; while controls showed a clear increase in DLPFC rCBF, patients did not (Figs. 3A,B and 4). The changes were regionally specific, involving only DLPFC. Autonomic arousal parameters (e.g. pulse, skin conductance, respiratory rate) measured during each rCBF procedure indicated that these DLPFC differences could not be explained on the basis of preferential arousal for one task

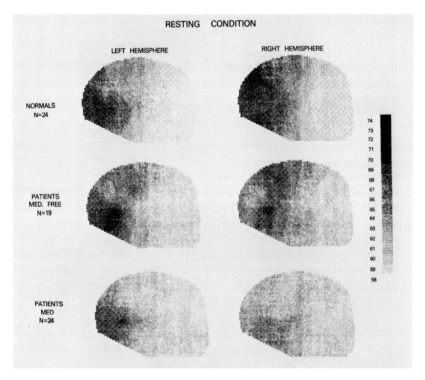

FIG. 2   *rCBF landscapes of left and right hemisphere gray matter blood flow (IS) during the resting state for 24 normal control subjects (top), 19 medication-free patients with chronic schizophrenia (center), and 24 patients treated with neuroleptic medication (bottom). rCBF values are attached to the vertical grey scale, and higher values are depicted as darker shades. The anterior pole of each hemisphere is at the left. After Weinberger et al. (52) and Berman et al. (53).*

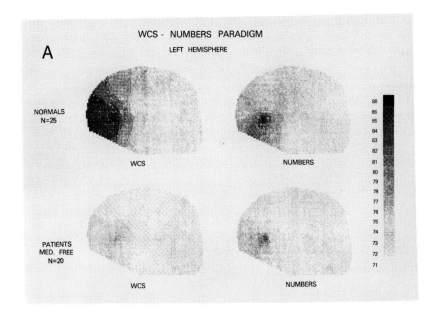

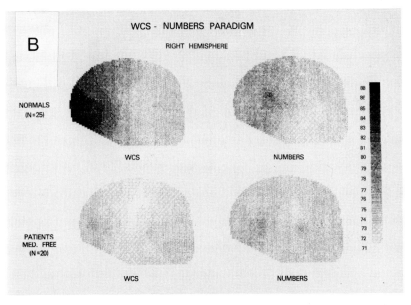

FIG. 3   *Left (A) and right (B) hemisphere rCBF landscapes for a group of medication-free patients and a group of normal control subjects during the Wisconsin Card Sort (WCS) and the numbers match control (NM) task. Note that controls show highest rCBF values in DLPFC during WCS, while patients do not. After Weinberger et al. (52).*

over the other. Furthermore, in patients, DLPFC rCBF correlated directly with WCS cognitive performance, suggesting that the better DLPFC was able to function, the better patients could perform. The pattern of WCS errors, similar to that of patients with known frontal lesions (75, 76), also supports the notion that the DLPFC finding is linked to regionally specific cognitive demand and is not a nonspecific epiphenomenon.

In a companion report (53), the NIMH group described two additional xenon-133 inhalation rCBF studies which further clarified the findings of DLPFC dysfunction. First, Berman and her colleagues compared 24 neuroleptic-treated patients to 25 normal controls all of whom underwent three rCBF procedures as described above: first while 'at rest,' then during the Wisconsin Card Sort and during a number matching control task. The results were qualitatively identical to those reported for medication-free patients (see Figs. 2 and 4), indicating that DLPFC dysfunction is

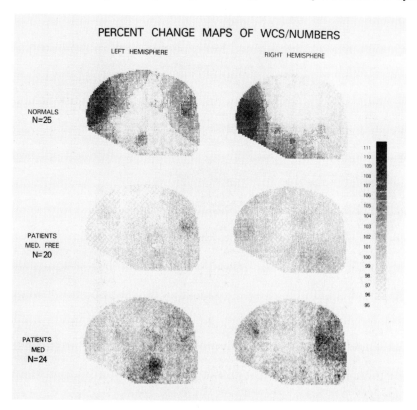

FIG. 4   *Left and right hemisphere maps of percent change in WCS rCBF from NM rCBF [(WCS/NM) × 100]. Data are for 25 normal control subjects (top), 20 medication-free patients, and 24 neuroleptic-treated patients. Note that control subjects, unlike either patient group, show striking rCBF increases during WCS over that during NM (i.e. darker shades) in an area corresponding to DLPFC. After Weinberger et al. (52) and Berman et al. (53).*

not reversed by neuroleptic treatment. In addition, these investigators determined rCBF while 18 medication-free patients and 17 normal control subjects each performed two versions of a visual Continuous Performance Task (CPT), an attentional task not specifically linked to DLPFC. No differences in DLPFC blood flow between the two groups were found during either CPT condition (see Fig. 5). Taken together, these data suggested that 'DLPFC, a cortical region selectively activated in normal subjects while performing the WCS, is not activated in patients with schizophrenia under similar circumstances. The degree to which patients successfully perform the test is linked to how much they increase metabolism to DLPFC. The findings do not appear to be epiphenomena of medication state, level of autonomic arousal, inattention, effort, or simply failing to perform well.' These authors echoed the speculations of others in suggesting that 'DLPFC pathophysiology appears to be linked to regionally specific cognitive function and may be an important neurobiologic aspect of schizophrenia.'

Comment

While some recurrent themes emerge from the studies reviewed above, there is no clear consensus as to the nature, or even the presence, of rCBF abnormalities in schizophrenia. Potential problems in research design and/or the application of CBF technology may, in part, account for this. Nonetheless, considered as a whole, this body of data does provide evidence relevant to some hypotheses of the neurologic

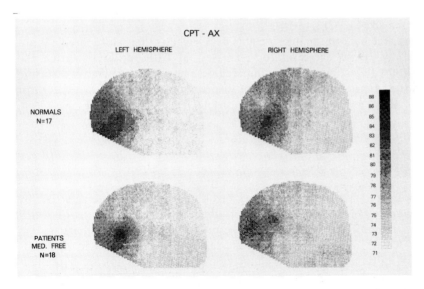

FIG. 5   *Maps of left and right hemisphere rCBF values during a visual continuous performance task (CPT) for a group of normal controls and a group of medication-free patients. Note that rCBF patterns for the two groups are strikingly similar. After Berman et al. (53).*

basis of schizophrenia. The CBF data supporting or refuting these theories will be considered in turn.

Alterations in whole brain mean CBF?

The question of whether schizophrenia is characterized by decreased whole brain mean blood flow, as are many degenerative disorders, is a potentially important one. While not entirely consistent, the bulk of the relevant data suggests that schizophrenia is not characterized by global decreases in blood flow.

Normal whole brain mean blood flow in schizophrenia was first demonstrated by Kety et al. in 1948 (67). With a similar technique, Hoyer and Oesterreich (45) found lower mean CBF in non-productive patients, but higher mean CBF in productive patients and no differences in patients with paranoia and simple schizophrenia. The data of Ingvar and Franzen (46, 68 – 71) also suggested that schizophrenia is not characterized by decreased mean CBF (at least in the dominant hemisphere) during resting and activation conditions. Like Hoyer and Oesterreich, they found that more actively disturbed patients had the highest blood flow.

The results of inhalation rCBF studies have been less consistent. While the data of several studies (43, 47, 54, 55) suggest decreased CBF, in each case the resting state was studied, the patient groups were medicated, and pCO_2 may have played a role (in two of these studies (47, 55) the difference in mean CBF was not statistically significant). In contrast, the data in four other reports (44, 52, 53, 74), which examined activation states as well as the resting condition, showed no decrease in mean hemisphere or whole brain CBF in either medication-free (52, 53, 74) or neuroleptic-treated (44, 53) patients.

In summary, the bulk of the interpretable data suggests that schizophrenia is not characterized by global decreases (or increases) in CBF, or at least that the magnitude of any reduction is slight compared with primary degenerative dementia of the Alzheimer type. This is perhaps not surprising in view of the fact that most neurological illnesses in which altered whole brain mean CBF has been demonstrated, are characterized by either gross structural or physiological pathology and unequivocal neurological signs.

Altered cerebral lateralization?

Some investigators have suggested that schizophrenia may be characterized by disordered cerebral lateralization. However, there is no agreement as to which hemisphere is implicated, or whether the aberration involves both. Similarly, it is unclear whether the abnormality involves increased or decreased activity in the affected side, or a decrease in one and an increase in the other. Thus, the hypothesis of cerebral lateralization abnormalities in schizophrenia is not decisively supported either on clinical grounds or by investigations into the neurobiology of this disorder.

Unfortunately, the existing rCBF data specifically addressing this confused issue are sparse and do little to help resolve this complicated question. Whole brain mean

CBF measurements are obviously of no help in this line of inquiry, and intracarotid xenon-133 studies only measure rCBF in the dominant hemisphere. Several regional inhalation studies of the resting condition in medicated patients addressed this issue a limited way (43, 54, 55) and found no laterality differences between patients and normals. Gur et al. (74) reported left hemisphere overactivation during the resting condition only in medication-free patients.

Only two inhalation rCBF studies (44, 74), both by Gur and colleagues, have been specifically designed to test for laterality differences. With activation conditions, findings that may be consistent with generalized left hemisphere overactivation emerged in both medicated (44) and medication-free (74) patients. However, it is worth noting that the lateralizing effects of these tasks was not robust in the normal population, and the interpretation of the effects in patients, whose response to the tasks may differ from that of controls, is not clear. Further studies of lateralized cerebral function in schizophrenia are necessary.

Hypofrontality?

Although not all studies have reported decreased frontal blood flow in schizophrenia, the rCBF evidence for frontal lobe dysfunction is nonetheless compelling. Reports of Ingvar et al. (46, 68 – 71) as well as five inhalation studies (47, 52 – 55), including one exclusively of medication-free patients (52), described frontal pathophysiology in patients. Of the remaining inhalation studies, while two using activation (44, 74) did not specifically address the frontality issue, three carried out during rest (43, 44, 74) did not find hypofrontality. However, a simple tally of positive versus negative studies may be misleading. While differences in instrumentation and methodology of rCBF measurements as well as in patient populations studied may explain some inconsistencies, there are additional conceptual issues to be considered.

First, in many studies the frontal lobe has been considered as a single, functionally homogeneous entity. Thus, blood flow to all regions anterior to the central sulcus has been considered as a whole, and not distinguished into more anatomically and physiologically discrete components. In some cases (44, 54, 74), this approach may have been mandated by the limited number of detectors used (and cortical regions surveyed), but this strategy does not do justice to the complexity of the frontal lobe. The frontal lobe is, in fact, a heterogeneous structure with respect to anatomy, physiology, and function (80, 81, 82); its gray matter is comprised not only of motor cortex, supplementary motor areas, frontal eye fields, and Broca's area, but also of a large association cortex. The role of non-association cortical regions may be less crucial in schizophrenia, and their inclusion in an overall 'frontal lobe rCBF' determination may dilute differences in more important association area rCBF, thus rendering group differences undetectable.

Moreover, even frontal association cortex is heterogeneous. It has traditionally been subdivided into orbitomedial and dorsolateral (DLPFC) components on anatomical and physiological bases. Many of the defect symptoms, the pattern of cognitive impairment, and minor ('soft') neurological signs characteristic of schizophrenia may implicate DLPFC in particular (52, 53, 83). In view of these considerations, normal blood flow to the entire frontal cortex, or hyperfrontality, may not rule out dysfunction of more distinct prefrontal cortical areas. Weinberger et al. (52) found that only DLPFC blood flow differentiated medication-free patients from controls. Nonetheless, even in studies that did discriminate between discrete frontal areas (52, 53), decreased DLPFC blood flow was not seen under all conditions. This observation suggests another important conceptual issue.

Patients with schizophrenia may not exhibit prefrontal deficit under all conditions. If such dysfunction is subtle or contingent upon physiological 'demand,' it may only become apparent if a physiological load is imposed on this brain region (i.e. if a 'prefrontal stress test' is carried out). Consistent with this notion are the data of Weinberger et al. (52) and Berman et al. (53). These studies found decreased DLPFC rCBF during a task which requires intact DLPFC function, i.e. the Wisconsin Card Sort, but not during a simple numbers matching task or CPTs (53). Unlike the WCS, the latter tasks may not be specifically linked to DLPFC. Prohovnik (42) suggested that there may be two varieties of frontal blood flow: (a) that which is ambient (or 'vegetative,' or necessary for 'housekeeping' functions), and (b) that which is specific to certain cognitive or behavioral activities (like the WCS, contingency planning, anticipatory drive, goal-orientation). These 'varieties' may correspond to activation of discrete anatomical and physiological prefrontal systems. The second variety possibly reflects DLPFC function, and perhaps only this component is deficient in some patients with schizophrenia. If patients with schizophrenia are unable to mobilize this variety, then the degree to which their rCBF will differ from normals will depend on how much the normals do mobilize this manner of cerebral physiological response. It follows that this difference would vary with the test conditions.

Studies of rCBF during resting, in particular, have resulted in variable findings. This may be because some individuals may respond to this situation with a 'prefrontal mode', e.g. contingency planning, divergent thinking, or anticipatory states (71, 78), while others do not. This may reflect the degree to which the subject is familiar with the testing environment or with the investigators, the ambient conditions in the laboratory, or a host of additional uncontrolled variables that become more critical in the absence of prescribed testing conditions. In the 'resting' study of Mathew et al., for example, perhaps attention to the task of breathing in time to a metronome precluded contingency planning, anticipatory state, divergent thinking, etc., thus lessening the physiological load on DLPFC and preventing the detection of group differences in prefrontal function. In contrast, the experience of having an intracarotid injection, as in the studies of Ingvar et al. (46, 68 – 71), might predispose to these behavioral modes and thus emphasize group differences.

In summary, failure to take into account the anatomically and physiologically diverse nature of the frontal lobe and lack of appreciation of the implications and importance of the testing condition in studies of frontal lobe function may account for some of the lack of concordance in rCBF studies of schizophrenia. Nonetheless, the majority of rCBF studies are consistent with frontal lobe dysfunction in this disorder. Those in which such findings did not emerge may not have examined discrete cortical areas and/or may have involved testing conditions in which the prefrontal cortex was not specifically taxed.

Summary and future directions

Regional cerebral blood flow (rCBF) is tightly coupled with local neuronal activity in the brain. Thus, rCBF can be measured as an indirect marker of local 'brain work.' rCBF techniques have been fruitfully applied to the search for pathophysiology in schizophrenia. However, the resulting studies, which are described above, do not always concur. Some possible explanations for the disconcerting lack of consensus in these data are suggested in previous sections of this chapter. The experiences of the past have paved the way for more enlightened approaches to the application of rCBF to schizophrenia research. For example, careful selection of patient and control populations and more standardized laboratory conditions will yield more consistent results. Most important, as emphasized in this chapter, are rigorous control of testing conditions, including the design and implementation of activation studies geared to investigate specific hypotheses (i.e. cerebral 'stress tests'), and thoughtful interpretation of the results.

The evidence to date, while not completely consistent, nonetheless indicates that while global whole brain metabolism may be normal in schizophrenia, there may be a deficit in frontal cortical function, particularly that of the dorsolateral aspect of prefrontal cortex and especially under circumstances that in normal persons specifically engage this area. Thus, the frontal lobe is a site meriting further investigation in this disorder.

REFERENCES

1. Deshmukh VD, Meyer JS (1978) *Noninvasive Measurement of Cerebral Blood Flow in Man.* Prentice Hall, New York.
2. Stump DA, Williams R (1980) The noninvasive measurement of regional cerebral circulation. *Brain Lang., 9,* 35.
3. Hoffman EJ, van der Stee M, Ricci AR, Phelps ME (1984) Prospects for both precision and accuracy in positron emission tomography. *Ann. Neurol., 15 (Suppl.),* S25.
4. Roland PE (1985) Blood flow imaging in behavioral neurophysiology: cortical field activation hypothesis. In: Sokoloff L (Ed), *Brain Imaging and Brain Function,* pp. 87 – 104. Raven Press, New York.
5. Roy CS, Sherrington CS (1896) On the regulation of the blood supply of the brain. *J. Physiol. (London), 11,* 85.
6. Barcroft J (1914) *The Respiratory Function of the Blood.* Cambridge University Press, London.
7. Schmidt C, Hendrix J (1938) Action of chemical substances on cerebral blood vessels. *Res. Publ. Assoc. Nerv. Ment. Dis., 18,* 229.
8. Kety SS (1985) Basic principles for the quantitative estimation of regional cerebral blood

flow. In: Sokoloff L (Ed), *Brain Imaging and Brain Function*, pp. 1 – 8. Raven Press, New York.

9. Raichle ME, Grubb RL, Gado MH, Eichling JO, Ter-Pogossian MM (1976) Correlation between regional cerebral blood flow and oxidative metabolism. *Arch. Neurol., 33,* 523.

10. Siesjo BK (1984) Cerebral circulation and metabolism. *J. Neurosurg., 60,* 883.

11. Kety SS, Schmidt CF (1945) The determination of cerebral blood flow in man by use of nitrous oxide in low concentrations. *Am. J. Physiol., 143,* 53.

12. Lassen NA, Munck O (1955) The cerebral blood flow in man determined by the use of radioactive krypton. *Acta Physiol. Scand., 33,* 30.

13. Munck O, Lassen NA (1957) Bilateral cerebral blood flow and oxygen consumption in man by the use of krypton. *Circ. Res., 5,* 163.

14. Ingvar DH, Lassen NA (1961) Quantitative determination of regional cerebral blood flow in man. *Lancet, 2,* 806.

15. Hoedt-Rasmussen K, Svensdottir E, Lassen NA (1966) Regional cerebral blood flow in man determined by intra-arterial injection of radioactive inert gas. *Circ. Res., 18,* 237.

16. Ingvar DH, Cronquist S, Ekberg K, Risberg J, Hoedt-Rasmussen K (1965) Normal values of regional cerebral blood flow in man including flow and weight estimates of gray and white matter. *Acta Neurol. Scand., 41 (S14),* 72.

17. Lassen NA (1985) Measurement of regional cerebral blood flow in humans with single-photon-emitting radioisotopes. In: Sokoloff L (Ed), *Brain Imaging and Brain Function,* pp. 9 – 20. Raven Press, New York.

18. Olesen J (1971) Contralateral focal increase of cerebral blood flow in man during arm work. *Brain, 94,* 635.

19. Ingvar DH (1976) Functional landscapes of the dominant hemisphere. *Brain Res., 107,* 181.

20. Lassen NA, Roland PE (1983) Localization of cognitive function with cerebral blood flow. In: Kerteaz A (Ed), *Localization in Neuropsychology,* pp. 141 – 152. Academic Press, New York.

21. Conn HL (1955) Measurement of organ blood flow without blood sampling (Abstract) *J. Clin. Invest., 34,* 916.

22. Veall N, Mallet BL (1965) The two-compartment model using Xe133 inhalation and external counting. *Acta Neurol. Scand., Suppl. 14,* 83.

23. Mallet BL, Veall N (1965) Measurement of regional cerebral clearance rates in man using ^{133}Xenon inhalation and extracranial recording. *Clin. Sci., 29,* 124.

24. Veall N, Mallet BL (1966) Regional cerebral blood flow determination by ^{133}Xenon inhalation and external recording: the effect of arterial recirculation. *Clin. Sci., 30,* 353.

25. Obrist WD, Thompson HK, King HC, Wang HS (1967) Determination of regional cerebral blood flow by inhalation of ^{133}Xenon. *Circ. Res., 20,* 124.

26. Obrist WD, Thompson HK, Wang HS, Cronquist S (1971) A simplified procedure for determining fast compartment rCBF by 133Xenon inhalation. In: Russell RWR (Ed), *Brain and Blood Flow,* pp. 11 – 15. Pitman Publishing Co., London.

27. Obrist WD, Thompson HK, Wang HS, Wilkinson WE (1975) Regional cerebral blood flow estimated by Xenon133 inhalation. *Stroke, 6,* 245.

28. Obrist WD, Wilkinson WE (1980) The noninvasive Xe133 method: evaluation of CBF indices. In: Bes A, Geraud G (Eds), *Cerebral Circulation,* pp. 119 – 124. Excerpta Medica, Amsterdam.

29. Risberg J, Ali Z, Wilson EM, Wills EL, Halsey JH (1975) Regional cerebral blood flow by ^{133}Xenon inhalation. *Stroke, 6,* 142.

30. Risberg J (1980) Regional cerebral blood flow measurements by 133Xe-inhalation: methodology and application in neuropsychology and psychiatry. *Brain Lang., 9,* 9.
31. Rosenblum WI (1965) Cerebral microcirculation: a review emphasizing interrelationship of local blood flow and neuronal function. *Angiology, 16,* 485.
32. Sokoloff L (1981) Relationships among local functional activity, energy, metabolism and blood flow in the central nervous system. *Fed. Proc.: Fed. Am. Soc. Exp. Biol.,* 2311.
33. Gur RC, Gur RE, Obrist WK, Hungerbuhler JP, Younkin D, Rosen AD, Skolnick BE, Reivich M (1982) Sex and handedness differences in regional cerebral blood flow during rest and cognitive activity. *Science, 217,* 659.
34. Eichling J (1979) Noninvasive methods of measuring regional cerebral blood flow. In: Price TR, Nelson B (Eds), *Cerebrovascular Diseases,* pp. 51 – 56. Raven Press, New York.
35. Prohovnik I (1980) *Mapping Brainwork.* Liber, Lund.
36. Prohovnik I (1984) Regional cerebral blood flow (rCBF). In: Morihisa JM (Ed), *Brain Imaging in Psychiatry,* pp. 28 – 40. APA Press, Washington, DC.
37. Berman KF, Weinberger DR, Morihisa JM, Zec ŘF (1984) Xenon-133 inhalation regional cerebral blood flow: application to psychiatric research. In: Morihisa JM (Ed), *Brain Imaging in Psychiatry,* pp. 42 – 64. APA Press, Washington, DC.
38. Shaw T, Meyer J (1982) Aging and cerebrovascular disease. In: Meyer JS, Shaw T (Eds), *Diagnosis and Management of Stroke.* Addison-Wesley Publishing Co., Menlo Park.
39. Naritomi H, Meyer JS, Sakai F, Yamaguchi F, Shaw T (1979) Effects of advancing age on regional cerebral blood flow. *Arch. Neurol., 36,* 410.
40. Shaw TG, Mortel KF, Meyer JS, Rogers RL, Hardenberg J, Cutaia MM (1984) Cerebral blood flow changes in benign aging and cerebrovascular disease. *Neurology, 34,* 855.
41. Mamo H, Meric P, Luft A, Seylaz A (1983) Hyperfrontal pattern of human cerebral circulation. *Arch. Neurol., 40,* 626.
42. Prohovnik I, Hakansson K, Risberg J (1980) Observations on the functional significance of regional cerebral blood flow in resting normal subjects. *Neuropsychologia, 18,* 203.
43. Mathew RJ, Duncan GC, Weiman ML, Barr DL (1982) Regional cerebral blood flow in schizophrenia. *Arch. Gen. Psychiatry, 39,* 1121.
44. Gur RE, Skolnik BE, Gur RC, Caroff S, Rieger W, Obrist WD, Younkin D, Reivich M (1983) Brain functions in psychiatric disorders I. Regional cerebral blood flow in medicated schizophrenics. *Arch. Gen. Psychiatry, 40,* 1250.
45. Hoyer S, Oesterreich K (1975) Blood flow and oxidative metabolism of the brain in patients with schizophrenia. *Psychiatr. Clin., 8,* 304.
46. Ingvar DH, Franzen G (1974) Abnormalities of cerebral blood flow distribution in patients with chronic schizophrenia. *Acta Psychiatr. Scand., 50,* 425.
47. Kurachi M, Kobayashi K, Matsubara R, Hiramatsu H, Yomaguchi N, Matsuda H, Maeda T, Hisada K (1985) Regional cerebral blood flow in schizophrenic disorders. *Eur. Neurol., 24,* 176.
48. Skinhoj E, Olesen J, Paulson O (1973) Influence of smoking and nicotine on cerebral blood flow and metabolic rate of oxygen in man. *J. Appl. Physiol., 35,* 820.
49. Mathew RJ, Barr DL, Weinman ME (1983) Caffeine and cerebral blood flow. *Br. J. Psychiatry, 143,* 604.
50. Wood F (1980) Theoretical, methodological, and statistical implications of the inhalation rCBF technique for the study of brain-behavior relationships. *Brain Lang., 9,* 1.
51. Jaccard J, Ackerman L (1985) Repeated measures analysis of means in clinical research.

J. Consult. Clin. Psychol., 53, 426.

52. Weinberger DR, Berman KF, Zec RF (1986) Physiological dysfunction of dorsolateral prefrontal cortex in schizophrenia: I. Regional cerebral blood flow (rCBF) evidence. *Arch. Gen. Psychiatry, 43,* 114.

53. Berman KF, Zec RF, Weinberger DR (1986) Physiological dysfunction of dorsolateral prefrontal cortex in schizophrenia: II. Role of neuroleptic treatment, attention, and mental effort. *Arch. Gen. Psychiatry, 43,* 126.

54. Ariel RN, Golden CJ, Berg RA, Quaife MA, Dirksen JW, Forsell T, Wilson J, Graber B (1983) Regional cerebral blood flow in schizophrenia with the [133]Xenon inhalation method. *Arch. Gen. Psychiatry, 40,* 258.

55. Mubrin Z, Knezevic S, Koretic D, Lazic L, Javorni K (1982) Regional cerebral blood flow patterns in schizophrenic patients. *rCBF Bull., 3,* 43.

56. Duara R, Barker W, Apicella A, Chang J, Siegel C, Finn R, Gilson A (1985) Resting cerebral glucose metabolism: intraindividual versus interindividual variability in young and elderly subjects. *Neurology, 35,* 138.

57. Duara R, Sevush S, Gross-Glenn K, Chang J, Barker W, Apicella A, Gilson A, Finn R (1985) Intraindividual reliability of cerebral glucose metabolism in the resting state and during psychological activation. *Neurology, 35,* 138.

58. Mazziotta JC, Phelps ME, Carson RE, Kuhl DE (1982) Tomographic mapping of human cerebral metabolism: sensory deprivation. *Ann. Neurol., 12,* 435.

59. Yamamoto M, Meyer JS, Sakai F, Yamaguchi F (1980) Aging and cerebral vasodilator responses to hypercarbia: responses in normal aging and in persons with risk factors for stroke. *Arch. Neurol., 37,* 489.

60. Maximillian VA, Prohovnik I, Risberg J (1980) Cerebral hemodynamic responses to mental activation in normo- and hypercapnia. *Stroke, 11,* 342.

61. Davis SM, Ackerman RH, Correia JA, Alpert NM, Chang J, Buonanno F, Kelley RE, Rosner B (1983) Cerebral blood flow and cerebrovascular CO_2 reactivity in stroke-age normal controls. *Neurology, 33,* 391.

62. Tominaga S, Strandgaard S, Uemura K, Ito K, Kutsuzawa T (1976) Cerebrovascular CO_2 reactivity in normotensive and hypertensive man. *Stroke, 7,* 507.

63. Olesen J, Paulson OB, Lassen NA (1981) Regional cerebral blood flow in man determined by the initial slope of the clearance of intra-arterial injected [133]Xe. *Stroke, 2,* 519.

64. Evans MC, Cameron IR (1981) Adaption of rCBF during chronic exposure to hypercapnia and to hypercapnia with hypoxia. *J. Cereb. Blood Flow Metab., 1,* 435.

65. Prohovnik I, Epersen JO, Christensen FK (1983) Development and initial evaluation of a helmet for rCBF measurements. *rCBF Bull., 6,* 107.

66. Prohovnik I, Knudsen E, Risberg J (1984) Accuracy of models and algorithms for determination of fast-compartment flow by non-invasive ^{133}Xe clearance. *rCBF Bull., 8,* 151.

67. Kety SS, Woodford RB, Harmel MH, Freyhan FA, Appel KE, Schmidt CF (1948) Cerebral blood flow and metabolism in schizophrenia: effects of barbiturate seminarcosis, insulin coma and electroshock. *Am. J. Psychiatry, 104,* 765.

68. Ingvar DH, Franzen G (1974) Distribution of cerebral activity in chronic schizophrenia. *Lancet, 2,* 1484.

69. Franzen G, Ingvar DH (1975) Abnormal distribution of cerebral activity in chronic schizophrenia. *J. Psychiatric Res., 12,* 199.

70. Franzen G, Ingvar DH (1975) Absence of activation in frontal structures during psychological testing of chronic schizophrenics. *J. Neurol. Neurosurg. Psychiatry, 38,* 1027.

71. Ingvar DH (1980) Abnormal distribution of cerebral activity in chronic schizophrenia: a neurophysiological interpretation. In: Baxter C, Melnechuk T (Eds), *Perspectives in Schizophrenia Research*, pp. 107–130. Raven Press, New York.

72. Mathew RJ, Meyer JS, Francis DJ, Schooler JC, Weinman M, Mortel KF (1981) Regional cerebral blood flow in schizophrenia: a preliminary report. *Am. J. Psychiatry, 138,* 112.

73. Kennedy C, Sakurada O, Shinohara M, Hehle J, Sokoloff L (1978) Local cerebral glucose utilization in the normal conscious macaque monkey. *Ann. Neurol., 4,* 293.

74. Gur RE, Gur RC, Skolnik BE, Caroff S, Obrist W, Resnick S, Reivich M (1985) Brain function in psychiatric disorders. III. Regional cerebral blood flow in unmedicated schizophrenics. *Arch. Gen. Psychiatry, 42,* 329.

75. Milner B (1963) Some effects of frontal lobectomy in man. In: Warren JM, Akert K (Eds), *The Frontal Granular Cortex and Behavior,* pp. 313–334. McGraw-Hill, New York.

76. Milner B (1963) Effects of different brain lesions on card sorting. *Arch. Neurol., 9,* 100.

77. Milner B (1971) Interhemispheric differences in the localization of psychological processes in man. *Br. Med. Bull., 27,* 272.

78. Milner B, Petrides M (1984) Behavioral effects of frontal lobe lesions in man. *Trends Neurosci., 7,* 403.

79. Stuss DT, Benson DF (1983) Frontal lobe lesions and behavior. In: Kertesz A (Ed), *Localization in Neuropsychology,* pp. 429–454. Academic Press, New York.

80. Luria AR (1980) *Higher Cortical Functions in Man.* Basic Books, New York.

81. Fuster J (1980) *The Prefrontal Cortex.* Raven Press, New York.

82. Stuss DT, Benson DF (1984) Neuropsychological studies of the frontal lobes. *Psychol. Bull., 95,* 3.

83. Berman KF, Weinberger DR (1985) Schizophrenic dementia. In: Jeste DV (Ed), *Dementia.* APA Press, Washington, DC.

CHAPTER 13

The use of positron emission tomography (PET) to image regional brain metabolism in schizophrenia and other psychiatric disorders: a review

LYNN ELEANOR DELISI

Major psychiatric disorders have been distinguished from other medical entities by their lack of association with specific pathologic lesions that can be detected by present-day histological or biochemical techniques, though the search for such abnormalities is ongoing. It is assumed, nevertheless, that psychiatric symptoms are associated with the brain; and thus, biologic studies have centered on descriptions of post-mortem brain specimens or peripheral biologic measures that are presumed to be generalizable to brain functioning.

As radiologic techniques were developed these too were used to determine if detectable anatomical abnormalities are associated with the psychoses. X-rays of the brain and tomograms of the skull showed no significant abnormalities but have been useful in state hospital settings to rule out enlargements of the pituitary fossa and related endocrine disease, subdural hematomas, and tumors, that may all masquerade as affective or schizophrenia-like disorders. Pneumoencephalography, the injection of air into the lumbar subarachnoid space, first described to visualize the ventricles of the brain by Dandy in 1919 (1), has been a useful technique to neurologists and neurosurgeons for localizing tumors, areas of infarction, or acute hemorrhage. It is a technique not without considerable risk and trauma to the patient, and additionally, technically difficult to perform on actively psychotic patients. Numerous early pneumoencephalographic studies of psychiatric patients found evidence for enlargement of the cerebral ventricles and other evidence of cerebral atrophy, which was largely overlooked by the mainstream of psychiatry (reviewed by Weinberger and Wyatt, Ref. 2).

With the development of Computed Axial Tomography (CAT or CT), less traumatic and more detailed descriptions of brain pathology in vivo were available. In 1976, Johnstone et al. (3) published the first CT study with evidence of ventricular enlargement in a small group of chronic schizophrenic patients. The majority of subsequent CT studies have confirmed their findings and some, in addition to describing the presence of cortical atrophy (reviewed by Weinberger and Wyatt, Ref. 2), have also shown evidence of atrophy of the vermis of the cerebellum (4,

Handbook of Schizophrenia, Vol. 1: The Neurology of Schizophrenia.
H.A. Nasrallah and D.R. Weinberger, editors.
© Elsevier Science Publishers B.V., 1986.

5), reversals of the normal frontal and occipital lobe asymmetries (6, 7), and decreased density of the tissue from several brain regions (8).

Evidence of cerebral atrophy is not, however, pathognomonic for schizophrenia, but is of particular interest relevant to the proposed biochemical hypotheses of schizophrenia and their assumed anatomical localizations. Several neurotransmitters and regulators have been proposed to be abnormally metabolized in schizophrenia and affective disorders, some of which are heavily concentrated in periventricular structures, such as the striatum and limbic systems. Moreover, recent post-mortem examinations have uncovered both morphologic and biochemical alterations in structures of the limbic system of schizophrenics that may be related

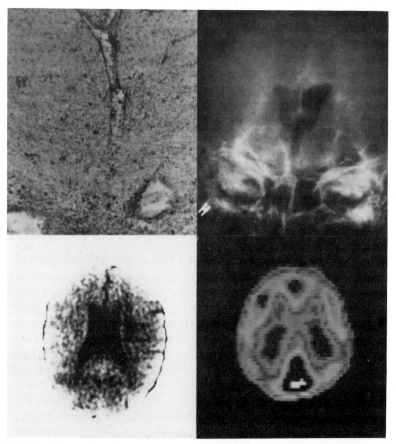

FIG. 1 *Examples of techniques employed over the years to describe brain abnormalities in schizophrenic patients. Upper left: histological specimen from Stevens (56) showing intense periventricular fibrillary gliosis. Histological findings in schizophrenic patients date back to 1900. Upper right: pneumoencephalographic evidence of enlarged ventricles (57). Lower left: CT evidence of enlarged ventricles. Lower right: PET evidence of 'hypofrontality'.*

to the radiologic findings (9, 10). Nevertheless, all the above techniques fail to directly measure metabolic activity of the brain in vivo.

Until the advent of positron emission tomography (PET), electro-encephalography was the only method to record actual brain activity. Interpretation of the brain waves generated from strategically placed scalp electrodes has been the mainstay of diagnosis in neurology. Schizophrenic patients have been found to have various EEG abnormalities (discussed in detail in Chapter 11); however, questions concerning the interpretation of these findings further confirm the necessity to enable more direct exploration of brain pathology.

PET evolved from the ability to combine the computerized tomographic methods, as used in CT, with the ability to quantitate brain metabolic activity. The latter was first developed by Kety and Schmidt (11) to determine average rates of glucose utilization in the brain as a whole from measurements of blood flow and the cerebral arteriovenous difference. The autoradiographic measurement of ^{14}C-labeled 2-deoxyglucose in animals developed 30 years later by Sokoloff et al. (12), formed the basis for the subsequent use of ^{18}F-fluorodeoxyglucose as a method to measure regional cerebral glucose use in man. This made possible the direct quantification of local cerebral glucose metabolism as well as metabolism of more specific labeled compounds, such as dopamine, or its antagonist, spiroperidol in vivo. It has been of extreme interest to research psychiatrists to explore the use of this technique, since it is the hope that subtle changes not visualized with previous techniques would be evident on PET; or alternatively, that if no anatomical lesion is present, perhaps a metabolic change would be found to be associated with specific psychiatric symptomatology.

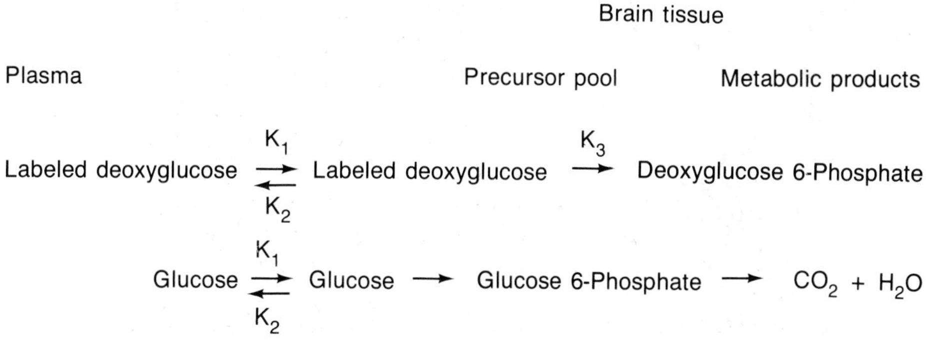

Brain tissue

| Plasma | | Precursor pool | | Metabolic products |

$$\text{Labeled deoxyglucose} \underset{K_2}{\overset{K_1}{\rightleftharpoons}} \text{Labeled deoxyglucose} \overset{K_3}{\longrightarrow} \text{Deoxyglucose 6-Phosphate}$$

$$\text{Glucose} \underset{K_2}{\overset{K_1}{\rightleftharpoons}} \text{Glucose} \longrightarrow \text{Glucose 6-Phosphate} \longrightarrow CO_2 + H_2O$$

$$\text{Rate of Reaction} = \frac{\text{Total label in tissue at time T } - \text{ label in precursor remaining in tissue at time T}}{\text{Isotope effect correction factor} \times [\text{Integrated plasma specific activity } - \text{ Correction for lag in tissue equilibration with plasma}]}$$

FIG. 2 *Basis for the mathematical model for calculation of the rate of deoxyglucose use in the brain (see ref. 12 for details).*

The technique of PET

Radioisotopes have long been used to measure rates of biochemical reactions in vitro, by labeling one of the reactants and then measuring the rate of accumulation of a labeled product. Quantitative autoradiography was an advancement that then made it possible to measure the local concentrations of isotopes in vivo. The rate of the reaction can be determined if the biochemical kinetics of the labeled substance and its metabolic products are known. The rate of disappearance of a labeled product from arterial blood can be directly measured by counting label in serial blood samples. This can be related to the rate of uptake into the brain and thus the cellular metabolic rate can be calculated by the mathematical model derived by Sokoloff et al. (12) based on the diagram in Figure 2.

The Sokoloff model is based on the following assumptions: that a steady state for glucose consumption exists throughout the experimental period; that a homogeneous tissue compartment exists within which the concentrations of deoxyglucose and glucose are uniform and exchange directly with plasma; and the concentrations of labeled deoxyglucose free in tissues is essentially zero. The rate constants crucial to this reaction have been derived from animal tissue studies by Sokoloff et al. and have been extrapolated to human studies. The K_1 represents the equilibrium constant for the transport of labeled deoxyglucose from plasma to brain tissue. The K_2 is the constant for the conversion of the labeled deoxyglucose to deoxyglucose-6-phosphate, while the K_3 is the constant associated with the conversion of tissue glucose to glucose-6-phosphate in brain tissue. While the above assumptions are most likely valuable in the animal model system when the animal is killed shortly after the experiment and the tissues immediately fixed, critics of Sokoloff's model have suggested that this may not be valid in the human situation, since the time from injection of the compound to time of starting and completing the emission tomography can be long enough to get appreciable removal of the labeled deoxyglucose from brain tissue. There then is a need for a further constant, the K_4, which estimates this rate. The Sokoloff et al. model has therefore been revised by Reivich et al. (13) for use in human studies.

There are two major methods in operation for the measure of energy metabolism by PET: one is based on glucose metabolism and the other on cerebral oxygen consumption. Since glucose is the major energy source for all aerobic metabolism in the brain and its kinetics and metabolic pathways are known, it is a workable model. In order, however, to enable application to emission tomography the labeled compound used is deoxyglucose. While deoxyglucose is taken up by tissues at the same rate as glucose, unlike glucose, which is metabolized to CO_2 and water and then cleared from tissues, deoxyglucose is only carried through the first step in glucose metabolism to deoxyglucose-6-phosphate and then accumulates in the tissues, disappearing at a slow rate; thus enabling measurement of its labeled product.

The steady-state cerebral oxygen consumption technique allows the measurement of cerebral blood flow by PET using oxygen-15 and measuring the oxygen-15 labeled carbon dioxide produced. When this is multiplied by the arterial oxygen content, the steady state delivery of oxygen for metabolic reactions can be calculated. The product of local oxygen extraction, blood flow and arterial oxygen content is the value for local O_2 consumption.

^{14}C and ^3H are the atoms used for autoradiographic studies in animals; however, for a variety of reasons, they are not appropriate for labeling compounds for human studies. Gamma- (or photon) emitting isotopes can be determined in humans with what is called single photon tomography. Fluorine-18 has been used in single photon tomography, although other popular gamma emitting isotopes have been bromine-77 and the isotopes of iodine. Fluorine-18 is actually a positron emitter, which means that it emits short-lived positrons, which annihilate, emitting two coincident gamma rays simultaneously of equal energy and traveling at almost 180 degrees to each other. PET takes advantage of these events and is capable of better spatial resolution than single photon tomography. Several detectors at different angles are able to pinpoint the point at which the positron decays. The number of these events at a single site is proportional to the concentration of the labeled substance at that site, and thus, the amount of labeled compound at that site. Other positron emitters, such as ^{11}C, have been used in these studies; however, they vary in tissue half-life. Thus the comparison of data obtained in independent studies using different isotopes may be difficult.

Positron-emitting atoms are produced in accelerators, the one of choice for biomedical application has been the cyclotron. The basic principle involves the bombardment of a stable daughter nuclide, such as oxygen-18 as a fluorine-18 precursor, nitrogen-15 as an oxygen-15 precursor and boron-11 for carbon-11, with a source of nuclear energy, such as protons or deuterons. The label is then attached to the experimental compound using standard chemical principles.

Finally, the clinical application of these chemical and physical techniques involves intravenous injection of the labeled compound into one arm of a patient with serial arterial blood sampling from the opposite arm for quantification of the disappearance of the label and quantification of the obtained tomograms. Allowing for a period for peak absorption of the compound into the brain (for deoxyglucose approximately 30 minutes), during which time the experimental environment is standardized, the patient is then scanned and tomographic slices are obtained. These are generally horizontal sections taken in series of 7 – 10, parallel to the canthomeatal or orbitomeatal line. The limit of resolution of present-day scanners is rapidly improving; however, in most of the studies presently published it is above 1 cm. The radioactivity is digitalized and can be converted by computer into color-coded images of activity in different regions of the brain. Accuracy of measurements is determined by the amount of resolution, uniformity of resolution, and amount of scatter present, and is also obtained by routine comparisons with standards (with known geometry and isotope concentration). Values are then standardized to those obtained with these known phantoms.

The limitations for interpretation of data generated by PET are several, and need to be considered before defining the significance of the observable abnormalities in disease versus normal states (see Table 1 for a listing of some sources of potential artifacts in PET). Imaging the brain with this prolonged and somewhat complex procedure is difficult to carry out in actively psychotic individuals; and thus the experience of patients may be different from the experience of normal controls, complicating the analysis of data (i.e. the paranoid patient exhibiting delusional fright during the procedure, fails to sit still, hold head still, or keep eyes closed, etc.).

TABLE 1 *Sources of potential artifacts related to final PET results and comparisons of clinical studies*

Compound used as tracer:
1. Half-life and breakdown rate of label
2. Purity of compound
3. Differences in oxygen vs. glucose use
4. Differences in positron emitting labels (i.e. 18-F vs. 11-C)

Experimental conditions:
1. Variation in anxiety and emotional state of normal subjects
2. Psychiatric state of patient (agitation, movements, distractibility)
3. Task performed during uptake
4. Variation in eye/ear closures, as well as other sensory inputs
5. Prolonged uptake period and thus inconsistent physiologic changes
6. Variation in blood sampling procedures (arterial vs. venous blood, etc.)
7. Failure to control for gender and age differences

PET instrumentation:
1. Limited resolution (spatial and temporal)
2. Non-uniform resolution
3. Scatter and partial volume effects
4. Inadequate number of planes for anatomic sampling
5. Need to standardize adequately to phantoms
6. Inability to standardize planes among individuals due to variation in head size and shapes
7. Movement of head in scanner
8. Change in distribution of tracer compound during scan procedure from first to last slice

Data analysis:
1. Inaccuracy of models to describe biochemical kinetics
2. No appropriate model for substances studied
3. Relating kinetic constants derived in animals to human studies
4. Difference in kinetics between white and grey matter
5. Difficulty in matching same slices among individuals
6. Undersampling of anatomical structures
7. Overinterpretation of assumed anatomical details
8. Computerized methods do not account for anatomical differences among individuals
9. Accounting for cortical folding
10. Lack of serial determinations of data in same individual over time to obtain normal variation

While the experimental variables that may lead to potential artifactual data need to be considered (Table 1), nevertheless, the following major findings have emerged in studies of psychiatric patients, and warrant further exploration for relationship to etiology, overall pathology, mental state, and prognosis.

PET studies of schizophrenia

Table 2 is a summary of the major PET studies to date of psychiatric patients. The first PET description of a psychotic patient was completed by Farkas et al. (14) and later expanded upon in a recent publication (Farkas et al., 15) in collaboration with the Brookhaven, N.Y. facility. He presented a chronic schizophrenic patient who displayed decreased frontal cortex glucose use (40%) that shifted towards normality subsequent to treatment with antipsychotic medication. Since cerebral blood flow is assumed from animal studies to be correlated with glucose use, this finding is consistent with the earlier work of Ingvar and Franzen (16), who used labeled xenon carotid artery injections for the measurement of cerebral blood flow. They found what they termed 'hypofrontality', a relative decrease in frontal vs. posterior blood flow in chronic schizophrenic patients. Several more recent studies have confirmed this finding, while others have not or have found it only under certain conditions (17 – 23).

Further PET studies confirming the Farkas et al. studies have been reported in a series of publications from three other major independent research institutions. Widen et al. (24), at the Karolinska Institute in Sweden, Buchsbaum et al. (25), at the National Institute of Mental Health, and Stahl et al. (26), at Stanford, have confirmed the finding of relative hypofrontality in chronic schizophrenic patients at rest and during a variety of neuropsychological tasks. Although Ingvar and Franzen (16) in their original blood flow studies found hypofrontality to be associated with the degree of psychopathology, and particularly with the severity of catatonic symptoms and withdrawal, correlations of clinical symptoms with relative hypofrontality on PET have not been found (27). In addition, The Swedish group more recently reported that they are unable to confirm their initial finding upon repeating their studies in a younger population of first-episode schizophrenic patients (28, 29). This new report is consistent with Sheppard et al. (30), who failed to find evidence for hypofrontality in 12 acute schizophrenic patients, most of whom had never been medicated with neuroleptics.

Other findings, such as temporal cortex alterations in metabolic activity and altered laterality in schizophrenia also await consistent replications. While DeLisi et al. (31) found bilateral increases in temporal cortex glucose use in chronic schizophrenics, and others have consistent findings in blood flow or EEG studies (16, 32), another group found decreased temporal cortical activity (Brodie et al., New York University, personal communication). Sheppard et al. (30) in their study found a decrease in the normal lateralization of oxygen utilization, while Buchsbaum et al. (33) failed to find any evidence of lateralization to metabolic activity in normal or schizophrenic patients in PET studies, and Gur et al. (22), using

315

TABLE 2   *Summary of published psychiatric PET studies*

Study (Ref.)	Compound	Subject characteristics	Conditions of procedure	Results
1. Farkas et al. (14)	^{18}F-deoxyglucose	1 schizophrenic, pre- and post-med.	Resting	Pre: Higher right than left hemisphere glucose use. 40% decrease in glucose use in frontal cortex, mid ventricular slice Post: shift towards normal
2. Widen et al. (24)	^{11}C-deoxyglucose	9 schizophrenics, medicated 2 controls	Eyes closed, quiet, resting	Frontal/temporal cortex decrease in mid ventricular slice
3. Buchsbaum et al. (33)	^{18}F-deoxyglucose	8 schizophrenics, medication-free for 2 wks 6 controls	Eyes closed, quiet, resting	Hypofrontal cortical pattern in patients: supraventricular slice; no asymmetry; increase in left auditory cortex; decreased caudate activity
4. Sheppard et al. (30)	^{15}O	12 schizophrenics (10/12 = 1st hosp.; 6 = never medicated 6 = 48-hrs medication free from 1–4 single doses)	Eyes closed, reclining, minimized sensory stimulation	No hypofrontality; no basal ganglia difference; decreased overall normal asymmetry in schizophrenics (normal = R > L)
5. Sedvall et al. (28)	^{11}C-deoxyglucose	13 schizophrenics (6 = 1st episode; 3 wks medication-free) 10 controls	Resting	Brodmann areas 32 and 39/40 decreased; no hypofrontality
6. Farkas et al. (15)	^{18}F-deoxyglucose	13 schizophrenics (7 = medication-free) 11 controls	Resting, eyes closed, quiet	Decreased frontal/post glucose use in schizophrenics

7. Phelps et al. (37)	18F-deoxyglucose	14 unipolar-depressed 15 bipolar-depressed 7 controls	Eyes open; ears open	Bipolar depressed had lower metabolic rate than bipolar manic, controls
8. Georgotas et al. (38)	18F-deoxyglucose	14 unipolar-depressed		25% increase in metabolic rate; hypofrontal pattern
9. Reiman et al. (58)	15O	10 Panic disorder 6 controls	Eyes closed	Decreased left vs. right parahippocampal gyrus metabolism, correlated with abnormal lactate response
10. Brodie et al. (36) Wolkin et al. (59)	18F-deoxyglucose	10 schizophrenics (medication-free)	Resting; eyes open; ears closed	Hypofrontality confirmed; decrease in frontal and temporal cortex
11. Stahl et al. (26)	18F-deoxyglucose	4 schizophrenics (medication-free for 2 wks) 4 controls	Eyes closed; auditory task	Hypofrontal, hypertemporal, and hyperoccipital metabolism
12. DeLisi et al. (27) DeLisi et al. (31) Buchsbaum et al. (33)	18F-deoxyglucose	21 schizophrenics (medication-free for 2 wks) 21 controls 11 affectives	Pain stimulation in right forearm; eyes closed; quiet room	Hypofrontal pattern, high slice; increased temporal cortex glucose use, low slice; no asymmetry

blood flow techniques, found evidence for a greater than normal left hemispheric lateralization of activity in schizophrenics during spatial tasks.

The effect of chronic neuroleptic treatment of these patients on overall brain metabolic activity has not yet thoroughly been investigated. While the results of animal autoradiographic studies may not be completely generalized to human physiology, nevertheless, some of these studies suggest associations that could be relevant to the understanding of the psychiatric studies. In one study, McCulloch et al. (34) found that haloperidol administrated in acute doses to rats, decreased glucose utilization in the majority of brain regions, while specifically increasing glucose utilization in the nucleus accumbens. However, no animal studies of chronic neuroleptic administration have been published, for comparison, nor has any animal study shown differences in gradients of activity from front to back.

The human studies of the effects of neuroleptics thus far completed have not been consistent with the original report by Farkas et al. (14). The metabolic gradient from front to back appears to remain unaffected by neuroleptic treatment in patients who have been studied both on and off medication and may even further decrease with the use of medication (26, 29, 35, 36, 59). Contrary to the study of McCulloch et al., neuroleptics were found to increase overall metabolic rates and increase activity specifically in the basal ganglia. Since these variables even further deviated from normal with medication and improvement in mental status, these results suggest a lack of direct correlation of PET findings thus far with disease pathology.

Studies of affective disorders

PET and blood flow studies of other psychiatric disorders have been less extensive than the studies of schizophrenia. The hypofrontal pattern described in chronic schizophrenic patients has also been found in affective disorders (33), although the studies of affective disorder conflict and may depend on clinical subdiagnosis (i.e. unipolar or bipolar) and mental state during the procedure. In one study (37), bipolar depressed patients had lower metabolic rates than bipolar manic, unipolars, or controls. Georgotas et al. (38) found a 25% increase in metabolic rates, as well as hypofrontality, in unipolar depressed patients when compared with controls. In contrast, Buchsbaum et al. (33) reported hypofrontality in predominantly bipolar patients and did not find changes in overall metabolic rate.

The parallel blood flow studies in affective disorder have even been less consistent. Johanson et al. (39) found a 10% reduction in mean hemispheric flow in 19 depressed patients after ECT, with the responders to ECT having higher pretreatment flows. Mathew et al. (40) reported lower gray matter flow in 12 severely depressed patients after a 2-week medication washout period, with significant negative correlations between regional cerebral blood flow and the Hamilton rating scale of depression. Gustafson et al. (41) also reported lower hemispheric mean flows for depressed patients. However, manic patients were even lower. Gur et al. (42) did not find evidence of hypofrontality or reduced flow in a group of 14 medicated depressed patients at rest; however, during specific cognitive tasks and when separated by gender, differences were evident. Depressed females had higher than normal flows in all conditions, while depressed males had lower than normal resting flows, which increased to normal during cognitive activity.

Similar to the studies of schizophrenia, these studies also have not ruled out effects of antidepressant or anti-manic medication. In one animal autoradiographic study (43) desmethylimipramine (DMI), a tricyclic antidepressant, was found to increase glucose utilization in 11 brain regions acutely, while chronic administration decreased glucose use in 7 of 30 brain regions. The regions affected included those of the occipital cortex, thalamus, limbic system, striatum, and hypothalamus. Phenelzine, a monoamine oxidase inhibitor, on the other hand, had relatively little effect on glucose utilization given either in acute or chronic doses. Phelps et al. (37) studied the effect of methylphenidate in 6 depressed patients and 7 controls. A worsening of the clinical state following methylphenidate administration resulted in an exaggeration of the left less than right metabolic asymmetry seen in the baseline study. Patients who became euphoric following the administration of methylphenidate tended to have a lower overall hemispheric metabolic rate than individuals who had a dysphoric response to the drug, and a positive clinical response to methylphenidate was correlated with a diminution in the baseline metabolic asymmetries of frontal and temporal cortex.

In another study, Brodie et al. (personal communication) have found a decrease in metabolic rates in unipolar depression that is even further decreased from normality in 12 patients after antidepressant medication. No studies of the effects of lithium on brain metabolic rate have been reported.

Studies of miscellaneous other disorders

PET and blood flow measurements of patients with neurologic diseases, that may be comparable in some aspects to psychiatric disorders, have also been done. In organic dementias, blood flow studies have shown an overall reduction in total blood flow that is proportional to the intellectual defect (44, 45). Alzheimer's dementia patients have specific reductions in parietal cortex that actually result in what appears to be relatively elevated frontal to posterior gradients (46). In other studies, adults who were diagnosed with childhood autism had increased overall metabolic activity (47), as did adult subjects with mongolism (48).

Few PET studies have been reported on patients with Parkinson's disease, a disorder thought to result from loss of dopaminergic neurons in the substantia nigra, and thus, dopamine concentrations. While global cerebral metabolism appears decreased in parkinsonian patients from one study (49), the relative distribution of glucose throughout the brain remains normal. Patients with Huntington's disease, on the other hand, were found to have decreased glucose utilization in the caudate and putamen, while metabolism appeared normal throughout the rest of the brain (49). The Parkinson patients in these studies were all receiving L-dopa, while the majority of the Huntington's chorea patients were medicated with neuroleptics.

Receptor visualization by PET

The use of PET to visualize more specific activity of cells, such as binding to receptors for neuroregulators, is now in progress. The use of both antagonists and agonists for dopamine receptors is now being employed for human use by a few PET centers. Bromine-77-labeled spiperone has been used in single photon studies (50); ^{11}C-spiperone and L-dopa have been used in PET studies (51, 52). These projects are only in the beginning stages and the initial reports of differences between patients and controls must await further analyses of normal data and substantiation of models to quantify the interaction between these substances, brain uptake, and receptor kinetics.

Tune et al. (53) reported decreased caudate to cerebellar ratios of spiperone activity on PET in a small group of medication-free schizophrenic subjects compared with controls; however, in a larger group this difference disappeared, and schizophrenic patients were undistinguishable from a control group with respect to spiperone binding in the caudate (Henry Wagner, Johns Hopkins Medical Center, personal communication, 1985).

On the other hand, Crow and colleagues (unpublished) have evidence of increased caudate dopamine receptor binding in 12 medication-free schizophrenics using Bromine-77-spiperone in single photon imaging.

Baron et al. (54) have published preliminary PET studies of 5 schizophrenic subjects using carbon-11-labeled pimozide to image dopamine receptors. No kinetic differences between schizophrenics and controls were noted. The significance of all these findings in terms of the dopamine hypothesis of schizophrenia is unclear.

Other receptors being focused on for future imaging studies are the cholinergic muscarinic receptor and endorphin receptor. Positron and gamma emitting labels attached to analogs specifically binding these receptors have already been visualized in initial studies in humans (Snyder et al., Johns Hopkin's University, unpublished data; Frost et al. (55); Eccleman et al., The National Institutes of Health, unpublished data).

At present PET is a relatively non-invasive research tool that may enable localization of brain metabolic defects in vivo. With ultimate improvement in the biochemical and physical technology that constitutes PET, better visualization of microscopic brain activity will be possible. This is a technique that potentially may lead to better understanding of brain metabolism in a variety of normal and diseased states.

REFERENCES

1. Dandy WE (1919) Roentgenography of the brain after the injection of air into the spinal cord. *Ann. Surg., 70,* 397.
2. Weinberger DR and Wyatt RJ (1982) Brain morphology in schizophrenia: in vivo studies. In: Henn FA, Nasrallah HA (Eds), *Schizophrenia as a Brain Disease,* pp. 148 – 175. Oxford University Press, New York.

3. Johnstone EC, Crow TJ, Frith CD, Husband J, Kreel L (1976) Cerebral ventricular size and cognitive impairment in chronic schizophrenia. *Lancet, 2,* 924.
4. Heath RG, Franklyn DE, Shraberg D (1979) Gross pathology of the cerebellum in patients diagnosed and treated as functional psychiatric disorders. *J. Nerv. Ment. Dis., 167,* 585.
5. Weinberger DR, Torrey EF, Wyatt RJ (1979) Cerebellar atrophy in chronic schizophrenia. *Lancet, 1,* 718.
6. Luchins DJ, Weinberger DR, Wyatt RJ (1982) Cerebral asymmetry in schizophrenia as determined by computed tomography. *Am. J. Psychiatry, 139,* 753.
7. Naeser MA, Levine HL, Benson DF, Stuss DT, Weir WS (1981) Frontal leukotomy size and hemispheric asymmetries on CT scans of schizophrenics with variable recovery. *Arch. Neurol., 38,* 30.
8. Golden CJ, Graber G, Coffman J, Berg R, Bloch S, Brogan D (1980) Brain density deficits in chronic schizophrenia. *Psychiatry Res., 3,* 179.
9. Bogerts B, Hantsch J and Herzer MA (1983) Morphometric study of the dopamine-containing cell groups in the mesencephalon of normals, Parkinson patients, and schizophrenics. *Biol. Psychiatry, 18,* 951.
10. Johnstone EC, Colter N, Crow TJ, Frith CD, Brown R, Corsellis JAN (1984) Changes in brain weight and structure in patients with functional psychosis. In: *Abstract Volume, 14th Collegium Internationale Neuropsychopharmacologicum, Florence, Italy. Clin. Neuropharmacol., 7, Suppl. 1,* 794, 1012.
11. Kety SS, Woodford RB, Harmel MH, Freyhan KE, Appel KE, Schmidt CF (1948) Cerebral blood flow and metabolism in schizophrenia. *Am. J. Psychiatry, 104,* 765.
12. Sokoloff L, Reivich M, Kennedy C, Des Rosiers MH, Patlack CS, Pettigrew KD, Sakvrada O, Shinohara M (1977) The [^{14}C]-deoxyglucose method for the measurement of local cerebral glucose utilization: theory, procedure and normal values in the conscious and anesthetized albino rat. *J. Neurochem., 28,* 897.
13. Reivich M, Kuhl D, Wolf A, Greenberg J, Phelps M, Ido T, Casella V, Fowler J, Hoffman E, Alavi A, Som P, Sokoloff L (1979) The [^{18}F]-fluoro-deoxyglucose method for the measurement of local cerebral glucose utilization in man. *Circ. Res., 44,* 127.
14. Farkas T, Reivich M, Alavi A, Greenberg JH, Fowler JS, MacGregro RR, Christman DR, Wolf AP (1980) The application of 18-fluoro-2-deoxyglucose and positron emission tomography in the study of psychiatric conditions. In: Passonneau JV, Hawkins RA, Lust WD, Welch FA (Eds): *Cerebral Metabolism and Neural Function,* p. 403. Williams and Wilkins, Baltimore, MD.
15. Farkas T, Wolf AP, Jaeger J, Brodie JD, Christman DR, Fowler JS (1984) Regional brain glucose metabolism in chronic schizophrenia. *Arch. Gen. Psychiatry, 41,* 293.
16. Ingvar DH and Franzen G (1974) Abnormalities of cerebral blood flow distribution in patients with chronic schizophrenia. *Acta Psychiatr. Scand., 50,* 425.
17. Kety SS and Schmidt CE (1948) The nitrous oxide method for the quantitative determination of cerebral blood flow in man: theory, procedure and normal values. *J. Clin. Invest., 27,* 476.
18. Gordon GS, Estess FM, Adams JE, Bowman KM, Simon A (1955) Cerebral oxygen uptake in chronic schizophrenic reaction. *Arch. Neurol. Psychiatry, 73,* 544.
19. Hoyer S, Oesterreich K (1975) Blood flow and oxidative metabolism of the brain in patients with schizophrenia. *Psychiatria Clin., 8/6,* 304.
20. Mathew RJ, Barr DL, Duncan GC, Weinman ML (1982) Regional cerebral blood flow in schizophrenia. *Arch. Gen. Psychiatry, 39,* 1121.

21. Ariel RN, Golden CJ, Berg RA, Quaife MA, Dirksen JW, Forsell T, Wilson J, Graber B (1982) Regional cerebral blood flow in schizophrenics: testing using the xenon (Xe-133) inhalation method. *Arch. Gen. Psychiatry, 40,* 258.

22. Gur RE, Skolnick BE, Gur RC, Caroff S, Rieger W, Obrist WD, Younkin D, Reivich M (1983) Brain function in psychiatric disorders: I. Regional cerebral blood flow in medicated schizophrenics. *Arch. Gen. Psychiatry, 40,* 1250.

23. Berman KF, Zec RF, Weinberger DR (1984) Impaired frontal cortical function in schizophrenia: rCBF evidence. In: *Abstract Volume, Society of Biological Psychiatry, 39th Annual Convention, Los Angeles, CA,* p. 60.

24. Widen L, Bergstrom M, Blomqvist G, Brismar T, Ehrin E, Elander S, Eriksson K, Eriksson L, Greitz T, Litton J-E, Malmborg P, Nilsson L, Sedvall G, Ugglas M (1981) Glucose metabolism in patients with schizophrenia: emission computed tomography measurements with 11-C-glucose. *J. Cereb. Blood Flow Metab., 1, Suppl. 1,* S455.

25. Buchsbaum MS, Ingvar D, Kessler R, Waters RN, Cappelletti J, van Kammen DP, King AC, Johnson JL, Manning RG, Flynn RW, Mann LS, Bunney WE, Sokoloff L (1982) Cerebral glucography with positron tomography. *Arch. Gen. Psychiatry, 39,* 251.

26. Stahl SM, Jernigan T, Pfefferbaum A, Berger P, Budinger T, Sargent T (1984) Positron emission tomography in schizophrenia. In: *New research Abstract Volume, American Psychiatric Association, Annual Meeting, Los Angeles, CA,* P. NR147.

27. DeLisi LE, Buchsbaum MS, Holcomb HH, Pickar D, Boronow J, Morihisa JM, van Kammen DP, Carpenter W, Kessler R, Margolin R, Cohen RM (1985) Clinical correlates of decreased anteroposterior gradients in positron emission tomography (PET) of schizophrenic patients. *Am. J. Psychiatry, 142,* 78.

28. Sedvall G, Blomquist G, DePaulis T, Ehrin D, Eriksson L, Farde L, Grietz T, Hedstrom DG, Ingvar DH, Litton J-E, Nilsson JGL, Stone-Elander S, Widen L, Wiesel F-A, Wik G (1983) PET-studies on brain energy metabolism and dopamine receptors in schizophrenic patients and monkeys. In: *Proceedings of the VII World Congress of Psychiatry, Vienna, July 11 – 16, 1983.* Plenum Press, New York.

29. Widen L, Blomqvist G, DePaulis T, Ehrin E, Eriksson L, Farde L, Greitz T, Hedstrom CG, Ingvar DH, Litton JE, Nilsson JLG, Ogren SO, Sedvall G, Stone-Elander S, Weisel F-A, Wik G (1984) Studies of schizophrenia with positron CT. In: *Abstract Volume, 14th Collegium Internationale Neuropsychopharmacologicum, Florence, Italy. Clin. Neuropharmacol., 7, Suppl. 1,* 538.

30. Sheppard G, Gruzelier J, Manchanda R, Hirsch SR, Wise R, Fracjowiak R, Jones T (1983) 15-O positron emission tomographic scanning in predominantly never-treated acute schizophrenic patients. *Lancet, 2,* 1448.

31. DeLisi LE, Buchsbaum MS, Holcomb HH, Langston KC, King AC, Kessler R, Pickar D, Carpenter W, Morihisa JM, Margolin R, Weinberger DR, Cohen R (1986) Increased temporal lobe glucose use in chronic schizophrenic patients. *Biol. Psychiatry,* in press.

32. Morihisa JM, Duffy FH, Wyatt RJ (1983) Brain electrical activity mapping (BEAM) in schizophrenic patients. *Arch. Gen. Psychiatry, 40,* 719.

33. Buchsbaum MS, DeLisi LE, Holcomb HH, Cappelletti J, King AC, Johnson J, Hazlett E, Dowling-Zimmerman S, Post RM, Morihisa J, Carpenter W, Cohen R, Pickar D, Weinberger DR, Margolin R, Kessler RM (1984) Anteroposterior gradients in cerebral glucose use in schizophrenia and affective disorders. *Arch. Gen. Psychiatry, 41,* 1159.

34. McCulloch J, Savaki HE, Sokoloff L (1982) Distribution of effects of haloperidol on energy metabolism in the rat brain. *Brain Res., 243,* 81.

35. DeLisi LE, Holcomb HH, Cohen RM, Pickar D, Carpenter W, Morihisa JM, King AC,

Kessler R, Margolin R, Buchsbaum MS (1985) Positron emission tomography (PET) in schizophrenic patients with and without neuroleptic treatment. *J. Cereb. Blood Flow Metab., 5,* 201.

36. Brodie JD, Christman DR, Corona JF, Fowler JS, Gomez-Mont F, Jaeger J, Micheels PA, Rotrosen J, Russell JA, Volkow ND, Wickler A, Wolf AP, Wolkin A (1984) Patterns of metabolic activity in the treatment of schizophrenia. *Ann. Neurol., 15 (Suppl),* S166.

37. Phelps ME, Mazziotta JC, Baxter L and Gerner R (1984) Positron emission tomographic study of affective disorders: problems and strategies. *Ann. Neurol., 15 (Suppl.),* S149.

38. Georgotas A (1984) Positron emission tomography studies in affective disorders. In: *Abstract Volume, 14th Collegium Internationale Neuropsychopharmacologicum, Florence, Italy. Clin. Neuropharmacol., 7, Suppl. 1,* 532.

39. Johanson M, Risberg J, Silfverskiold P et al (1979) Regional cerebral blood flow related to acute memory disturbance following electroconvulsive therapy in depression. *Acta Neurol. Scand., 60 (Suppl 72),* 534.

40. Mathew RJ, Meyer JS, Frances DJ, Semchuch KN, Mortel K, Claghorn JL (1980) Regional cerebral blood flow in depression. *Am. J. Psychiatry, 137,* 1449.

41. Gustafson L, Risberg J, Silfverskiold P (1981) Regional cerebral blood flow in organic dementia and affective disorders. *Adv. Biol. Psychiatry, 6,* 109.

42. Gur RE, Skolnick BE, Gur RC, Caroff S, Rieger W, Obrist WD, Younkin D, Reivich M (1984) Brain function in psychiatric disorders. II. Regional cerebral blood flow in medicated unipolar depressives. *Arch. Gen. Psychiatry, 41,* 695.

43. Gerber JC, Choki J, Brunswick DJ, Reivich M, Frazer A (1983) The effect of antidepressant drugs on regional cerebral glucose utilization in the rat. *Brain Res., 269,* 319.

44. Freyhan FA, Woodford RB, Kety SS (1951) Cerebral blood flow and metabolism in psychoses of senility. *J. Nerv. Ment. Dis., 113,* 449.

45. Lassen NA, Feinberg I, Lane MH (1960) Bilateral studies of cerebral oxygen uptake in young and aged normal subjects and in patients with organic dementia. *J. Clin. Invest., 39,* 491.

46. Chase TN, Foster NL, Fedio P, Brooks R, Mansi L, DiChiro G (1984) Regional cortical dysfunction in Alzheimer's disease as determined by positron emission tomography. *Ann. Neurol., 15 (Suppl),* S170.

47. Rumsey JM, Duara R, Grady C, Rapoport JL, Margolin RA, Rapapport SI, Cutler N (1986) Brain metabolism in autism: resting cerebral glucose utilization as measured with positron emission tomography (PET). *Arch. Gen. Psychiatry,* in press.

48. Schwartz M, Duara R, Haxby J, Grady C, White BJ, Kessler RM, Kay AD, Cutler NR, Rapapport SI (1983) Down's syndrome in adults: brain metabolism. *Science, 221,* 781.

49. Kuhl DE, Metter EJ, Riege WH, Markham CH (1984) Patterns of cerebral glucose utilization in Parkinson's disease and Huntington's disease. *Ann. Neurol., 15 (Suppl),* S119.

50. Owen F, Poulter M, Mashal RD, Crow TJ, Veall N, Zanelli GD (1983) [77]Br-p-bromospiperone: a ligand for in vivo labelling of dopamine receptors. *Life Sci., 33,* 765.

51. Wagner HN, Burns HD, Dannals RF, Wong DF, Langstrom B, Duelfer T, Frost JJ, Ravert HT, Links JM, Rosenbloom SB, Lukas SE, Kramer AV, Kuhar MJ (1983) Imaging dopamine receptors in the human brain by positron emission tomography. *Science, 221,* 1264.

52. Garnett ES, Firnau G, Nahmias C (1983) Dopamine visualized in the basal ganglia of living man. *Nature (London), 305,* 137.
53. Tune L (1984) Preliminary findings from in vivo dopamine-2 receptor binding in schizophrenic patients. In: *Abstract Volume, Society of Biological Psychiatry, 39th Annual Convention and Scientific Program, Los Angeles, CA,* p. 44.
54. Baron JC, Comar D, Zarifian E, Agid Y, Crouzel C, Loo H, Deniker P, Kellershohn C (1985) Dopamine receptor sites in human brain: positron emission tomography. *Neurology, 35,* 16.
55. Frost JJ, Dannals RF, Duelfer T, Burns D, Ravert HT, Langstrom B, Balasubramanian V, Wagner HN (1984) In vivo studies of opiate receptors. *Ann. Neurol., 15 (Suppl),* S85.
56. Stevens JR (1982) Neuropathology of schizophrenia. *Arch. Gen. Psychiatry, 39,* 1131.
57. Haug JO (1962) Pneumoencephalographic studies in mental disease. *Acta Psychiatr. Scand., 38 (Suppl.), 165,* 58.
58. Reiman EM, Raichle ME, Butler FK, Herscovitch P, Robins E (1984) A focal brain abnormality in panic disorder, a severe form of anxiety. *Nature (London), 310,* 683.
59. Wolken A, Jaeger J, Brodie JD, Wolf AP, Fowler J, Rotrosen J, Gomez-Mont F, Cancro R (1985) Persistence of cerebral metabolic abnormalities in chronic schizophrenia as determined by positron emission tomography. *142,* 564.

CHAPTER 14

Anatomical neuropathology in schizophrenia: post-mortem findings

DARRELL G. KIRCH AND DANIEL R. WEINBERGER

In marked contrast to many of the technological approaches discussed elsewhere in this volume, the direct examination of post-mortem brain tissue in the study of schizophrenia may be traced back as far as, and even beyond, the concept of 'schizophrenia' itself. Hecker in 1871 (1) and Kahlbaum in 1874 (2), examining cases of 'hebephrenia' and 'catatonia' respectively, reported finding anatomical pathology in the brain. In the past century there have been hundreds of studies searching for gross and microscopic central nervous system anatomical abnormalities in schizophrenia.

Unfortunately, these years of intense study have failed to yield a consensus regarding any neuropathological lesion. This is not to say that findings have been lacking. As will be reviewed in some detail, there has been no shortage of reported pathology. Every area of the central nervous system, including the spinal cord (3), has been identified as showing structural abnormalities in schizophrenia. A number of excellent efforts to summarize and synthesize these findings have been published over the years. These include reviews by Hassin in 1918 (4), Buscaino in 1921 (5), Josephy in 1930 (6), Spielmeyer in 1930 (7), Conn in 1934 (8), Peters in 1956 (9), David in 1957 (10), Dastur in 1959 (11), Corsellis in 1976 (12), Stevens in 1982 (13), and Weinberger et al. in 1983 (14).

Although they will not be the subject of the present discussion, there have also been numerous reports of anatomical pathology in other organ systems (11, 12). The heart has been described as small and the vascular bed as underdeveloped (15, 16). Inflammatory or sclerotic involvement of the gastrointestinal tract was noted by Buscaino (17), who also observed hepatic cellular changes and cell loss. Endocrine abnormalities have been reported in testes and ovaries, thyroid, and adrenal glands (15, 18). Often these systemic findings have been linked to observed brain abnormalities. For example, Buscaino (19) felt that hepatic changes and cortical neuron loss were both related to a process of 'autointoxication' by amines from the gastrointestinal tract.

Our initial focus in the present chapter will be an attempt to identify certain theoretical and methodological issues which are crucial to any analysis of post-mortem neuropathological studies of schizophrenia. This will be followed by a review of reported findings, in general proceeding chronologically, but also group-

Handbook of Schizophrenia, Vol. 1: The Neurology of Schizophrenia.
H.A. Nasrallah and D.R. Weinberger, editors.
© Elsevier Science Publishers B.V., 1986.

ing similar studies together with attempts (both successful and not) to replicate them. The discussion will close with our own effort to synthesize the findings to date and with some thoughts regarding future research in this area.

Theoretical issues

The 'lesion' in schizophrenia

Classical neuropathology has been a powerful tool in understanding both neurological disorders and the normal function of specific brain structures. While the failure to identify a distinct anatomical lesion in schizophrenia has been frustrating, it is not entirely surprising. The search for a pathognomonic finding in the brain in association with any illness is based upon the assumption that the illness is a singular entity with respect, at least, to pathology, if not etiology. If schizophrenia were clinically and pathologically homogeneous, a single 'disease,' it would be logical to expect such a lesion.

In spite of Kraepelin's early insistence that dementia praecox represents 'the expression of a single morbid process' (20), there is much clinical and research evidence to the contrary. Bleuler (and many who followed) presented the alternate hypothesis that schizophrenia may very well represent a 'group of diseases' (21). The symptomatic heterogeneity and changing diagnostic 'subtypes' of schizophrenia complicate any comparisons of neuropathological findings between cases or studies. It is exceedingly common in almost any area of schizophrenia research to find the variance within the subject group to be greater than that of the controls, a tribute to this heterogeneity. Moreover, the nosological confusion of the early part of this century is not entirely resolved, and diagnostic criteria continue to evolve.

Experience in other areas of neurology has shown that even a syndrome which appears to be relatively distinct may result from varied causes. As an example one need only look at the inflammatory, vascular, toxic, pharmacological, and idiopathic forms of parkinsonism.

All this should engender a measure of humility as we review the neuropathology of schizophrenia, or perhaps more accurately 'the schizophrenias.' The clinical heterogeneity of schizophrenia itself may be crucial in explaining the heterogeneity of reported anatomical findings in this disorder. Obviously this note of caution applies to techniques other than post-mortem neuropathology, as well. As Dastur observed in 1959 (11), reviewing the failure of neuropathology to find a consistent lesion and anticipating the oncoming wave of neurochemical studies in schizophrenia:

> At the risk of sounding pessimistic, it appears to me that it is the lesson of the past that history repeats itself. One need not be shocked, therefore, if the current notion of there being a distorted molecule behind a distorted thought is as difficult to demonstrate as the older belief of a defective neuron behind a defective thought.

Functional understanding of brain structure

In terms of fully appreciating the implications of an observed neuropathological abnormality, one obvious limiting factor is how much is known about the normal
function of the structure involved. With regard to studies of the brain, structural
and functional understanding usually have advanced in tandem. Research in mapping the functional areas of the central nervous system has consistently benefited
from linking clinical observations to the post-mortem identification of focal lesions.

As will be reviewed, the brain area initially emphasized in neuropathological
studies of schizophrenia was the neocortex, a reasonable choice in view of its
primary role in higher cognitive functions and the profound functional deterioration
observed in this illness. It was logical that early researchers looking at dementia
praecox should emphasize the same area of the brain so clearly damaged in other
dementias (22).

In recent years, however, the anatomical focus has shifted. The expansion of
knowledge regarding 'deeper' structures, in particular the diencephalon and limbic
system (23, 24), has been accompanied by more neuropathological emphasis on
these structures in schizophrenia (14). The fact that much remains unknown about
the function of these areas confounds interpretation of pathological findings in
them.

Methodological issues

In reviewing studies of the neuropathology of schizophrenia (and any other neuropsychiatric disorder as well) certain key methodological factors must be taken into
account, as summarized in Table 1.

TABLE I   *Methodological issues in post-mortem neuropathological studies*

Subject selection:
- Use of rigorous diagnostic criteria
- Prospective pre-mortem assessment preferable to post-mortem chart review

Control subjects:
- Matching by 'demographic' variables (e.g. age, gender, race)
- Matching by 'peri-mortem' variables (e.g. coexisting illnesses, agonal events, interval be-
  tween death and autopsy)

Sources of artifacts:
- Pre-mortem nutrition and somatic treatments
- Agonal events
- Interval between death and autopsy
- Fixation, sectioning, staining of tissue

Quantification:
- Measurement (e.g. cell count, volume) by blind observers
- Assessment of validity, reproducibility, reliability of measures

Subject selection

The problem of diagnosis has long been a particularly difficult one in schizophrenia research. Diagnostic criteria have changed and will continue to do so. Insofar as this is the case, caution must be exercised when making comparisons between studies, especially those employing different diagnostic concepts. This is particularly true of studies from the first half of this century. Moreover, post-mortem specimens from well-diagnosed subjects are not easy to obtain, and the price paid for a larger number of subjects in any given study may be that of less stringent diagnostic criteria or accepting cases lacking an adequate history. The ideal situation would be one in which all subjects had undergone a consistent pre-mortem research diagnostic evaluation and examination, clearly a difficult condition to meet.

Controls

Although now regarded as crucial to good research design, tissue samples from control subjects were conspicuously lacking in many early studies. There are considerable practical problems, however, involved in obtaining brain specimens from individuals 'matched' to patients with schizophrenia. Not only must the usual factors such as age and gender be taken into account, but issues of coexisting illnesses, agonal events, and interval between death and autopsy must be considered. The ideal match may be exceedingly difficult to obtain.

Artifacts

Not all abnormalities observed in studies of this type involve lesions which are directly related to the illness itself. Many secondary processes may be incorrectly mistaken for a primary 'neuropathology of schizophrenia.' For example, pre-mortem factors such as patient nutrition, pharmacological treatment, and somatic or surgical therapies (including leukotomy) may alter the anatomical picture. Agonal events, in particular trauma, hypoxia, and infection, may cause histopathological changes. The interval between death and autopsy and the process of fixation, sectioning, and staining of individual specimens may introduce distortions in tissue, neuronal inclusions, vacuoles, and other artifactual 'lesions.' These parameters may be difficult to control from one tissue specimen to another in the same case, not to mention from case to case and study to study.

Quantification

The pioneers of classical neuropathology reported primarily qualitative impressions of the material they examined. It was many years before attempts at more quantitative assessment (e.g. cell counting) were made. Quantitative analysis is an attractive approach to studying subtle brain illnesses such as schizophrenia. While it cannot provide evidence of a pathognomonic lesion in the sense of an inclusion body or of an infiltrate, it can show that a pathological process has occurred.

As graphically illustrated by David in 1957 (10), the actual number of neurons that can practically be examined in a brain is exceedingly small. He estimated that 'a random sample of even 1% of the total volume of the brain would contain 20 000 000 microscopical fields' (10). Obviously the search for neuropathological changes in schizophrenia must rely on more than qualitative impressions of random samples. A well-designed study would clearly demarcate the structural area of interest (e.g. nucleus, tract, cortical layer). Multiple samples of the area would be obtained and the element of interest (e.g. neuron size, cell count, intensity of glial staining, or volume of a specific structure) then quantified in both patient and matched control specimens. Observers (whether using 'manual' or computer-assisted quantification) would be blind to diagnosis. Reproducibility and inter-observer reliability would be assessed. As will be reviewed, in many studies the conditions obtained fall far short of the methodological ideal.

Neuropathological studies of schizophrenia

The nineteenth century and evolution of the concept of schizophrenia

The latter half of the nineteenth century was a period of intense activity in both the classification of neuropsychiatric disorders and the microscopic study of normal and pathological neuroanatomy. During this period attention turned toward a particular type of psychotic illness with onset typically occurring in adolescence, followed by a chronic deteriorating course. Morel introduced the term 'démence précoce' in 1860 (25) to describe this disorder, and what followed were a number of attempts to classify what now is considered to be schizophrenia.

In 1871 Hecker (1) described the symptoms of hebephrenia and in addition reported post-mortem findings in a single case. The gross abnormalities he noted included darkening of cortex, pial and cerebellar hyperemia, and ventricular enlargement. Given the current interest in radiologic studies of ventricular enlargement, it is interesting to see how long a history this finding has.

The diagnostic term 'Katatonie' was introduced by Kahlbaum in 1874 (2). He associated acute cases of catatonia with brain tissue and arachnoidal exudates and chronic cases with retraction of cerebral tissue and organized ependymal exudates. Moreover, he emphasized the distinctly different neuropathology seen in catatonia versus that seen in general paralysis.

Meynert, the eminent neuropathologist and psychiatrist, in 1884 (26) noted an occasional association between psychosis and frontal cortical atrophy.

Attempts at nosological systematization and histopathological correlation reached a peak before the turn of the century with Kraepelin's delineation of the concept of dementia praecox (a term used originally by Morel, as noted above). Kraepelin, who had also been trained in neuropathology, cited numerous authorities (including Alzheimer and Nissl) as supporting his view that dementia praecox is 'a severe and widespread disease of the nervous tissue' (20). In 1897 Alzheimer (22) noted the loss

329

of cerebral cortical neurons in cases of psychosis, emphasizing in particular disorganization of ganglion cells in deeper cortical layers, with an accompanying glial reaction. Similarly, Kraepelin noted reports by Nissl of 'lipoid decomposition' of neurons, particularly in layers II and III of the cortex, and he also cited Sioli, Mariyasu, Wada, and Goldstein as having also observed distortions and loss of cortical neurons in dementia praecox (20).

Thus, by the turn of the century a school of thought regarding the neuropathology of schizophrenia had become predominant in Europe. Specifically, the idea of the time was not only that dementia praecox was a distinct disease process, but also that it involved areas of neuronal loss in specific layers of neocortex. While some observers reported an accompanying glial response, this was neither prominent nor consistently found. It should be noted that neuronal loss without gliosis is difficult to interpret and often suggests agonal changes. An alternative and rarely considered interpretation of neuronal loss in the absence of gliosis is that of an early developmental deficit.

The early twentieth century and further specific findings

In 1913 Alzheimer (27) published findings from a study of 55 patients with dementia praecox. Again, he noted changes in cortical neurons, including disorientation of neuronal apical processes, lipoid degeneration, and areas of cell loss. Pyramidal cells in layers II and III of the frontal cortex were noted to show the greatest changes. These neurons project primarily intra-cortically.

In a series of studies around the time of World War I, Southard (28 – 30) also emphasized loss of cortical neurons and accompanying gliosis as the primary microscopic histopathology of dementia praecox. He went beyond this general finding, however, and presented a 'topographical' analysis of specific types of symptoms. In his view, delusions, catatonia, and auditory hallucinations were associated with frontal, parietal, and temporal lobe lesions respectively. These claims were curiously consistent with now outdated oversimplifications about the function of these brain areas.

These studies by Alzheimer and Southard represented further arguments in support of both the unity of the concept of dementia praecox and the idea that its organic substrate was in specific layers of cortical neurons. In fact, Alzheimer (22) noted an absence of such changes in melancholia and Southard saw no lesions in cases of pure paranoia (8, 30).

Diagnostic and neuropathological diversity

Not all researchers, however, agreed with the relatively unitary concept of dementia praecox as proposed by Kraepelin. Questions were raised as to whether the numerous reports of damage to cortical neurons and specific cell loss as cited above were indeed the consistent anatomical expression of a single disease entity. Moreover, reports of similar anatomical changes in other illnesses began to appear, raising questions about the specificity of the cortical findings noted above. Hassin in 1918 (4) agreed that in cases of dementia praecox there were neuronal changes localized to cortical layers II and III, especially in the frontal lobe, but he noted that similar changes were also found in encephalitis, dementia paralytica, and other neurological disorders. While such findings did not diminish the importance of the observations in schizophrenia, they did dishearten those who sought a qualitatively distinct 'lesion.'

The clinical picture was said to be dependent upon the stage of pathology by Gurd in 1920 (31), who noted severe fatty degeneration in neurons and glia in cases of acute catatonia. In cases of longer duration, chromatolysis and loss of pyramidal cells predominated, and glial proliferation was more pronounced.

In 1922 Buscaino (32) described 'grape-like' neuronal degeneration focused primarily in the white matter, basal ganglia, and thalamus rather than in the cerebral cortex. He associated pallidal lesions with catatonia and lesions in the dentate nucleus of cerebellum with catalepsy. He clearly did not agree with the frontal, parietal, temporal distinctions of Southard (29) or the emphasis on cortical lesions.

In the same year, Mott (33) reported a case of advanced dementia praecox in which cortical tissue (area unspecified) showed swelling of nuclei, lipoid degeneration, and glial proliferation, but in which similar changes were observed in basal ganglia, pons, and medulla. Both Buscaino (17) and Mott (18) also emphasized pathology in other organ systems, the former focusing on liver, reticulo-endothelial system, and gastrointestinal tract, while the latter cited endocrine and testicular abnormalities.

Observations from 50 cases of schizophrenia were reported by Josephy in 1923 (34). He felt that there was prominent cortical neuron loss in layers III and V, primarily in frontal areas, but also cited an absence of accompanying inflammation or glial proliferation. This lack of gliosis was one factor that led Josephy (6) to doubt whether neuronal loss was a primary neuropathological process in schizophrenia.

Localization of changes to the frontal lobe corresponded with a report by Rawlings in 1920 (35) that cited frontal atrophy as a gross anatomical finding in 10 of 12 cases. Lewis in 1923 (15) had studied several hundred autopsies and reported that brain size was decreased in dementia praecox. In a subsequent review (36) he emphasized his view that the key lesion was vascular hypoplasia on a 'constitutional' basis. Other observers had reported decreased brain weight in cases of schizophrenia (37 – 39). In contrast, Bamford (40) identified the brain as macrocephalic (mean weight 1500 g) in 6 cases of catatonia in young patients. This report stands out as an exception to the usual finding of atrophy. Bamford, however, was reporting on somewhat atypical and, indeed, questionable cases of dementia praecox in which there was 'a rapid and acute course, ending in comparatively early death' (40).

By the end of World War I, although abnormalities were frequently reported, it had become unclear as to whether histopathological changes in schizophrenia were actually limited to the cortex (or even the central nervous system) and also whether the findings were at all specific. The inconsistent nature of the observations from one case to another and from one study to another began to raise doubts about the meaning of the findings. Commenting on this state of affairs, Adolf Meyer summarized it by saying, 'I doubt whether many of us would dare to make our diagnoses from sample sections of the nervous system' (41).

Dissenting opinions

One of the most careful studies in the neuropathology of schizophrenia was that by Dunlap in 1924 (42). In an effort to replicate the findings of his predecessors, he undertook a study which was the first to address some key methodological issues. He selected cases in which the diagnosis of dementia praecox was 'acceptable to even the most critical.' In all cases the subject had to be under 40 years of age, suffering an acute death, and with the autopsy done immediately after death. Moreover, working with a medical examiner he obtained well-matched control cases. Fixation and sectioning of all specimens were standardized. Multiple cell counts by different blind observers were averaged, using photographs of microscopic sections. His rigorous methodology was clearly ahead of its time. Indeed, in some of his eight selected cases of dementia praecox, he observed some of the abnormalities previously reported, including lipoid degeneration, distorted nuclei, and sclerotic cells. These changes were also present, however, in some control cases. Moreover, he showed that some changes (e.g. lipoid findings) could be artifacts of alcohol fixation. Using quantitative cell counts of frontal cortical neurons, there were no significant differences between control and patient specimens. Dunlap concluded that the reported histopathological changes in dementia praecox were probably secondary to agonal processes or fixation artifacts. The only clear shortcomings of this study were the small sample sizes (eight schizophrenic and five control subjects) and the fact that only a small region of cortex was examined.

In a critical review in 1934, Conn (8) presented evidence that focal cortical neuron loss may well be a result of agonal events such as ischemia. Spielmeyer (7) supported this view by pointing out that agonal hypoperfusion caused cellular changes and even cell loss. A few years later Peters (43) compared tissue from schizophrenic subjects with samples from non-psychotic executed criminals (a dubious control population), showing no significant differences between groups. As a result of these better controlled studies, Wertham and Wertham stated in 1934 (44) that 'it is impossible to avoid the conclusion that all the neurohistological data described for schizophrenia are irrelevant.' While this view can be argued, in retrospect it seems premature considering the relatively small number of negative studies and the myopic preoccupation with cortical neurons drawn from a relatively limited region of cortex.

Further positive findings

In spite of the cautionary note regarding methodology and controls sounded in 1924 by Dunlap (42) (and subsequently by others as cited above), work in this area continued to flourish, especially in Europe. Even Bleuler (45) remained enthusiastic about finding some 'uniformity' of histopathological changes in schizophrenia.

Füngfeld in 1927 (46) examined 11 patients and 20 controls and found (non-quantitatively) cell loss in layers III and V and glial reaction in layer VI in the cortex of these patients. He did acknowledge that some control cases showed similar findings.

In a study of three patients, Bouman (47) noted neuron loss in cortical layer III, primarily in the frontal and temporal lobes, without inflammation or glial reaction. He also noted some white matter abnormalities.

Even Spielmeyer, who was a cautious voice regarding artifacts caused by agonal events (7), stated that lipoid degeneration in cortical layer III was a definite feature of carefully selected cases of dementia praecox (48).

A new focus of study emerged during this period, as attention shifted to the diencephalon. In 1934, Dide (49) reported neuronal abnormalities and glial plaques in the hypothalamus. Similarly, Morgan and Gregory (50) noted degenerative changes and neuronal loss in the area of the tuber cinereum.

As a result of the application of psychosurgery, biopsy specimens of brain tissue became available. One of the more unique and controversial findings was reported by Papez and Bateman (51). Using dark-phase microscopy and tissue samples obtained at biopsy, 'inclusion bodies' were identified in cortical neurons. These bodies were approximately one micron in diameter and were thought to represent 'pleomorphic organisms.' They were described, on occasion, as being motile. Kirschbaum and Heilbrunn (52) noted degenerative neuronal and glial changes in 10 of 11 schizophrenic frontal lobe biopsy specimens. Hyden and Hartelius (53) examined specimens from 10 patients and noted both shrinking and swelling of cortical neurons with an accompanying decrease in nucleoprotein. Unfortunately, these studies lacked controls and artifacts were noted by other investigators (54, 55) to be common in biopsy preparations.

Counterbalancing these positive reports were negative results from attempts to replicate earlier post-mortem tissue findings. Wohlfahrt (56) examined Nissl-stained cortex, thalamus, basal ganglia, and cerebellum in normal controls and patients and found no differences. Using quantification of brain thickness and cortical neurons in frontal specimens from psychotic patients, Rowland and Mettler in 1949 (57) noted no abnormalities. They did not, however, use specimens from normal controls for comparison.

Thus, despite greater emphasis on the use of controls and an increased awareness of artifacts, both positive and negative findings continued to be reported. Moreover, to add to the controversy, case reports appeared in which the clinical diagnosis was schizophrenia but the autopsy revealed distinct and unusual neuropathology. In two reports detailing three cases diagnosed as schizophrenia, Ferraro (58, 59) noted diffuse cortical encephalopathy and widespread demyelination with marked gliosis and inflammation. Roizin et al. (60) reported a case of acute catatonia accompanied by symmetrical lobar demyelination. These reports undoubtedly represented leukoencephalopathies, the clinical manifestations of which masqueraded as schizophrenia.

Obviously, by the time of World War II and after nearly 80 years of published research, no consensus had been reached regarding the neuropathology of schizophrenia, and questions continued to be raised about the diagnostic classification itself.

The First International Congress of Neuropathology

In 1952, the First International Congress of Neuropathology convened in Rome. In attendance were many of the key figures involved in studying the histopathology of schizophrenia during the first half of this century. The meeting represented the highwater mark in this area of research. Failure by the participants to reach a consensus, coupled with the dramatic emergence of developments in pharmacology and neurochemistry, turned schizophrenia research away from neuropathology.

Among the most prominent attendees were Cecil and Oskar Vogt, whose efforts to rigorously collect and examine control and patient material spanned several decades. They had developed a unique method of preparing thin $(10-20 \mu m)$ serial sections of complete human brains. In addition, they placed great emphasis on establishing the range of normal central nervous system histology across the lifespan, collecting specimens from hundreds of subjects (ranging in age from embryos to over 100 years old). No other group of investigators, before or since, has studied as carefully controlled and prepared specimens. Furthermore, there are distinct advantages to serial sectioning over random sampling, especially in the search for subtle pathology.

The Vogts (61) summarized their findings by reporting that all cases of schizophrenia showed anatomical abnormalities, primarily in the form of 'gaps' in cortical neurons (rather than diffuse loss). In addition to these areas of focal neuronal loss, they listed a variety of specific degenerative neuronal changes. These included 'dwarf cells,' cytoplasmic vacuolation, lipoid sclerosis, cell shrinkage, and pale 'balloon cells'. Deficits were varied in location, including frontal and temporal cortex, thalamus, and basal forebrain, leading the Vogts to restate the belief that specific psychotic symptoms might be localized in specific cortical regions.

Bruetsch (62) presented the view that different 'sub-groups' of patients with schizophrenia may have different neuropathology. He stated that approximately 9% of patients at autopsy had rheumatic occlusive endarteritis in meningeal and cortical vessels. He cited this as a potential sub-group of patients with a distinct underlying organic pathology.

Van der Horst (63) reported on his study of patients 'unreservedly' diagnosed as having schizophrenia. The lesions he noted were alterations around blood vessels (such as plasma exudate and fibrinoid deposits), neuronal degeneration accompanied by glial reaction, and demyelination (both cerebral and cerebellar). He regarded these changes as being associated with rheumatic endocarditis.

In summarizing over 30 years of research, Buscaino (19) reviewed his theory that schizophrenia was the result of toxicity from amines of intestinal origin that are not cleared by the liver and that act on a vulnerable nervous system. The brain findings of focal cell loss and demyelination, in his view, were the consequence of this 'aminic toxicosis.'

De Vries (64) lent his support to the recurrently reported finding of loss of cortical neurons in layer III as the primary abnormality in schizophrenia. He viewed this as possibly being a form of congenital hypoplasia.

Scharenberg (65) cited degenerative changes of both neurons and glia in cases of catatonia, but did not view these changes as 'pathognomonic.'

The dissenters were also represented. Peters (66) restated his view that focal areas of neuronal loss were due to 'peri-mortem' events. In support of the idea that these changes were agonal, he noted that most observers did not see an accompanying glial reaction as would be expected in a more chronic process. Peters did not address the possibility that the changes might have occurred early in development and therefore might not be associated with gliosis.

Another pioneer in the field, Adolph Meyer (54), observed that 'some of the speakers have been anxious to establish a somatic pathology lest victory go to the protagonists of a psychogenic etiology.' He again reported that his research, most of which appears to have been anecdotal, had failed to find a *consistent* neuropathology and attributed the varied findings of other observers to 'coincidental' factors such as age, complications, and prior treatment. Meyer perhaps neglected to consider his own impatience to establish schizophrenia as a 'reactive' disorder.

Perhaps the best summary of the efforts up to that point was that of Ferraro (67):

> At the present stage of our knowledge, I do not think therefore that we have succeeded in establishing the specific pathology of schizophrenia. We have only succeeded in establishing concomitant structural pathology in the course of the schizophrenic syndrome.

Recent findings

The 1952 International Congress of Neuropathology highlighted both the lack of consensus regarding the central nervous system pathology of schizophrenia and the curious tendency for idiosyncratic theories to affect the collection and interpretation of data. Moreover, the meeting was followed by a wave of basic and clinical research in biochemistry and pharmacology which served to divert attention away from more traditional investigations of histopathology. Since 1952, studies regarding the neuropathology of schizophrenia have tended to be more focused. There has been a trend toward examination of a single well-delimited region or nucleus, often involving the deeper midline structures of the diencephalon and limbic system, rather than the neocortex. Rather than search for a pathognomonic lesion, several groups have concentrated on quantitative techniques in an effort to consider that the pathological process might involve only subtle changes. Other studies have utilized newer specialized stains or advanced technology such as the electron

335

TABLE 2   *Post-mortem neuropathological abnormalities in schizophrenia: 1964 – 1985*

Study	Ref. no.	No. of schizo-phrenic sub-jects/controls	Reported abnormality
Tatetsu (1964)	69	41/55	Thickened, densely staining axons and dendrites in multiple cortical areas
Wildi et al. (1967)	70	75/638	Elderly schizophrenics showed greater overall atrophy not related to senile changes
Nieto Escobar (1972)	71	10/3	Gliosis in reticular formation, hypothalamus, thalamus, peri-aqueductal gray matter, hippocampus
Colon (1972)	72	3/unspecified	Decreased neurons (maximal in layers IV and V) in cortical areas 10, 4, 24
Miyakawa et al. (1972)	73	5/4	Ultrastructural abnormalities in frontal gyrus neurons and glia (by electron microscopy)
Fisman (1975)	74	7/24	6 of 7 schizophrenics showed brainstem glial knots and peri-vascular infiltration
Weinberger et al. (1980)	75	12/35	More frequent cerebellar ver-mian atrophy
Kovelman Scheibel (1981, 1984)	76, 77	10/8(77)	Pyramidal cell disorientation in hippocampus (not confirmed by Weinberger et al. (78))
Averback (1981)	79	13/35	Degeneration of nucleus of the ansa peduncularis in the substantia innominata
Dom et al. (1981)	80	5/5	Decreased cell diameter in Golgi Type II neurons in neostriatum and nucleus accumbens
Stevens (1982)	13	25/48	Increased fibrillary gliosis in periventricular diencephalon, periaqueductal gray matter, and basal forebrain
Bogerts et al. (1983)	83	6/9	Decreased volume of lateral substantia nigra

TABLE 2 *(continued)*

Study	Ref. no.	No. of schizophrenic subjects/controls	Reported abnormality
Benes et al. (1984)	87	10/9	Decreased cortical neurons in layers VI (prefrontal), V (cingulate), III (motor)
Bogerts et al. (1984, 1985)	84, 85	13/9(85)	Decreased volume of amygdala, hippocampal formation, parahippocampal gyrus, and pallidum internum
Brown et al. (1986)	86	41/29	Decrease in brain weight and parahippocampal gyral width and increased area of temporal horn of lateral ventricle (compared to affective disorders)

microscope. The methodological issues of patient selection, matching controls, and elimination of artifacts tended to receive greater emphasis. Table 2 contains an overview of the positive findings reported in more recent studies.

Using material from the Vogt collection, von Buttlar-Brentano (68) focused specifically on the area of the basal forebrain known as the substantia innominata. This area includes the nucleus basalis of Meynert and consists largely of cholinergic neurons with widespread cortical connections. Von Buttlar-Brentano found these cells to be reduced in size in the brains of schizophrenic subjects, referring to this alteration as an expression of 'congenital dwarfism.'

Tatetsu (69) examined the prefrontal cortex (area 10) and multiple other cortical regions in 41 schizophrenic patients. Using a silver stain to facilitate examination of cellular processes, he identified thickened, more densely stained dendrites and axons as being more common in patients than in controls, attributing these changes to disordered neuronal metabolism.

Wildi et al. (70) emphasized quantitative morphology, including brain weight, brain measurements, and ventricular size, in their study of 75 elderly schizophrenic patients and 638 control subjects. They were particularly attentive to issues of consistent diagnosis and tissue handling. Overall brain atrophy not related to senile changes was noted to be more frequent in patients than in controls.

Nieto and Escobar (71) utilized a lithium-silver carbonate staining technique to identify glial fibrils in 10 younger (age 29 to 52 years) schizophrenic patients. A degree of gliosis not seen in four control cases was identified in the reticular formation, hypothalamus, septum, medial and anterior thalamus, periaqueductal gray matter, and hippocampus of the schizophrenic subjects.

Colon (72) developed a technique for quantifying cortical morphological features such as numbers of neurons, nuclear volume, and cell depth. In three older (60 – 62 years) schizophrenic patients there were decreased numbers of cortical neurons in layers IV and V and an overall decrease in cortical thickness. Cortical samples were taken from areas 10, 4, 24, and 17, with the latter posterior area showing 'minimal' cell loss in comparison to the other more anterior areas. Colon felt that this cell loss may have been related to clinical features of 'dementia' in these cases, and not specific to schizophrenia.

The use of electron microscopy to examine cellular ultrastructure is limited by the need for biopsy material. Using frontal gyrus specimens from schizophrenic and control subjects, Miyakawa et al. (73) noted ultrastructural abnormalities in both neurons and oligodendroglia in the schizophrenic subjects. Findings included prominent Golgi bodies, abnormal tubular membranous structures, and synaptic distortions. These ultrastructural changes were attributed to enzymatic disturbances, though their true meaning is unknown.

In an examination of the brainstem for evidence of gliosis, Fisman (74) found glial proliferation (especially prominent in the medial reticular area of the pons) in 6 of 7 schizophrenic subjects and in only 1 of 24 controls. The observed abnormalities were similar to changes seen in herpes encephalitis.

Using material from the Yakovlev collection at the Armed Forces Institute of Pathology in Washington, DC, Weinberger et al. (75) examined the cerebellar vermis, finding significantly more frequent atrophy using quantitative techniques in 12 schizophrenic subjects as compared with 35 controls.

Another area of repeated recent interest has been the hippocampus. Scheibel and Kovelman (76, 77) examined the spatial orientation of the apical processes of hippocampal pyramidal cells using Golgi preparation. They found dendritic disarray to be more common in schizophrenic subjects than in controls, attributing this to a congenital failure of these cells to properly orient. In an effort to replicate this finding, Weinberger et al. (78) examined the hippocampus in brains from the Yakovlev collection (using brains prepared with a Nissl stain that is less specific for these dendritic structures). No greater disorientation was found in schizophrenic patients than in controls.

The nucleus of the ansae peduncularis, a group of ganglionic cells in the substantia innominata, was examined by Averback (79). Neuronal abnormalities (degeneration and cytoplasmic vacuolation) were found in 11 out of 13 cases. These alterations may be common in elderly individuals, but the patients in this study had a mean age of 47.4 years.

Dom et al. (80) performed quantitative morphological assessments of the caudate, putamen, thalamus, and nucleus accumbens. Using material from the Vogt collection, no decrease in cell numbers was observed in five catatonic schizophrenic subjects compared with controls. However, the former did show decreased cell diameter in Golgi Type II microneurons in the neostriatum and nucleus accumbens compared with controls.

In one of the more exhaustive recent neuropathological studies, Stevens (13) examined material from 25 schizophrenic subjects obtained from the collection at Saint Elizabeth's Hospital in Washington, DC and from matched non-schizophrenic psychiatric patients and normal controls. A Holzer's stain for glial fibrils revealed evidence of 'pathological' gliosis in 75% of the schizophrenic subjects. Involved sites included the periventricular diencephalon, periaqueductal mesencephalon, and the substantia innominata in the basal forebrain. The control specimens contained much less evidence of similar gliotic changes. Other chronic degenerative changes (e.g. calcifications in globus pallidus) were also found more frequently in schizophrenic cases.

In a preliminary quantitative assessment of the nucleus basalis of Meynert, Kirch et al. (81) found decreased numbers of large neurons in some older schizophrenic subjects. The cell loss in sections from the midportion of the nucleus was not as profound as that observed in Alzheimer's disease (82), and subsequent examination of a greater number of subjects indicated that most older schizophrenic patients (regardless of degree of cognitive impairment) had cell counts in the nucleus basalis of Meynert similar to that seen in age-matched normal controls (unpublished data).

More recent reports have quantitatively examined material from the Vogt collection (83 – 85). In an initial study, Bogerts et al. (83) found a significant decrease in volume of the lateral substantia nigra and a decrease in the mean volume of glial nuclei in 6 schizophrenic patients. Subsequently, planimetric volume estimates were made of basal ganglia and limbic structures in 13 schizophrenic and 9 control subjects. The amygdala, hippocampal formation, and pallidum internum were significantly decreased in volume in the schizophrenic group. The pallidum externum showed a trend toward decreased volume. The volume of putamen, caudate, nucleus accumbens, and bed nucleus of the stria terminalis did not differ in the two groups.

Brown et al. (86) examined post-mortem brain specimens from 41 patients with schizophrenia and 29 with affective disorder. The former were found to have decreased brain weight and parahippocampal gyral cortical width, and increased cross-sectional area of the temporal horn of the lateral ventricle. Moreover, the difference in parahippocampal cortex thickness was greater in the left hemisphere.

Finally, the frontal cortex is still an area in which abnormalities are reported. Benes et al. (87) examined prefrontal, anterior cingulate, and motor cortex in 10 schizophrenic patients and 9 control subjects. Significantly lower neuron counts were observed in layer VI of prefrontal, layer V of cingulate, and layer III of motor cortex in the schizophrenic patients.

Overview and synthesis

Over the last century almost every area of the brain has been implicated as showing anatomical pathology in schizophrenia. Almost as impressive, however, have been the numerous failures to replicate specific findings and the elaboration of multiple potential sources of error.

No consistent finding has emerged as 'the lesion' of schizophrenia. As discussed at the outset, however, the heterogeneity of schizophrenia may make an attempt to identify such a lesion inherently futile. Moreover, given the profound behavioral and affective deficits and the subtle cognitive impairments which are the clinical manifestations of the disorder, it would seem unrealistic to expect a single, well-delimited lesion. By way of reinforcing this point one need only observe the vast number of diverse neurological disorders with varied etiologies (infectious, auto-immune, neoplastic, traumatic, metabolic, degenerative, vascular, and so on) which clinically may mimic schizophrenia (88). It should not surprise us, therefore, were the post-mortem neuropathology of schizophrenia to involve multiple lesions in diverse sites.

Although we cannot identify a pathognomonic lesion in schizophrenia, the conclusion that no brain pathology exists is far from warranted. There are too many studies employing rigorous methodology that have cited positive findings. In reviewing these positive reports, certain recurrent themes seem to emerge. At the risk of oversimplification, these themes will be identified as *brain atrophy, cortical dysmorphism, and limbic-diencephalic dysmorphism and gliosis.*

Brain atrophy

From Hecker's 1871 (1) report of ventricular enlargement in a case of hebephrenia to Bogerts' 1985 (85) volumetric study showing decreased size in several limbic and diencephalic structures, the persistent finding of brain atrophy in one form or another is difficult to ignore. Decreased tissue mass has been identified in several forms, including decreased brain weight (15, 37 – 39, 70), gross cortical atrophy (especially in the frontal lobe) (35), and decreased volume in deeper midline and limbic structures (83 – 86). As discussed in detail elsewhere in this volume, advances in in vivo radiologic imaging procedures lend extra credence to these findings by presenting evidence of frontal atrophy, enlargement of the lateral and third ventricles, and cerebellar vermian atrophy. Insofar as these neuropathological and radiological findings imply damage to prefrontal cortex and limbic diencephalic structures, they are wholly consistent with the profound attentional, behavioral, and affective disturbances which chronically debilitate the patient with schizophrenia.

Two notes of caution are necessary. Atrophy is a generic term, by definition indicating a 'wasting' of tissue. In fact, as postulated by some researchers (68), the process actually may be one of a congenital failure to develop. Secondly, the range of normal variation is great, and a smaller brain or nucleus is not necessarily dysfunctional. In spite of the heroic efforts of pioneers such as Cecil and Oskar Vogt in Germany and Paul Yakovlev in the United States to accumulate standardized collections of normal brain tissue, much remains obscure regarding normal central nervous system anatomical variation. A simple illustration that puts this issue in some perspective is the recent preliminary examination of the brain of Albert Einstein (89). In the inferior parietal region (area 39) of Einstein's brain, the neuronal/glial ratio was significantly smaller than in a group of matched controls. Whether this is interpreted as 'gliosis,' 'cell loss,' or 'failure to develop,' the result was obviously far from 'pathological.'

Accepting for the moment that these findings of decreased brain weight, frontal atrophy, ventricular enlargement, and decreased volume of some nuclei are indeed real, the questions then become which elements are specifically damaged or missing (e.g. neurons, glia, or neuropil), and what is the cause.

Cortical dysmorphism

The focus on cortical neurons in the early neuropathological studies of schizophrenia was not surprising, given the extensive cortical changes observed in senile dementia. It was quite logical to pursue the lesion of dementia praecox in the same anatomical substrate. Observers differed in terms of which layers of neocortex were most involved. Moreover, cell loss was not the only finding cited, with some investigators emphasizing various distortions of size and shape, for example, distortions of apical dendrites as noted by Alzheimer (27) or the 'dwarf cells' and cytoplasmic vacuolation observed by the Vogts (61).

The problem of lack of controls in these early studies was brought to the fore by Dunlap (42), and the potential for neuronal damage by agonal hypoxia was emphasized by Spielmeyer (7) and Conn (8). Nevertheless, subsequent researchers continued to report neuronal loss in some layers of neocortex even when attempting to rigorously employ controls and limit artifacts. One of the most recent reports in this area (87) once again noted decreased cell numbers in specific layers of prefrontal, cingulate, and motor cortex, though the relationship of these recent findings to earlier reports is unclear.

Thus, evidence remains that cannot be summarily dismissed that cortical neurons, especially those in the frontal cortex, are altered in some patients with schizophrenia. These alterations may include somatic distortions, changes in cell size, or actual decreases in cell numbers, all grouped together here under the term 'dysmorphism.' In which patients, by what means, and whether by cell destruction or congenital failure to develop, are questions that remain to be rigorously examined.

Although cortical neuronal damage has long been claimed to be a consistent feature of advanced presenile and senile dementia of the Alzheimer type, it has become clear that the cortical lesions are far from the sole neuropathology in these dementias. Recent findings regarding alterations in the cholinergic neurons of the basal forebrain and other neurotransmitter systems illustrate the fact that dementia of this type is a disorder of multiple systems involving complex cortical-limbic-diencephalic-brainstem interconnections (82). Whether cortical neurons or deeper midline centers are damaged in primary or secondary fashion is far from clear. The same considerations may affect interpretations of cortical findings in schizophrenia.

If cortical neuronal dysmorphism is confirmed in schizophrenia, this is only a starting point. Attention must then be devoted to the central nervous system interconnections of these cortical neurons. Insofar as the prefrontal cortex has in particular been implicated in schizophrenia, other brain areas which send and receive prefrontal projections (e.g. thalamus, hypothalamus, and amygdala, in addition to diffuse areas of neocortex) must be given equal attention (90).

Limbic-diencephalic dysmorphism and gliosis

It was only after the initial wave of research citing cortical lesions in schizophrenia had passed, that attention began to turn toward deeper midline structures. Although the term 'limbic' was used by Broca in 1878 (91) to designate the lobe of tissue beneath the neocortex and surrounding the brain stem, the early emphasis was on the olfactory connections of the system as observed in lower animals (24). The work of Papez (92) and MacLean (23) expanded the concept of the limbic system to involve much more complex affective, behavioral, and cognitive functions attributed to structures such as the amygdala, hippocampus, septum, and hypothalamus. From Dide's 1934 (49) report of cellular distortions and glial plaques in the hypothalamus to Stevens' (13) observation of glial fibrillary proliferation in several limbic-diencephalic structures, numerous reports of pathology in this region in cases of schizophrenia have appeared. Not only have neuronal changes (both cellular distortions and decreased cell numbers) been cited, but an accompanying glial reaction has frequently been noted.

Gliosis is a non-specific finding, a marker for cellular damage that does not reveal etiology. It may reflect infection, auto-immune process, trauma, vascular injury, and numerous other insults to the central nervous system. It is of interest to note that, in reviewing neuropathological studies of schizophrenia, glial reaction may be a more prominent finding in limbic-diencephalic structures, this in contrast to findings in neocortex. Insofar as special glial stains have been developed more recently, this observation may not be a reflection of the disease process, but rather the result of a greater recent focus on deep structures. Nevertheless, it is tempting to speculate that a propensity toward limbic-diencephalic glial reaction may indicate a 'primary' site of injury, while changes in neocortex tend to be 'secondary.' Such a distinction obviously requires much further study before it merits firm support. The findings of Bogerts et al. (84, 85) and Brown et al. (86) of reduced volume in certain deep structures are consistent with the findings of Stevens (13) and others. However, the brain elements involved cannot be determined from volumetric observations alone, and changes in glial or neuropil concentrations could be responsible.

Summary

Over a century of post-mortem research on the brains of patients with schizophrenia has yet to reveal a consistent lesion, and we are still far removed from understanding the cause or causes of this disorder. Moreover, even if the numerous reported neuropathological findings are 'real' and not simply artifacts, it would remain to be determined whether they are causally linked to schizophrenia or in fact associated with some other pathophysiological process. Nevertheless, there are three general findings in the research to date which are strikingly prominent: atrophy (especially of the frontal lobe and periventricular structures); cortical neuronal abnormalities (again especially frontal); and limbic-diencephalic abnormalities (involving decreased tissue volume and cellular disarray and gliosis). Taken together, these observations suggest that the brain in schizophrenia is not structurally normal, but rather that it manifests a condition of subtle cortico-limbic structural deficit.

Future research directions

Given the lack of resolution in research to date and the ongoing surge of technological advances in the neurosciences, it is reasonable to make a proposal for new 'state-of-the-art' neuropathological examinations of the central nervous system in schizophrenia. The basic methodological standards outlined earlier in this chapter must remain a cornerstone of any such effort. Diagnostic criteria must be strictly applied and patients carefully matched to control subjects. Rapid autopsy and standardized tissue handling and fixation are crucial to minimizing artifacts. Quantitative data gathered in 'blind' fashion, rather than global qualitative impressions, are essential.

Given the data distortions which may result from post-mortem chart reviews and retrospective diagnosis, the best design would be one in which resources are initially devoted to prospective examination of a large number of subjects with chronic schizophrenia. This would allow concurrent psychiatric and neurological examinations and facilitate obtaining pre-mortem permission for later autopsy and brain removal. Following this group of patients until death would also provide critical data regarding course of illness, severity of symptoms, coexisting movement disorders, and other neurological findings. Such a system could be designed to minimize the interval between death and autopsy and allow tissue handling in standard fashion for both patient and control material. The help of citizen advocacy groups such as the National Alliance for the Mentally Ill might be enlisted to maintain follow-up and even secure autopsies.

Advances in computer-based systems for image analysis make new levels of data quantification possible. Not only may routine neuron counts be performed on large numbers of tissue sections in semi-automated fashion, but one may also differentiate cell types, perform volumetric estimates of discreet structures, three-dimensionally reconstruct areas of the brain, and make density evaluations of 'staining' (including autoradiography and immunohistofluorescence).

Neuropathological studies should no longer be performed in isolation. Much could be gained by alternately allocating tissue (e.g. by random assignment of hemispheres or serial sections) to fixation, freezing, or fresh preparations for different analytical methods. In this fashion, histopathology may be correlated with data from biochemical and enzymatic assays, antibody probes, premortem cerebral imaging, and other techniques described in this volume. The potential interfaces between neuropathology and other neuroscientific disciplines continue to expand. It is likely that structural and ultrastructural anatomical studies of the brain will remain a key element in our attempts to understand schizophrenia.

REFERENCES

1. Hecker E (1871) Die Hebephrenie. *Arch. Pathol. Anat. Physiol. Klin. Med., 52,* 394.
2. Kahlbaum K (1874) *Die Katatonie oder der Spannungsirresein.* Hirschwald, Berlin.
3. Goldstein K (1910) Zur pathologischen Anatomie der Dementia praecox. *Arch. Psychiatr. Nervenkr., 46,* 1062.
4. Hassin GB (1918) The present status of the histopathology of dementia praecox. *Dement. Praecox Stud., 1,* 7.
5. Buscaino VM (1921) I dati attuali sull'anatomia pathologica del sistema nervoso dei dementi precoci. *Riv. Patol. Nerv. Ment., 26,* 87.
6. Josephy H (1930) Dementia praecox (Schizophrenie). In: Bumke O (Ed), *Handbuch der Geisteskrankheiten, 2nd Ed, Vol 11,* pp. 763 – 778. Springer-Verlag, Berlin.
7. Spielmeyer W (1930) The problem of the anatomy of schizophrenia. *J. Nerv. Ment. Dis., 72,* 241.
8. Conn JH (1934) An examination of the clinico-pathological evidence offered for the concept of dementia praecox as a specific disease entity. *Am. J. Psychiatry, 13,* 1039.
9. Peters G (1956) Dementia praecox. In: Lubarsch O, Henke F, Rossle R (Eds), *Erkrankungen des zentralen Nervensystem, Handbuch der speziellen pathologischen Anatomie und Histologie, Vol 13, Pt 4, Ch 9,* pp. 1 – 52. Springer-Verlag, Berlin.
10. David GB (1957) The pathological anatomy of the schizophrenias. In: Richter D (Ed), *Schizophrenia: Somatic Aspects,* pp. 93 – 130. Macmillan, New York.
11. Dastur DK (1959) The pathology of schizophrenia. *Arch. Neurol. Psychiatry, 81,* 601.
12. Corsellis JAN (1976) Psychoses of obscure pathology. In: Blackwood W, Corsellis JAN (Eds), *Greenfield's Neuropathology, 3rd Ed, Ch 20,* pp. 903 – 915. Edward Arnold, London.
13. Stevens JR (1982) Neuropathology of schizophrenia. *Arch. Gen. Psychiatry, 39,* 1131.
14. Weinberger DR, Wagner RL, Wyatt RJ (1983) Neuropathological studies of schizophrenia: a selective review. *Schizophr. Bull., 9,*193.
15. Lewis NDC (1923) *The constitutional factors in dementia praecox with particular attention to the circulatory system and to some of the endocrine glands.* Monograph Series No 35, Nervous and Mental Disease Publishing Company, Washington.
16. Shattock FM (1950) Somatic manifestations of schizophrenia: a clinical study of their significance. *J. Ment. Sci., 96,* 32.
17. Buscaino VM (1953) Extraneural pathology in schizophrenia: liver, digestive tract, reticuloendothelial system. *Acta Neurol., 8,* 1.
18. Mott FW (1919) Normal and morbid conditions of the testis from youth to old age in 100 asylum and hospital cases. *Br. Med. J., 2,* 737.
19. Buscaino VM (1952) Extraneural pathology of schizophrenia (liver, digestive tract, reticulo-endothelial system). In: *Proceedings of the First International Congress of Neuropathology, Rome, Vol I,* pp. 545 – 577. Rosenberg and Sellier, Turin.
20. Kraepelin E (1919) *Dementia Praecox and Paraphrenia.* (Edited in 1971 by Robertson GM). Robert E. Krieger Publishing Company, Huntington, New York.
21. Bleuler E (1911) *Dementia Praecox or the Group of Schizophrenias.* International Universities Press, New York.
22. Alzheimer A (1897) Beiträge zur pathologischen Anatomie der Hirnrinde und zur anatomischen Grundlage einiger Psychosen. *Monatsschr. Psychiatr. Neurol., 2,* 82.
23. MacLean PD (1952) Some psychiatric implications of physiological studies on frontotemporal portion of limbic system (visceral brain). *Electroencephalogr. Clin.*

Neurophysiol., 4, 407.

24. Isaacson RL (1982) *The Limbic System, 2nd Ed.* Plenum, New York.
25. Morel BA (1860) *Traitement des Maladies Mentales.* Victor Masson, Paris.
26. Meynert T (1884) *Psychiatrie.* W. Braumüller, Vienna.
27. Alzheimer A (1913) Beiträge zur pathologischen Anatomie der Dementia Praecox. *Allg. Z. Psychiatr. Psychischgericht. Med., 70,* 810.
28. Southard EE (1914) On the topographical distribution of cortex lesions and anomalies in dementia praecox, with some account of their functional significance. *Am. J. Insanity, 71,* 383.
29. Southard EE (1915) On the topographical distribution of cortex lesions and anomalies in dementia praecox, with some account of their functional significance. *Am. J. Insanity, 71,* 603.
30. Southard EE (1919) On the focality of microscopic brain lesions found in dementia praecox. *Arch. Neurol. Psychiatry, 1,* 172.
31. Gurd AE (1920) The structural brain lesions of dementia praecox. *Am. J. Insanity, 77,* 201.
32. Buscaino VM (1922) New data concerning the distribution and production of the 'clustered areas of disintegration' in dementia praecox. *Dement. Praecox Stud., 5,* 1.
33. Mott FW (1922) The genetic origin of dementia praecox. *J. Ment. Sci., 68,* 333.
34. Josephy H (1923) Beiträge zur Histopathologie der Dementia praecox. *Z. Gesamte Neurol. Psychiatr., 86,* 391.
35. Rawlings E (1920) The histopathologic findings in dementia praecox. *Am. J. Insanity, 76,* 265.
36. Lewis NDC (1925) Pathology of dementia praecox. *J. Nerv. Ment. Dis., 62,* 225.
37. Crichton-Browne J (1879) On the weight of the brain and its component parts in the insane. *Brain, 2,* 42.
38. Southard EE (1910) A study of the dementia praecox group in the light of certain cases showing anomalies or sclerosis in particular brain regions. *Am. J. Insanity, 67,* 119.
39. Kure S, Shimoda M (1923) On the brain of dementia praecox. *J. Nerv. Ment. Dis., 58,* 338.
40. Bamford C (1929) Considerations on dementia praecox as a physical disease. *J. Ment. Sci., 75,* 120.
41. Meyer A (1922) Constructive formulation of schizophrenia. *Am. J. Psychiatry, 1,* 355.
42. Dunlap CB (1924) Dementia praecox: some preliminary observations on brains from carefully selected cases, and a consideration of certain sources of error. *Am. J. Psychiatry, 3,* 27.
43. Peters G (1938) Anatomisch-pathologische Bemerkungen zur Frage der Schizophrenie. *Allg. Z. Psychiatr. Grenzgeb., 108,* 274.
44. Wertham F, Wertham F (1934) *The Brain as an Organ.* Macmillan, New York.
45. Bleuler E (1930) The physiogenic and the psychogenic. *Am. J. Psychiatry, 10,* 203.
46. Füngfeld E (1927) Über die pathologische Anatomie der Schizophrenie und ihre Bedeutung für die Abtrennung 'atypischer' periodisch verlaufender Psychosen. *Monatsschr. Psychiatr. Neurol., 63,* 1.
47. Bouman KH (1928) Die Pathologische Anatomie des Zentralnervensystems bei Schizophrenie. *Psychiatr. Neurol. Bladen, 32,* 517.
48. Spielmeyer W (1929) The problem of the anatomy of schizophrenia. *Res. Publ. Assoc. Res. Nerv. Ment. Dis., 10,* 105.
49. Dide MM (1934) Les syndromes hypothalamiques et la dyspsychogénèse. *Rev. Neurol., 6,* 941.

50. Morgan LO, Gregory HS (1935) Pathological changes in the tuber cinereum in a group of psychoses. *J. Nerv. Ment. Dis., 82,* 286.

51. Papez JW, Bateman JF (1951) Changes in nervous tissues and study of living organisms in mental disease. *J. Nerv. Ment. Dis., 114,* 400.

52. Kirschbaum WR, Heilbrunn G (1944) Biopsies of brain of schizophrenic patients and experimental animals. *Arch. Neurol. Psychiatry, 51,* 155.

53. Hyden H, Hartelius H (1948) Stimulation of nucleoprotein production in nerve cells by malononitrile and its effect on psychic functions in mental disorders. *Acta Psychiatr. Neurol., Suppl. 48,* 1.

54. Meyer A (1952) Critical evaluation of histopathological findings in schizophrenia. In: *Proceedings of the First International Congress of Neuropathology, Rome, Vol 1,* pp. 649 – 666. Rosenberg and Sellier, Turin.

55. Wolf A, Cowen D (1952) Pathology. In: Mettler FA (Ed), *Some Problems of the Human Frontal Lobe, Ch 27.* Paul B. Hoeber, New York.

56. Wohlfahrt S (1936) Die Histopathologie der Schizophrenie. *Acta Psychiatr. Neurol., 11,* 687.

57. Rowland LP, Mettler FA (1949) Cell concentration and laminar thickness in the frontal cortex of psychotic patients; studies on cortex removed at operation. *J. Comp. Neurol., 90,* 255.

58. Ferraro A (1934) Histopathological findings in 2 cases of clinically diagnosed dementia praecox. *Am. J. Psychiatry, 13,* 883.

59. Ferraro A (1943) Pathological changes in the brain of a case of clinically diagnosed dementia praecox. *J. Neuropathol. Exp. Neurol., 2,* 84.

60. Roizin L, Moriarty JD, Weil AA (1945) Schizophrenic reaction syndrome in course of acute demyelination of central nervous system: clinicopathologic report of a case, with brief review of the literature. *Arch. Neurol. Psychiatry, 54,* 202.

61. Vogt C, Vogt O (1952) Altérations anatomiques de la schizophrénie et d'autres psychoses dites fonctionelles. In: *Proceedings of the First International Congress of Neuropathology, Rome, Vol 1,* pp. 515 – 532. Rosenberg and Sellier, Turin.

62. Bruetsch WL (1952) Specific structural neuropathology of the central nervous system (rheumatic, demyelinating, vasofunctional, etc.) in schizophrenia. In: *Proceedings of the First International Congress of Neuropathology, Rome, Vol 1,* pp. 487 – 499. Rosenberg and Sellier, Turin.

63. Van der Horst L (1952) Histopathology of clinically diagnosed schizophrenic psychoses or schizophrenia-like psychoses of unknown origin. In: *Proceedings of the First International Congress of Neuropathology, Rome, Vol 1,* pp. 501 – 513. Rosenberg and Sellier, Turin.

64. De Vries E (1952) Discussion. In: *Proceedings of the First International Congress of Neuropathology, Rome, Vol 1,* pp. 579 – 583. Rosenberg and Sellier, Turin.

65. Scharenberg K (1952) Discussion. In: *Proceedings of the First International Congress of Neuropathology, Rome, Vol 1,* pp. 611 – 623. Rosenberg and Sellier, Turin.

66. Peters G (1952) Discussion. In: *Proceedings of the First International Congress of Neuropathology, Rome, Vol 1,* pp. 624 – 629. Rosenberg and Sellier, Turin.

67. Ferraro A (1952) Discussion. In: *Proceedings of the First International Congress of Neuropathology, Rome, Vol 1,* pp. 630 – 636. Rosenberg and Sellier, Turin.

68. Von Buttlar-Brentano K (1952) Pathohistologische Feststellungen am Basalkern Schizophrener. *J. Nerv. Ment. Dis., 116,* 646.

69. Tatetsu S (1964) A contribution to the morphological background of schizophrenia:

with special reference to the findings in the telencephalon. *Acta Neuropathol., 3,* 558.

70. Wildi E, Linder A, Costoulas G (1967) Schizophrénie et involution cérébrale sénile. *Psychiatr. Neurol., 154,* 1.
71. Nieto D, Escobar A (1972) Major psychoses. In: Minkler J (Ed), *Pathology of the Nervous System, Vol 3, Ch 189,* pp. 2654 – 2665. McGraw-Hill, New York.
72. Colon EJ (1972) Quantitative cytoarchitectonics of the human cerebral cortex in schizophrenic dementia. *Acta Neuropathol., 20,* 1.
73. Miyakawa T, Sumiyoshi S, Deshimaru M, Suzuki T, Tomonari H, Yasuoka F, Tatetsu S (1972) Electron microscopic study on schizophrenia: mechanism of pathological changes. *Acta Neuropathol., 20,* 67.
74. Fisman M (1975) The brain stem in psychosis. *Br. J. Psychiatry, 126,* 414.
75. Weinberger DR, Kleinman JE, Luchins DJ, Bigelow LB, Wyatt RJ (1980) Cerebellar pathology in schizophrenia: a controlled postmortem study. *Am. J. Psychiatry, 137,* 359.
76. Scheibel AB, Kovelman JA (1981) Disorientation of the hippocampal pyramidal cell and its processes in the schizophrenic patient. *Biol. Psychiatry, 16,* 101.
77. Kovelman JA, Scheibel AB (1984) A neurohistological correlate of schizophrenia. *Biol. Psychiatry, 19,* 1601.
78. Weinberger DR, Luchins DJ, Kleinman JE, Wyatt RJ (1980) The hippocampus in schizophrenia: a controlled post-mortem study. Presented at the 35th Annual Meeting of the Society for Biological Psychiatry, Boston, MA.
79. Averback P (1981) Lesions of the nucleus ansae peduncularis in neuropsychiatric disease. *Arch. Neurol., 38,* 230.
80. Dom R, De Saedeleer J, Bogerts J, Hopf A (1982) Quantitative cytometric analysis of basal ganglia in catatonic schizophrenics. In: Perris C, Struwe G, Jansson B (Eds), *Biological Psychiatry, 1981.* Elsevier, Amsterdam.
81. Kirch DG, Shelton R, Fan K-J, Kanhouwa S, Kleinman J, Wyatt RJ (1984) Nucleus basalis neuron loss in schizophrenia. Presented at the 137th Annual Meeting of the American Psychiatric Association, Los Angeles, CA.
82. Coyle JT, Price DL, DeLong MR (1983) Alzheimer's disease: a disorder of cortical cholinergic innervation. *Science, 219,* 1184.
83. Bogerts B, Häntsch J, Herzer M (1983) A morphometric study of the dopamine-containing cell groups in the mesencephalon of normals, parkinson patients, and schizophrenics. *Biol. Psychiatry, 18,* 951.
84. Bogerts B (1984) Zur Neuropathologie der Schizophrenien. *Fortschr. Neurol. Psychiatr., 52,* 428.
85. Bogerts B, Meertz E, Schönfeldt-Bausch R (1985) Basal ganglia and limbic system pathology in schizophrenia. *Arch. Gen. Psychiatry, 42,* 784.
86. Brown R, Colter N, Corsellis JAN, Crow TJ, Frith CD, Jagoe R, Johnstone EC, Marsh L (1986) Brain weight and parahippocampal cortical width are decreased and temporal horn area is increased in schizophrenia by comparison with affective disorder. *Arch. Gen. Psychiatry, 43,* 36.
87. Benes FM, Davidson J, Bird ED (1984) Quantitative morphometric studies of schizophrenic cortex. In: *Clinical Neuropharmacology, Vol 7, Suppl 1,* S498. Raven Press, New York.
88. Davison K, Bagley CR (1969) Schizophrenia-like psychoses associated with organic disorders of the central nervous system. In: Herrington RN (Ed), *Current Problems in Neuropsychiatry. Br. J. Psychiatry, Suppl. 4,* pp. 113 – 184.

89. Diamond MC, Scheibel AB, Murphy G, Harvey T (1985) The brain of a scientist: Albert Einstein. Presented at the 18th Annual Winter Conference on Brain Research, Vail, CO.
90. Fuster JM (1980) *The Prefrontal Cortex: Anatomy, Physiology, and Neuropsychology of the Frontal Lobe.* Raven Press, New York.
91. Broca P (1878) Anatomie comparée des circonvolutions cérébrales. *Rev. Anthropol., Series 3, 1,* 385.
92. Papez JW (1937) A proposed mechanism of emotion. *Arch. Neurol. Psychiatry, 38,* 725.

CHAPTER 15

Postmortem neurochemistry studies in schizophrenia

JOEL E. KLEINMAN

The study of postmortem neurochemistry of schizophrenic brain specimens provides opportunities to test a number of hypotheses. Over the last decade a number of laboratories have utilized this research strategy with at least some success. Although there has been no shortage of findings there have been problems with replications and interpretations of data. Inter-laboratory differences may be the result of methodological variables which are inherent to postmortem studies. Some of these variables include postmortem intervals, age of the subjects, psychiatric diagnosis, differences in dissection and prior neuroleptic treatment. Since these variables are formidable and inter-laboratory differences are all too common, there is a tendency to disregard many of the results from this area of schizophrenia research. Nevertheless, there is a surprising convergence of postmortem neurochemical results with regard to which brain areas are involved in the schizophrenic syndrome.

Although most reviews of this topic concentrate on neurochemical findings and the methodological problems inherent in these studies (1 – 4), this chapter will be organized around neuroanatomical regions. Four broadly defined brain areas will be considered, including the basal ganglia, the limbic system, the cerebral cortex and the brainstem. The notions underlying this method of review are relatively simple. In the first place, there is a preponderance of findings in the basal ganglia and the limbic system. Secondly, the innervation of these structures are in part from the cerebral cortex and the brainstem. Since this oversimplification leaves out major structures such as the thalamus and cerebellum it will be necessary to add a fifth area to cover structures omitted from the four major areas of discussion.

The basal ganglia

The definition of the basal ganglia varies considerably among textbooks of neuroanatomy (5, 6). For the purpose of this review the basal ganglia will be restricted to the caudate, the putamen and the globus pallidus. Although the basal ganglia are classically thought to be involved in movement disorders, there is a surprisingly high frequency of psychiatric symptoms associated with disorders of the basal ganglia such as Huntington's disease, Parkinson's disease, Wilson's disease, and the Lesch-Nyhan syndrome. Whether these psychiatric symptoms are the result

Handbook of Schizophrenia, Vol. 1: The Neurology of Schizophrenia.
H.A. Nasrallah and D.R. Weinberger, editors.
© Elsevier Science Publishers B.V., 1986.

of basal ganglia pathology or are related to pathology of other structures associated with these disorders is a subject not easily determined and unfortunately beyond the scope of this review. Nevertheless, it should not come as a surprise that there are a number of postmortem findings in schizophrenic brains in this area.

Studies of the basal ganglia in schizophrenia include measurements of catecholamines, indoleamines, neuropeptides, amino acids, their binding sites and the enzyme of synthesis and degradation. The most relevant positive findings relate to dopamine receptors in the basal ganglia. A number of laboratories (see Table 1) have demonstrated increases in dopamine receptors (Type II − those linked to a decrease in adenylate cyclase with dopamine stimulation) in the putamen and caudate nucleus (7 − 12). There seems to be little dispute that this finding is replicable, but there is considerable controversy over its significance (13, 14). Since drugs which are effective in the treatment of schizophrenia block dopamine type II receptors in proportion to their antipsychotic properties (15), this finding has the potential to be of major clinical relevance.

The proponents of the notion that dopamine receptors are pathologically increased in the basal ganglia have several lines of argument. First, in those subjects who have no known history of neuroleptic treatment, there are similar increases in dopamine receptor numbers (7, 8). Second, positive psychotic symptoms have been shown to correlate with the number of dopamine receptors (16). Third, there appears to be a bimodal distribution of dopamine receptors which is thought to be unrelated to prior neuroleptic treatment (12). As compelling as these arguments are, there is the alternative hypothesis that dopamine receptor increases are a supersensitivity phenomenon secondary to receptor blockade from prior neuroleptic treatment (13).

Equally compelling arguments to suggest the idea that dopamine receptor increases are a result of prior neuroleptic treatment have been proposed. Subjects who have been drug-free for one month or longer have dopamine receptor numbers similar to controls (13). Also, the correlation of positive psychotic symptoms with increased dopamine receptor numbers may be a function of increased neuroleptic

TABLE 1   *Dopamine Type II receptors in basal ganglia and limbic system*

	Caudate	Putamen	Nucleus accumbens
Lee et al., 1978 (7), 1980 (9)	↑	↑	↑
Owen et al., 1978 (8)	↑	↑	↑
Reisine et al., 1980 (10)	↑	↑	
MacKay et al., 1980 (13)	NC		NC
Reynolds et al., 1980 (14)		NC	
Kleinman et al., 1982 (11)	↑		
Seeman et al., 1984 (12)	↑	↑	↑

↑ = increased; NC = no change

treatment in order to treat symptomatic patients (4). Finally, in the study which demonstrates a bimodal distribution for dopamine receptors, almost all of the patients who were drug-free for six months or longer had dopamine receptor numbers in the range of the control population (12). The data can be interpreted, however, in at least two ways. On the one hand, since drug-free subjects appear to have normal numbers of dopamine receptors, a neuroleptic effect may very well account for those subjects with increased numbers of receptors. On the other hand, it may be that the only subjects who could exist off of neuroleptics are those with few positive psychotic symptoms who may have fewer dopamine receptors.

What can be said about dopamine Type II receptors in the basal ganglia of schizophrenic patients? First, the numbers of drug-naive or even one month drug-free subjects is relatively small in any of the aforementioned studies. Larger numbers may need to be obtained to resolve this issue. Second, there are increases in dopamine receptor numbers in the basal ganglia of schizophrenic subjects. At the least these increases suggest that neuroleptic have an effect on the dopamine receptors in the basal ganglia. At the most, increased dopamine receptors are related to some of the psychopathology of the schizophrenic syndrome.

Dopamine Type I receptors (those linked to an increase in adenylate cyclase activity with dopamine stimulation) have also been measured in basal ganglia. They have not attracted as much attention for two reasons. In the first place, there is not as good a correlation between antipsychotic activity and blockade of dopamine Type I receptor primarily because butyrophenones are effective antipsychotics with relatively weak abilities to block this receptor. Secondly, initial studies demonstrated no increases in this receptor (17). As a matter of fact, since some animal studies indicate that neuroleptics cause an increase in dopamine Type I receptors, the lack of an increase in postmortem studies has been taken as evidence that increases in dopamine Type II receptors are not a neuroleptic effect (9). More recently, however, increased responsiveness of dopamine sensitive adenylate cyclase activity (Type I receptor) has been demonstrated in the caudate nucleus of schizophrenic patients (18). The significance of this finding cannot be determined as yet, since a neuroleptic effect has not been ruled out.

A number of other receptors have been studied in the basal ganglia of schizophrenic patients. Although there have been occasional positive findings (10),

TABLE 2 *Other receptors in basal ganglia in schizophrenia*

Reisine et al., 1980 (10)	↓ ^{3}H-naloxone binding in caudate
Kleinman et al., 1982 (11)	Normal ^{3}H-naloxone, WB 4101 (α-receptors), dihydro-alprenolol (β-receptors), QNB (muscarinic receptors), GTP, diazepam in caudate
Owen et al., 1981 (19)	Normal ^{3}H-ADN, 5HT, LSD, QNB, GABA, diazepam in caudate and putamen
Ferrier et al., 1985 (20)	Normal ^{3}H-naloxone binding in caudate

these have not been replicable (11, 19, 20; see Table 2). A similar picture can be seen with regard to a number of enzymes including each of the enzymes of synthesis and degradation of catecholamines which have been studied in basal ganglia and numerous other brain regions (21 – 38).

With regard to the proposed neurotransmitters, neuromodulators and their metabolites, there have been a number of negative or unreplicable findings in the basal ganglia (35, 39 – 42; see Table 3). Possible exceptions include increased serotonin in the putamen (35, 41) and globus pallidus (40, 41) as well as decreased met-enkephalin in the caudate nucleus of chronic paranoid schizophrenic patients (42). The latter finding has not been studied by any other laboratory, while increases in serotonin concentrations are of dubious significance since increases in its metabolite, 5-hydroxyindoleacetic acid, have been reported by only one group (40) and not confirmed by another (41).

The limbic system

As difficult as it is to define the basal ganglia, the limbic system may be harder. For the purposes of this review, the following structures will be included: nucleus accumbens, hypothalamus, ventral septum, mammillary bodies, bed nucleus of the stria terminalis, olfactory area, amygdala, and hippocampus. The very notion of the limbic system as a network of neurons involved in emotions suggests the importance of these structures in the schizophrenic syndrome.

Although the number of structures is large, the task of reviewing findings in this area is made simpler by the fact that researchers have concentrated on only several of these structures, i.e. the nucleus accumbens, the hypothalamus, the amygdala and the hippocampus. The accumbens in particular has been a hotbed of research activity with the first report of increased dopamine concentrations in schizophrenic brains (43). This initial report has not been confirmed by others (11, 35, 40, 44, 45).

TABLE 3   *Basal ganglia catecholamines, indoleamines, neuropeptides and metabolites in schizophrenia*

Crow et al., 1979 (35)	↑ DA in caudate nucleus; ↑ 5HT in putamen
Joseph et al., 1979 (39)	NC in 5HT or 5HIAA in basal ganglia
Farley et al., 1980 (40)	↑ 5HT and 5HIAA in globus pallidus
Korpi et al., in press (41)	↑ 5HT in globus pallidus and putamen; NC in 5HT in caudate nucleus or 5HIAA in basal ganglia
Kleinman et al., 1983 (42)	↓ Met-enkephalin in caudate nucleus; NC in met-enkephalin in putamen and globus pallidus.

↑ = increased; NC = no change; ↓ = decreased; DA = dopamine; 5HT = serotonin; 5HIAA = 5-hydroxyindoleacetic acid.

Moreover, there have been no reports of increases in dopamine metabolites in the accumbens (11, 35, 44 – 46). There have, however, been two reports of increased norepinephrine in the nucleus accumbens of chronic paranoid schizophrenic patients (11, 47) and one report of increased 3-methoxy-4-hydroxyphenylglycol, a major metabolite of norepinephrine (11). Failures to demonstrate increases in norepinephrine in the accumbens may be a function of other groups (35, 48) looking at all schizophrenic patients together rather than at the paranoid subtype, in particular. For a summary see Table 4. Moreover, the failure to find similar increases in chronic undifferentiated schizophrenic patients and other neuroleptic treated psychotic controls suggests that this may not be a neuroleptic effect (11).

The nucleus accumbens has proven a fruitful site for studying dopamine receptors as well. Increases in both types of dopamine receptors have been demonstrated in the accumbens (7 – 9, 12) although the significance of these findings is as difficult to determine here as it has been in the basal ganglia (13) (see Table 1). Finally, a number of enzymes, indoleamines and their metabolites, binding sites, amino acids and neuropeptides have been studied in the accumbens with essentially negative results (40 – 42, 49 – 51).

There have also been a number of studies on the neurochemistry of the hypothalamus in schizophrenia. Typical of results in this area are findings of increased serotonin by one group (40), decreased serotonin by another (52) and no change by still a third (41). A similar picture can be seen with norepinephrine (11, 47). Perhaps, the neurochemical heterogeneity and relatively imprecise boundaries of the hypothalamus may be responsible for these discrepancies. For instance, increases in serotonin were reported in lateral hypothalamus (40), while contrary reports involved the whole hypothalamus (41, 52).

Surprisingly, there have been very few positive findings in the amygdala. Increased dopamine in the left amygdala of schizophrenic patients is certainly one of the more intriguing ones (53). Unfortunately, a study of the central nucleus of the amygdala, the major locus of dopamine in the amygdala does not confirm this (54).

TABLE 4 *Nucleus accumbens catecholamines and metabolites in schizophrenia*

	DA	HVA	DOPAC	NE	MHPG
Bird et al., 1977 (43) and 1979 (48)	↑			NC	
Farley et al., 1977 (44) and 1978 (47)	NC	NC		↑	
Crow et al., 1979 (35)	NC	NC	NC	NC	
Bacopoulos et al., 1979 (46)		NC			
Kleinman et al., 1982 (11)	NC	NC	NC	↑	↑
Toru et al., 1982 (45)	NC	NC	NC		

NC = no change; ↑ = increased; DA = dopamine; HVA = homovanillic acid; DOPAC = dihydroxyphenylacetic acid; NE = norepinephrine; MHPG = 3-methoxy-4-hydroxyphenylglycol.

Regardless, there does not appear to be any increase in dopaminergic activity in the amygdala as determined by measurements of dopamine metabolites (53).

A second positive study of the amygdala involves decreases in two neuropeptides, cholecystokinin and somatostatin, in negative symptom schizophrenic patients (55). These changes were also seen in the hippocampus (55). A study that failed to replicate findings with cholecystokinin examined younger patients with fewer negative symptoms (56). Similar problems may account for the failure to replicate decreases in amygdala somatostatin (57). Other studies have yet to look at hippocampal somatostatin. Finally, decreased cholecystokinin binding in the hippocampus has been recently reported (58).

Before leaving the limbic system, several other intriguing neurochemical findings in schizophrenia need to be mentioned. These include the following: (1) increased dopamine in the anterior perforated substance (43, 48); (2) increased norepinephrine in the ventral septum, mammillary bodies and the bed nucleus of the stria terminalis (47); and (3) increased serotonin in the medial olfactory area (40). As yet, no attempt has been made to replicate these findings.

The cerebral cortex

Few would question the statement that the development of the cerebral cortex distinguishes the human brain from other mammals. Coupling this notion with the observation that schizophrenia may be a peculiarly human condition, it is tempting to implicate the cerebral cortex in the schizophrenic syndrome. This idea has received considerable support from studies of schizophrenic patients using computerized electroencephalograms, positron emission tomography, cerebral blood flow and computerized tomographic scans reviewed in other chapters in this book. Surprisingly little support comes from postmortem neurochemical studies of schizophrenic brains.

Four recent findings in cerebral cortex of schizophrenic patients are relevant. These include the following: (1) decreased cholecystokinin and somatostatin in temporal cortex (55); (2) decreased cholecystokinin binding in frontal cortex (58); (3) increased neurotensin concentrations in frontal cortex (Brodmann area 32) (57); and (4) increased kainic acid binding in prefrontal cortex (Brodmann areas 8, 9, 10 and 46) (59). Only one of these findings has been tested for reproducibility. In the hands of another group (56), cholecystokinin appears to be normal in temporal cortex

TABLE 5 *Positive findings in cerebral cortex*

Ferrier et al., 1983 (55)	↓ Cholecystokinin and somatostatin in temporal cortex
Farmery et al., 1985 (88)	↓ Cholecystokinin binding in frontal cortex
Nemeroff et al., 1983 (57)	↑ Neurotensin in frontal cortex
Nishikawa et al., 1983 (59)	↑ Kainic acid binding in prefrontal cortex

↑ = increased; ↓ = decreased.

although it is very unlikely that both studies are examining the same portion of temporal cortex. Other cortex studies have looked at indoleamines and metabolites (41, 52), LSD receptors (60, 61), amino acids (62), homovanillic acid (46), gamma-aminobutyric acid receptors (60) and glutamic acid dehydrogenase (60). These have been negative.

Caution in interpreting the significance of these findings is warranted for at least two reasons. In the first place, none of these studies has been replicated. In the second place, a neuroleptic effect cannot be excluded at this time. Nevertheless, each of these findings has one common factor. Cholecystokinin, neurotensin and kainic acid binding (presumably a measure of glutamate binding) have each been hypothesized to interact with dopaminergic neurons. This, in turn, potentially implicates each of these findings with one of the major neurochemical theories of the schizophrenic syndrome, the dopamine hypothesis.

Reviews of the postmortem neurochemistry of the basal ganglia and limbic system lend some support to the notions of increased dopaminergic and/or noradrenergic activity in schizophrenic brains. In the case of the basal ganglia, there are several known innervations which include amygdala, thalamus, substantia nigra and cerebral cortex. Moreover, lesions in prefrontal cortex in rats lead to increases in dopamine as well as dopamine receptors in corpus striatum (63). Findings of changes in cortex in schizophrenic brains may then be worth pursuing not just on their own merit, but in relationship to changes in the basal ganglia and limbic system.

The brainstem

A major input to the basal ganglia comes from the substantia nigra. Similarly, input to the limbic system come from the ventral tegmentum, the locus ceruleus and the raphe neurons. Few neurochemical studies of schizophrenic brains have attempted to examine these structures. Still fewer positive findings have emerged from these efforts.

Positive findings from studies of brainstem structures include decreased serotonin in the medulla and mesencephalon (52) and increased norepinephrine in the pons (64) of schizophrenic patients. Neither has been replicated, nor have neuroleptic effects been ruled out.

Other brain regions

Although there have been no consistent positive findings in other brain regions, structures such as thalamus and cerebellum give inputs to the basal ganglia and the limbic system as well as to the brainstem and deserve further study. Initial reports of decreased gamma-aminobutyric acid in thalamus (51) were not confirmed (49) although both groups found normal glutamic acid dehydrogenase activity (49, 51). Recently, there was a report of increased somatostatin concentrations in the lateral thalamus of schizophrenic subjects (35).

Conclusion

This review of the postmortem neurochemistry of schizophrenia should make it abundantly clear that the bulk of positive findings are in the basal ganglia and the limbic system. Perhaps, this is because researchers have concentrated on these structures. In the case of the limbic system this is not surprising, since its hypothesized functions relate to emotions and behavior. This is not, however, the major function of the basal ganglia which are usually thought to be involved with motor behavior. However, the basal ganglia are easily identified and relatively easy to dissect, factors which could predispose investigators to study them. Nevertheless, there is the very real possibility that some of the psychopathology of the schizophrenic syndrome may be related to the basal ganglia and the limbic system.

Should schizophrenia prove to be related to basal ganglia – limbic neurochemical abnormalities, then one obvious question is are the inputs to or outputs from these systems malfunctioning? Structures such as the frontal cortex, thalamus, substantia nigra, ventral tegmentum, locus ceruleus, raphe neurons and anterior vermis of the cerebellum appear to be worthy of further postmortem neurochemical studies, if not for their own sake, then for their potential effects on the basal ganglia and the limbic system. Hopefully, research in this direction will lead to a better understanding and new treatments of the schizophrenic syndrome.

REFERENCES

1. Spokes EGS (1980) Neurochemical alterations in Huntington's chorea: A study of postmortem human tissue. *Brain, 103,* 179.
2. Perry EK, Perry RH (1983) Human brain neurochemistry: Some post-mortem problems. *Life Sci., 3,* 1733.
3. Rossor M (1984) Biological markers in mental disorders: post-mortem studies. *J. Psychiatr. Res., 18,* 457.
4. Bracha HS, Kleinman JE (1984) Postmortem studies in psychiatry. *Psychiatr. Clin. N. Am., 7,* 473.
5. Carpenter MB (1978) Corpus striatum and related nuclei. In: Carpenter MB (Ed), *Core Text of Neuroanatomy,* Ch 11, pp. 236 – 257. Williams and Wilkins, Baltimore – London.
6. Heimer L (1983) Basal ganglia in the human brain and spinal cord. In: Heimer L (Ed.), *Functional Neuroanatomy and Dissection Guide,* pp. 199 – 210. Springer-Verlag, New York.
7. Lee T, Seeman P, Tourtelotte WW, Hornykiewicz O (1978) Binding of ^{3}H-neuroleptics and ^{3}H-apomorphine in schizophrenic brains. *Nature (London), 274,* 897.
8. Owen F, Cross AJ, Crow TJ, Longden A, Poulter M, Riley GJ (1978) Increased dopamine-receptor sensitivity in schizophrenia. *Lancet, 2,* 223.
9. Lee T, Seeman P (1980) Elevation of brain neuroleptic/dopamine receptors in schizophrenia. *Am. J. Psychiatry, 137,* 191.
10. Reisine TD, Rossor M, Spokes E, Iversen LL, Yamamura HI (1980) Opiate and neuroleptic receptor alterations in human schizophrenic brain tissue. In: Pepeu G,

Kuhar MJ, Enna SJ (Eds), *Receptors for Neurotransmitters and Peptide Hormones,* pp. 443 – 450. Raven Press, New York.

11. Kleinman JE, Karoum F, Rosenblatt JE, Gillin JC, Hong J, Bridge TP, Zalcman S, Del Carmen R, Wyatt RJ (1982) Postmortem neurochemical studies in chronic schizophrenia. In: Usdin E, Hanin I (Eds), *Biological Markers in Psychiatry and Neurology,* pp. 67 – 76. Pergamon Press, Oxford – New York.

12. Seeman P, Ulpian C, Bergeron C, Riederer P, Jellinger K, Gabriel E, Reynolds GP, Tourtelotte WW (1984) Bimodal distribution of dopamine receptor densities in brains of schizophrenics. *Science, 225,* 728.

13. Mackay AVP, Bird O, Bird ED, Spokes EG, Rossor M, Iversen LL, Creese I, Snyder SH (1980) Dopamine receptors and schizophrenia: drug effect or illness? *Lancet, 2,* 915.

14. Reynolds GP, Reynolds LM, Riederer P, Jellinger K, Gabriel E (1980) Dopamine receptors and schizophrenia: drug effect or illness? *Lancet, 2,* 1251.

15. Creese I, Burt DR, Snyder S (1976) Dopamine receptor binding predicts clinical and pharmacological potencies of antischizophrenic drugs. *Science, 192,* 481.

16. Crow TJ, Johnstone EC, Owen F (1979) Research on schizophrenia. In: Granville-Grossman K (Ed), *Recent Advances in Clinical Psychiatry,* pp. 1 – 36. Churchill-Livingstone, London.

17. Carenzi A, Gill JC, Guidotti A, Schwartz MA, Trabucchi M, Wyatt RJ (1975) Dopamine sensitive adenylyl cyclase in human caudate nucleus – a study in control subjects and schizophrenic patients. *Arch. Gen. Psychiatry, 32,* 1056.

18. Memo M, Kleinman JE, Hanbauer (1983) I. Coupling of dopamine D1 recognition sites with adenylate cyclase in nuclei accumbens and caudatus of schizophrenics. *Science, 221,* 1304.

19. Owen F, Cross AJ, Crow TJ, Lofthouse R, Poulter M (1981) Neurotransmitter receptors in brain in schizophrenia. *Acta Psychiatr. Scand., 63, Suppl. 291,* 20.

20. Owen F, Bourne RC, Poulter M, Crow TJ, Paterson SJ, Kosterlitz WW (1985) Tritiated etorphine and naloxone binding to opioid receptors in caudate nucleus in schizophrenia. *Br. J. Psychiatry, 146,* 507.

21. Birkhauser H (1941) Cholinesterase und Mono-aminoxydase im zentralen Nervensystem. *Schweiz. Med. Wochenschr., 71,* 750.

22. Utena H, Kanamura H, Suda S, Nakamura R, Machiyama Y, Takahashi R (1968) Studies on the regional distribution of the monoamine oxidase activity in the brains of schizophrenic patients. *Proc. Jpn. Acad., 44,* 1078.

23. Vogel WH, Orfei V, Century B (1969) Activities of enzymes involved in the formation and destruction of biogenic amines and in various areas of human brains. *J. Pharmacol. Exp. Ther., 165,* 195.

24. Domino EF, Krause RR, Bowers J (1973) Various enzymes involved with putative neurotransmitters. *Arch. Gen. Psychiatry, 29,* 195.

25. Wise CD, Stein L (1973) Dopamine-B-hydroxylase deficits in the brains of schizophrenic patiens. *Science, 181,* 344.

26. Nies A, Robinson DS, Harris LS, Lamborn KR (1974) Comparison of monoamine oxidase substrate activities in twins, schizophrenics, depressives and controls. In: Usdin E (Ed), *Neuropsychopharmacology of Monoamines and Their Regulatory Enzymes,* pp. 59 – 70. Raven Press, New York.

27. Schwartz MA, Aikens AM, Wyatt RJ (1974) Monoamine oxidase activity in brains from schizophrenic and mentally normal individuals. *Psychopharmacologia (Berlin), 38,* 319.

28. Schwartz MA, Wyatt RJ, Yang H-YT, Neff NH (1974) Multiple forms of brain

357

monoamine oxidase in schizophrenic and normal individuals. *Arch. Gen. Psychiatry,* *31,* 557.

29. Wise CD, Baden MH, Stein L (1974) Postmortem measurements of enzymes in human brain: evidence of a central noradrenergic deficit in schizophrenia. *J. Psychiatr. Res.,* *11,* 185.

30. Wise CD, Stein L (1975) Dopamine-B-hydroxylase activity in brains of chronic schizophrenic patients. *Science, 187,* 370.

31. Wyatt RJ, Schwartz MA, Erdelyi E, Barchas JD (1975) Dopamine-B-hydroxylase activity in brains of chronic schizophrenic patients. *Science, 187,* 368.

32. McGeer PL, McGeer EG (1977) Possible changes in striatal and limbic cholinergic systems in schizophrenia. *Arch. Gen. Psychiatry, 34,* 1319.

33. Cross J, Crow TJ, Killpack WS, Longden A, Owen F, Riley GJ (1978) The activities of brain dopamine-B-hydroxylase and catechol-O-methyltransferase in schizophrenics and controls. *Psychopharmacology (Berlin), 59,* 117.

34. Wyatt RJ, Erdelyi W, Schwartz M, Herman M, Barchas JD (1978) Difficulties in comparing catecholamine-related enzymes from the brains of schizophrenics and controls. *Biol. Psychiatry, 13,* 317.

35. Crow TJ, Baker HF, Cross AJ, Joseph MH, Lofthouse R, Longden A, Owen F, Riley GJ, Glover V, Killpack WS (1979) Monoamine mechanisms in chronic schizophrenia: Postmortem neurochemical findings. *Br. J. Psychiatry, 132,* 249.

36. Eckert B, Gottfries CG, von Knorring L, Oreland L, Wiberg A, Winblad B (1980) Brain and platelet monoamine oxidase in schizophrenics and cycloid psychotics. *Progr. Neuropsychopharmacol., 4,* 57.

37. Fowler CJ, Carlsson A, Winblad A (1981) Monoamine oxidase-A and -B activities in the brain stem of schizophrenics and non-schizophrenic psychotics. *J. Neural Transm., 52,* 23.

38. Reveley MA, Glover V, Sandler M, Spokes EG (1981) Brain monoamine oxidase activity in schizophrenics and controls. *Arch. Gen. Psychiatry, 38,* 663.

39. Joseph MH, Baker HF, Crow TJ, Riley GJ, Risby D (1979) Brain tryptophan metabolism in schizophrenia: a postmortem study of metabolites on the serotonin and kynurenine pathways in schizophrenic and control subjects. *Psychopharmacology, 62,* 279.

40. Farley IJ, Shannak KS, Hornykiewicz O (1980) Brain monoamine changes in chronic paranoid schizophrenia and their possible relation to increased dopamine receptor sensitivity. In Pepeu G, Kuhar MJ, Enna SJ (Eds), *Receptors for Neurotransmitters and Peptide Hormones,* pp. 427 – 433. Raven Press, New York.

41. Korpi ER, Kleinman JE, Goodman SI, Phillips I, Delisi LE, Linnoila M, Wyatt RJ (1986) Serotonin and 5-hydroxyindoleacetic acid concentrations in different brain regions of suicide victims: comparison in chronic schizophrenic patients with suicides as cause of death. *Arch. Gen. Psychiatry* (in press).

42. Kleinman JE, Hong J, Iadarola M, Govoni S, Gillin JC (1985) Neuropeptides in human brains – postmortem studies. *Progr. Neuro-Psychopharmacol., 9,* 91.

43. Bird EO, Spokes EG, Barnes J, Mackay AV, Iversen LL, Shepherd M (1977) Increased brain dopamine and reduced glutamic acid decarboxylase and choline acetyltransferase activity in schizophrenia and related psychoses. *Lancet, 2,* 1157.

44. Farley IJ, Price KS, Hornykiewicz O (1977) Dopamine in the limbic regions of the human brain: normal and abnormal. *Adv. Biochem. Psychopharmacol., 16,* 57.

45. Toru M, Nishikawa T, Matag N (1982) Dopamine metabolism increases in post-mortem schizophrenic basal ganglia. *J. Neural Transm., 54,* 181.

46. Bacopolous NC, Spokes EG, Bird EO, Roth RH (1979) Antipsychotic drug action in schizophrenic patients: effects on cortical dopamine metabolism after long-term treatment. *Science, 205,* 1405.
47. Farley IJ, Price KS, McCullough E, Deck JHN, Hordynski O, Hornykiewictz O (1978) Norepinephrine in chronic paranoid schizophrenia: above-normal levels in limbic forebrain. *Science, 200,* 456.
48. Bird EO, Spokes EG, Iversen LL (1979) Brain norepinephrine and dopamine in schizophrenia. *Science, 204,* 93.
49. Cross AJ, Crow TJ, Owen F (1979) Gamma-aminobutyric acid in the brain in schizophrenia. *Lancet, 1,* 560.
50. Iversen LL, Bird EO, Spokes EG, Nicholson SH, Suckling DJ (1979) Agonist specificity of GABA binding sites in human brain and GABA in Huntington's disease and schizophrenia. In: Krogsgaard-Larsen P, Scheel-Kruger J, Kofod H (Eds), *GABA-Neurotransmitters: Pharmacochemical, Biochemical and Pharmacological Aspects,* pp. 177 – 190. Academic Press, New York.
51. Perry TL, Kish SJ, Buchanan J, Hansen S (1979) Gamma aminobutyric-acid deficiency in brain of schizophrenic patients. *Lancet, 1,* 237.
52. Winbald B, Bucht G, Gottfries CG, Roos BE (1979) Monoamines and monoamine metabolites in brains from demented schizophrenics. *Acta Psychiatr. Scand., 60,* 17.
53. Reynolds G (1983) Increased concentrations and lateral asymmetries of amygdala dopamine in schizophrenia. *Nature (London), 306,* 527.
54. Bird EO, Spokes EG, Iversen LL (1979) Increased dopamine concentration in limbic areas of brain from patients dying with schizophrenia. *Brain, 102,* 347.
55. Ferrier IN, Roberts GW, Crow TJ, Johnstone EC, Owens BG, Lee YC, O'Shaughnessy D, Adrian TE, Polak JM, Bloom SR (1983) Reduced cholecystokinin-like and somatostatin-like immunoreactivity in limbic lobe is associated with negative symptoms in schizophrenia. *Life Sci., 33,* 475.
56. Kleinman JE, Iadarola M, Govoni S, Hong J, Gillin JC, Wyatt RJ (1983) Postmortem measurements of neuropeptides in human brain. *Psychopharmacol. Bull., 19,* 375.
57. Nemeroff CB, Youngblood WW, Manberg PJ, Prange AJ, Jr, Kizer JS (1983) Regional brain concentrations of neuropeptides in Huntington's chorea and schizophrenia. *Science, 221,* 972.
58. Farmery SM, Owen F, Poulter M, Crow TJ (1985) Reduced high affinity cholecystokinin binding in hippocampus and frontal cortex of schizophrenia patients. *Life Sci., 36,* 472.
59. Nishikawa T, Takashima M, Toru M (1983) Increased [3H] kainic acid binding in the prefrontal cortex in schizophrenia. *Neurosci. Lett., 40,* 245.
60. Bennett JP, Enna SJ, Bylund DB, Gillin JC, Wyatt RJ, Snyder SH (1979) Neurotransmitter receptors in frontal cortex of schizophrenics. *Arch. Gen. Psychiatry, 36,* 927.
61. Whitaker PM, Crow TJ, Ferrier IN (1981) Tritiated LSD binding in frontal cortex in schizophrenia. *Arch. Gen. Psychiatry, 38,* 278.
62. Perry T, Hansen S (1985) Interconversion of serine and glycine is normal in psychiatric patients. *Psychiatry Res., 15,* 109.
63. Pycock CJ, Kerwin RW, Carter RJ (1980) Effect of lesion of cortical dopamine terminals on subcortical dopamine receptors in rats. *Nature (London), 286,* 74.
64. Carlsson A (1980) The impact of catecholamine research in medical science and practice. In: Usdin E, Kopin I, Barchas JD (Eds), *Catecholamines: Basic and Clinical Frontiers, Vol 1,* pp. 4 – 19. Pergamon Press, New York.

CHAPTER 16

Schizophrenia and neuroviruses

E. FULLER TORREY AND CHARLES A. KAUFMANN

The idea that schizophrenia might be an infectious disease was noted as early as 1845 by Jean Esquirol: 'Many authors assure us that mental alienation is epidemic. It is certain that there are years when, independently of moral causes, insanity seems suddenly to extend to a great number of individuals' (1). Increased interest in this theory followed the pandemic of influenza and the subsequent outbreak of Von Economo's encephalitis in the early years of this century when many postencephalitic patients presented with schizophrenia-like symptoms. Karl Menninger typified such thinking in 1922 when he wrote: 'I am persuaded that dementia praecox (schizophrenia) is at least in most instances a somato-psychosis, the psychic manifestations of an encephalitis' (2).

In the past ten years infectious agents have come under increasing scrutiny as possible etiological agents in many chronic diseases, both those of the brain (e.g. multiple sclerosis, Alzheimer's disease, Parkinson's disease) as well as those of other organs (e.g. rheumatoid arthritis, Type I diabetes, some cancers). Most research attention has been directed toward viruses and viral-like agents (e.g. 'slow' viruses, prions) but diseases caused by bacteria (e.g. legionnaires' disease, Lyme arthritis, cat scratch disease) and fungi (e.g. Balkan nephropathy) continue to come to light as well.

Adult-onset schizophrenia appears to be a brain disease whose etiology is widely assumed to be multifactorial. Recent research has focused most sharply on genetic aspects of the disease and on possible abnormalities in brain neurotransmitters such as dopamine. It is known that infectious agents may be vertically transmitted on genes, and that there is a genetic susceptibility to many infectious diseases. It is also known that infectious agents may alter dopamine turnover in the brains of laboratory animals (3). Thus, neither the genetic nor the dopamine hypotheses of schizophrenia's etiology are incompatible with infectious theories.

This chapter will examine evidence that some cases of schizophrenia may have an infectious etiology. It will review clinical and epidemiological studies suggesting (a) *perinatal transmission* and (b) *adult transmission*, and summarize (c) *laboratory findings bearing on this hypothesis*. Viruses remain the infectious agents of greatest interest because of their frequent neurotropism, their ability to remain latent in brain tissue for many years, their propensity to relapse and remit, and ability to alter enzymatic processes in brain cells without causing visible structural damage (4).

Handbook of Schizophrenia, Vol. 1: The Neurology of Schizophrenia.
H.A. Nasrallah and D.R. Weinberger, editors.
© Elsevier Science Publishers B.V., 1986.

Perinatal transmission

It is well known that some viruses are neurotropic and can affect the central nervous system of the developing fetus. A variety of clinical and epidemiological observations of schizophrenia suggest that an environmental agent may affect the brains of some persons who later develop this disease; viruses are attractive candidates for that role. The clinical and epidemiological observations include the following:

Physical anomalies

Physical anomalies may arise from damage to the growing fetus. A recent study showed significantly more minor physical anomalies in 40 adult patients with schizophrenia compared with normal controls (5). Patients with schizophrenia with higher anomaly scores also had had poorer premorbid adjustments. Minor physical anomalies include such things as low-set ears, hypertelorism (greater distance between eyes), and a single transverse palmar crease, and are thought to originate in the first trimester of pregnancy. Higher scores have been reported previously in patients with epilepsy, mental retardation, learning disabilities, autism, and childhood schizophrenia and are thought to be due to genetic abnormalities, dietary deficiencies, anoxia, or infections. A criticism of this study of adult schizophrenics is its use of previously published normative data rather than a specific control group; the study needs to be replicated with such a control group.

Dermatoglyphics

Like physical anomalies, alterations in dermatoglyphics may arise from insults to the fetus in utero. At least since 1935 studies have been done on the epidermal ridge patterns of fingers, palms, and soles in patients with schizophrenia. Thirteen such studies have been reported since 1962. Of these, one found no dermatoglyphic abnormalities (6) while 11 reported statistically significant deviations (7–17). The positive studies included over 4,000 schizophrenic patients, and were done in Denmark, Sweden, Germany, Italy, Spain, England, Australia, India, Chile, Mexico, and the United States. The abnormalities described are not consistent from study to study, and thus there is no typical schizophrenic dermatoglyphic picture. There are many methodological shortcomings to these studies, especially in the selection of controls.

Dermatoglyphic patterns were at one time thought to be exclusively genetically determined. More recently it has been found that in utero viral infections (e.g. rubella, cytomegalovirus, polio) during the first six months of pregnancy may also alter them, and dermatoglyphics has been proposed 'as a useful marker of a deleterious intra-uterine experience' (18). Rubella infection has been studied extensively, and like schizophrenia it produces a 'marked variability of dermatoglyphics and the failure to find a pathognomonic alteration' (18). Several other diseases have been reported as having altered dermatoglyphics including congenital diseases,

Down's syndrome, phenylketonuria, Huntington's disease, Wilson's disease, mitral valve prolapse, myasthenia gravis, psoriasis, neurofibromatosis, epilepsy, and childhood schizophrenia. Further research on the dermatoglyphics of schizophrenia is indicated; computerized readings are now available which will improve methodology and allow correlation with other measures that might reflect early developmental insult, such as premorbid asociality and brain atrophy on CT scans.

Pregnancy and birth complications

Four studies have been carried out on the occurrence of pregnancy and birth complications (PBCs) in persons who later develop schizophrenia. An American study utilized retrospective histories from the mothers plus birth records and compared the patients with schizophrenia with normal sibling controls; the study found significantly more complications with pregnancy and birth among the patients with schizophrenia (19). Two Scandinavian studies used midwife and hospital records exclusively and blindly rated the PBCs in patients with schizophrenia and matched controls; one reported significantly more PBCs among patients with schizophrenia (20) and the other found both significantly more PBCs and more severe PBCs among the patients with schizophrenia (21). Finally a prospective study rated PBCs on high-risk children born to mothers with schizophrenia; 12 children who developed schizophrenia had more PBCs than 39 who did not, but the difference did not achieve statistical significance (22). The general direction of these studies is consistent with observations in twin studies of schizophrenia that the affected twin has more PBCs; twin studies are unsatisfactory for studying PBCs, however, since twin births themselves are PBCs.

Increased PBCs are found in persons with a variety of central nervous system conditions, including epilepsy, mental retardation, autism, childhood schizophrenia, and in hospitalized psychiatric patients with personality disorders. The causes of PBCs are thought to include genetics, nutritional status, and trauma; Mednick has speculated that PBCs may lead to schizophrenia by producing hypoxia of the hippocampus (23). Infectious agents are also widely suspected of causing PBCs, as 3 percent of normal newborns are known to have active (usually occult) infections. Psychosocial explanations must also be considered; Shields and Gottesman postulated that parents treat children who have experienced PBCs differently (24).

Seasonality of birth

Many infectious agents have a seasonal occurrence; if such agents affect the fetus transplacentally or the newborn child directly and produce changes leading to disease many years later, then one might find a seasonality in the birth pattern of individuals with the disease. It has been consistently observed that persons who develop schizophrenia as adults are born disproportionately more often during the late winter and spring months. Methodologically adequate studies have shown this to be true in every northern hemisphere country which has been studied, including

363

England and Wales (25, 26), Ireland (27), Denmark (28), Norway (29), Sweden (30), the United States (31 – 33), Japan (34), and the Philippines (35). The excess of births which develop schizophrenia ranges between 5 and 15%. Studies have also been carried out in southern hemisphere countries such as South Africa, Australia, and New Zealand where the seasons are reversed. Although the results are less conclusive, the general direction of findings indicate an excess number of births which develop schizophrenia during their winter and spring months (30, 36 – 38). Especially noteworthy was a study in Western Australia in which the seasonal excess of births which developed schizophrenia was 102% for males and 89% for females (39).

Studies in Japan, the United States, England and Wales suggest that the seasonality of births which developed schizophrenia is not a fixed phenomenon, but may shift over time (40 – 42). The seasonality may also differ for different parts of a country; e.g. northern states in the U.S. show it much more prominently than southern states, and in June the northern part of Sweden has a 17% excess of births which develop schizophrenia, which is not seen in the southern part of the country (30, 31).

Other aspects of the seasonality question have yielded less consistent results. Studies in Sweden (43), Japan (40), and England and Wales (25) indicate that patients with manic-depressive disorders have a seasonality of birth similar to that seen in schizophrenia; a study in Denmark (28) found the opposite. Five studies failed to show any birth seasonality for persons diagnosed with neuroses (30, 39, 42, 44, 45); a sixth reported that inpatients with anxiety neurosis had an excess of spring births (46). Attempts to correlate birth seasonality for schizophrenia with subgroups of patients (male vs. female (30, 32, 36, 39, 42, 47), black vs. white (48), paranoid vs. non-paranoid (30, 31, 49), early vs. late onset (32, 50), brief vs. prolonged hospitalization (30, 32, 33), and family history for schizophrenia present vs. absent (51 – 53)) have also yielded inconsistent results.

Many explanations have been proposed for the birth seasonality of schizophrenia, but current thinking focuses on environmental factors. The possibilities that seasonality is a statistical artifact or merely an accentuation of the seasonality observed for general births have been considered and refuted (32, 54 – 56). Also considered was the possibility that parents who themselves have schizophrenia, or are genetically predisposed to give birth to offspring who will develop schizophrenia, might have an idiosyncratic conception pattern. Four separate studies have looked at this by examining the birth pattern of schizophrenics' siblings; 1 study reported a statistically insignificant trend toward a schizophrenic pattern (57) but 3 studies found no difference from the general population (58 – 60). The net weight of the evidence is against an idiosyncratic conception pattern as an explanation.

Environmental factors which have been proposed to explain the birth seasonality of schizophrenia include infectious agents, nutritional factors, temperature variations, environmental contaminants, or some interaction of these factors with genetic predisposition. Infectious agents have received the most attention because of the well-known seasonality of some viral diseases of the central nervous system, e.g. the seasonality of births of children with congenital rubella. Two attempts have been made to look for correlations between the birth seasonality of schizophrenia and infectious agents. In Australia it was noted that the greatest increase in seasonality in male births which developed schizophrenia occurred during 1915 – 1924, a period when Von Economo's disease (with a presumed viral etiology) was at its peak (38). In Minnesota the variations in 5 bacterial (diphtheria, pneumonia, scarlet fever, pertussis, typhoid fever) and 3 viral (influenza, measles, polio) diseases were compared with the seasonal pattern of births between 1915 and 1959 of persons who later developed schizophrenia; the birth seasonality in those who developed schizophrenia was found to be significantly greater 'in the years directly following those marked by high levels of infectious disorders', most marked for diphtheria, pneumonia and influenza (33).

Other environmental factors have received less attention but must still be considered. Proposed nutritional theories include a summer protein deficiency (at the time of conception) or a winter vitamin K deficiency (leading to intracerebral hemorrhages at the time of birth) but neither has been tested. Several studies have attempted to correlate the birth seasonality of persons who developed schizophrenia with temperature at the time of conception (33, 61 – 64) or at the time of birth (33, 41, 61, 63) but the results have been contradictory. Environmental contaminants such as lead poisoning have a known summer peak and must also be considered. Finally any one of these factors might interact with genetic predisposition, e. g. some researchers have proposed that the genotype predisposing to schizophrenia might confer increased robustness and resistance to infection on the developing fetus leading to increased survival for those born in the winter and spring months.

Adult transmission

In recent years a few researchers have suggested that schizophrenia may be transmitted among adults, and that an infectious agent would be the most likely explanation for this if it occurs. The studies bearing on this include the following:

Adult case clusters

Although anecdotal reports of schizophrenia case clusters are occasionally encountered among clinicians who work with these patients, there is only one such report in the literature. Kazanetz, working in Moscow apartment blocks between 1952 and 1977, analyzed all new cases of schizophrenia and showed that they had statistically more contact with preexisting cases than chance would predict (65). He concluded that 'these contacts play their part in transmitting an infectious agent from persons with schizophrenia to healthy people, the said agent causing new secondary cases of the disease.' The work can be criticized methodologically on many grounds, especially for failing to rule out a 'social drift' phenomenon whereby people developing schizophrenia tend to drift to like-minded individuals. It needs to be replicated but should serve as an impetus for further studies in this area.

Twins studies

Crow in England had reanalyzed previously published studies in which one or both twins develop schizophrenia, and initially claimed that these studies suggest adult transmission of an infectious agent (66). Twin pairs (and sibling pairs) in which both are of the same sex are said to have a higher concordance for the disease than pairs in which they are opposite sexed, suggesting that 'what matters is physical proximity' (e.g. sharing a bedroom). Similarly he reasons that dizygotic twin and full siblings share the same set of genes, yet dizygotic twins have a higher concordance rate for schizophrenia than do siblings; this also suggests physical proximity in transmission. Finally, he analyzes 57 monozygotic twin pairs and shows that onset of illness in the second twin, once the first twin had developed schizophrenia, occurred more rapidly if the twins were living together than apart. Crow concluded: 'The findings suggest either that both twins are exposed to a pathogenic agent at the same time, or that such an agent is passed from one twin to the other.' Others have disputed these conclusions, claiming that the twin studies are flawed methodologically and that the proximate onset of schizophrenia in monozygotic twins living together might be due to their having a more severe form of the illness (as manifested by more schizoid traits) or due to the stress of living closely with a twin who has developed the disease (67). More recently, Crow himself has been more skeptical of the findings and called for further studies to settle the issue.

Seasonality of hospitalization

Since many infectious diseases have a seasonality of occurrence, those which produce disease immediately (i.e. without a lag period) may also exhibit a seasonality of hospitalization for the disease. Esquirol noted a summer peak in psychiatric admissions and readmissions to the Salpetrière as early as 1806 – 1814 (1); later studies in Zürich (1900 – 1920) and in Wisconsin (1923 – 1932) claimed that the summer admission peak was for patients with schizophrenia only (68). In recent years studies have been done in Japan (68), Germany (69), England and Wales (70), and Canada (71); the first 3 found a statistically significant excess of admissions and readmissions for schizophrenia in the summer months and in the fourth study it was in the spring. Two of the studies also showed that manic depressive (bipolar) disorder had an even greater summer seasonal admission and readmission pattern than schizophrenia; the other 2 showed seasonal patterns of admission and readmission for various depressive syndromes ('endogenous depression', 'neurotic depression', 'periodic depression', 'depression of involution'). In these studies, patients with diagnoses of neuroses (other than depression) and personality disorders showed no seasonal pattern of admission and readmission.

Despite methodological problems with these studies (e.g. comparability of diagnoses), the uniformity in findings is impressive. Possible explanations for this seasonal pattern include the same environmental factors discussed under seasonality of birth: infectious agents, nutritional factors, temperature variations, or environmental contaminants. Viruses in particular could account for it by seasonality of primary infection or reactivation of infection such as found in herpes simplex 1 (HSV-1) infections. Non-environmental explanations such as seasonal availability of hospital beds or tolerance of deviant behavior should also be considered in future research efforts.

Laboratory evidence

A variety of laboratory abnormalities in schizophrenia provide indirect support for an infectious or inflammatory etiology. These include neuropathological and immunological (both humoral and cell-mediated) changes. More direct evidence of viral infection, such as virus isolation and detection of viral antigen or genome are currently under investigation.

Neuropathological

There have been more than 30 ante-mortem studies of brains of patients with schizophrenia using computed tomography (CT) since 1976. The vast majority of those studies with adequate samples have revealed cerebral abnormalities in a subgroup of approximately one-third of patients. Prevalent abnormalities, including increased lateral and third ventricular size and cortical atrophy, parallel earlier findings using pneumoencephalography (72). These abnormalities are not explained by past treatment, may antedate the onset of illness in late adolescence (appearing in some first-break patients with schizophrenia), and are at least consistent with a chronic inflammatory process. More recent studies measuring radiodensities of periventricular structures (caudate, thalamus, medial temporal lobe) (73) have found enhanced density in patients with chronic schizophrenia consistent with subcortical gliosis. These results are consonant with post-mortem findings of glial nodules in 6 of 7 patients with 'schizophreniform features' (74), diencephalic gliosis in 10 patients with chronic schizophrenia (75), and enhanced periventricular fibrillary gliosis in 25 patients with schizophrenia compared with 28 mentally ill, non-schizophrenic controls (76). Although such gliosis is non-specific and may follow any of several brain insults, it was notably present even in the brain of patients who had not been treated with drugs or ECT. Ventricular enlargement is commonly found in congenital and chronic central nervous system infections, and gliosis frequently accompanies infectious or immunologic disorders.

Immunological

Humoral. Infectious agents are antigens which elicit a humoral immune response. Several researchers have examined serum and CSF from patients with schizophrenia for antibodies to various viruses. Early reports of increased HSV-I antibody in serum have not been replicated (77). More recently, a survey of serum for 8 viruses reported mumps antibody to be significantly low (78). One study found cytomegalovirus (CMV) antibody to be significantly elevated in the CSF of patients with schizophrenia compared to serum (CSF/serum ratio) (79). Another study found an absolute elevation in CSF CMV-IgM antibody (80); this finding was replicated in two other studies (81 – 82) but not in a third (S. Shrikhande, S.R. Hirsch, J.C. Coleman et al., 1984, unpublished). Patients with the presence of CSF CMV-IgM antibody were more likely to have brain atrophy on CT scan (81) and lower levels of CSF homovanillic acid (Kaufmann C.A., unpublished observation) than those without the antibody. The CSF CMV-IgM antibody elevation was also found in patients with bipolar disorder so it is not specific to schizophrenia. The CMV antibody studies controlled for age, length of institutionalization, permeability of the blood-brain-barrier, and neuroleptic medication; the last is especially important to assess since neuroleptics are known to affect the immune system potentially producing antibody changes. The CMV findings in schizophrenia must be interpreted with caution because CMV is a known opportunistic virus which frequently invades secondary to any immune dysfunction. Moreover, it may conceivably be reactivated by a variety of non-specific stimuli, including the stress of psychosis itself. Furthermore, CMV antibody may also be reactivated by non-specific polyclonal B-cell stimulation. A similar mechanism has been invoked to account for the production of HSV-1 antibodies following cerebral infarction (83). Current humoral immunological research in schizophrenia, therefore, may be likened to that in multiple sclerosis wherein a variety of viral and immunological abnormalities have been described but there is no certainty as to what is primary and what is secondary.

Cell-mediated.   Infectious agents also elicit cell-mediated responses which are directed primarily against infected cells. When immune cells become infected such responses may affect their morphology, number, or function. The interpretation of studies in this field is therefore complex as elevations in activity may reflect active infection while depressions in activity may result from infection of lymphoid tissue, in turn enhancing host susceptibility, and/or allowing the virus to persist; moreover neuroleptics may affect the cell-mediated response in a variety of ways.

Alterations in T-lymphocyte morphology, with increased numbers of atypical cells similar to those found in viral mononucleosis, have been described in schizophrenia. Earlier studies speculated that this abnormality was caused by neuroleptics but a recent study reported more atypical lymphocytes in patients drug-free for more than a year (84). Alterations (both increases and decreases) have also been reported in the total number and percentage of T-lymphocytes in patients with schizophrenia (85); these changes may be seen in some drug-naive patients (86) although neuroleptic effects have not been conclusively ruled out. Studies of T-lymphocyte subsets, such as suppressor/cytotoxic cells, have not yielded consistent results (87; Kaufmann et al., unpublished); such subsets are altered in known viral infections (88), and in disorders of presumed viral etiology such as multiple sclerosis.

In terms of lymphocyte activity, patients with schizophrenia have been found to show diminished T-cell transformation to mitogens like phytohemagglutinin, although a drug effect has not been ruled out (89); similar reductions are seen in some viral infections. Diminished activity of the lymphocyte natural killer (NK) cells has also been reported in patients with schizophrenia, and is apparently unrelated to neuroleptics (90); such diminished activity may enhance susceptibility to infection (especially by herpesviruses) and is known to occur in some viral infections. Infected cells may also release interferon, and a recent study found serum interferon to be significantly elevated in 24% of patients with schizophrenia compared with 3% of normal controls; a drug effect was ruled out and in fact the highest interferon level was found in a never treated patient (O.T. Preble and E.F. Torrey, unpublished). Elevated serum interferon has previously been reported in patients with schizophrenia as well as in other psychiatric patients (91). Such elevations have also been found in patients with rheumatoid arthritis, systemic lupus erythematosis, and acquired immunodeficiency syndrome.

Virus isolation and transmission

In one study, CSF from 35% of patients with schizophrenia (versus 13% of patients with general medical conditions) has demonstrated cytopathic effects (CPE) when inoculated into cell cultures of human embryonic fibroblasts (92). Viruses are known to produce similar CPE. This finding is not specific to schizophrenia, however, as CSF from patients with affective disorders produce similar CPE with approximately the same frequency. It is not yet known whether the CPE is due to a toxin or due to replicating virus; the inability to date to pass the CPE from culture to culture, and its persistence in the presence of DNA, RNA, and protein synthesis inhibitors, suggests the former. Attempts to replicate this work in a second laboratory were unsuccessful (D.R. Weinberger and C.A. Kaufmann, unpublished), although CSF from less acutely ill patients was studied.

Efforts have also been made to transmit the putative schizophrenia-causing agent to laboratory animals. CSF known to cause CPE from patients with schizophrenia has been injected intracerebrally into marmosets and produced behavioral alterations such as diminished activity and social withdrawal reminiscent of the deficit symptoms of schizophrenia; injection of CPE-negative CSF had no such effects (93). Other attempts to transmit schizophrenia to laboratory animals via direct intracerebral inoculation of post-mortem brain tissue from patients with schizophrenia have been unsuccessful (C.A. Kaufmann, unpublished observation). It should be noted that while such techniques have proven effective in demonstrating replicating, filterable agents in 'slow virus' disease (kuru, Creutzfeldt-Jakob disease), they have not been useful in demonstrating more conventional viruses in known chronic infections of the CNS (progressive multifocal leukoencephalopathy, subacute sclerosing panencephalitis).

Detection of viral antigen or genome

If replicating virus is present in the brains of patients with schizophrenia, viral antigens might be detected with immunohistochemical probes. If the virus is present in a non-replicating form (chromosomal or extrachromosomal), viral genome might be detected with genome hybridization probes. Preliminary studies along these lines have been carried out. An immunohistochemical study which looked for various herpesviruses (HSV-1, HSV-2, CMV) in specific regions of post-mortem brain from 12 patients with chronic schizophrenia and controls, failed to detect viral antigen (94). Genome hybridization studies on patients with schizophrenia and controls have failed to detect CMV genome in specific limbic system structures in 10 patients in one study (94), in the hippocampi of 6 patients in another study (95), and in the temporal cortex of 32 patients in a third study (96). Other studies are in progress utilizing other areas of the brain and looking for other viruses; more post-mortem brain tissue from acutely ill patients is also needed. Rapidly improving sensitivity of these probes, new techniques combining hybridization with autoradiography, and expanding banks to collect post-mortem brain tissue all suggest that this is the research frontier on which the hypothesis that schizophrenia is an infectious disease will ultimately be tested.

Discussion

Clinical and epidemiological observations of schizophrenia suggest that environmental factors may be etiologically involved in some cases of the disease. Infectious agents, especially viruses, are attractive candidates because of their explanatory power for the disparate data. In addition, laboratory findings in schizophrenia suggest infection and/or immune dysfunction in some patients, although it is not yet possible to determine which of these is primary and which secondary. A subgroup of only 10 – 20% of patients with schizophrenia could theoretically account for the findings reported to date.

If an infectious agent is etiologically involved, it is more likely that it is originally transmitted perinatally rather than in later years. There is less evidence that the theoretical infectious agent is transmitted to adults; even the strongest evidence supporting adult transmission – the seasonality of admission findings – can be explained as a seasonal reactivation of a pre-existing infection. It is also possible that more than one infectious agent is involved synergistically (e.g. the suspected role of retroviruses in some chronic neurological diseases) (97), that there are multiple infectious subgroups, or that an infectious agent interacts with other environmental factors (e.g. nutritional status, temperature) and/or with a genetic predisposition in the individual.

An infectious etiology for a subgroup of patients with schizophrenia is compatible with many other aspects of the disease. It might explain the brain damage measured clinically (e.g. soft neurological signs), radiographically (e.g. ventricular enlargement) and neurophysiologically (EEG and evoked potential abnormalities). As mentioned previously, it is also compatible with biochemical theories of dopamine pathway abnormalities. An infectious etiology might also explain prevalence differences reported for various parts of the world which appear to be at least fifteenfold from low-prevalence to high-prevalence areas (98).

There are, of course, methodological problems with much of the research bearing on infectious theories. Diagnostic comparability has plagued these studies as it has much of schizophrenia research; the widespread utilization of DSM-III diagnostic criteria should make future studies more reliable. In closing, it should be noted that research on an infectious etiology need not be confined to high technology laboratories with state-of-the-art equipment; hospital and birth records can be brought to bear on many unanswered questions.

Summary

Evidence for an infectious etiology of schizophrenia is reviewed. Reports of minor physical anomalies, abnormal dermatoglyphics, frequent complications of pregnancy and birth and seasonality of birth (late winter-early spring predominance) among schizophrenics are consistent with a perinatal viral insult. Epidemiologic evidence for adult transmission (case clusters, twin studies, seasonality of hospitalization) is less conclusive. A variety of laboratory abnormalities (neuropathological, immunological, and biochemical) provide further indirect support for past or present viral infection. Studies seeking direct evidence of viral infection (virus isolation and transmission, detection of viral antigens and genomes) are underway. More research is needed, not only using emerging neurobiological techniques but hospital and birth records as well.

REFERENCES

1. Esquirol JE (1845) *Mental Maladies, a Treatise on Insanity.* Lea and Blanchard, Philadelphia.
2. Menninger KA (1922) Reversible schizophrenia. *Am. J. Psychiatry, 1,* 573.
3. Lycke E, Roos BE (1968) Effect on the monoamine metabolism of the mouse brain by experimental herpes simplex infection. *Experientia, 24,* 687.
4. Johnson RT (1982) *Viral Infections of the Nervous System.* Raven Press, New York.
5. Guy JD, Majorski LV, Wallace CJ, Guy MP (1983) The incidence of minor physical anomalies in adult male schizophrenics. *Schizophr. Bull., 9,* 571.
6. Veliscu C, Scripcaru GH, Pirozynski T, Alexandrescu L (1968) Aspect dermatoglifice in schizofrenie. *Rev. Med.-Chir. Soc. Med. Nat. Din Iasi, 72,* 631.
7. Raphael T, Raphael LG (1962) Fingerprints in schizophrenia. *J. Am. Med. Assoc., 180,* 215.
8. Beckman L, Norring A (1963) Finger and palm prints in schizophrenia. *Acta Genet., 13,* 170.

9. Singh S (1967) Dermatoglyphics in schizophrenia. *Acta Genet., 17,* 348.
10. Mellor CS (1968) Dermatoglyphics in schizophrenia. *Br. J. Psychiatry, 114,* 1387.
11. Rosner F, Steinberg FS (1968) Dermatglyphic patterns of negro men with schizophrenia. *Dis. Nerv. Syst., 29,* 739.
12. Stowens D, Sammon JW, Proctor A (1970) Dermatoglyphics in female schizophrenia. *Psychiatr. Quart., 44,* 516.
13. Zauala C, Nunez C (1970) Dermatoglyphics in schizophrenia. *J. Genet. Hum., 18,* 407.
14. Rothhammer F, Pereira G, Comousseight B, Benado M (1971) Dermatoglyphics in schizophrenic patients. *Hum. Hered., 21,* 198.
15. Polednak AP (1972) Dermatoglyphics of negro schizophrenic males. *Br. J. Psychiatry, 120,* 397.
16. Kemali, Polani N, Polani PE, Amati A (1976) A dermatoglyphic study of 219 Italian schizophrenic males. *Clin. Genet., 9,* 51.
17. Murthy RS, Wig NN (1977) Dermatoglyphics in schizophrenia: the relevance of family history. *Br. J. Psychiatry, 130,* 56.
18. Alter M, Schulenberg R (1966) Dermatoglyphics in the rubella syndrome. *J. Am. Med. Assoc., 197,* 93.
19. Woerner MG, Pollack M, Klein DF (1973) Pregnancy and birth complications in psychiatric patients: a comparison of schizophrenic and personality disorder patients with their siblings. *Acta Psychiatr. Scand., 49,* 712.
20. McNeil TF, Kaij L (1978) Obstetric factors in the development of schizophrenia: complications in the births of preschizophrenics and in reproduction by schizophrenic parents. In: Wynne LC, Cromwell RL, Matthysse S (Eds), *The Nature of Schizophrenia.* John Wiley and Sons, New York.
21. Jacobsen B, Kinney DK (1980) Perinatal complications in adopted and non-adopted schizophrenics and their controls: preliminary results. *Acta Psychiatr. Scand. Suppl., 285.*
22. Parnas J, Schulsinger F, Teasdale T, Schulsinger H, Feldman PM, Mednick SA (1982) Perinatal complications and clinical outcome within the schizophrenia spectrum. *Br. J. Psychiatry, 140,* 416.
23. Mednick SA (1970) Breakdown in individuals at risk for schizophrenia; possible predispositional perinatal factors. *Ment. Hyg., 54,* 50.
24. Shields J, Gottesman II (1977) Obstetric complications and twin studies of schizophrenia: clarifications and affirmations. *Schizophr. Bull., 3,* 351.
25. Hare E, Price J, Slater E (1974) Mental disorder and season of birth. *Br. J. Psychiatry, 124,* 81.
26. Hare E (1975) Season of birth in schizophrenia and neurosis. *Am. J. Psychiatry, 132,* 1168.
27. O'Hare A, Walsh D, Torrey F (1980) Seasonality of schizophrenic births in Ireland. *Br. J. Psychiatry, 137,* 74.
28. Videhech T, Wecke A, Dupont A (1974) Endogenous psychoses and season of birth. *Acta Psychiatr. Scand., 50,* 202.
29. Odegard O (1977) Season of birth in the population of Norway with particular reference to the September birth maximum. *Br. J. Psychiatry, 131,* 339.
30. Dalen P (1975) *Season of Birth – A Study of Schizophrenia and Other Mental Disorders.* Elsevier, Amsterdam.
31. Torrey EF, Torrey BB, Peterson MR (1977) Seasonality of schizophrenic births in the United States. *Arch. Gen. Psychiatry, 34,* 1065.

32. Pulver AE, Stewart W, Carpenter WT, Jacobs L (1983) Risk factors in schizophrenia: season of birth in Maryland, USA. *Br. J. Psychiatry, 143,* 389.
33. Watson CG, Kucala T, Tilleskjor C et al. (1984) Schizophrenic birth seasonality in relation to the incidence of infectious diseases and temperature extremes. *Arch. Gen. Psychiatry, 41,* 85.
34. Shimura M, Nakamura I, Miura T (1977) Season of birth of schizophrenics in Tokyo, Japan. *Acta Psychiatr. Scand., 55,* 225.
35. Parker G, Balza B (1977) Season of birth and schizophrenia − An equatorial study. *Acta Psychiatr. Scand., 56,* 143.
36. Parker G, Neilson M (1976) Mental disorder and season of birth − A southern hemisphere study. *Br. J. Psychiatry, 129,* 355.
37. Parker G (1978) Schizophrenia and season of birth: further southern hemisphere studies. *Aust. N. Z. J. Psychiatry, 12,* 65.
38. Jones IH, Frei D (1979) Seasonal births in schizophrenia. *Acta Psychiatr. Scand., 59,* 164.
39. Syme GJ, Illingworth DJ (1978) Sex differences in birth patterns of schizophrenics. *J. Clin. Psychol., 34,* 633.
40. Shimura M, Miura T (1980) Season of birth in mental disorders in Tokyo, Japan, by year of birth, year of admission and age of admission. *Acta Psychiatr. Scand., 61,* 21.
41. Torrey EF, Torrey BB (1979) A shifting seasonality of schizophrenic births. *Br. J. Psychiatry, 134,* 183.
42. Hare EH (1978) Variations in the seasonal distribution of births of psychotic patients in England and Wales. *Br. J. Psychiatry, 132,* 155.
43. Dalen P (1979) Month of birth and mental disorders. In: Tromp SW, Bouma JJ (Eds), *Biometeorological Survey.* Heyden and Son, London.
44. Greenberg ED (1981) Obsessive-compulsive neurosis and season of birth. *Biol. Psychiatry, 16,* 513.
45. Shimura M (1981) Mental disorder and season of birth − Variation by birth year. *Teikyo Med. J., 4,* 127.
46. Parker G (1978) The season of birth of anxiety neurotics. *Aust. N. Z. J. Psychiatry, 12,* 69.
47. Torrey EF, Torrey BB (1980) Sex differences in the seasonality of schizophrenic births. *Br. J. Psychiatry, 137,* 101.
48. Gallagher BJ, McFalls JA, Jones BJ (1983) Racial factors in birth seasonality among schizophrenics: a preliminary analysis. *J. Abnorm. Psychol., 92,* 524.
49. Nasrallah HA, McCalley-Whitters M (1984) Seasonality of birth in subtypes births of chronic schizophrenia. *Acta Psychiatr. Scand., 69,* 292.
50. Corgiat MD, Regier MW, Templer DI (1983) Seasonality of schizophrenia and age of onset. *J. Orthomol. Psychiatry, 12,* 268.
51. Kinney DK, Jacobsen B (1978) Environmental factors in schizophrenia: new adoption study evidence and its implications for genetic and environmental research. In: Wynne LC, Cromwell RL, Matthysse S (Eds), *The Nature of Schizophrenia.* John Wiley and Sons, New York.
52. Shur E (1982) Season of birth in high and low genetic risk schizophrenics. *Br. J. Psychiatry, 140,* 410.
53. Machon RA, Mednick SA, Schulsinger F (1983) The interaction of seasonality, place of birth, genetic risk and subsequent schizophrenics in a high risk sample. *Br. J. Psychiatry, 143,* 383.

54. Watson CG, Kucala T, Angulski G, Brunn C (1982) Season of birth and schizophrenia: a response to the Lewis and Griffin critique. *J. Abnorm. Psychol., 91,* 120.
55. Shur E, Hare E (1983) Age-prevalence and the season of birth effect in schizophrenia: a response to Lewis and Griffin. *Psychol. Bull., 93,* 373.
56. Torrey EF (1978) Schizophrenic births. *Lancet, 1,* 882.
57. McNeil T, Kaij L, Dzierzykray-Rogalska M (1976) Season of birth among siblings of schizophrenics. *Acta Psychiatr. Scand., 54,* 267.
58. Hare E (1976) The season of birth of siblings of psychiatric patients. *Br. J. Psychiatry, 129,* 49.
59. Buck C, Simpson H (1978) Season of birth among sibs of schizophrenics. *Br. J. Psychiatry, 132,* 358.
60. Larson CA, Nyman GE (1976) Birth month of schizophrenics and their sibs. *IRCS Med. Sci., 4,* 56.
61. Templer DI, Austin RK (1980) Confirmation of relationship between temperature and the conception and birth of schizophrenics. *J. Orthomol. Psychiatry, 9,* 220.
62. Pasamanick B and Knobloch H (1961) Epidemiologic studies on the complications of pregnancy and the birth process. In: Caplan G. (Ed), *Prevention of Mental Disorders in Children.* Basic Books, New York.
63. Hare E, Moran P (1981) A relation between seasonal temperature and the birth rate of schizophrenic patients. *Acta Psychiatr. Scand., 63,* 396.
64. McNeil T, Dalan P, Dzierzykray-Rogalska M, Kaij L (1975) Birthrates of schizophrenics following relatively warm versus relatively cool summers. *Arch. Psychiatr. Nervenkr., 221,* 1.
65. Kazanetz EF (1979) Tecnica per investigare il ruolo di fattori ambientali sulla genesis della schizofrenia. *Rev. Psicol. Anal., 10,* 193.
66. Crow TJ (1983) Is schizophrenia an infectious disease? *Lancet, 1,* 173.
67. Murray RM, Reveley AM (1983) Schizophrenia as an infection. *Lancet, 1,* 583.
68. Abe K (1963) Seasonal fluctuation of psychiatric admissions, based on the data for seven prefectures of Japan for a seven-year-period 1955-1961, with a review of the literature. *Folia Psychiatr. Neurol., 17,* 101.
69. Faust V, Sarreither P (1975) Jahreszeit und psychische Krankheit. *Med. Klin., 70,* 467.
70. Hare EH and Walter SD (1978) Seasonal variation in admissions of psychiatric patients and its relation to seasonal variation in their births. *J. Epidemiol. Comm. Health, 32,* 47.
71. Eastwood MR, Stiasny S (1978) Psychiatric disorder, hospital admission, and season. *Arch. Gen. Psychiatry, 35,* 769.
72. Haug JO (1962) Pneumoencephalographic studies in mental disease. *Acta Psychiatr. Scand., 38 (Suppl. 165),* 1.
73. Dewan MJ, Pandurangi AK, Lee SH, Ramachandran T, Levy B, Boucher M, Yozawitz A, Major LF (1983) Central brain morphology in chronic schizophrenic patients: a controlled CT study. *Biol. Psychiatry, 18,* 1133.
74. Fisman M (1975) The brain stem in psychosis. *Br. J. Psychiatry, 126,* 414.
75. Nieto D, Escobar A (1972) Major psychoses, In: Minckler J (Ed), *Pathology of the Nervous System,* pp. 2654–2665. McGraw Hill, New York.
76. Stevens JR (1982) Neuropathology of schizophrenia. *Arch. Gen. Psychiatry, 39,* 1131.
77. Libikova H, Pogady J, Mucha V (1982) Enveloped viruses and viral immunity in schizophrenia and senile dementia. In: Perris C, Struwe G, Jansson B (Eds), *Biological Psychiatry 1981,* pp. 69–72. Elsevier-North Holland, Amsterdam.

78. King DJ, Cooper SJ, Earle JAP, Martin SJ, McFerran NV, Rima BK, Wisdom GB (1986) A survey of serum antibodies to eight common viruses in psychiatric patients. In press.
79. Albrecht P, Torrey EF, Boone E, Hicks JT, Daniel N (1980) Raised cytomegalovirus antibody level in cerebrospinal fluid of schizophrenic patients. *Lancet, 2,* 769.
80. Torrey EF, Yolken RH, Winfrey CJ (1982) Cytomegalovirus antibody in cerebrospinal fluid in schizophrenic patients detected by enzyme immunoassay. *Science, 216,* 892.
81. Kaufmann CA, Weinberger DR, Yolken RH, Torrey EF, Potkin SG (1983) Viruses and schizophrenia. *Lancet, 2,* 1136.
82. Van Kammen DP, Mann L, Scheinen M, Van Kammen WB, Linnoila M (1984) Spinal fluid monoamine metabolites and anti-cytomegalovirus antibodies and brain scan evaluation in schizophrenia. *Psychopharmacol. Bull., 20,* 519.
83. Rostrom B, Link H, Norrby E (1981) Antibodies in oligoclonal immunoglobulins in CSF from patients with acute cerebrovascular disease. *Acta Neurol. Scand., 64,* 225.
84. Hirata-Hibi M, Higashi S, Tachibana T, Watanabe N (1982) Stimulated lymphocytes in schizophrenia. *Arch. Gen. Psychiatry, 39,* 82.
85. Nyland H, Naess A, Lunde H (1980) Lymphocyte sub-populations in peripheral blood from schizophrenic patients. *Acta Psychiatr. Scand., 16,* 313.
86. Coffey CE, Sullivan JL, Rice JR (1983) T-lymphocytes in schizophrenia. *Biol. Psychiatry, 18,* 113.
87. DeLisi LE, Goodman S, Neckers L, Wyatt RJ (1982) Lymphocyte subpopulations in chronic schizophrenic patients. *Biol. Psychiatry, 17,* 1003.
88. Rinaldo CR, Levin MJ, Carney WP, Black PH, Hirsch MS (1979) Interactions of lymphocytes with cytomegalovirus. In: Proffitt MR (Ed), *Virus Lymphocyte Interactions: Implications for Disease.* Elsevier/North-Holland, Amsterdam.
89. Vartanian ME, Kolyaskina GI, Lozofsky DV, Burbaeva GS, Ignatov SA (1978) Aspects of humoral and cellular immunity in schizophrenia. In: Bergsma D, Goldstein AI (Eds), *Neurochemical and Immunological Components of Schizophrenia,* pp. 339–354. Liss, New York.
90. DeLisi LE, Ortaldo JR, Maluish AE, Wyatt RJ (1983) Deficient natural killer cell (NK) activity and macrophage functioning in schizophrenic patients. *J. Neurol. Transm., 58,* 99.
91. Libikova H, Breier S, Kocisova M, Pogady J, Stunzner D, Ujhazyova D (1979) Assay of interferon and viral antibodies in the cerebrospinal fluid in clinical neurology and psychiatry. *Acta Biol. Med. Ger., 38,* 879.
92. Tyrrell DAJ, Parry RP, Crow TJ, Johnstone E, Ferrier IN (1979) Possible virus in schizophrenia and some neurological disorders. *Lancet, 1,* 839.
93. Baker HF, Ridley RM, Crow TJ, Bloxam CA, Parry RP, Tyrrell DAJ (1983) An investigation of the effects of intracerebral injection in the marmoset of cytopathic cerebrospinal fluid from patients with schizophrenia or neurological disease. *Psychol. Med., 13,* 499.
94. Stevens JR, Langloss JM, Albrecht P, Yolken R, Wang YN (1984) A search for cytomegalovirus and herpes viral antigen in brains of schizophrenic patients. *Arch. Gen. Psychiatry, 41,* 795.
95. Aulakh GS, Kleinman JE, Aulakh HS, Albrecht P, Torrey EF, Wyatt RJ (1981) Search for cytomegalovirus in schizophrenic brain tissue. *Proc. Soc. Exp. Biol. Med., 167,* 172.
96. Taylor GR, Crow TJ, Higgins T, Reynolds G (1985) Search for cytomegalovirus in postmortem brain tissue from patients with Huntington's chorea and other psychiatric

disease by molecular hybridization using cloned DNA. *J. Neuropath. Exp. Neurol., 44,* 176.

97. Viola MV, Frazier M, White L, Brody J, Spiegelman S (1975) RNA-instructed DNA polymerase activity in a cytoplasmic particulate fraction in brains from Guamian patients. *J. Exp. Med., 142,* 483.

98. Torrey EF (1980) *Schizophrenia and Civilization.* Jason Aronson, New York.

CHAPTER 17

Neuroimmunology: clinical studies of schizophrenia and other psychiatric disorders

LYNN ELEANOR DELISI

Credit for the hypothesis that neuropsychiatric disorders are associated with immune system dysfunction belongs to the Russian investigators who have been pursuing research along these lines since the beginning of the twentieth century (1, 2). Experimental evidence, however, paralleled the much later sophistication and development of the field of immunology.

Leukocytosis: Early studies

Nevertheless, increased leukocyte counts were reported in psychotic patients as early as the late 19th century (reviewed by Malis, Ref. 1). In 1903 and 1904 Bruce and Peebles (3, 4) reported that leukocytosis, monocytosis, and elevated temperature were associated with acute psychoses (catatonia and hebephrenia) and then declined with the onset of chronic dementia. Several other studies followed, confirming acute elevations in total leukocyte counts due to increased neutrophils and eosinophils followed by other changes associated with either improvement or chronic dementia (see Table 1). One study of the histological picture of the blood forming elements in the bone marrow of schizophrenics (5) found marked decreases in the maturation of young neutrophils and a general depression of leukocytosis, while another study of the bone marrow (6) focused on abnormal lymphocytes and increased reticular cells. All these studies have been largely ignored in present day literature. While routine blood counts are performed on admissions to most psychiatric hospitals today, no changes, such as those seen in these earlier publications, have been reported to be associated with schizophrenia. When present, leukocytosis in a psychotic patient has been attributed to concurrent infection not related to the psychosis. The earlier findings may have represented the easy spread of infectious diseases in institutional settings and the presence among the psychoses of undiagnosed primary bacterial, parasitic, or viral diseases. One recent publication (7), however, describes increases in circulating neutrophils and decreased numbers of lymphocytes in patients with a major depressive disorder compared with schizophrenics from the same institution. This finding could have resulted from actual abnormalities in percentages of these cells among the schizophrenic patients. The lack of diagnostic specificity of leukocyte differentials is partially the reason why these studies have

---

TABLE 1 *Historical associations of abnormalities in leukocyte differentials in schizophrenia. Note that diagnostic criteria are uncertain and varied from study to study*

Study	Ref.	Findings
1. Macphail (1885)	82	Decreased hematocytes with no change in white/red cell ratios.
2. Bruce and Peebles (1903)	3	In catatonic schizophrenia: increased leukocytes and monocytes (acute stage); decreased leukocytes with decreased neutrophils (chronic stage)
3. Bruce and Peebles (1904)	4	In hebephrenia: initially increased leukocytes, followed by increased neutrophils and eosinophils.
4. Dide (1905)	83	Increased monocytes and decreased neutrophils
5. Lundvall (1907)	84	Leukocytic crises in psychotic excitement
6. Sandri (1907)	85, 86	Increased leukocytes due to increased neutrophils and monocytes
7. Lepine and Popoff (1908)	87	Increased leukocytes. Good prognosis associated with increases in neutrophils, monocytes, eosinophils
8. Ermakov (1910)	88	Only slight increase in leukocytes
9. Graziani (1910)	89	Increased leukocytes in acute stage
10. Krueger (1912)	90	Increased leukocytes in 70% of hebephrenics and in 44% of catatonics.
11. Pfoertner (1912)	91	Decreased leukocytes
12. Schultz (1913)	92	Increased leukocytes due to increased neutrophils. Increased leukocytes, neutrophils and eosinophils = good prognosis Increased lymphocytes = poor prognosis
13. Itten (1914)	93	Increased leukocytes due to neutrophils, acute Increased lymphocytes, chronic Improvement preceded by increased neutrophils and eosinophils
14. Jackson (1914)	94	Increased neutrophils and eosinophils = improvement; decreased = deterioration
15. Zimmermann (1914)	95	Increased leukocytes = improvement
16. Prusenko (1915)	96	Increased leukocytes due to neutrophils and eosinophils in acute psychosis Increased leukocytes due to lymphocytes and basophils, but decreased neutrophils in chronic psychosis Increase in neutrophils and decrease in lymphocytes preceded improvement.
17. Wuth (1922)	97	No changes in the blood of the 37/40 schizophrenics No association of prognosis with blood morphology

TABLE 1   *(Continued)*

Study	Ref.	Findings
18. Granskaya (1927)	98	Decreased leukocytes Increased eosinophils associated with improvement
19. Berger (1927)	99	Toxic changes in cytoplasm and nucleus of neutrophils
20. Zalkind (1929)	100	Marked variation in leukocyte differentials in schizophrenics serially within 24 hours
21. Dameschek (1930)	101	Increased lymphocytes, decreased neutrophils, increased eosinophils
22. Sagel (1930)	102	Increased leukocytes, followed in time by increased monocytes and ultimately increased lymphocytes with recovery Acute cases associated with increased eosinophils; chronic cases showed increased neutrophils, lymphocytes and monocytes
23. Shekhonin (1939)	103	Toxic changes in nucleus and cytoplasm of neutrophils
24. Ederle (1941)	104	Toxic granularity in neutrophils
25. Ferroni (1942)	105	Decreased leukocytes
26. Chistovich (1945)	106	Acute increased leukocytosis, followed by decreased leukocytes and lymphocytosis

(Adapted from Malis (1))

not been pursued further. Nevertheless, they remain markers that may be associated with the etiology of illness in a subgroup of patients.

Other studies of historical interest

Lehmann-Facius (8, 9) was the first to report evidence for the presence of antibrain antibodies in a population of schizophrenic patients by demonstrating a lipid extracted fraction of serum from schizophrenic patients that forms a precipitate with human brain extract from schizophrenics. Other early scattered reports suggesting compromised immune functioning in schizophrenic patients included a study by Molholm (10) describing decreased delayed hypersensitivity to guinea pig serum, and a report from Vaughan et al. (11) showing decreased responsivity to pertussis vaccine in schizophrenic patients, and the numerous studies showing increased leukocyte counts in these patients (reviewed by Malis, Ref. 1). These studies taken together are not only of historical interest, but are the major evidence that immune dysfunction existed in schizophrenic patients prior to the widespread use of chronic neuroleptic treatment for these patients.

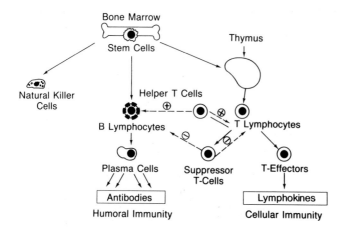

Bone Marrow

Stem Cells

Thymus

Natural Killer
Cells

Helper T Cells

B Lymphocytes

T Lymphocytes

Plasma Cells

Suppressor
T-Cells

T-Effectors

Antibodies

Lymphokines

Humoral Immunity

Cellular Immunity

FIG. 1   *Schematic description of the major functional components of the immune system. Solid arrows indicate the direction of derivation, broken arrows indicate influence, (−) inhibition and (+) enhancement.*

Components of immunity

The immune system can be broken down into a few major components, the lymphocyte being the central cell to immunity, but one that differentiates into several heterogeneous cell populations (see Fig. 1). The B-cells are responsible for immunoglobulin production, or humoral immunity, while some T-cells produce lymphokines, such as interferon, transfer factor, and others primarily regulate the functioning of other lymphocytes as 'helper' or 'suppressor' cells. The natural killer (NK) cells are unique lymphocytes known to have a specific function with regard to defence against cancer cell growth and specifically herpes class viral infections.

Studies of lymphocyte histology

In the early 1960s, several histopathologic studies were published reporting morphological changes in the shape of circulating lymphocytes from schizophrenics, including changes in nuclear lobulation and abnormal nuclear and cytoplasmic basophilic staining (12, 13) corresponding to changes seen in the bone marrow cells (6). These findings were eventually thought to be a result of neuroleptic medication (14). Recently, however, Hirata-Hibi et al. (15) reopened this controversy in an extensive histological study of atypical lymphocyte structure in schizophrenic patients, many of whom had never been given neuroleptic medication. They found a significantly higher percentage of atypical lymphocytes (thought to be stimulated lymphocytes and classified as the 'P'-cell) in schizophrenic patients not receiving neuroleptic medication for at least one year compared with other psychiatric patients and normal controls (see Figs 2a and b). In three independent further studies,

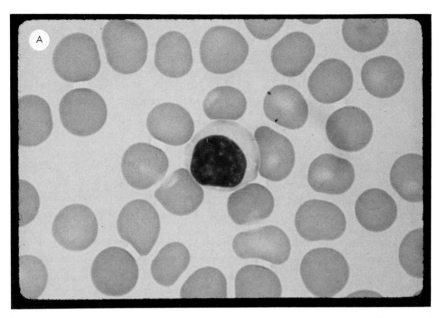

FIG. 2a *Normal lymphocyte (May-Grünwald Giemsa stain). Regular shaped nucleus, smooth chromatin, and clear cytoplasm.*

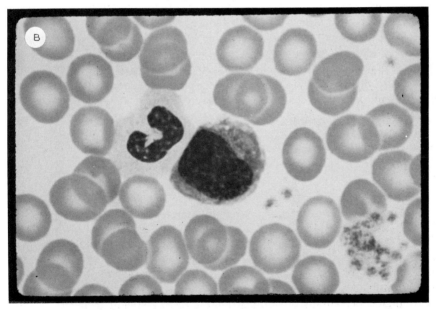

FIG. 2b *Typical P-type atypical lymphocyte. These cells are distinguished by the irregular shape of the nucleus, showing lobulation or deep indentation and fine chromatin clumping. Their cytoplasm is deeply basophilic, and these cells are generally larger than other lymphocytes. Reproduced by courtesy of Dr. Hirata-Hibi.*

however, of psychiatric patients at Saint Elizabeth's Hospital in Washington, DC and The National Institute of Mental Health, this finding has not been confirmed. In one study of chronic schizophrenic patients on a research unit, the patients did not have increased numbers of atypical lymphocytes (16), whereas in a study of more acute admissions on and off medication, schizophrenics had higher percentages of circulating atypical lymphocytes than controls, but so had similarly medicated Huntington's chorea patients (17). Another unpublished study of schizophrenics with familial schizophrenia and their family members, carried out in our laboratory, resulted in atypical lymphocytes reported sporadically over time in a small group of patients and their well family members. Atypical lymphocyte counts were not related to exacerbations of symptoms and did not remain consistent with time. Nevertheless, since the lymphocyte is the central cell of the immune system, confirmation of the Hirata-Hibi finding by others would be important evidence for immune system disturbance in some forms of schizophrenia.

The histological characteristics of lymphocytes generally suggest little about the functional capacity of these cells, and it is unknown which functional subtypes of lymphocytes become 'atypical' lymphocytes with stress.

Natural killer cell activity

Natural killer (NK) cells are the one functional subtype of lymphocytes that have

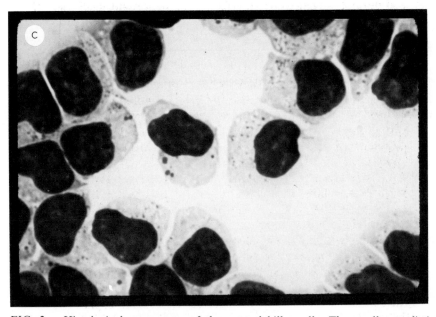

FIG. 2c *Histological appearance of the natural killer cells. These cells are distinguished from others by their large size, reniform shaped nucleus, deep basophilic cytoplasm with granules, and high cytoplasmic-to-nuclear ratio.*

correlated histological features (see Fig. 2c). They have been shown to have irregularly shaped, large granular nuclei with chromatin clumps and deep basophilic cytoplasmic staining (18), much like the atypical lymphocytes described by Hirata-Hibi (Fig. 2b). In addition, NK cells are also important in the first-line defense against viruses, particularly of the Herpes class (19), implicated in the etiology of schizophrenia (20, 21). In an initial study of NK activity in 27 schizophrenic patients compared with normal controls (16), a subgroup of 15% had NK activity lower than the control range, while none of the patients had NK activity elevated above controls. Manual counts of NK cells from histopathology smears revealed low normal percentages of NK cells. Macrophages, cells related functionally to NK cells, also showed deficient activity in 33% of the patients, although these NK and macrophage deficiencies appeared independent. Neither activity was inhibited by a range of doses of haloperidol equivalent to therapeutic blood levels (DeLisi and Maluish, unpublished data), although the effects of chronic neuroleptic medication on the development and activity of these cells are unknown. Nevertheless, 20 Huntington's chorea patients, 12 of whom were medicated with neuroleptic medication similar to the schizophrenics did not have abnormal NK activity, although they also had deficient macrophage functioning. We were, however, unable to establish an association between the increased atypical lymphocytes, as reported by Hirata-Hibi and colleagues, and NK cells.

NK activity has also recently been reported to be low in patients with major depression, and did not appear to be an effect of antidepressant medication (22).

B- and T-lymphocytes

Other functional aspects of lymphocytes not associated with specific histological descriptions have also been studied. While we and others have reported elevated percentages of B-cells (the cells responsible for humoral immunity) per total lymphocytes, decreased percentages of T-cells (the cells responsible for cellular immunity) have also been found by some, but not all investigators (2, 23 – 25). Elevated T-suppressor cell percentages were found in one study (24), while Kolyaskina et al. (26) reported low suppressor cell percentages compared with normals. These inconsistencies are not surprising given the heterogeneity of the schizophrenic disorders, the difference in length of illness, mental status, and diagnostic criteria of subjects sampled in the different studies. The change in the proportions of circulating lymphocyte subtypes has been used as a marker in immunology to determine the relative ability of the integrated immune system to respond to stress, and with various physical stresses these proportions are known to vary (27).

In other studies, Vartanian et al. (2) have reported decreased in-vitro cellular functioning of both total B- and T-lymphocytes from schizophrenic patients, as evidenced by lack of sufficient response of lymphocytes from schizophrenic patients in mitogen stimulation and thymidine incorporation studies. In addition, Fudenberg and colleagues (University of South Carolina, personal communication) have studied suppressor cell functioning in vitro and found schizophrenic patients to have lower activity of these cells than normal controls. They have further hypothesized that some schizophrenia may be due to a specific suppressor cell defect and have been presently treating a group of these patients with pharmacologic agents known to stimulate suppressor cell activity. Some initial success with this treatment has been reported (Fudenberg et al., personal communication).

General immune suppression, using a variety of markers of cellular immunity, has also been reported during acute stages of depression and psychiatric stress, such as that occurring from job loss or during mourning (7, 28, 29). These deficiencies in immune response may be related to the associated subsequent increased prevalence of physical illness.

Immunoglobulins

To further explore the capacity of the humoral immune system, immunoglobulins in serum and cerebrospinal fluid have been quantified in populations of schizophrenic patients. Several investigators report generalized increases in the three major classes of immunoglobulins in both acute and chronic schizophrenics (23, 30 – 33) while at least two others, including a study from our research group, report significantly lower levels in schizophrenic patients compared with controls (34, 35). We found a generalized decrease in IgG, IgA, and IgM in the plasma and CSF of institutionalized chronic schizophrenic patients. A subgroup of these patients (16%) also had decreases in the [serum/CSF] IgG ratio that was further associated with increased immunoglobulins to cytomegalovirus. In another study of non-institutionalized acute consecutive admissions (predominantly for depression) to a private psychiatric hospital, significantly lower than normal IgM was noted in these patients with a trend towards lower levels of circulating IgG and IgA as well (36). While in the first study the effects of chronic institutionalization and years of neuroleptic medication on circulating immunoglobulin levels have not been ruled out, these were not presented in the second study, thus suggesting that other factors may be involved. Recently we have also studied circulating immunoglobulin levels in 10 families with both schizophrenic (at least 2) and well members. We found IgG, IgA, and IgM immunoglobulin levels to be stable with time and highly heritable within families. There was no association, however, of lower or higher levels of these antibodies with schizophrenia when the schizophrenic members were compared with the well members within each family. Other studies in the literature confirm the familial contribution to circulating immunoglobulin levels (37 – 39). The clinical significance of the wide variation in these values remains unknown.

Autoantibody production

Specific types of pathological antibody production have also been investigated. The hypothesis that schizophrenia may be an autoimmune disease has prompted the search for autoantibody production in schizophrenic patients. While several studies report increased antinuclear antibodies in hospitalized psychiatric patients (23,

40 – 42), none have found antibodies to native DNA in schizophrenics, a finding characteristic of the autoimmune disease lupus erythematosus. Whether neuroleptic medication and/or lithium stimulates antinuclear antibody production is controversial. While Johnstone and Whaley (41), Gallien et al. (40), and Zarrabi et al. (23), find correlations of antinuclear antibody titers with length of pharmacologic treatment, we have found increased antinuclear antibody titers in first episode schizophrenic patients prior to the onset of treatment (42). Increased antinuclear antibody titers have also been found in patients with major affective disorders, as well as schizophrenia in some (41, 43), but not all studies (44). Von Brauchitsch (45) found increased titers only in affective disorders and not in schizophrenia.

Perhaps more relevant to schizophrenia has been the search for circulating antibrain antibodies in sera or cerebrospinal fluid from these patients. Although Lehmann-Facius (8, 9) first published data suggestive of an autoimmune process in schizophrenia, it was not until the 1960s that further studies were designed to address this issue. Burch (46) compiled mathematical analyses of epidemiological data for psychiatric hospital admissions compared with known mathematical predictions for autoimmune disorders and, based on this, he proposed that the development of schizophrenia, similar to autoimmune disorders, was dependent on the accumulation of two somatic mutations that increase the probability that a clone of immunologically competent cells will carry cell-bound autoantibodies.

Several other investigators reported more direct data in support of the existence of antibrain antibodies in schizophrenic patients (47 – 49). In the most extensive series of investigations, Heath and co-workers (50, 51) isolated a factor from the serum of schizophrenic patients which produced catatonia and abnormal brain wave tracings when injected into normal monkeys and humans. They called this substance

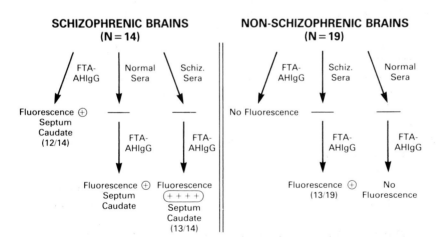

FIG. 3   *Results from the studies of Heath and Krupp (49), suggesting the presence of an antibody in serum from schizophrenics binding to an antigen specifically present in schizophrenic brain.*

'Taraxein'. Both the behavioral symptomatology and the EEG abnormalities were similar to those also described in schizophrenic patients. In other studies of post-mortem brain regions (49), they demonstrated fluorescent antibody staining most pronounced in human brain from schizophrenic patients that was first incubated with sera from similar patients (see Fig. 3). Sera from normal controls did not produce fluorescence. In further studies with preparations of antibrain antibodies, they reported the production of signs and symptoms similar to those produced by Taraxein in monkeys and humans (51). While a few investigators have been able to confirm portions of Heath's work (52 – 54), others have not (55 – 57). These studies began to fall into disrepute when new evidence suggested that Taraxein did not have the chemical characteristics of an immunoglobulin, but rather of a small peptide, at best a carrier molecule for immunoglobulins (54).

More recently, Baron et al. (58), employing a radioimmune assay which is more specific and sensitive than the fluorescent antibody techniques employed by Heath and others, found an increased prevalence of antibrain antibodies in schizophrenics compared with normal controls. Pandey et al. (59) confirmed this in a study using a less sensitive hemagglutinin method. In both studies there was a familial tendency for increased antibrain antibody titers as well. In addition, the investigations of Vartanian and co-workers (2), quantifying titers of antithymic antibodies (antibodies to lymphocytes), which cross-react with brain tissue, found elevated titers in schizophrenic patients and their family members. In contrast, however, in our studies of nuclear families with two or more schizophrenics, there was a notable lack of autoantibody production (antinuclear antibodies) among the schizophrenics and their healthy family members (0 increased titres in schizophrenics and 2 well relatives among 11 families).

The assay developed in our laboratory to detect antibodies in plasma to human brain tissue (caudate membranes) is a radioimmune assay similar to that used by Baron (58). Preliminary screening of 69 psychiatric patients and 58 controls showed immunoglobulin binding to brain tissue in both normal individuals and severely disordered psychiatric patients (58 chronic schizophrenics, 11 major affective disorder patients) (60). Only 2 patients had levels of binding higher than any controls. Five patients (3 schizophrenic and 2 affective) were considered to have high levels (higher than 50% above control brain membranes not incubated with serum), although 2 normal subjects also had elevations. Increased antinuclear antibody titers were also present in the patients with the highest antibrain antibody binding. In addition, antibody binding appeared to be not specific to caudate membranes and occurred in other brain regions as well. It also appeared to cross-react with antigens on at least one other tissue (kidney) and with membranes prepared from rat brain. Therefore, our studies indicate that if antibodies directed against brain tissue play any role in psychiatric disorders, they are non-specific and are only present among a small percentage of patients. Nevertheless, visualization of the binding of antibody in patients' plasma on rat brain sections using fluorescent antibody techniques (Rogon and Delisi, unpublished) shows a specific pattern of binding appearing to circumscribe the inner rim of some brain cells in clusters, while not of others. This would not appear to be characteristic of a non-specific binding reaction.

In another approach to this problem, but exploring cellular hypersensitivity to brain antigens, Jankovik et al. (61) completed a series of extensive experiments, injecting normal volunteers and psychiatric patients intradermally with antigens prepared from the S100 protein fraction (membrane fraction richest in receptors) from normal human brain tissue. Measurement of the subsequent skin delayed hypersensitivity reaction revealed greater reactions in the psychiatric patients than in controls, indicating prior sensitization and cellular immune recognition of brain membranal protein in these individuals. This work, however, has not been repeated by other investigators and remains controversial.

Taken together, these studies indicate the need for further investigation of the autoimmune hypothesis to the development of mental disorders. Studies are presently in progress to determine if antibodies to brain tissue specific to certain crucial receptors are present in psychotic patients and not in healthy individuals. Todd and Ciaranello (62), for example, have found evidence for the presence of antibodies to the serotonin receptor in some autistic children. Similar mechanisms may be operating in other psychiatric disturbances as well.

Viral-specific antibody titers

Since abnormal immune functioning may suggest the presence of an infectious agent, increased antibody titers to specific viruses have been searched for in sera and CSF from these patients. The data from these studies are controversial and contradictory. Nevertheless, there is a suggestion in the literature as a whole that antibodies to some types of herpes class viruses may be increased in both schizophrenic and depressed patients (63 – 65). Some of these increases have only been found in CSF. Torrey et al. (66) have reported elevated CSF IgM titers to cytomegalovirus, suggesting the presence of active infection. Others, however, have not been able to confirm this finding (67). The search for evidence of possible retrovirus infection in association with schizophrenia (68) led us to determine if schizophrenic patients had positive titers of antibodies to the enzyme, reverse transcriptase, an enzyme only coded for by the viral nucleoprotein, and known to be positive in patients who have or have had retrovirus associated illness. No positive titers were found in 15 severely symptomatic chronic schizophrenic patients and 15 matched controls (69).

Other immunoglobulin evidence for infection may be the presence of oligoclonal antibodies in CSF, as has been found in several studies of multiple sclerosis patients. No such findings, however, have been published for the psychiatric disorders.

Allergies

Allergic reactions entail disordered immune functioning and much controversy exists concerning allergies to various food substances and psychiatric disorders. Studies suggest that schizophrenics have an increased history of allergies in childhood and prevalence of specifically wheat intolerance. In countries where schizophrenia is rare, wheat grain is also scarce (70). Some investigators have promoted the idea that the pathogenesis of schizophrenia is related to these food sensitivities and have proclaimed dramatic improvement of schizophrenic symptoms when their patients are placed on various restrictive diets. A few double-blind scientific studies of this issue have been negative, and thus no clearly positive evidence exists in support of these diets.

Discussion

Taken together, several published studies suggest signs of immune system abnormalities in at least some patients with major psychiatric disorders. We have studied several measures of immunity in a total of 79 patients at St. Elizabeth's Hospital in Washington, DC. Decreased immunoglobulin concentrations, decreased natural killer cell activity, decreased macrophage functioning, increased B-cell percentages, increased suppressor cell percentages, and autoantibodies have been found in different subgroups of schizophrenic patients, although other diagnostic groups were not examined.

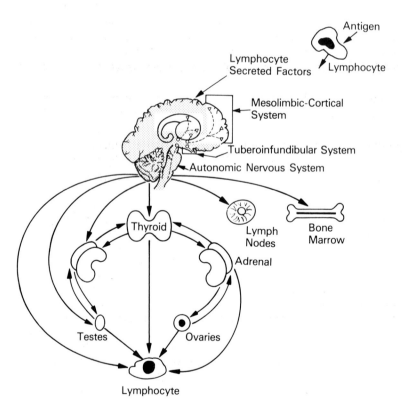

FIG. 4 *Schematic description of the interaction of the central nervous and immune systems.*

The significance of these findings is far from clear. Limitations in assay specificity and thus the diagnostic usefulness of these determinations may simply be reflected by these results. Alternatively, if it is assumed that the summation of reports from our group and others over the past several years suggests immune dysfunction in some psychiatric patients, one explanation, or a combination of several, is possible.

Neuroleptics are known to alter the immune system in several ways (71, 72), and this could increase vulnerability towards the development of opportunistic viral or other infections, as well as cancer; or it can result in clinically insignificant laboratory alterations such as those mentioned above. Lithium, on the other hand, is known to generally enhance the immune response (reviewed by Horrobin and Lieb, Ref. 73), while at least one report exists of a suppressive effect of tricyclic antidepressants on the responsiveness of lymphocytes (74). These three classes of drugs used in psychiatric treatment may have multiple side effects with longterm usage and may confuse the ability of researchers to determine which abnormalities noted are associated with the development of a disorder.

Viruses, on the other hand, could cause a number of psychiatric symptoms directly, or cause alterations through the immune system, such as increased autoantibody production, which could then be responsible for the illness pathogenesis. The several laboratory indicators of immune system alterations mentioned in this manuscript can all be the necessary laboratory signs of an infectious illness, and aside from the actual isolation of viral particles, or viral specific antibodies, this remains the best present evidence for the 'viral hypothesis' of schizophrenia (reviewed in reference 21).

A genetic basis for schizophrenia and other major psychiatric disorders is strongly suggested from several family and adoption studies. An inherited primary defect in the immune system could either produce the psychiatric disorder directly (i.e. through the production of antibrain antibodies) or increase vulnerability towards the establishment of an unknown viral infection responsible for the illness. Histocompatibility antigens (HLA) are genetically determined markers present on

TABLE 2 *Regulation of lymphocyte activity by hormones and neuroregulators: effect on the immune response*

Neuroregulators		Hormones	
Stimulation	Suppression	Stimulation	Suppression
α-Adrenergic antagonists	α-Adrenergic antagonists	Growth hormone	Progesterone
Substance P	Epinephrine	Thyroxin	Corticosteroids
	Norepinephrine	Insulin	Testosterone
	Somatostatin	Prolactin	Estrogen
	Opioids	Estrogen	(cellular
	cAMP	(humoral	response)
		response)	

the surface of lymphocytes that are now known to determine the heterogeneity and variability in immune response. Their genes are located in a concentrated area on chromosome 6 and divided into 4 major loci (A, B, C and D_r). These antigens have several polymorphic variants representing the diversity in immune response. They are of particular interest, not only as gene markers that may be linked to a 'psychosis gene', but because of their determination of components of the immune response. Increased frequencies of specific HLA antigens have been found in association with certain medical disorders. Especially notable is the association of the B27 antigen with autoimmune disorders (reviewed in Ref. 75).

Associations of specific HLA antigens with major psychiatric illness have not been shown. While there have been extensive studies of this phenomenon, no consistent findings have emerged. Moreover, each population study has resulted in different associations (reviewed in Ref. 76). One family pedigree study shows linkage of the HLA gene to schizophrenia, although no single haplotype distinguished schizophrenics in all families (77). Two other family linkage studies of HLA antigens to schizophrenia were clearly negative (Ref. 78; and Goldin and DeLisi, unpublished data). The HLA data for affective disorders is similarly inconsistent (76).

Finally, a primary defect in neurotransmitter metabolism may, through central nervous system control of the immune system (see Fig. 4), lead to the abnormalities in immune functioning that have been presented in this review. Stein et al. (79) have published a series of experiments in animals, showing that lesions in specific nuclei of the anterior hypothalamus suppress immune response. Anaphylaxis has been frequently used as a model of the effect of the hypothalamus on the humoral immune response. It appears from several published independent studies (reviewed in ref. 79) that anterior hypothalamic lesions inhibit lethal anaphylactic shock in animals. This effect can be explained by both antigen-specific and non-specific changes in the immune system, changes in tissue factors or target organ responsivity.

Cell-mediated immunity (as measured by delayed hypersensitivity reactions and in vitro T-cell stimulation tests) is also suppressed by anterior hypothalamic lesions, and enhanced by stimulation. These effects of the hypothalamus appear to be regulated through a complex and not well worked out interaction between neurotransmitter and endocrine systems. The effects of several of these on overall cellular and humoral immune response are listed in Table 2. Although there may be a much more complex interaction occurring than had been previously thought, attempts have been made to establish a link between elevated circulating cortisol production and immune suppression in depression. In vitro assays of lymphocytes also have shown receptors on the surface of lymphocytes for several of the neurotransmitters and peptides (80) (corticosteroids, opiates, insulin, prolactin, growth hormone, oestradiol, testosterone, beta-adrenergic agents, acetylcholine), and have shown that lymphocytes secrete substances for which receptors are present on brain cells (i.e. histamine, serotonin, prostaglandins, and endorphins). Their functions remain unknown, but of interest. Both the presence of receptors for neuroregulators and the production of these substances by lymphocytes suggest humoral mechanisms for direct brain regulation of the immune system. In addition, there is direct innervation of several organs associated with the immune system (the thymus, spleen and lymph nodes). These neuronal connections have been shown to be primarily catecholamine containing neurons of the autonomic nervous system (81).

Abnormalities in immune system functioning seen in psychiatric patients, while not specific to one disorder or present in all individuals with a specific disorder, may represent a by-product of the agent producing the symptoms. That these signs of disordered immunity exist, is of clinical interest. If these aberrant values produce vulnerability towards the development of infections and neoplasms, regardless of their etiology, then pharmacologic agents designed to stimulate immune response may be the indicated treatment for psychiatric patients with these findings.

REFERENCES

1. Malis GYu (1961) *Research on the Etiology of Schizophrenia,* pp. 11 – 40. Consultants Bureau Enterprises, Inc., New York.
2. Vartanian ME, Kolyaskina GI, Lozovsky DV, et al. (1978) Aspects of humoral and cellular immunity in schizophrenia. In: Bergsma D, Goldstein AL (Eds), *Neurochemical and Immunological Components of Schizophrenia, Vol. 18 (Series: Birth Defects),* pp. 339 – 364. Alan R. Liss, Inc., New York.
3. Bruce LC Peebles AMS (1903) Clinical and experimental observations on catatonia. *J. Ment. Sci., 49,* 614.
4. Bruce LC Peebles AMS (1904) Quantitative and qualitative leukocyte counts in various forms of mental disease. *J. Ment. Sci., 50,* 409.
5. Lyubovskaya PI, Rokhlenko SZ (1957) The condition of the bone marrow in schizophrenia. *Vrach. Delo, 12.*
6. Hirata-Hibi M, Fessel WJ (1964) The bone marrow in schizophrenia. *Arch. Gen. Psychiatry, 10,* 414.
7. Kronfol Z, Silva J, Greden J, Dembinski J, Gardner R, Carroll B (1983) Impaired lymphocyte function in depressive illness. *Life Sci., 18,* 241.
8. Lehmann-Facius H (1937) Uber die Liquordiagnose der Schizophrenien. *Klin. Wochenschr., 16,* 1646.
9. Lehmann-Facius H (1939) Serologisch-analytische Versuche mit Liquoren und Seren von Schizophrenien. *Alg. Z. Psychiatr., 110,* 232.
10. Molholm HB (1942) Hyposensitivity to foreign protein in schizophrenic patients. *Psychiatric Q., 16,* 565.
11. Vaughan WT, Sullivan JC, Elmadjian F (1949) Immunity and schizophrenia. *Psychosom. Med., 11,* 327.
12. Fessel WJ, Hirata-Hibi M (1963) Abnormal leukocytes in schizophrenia. *Arch. Gen. Psychiatry, 9,* 601.
13. Kamp HV (1962) Nuclear changes in the white blood cells of patients with schizophrenic reactions. *J. Neuropsychiatry, 4,* 1.
14. Fieve RR, Blumenthal B, Little B (1966) The relationship of atypical lymphocytes, phenothiazines, and schizophrenia. *Arch. Gen. Psychiatry, 15,* 529.
15. Hirata-Hibi M, Higashi S, Tachibana T, Watanabe N (1982) Stimulated lymphocytes in schizophrenia. *Arch. Gen. Psychiatry, 39,* 82.
16. DeLisi LE, Ortaldo JR, Maluish AE, Wyatt RJ (1983) Deficient natural killer cell (NK)

activity and macrophage functioning in schizophrenic patients. *J. Neural Trans., 58*, 96.

17. Torrey EF, DeLisi LE, Kaufmann CA (1986) Atypical lymphocytes and schizophrenia. Submitted for publication.
18. Timonen T, Ortaldo JR, Herberman RB (1981) Characteristics of human large granular lymphocytes and relationship to natural killer cells and K cells. *J. Exp. Med., 153*, 569.
19. Herberman RB Ortaldo JR (1981) Natural killer cells: their role in defences against disease. *Science, 214*, 24.
20. Torrey EF, Peterson MR, Brannon WL et al. (1978) Immunoglobulins and viral antibodies in psychiatric patients. *Br. J. Psychiatry, 132*, 342.
21. Morozov PV (Ed) (1983) *Research on the Viral Hypothesis of Mental Disorders, Vol. 12 (Series: Advances in Biological Psychiatry)*, pp. 1 – 175. Karger Press, Basel, New York.
22. Nasrallah H, Ballas Z, Chapman S, Kronfol Z (1984) Natural killer cell activity in major depression. *Abstr. First World Conf. Virus Dis. Ment. Health, Montreal.*
23. Zarrabi MH, Zucker S, Miller F et al. (1979) Immunologic and coagulation disorders in chlorpromazine-treated patients. *Ann. Int. Med., 91*, 194.
24. DeLisi LE, Goodman S, Neckers LM, Wyatt RJ (1982) Lymphocyte subpopulations in schizophrenic patients. *Biol. Psychiatry, 17*, 1003.
25. Coffee CE, Sullivan JL, Rice JR (1983) T Lymphocytes in schizophrenia. *Biol. Psychiatry, 18*, 113.
26. Kolyaskina GI (1983) Blood lymphocytes in schizophrenia: immunological and virological aspects. In: Morozov PV (Ed), *Research on the Viral Hypothesis of Mental Disorders (Series: Advances in Biological Psychiatry), Vol. 12*, pp. 142 – 149. Karger Press, Basel, New York.
27. Hedfors E, Holm G, Ivansen M, Wahren J (1983) Physiological variation of blood lymphocyte reactivity: T-cell subsets, immunoglobulin production, and mixed-lymphocyte reactivity. *Clin. Immunol. Immunopathol., 27*, 9.
28. Bartrop RW, Lazarus L, Luckhurst E et al. (1977) Depressed lymphocyte function after bereavement. *Lancet, 1*, 834.
29. Schleifer SJ, Keller SE, Comerino M, Thornton JC, Stein M (1983) Suppression of lymphocyte stimulation following bereavement. *J. Am. Med. Assoc., 250*, 374.
30. Amkraut A, Solomon GF, Allansmith M et al. (1973) Immunoglobulins and improvement in acute schizophrenic reactions. *Arch. Gen. Psychiatry, 28*, 673.
31. Domino EF, Krause RR, Thiessen MM, Batsakis JG (1975) Blood protein fraction comparisons of normal and schizophrenic patients. *Arch. Gen. Psychiatry, 32*, 717.
32. Solomon GF, Allansmith M, McGlellan B, Amkraut A (1969) Immunoglobulins in psychiatric patients. *Arch. Gen. Psychiatry, 20*, 272.
33. Strahilevitz M, Fleishman JB, Fischer GW et al. (1976) Immunoglobulin levels in psychiatric patients. *Am. J. Psychiatry, 133*, 772.
34. Bock E, Week B, Rafaelson OJ (1970) Immunoglobulins in schizophrenic patients. *Lancet, 2*, 523.
35. DeLisi LE, Neckers LM, Weinberger DR et al. (1981) Quantitative determination of immunoglobulins in CSF and plasma of chronic schizophrenic patients. *Br. J. Psychiatry, 139*, 513.
36. DeLisi LE, King AK, Targum S (1984) Serum immunoglobulin concentrations in patients admitted to an acute psychiatric inpatient service. *Br. J. Psychiatry, 145*, 661.
37. Allansmith M, McClellan B, Butterworth M (1969) The influence of heredity and environment on human immunoglobulin levels. *J. Immunol., 102*, 1504.

38. Agrawal S, Bhalla V (1981) Isoagglutinin levels in twins and families: a study of the naturally occurring antibodies in human serum. *Acta Genet. Med. Genellol, 30,* 289.
39. Escobar V, Corey LA, Bixler D et al. (1979) The human X-chromosome and the levels of serum immunoglobulin. *Clin. Genetics, 15,* 221.
40. Gallien M, Schnetzler JP Morin J (1975) Anticorps antinucléaires et lupus induits per les phénothiazines chez six cents malades hospitalisés. *Ann. Med. Psychol., 1, 237.*
41. Johnstone EC, Whaley K (1975) Antinuclear antibodies in psychiatric illness: their relationship to diagnosis and drug treatment. *Br. Med. J., 28,* 724.
42. DeLisi LE, Wyatt RJ (1982) Abnormal immune regulation in schizophrenic patients. *Psychopharmacol. Bull., 18* 158.
43. Deberdt R, VanHooren J, Biesbrouck M, Amery W (1976) Antinuclear factor-positive mental depression. A single disease entity? *Biol. Psychiatry, 11,* 69.
44. Shopsin B, Sathananthan GL, Chan TL, Kravitz H, Gershon S (1973) Antinuclear factor in psychiatric patients. *Biol. Psychiatry, 7,* 81.
45. Von Brauchitsch H (1972) Antinuclear factor in psychiatric sorders. *Am. J. Psychiatry, 128, 102.*
46. Burch PRJ (1964) Schizophrenia: some new etiological considerations. *Br. J. Psychiatry, 110,* 818.
47. Kuznetoza NI, Semenov SF (1961) Detection of antibrain antibodies in the sera of patients with neuropsychiatric disorders. *Zh. Neuropatol. Psikhiatr., 61,* 869.
48. Fessel WJ (1962) Autoimmunity and mental illness: preliminary report. *Arch. Gen. Psychiatry, 6, 320.*
49. Heath RG Krupp IM (1967) Schizophrenia as an immunological disorder I. Demonstration of antibrain globulins by fluorescent antibody techniques. *Arch. Gen. Psychiatry, 16, 1.*
50. Heath RG, Krupp IM, Byers LW, Liljekvist JI (1967) Schizophrenia as an immunologic disorder. II. Effects of serum protein fractions on brain function. *Arch. Gen. Psychiatry, 16, 10.*
51. Heath RG, Krupp IM, Byers LW, Liljekvist JI (1967) Schizophrenia as an immunologic disorder. III. Effects of antimonkey and antihuman brain antibody on brain function. *Arch. Gen. Psychiatry, 16,* 24.
52. Martens S, Vallbo S, Melander B (1959) A comparison between taraxein and some psychotomimetics. *Acta Psychiatr. Scand. (Suppl), 136,* 361.
53. Meckler LB, Laptera NN, Lozovskii DV, Balezinc TI (1960) On the chemical and biological properties of taraxein, a toxic protein observed in the blood serum of schizophrenic patients. *Proc. Acad. Sci. USSR, 130,* 1148.
54. Bergen JR, Grinspoon L, Pyle HM, et al (1980) Immunologic studies in schizophrenic and control subjects. *Biol. Psychiatry, 15,* 369.
55. Whittingham S, Mackay IR, Jones IH, Davies B (1968) Absence of brain antibodies in patients with schizophrenia. *Br. Med. J., 1,* 347.
56. Logan DG, Deodhar SD (1970) Schizophrenia, an immunologic disorder? *J. Am. Med. Assoc., 212,* 1703.
57. Boehme DH, Cottrell JC, Dohan FC, Hillegass LM (1974) Demonstration of nuclear and cytoplasmic fluorescence in brain tissues of schizophrenic and nonschizophrenic patients. *Biol. Psychiatry, 8,* 89.
58. Baron M, Stern M, Anavi R, Witz JP (1977) Tissue binding factor in schizophrenic sera: a clinical and genetic study. *Biol. Psychiatry, 12,* 199.
59. Pandey RS, Gupta AK, Chaturvedi VC (1981) Autoimmune model of schizophrenia

with special reference to antibrain antibodies. *Biol. Psychiatry, 16,* 1123.

60. DeLisi LE, Weber R, Pert C (1985) Are there antibodies against brain in sera from schizophrenic patients? Review and Prospectus. *Biol. Psychiatry, 20,* 94.

61. Jankovik BD, Jakulic S, Horvat J (1979) Cell mediated immunity and psychiatric diseases. *Period. Biol., 81,* 219.

62. Todd RD, Ciaranello RD (1985) Demonstration of inter- and intraspecies binding sites by antibodies from an autistic child. *Proc. Natl. Acad. Sci., 82,* 612.

63. Rimon R, Halonen P (1969) Herpes simplex virus infection and depressive illness. *Dis. Nerv. Syst., 30,* 338.

64. Cappel R Sprecher S (1983) Are herpes viruses responsible for neuropsychiatric diseases? In: Morozov P. (Ed), *Research on the viral Hypothesis of Mental Disorders (Series: Advances in Biological Psychiatry), Vol. 12,* pp. 168 – 173. Karger, New York, Basel.

65. Libikova, H (1983) Schizophrenia and viruses: principles of aetiological studies. In: Morovov P (Ed) *Research on the Viral Hypothesis of Mental Disorders (Series: Advances in Biological Psychiatry), Vol. 12.* pp. 20 – 51.

66. Torrey EF, Yolken RH, Winfrey CJ (1982) Cytomegalovirus antibody in cerebrospinal fluid of schizophrenic patients detected by enzyme immunoassay. *Science, 216,* 892.

67. Shrikhande S, Hirsch SR, Coleman JC, Reveley MA, Dayton R (1985) Cytomegalovirus and schizophrenia. *Br. J. Psychiatry, 146,* 503.

68. Crow TJ (1984) A re-evaluation of the viral hypothesis: is psychosis the result of retroviral integration at a site close to the cerebral dominance gene? *Br. J. Psychiatry, 145,* 243.

69. DeLisi LF and Sarin P (1985) Lack of evidence for retroviral infection in schizophrenia. *Br. J. Psychiatry, 146,* 674.

70. Dohan FC, Harper EH, Clark MH, Rodrigue RB, Zigas V (1984) Is schizophrenia rare if grain is rare? *Biol. Psychiatry, 19,* 385.

71. Ferguson RM, Schmidtke JR, Simmons RL (1978) Effects of psychoactive druge on in vitro lymphocyte activation. In: Bergsma D, Goldstein AL (Eds) *Neurochemical and Immunological Components of Schizophrenia (Series: Birth Defects), Vol. 18.* pp. 379 – 402. Alan R. Liss, New York.

72. Lovett CL, Urlich JT, Simms BG, Goldstein AL (1978) In: Bergsma D, Goldstein AL (Eds), *Neurochemical and Immunological Component of Schizophrenia, Vol. 18 (Series: Birth Defects),* pp. 407 – 422. Alan R. Liss, Inc., New York.

73. Horrobin DF and Lieb J (1981) A biochemical basis for the actions of lithium on behavior and on immunity: relapsing and remitting disorders of inflammation and immunity such as multiple sclerosis or recurrent herpes as manic-depression of the immune system. *Med. Hypotheses, 7,* 891.

74. Audus KL, Gordon, MA (1982) Tricyclic antidepressant effects on the murine lymphocyte mitogen response. *J. Immunopharmacol., 41 – 2,* 13.

75. Thomson G (1981) A review of theoretical aspects of HLA and disease associations. *Theor. Popul. Biol., 20,* 168.

76. Goldin LR, Gershon ES (1983) Association and linkage studies of genetic marker loci in major psychiatric disorders. *Psychiatr. Dev., 4,* 387.

77. Turner W (1979) Genetic markers for schizotaxia. *Biol. Psychiatry, 14,* 177.

78. McGuffin P, Festenstein H, Murray R (1983) A family study of HLA antigens and other genetic markers in schizophrenia. *Psychol. Med., 13,* 31.

79. Stein M, Keller S, Schleifer S (1981) The hypothalamus and the immune response. In: Werner H, Hofer MA, Stunkard AJ (Eds), *Brain, Behavior, and Bodily Disease,* pp.

45 – 65. Raven Press, New York.

80. Besedovsky HO, deRey A, Sorkin E (1983) In: Fabris W, Garaci E, Hadden J, Mitchison NA (Eds), *Immunoregulation*, pp. 315 – 339. Plenum Press, London.

81. Felton D (1984) Stress and the immune system: an interactive relationship. Presented at the Annual Meeting of the American College of Neuropsychopharmacology, Puerto Rico.

82. Macphail SR (1885) Clinical observations on the blood of the insane. *J. Ment. Sci., 30,* 378.

83. Dide M (1905) La demence précoce est un syndrome mental toxi-infectieux subaigu ou chronique. *Rev. Neurol., 13,* 381.

84. Lundvall H (1907) Researches on the blood of the insane. *Hygiea, 2 7,* 1142.

85. Sandri O (1907) Criteri diagnostici differziali desunti da leostudio della formula emoleucocitario in diverse malate mentale. *Riv. Pat. Nerv., 12,* 400.

86. Sandri O (1907) La formula emoleucocitaria nelle psicosi acute confusionali. *Riv. Pat. Nerv., 12,* 73.

87. Lepine J, Popoff, V-St. (1908) Recherches sur les variations sérologiques du sang chez les aliénés. *Encéphale, 2,* 574.

88. Ermakov J (1910) Investigation of the blood in some forms of mental disorder. *Arch. Int. Neurol., 2,* 369.

89. Graziani A (1910) Ricerche sulle modificazioni citologiche del sangrie nelle principali psicosi. *Riv. Sper. Freniat., 36,* 878.

90. Krueger H (1912) Ueber die Cytologie des Blutes bei Dementia praecox. *Z. Gesamte Neurol. Psychiatr., 14,* 97.

91. Pfoertner (1912) Die weissen Blutkörperchen beim Jugendirresein. *Arch. Psychiatr., 50,* 574.

92. Schultz JH (1913) Haematologische Untersuchungsmethoden im Dienste der Psychiatrie. *Dtsch. Med. Wochenschr., 39,* 1399.

93. Itten W (1914) Zur Kenntnis haematologischer Befunde bei einigen Psychosen. *Z. Ges. Neurol. Psychol., 244,* 341.

94. Jackson DL (1914) The clinical value and significance of leukocytosis in mental disease. *J. Mental Sci., 60,* 56.

95. Zimmermann R (1914) Beitrag zur Kenntnis der Leukocytose bei der Dementia praecox. *Z. Ges. Neurol. Psychiatr., 22,* 266.

96. Prusenko AI (1915) The morphology of the blood in dementia praecox. *Zh. Nevropatol. Psikhiatr., 15,* 118.

97. Wuth O (1922) Untersuchungen ueber die koerperlichen Stoerungen bei der Schizophrenie. *Z. Ges. Neurol. Psychiatr., 78,* 532.

98. Granskaya NA (1927) Mental condition in dementia praecox. *J. Nevropat. Psikhiatr., 20,* 139.

99. Berger IA (1927) Toxicity of the blood in dementia praecox. *Z. Nevropat. Psikhiatr., 20,* 295.

100. Zalkind EM (1929) Dynamics of the leukocytosis in some nervous diseases and personality defects. Reported in Malis (Ref. 1), p. 17.

101. Dameschek W (1930) The white blood cells in dementia praecox and dementia paralytica. *Arch. Neurol. Psychiatry, 24,* 855.

102. Sagel W (1930) Einige Erfahrungen ueber das weisse Blutbild und seinen Wert fuer die Psychiatrie. *Z. Ges. Neurol. Psychiatr., 125,* 436.

103. Shekhonin VP (1939) The reaction of the barrier apparatus in schizophrenia. *Nevropat.*

Psikhiatr., 7.

104. Ederle W (1941) Somatische Stoerungen bei Schizophrenen. *Allg. Z. Psychiatr., 118,* 239.
105. Ferroni A (1942) Sull'esistenza di una sindrome perniciose − forme nelle psicose schizophreniche. *Rev. Patol. Nerv. Ment., 60,* 298.
106. Chistovich L (1945) Changes in the white blood cells in mental diseases. Collection from the Departments of Nervous Diseases and Psychiatry. Reported in Malis (Ref. 1), pp. 18 − 19.

CHAPTER 18

The pathogenesis of schizophrenia: a neurodevelopmental theory

DANIEL R. WEINBERGER

Any theory about the pathogenesis of schizophrenia must address two inescapable facts about this illness: first, the very high probability that it will become clinically apparent in late adolescence, and second, the therapeutic efficacy of neuroleptic drugs. Psychosocial theories, by emphasizing the intrapsychic conflicts and social stresses associated with sexual maturity, offer at least a coherent explanation for the former but fail to address the latter. Biochemical theories such as the dopamine hypothesis are, for the most part, based on the second fact, in that the degree to which neuroleptic drugs antagonize dopaminergic function correlates with their clinical potency in ameliorating psychotic symptoms. As valuable as these biochemical theories have been in generating basic research into neurochemistry and neuropharmacology, they have produced virtually no insight into the first inescapable fact about schizophrenia. Efforts to cover both bases by combining the approaches into a 'biopsychosocial' model lose something in the process, as it is unclear how the two theoretical schools relate to each other.

 The chapters in this volume detail the results of various neurologic investigations of the brain in schizophrenia. The underlying premise of these investigations is that the pathogenesis of this illness involves dysfunction of the central nervous system. While this is far from a novel speculation, it is one that has gained increasing momentum in the past decade. The advent of incisive techniques for direct observation of cerebral structure and physiology during life as well as enlightened approaches to post-mortem examination of brain structure and biochemistry have provided compelling evidence that replicable pathology of the brain is associated with schizophrenia. While the possibility that all these findings are epiphenomena or artifacts has not been definitively ruled out, the striking convergence of data from diverse approaches weighs against this possibility. The following discussion is an attempt to synthesize this recent evidence into a theory of the pathogenesis of schizophrenia that is based on two traditional neurologic principles: neuroanatomical localization of function, and the implications of the state of brain maturation for the clinical manifestations of a lesion. The theory is only peripherally about etiology. It proposes that the critical pathogenic issues are the areas of the brain that appear to be pathological and the fact that these areas normally reach functional maturity during adolescence. This theory is not original. It is a compila-

Handbook of Schizophrenia, Vol. 1: The Neurology of Schizophrenia.
H.A. Nasrallah and D.R. Weinbergr, editors.
© Elsevier Science Publishers B.V., 1986.

tion and restatement of the thoughts of many psychiatric and neurologic investigators who have contemplated this problem. One of its most appealing features is that it provides a framework for understanding in neurobiological terms the two inescapable clinical facts.

Where is the lesion?

The brain lesion in schizophrenia appears to involve a system of interconnected limbic and diencephalic nuclei and prefrontal cortex. Since all areas of the brain are not equipotential with respect to where a lesion might produce symptoms characteristic of schizophrenia, some regions within this system are possibly more critical than others. For example, subcortical connections to the dorsolateral prefrontal cortex may be crucial. Nevertheless, most of the evidence detailed in this volume suggests that the lesion in schizophrenia is not finely circumscribed. There is clearly no single nucleus, cortical region, or major pathway that is implicated all by itself. Instead, the evidence favors involvement of a system of anatomically and neurochemically related cortical and subcortical regions. The components of this system include various periventricular limbic and diencephalic nuclei such as hypothalamus, nucleus accumbens, substantia innominata, medial pallidum, and amygdala, as well as 'limbic cortex,' i.e. hippocampal formation, and neocortex, i.e. dorsolateral prefrontal cortex.

The evidence supporting involvement of periventricular nuclei is reviewed in Chapters 9, 14 and 15 and on post-mortem studies. Several recent controlled quantitative studies of post-mortem brain tissue have reported evidence of pathology in these areas. A much larger number of controlled CT investigations have found quantitative evidence of brain pathology in the form of enlarged third and lateral ventricles. The CT findings are consistent with, but not proof of, periventricular pathology. This is because ventricular enlargement may reflect local as well as distant reductions in tissue mass. However, to the extent that they are consistent with the post-mortem studies, the CT findings enhance the credibility of the post-mortem observations because CT studies are well controlled and much less susceptible to artifacts.

The evidence for cortical involvement comes from CT, MRI, rCBF, PET, EEG, and post-mortem studies and is reviewed in Chapters 5, 9, 11, 12, 13, 14 and 15. Numerous CT studies have reported increased cortical markings suggestive of reduced gyral mass and several of these studies have selectively implicated prefrontal cortex. The in-vivo physiological approaches have provided complementary functional data and quantitative post-mortem, neuroanatomical, and neurochemical evidence has also been reported. Hippocampal pathology has been observed in several post-mortem neuroanatomical studies.

The cortical and subcortical components of the system are linked functionally and anatomically. In addition to interconnections of both known and as yet uncharacterized neurotransmitter types, most of the subcortical components receive projections from mesolimbic dopamine neurons, while the cortical components are innervated by mesocortical dopamine neurons. That the lesion in schizophrenia involves connections between these components is suggested by the research finding of a correlation between periventricular pathology (enlarged ventricles) and prefrontal physiological dysfunction (rCBF).

What is the lesion?

The lesion involves a subtle reduction of tissue mass. In the quantitative post-mortem studies, the magnitude of the differences between patients with schizophrenia and controls is not so extreme as to be qualitatively obvious. Most studies rely on statistical comparisons of means in order to observe differences, and considerable overlap between the groups invariably exists. Indeed, this may explain the failure of some investigators during the first half of this century to observe or appreciate differences. The qualitative post-mortem studies reporting gliosis are consistent with the notion of a subtle, static process. For the most part, the magnitude of the gliosis is not severe enough to be appreciated with routine staining techniques. Gliosis is a tombstone of pathological degeneration; it is typically seen in association with conditions of atrophy. Both the quantitative and qualitative studies suggest that the observed changes are old and associated with an inactive pathological process. Whether the process was truly degenerative or dysplastic is impossible to surmise from the available evidence. While gliosis is most consistent with a degenerative process, earlier studies which did not consistently observe gliotic involvement could be interpreted as being consistent with a congenital deficit. By either assumption, the pathology appears to occur a long time before the post-mortem observations and probably before the clinical diagnosis is made. The available evidence does not imply more about the specific nature of the pathological process, i.e. whether it was infectious, metabolic, toxic, traumatic, immunologic, or vascular. All of these processes could produce the changes.

The results of the post-mortem neurochemical studies do not shed additional light on this matter. The findings, however, are not inconsistent with any of these assumptions. A reduction in nuclear mass that, for example, spares dopamine terminals could result in increased concentrations of dopamine and its metabolites when expressed as a percentage of tissue mass or protein concentration. Likewise, increased dopamine receptor activity could reflect deafferentation and/or loss of modulating-inhibitory systems. Findings of reductions in peptide concentrations are consistent with loss of neuronal populations.

The data from CT studies also suggest that the lesion is old, non-progressive, and characterized by a subtle reduction in brain mass. Ventricular enlargement has been reported in first episode schizophreniform patients, a finding which implicates early developmental pathology since ventricular enlargement would be unlikely to develop acutely in adolescence without concomitant traditional neurological symptoms. The majority of the CT studies have not found a relationship between ventricular enlargement and length of illness, a correlation that would be expected if the pathological process were progressive. The argument that its rate of progression is too slow to be correlated with ventricular size is untenable as normal aging and ventricular size are usually seen to correlate in most studies. A degenerative process that progresses less rapidly than normal aging is unlikely to be clinically important. Ventricular enlargement and increased cortical markings are hallmarks of brain atrophy and therefore reflect diminished tissue mass. Like the post-mortem morphometric findings, however, the CT evidence rests on statistical comparisons with considerable overlap between groups.

In the absence of more conclusive data about the pathological process responsible for these findings in schizophrenia, the most coherent interpretation seems to be as follows. The lesion reflects a short-lived, histopathologically non-specific process that occurs early in development and results in a subtle structural deficit involving certain brain regions critical for normal human psychological and intellectual development.

Clinical-pathological relationships

The clinical features of schizophrenia are at least theoretically consistent with dysfunction of the brain areas implicated as the site of the lesion. Hallucinations and perceptual distortions may reflect dysfunction of periventricular limbic diencephalic nuclei, while flat affect, poor motivation and insight, social ineffectiveness, and the characteristic pattern of intellectual impairment suggest dysfunction of dorsolateral prefrontal cortex. From depth electrode studies in man, it is apparent that psychotic experiences such as hallucinations, ineffable and strange experiences, as well as perceptual distortions can result from electrical discharges in either temporal cortex, amygdala, or hippocampus (1). Neurological diseases such as tumors, trauma, and infections are associated with schizophreniform symptomatology much more frequently when they involve the limbic system and diencephalon than when they present in other brain areas (2). These clinical analogies suggest that so-called positive psychotic symptoms represent dysfunction in these subcortical sites.

While hallucinations and delusions are perhaps the most dramatic clinical features of schizophrenia and the cornerstones of current diagnostic criteria, it is doubtful that they are the most disabling features. This distinction is reserved for what are called the defect or negative symptoms and for the intellectual impairment that characterizes the majority of individuals with the disorder. These subtle and difficult to define features bear a remarkable similarity to symptoms seen in patients with lesions of the dorsolateral prefrontal cortex. This is particularly true of the pattern of cognitive impairment, motivational difficulties, and deficits in social functioning and insight (3). In the case of schizophrenia, there is compelling evidence from recent rCBF studies that the degree of characteristic intellectual deficit is linked to a failure of dorsolateral prefrontal cortex physiological activation.

The role of dopamine

The relationship of dopamine activity to the positive psychotic phenomena is a familiar theoretical argument. Dopamine agonist drugs are psychotogenic, and this effect is thought to be mediated by the mesolimbic dopamine system that projects from ventral tegmental area to nucleus accumbens, hypothalamus, and amygdala. It remains to be determined whether mesolimbic dopamine hyperactivity is a primary pathogenic event in the development of psychosis or a secondary manifestation of defective inhibitory activity. According to the theory put forth in this discussion, mesolimbic dopamine hyperactivity is assumed to be a secondary event that reflects a state of disinhibition. In light of the pathological lesion described above, for the mesolimbic dopamine system (i.e. the VTA dopamine neurons as well as their terminal fields) to be overactive, it must be relatively spared by the primary pathological process. The efficacy of neuroleptic drugs in reducing positive symptoms is thought to be related to their reducing dopamine activity in this system.

The role of dopamine in the dorsolateral prefrontal cortex related symptoms is more speculative. Nevertheless, there is circumstantial evidence to suggest that *decreased* activity in the mesocortical system contributes to these features. In the monkey, cognitive functions mediated by the dorsolateral prefrontal cortex (e.g. delayed response tasks) can be impaired by selective ablation of ascending dopamine afferents to dorsolateral prefrontal cortex (4). Clinical symptoms phenomenologically similar to the defect symptoms of schizophrenia are found in patients with Parkinson's disease, where they are thought to directly reflect loss of mesocortical dopamine neurons. In schizophrenia, evidence of diminished dopamine metabolism as determined by homovanillic acid concentrations in cerebrospinal fluid have been linked directly with defect symptoms (5) as well as with the presence of signs of atrophy on CT (6), which also have been linked to defect features. These studies in schizophrenia may turn out to be more informative than at first appreciated, as recent evidence in monkeys indicates that cerebrospinal fluid homovanillic acid concentrations reflect primarily mesocortical dopamine metabolism (7). Finally, while dopamine agonists tend to exacerbate positive psychotic symptoms, consistent with the presumed relationship of these symptoms to mesolimbic dopamine hyperactivity, they generally have little impact on and may even improve defect symptoms. The inverse of this is seen with neuroleptic agents, which diminish presumed mesolimbic hyperactivity and positive psychotic symptoms, but perhaps compound mesocortical dopamine hypoactivity as suggested by their tendency to occasionally exacerbate defect symptoms.

These observations and inferences suggest that a state of conflicting dopaminergic activity may exist in the brain in schizophrenia. While the VTA cell bodies that project within the limbic system are functionally intact and possibly disinhibited, projections to the prefrontal cortex are functionally deficient. It is unknown whether any single lesion or pathological condition of the human brain could produce such a peculiar physiological state. In the rat, however, this state has been described. A prefrontal lesion that destroys the dopamine afferentation of the prefrontal cortex results in a state of chronic hyperactivity in subcortical dopamine systems (8). It appears that at least in the rat, mesocortical dopamine neurons synapse with prefrontal cortical neurons that exert feedback inhibitory control over mesolimbic dopamine activity (9).

Other unique aspects of the mesocortical dopamine system may be relevant to the theory presented here. In particular, this system in rats appears to be much more sensitive to the effects of both environmental (e.g. foot shock) (10) and pharmacological (e.g. beta carboline anxiety model) (11) stress than are the other dopamine systems. These stress models cause dramatic increases of mesocortical dopamine metabolism not seen in either nigrostriatal or mesolimbic regions. These observations in animals may provide a clue as to why stress is associated with clinical decompensation in schizophrenia. One possibility, based on the dopamine hypothesis of excessive dopamine activity, is that patients with schizophrenia are unusually sensitive to stress because they cannot handle an excessive stress-induced dopamine load. An alternative possibility must be considered, however, in view of the evidence of *diminished* mesocortical activity in schizophrenia. Rather than regarding the normal stress response as potentially overwhelming to the patient with schizophrenia, it might be viewed as an important adaptation that the patient is unable to make. In other words, stress-related decompensation may represent failure to respond, not excessive response. Perhaps mesocortical dopamine projections evolved as a means of increasing prefrontal cortical function when there is a critical need for it. A lesion that disrupts the normal dopamine afferentation of the prefrontal cortex might render an individual physiologically incapable of making appropriate cognitive responses to stress and, because of the feedback interruption, predisposed to unmodulated mesolimbic dopamine overactivity and psychosis.

The natural course of psychotic and defect symptoms may be a manifestation of an interaction between this state of cortical dopamine deficiency and subcortical overactivity and the effects of normal aging. Over the natural history of schizophrenia, hallucinations tend to become less florid, while defect symptoms become more apparent. Normal aging is associated with a reduction in subcortical dopamine receptor activity (12) and a loss of dopamine from prefrontal cortex (13). In fact, the magnitude of these losses may be greatest between the second and fourth decades (12), around the time when patients with schizophrenia begin to 'burn out.' A reduction in subcortical receptor activity should counteract the effects of unmodulated mesolimbic dopamine activity while loss of prefrontal dopaminergic function would compound the effects of a mesocortical deficit.

In summary, schizophrenia is presumed to involve a subtle, static brain lesion that interrupts connections between certain periventricular limbic nuclei and dorsolateral prefrontal cortex. Among its effects, this lesion deafferents prefrontal cortex of its dopaminergic innervation. While this lesion may be consistent with the research reviewed in this volume and may provide a theoretical framework for understanding many of the clinical features of schizophrenia, it is far from a unique or specific lesion. It is certainly not by itself a sufficient explanation for the illness because other disorders that are associated with similar lesions do not necessarily present as schizophrenia. For example, psychosis is exceedingly rare in untreated Parkinson's disease, despite the mesocortical dopamine deficit (though it might be argued that psychosis is rare because of concomitant degeneration of the mesolimbic system). Some cases of trauma, tumor, and demyelinating disorders probably effect the systems involved in schizophrenia, yet relatively infrequently do such cases present with schizophrenia-like symptoms. It appears that even if the proposed lesion in schizophrenia were a necessary condition for the development of the syndrome, it must exist in combination with other factors for it to be clinically apparent.

The role of brain maturation

The final step in the evolution of this theory is to consider the role of normal brain development and maturation in the expression of the schizophrenia lesion. It will be suggested that what is unique about the lesion is not its location, histopathological appearance, neurochemistry, or etiology, but its interaction with the changes that occur in the brain at the time of sexual maturity.

The relationship between the time of life when a brain lesion presents and the manner of psychopathology that it causes is underemphasized in adult psychiatry. In a number of neurologic disorders that frequently present with psychiatric symptoms, the psychopathology seems to be determined more by the age of the patient than by the characteristics of the neuropathology. For example, Huntington's disease is an hereditary encephalopathy with a variable age of onset that frequently begins with changes in behavior. Although the neuropathological features do not appear to vary consistently with age of onset, the psychiatric symptoms do. Behavioral manifestations are rare in childhood cases; adolescent onset is more likely to be associated with psychosis than are cases of later onset; onset in the late third decade and in the fourth decade is more likely to be associated with depression; and later-onset cases typically present with dementia as the psychiatric concomitants (14). A similar age-related pattern of behavioral change is also seen in other neurologic disorders that have a variable age of onset, such as Wilson's disease, metachromatic leukodystrophy, ceroid lipofuscinosis, herpes encephalitis, systemic lupus erythematosus of the central nervous system, Creutzfeldt-Jacob disease, trauma and tumor. In each illness, if psychosis develops it tends to do so more frequently during the late second and early third decades of life than at any other time. Since the neuropathology is each disorder does not vary systematically with age, the predictable behavioral variation appears to represent an interaction between the lesion and age-related aspects of brain physiology.

In childhood, classic examples of this interaction are illustrated by the changing manifestations of certain fixed congenital lesions. Perinatal hypoxic encephalopathy may cause cerebral palsy with spastic diplegia or hemiparesis in a two-year-old. At four, athetosis may develop, and seizures may follow in a few years. The lesion itself is static, but its effects on neurological function change. This is thought to reflect the fact that the pathways mediating athetosis, as an example, do not come 'on line' until after a few years of life. In other words, if a lesion involves a brain structure or region that has yet to mature functionally, the effects of the lesion may remain silent until the structure or system matures (15). Another example of this phenomenon, one that is closer to the issue of schizophrenia, is the changing pattern of seizures that result from a congenital scar in the temporal lobe. During childhood, the clinical manifestations of epileptic discharges from the temporal lobe usually include only autonomic phenomena and lapses in consciousness. At adolescence, psychic experiences begin to appear.

It is now necessary to make an assumption that analogous to the case of congenital athetosis the brain system mediating the schizophrenic syndrome does not mature functionally until adolescence. There are several lines of evidence in support of this assumption. The neurological disorders already discussed suggest that the physiological mechanism responsible for psychosis is maximally active during this age period and regresses with advancing age. This may relate to hormonal influences on dopamine neurons and receptors or reflect more simply the natural history of subcortical dopamine activity. Results from recent in-vivo studies of subcortical dopamine activity suggest that it peaks at around age twenty (12). Thus the limbic components of the schizophrenic lesion may go relatively unnoticed until this time of life when the structures it involves become functionally critical for certain aspects of behavior.

The same considerations apply to understanding the implications of the prefrontal component of the lesion. Several lines of evidence suggest that the dorsolateral prefrontal cortex also comes functionally 'on line' around the time of sexual maturity. It only begins to myelinate during the second decade of life and continues its myelogenic cycle well into the third decade (16). Cognitive functions attributed to dorsolateral prefrontal cortical processing are similar to Piaget's formal operations which begin in early adolescence. In experiments with monkeys, perinatal dorsolateral prefrontal cortical ablations remain clinically silent until sexual maturity when the animals appear to 'develop' cognitive deficits that clearly distinguish them from their peers (17). If the monkey model is applicable to humans, it means that an early developmental lesion involving dorsolateral prefrontal cortex could be inapparent until this region becomes essential for certain behaviors, at which time the existence of the lesion would become clinically manifest.

According to the model proposed here, both the florid psychotic and the defect symptoms of schizophrenia have a characteristic time of onset, not because the brain lesion associated with the illness begins then, but because the brain areas it involves become functionally mature at this time. It is probably an oversimplification to assume that the lesion is totally clinically silent before adolescence. It more likely than not produces subtle behavioral abnormalities, perhaps social awkwardness, shyness, and other personality traits that have been regarded as premorbid characteristics of schizophrenia. A recent study of the premorbid personality features of patients with Parkinson's disease found similar traits (18), suggesting at least the possibility of a correlation between the degree of mesocortical dopamine deficiency and the severity of defect-like symptoms.

What is the etiology of the lesion?

The etiology of the lesion is unknown. Any of the potential etiologies discussed in this volume and elsewhere, such as an hereditary encephalopathy, infection or post-infectious state, a primary immunological disorder, perinatal trauma or encephalopathy, toxin exposure, primary metabolic disease, etc., could cause the lesion. The fact that it is neuropathologically non-specific suggests that no single etiology has a monopoly on it. Indeed, it is appealing to consider that there may be many causes of the lesion, and thus of schizophrenia. If there are multiple etiologies for the lesion, then the extent of it is likely to vary from one individual to another. This could help explain the clinical heterogeneity of the illness. Patients who have an extensive lesion involving both the periventricular and prefrontal systems would be expected to have a poorer prognosis and more evidence of a 'brain disease.' In contrast, patients who have a relatively limited lesion, perhaps confined to a few limbic sites, some of the corticofugal feedback projections, with little prefrontal involvement would have a better prognosis, primarily positive psychotic symptoms, and less evidence of 'brain disease.' This approach to clinical heterogeneity differs from more familiar subgrouping schemes which tend to view schizophrenia as comprised of distinct subtypes. Clinical and biological differences between patients are seen here as manifestations of differences in the extent of the lesion. Patients who have a more extensive lesion have more defect symptoms, greater neurological impairment and, not surprisingly, a poorer prognosis. Whether the extent of the lesion can be consistently linked to a specific etiology will have to await future research.

Summary

A theory of the pathogenesis of schizophrenia is outlined as follows. Schizophrenia is associated with a subtle, static structural brain lesion that involves a diffuse system of periventricular limbic and diencephalic nuclei and their connections to the dorsolateral prefrontal cortex. Defect symptoms relate to physiological dysfunction of the dorsolateral prefrontal cortex, in part mediated by diminished mesocortical dopamine activity. Positive psychotic symptoms relate to physiological dysfunction of limbic nuclei and mesolimbic dopamine overactivity, in part because of disruption of prefrontal corticofugal inhibitory feedback. An intact mesocortical-mesolimbic dopamine system feedback loop is important for normal behavioral responses to stress. The onset of the symptoms of schizophrenia is not a function of the time of onset of the lesion, which is presumed to have occurred early in development. Rather, it is a manifestation of the time at which the brain areas involved by the lesion reach physiological maturity. The etiology of the lesion is unknown but presumed to be multiple, accounting for the variability of the extent of the lesion and the clinical and biological heterogeneity of the syndrome.

REFERENCES

1. Gloor P, Olivier A, Quesney LF, Anderman F, Horowitz S (1982) The role of the limbic system in experiential phenomena of temporal lobe epilepsy. *Ann. Neurol., 12,* 129.

2. Davison K, Bagley CR (1969) Schizophrenia-like psychoses associated with organic disorders of the central nervous system. In: Herrington RN (Ed), *Current Problems in Neuropsychiatry,* pp. 113 – 184.
3. Stuss DT, Benson DF (1984) Neuropsychological studies of the frontal lobes. *Psychol. Bull., 95,* 3.
4. Brozoski TJ, Brown RM, Rosvold HE, Goldman PS (1979) Cognitive deficit caused by regional depletion of dopamine in prefrontal cortex of rhesus monkey. *Science, 205,* 929.
5. Lindstrom LH (1985) Low HVA and normal 5HIAA CSF levels in drug-free schizophrenic patients compared to healthy volunteers: correlations to symptomatology and family history. *Psychiatry Res., 14,* 265.
6. Van Kammen DP, Mann LS, Sternberg DE, Scheinin M, Ninan PT, Marder SR (1983) Dopamine-beta-hydroxylase activity and homovanillic acid in spinal fluid of schizophrenics with brain atrophy. *Science, 220,* 974.
7. Elsworth JD, Roth RH, Redmond Jr De (1983) Does HVA concentration in CSF or plasma reflect central dopamine function in primates? *Prog. Neuropsychopharmacol. Biol. Psychiatry, 125, Suppl.,* 128.
8. Pycock CJ, Kerwin RW, Carter CJ (1980) Effect of lesion of cortical dopamine terminals on subcortical dopamine in rats. *Nature (London), 286,* 74 – 77.
9. Glowinski J, Tassin JP, Thierry AM (1984) The mesocortical-prefrontal dopaminergic neurons. *Trends Neurosci., 7,* 415.
10. Herman JP, Guilloneau D, Dantzer R (1982) Differential effects of inescapable foot shocks and of stimuli previously paired with inescapable foot shocks on dopamine turnover in cortical and limbic areas of the rat. *Life Sci., 30,* 2207.
11. Tam S-Y, Roth RH (1985) Selective increase in dopamine metabolism in the prefrontal cortex by the anxiogenic beta-carboline FG 7142. *Biochem. Pharmacol., 34,* 1595.
12. Wong DF, Wagner Jr HN, Dannals RF (1984) Effects of age on dopamine and serotonin receptors measured by positron emission tomography in the living human brain. *Science, 226,* 1393.
13. McGeer PL, McGeer EG (1981) Neurotransmitters in the aging brain. In: Darrison AM, Thompson RHS (Eds), *The Molecular Basis of Neuropathology,* pp. 631 – 648. Edward Arnold, London.
14. Lishman WA (1978) *Organic Psychiatry,* pp. 549 – 557. Blackwell Scientific Publications, Oxford.
15. Adams RD, Lyon G (1982) *Neurology of Hereditary Metabolic Diseases of Children,* pp. 5 – 6, 376 – 381. McGraw-Hill Book Co., New York.
16. Yakovlev P, LeCours A-R (1964) The myelogenetic cycles of regional maturation of the brain. In: Minkowski A (Ed), *Regional Development of the Brain in Early Life,* pp. 3 – 70. Blackwell Scientific Publications, Oxford.
17. Goldman-Rakic PS, Isseroff A, Schwartz ML, Rugbee NM (1983) The neurobiology of cognitive development. In: Mussen P (Ed), *Handbook of Child Psychology: Biology and Infancy Development,* pp. 281 – 344. J. Wiley, New York.
18. Todes CJ, Lees AJ (1985) The pre-morbid personality of patients with Parkinson's disease. *J. Neurol., Neurosurg. Psychiatry, 45,* 97.

Subject index

413